COMMERCIAL LAW
PROBLEMS AND MATERIALS
ON SALES AND PAYMENTS

■ ■ ■

By

Linda J. Rusch
Professor of Law
Co-director, Commercial Law Center,
Gonzaga University School of Law

Stephen L. Sepinuck
Professor of Law
Co-director, Commercial Law Center,
Gonzaga University School of Law

AMERICAN CASEBOOK SERIES®

WEST®
A Thomson Reuters business

Mat #41194404

American Casebook Series is a trademark registered in the U.S. Patent and Trademark Office.

© 2012 Thomson Reuters
610 Opperman Drive
St. Paul, MN 55123
1–800–313–9378
Printed in the United States of America

ISBN: 978–0–314–27817–3

To Doug, Kari, and Anna

　　LJR

To Sandra, Ben, and Jacob

　　SLS

PREFACE

This book is designed to help the student learn the law governing: (i) sales and leases of goods; and (ii) payment systems. This book is also designed to teach the art and skill of statutory reading. Much of the law school curriculum, particularly in the first year, is designed to teach the skill of case analysis and the art of argument, both based largely on techniques of analogy and distinction. While those skills are undoubtedly important, this book instead focuses on the equally important skills of statutory reading and analysis. These skills require close attention to each word of the statute or regulation, careful review of the applicable commentary, and an appreciation of how the different provisions of the statute or regulation interact and interrelate. Reading and rereading the text of and comments to a statute is critical to this process of textual interpretation. Accordingly, whenever this book instructs students to read a specified statutory or regulatory section, you should thoroughly study that section and its commentary.

Armed with what you have learned from careful reading of the overview of the law in this book, along with the statutory text and commentary, you will then be tasked with solving various problems. Some of these problems will require that you list or diagram the elements of a particular statutory provision and some require you to draft contractual language. Most require you to apply the statutory language to a given set of facts. Particularly for problems of this last type, students should map out their reasoning based upon the statutory language or commentary. In other words, write out your reasoning steps for each problem. This will help solidify your understanding of the required methodology. As when learning case analysis and reasoning, the final result is not nearly as important as mastering the method.

Confronting a complex and interrelated statutory regime can be daunting. It is often necessary to learn all the fine details while simultaneously understanding the larger picture created by those details, because each informs the other. This can be exceedingly difficult. This book attempts to address that difficulty by using textual overviews to provide a sense of the big picture and then moving on to the details through assigned problems that function as building blocks for learning the law as it applies to typical factual scenarios.

The problem-solving orientation of this book is based on our judgment that most lawyers use the skills developed in law school to solve problems. These problems may be from clients in a practice setting, from constituents in a legislative setting, from executives in a corporate setting, or from policy makers in an administrative setting. Using the tools of critical analysis and linear logical thinking to solve problems is the hallmark of a lawyer. Thus, this book provides repeated opportunities for students to practice their problem-solving skills.

One occasionally frustrating aspect of complex statutory regimes is that learning even the smallest detail may require the reader to study not only the provisions that seem the most relevant to the issue, but also one or more other provisions that impact the situation, as well as any number of statutory definitions. Students, who often do not know if there are other relevant provisions, let alone where to look for them, often expect the text or the teacher to alert them to everything that may be relevant. Some also resent the time it takes to thoroughly read the necessary sections and prepare the problems for the class. However, practicing lawyers often have no one to guide them when they tackle a new statutory or regulatory regime and thus law students need to learn the skill of how to do so for themselves. We have tried to strike an appropriate balance between providing help and letting students fend for themselves. If we have erred in that judgment, please let us know. We can say with some confidence, however, is that it gets easier with practice. Some of us even learn to prefer statutes to cases.

SUMMARY OF CONTENTS

TABLE OF CONTENTS

TABLE OF CASES

TABLE OF STATUTES, REGULATIONS AND RESTATEMENTS

COMMERCIAL LAW
PROBLEMS AND MATERIALS
ON SALES AND PAYMENTS

CHAPTER ONE

INTRODUCTION TO COMMERCIAL TRANSACTIONS

SECTION 1. THE STUDY OF COMMERCIAL LAW

A. Transactional Law and the Commercial Lawyer

Millions of "deals" occur each day in the United States and around the world. Many are between businesses, many are between consumers, and many are between a business and a consumer. These deals range in value and complexity from the purchase of a candy bar at the local market to the leveraged buyout of a multi-national business empire. They include purchases and leases of goods, licenses of intellectual property, sales of receivables, service contracts, and all manner of loans.

These deals are conducted with a varying degree of negotiation about terms. Sometimes lawyers are involved in negotiating and documenting the deal, but often the negotiation (if any) occurs without involvement of legal counsel. Particularly in the business-to-consumer context, it is customary for the business to conduct business through the use of standard written forms or dialog boxes on web pages. Standard forms and dialog boxes are also used in varying degrees in business-to-business transactions. However, even when they are not involved in negotiating or documenting a particular transaction, lawyers are often involved in drafting standard forms and advising their clients on how to use them.

To grossly oversimplify, transactions typically have at least two distinct phases: the pre-transaction stage and the performance stage. In the pre-transaction stage, the parties contemplate entering into the deal, may negotiate terms, and may prepare and execute the documentation for the deal. In the performance stage, the parties either perform their contractual obligations or fail to perform in some way or another. In some circumstances, a party may be excused from performing its contractual obligation.

The role of lawyers in the pre-transaction phase differs depending on whether they are negotiating and documenting a particular deal or drafting a standard form for repeated use in multiple transactions. In a negotiated deal, the lawyers try to document the deal that has been negotiated – often by the parties themselves – and to allocate the risks associated with that transaction. In other words, they try to faithfully put on paper the parties' basic understanding of the deal, imagine everything that might go wrong, and consider which of those contingencies to provide for in the transaction documents. In these negotiated transactions, the lawyers and client will usually discuss the various risks and determine which risks the document terms should address. In such situations, both the parties and their lawyers have an incentive to try and make the deal happen in accord with the parties' objectives. In drafting standard forms for use in multiple transactions, lawyers try to construct a form that will allocate risks in transactions with as yet unknown parties based not only on the legal issues that might arise but also taking into account the client's perspective on what will work in the market place.

Some transactions have a third phase: dispute resolution. This occurs when one of the parties fails – or is claimed by the other party to have failed – to adequately perform one or more contractual obligations to which it has agreed. The parties in this stage of a transaction may disagree about what their respective obligations were, which (if any) of those obligations were not fulfilled, or what remedy for the aggrieved party is appropriate. Fortunately, the number of transactions that enter this third stage is quite small compared to the numerous deals agreed to.

Many courses in law school – including most courses on sales of goods – are taught in the context of this third stage, when something goes wrong. The question usually posed to a student is "what are the rights and liabilities" of the parties in the transaction gone wrong? To answer that question, students are often referred to the applicable statute, as interpreted by judicial decisions. While ascertaining how disputes may be resolved is important, for two main reasons it is not the principal focus of this book. First, as just noted, the portion of deals that enter the dispute phase is small. The percentage that are litigated is significantly smaller. The portion that yield a published opinion is even tinier. As a result, even though those decisions may be relevant in analyzing the parties' legal rights and responsibilities, it is far from clear that those decisions play a major role in dispute resolution. Indeed, there is a substantial body of scholarship that suggests that the law itself may have little relevance to how parties resolve their disputes.[1] Second, particularly if you consider the role of the lawyer in drafting standardized forms and procedures, lawyers are far more likely to be involved in a deal at the pre-transaction phase than in the dispute resolution phase. Moreover, even if we are wrong in this assessment,

---

[1] *See, e.g.,* Lisa Bernstein, *Merchant Law in A Merchant Court: Rethinking the Code's Search for Immanent Business Norms,* 144 U. PA. L. REV. 1765 (1996); Lisa Bernstein, *Opting Out of the Legal System: Extralegal Contractual Relations in the Diamond Industry,* 21 J. LEGAL. STUD. 115 (1992); Stewart Macaulay, *An Empirical View of Contract,* 1985 WIS. L. REV. 465, 476–68.

we strongly believe that law schools need to do more to provide their students with the skills necessary to be transactional lawyers. Learning how to anticipate and resolve issues before they become the subject of a dispute is significantly better for the client than having deals go sour and spending client's resources on resolving the situation.

A transactional lawyer's responsibility is to consider how to accomplish creatively the contracting parties' objectives within the boundaries of the applicable legal rules. This perspective requires the lawyer to imagine all the possible risks to the client and advise the client on how to manage those risks prospectively. To pick a common example in the sale of goods context, consider a client who sells small kitchen appliances and who wants the lawyer to draft a standard sales agreement that will work for all types of those appliances. The client wants to give a warranty on the products it sells as a way of enhancing sales. One of the things the lawyer will need to do is to determine what specifically the client wants to warrant about the goods. Is it that the goods will be free from defects in material and workmanship at the time of sale, that the goods will function properly at the time of sale, or that the goods will function properly for a certain period of time? Each of these promises about the quality of the goods exposes the seller to a different type of risk under the law governing remedies for breach. In connection with this, the lawyer will need to consider the potential problems that may arise. For example, if one of the small appliances is a toaster, in all likelihood, the client expects that the toasters it sells will be fit for their ordinary purpose, will readily acknowledge that a toaster that does not make toast is not fulfilling its ordinary purpose, and would be happy to repair or replace such a malfunctioning toaster. But suppose a toaster lacks a temperature control shut off mechanism or has one that fails to work. As a result, the toaster overheats and causes a fire. If the client warranted that the toaster was "fit for its ordinary purpose," would the warranty be breached? Is toasting bread without roasting the house the ordinary purpose of the toaster? If so, does the client really want liability for the full value of the house and its contents? If not, the lawyer should find a different way to phrase the warranty or some other way to limit the client's liability.

Restricting potential liability for malfunctioning products sold is just one of the many clauses the transactional lawyer must consider. Should the documentation contain clauses governing how disputes are handled, such as an arbitration clause, a choice-of-law clause, a choice-of-forum clause, or an attorney's fees clause? If so, how should those clauses be drafted? Are they enforceable? If the law of a particular jurisdiction is chosen, what legal rules are being chosen? Are all the legal rules of that jurisdiction appropriate for the particular type of transaction?

The issue underlying all these questions is risk allocation. To identify and appreciate the relevant risks, a transactional lawyer must have intimate knowledge of the underlying legal principles, the client's business, and the activities of the client's counter-parties as they relate to your client's interaction with them. The transactional lawyer must also have the ability to imagine or anticipate problems that have, as yet, not arisen. The transactional lawyer must then be able to clearly articulate the issues to the client, generate options for dealing with the identified issues and risks, help the client decide among the various options, and at least in some situations, negotiate the deal points and documentation with the client's counter-party. In doing this, the transactional lawyer also has to pay meticulous attention to the language used in any agreement to ensure that it means what the parties intend. A transactional lawyer thus must have many skills in addition to the knowledge of legal rules and principles applicable to a particular transaction.[2]

This book is designed to assist students of the law in several ways. First, it will help students learn the legal rules and principles applicable to transactions in goods. Second, it will help students acquire the skills essential to a transactional practice, including the skill of statutory construction. Third, it will help students learn how to deal with disputes that often arise in goods transactions. These three goals are not mutually exclusive. Certainly, knowledge of the operative legal principles is critical to practice from both a transactional and a dispute resolution perspective. Understanding how the dispute is likely to be resolved helps a transactional lawyer determine how to structure the transaction to avoid the dispute or to minimize a potential dispute's negative impact. Understanding how the transaction arises and is structured, including the documentation that is part of the transaction, helps the lawyer in the dispute resolution phase to craft the arguments and strategy to help the client resolve the dispute. In much of the material that follows, we will ask the student to try out both roles, how they would approach an issue as a transactional lawyer and how they would approach the issue if there was a dispute in a transaction. Keeping these two roles in mind will, we hope, result in an in-depth understanding of the legal principles and policies that operate in this area of law, as well as the development of the essential skills needed to represent clients effectively in transactional and dispute resolution work.

---

[2] *See generally*, Tina L. Stark, *Thinking Like a Deal Lawyer*, 54 J. LEGAL EDUC. 223 (2004).

B. The Uniform Commercial Code: Structure & Scope

1. *A Very Short History*

The principal source of commercial law in this country – at least the principal source applicable to sales of goods – is the Uniform Commercial Code. The UCC is the joint product of two organizations: the National Conference of Commissioners on Uniform State Laws (NCCUSL)[3] and the American Law Institute (ALI). In reality, however, the UCC is not law; it is merely a model for state legislatures to enact. Originally drafted in the early 1950s,[4] by 1968, the UCC had been enacted in every state except Louisiana.[5] A "Permanent Editorial Board" (PEB) was established by the sponsoring organizations to comment on problems that arise and consider the wisdom of proposed amendments to the UCC.[6]

Over the years, NCCUSL and the ALI have modified the UCC to adjust it to changes in commercial practices. The most recent round of revisions started in the late 1980s. They added Articles 2A and 4A and made major revisions to all the other Articles. Most of the revisions have been widely adopted. However, some of the substantive changes have generated significant opposition. Even the revision process itself has not been without controversy,[7] with concerns expressed that this unique "private" law making process may not always produce rules that are "consonant with democratic values."[8] In particular, the 2003 amendments to Article 2 (Sales of Goods) and Article 2A (Leases of Goods) (finished in 2003) were

---

[3] In 2008, NCCUSL also became known as the Uniform Law Commission.

[4] The drafting process is discussed extensively in a symposium to which five drafters contributed. *See* Symposium, *Origins and Evolution: Drafters Reflect Upon the Uniform Commercial Code,* 43 OHIO ST. L.J. 535–84 (1982).

[5] Louisiana has now adopted most of the Articles of the UCC, except for Articles 2 and 2A.

[6] *See PEB Commentaries on the Uniform Commercial Code,* some of which are reprinted in THOMSON/WEST, SELECTED COMMERCIAL STATUTES issued every year for classroom use.

[7] *See* Robert E. Scott, *The Rise and Fall of Article 2,* 62 LA. L. REV. 1009 (2002); Symposium, *Perspectives on the Uniform Laws Revision Process,* 52 HASTINGS L.J. 603–701 (2001).

[8] *See* David V. Snyder, *Private Lawmaking,* 64 OHIO ST. L.J. 371, 448 (2003). *See also* Amelia H. Boss, *The Future of the Uniform Commercial Code Process in an Increasingly International World,* 68 OHIO ST. L.J. 349 (2007).

subject to extensive lobbying and political compromise, and no state has yet adopted them. In 2011, these amendments were withdrawn from the Official Text of the UCC.

2. The Structure of the UCC

The Code is now divided into eleven substantive articles. The first is a general article bearing on various aspects of the entire Code. The remaining ten articles each address a somewhat unique part of commercial law. What follows is a brief description of each article of the UCC and the fate of the most recent round of proposed revisions to each article.

Article 1: General Provisions. Article 1 contains definitions and general rules applicable to transactions governed by other articles of the UCC. UCC § 1-102. Article 1, therefore, is not a free-standing Article; if a substantive transaction is not governed by the Code, Article 1 does not apply. In 2001, NCCUSL and the ALI approved a revised Article 1, which 40 states have enacted to date.[9] The remaining states have former Article 1. Except where otherwise indicated, the references in these materials to Article 1 are to revised Article 1.

Article 2: Sales. Article 2 applies to "transactions in goods," UCC § 2-102, but deals almost exclusively with the formation, adjustment, construction, performance, and enforcement of contracts for the sale of goods. Every state but Louisiana has enacted Article 2. The major innovations of Article 2 were the de-emphasis of title in deciding issues regarding performance and enforcement of sales contracts and several novel provisions on the formation of sales agreements. It has also proven to be a major force in moving contract law from a subjective theory of contract to a more objective one. In 2002, NCCUSL approved a set of amendments to Article 2 and in 2003, the ALI approved those same amendments. However, to date no state has enacted those amendments and those amendments were withdrawn from the official text in 2011. These materials focus on pre-amended Article 2, which remains the law of the land. The Appendix to this book (which is available on line) contains a discussion of the major differences between the pre-amended version and the 2003 version of Article 2.

---

[9] NCCUSL maintains a website where the current enactments are tracked: www.nccusl.org. In addition, the UNIFORM LAWS ANNOTATED series also tracks the enactments.

Article 2A: Leases. Article 2A was originally promulgated in 1987 to deal with leases of goods, a type of business transaction that has existed for a long time but which was increasing almost exponentially (largely for tax reasons) both in numbers and in dollar amounts. Article 2A's rules and principles are drawn from Article 2, but with variations to accommodate the fact that the transactions it governs involve the transfer of a property interest for a limited period of time (a lease) as opposed to the transfer of complete ownership (a sale). Every state but Louisiana has enacted Article 2A. Article 2A amendments were also approved in 2002 by NCCUSL and in 2003 by the ALI.[10] To date no state has enacted the 2003 amendments to Article 2A and those amendments were withdrawn from the official text in 2011. These materials deal with Article 2A prior to its amendment in 2003. The Appendix to this book (available online) contains a discussion of the major differences between the pre-amended and 2003 versions of Article 2A.

Article 3: Negotiable Instruments. Article 3 deals with checks, drafts, promissory notes, certificates of deposit, and other types of commercial paper. It provides rules on negotiability, the rights of holders, and the liabilities of issuers and endorsers. Article 3 governs these types of items only if they are "in writing" and thus does not apply to the electronic equivalent of these items.[11] NCCUSL and the ALI revised Article 3 in 1990 and every state except New York has adopted those revisions. Another minor set of amendments to Article 3 was promulgated in 2002. To date, ten states have enacted the 2002 amendments. Because those amendments are not particularly controversial and are likely to be uniformly adopted, the references to Article 3 in this book are to Article 3 as amended in 2002.

Article 4: Bank Deposits and Collections. Article 4 deals with checks and other demand instruments that are drawn on a bank and collected through the banking system. Article 4 covers the contractual relationship between the drawer and the payor bank, the relationship between the payee and the depositary bank, and the relationship among the banks in the collection process, including the responsibilities of the payor bank when a check is presented for payment.[12] Article

---

[10] In 1994, the Article 2A Drafting Committee was appointed and charged with considering the Article 2 revision to the extent those revisions made sense for leasing transactions.

[11] In states that have enacted the Uniform Electronic Transactions Act (UETA), promissory notes, if created electronically, are governed by UCC Article 3 to the extent of rights of holders of these electronic notes. UETA § 16.

[12] Article 4's provisions are supplemented and in some cases superseded by federal

4 also applies only to items that are "written" and generally does not apply to electronic collection of payments that started out as a written item.[13] Every state except New York has enacted Article 4 as revised in 1990. A small set of amendments to Article 4 were adopted in 2002. To date, ten states have enacted the 2002 amendments. These materials refer to Article 4 as amended in 2002.

Article 4A: Funds Transfers. Article 4A was promulgated in 1989 and governs the transfer of funds from one bank account to another bank account as long as the bank accounts are not consumer bank accounts covered by federal regulation.[14] Such a transfer is initiated by a customer's payment order (given in any manner, orally, in writing, or electronically) to its bank and concluded when the beneficiary's bank accepts the payment order for the benefit of the beneficiary. The payment orders are communications that are followed in very short order by the transfer of credits from the originator to the beneficiary in settlement of the payment order. Article 4A has been enacted in every state.[15]

Article 5: Letters of Credit. A letter of credit is a written promise by the issuer – typically a bank – to pay a specified sum of money to the beneficiary upon a presentation of specified documents. The bank's letter of credit is issued at the request of an applicant, usually in furtherance of some business relationship between the applicant and the beneficiary. The bank's obligation to pay on the letter of credit is conditioned on the beneficiary presenting the documents required and those documents "strictly complying" with the terms of the letter of credit. The issuing bank's obligation on the letter of credit is independent of the applicant's

---

regulations. For example, Federal Reserve Regulation J, 12 C.F.R. Part 210, governs check collection through use of the federal reserve banks. Similarly, the Federal Expedited Funds Availability Act, 12 U.S.C. § 4001 *et seq.*, and its accompanying Regulation CC, 12 C.F.R. Part 229, preempts Article 4 on questions of when deposited funds are available for withdrawal as a matter of right and some of Article 4 on the check return process after a check presented for payment has been dishonored.

[13] Article 4 does apply if a payor bank agrees to accept electronic presentments. UCC § 4-110.

[14] If any part of the funds transfer is governed by the federal Electronic Fund Transfer Act, 15 U.S.C. § 1693 *et seq.* and its implementing Regulation E, 12 C.F.R. Part 205, Article 4A does not apply. UCC § 4A-108. The federal act and regulation, not Article 4A, govern electronic funds transfers to or from a consumer's bank account.

[15] Federal Reserve Regulation J, 12 C.F.R. Part 210, governs payment orders transmitted through the federal reserve banks, and it adopts many parts of Article 4A.

obligation to the beneficiary on the underlying business transaction. Letters of credit are designed to substitute the creditworthiness of the issuer for that of the applicant and are commonly used in international sales of goods when the seller wants assurance that the goods will be paid for. Article 5 was revised in 1995 and every state has enacted those revisions.[16]

Article 6: Bulk Sales. Article 6 deals with bulk transfers by a seller. It is designed to protect the creditors of a business that sells in bulk all or virtually all of its inventory by requiring advance notice to the creditors of the sale. NCCUSL and the ALI have recommended repeal of Article 6, largely because the modern Bankruptcy Code and various laws governing fraudulent transfers have made the Article – and its rather cumbersome rules – unnecessary. To date, 45 states have repealed Article 6 and two states have revised Article 6.

Article 7: Documents of Title. Article 7 applies to documents of title, which are documents issued by a bailee of goods by which the bailee promises to deliver the goods to the holder of the document.[17] To qualify as a document of title, it must be issued by or to a bailee and be recognized in the commercial world as a document that entitles the holder to possession of the goods covered by the document. Documents of title include warehouse receipts, which are issued by warehouses, and bills of lading, which are issued by carriers. A document of title should not be confused with "certificates of title" that are issued by state licensing authorities and cover motorized vehicles of various sorts. Article 7 was revised in 2003 and to date 40 states have enacted those revisions. References in these materials to Article 7 are to the revised version.[18]

Article 8: Investment Securities. Article 8, often called the "negotiable instruments" law for investment securities, defines the rights and liabilities of

---

[16] In many instances, the parties agree that the letter of credit will be governed by the Uniform Customs and Practices (UCP) 600 or International Standby Practices (ISP) 98, both promulgated by the International Chamber of Commerce. Article 5 allows the parties to choose non-Article 5 principles.

[17] Federal law also plays a role in governing documents of title through the United States Warehouse Act (codified at 7 U.S.C. § 241 *et seq.*) and the Carriage of Goods by Sea Act, *see* 46 U.S.C. § 30701 *et seq.*, among others.

[18] As part of the Article 7 revision process, conforming amendments to other articles of the UCC were promulgated. As states enact the Article 7 revision, they also amend the other UCC articles with those conforming amendments. References in these materials to the other UCC articles are to the versions as amended by the Article 7 conforming amendments.

issuers, transferors, and transferees of securities and securities entitlements. Article 8, however, does not supersede state or federal regulatory laws governing the issuance of securities. Article 8 was last revised in 1994. The 1994 revision has been enacted in all states.

Article 9: Secured Transactions. Article 9 deals with the creation, perfection, priority, and enforcement of security interests in personal property. In 1999, NCCUSL and the ALI completed a major revision of Article 9, which every state has adopted. In 2010, several amendments to Article 9 were promulgated, with a delayed effective date of 2013. To date, nine states have adopted the amendments. This book references Article 9 prior to the 2010 amendments.

3. The UCC in Context

As you can see by the brief descriptions of each UCC article, the scope of the UCC is broad, applying to a wide range of transactions. There is not, in the UCC, a single "scope" provision which defines the *subject matter* to which the *entire* UCC applies. Instead, the UCC is divided into several articles as described above. The precise scope of each article must usually be determined by examining not merely a specific "scope" provision within the article (if there is one) but other provisions as well, some of which are definitions. While many of the articles of the UCC can, in relation to some kinds of transactions, apply separately and alone, frequently provisions from more than one article will be applicable to the transaction at hand. The UCC recognizes the possibilities of conflict between Articles, and includes provisions governing such possibilities. *See, e.g.,* UCC §§ 2-102, 3-102, 4-102(a), 8-103(d), 9-109, 9-110.

Despite its seemingly wide sweep, the UCC is far from comprehensive. There are some transactions it does not govern at all. There are also many aspects of covered transactions which, for the reasons noted below, the UCC instead defers to some other source of law.

First, the parties can generally make their own "law." They do so expressly through agreement, implicitly through their actions and course of dealing, and collectively through custom and resultant usage of trade.[19] By their own agreement,

---

[19] Commercial law, by definition, concerns commercial enterprise where customs and modes of interaction between business people evolve over time. This history has an effect on how people understand the agreements they have made and also influences the development of the commercial law itself.

then, the parties to a commercial deal can vary the effect of many of the provisions of the UCC. *See* UCC §§ 1-302, 1-303.

Second, the UCC by its own terms does not purport to control many types of transactions that can fairly be called commercial. For example, it does not apply to sales of commercial realty or to security interests therein. It does not apply to the formation, performance, and enforcement of insurance contracts. It does not apply to suretyship transactions (except where a surety is a party to a negotiable instrument or involved in a secured transaction). It does not encompass the law of bankruptcy. It does not govern legal tender.

Third, there are state statutes, most of which are regulatory in nature, which either supplement or supersede UCC provisions altogether. *See* UCC §§ 2-102, 9-201(b), (c) (referencing the possible existence of such statutes). Usury laws and so-called "Lemon Laws" are common examples.[20]

Fourth, the Uniform Commercial Code is *state* law. There is a large body of *federal* law that supplements state commercial law in general and the UCC in particular.[21] More important, several federal statutes and treaties supercede or preempt portions of the UCC.[22] Of particular note to the sale of goods is the United Nations Convention on the International Sale of Goods (CISG), which has been ratified by the United States and over 70 other countries, including Canada and Mexico. Unless otherwise agreed, the CISG applies to contracts for sale of goods between private commercial parties (not consumers) whose places of business are

---

[20] Lemon laws are discussed in Chapter Eight. Another fairly common example is the right of consumers to rescind certain transactions for a brief period of time. *E.g.*, Va. Code Ann. § 59.1-21.3 (involving in-home sales); *see also* 16 C.F.R. § 429.1 (providing a similar rule for door-to-door sales of consumer goods and services). Others are less common state and local rules, for which careful lawyers must always be on the lookout. *See, e.g.*, *Consolidated Aluminum Corp. v. Krieger*, 710 S.W.2d 869 (Ky. Ct. App. 1986) (in an Article 2 transaction, applied a statute that invalidates contract clauses printed below the signature line unless referenced above the signature line).

[21] For example, the federal Food, Drug, and Cosmetic Act (codified at 21 U.S.C. § 301 *et seq.*) imposes controls on the quality of goods sold and on the ways they are marketed. The Robinson-Patman Act (codified at 15 U.S.C. §§ 13a, 13b and 21a) operates to regulate the price of some goods.

[22] Thus, for example, the federal Consumer Credit Protection Act (codified at 15 U.S.C. §§ 1601–1693r), the Magnuson-Moss Warranty Act (codified at 15 U.S.C. §§ 2301–2312), and the federal Insecticide, Fungicide, and Rodenticide Act (codified at 7 U.S.C. §§ 136–136v) all preempt parts of Article 2.

in different nations, if both nations have ratified the convention. *See* CISG Art. 1(a). Thus, the CISG, and not the UCC, would apply when an Illinois corporation buys goods from a Canadian supplier or sells goods to a Mexican buyer, unless the parties opt out of application of the CISG. CISG Art. 6. The CISG, however, does not purport to be a complete statement of international law principles that govern an international sale of goods.[23] CISG Art. 7(2). Thus, some domestic principles of law may apply even in a transaction otherwise governed by the CISG.[24]

Other international conventions or model laws may have an effect on commercial transactions.[25] Of particular note for the subject of international sales contracts is the UNIDROIT Principles of International Commercial Contracts, a statement of international contract law principles. These principles were originally promulgated in 1994 and updated and reissued in 2004. These principles are not a treaty but represent a body of rules that parties can choose by agreement to apply to their transaction. A working group is currently considering additional provisions.

Fifth, the UCC does not even purport to govern exhaustively all aspects of the transactions to which its provisions do apply. Resort to supplemental common-law doctrines and equitable principles outside the UCC is often necessary and is expressly authorized. *See generally* UCC § 1-103. The importance of this cannot

---

[23] *See* Franco Ferrari, *What Sources of Law for Contracts for the International Sale of Goods? Why One has to Look Beyond the CISG*, 25 INT'L REV. L. & ECON. 314 (2005); Filip De Ly, *Sources of International Sales Law: An Eclectic Model*, 25 J. L. & COM. 1 (2005).

[24] For an example of a court considering whether certain legal or equitable principles are preempted by the CISG, *see Geneva Pharms. Tech. Corp. v. Barr Labs., Inc.*, 201 F. Supp. 2d 236, 286–87 (S.D.N.Y. 2002) (promissory estoppel as alleged in case not preempted by the CISG even though the CISG was governing law), *rev'd in part on other grounds*, 386 F.3d 485 (2d Cir. 2004).

[25] Four ready examples are: (i) the Convention on the Limitation Period in the International Sale of Goods (1974) as amended by the Protocol of April 11, 1980 (ratified by 20 countries, including the United States); (ii) the Convention on International Financial Leasing (ratified by ten countries, signed but not yet ratified by ten more, including the United States); (iii) the Convention on the Use of Electronic Communications in International Contracts (signed by 18 countries but not yet ratified by any); and (iv) the UNIDROIT Draft Model Law on Leasing, finalized in November, 2008. To view these and other international conventions and to determine what countries are bound by them, *see* http://www.uncitral.org and http://www.unidroit.org.

be overstated.[26] Dozens of doctrines and centuries of jurisprudence remain relevant. In some places the UCC text or comments expressly note this.[27] In others, the point is implicit though the UCC's adoption of a common-law term.[28] Nevertheless, even when there is no explicit or implicit reference to other legal concepts in the UCC, supplemental rules of law may apply.[29]

Finally, and most important, is a point that relates to all the others. Commercial transactions do not fall neatly under one legal regime. In the real world, even simple transactions do not necessarily fall within the scope of a single law school course. Commercial law may be based upon contract law and principles, but it is far broader. It encompasses property-law concepts, tort rules, and agency principles. It also includes a whole host of national and international regulations.

To illustrate the breadth of legal principles that a simple commercial transaction may implicate, assume a manufacturer agreed to sell a warehouse full of toasters to

---

[26] The authors of the main hornbook on the UCC have stated, in an earlier edition, that "[s]ection 1-103 is probably the most important single provision in the Code." JAMES J. WHITE & ROBERT S. SUMMERS, UNIFORM COMMERCIAL CODE § 2, at p. 6 & § 5, at p. 19 (3d ed. 1988). In addition to substantive legal principles outside of the UCC, the procedural law relevant to resolving disputes is an important part of the practice of commercial law. In the event there is a dispute in a transaction, the resolution of that dispute may be as much a matter of having the relevant evidence and the allocation of the burden of proof as it is of determining and applying the legal principles. Knowledge of the rules of evidence and civil procedure thus will also influence the transactional lawyer as well as the lawyer involved in dispute resolution. For the most part, the UCC does not deal with such evidentiary and procedural issues.

[27] *See, e.g.,* UCC § 1-204 (defining "value" to include "any consideration sufficient to support a simple contract"), § 1-308(b) & cmt. 3 (referencing the doctrine of accord and satisfaction); § 2-318 cmt. 3 (referring to the common-law rules on privity of contract).

[28] *See, e.g., D.O.M. Farms v. Nakamoto,* 718 P.2d 262 (Colo. Ct. App. 1986) (concerning "breach"); *Neptune Research & Development, Inc. v. Teknics Indus. Systems, Inc.,* 563 A.2d 465 (N.J. Super. Ct. App. Div. 1989) ("substantial impairment" means the same as "material breach" in the RESTATEMENT (SECOND) OF CONTRACTS, and thus can include delay if time is of the essence, even though the contract did not say it was); *Mullan v. Quickie Aircraft Corp.,* 797 F.2d 845 (10th Cir. 1986) (because "unconscionable" is undefined in the UCC, courts must look to the common law).

[29] *See, e.g., Hopper Dev., Inc. v. John T. Arnold & Assocs., Inc.,* 163 P.3d 385 (Kan. Ct. App. 2007) (promissory estoppel principles may provide an exception to the writing requirement of the statute of frauds).

a retailer. What legal issues may arise in this very simple transaction? At what point does the retailer acquire property rights in the toasters? This point might be particularly important if the retailer purported to sell the toasters before paying the manufacturer for them. Does the manufacturer incur tort liability to persons other than the retailer, such as buyers and users of the toasters, when the retailer further distributes the toasters and those persons are injured when the toasters malfunction? Under what circumstances would the retailer's agent or employee incur liability to the manufacturer if the retailer fails to pay? What if the manufacturer or retailer wants to sell the toasters outside the country in which the toasters are manufactured? Are there export restrictions in the country of manufacture? Are there import restrictions in the country to which the toasters will be sent? A transactional lawyer must be able to think beyond one area of law and see how issues may arise under a multitude of areas of law that are separately studied in law school.

C. Statutory Interpretation

Using a statute such as the UCC to help structure a transaction or to anticipate issues that may arise in litigation can be a challenging endeavor. The methodology of statutory interpretation is both similar to and different from the process you have used in reading cases to understand common-law principles. It is similar in that it requires attention to detail and nuances of language. But it is different in that there is often a lot less explanation of what the text means. Most judicial opinions, no matter how complex the issues, have three main components: a brief story, after which the court says what it is doing and identifies the reasons for its actions. In other words, most judicial opinions provide context, apply a rule to that context, and explain why. Statutes, on the other hand, give you only one-third of this: they tell you merely the rule. They typically provide no obvious context for their application. They also usually provide no rationale for their rules or guidance on how to apply them. Yet without those additional things, you cannot truly understand the statute. You need to understand the context and appreciate the purpose of each rule, yet you have to supply those things for yourself.

So how do you begin? Not surprisingly, you should start with the text of the statute. The paramount rule of statutory interpretation is read it all, then read it again. Pay attention to each word. Parse out each provision, so that you understand it grammatically. Understand the syntax (to which clause, phrase, or word does each modifier relate). Sometimes the cadence (where to pause) of a clause is not clear, so try different possibilities. As you do so, the meaning may become more clear.

Once you have a linguistic understanding of a clause or phrase, try to provide the relevant context. Hypothesize. Imagine a situation to which the provision at issue might apply. Then test that paradigm against the language of the statute. Then pause to make sure the result makes sense. If not, there is a strong possibility – although by no means a certainty – that you are misreading the provision.

Now discard your initial paradigm. Imagine other situations to which the provision might also apply. This helps to make sure that your initial paradigm is not too limited. Then imagine similar or related situations to which the provision does not apply. Test these against the language of the statute and question whether it makes sense for the small differences in facts to yield a different result. This helps ensure that your initial paradigm is not too broad.

To take an example that seems simple on its face, but is more complex the deeper you go, read UCC § 2-102 up to the semicolon. What is a "transaction in goods"? In thinking about those three words, what questions do you need to ask and answer? Perhaps, what is a "transaction"?, what are "goods"?, and what is a "transaction *in* goods?" How do you begin to track down more information that would help you answer those questions? The temptation to think that you know what a word means and that this meaning applies to the word when used in the statute should be resisted.

This leads directly to the second rule of statutory interpretation: find the definitions. Beginners to the UCC (or to statutory construction in general) sometimes overlook the possibility that terminology in a particular section may be defined elsewhere in that section, in another section, or even in another Article. In fact, the UCC includes more than the usual quota of definitions and even a relatively mundane word may be statutorily defined, occasionally in a surprising way. For example, in the UCC "purchase" includes a gift, *see* UCC § 1-201(b)(29), and "goods" can include the unborn offspring of animals, *see* UCC § 2-105(1). Thus, the first step in interpreting or construing a statutory provision is to define the key terms.

There are a number of places in the UCC to check for such definitions. Section 1-201 contains 43 definitions, and is applicable to every article of the Code. Additionally, each article contains definitions of terms for purposes of that article; such definitions usually are near the beginning of the article. *E.g.,* UCC §§ 2-103, 2-104, 2-105, 2-106. *See also* UCC §§ 2A-103, 3-103, 4-104, 4-105, 9-102, 9-103, 9-104, 9-105, 9-106 & 9-107. Finally, in Articles 2 and 2A, there are cross references at the end of the "Official Comment" to each section. However, you should not depend on these references to be exhaustive. For example, section 2-316(2) details when the implied warranty of merchantability may be disclaimed and requires that written exclusions or modifications of the warranty be "conspicuous." The definitional cross references neglect to indicate that "conspicuous" is defined in section 1-201(b)(10). Do not assume that a word is undefined. Reach that conclusion reluctantly, only after you look in all the places the word may be defined and find nothing.

This process of determining the meaning of statutory language must be done in reference to the purposes of the entire statute or the particular statutory provision. Overall, the UCC "must be liberally construed and applied to promote its underlying purposes and policies which are: (1) to simplify, clarify, and modernize the law governing commercial transactions; (2) to permit the continued expansion of commercial practices through custom, usage, and agreement of the parties; and (3) to make uniform the law among the various jurisdictions." UCC § 1-103. Thus, if you reach an interpretation that would seem to run contrary to these stated objectives, you should reconsider it. Similarly, if your interpretation would frustrate the parties' reasonable expectations or put a loss on the party least able to avoid it, there may be a better interpretation.

Next, you should consider how the section you are analyzing fits in with the other sections in the same statute. A statutory scheme such as the UCC is an interrelated set of rules. Each section has a relationship to the other sections of the same statutory scheme. The job of a careful lawyer is to figure out how each section relates to all of the other sections in that enactment. The lawyer must build a blueprint of how the entire statutory structure fits together. This is important in order to come to a complete understanding of even the seemingly most simple section that may apply to a particular set of facts.

Finally – after your own textual analysis, not before – you should look for interpretations of the relevant statutory language in court or administrative decisions, legislative history, and legal scholarship. This inquiry may provide information about how the language has been perceived by those who wrote it, enacted it, applied it, or thought about it. Language has inherent ambiguity of varying degrees and this research may help you identify those ambiguities. It may confirm your initial understanding or lead to a change in your thinking. However, no matter what those sources say or fail to say, they do not excuse you from considering problems the statutory text may pose in light of the fact situation you are concerned about, whether that fact situation be litigation you are involved in or a transaction that you are attempting to structure.

A word of caution. Study of the UCC in law school is of the uniform version. However, the UCC is merely a model designed for enactment at the state level. Each state legislature, as it considers an article of the UCC for enactment, decides whether to adopt the uniform version or whether it should enact a modified version of the uniform text. As you study the UCC in its uniform version, remember that the law in any particular state may be different. When you give advice to a client, you should never rely on the uniform version, but always look at the version as enacted by the applicable state. Given that the UCC has a uniform version and slightly non-uniform versions that are enacted by each state, it is somewhat unique in that there are several kinds of "legislative history" relevant to interpreting it, each posing its own special problems. The four types of such history are: (1) Official Comments, (2) prior versions of the UCC, (3) legislative hearings and reports made prior to enactment in specific states, and (4) books and articles by the UCC drafters.

Official Comments. As promulgated by the ALI and NCCUSL, the Official Text of the UCC appears with comments on each section. These comments often provide valuable information about the purpose or scope of a particular provision. Bear in mind, however, that state legislators enact only the statutory text (with whatever amendments they choose to make to the Official Text), not the Official Comments. Indeed, some of the comments were not yet written when the sections to which they relate were enacted. Similarly, the Permanent Editorial Board occasionally modifies a comment long after the statutory text has been enacted. Accordingly, the Official Comments do not have the force of law and, in the event of a conflict between the Official Text and the comments, the Official Text controls. In a conflict between the Official Text and the state-enacted statutory text, the state-enacted text controls.

Even when there is no conflict, the comments should not be blindly accepted at face value. For some important portions of the UCC, the person who drafted the comments was not the person who drafted the statutory text to which they relate. Perhaps most telling, the reporter and chair of the drafting committee have control over the comments but the drafting committee has control over the statutory text. Thus, on occasion, the reporter may put into a comment a point that the drafting committee expressly rejected from the text.[30]

---

[30] Karl N. Llewellyn, *Why A Commercial Code?*, 22 TENN. L. REV. 779, 782, 784 (1953) ([W]hen we weren't allowed to put in where we wanted to go . . . , we at least got the thing set up so that we are allowed to state in accompanying comments where the particular sections are trying to go. . . . I am ashamed of it in some ways; there are so many pieces that

Still, the Comments have influenced many judicial decisions and will continue to do so.[31] That they are not entitled to exactly the same weight as true legislative history may, therefore, be unimportant.

Earlier Versions of the UCC. Earlier versions of the UCC may serve as a source of guidance in resolving problems of interpretation and construction. However, inferences based on changes in the language of successive revisions of UCC sections are inherently unreliable; the change in language may or may not indicate a change in meaning. Indeed, a comment to a section in the 1952 text expressly noted that "[p]rior drafts of text and comments may not be used to ascertain legislative intent" because "frequently matters have been omitted as being implicit without statement and language has been changed or added solely for clarity." Ironically, this section itself was eventually deleted from the Official Text of the UCC. It should have been left in.[32]

Despite this admonition, lawyers should be aware of the existence and content of earlier drafts. In particular, it is worth noting that shortly after the UCC was proposed, between 1953 and 1955, the New York Law Revision Commission made a thorough study of the UCC and recommended many changes in the official text. In 1956, the Editorial Board of the UCC revised the earlier Official Text, drawing largely from the criticisms made at the New York Law Revision Commission Hearings. This history, in particular, can be a useful interpretive tool.[33]

I could make a little better, there are so many beautiful ideas I tried to get in that would have been good for the law, but I was voted down"). *See generally* Robert H. Skilton, *Some Comments on the Comments to the Uniform Commercial Code,* 1966 WIS. L. REV. 597; Grant Gilmore, *On the Difficulties of Codifying Commercial Law*, 57 YALE L. J. 1341 (1948).

[31] *See* Sean M. Hannaway, Note, *The Jurisprudence and Judicial Treatment of the Comments to the Uniform Commercial Code*, 75 CORNELL L. REV. 962 (1990).

[32] For a view that the legislative history is critical to interpretation of the UCC, *see* John M. Breen, *Statutory Interpretation and the Lessons of Llewellyn*, 33 LOY. L.A. L. REV. 263 (2000). Access to prior versions of uniform acts as they go through a revision process is now facilitated by the internet. For example, earlier drafts of Article 2 as it went through the decades-long revision provision can be accessed through http://www.law.upenn.edu/bll/ulc/ulc_frame.htm. Final versions of the revised UCC articles may be obtained from the ALI or are available in commercially printed statutory compilations.

[33] *See generally* Robert Braucher, *The Legislative History of the Uniform Commercial Code,* 58 COLUM. L. REV. 798 (1958). An extensive treatment of the major research sources on the UCC is Igor I. Kavass, *Uniform Commercial Code Research: A Brief Guide to the Sources,*

Legislative History of Enactment in Particular State. Another relevant resource in resolving problems of UCC interpretation are the records of legislative hearings, committee reports, and state bar association reports. These do not exist in each state, but where they do, they form the more immediate background of UCC enactment in the state in which they arose. They can be particularly valuable in ascertaining the purpose of any nonuniform amendments.

Books and Other Commentary. As is true for any legal issue, books and articles authored by experts – those who teach the subject and those who practice in the area – can be useful in resolving interpretive problems. For the UCC, this type of scholarship is accompanied by books and articles written by those involved in the drafting. Almost every dispute that reaches an appellate court is accompanied by citations to treatises or law review articles expressing opinions on the issue.[34]

Once you have completed your own textual analysis and exhausted your research, there may still be interpretive questions that remain. Sometimes none of the sources you have found addresses the problem you have identified. Other times the authorities disagree or do not provide a convincing analysis. In these cases, you should look for a tie-breaker, a structuring policy that you can resort to solve the issue. This policy might be found in the policies stated in UCC § 1-103 or those immanent in contemporary views of social welfare or justice.

SECTION 2.   TRANSACTION TYPES

One of the first tasks for a lawyer involved in a commercial transaction – whether in the pre-transaction phase or the dispute resolution phase – is to ascertain what law or laws govern. This is critical because it can affect almost every aspect of the transaction and significantly impact the parties' rights and responsibilities. If the lawyer reaches a wrong conclusion about the law that applies, almost every decision the lawyer makes will be wrong or at least questionable.

---

88 COM. L.J. 547 (1983). *See also* ELIZABETH SLUSSER KELLY, UNIFORM COMMERCIAL CODE DRAFTS (1984).

[34] *See* JAMES J. WHITE AND ROBERT S. SUMMERS, THE UNIFORM COMMERCIAL CODE (5th ed. 2006 & Supp. 2008); WILLIAM D. HAWKLAND, UNIFORM COMMERCIAL CODE SERIES (2008).

As you can see from the description of the various UCC articles, there are often several possibilities just within the UCC itself, let alone all the other possible sources of law. So what should a lawyer consider in deciding what law governs? Four principal factors:

(i) The type of property or other subject matter of the transaction (*e.g.,* goods, real estate, services, intellectual property, accounts receivable);

(ii) The nature or extent of the rights being transferred (*e.g.,* a sale, lease, license, lien, bailment, gift);

(iii) The location of the parties to the transaction; and

(iv) What, if anything, the parties' agreement says about governing law.

The following chart summarizes *some* of the possibilities based on the first two factors.

THE LAW GOVERNING VOLUNTARY
TRANSFERS OF PROPERTY RIGHTS

Type of Transfer	Type of Property				
	Real Estate	Goods	Securities (stocks & bonds)	Commercial Paper	Intellectual Property
Sale	real estate law	UCC Art. 2 or CISG	UCC Art. 8 or securities laws	UCC Arts. 3 & 4	UCC Art. 2, state common law, or federal
Gift	real estate law	common law	UCC Art. 8	UCC Arts. 3 & 4	state common law or federal law
Lease or License	real estate law	UCC Art. 2A	UCC Art. 8 or federal law	N/A	state common law or federal law
Security Interest or Mortgage	real estate law	UCC Art. 9	UCC Art. 9	UCC Arts. 3, 4 & 9	UCC Art. 9 or federal law
Bequest or Devise	real estate law or law of wills	law of wills	UCC Art. 8 or law of wills	law of wills	law of wills or federal law

In analyzing a transaction or proposed transaction, we suggest that you examine these factors in the order presented. And for the moment, let us focus on the first factor: the nature of what is being transferred. Most of the time, this will be easy to ascertain. On occasion, however, it can be exceptionally difficult and even controversial. Consider the following example.

Example

You are the lawyer for Steadman Appliances, Inc., which is located in Dearborn, Michigan. You have been asked to draft a standard form purchase agreement for your client's use in its business. Steadman wants to use the form for a typical transaction such as selling and installing new gas stoves and refrigerators in individual customers' houses. Most of the customers are located in Michigan, but some are in nearby Ohio or Indiana, and some are located in Ontario, Canada. The stoves and refrigerators have software as part of the control circuitry. They also come with a one-year, in-home service warranty. Steadman typically supplies the new stove and refrigerator selected by the customer and delivers it to the house, placing it in the location the customer designates. Sometimes Steadman will have to run a gas line to the stove location or run a water pipe to the refrigerator location in order to supply water for the automatic ice maker.

In order to draft the standard form, you need to determine the governing law so that you have the right set of rules to guide the risk allocation you need to think about. The possibilities include UCC Article 2, UCC Article 2A, non-UCC domestic law (such as real estate law or the common law of contracts), the CISG, and Canadian law (at least as to Canadian customers). Is the subject matter of the transaction goods, software, or services? The first step is to read the scope provisions of the possibly applicable statutes and treaties to determine if the transaction falls within any of them. If none of the statutes or treaties applies, then you must consider what other law will govern, such as some state's common law or Canadian law.

Let's start with Article 2. Read section 2-102 which states that Article 2 applies to "transactions in goods." What do you need to think about to determine if Article 2 will govern this type of contract? First consider "goods." Is there any doubt that stoves and refrigerators in Steadman's inventory are goods? There should be. After all, in many cases the appliances will become fixtures of the customer's real estate upon installation. When you deal with a statute, such as the UCC, you must be careful and look for definitions. Read section 2-105(1), which defines "goods." Note how opaque the definition is. Among other things, it refers to things that are movable "at the time of identification to the contract for sale." What does this mean? When is property "identified to the contract"? That question is answered in section 2-501. Statutes often have many interrelated provisions, and you need to review all of them to reach reliable conclusions. You might ask, "but how was I supposed to know to look to at section 2-501?" See the cross-references after the comments to section 2-105. Section 2-501 is listed there in reference to "point 1."

But even after all this, you should not be done. Consider how the client may conduct its business. Perhaps on occasion Steadman will purport to sell an appliance that has been backordered and has not yet been manufactured. Would Article 2 apply to such a transaction? Read sections 2-105(2) and 2-106(1). Collectively, they refer to four concepts: a present sale, a future sale, existing goods, and future goods. The intersection of those four concepts creates at least four possible transactions: (i) a present sale of existing goods; (ii) a purported present sale of future goods, (iii) a future sale of existing goods, and (iv) a future sale of future goods. Are all of these transactions within the scope of Article 2?

Okay, now it is time for a few problems.

Problem 1-1

A. Adroit Industries Inc. sells medical supplies to hospitals and recently converted to a totally green environment by installing solar panels for its power needs. To which of the transactions, if any, does Article 2 apply?
   1. Selling radioactive isotopes suspended in solution for the purpose of nuclear imaging.
   2. Selling oxygen to fill the hospital's oxygen tanks.
   3. Selling to the local utility the excess electricity generated from Adroit's solar panels.

B. Benjamin recently purchased the following four items in four separate transactions. To which of the transactions, if any, does Article 2 apply?
   1. A 1908 Indian Eagle $2.5 gold coin for $2,500.00.

2. 500 euros (ten 50-euro notes) from Bank for use on an upcoming vacation in Florence, Italy.
3. 100,000 Japanese yen through his investment broker. The yen are credited to Benjamin's brokerage account.
4. 1,000 shares of Microsoft stock, in certificated form. Benjamin has possession of the certificate.

C. Cheyenne Industries, Inc. recently purchased the following four items in four separate transactions. To which of the transactions, if any, does Article 2 apply?
   1. A building from Lumber Yard. Lumber Yard is responsible for removing the building from its concrete foundation and putting it on skids. Cheyenne Industries is responsible for hauling the building away. *See* UCC § 2-107(1).
   2. All the timber standing on Forester's land. Cheyenne Industries is responsible for cutting and removing the timber. *See* UCC § 2-107(2).
   3. All the oil and natural gas that Cheyenne can find and remove underneath Jed Clampett's property.
   4. 20 gallons of gasoline from Service Station for one of Cheyenne's trucks.

Let us return to the example of Steadman Appliances. Even if you conclude that the stoves and refrigerators it sells are normally "goods" within the meaning of Article 2, does it matter that Steadman is not merely selling the items but also providing the service of installing them and promising to repair them if necessary? If the transaction were for services, only – such as if Steadman were hired to install appliances that its customers acquired from someone else or to fix appliances the customer already owned – then Article 2 would not apply.[35] In that circumstance, the common law of contracts would apply to the services.

---

[35] If you question this statement by noting that Article 2 applies to "transactions in goods," *see* UCC § 2-102, and posit that installation or repair services might well be a "transaction in goods," then you are on the right track. In fact, though, while Article 2 does apply to transactions in goods, most of its provisions apply only to sales of goods. *See* UCC § 2-106(1).

This difference in applicable law would not matter except for the fact that the rules in Article 2 and the rules at common law are likely to differ in some significant respects. These differences may include the rules on whether and when a contract is formed, the standard for measuring the quality of the promised performance, and what the applicable remedies are for non-performance or substandard performance. So, how then are we to deal with mixed transactions involving both a sale of goods and the provision of services? Does Article 2 apply to the whole transaction, part of the transaction, or not at all?

This is one issue on which the Code itself is silent. Most courts apply what is known as the "predominant purpose test." Under this test, courts ask whether the predominant purpose of the transaction was the provision of goods, in which case Article 2 applies, or the provision of services, in which event Article 2 does not apply. Factors that courts tend to recite as relevant to that inquiry include: (i) the contract language; (ii) the nature of the supplier's business; and (iii) the value of the materials and services provided under the contract. For the most part, courts state the facts and then declare an answer, without providing an analysis that is useful to other fact patterns. Perhaps because of this, they have reached conflicting results.[36]

Another type of mixed transaction is one involving both the provision of goods and software. Some courts have held that software is a "good" and thus a transfer of software is covered by Article 2. Others have disagreed.[37] This problem is also complicated by the increase in so called "smart goods": goods with one or more computer chips and integrated software. Many cars now come equipped with a computer to monitor and run various systems of the car. Smaller smart goods have become ubiquitous. Virtually all hand-held data organizers, cell phones, digital cameras, and microwave ovens have built-in software. Should the predominate purpose test be used to determine whether Article 2 governs a transaction in which

---

[36] *See* WILLIAM D. HAWKLAND, UNIFORM COMMERCIAL CODE SERIES § 2-102:4 (2008).

[37] On the side of applying Article 2, *see, e.g., Olcott Intern. & Co. v. Micro Data Base Sys., Inc.*, 793 N.E.2d 1063 (Ind. Ct. App. 2003); *Sagent Tech., Inc. v. Micros Sys., Inc.*, 276 F. Supp. 2d 464 (D. Md. 2003); *Micro Data Base Sys., Inc. v. Dharma Sys., Inc.*, 148 F.3d 649 (7th Cir. 1998); *Advent Sys., Ltd. v. Unisys Corp.*, 925 F.2d 670 (3d Cir. 1991). On the side of not applying Article 2, *see, e.g., Specht v. Netscape Communic'ns Corp.*, 306 F.3d 17 (2d Cir. 2002) (doubting whether Article 2 applied to downloaded software); *Pearl Inv. LLC v. Standard I/O, Inc.*, 257 F. Supp. 2d 326 (D. Me. 2003); *Multi-Tech Sys., Inc. v. Floreat, Inc.*, 2002 WL 432016 (D. Minn. 2002).

both goods and software are provided?[38] Even if Article 2 would apply to the software, federal intellectual property law will also apply to any license of software that is the subject of a patent or a copyright.

Problem 1-2

Danielle recently purchased the following four items in four separate transactions. To which of the transactions, if any, does Article 2 apply?

A. New book from Bookstore.

B. A new music CD from Music Retailer.

C. A song downloaded onto her MP3 player from Internet Company.

D. New word processing software (to replace the software she currently uses but hates) from Software Retailer. The software comes on three CDs in a box with a manual.

Not every jurisdiction has adopted the "predominant purpose" test to deal with transactions involving both goods and services. The most notable alternative —sometimes called the "gravamen of the claim test" – was formulated in *Anthony Pools v. Sheehan*, 455 A.2d 434, 441 (Md. 1983).[39] In essence, that test asks whether the claim relates to the goods or to the services. If it relates to the goods,

---

[38] *See* PRINCIPLES OF THE LAW OF SOFTWARE CONTRACTING § 1.07 (Tentative Draft No. 1, March 24, 2008). The American Law Institute has sponsored production of the "Principles of the Law of Software Contracting" which addresses contract principles in the context of software licensing. As a "principles" project, it does not have the force of law and instead is primarily a statement of principles that courts can consider when confronted with legal issues germane to software contracting. For a discussion of that project see Maureen A. O'Rourke, *An Essay on the Challenges of Drafting a Uniform Law of Software Contracting*, 10 LEWIS & CLARK L. REV. 925 (2006).

[39] *See also J.O. Hooker & Sons, Inc. v. Roberts Cabinet Co.*, 683 So.2d 396, 400 (Miss. 1996) (stating that the test in a mixed transaction – a construction contract – turned on the nature of the contract and "upon whether the *dispute* in question primarily concerns the goods furnished or the services rendered under the contract").

Article 2 applies; if it relates to the services, Article 2 does not apply. More specifically, the court ruled that even when services predominate, if the goods supplied (a diving board) were unmerchantable and caused loss (personal injuries), Article 2 could be applied both to impose an implied warranty of merchantability and to determine whether a clause purporting to disclaim the implied warranty of merchantability was enforceable. The court stressed that the goods had to be supplied under a commercial transaction, rather than a contract for professional services, and must "retain their character . . . after completion of the performance promised." *Id.*

While the gravamen of the claim test has some appeal, it is subject to the same major criticism frequently leveled on the predominant purpose test: it is difficult to apply. Specifically, how are courts and parties to determine if the claim relates to the goods or to the services? For example, if your new contact lenses irritate your eyes, is it because the lenses are defective or the optometrist erred in measuring your eyes? Moreover, what if the dispute does not involve damages from an allegedly nonconforming tender, but something entirely different, such as contract formation, parol evidence, or the Statute of Frauds? Should Article 2 apply then or not? Perhaps for these reasons, the gravamen of the claim test has not had much traction; the predominant purpose test remains the prevailing approach in most states.

Problem 1-3

A. Are Steadman Appliance's contracts with its U.S. customers governed by Article 2? Which of the facts provided are the most significant to the analysis of this question? What facts that you do not know would also be significant?

B. Superior Robotics, Inc. has agreed to design, build, and install a robotic welder in Bonneville Motors' assembly plant. The robot will be equipped with and controlled by custom software that Superior Robotics must write. Is this agreement governed by Article 2? Why or why not?

Now consider the phrase "unless the context otherwise requires" which is at the beginning of section 2-102. What does that phrase mean? Does it mean that even if the transaction is a "transaction in goods," there are contexts in which the court should not apply Article 2? As you study Article 2's substantive provisions, consider when it might be inappropriate to apply Article 2 to a transaction that otherwise concerns goods. For example, should Article 2 apply to a bailment of goods (where goods are deposited with a bailee for storage, transport, or other specified purpose) or to a lease of goods?

To continue our painstaking look at the language of section 2-102, consider the language after the semicolon. Article 2 does not apply to a transaction in goods "intended to operate only as a security transaction." Does the Official Comment explain what that phrase means?

Other law. The entire discussion so far on the scope of Article 2 has focused on section 2-102 and its reference to "transactions in goods." However, sometimes other law – outside the UCC – can affect or limit the coverage of Article 2. We have already seen that various state and federal laws supplement Article 2, often in important ways.[40] Indeed, section 2-102 recognizes this possibility in its last clause, which expressly provides that Article 2 does not "impair or repeal any statute regulating sales to consumers, farmers or other specified classes of buyers." More significantly, sometimes other laws render Article 2 wholly inapplicable. Consider the following problem, consulting the statutes that follow it as necessary.

Problem 1-4

A. Blood Bank, located in Washington, enters into an agreement with Hospital, located in Alaska, to supply Hospital with all the whole blood, plasma, and similar blood products it needs to perform surgeries and other medical procedures for the next three years. Is that agreement governed by Article 2?

B. Shylock, a resident of Kentucky, offers to sell one of her kidneys to the highest bidder, advertising that offer through an online auction website. The terms of the offer provide that the location of the surgery will be determined by mutual agreement, but that the high bidder must pay all of Shylock's expenses of traveling to that location. Is this transaction governed by Article 2? Does it matter if the high bidder is located in a different state, such as California?

---

[40] *See supra* notes 20–25 and accompanying text.

Alaska Statutes
§ 45.02.316 Exclusion or modification of warranties.
* * *

(e) Implied warranties of merchantability and fitness are not applicable to a contract for the sale of human blood, blood plasma or other human tissue or organs from a blood bank or reservoir of tissue or organs. The blood, blood plasma, tissue, or organs may not, for the purposes of this chapter, be considered commodities subject to sale or barter, but shall be considered medical services.

Revised Code of Washington
§ 70.54.120. Immunity from implied warranties and civil liability relating to blood, blood products, tissues, organs, or bones – Scope – Effective date.

The procurement, processing, storage, distribution, administration, or use of whole blood, plasma, blood products and blood derivatives for the purpose of injecting or transfusing the same, or any of them, or of tissues, organs, or bones for the purpose of transplanting them, or any of them, into the human body is declared to be, for all purposes whatsoever, the rendition of a service by each and every person, firm, or corporation participating therein, and is declared not to be covered by any implied warranty under the Uniform Commercial Code, Title 62A RCW, or otherwise, and no civil liability shall be incurred as a result of any of such acts, except in the case of wilful or negligent conduct: *Provided, however,* That this section shall apply only to liability alleged in the contraction of hepatitis, malaria, and acquired immune deficiency disease and shall not apply to any transaction in which the donor receives compensation: *Provided further,* That this section shall only apply where the person, firm or corporation rendering the above service shall have maintained records of donor suitability and donor identification: *Provided further,* That nothing in this section shall be considered by the courts in determining or applying the law to any blood transfusion occurring before June 10, 1971 and the court shall decide such case as though this section had not been passed.

Kentucky Revised Statutes

§ 311.171 Prohibitions and restrictions relating to transplantable organs.

(1) No person shall sell or make a charge for any transplantable organ.

(2) No person shall offer remuneration for a transplantable organ.

(3) No person shall broker for the sale or transfer of a transplantable organ.

(4) No person shall charge a fee associated with the transplantation of a transplantable organ in excess of the direct and indirect costs of procuring, preserving, distributing, or transplanting the transplantable organ.

(5) Nothing in this section shall be construed in any way to relate to the use, sale, distribution, procurement, preservation, distribution, experimentation, research, drug manufacture, or other treatment of any human or nonhuman part other than transplantable organs.

California Penal Code

§ 367f. Sale of human organ for transplantation; removal or transplant of organ with knowledge of sale; definitions; application; exceptions; punishment.

(a) Except as provided in subdivisions (d) and (e), it shall be unlawful for any person to knowingly acquire, receive, sell, promote the transfer of, or otherwise transfer any human organ, for purposes of transplantation, for valuable consideration.

(b) Except as provided in subdivisions (d), (e), and (f), it shall be unlawful to remove or transplant any human organ with the knowledge that the organ has been acquired or will be transferred or sold for valuable consideration in violation of subdivision (a).

(c) For purposes of this section, the following definitions apply:

(1) "Human organ" includes, but is not limited to, a human kidney, liver, heart, lung, pancreas, or any other human organ or nonrenewable or nonregenerative tissue except plasma and sperm.

(2) "Valuable consideration" means financial gain or advantage, but does not include the reasonable costs associated with the removal, storage, transportation, and transplantation of a human organ, or reimbursement for those services, or the expenses of travel, housing, and lost wages incurred by the donor of a human organ in connection with the donation of the organ.

* * *

(e) This section shall not apply to the person from whom the organ is removed, nor to the person who receives the transplant, or those persons' next-of-kin who assisted in obtaining the organ for purposes of transplantations.

* * *

(g) Any person who violates subdivision (a) or (b) shall be punished by a fine not to exceed fifty thousand dollars ($50,000), or by imprisonment in the state prison for three, four, or five years, or both.

CISG. In addition to preemptive state laws, there may be federal law that preempts Article 2. Recall the discussion of the CISG.[41] To what transactions involving goods does the CISG apply? Read Articles 1 through 6, and Article 10 of the CISG. Does Steadman Appliances have to worry about the CISG?

Problem 1-5

In each of these transactions, determine whether Article 2, the CISG, or some other law applies to the transaction. Detail all of your analytical steps.

A. Ahmad, a United States resident, placed a telephone order for a new computer from a Canadian manufacturer. The manufacturer agreed to ship the computer to Ahmad's home in Lansing, Michigan.

B. Bethlehem Steel, located in Pennsylvania, agreed to sell 500 steel frames to a Canadian building contractor. The goods are to be shipped by rail within ten days.

C. Controlled Heating Corp., a New York company, agreed to manufacture and install new heating units for Northern Lights, Inc., a Canadian company, at Northern Lights' office in Detroit, Michigan.

D. What difference, if any, would it make to the analysis of Part B if the parties had expressly provided that the law of Pennsylvania would govern the transaction? *See* UCC § 1-301.[42]

---

[41] *See supra* notes 23–24 and accompanying text.

[42] *See Travelers Prop. Cas. Co. of Am. v. Saint-Gobain Technical Fabrics Canada Ltd.*, 474 F. Supp. 2d 1075 (D. Minn. 2007) (selecting Minnesota law did not exclude application of CISG as part of the law of Minnesota).

SECTION 3.   STRUCTURING TRANSACTIONS

As mentioned above, transactional lawyers are often involved in preparing documentation to reflect the deal the parties have made. While the lawyer may inform the client of the applicable legal rules and advise the client how to comply with them, the lawyer must be prepared and have the drafting skills necessary to accurately and clearly reflect the deal the parties wish to make and to make sure that the documentation complies with applicable legal rules.

What are the hallmarks of good drafting? First and foremost, you must understand the deal. That means you must understand the client's business, what the client hopes to achieve, and any relevant usage of trade. You must know the difference between representations, warranties, covenants, and conditions, and be able to determine which of those should be used for each term of the deal.

Second, you must know the legal rules and the options that are available for allocating the risks of the transaction in accordance with the legal rules.

But this is merely the beginning. It relates only to the substance of the transaction. Good drafting is a skill that requires close attention to every word used, to make sure that the point expressed is the point intended. This, in turn, requires compliance with several important principles.

- Avoid ambiguity. Clauses should not be subject to multiple and different meanings. To help ensure this, observe the rules of grammar and punctuation. Tabulation and other formatting conventions can also help avoid confusion and make the meaning clear.
- Use consistent language. Always use the same words when you mean the same thing and never say the same thing if you mean something different.
- Provide a logical structure for the document; its provisions should relate to each other in a logical and cohesive manner. This helps avoid contradiction, which should never exist.
- Clearly identify and distinguish general rules from exceptions.
- Avoid legalese and convoluted language. Use short sentences with simple sentence structure.
- Use the active voice.

This book will provide you with several opportunities to draft contract clauses and to practice applying these seemingly simple principles. Here is the first such opportunity.

Problem 1-6

Return to the example with Steadman Appliances. Draft a choice-of-law clause for inclusion in the form agreement that will make Washington's UCC Article 2 apply to the transaction in its entirety, no matter who the customers are and no matter how the transaction is structured.

CHAPTER TWO

CONTRACT FORMATION AND BASIC TERMS

Once you determine what law governs a particular transaction (such as the common law of contracts, UCC Article 2, or the CISG), the next step is to determine whether an agreement was formed, if the parties have already dealt with one another, or how to form one, if you are planning a future transaction. If an agreement was or will be formed, the next issue is to determine if that agreement is in fact enforceable. That is, does the agreement form the basis of an enforceable contract? In connection with this, you need to ascertain what the terms of the agreement are.

Lawyers, particularly transactional lawyers, need to be aware of the rules and principles that govern these three issues – formation, enforceability, and terms – bearing in mind that the different potentially applicable bodies of law are likely to have different rules on these subjects. From a transactional perspective, the lawyer wants to be able to advise his or her client what is required to have an enforceable agreement and, just as important, how to avoid entering into an enforceable agreement.

This Chapter considers formation, enforceability and some very basic terms issues under both UCC Article 2 and the CISG. With this basic understanding, Chapters Three through Five then examine additional rules on contract terms in UCC Article 2 and the CISG. Later in this book, in Chapter Eleven, we investigate how UCC Article 2A deals with these issues in the context of leases.

SECTION 1.   CONTRACT FORMATION PRINCIPLES

A. Contract Formation under UCC Article 2

1. Basic Concepts

The place to begin any study of the principles of contract formation under the UCC is the definitions of "agreement" and "contract" in section 1-201. The two terms are related, but are different in several important respects. An *agreement* is the "bargain of the parties in fact." That bargain is typically evidenced by the parties' communications with each other. However, as suggested by the reference to course of performance, course of dealing, and usage of trade, their bargain may also be evidenced by the parties' conduct (either in the transaction at issue or in prior transactions between them) or from their participation in a common trade. *See* UCC § 1-303.

The *contract* consists of the parties' legal obligations resulting from their agreement. This can be both less and more than their agreement. A contract encompasses more than the agreement from which it arises whenever the law adds a term to the parties' bargain. For example, the warranty of merchantability may arise as a matter of law if the seller is a merchant with respect to the kind of goods sold in the transaction. *See* UCC §§ 2-314, 2-316. Article 2 has a variety of other "gap filler" rules designed to add detail to the parties' agreement. *See, e.g.,* UCC §§ 2-307, 2-308, 2-309, 2-310, 2-312, 2-315.

The contract is less than the agreement whenever all or part of the agreement is unenforceable. Thus, for example, an agreement for the sale of contraband is not a contract because it is not enforceable. Neither is an agreement that fails to satisfy the statute of frauds. *See* UCC § 2-201. An agreement with an unconscionable term may not be enforceable at all or may be enforceable without the offending term. *See* UCC § 2-302(1). In either case, the parties' contract is something less than their agreement.

It is worth noting that both "agreement" and "contract," because they are based on the parties' bargain, are broader than what the common law would traditionally regard as a contract. For example, the Restatement (Second) of Contracts defines a contract as a "promise or a set of promises for the breach of which the law gives a remedy." RESTATEMENT (SECOND) OF CONTRACTS § 1 (1981). Certainly the parties' bargain may consist of an exchange of explicit or implied promises. However, a bargain may also include the parties' consummated transaction. Consider the following.

Illustration

You go to a supermarket, select the items you want, proceed to the checkout counter, and pay for them. Arguably, at no time did either you or the store promise anything to the other. You tendered payment and completed a transaction, but arguably there were no promises. Thus, the common law would not regard this as a contract. The UCC does. There may not have been a promise, but there was a "bargain." Hence there was an "agreement." As long as there was no bar to enforceability – such as might be true if you were a minor purchasing cigarettes or alcohol – there would also be a "contract" within the meaning of the UCC.

At what point in time will the parties have engaged in enough discussion or conduct to create a "bargain in fact" which may be enforceable as a contract? The common-law construct with which you are familiar is that a contract is formed when there is an offer that is accepted, provided the promise is supported by consideration.[1] The rules regarding offer, acceptance, and consideration can be somewhat technical. They were no doubt explored in your contracts course, and that coverage will not be repeated here.

Article 2 begins with this common-law foundation to determine when a contract is formed. This reliance on the common law is evidenced by Article 2's failure to provide a complete set of rules on contract formation. Therefore, the common-law principles of offer and acceptance remain important for transactions governed by Article 2. Article 2 then builds upon this common-law foundation. The common law provides general principles governing contract formation, with several provisions of Article 2 providing different rules on a few points. These different rules are needed, at least in part, to account for the fact that Article 2's notion of a contract is based on the broader concept of a "bargain," rather than the more narrow concept of a "promise."

Article 2's rules on contract formation are contained in sections 2-204 *through* 2-207, and the starting point for examining them is section 2-204. Subsection (1) provides that a contract can be formed in any manner sufficient to show agreement.[2] Thus, while the parties may engage in offer and acceptance, as under the common law, there is no need for the parties to follow the formalities of an offer and acceptance to form an agreement, the bargain in fact of the parties. Subsection (2) then adds that we need not be able to point to the precise moment of formation, as long as we have agreement. This accounts for the fact that when parties have actually engaged in offer and acceptance, it is usually fairly easy to identify those communications, but when their bargain is evidenced in some other manner, such as by performance, it may be difficult to identify the precise moment when they reached agreement. Subsection (3) then adds an extremely important rule. It allows

---

[1] *See* RESTATEMENT (SECOND) OF CONTRACTS §§ 3, 17, 22.

[2] For an example of the factual nature of this inquiry, *see E.C. Styberg Eng'g Co. v. Eaton Corp.*, 492 F.3d 912 (7th Cir. 2007).

for a contract to be formed even though one or more terms of the transaction are left open, as long as there is a reasonable basis for providing a remedy in the event of breach. This represents a substantial deviation from the common law, which typically conditions formation of a contract on the parties having reached agreement on all the material terms.[3] In Chapters Three through Five we will examine the "gap filler" rules that UCC Article 2 uses to supplement an incomplete agreement.

These gap filler provisions are often critical to the requirement in section 2-204(3) that there be a "reasonably certain basis for giving an appropriate remedy" in order to create an enforceable agreement. Keep in mind that the need to resort to gap filler provisions arises only if the parties' bargain, as supplemented by applicable usage of trade, course of dealing, and course of performance, does not deal with a particular term. At common law, which lacks gap filler provisions, enforceable contracts require agreement on all the material terms.

Now read section 2-205. Under the common law, the offeror may generally revoke an offer any time before the offeree has accepted. A promise to keep an offer open is normally enforceable only if supported by consideration (so that there is, in essence, an option contract).[4] Section 2-205 provides an additional basis for making enforceable the promise to keep the offer open. Notice, this section does not purport to define what an offer is, and therefore implicitly relies on the common law to determine what qualifies as an offer.

Now read section 2-206. It too implicitly relies on the common-law rules regarding what constitutes an offer but contradicts old common-law rules on what qualifies as an acceptance. Specifically, paragraph (1)(a) abrogates the rules that presumed that an acceptance has to be sent in the same manner and medium as the offer.[5] An offeror may still specify the manner and medium of an acceptance. Paragraph (a) does not abrogate the common-law rule that the offeror is "master of its offer," it merely does away with the presumption that the acceptance must be transmitted in the same manner and medium as the offer. Paragraph (1)(b) does something more significant. It allows an offer to buy to be accepted either by a return promise or by performance: the shipment of goods. Even shipment of nonconforming goods can constitute an acceptance. By allowing the shipment of nonconforming goods to qualify as an acceptance, section 2-206 slightly modifies

---

[3] *See* RESTATEMENT (SECOND) OF CONTRACTS § 33.

[4] *See* RESTATEMENT (SECOND) OF CONTRACTS § 17(1). *Cf.* § 87.

[5] *Compare* RESTATEMENT (SECOND) OF CONTRACTS §§ 30, 60, 65.

the common-law distinction between a counter-offer and an acceptance.[6] Finally, subsection (2) gives the offeror the ability to treat the offer as lapsed if not notified of the acceptance within a reasonable time.[7]

Even though sections 2-204 through 2-206 provide rules regarding how a contract is formed, the parties are free to specify the circumstances that must exist in order to have an enforceable contract. *See* UCC § 1-302. For example, the parties may agree that they will not have a contract until both parties execute a writing containing all of the final terms.[8] Thus, Article 2 does not alter the fundamental contract principle that the parties may expressly determine the manner in which they will form an enforceable contract. Remember that we are addressing contract formation assuming the transaction is covered by Article 2. Later on we will consider contract formation using CISG principles. Now it is time for a few problems.

Problem 2-1

A. After reading Seller's catalogue of hi-fi equipment, Buyer orders a $470 amplifier by completing the order form included in the catalogue and faxing it to Seller. Upon Seller's receipt of the fax but prior to acknowledgment or shipment, is there an agreement?

B. Buyer faxes Seller an order for "1,000 lbs. of Grade A bananas at 25¢/lb., delivery by November 15, payment within 30 days after delivery."

   1. Seller faxes back a response that says, "Received your order. Expect to ship for delivery on November 10." Is there an agreement? If so, when is payment due?

   2. Instead of sending the response, Seller shipped Buyer 1,000 lbs. of Grade A bananas for delivery on November 10. Prior to delivery,

---

[6] *Compare* RESTATEMENT (SECOND) OF CONTRACTS §§ 39, 59, 61.

[7] *Compare* RESTATEMENT (SECOND) OF CONTRACTS § 56. *See also Scoular Co. v. Denney*, 151 P.3d 615 (Colo. Ct. App. 2006) (buyer's actions in reselling the goods was not the beginning of performance of the contract with the seller).

[8] *See, e.g., Flanagan v. Consolidated Nutrition, L.C.*, 627 N.W.2d 573 (Iowa Ct. App. 2001).

is there an agreement? If so, what are the payment terms? What if Seller shipped apples instead of bananas?

C. Seller faxes Buyer the following:

> Pleased to offer you 1,000 lbs. of Grade A cherries at 43¢/lb., delivery by November 15, payment within 30 days after delivery. E-mail or call me by end of the day if that's okay.

Buyer responds two days later with the following e-mail message:

> That sounds great. Look forward to delivery.

Is there an agreement? What if, after receiving Buyer's response, Seller ships the cherries?

D. Seller faxes Buyer the following:

> Pleased to offer you 500 lbs. of dates at 94¢/lb., delivery by November 15, payment within 30 days after delivery.

Buyer responds with the following message, also sent by fax:

> Price too high. Can't buy for more than 68¢/lb.

Is there an agreement? What if, after receiving Buyer's response, Seller ships the dates?

Problem 2-2

Sedgwick manufactures and sells bolts for use in airplane manufacture. The bolts are customarily sold by "lot," a term based on total weight.

A. On March 1, after some negotiations with Butler, but before Sedgwick had manufactured any bolts for Butler, Sedgwick sent Butler the following form in the mail:

> Will sell you ten (10) lots of No. 6 bolts for $2,000 per lot. This offer will be held open until March 15.

On March 14, Butler telephoned Sedgwick to accept the offer, but before Butler could say anything, Sedgwick said, "That offer I sent you is off the table. I can't sell you the bolts for that price." Butler protested that Sedgwick had promised to keep the offer open. Butler then stated she accepted the offer. Has a contract been formed?

B. On April 1, after some negotiations with Barker but before Sedgwick had manufactured any bolts for Barker, Sedgwick sent Barker a signed letter that stated:

> Will sell you ten (10) lots of No. 8 bolts for $2,000 per lot. This offer will be held open until April 15.

At the bottom of the letter was a line for the buyer to signify acceptance by affixing a signature. Barker signed the form on that line and mailed the form back to Sedgwick on April 6. On April 10, Barker bought bolts from another supplier and called Sedgwick, leaving a message on the answering machine that he would not be buying any bolts from Sedgwick. Is there a contract between Sedgwick and Barker?

C. On May 1, after some negotiations with Baxter but before Sedgwick had manufactured any bolts for Baxter, Sedgwick sent Baxter a preprinted form in the mail. The form had several paragraphs of standard sales terms. In the middle of the form was the following handwritten sentence:

> Baxter will buy ten (10) lots of No. 7 bolts for $2,000 per lot. This offer will be held open until May 15.

At the bottom of the form was a line for the buyer's signature. Baxter signed the form on that line and sent the form back to Sedgwick by mail on May 6. On May 10, Baxter bought bolts from another supplier and called Sedgwick, leaving a message on the answering machine that he would not be buying any bolts from Sedgwick. On May 11, Sedgwick called Baxter and purported to accept Baxter's offer to buy the bolts. Is there a contract between Sedgwick and Baxter?

D. After negotiation with Baker regarding the bolts that Baker needed for the type of plane that Baker makes, Sedgwick started to retool her manufacturing process to produce those bolts. About a week after that retooling process was started, Baker called Sedgwick to tell her that he was buying the bolts from someone else. Sedgwick sued Baker for breach of contract, arguing that by starting the retooling process, she had begun the requested performance and thereby accepted the offer to buy that Baker had made during the course of their negotiations. Assume that Baker indeed made an offer to buy. Is Sedgwick correct?

Problem 2-3

Stable Earth, Inc., a manufacturer of fertilizer, and Brittany, a farmer, had done business with each other for five years. When fertilizer was needed, Brittany would call the Stable Earth order desk and order a specific quantity and quality of fertilizer. Stable Earth's order desk would send that order to the warehouse, where personnel would ship the goods to Brittany by carrier, accompanied by a bill based on Stable Earth's current wholesale price. Frequently, Stable Earth would ship less or more than the amount Brittany ordered, depending upon what Stable Earth had on hand in the warehouse, but the deviation never exceeded 15%. The bill reflected the quantity actually shipped and Brittany invariably accepted and paid for what was actually shipped without objection. On July 10, during a time of price instability in the fertilizer market, Brittany used the website to order 500 bags of a specified fertilizer "for prompt shipment." The wholesale price on that date was $18 per bag. On July 12, Stable Earth shipped 400 bags of fertilizer to Brittany and mailed an invoice for the wholesale price on that date, $20 per bag. On July 15, while the goods were still in transit and the wholesale price was $25 per bag, Stable Earth notified Brittany that the order had been rejected and diverted the shipment to Carl, who agreed to pay $26 per bag. Brittany sued Stable Earth for breach of contract. Is there a contract between Brittany and Stable Earth? If so, what is the price per bag under the contract?

Problem 2-4

After reading Seller's catalogue of unique and expensive items, Buyer telephones Seller to order a brass eagle designed for mounting at the top of Buyer's flagpole. The price is $675, which Buyer pays by giving Seller Buyer's credit card number. Seller's catalogue contains the following in fairly large print on the order form, just below Seller's phone number:

> Seller warrants all its products will be as described in this catalogue. In the event of any problem with a shipment, customer must notify Seller in writing of such problem within 20 days of receipt or be barred from any remedy.

Prior to shipment, is there an agreement? If so, are the terms in the catalogue part of the agreement?

2. Battle of the Forms

The rules of sections 2-204 though 2-206 were arguably only minor variations from the prevailing common law when Article 2 was adopted in the 1950s and 1960s. The common-law rules today are generally in accord with these provisions of Article 2.[9] In contrast, section 2-207 was and remains a far more significant deviation of the common law. Consider this following typical scenario:

Illustration

Buyer sends Seller an order form which is an offer to buy. The form has on it numerous terms, including the description, quantity, and price of the desired goods. Seller responds by sending an order acknowledgment form which contains numerous terms, some different from those on the Buyer's form and some additional terms. The two forms match on the major transaction-specific terms: the description of the goods, quantity, and price.

At common law, Seller's responsive form was a counter-offer, not an acceptance. Thus, even though the parties may have thought they had an agreement – a likely situation given that neither party was apt to scrutinize and compare the terms on the two standardized forms – they did not. Accordingly, if at this point either reneged on their apparent deal, the other would have no legal recourse. On the other hand, if Buyer, thinking they had a deal, followed their communications by sending payment, Buyer would be deemed to have accepted Seller's counter-offer and a contract would be formed based on the terms in Seller's acknowledgment form. Alternatively, and probably more likely, if Seller (also thinking they had a deal) shipped the goods and Buyer accepted them, Buyer's conduct would again be an acceptance of the terms of Seller's counter-offer. Thus, in either case, the terms on Seller's form would control. Note, this result was not based on Seller's role in the transaction, but on the sequence of their communications. If Seller had sent the first offer and Buyer had responded with a form that included slightly different or additional terms, then subsequent performance by the parties would generate a contract based on the terms in Buyer's form. In short, the terms of the last communication before performance would be the ones that controlled. This was

---

[9] *See* RESTATEMENT (SECOND) OF CONTRACTS §§ 39, 58, 59, 61.

called the "last shot" rule, and most legal scholars thought it was arbitrary and produced a result that frequently bore no relationship to what the parties expected.

Section 2-207 tries to deal with this "battle of the forms" scenario. It does so by addressing two different but related issues: (1) when and how an agreement is formed; and (2) what the terms of the resulting agreement are. Unfortunately, section 2-207 is a bit confusing and has generated a significant amount of litigation. To understand the issues that the section raises, you must understand how the section works. Read Section 2-207.

The most important thing to understand about section 2-207 is that each of its three subsections deals with something different. Subsection (1) deals with when the parties' communications form an agreement. It abrogates the common-law mirror image rule by allowing a response that contains different or additional terms to nevertheless function as an acceptance. Subsection (2) provides guidance on the terms of an agreement formed under subsection (1). Thus, subsection (2) applies only if there is an agreement formed under subsection (1). Notice, subsection (2) provides two different rules for dealing with additional terms in an acceptance, one rule for communications "between merchants" and another rule for all other situations. As to who is a merchant, *see* UCC § 2-104. Subsection (3) then deals with situations in which no agreement is formed under subsection (1). It provides rules for: (i) when agreements are created not through the parties' "writings" but through their conduct; and (ii) what the terms for such agreements are.

The flow chart on the next page is one way to diagram the basic steps in the analysis. Although not reflected in the flow chart, notice that subsection (1) applies to "confirmations" as well as acceptances. A confirmation differs from an acceptance in that it confirms a pre-existing agreement. In other words, whereas an acceptance might begin "I agree," a confirmation might begin, "as we have already agreed" or "this note is to memorialize our agreement that." *See* UCC § 2-207 cmt. 1. When you think about it in those terms, subsection (1) seems to be written in Orwellian doublespeak: "a written confirmation . . . operates as an acceptance." This bit of alchemy treats a confirmation – which under the common law would have little or no relevance to whether an agreement exists or what the terms of any agreement are – as if it were part of the offer and acceptance process.

Notice also that the flow chart does not cover most of subsection (2). That is partly to keep it simple and partly because there is disagreement over how subsection (2) applies to different terms. That disagreement is a function of some rather unfortunate drafting. Reread subsections (1) and (2) and comments 3 and 6. Then consider the case that follows. It is a classic.

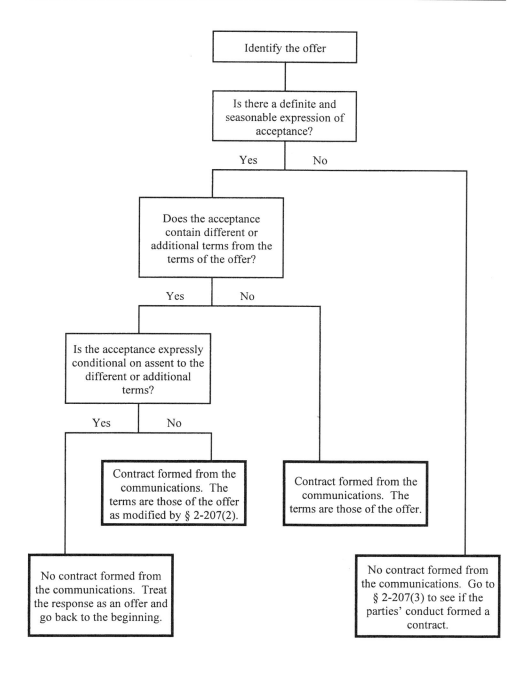

DAITOM, INC. V. PENNWALT CORP.
741 F.2d 1569 (10th Cir. 1984)

William E. Doyle, Circuit Judge

[On September 7, 1976, the seller (Pennwalt), after negotiations with the buyer (Daitom), submitted a proposal for the sale of two rotary vacuum dryers with dust filters. The proposal was made in a typewritten writing to which pre-printed form conditions were attached and explicitly made part of the proposal. One term in the form conditions imposed a one year period after delivery within which Daitom could bring a law suit. On October 5, 1976, Daitom issued a purchase order, which consisted of a pre-printed form and 17 standard terms and conditions on the back. One of the terms of the "boilerplate" reserved to Daitom "all of its rights and remedies available at law." Pennwalt delivered the goods in May, 1977 but, because the plant in which they were to be installed was under construction, left the crates outside. On June 15, 1978, the goods were finally installed and operated. Serious defects were discovered, of which Pennwalt was notified on June 17, 1978. When Pennwalt was unable to repair the defects, Daitom brought suit for breach of warranty on March 7, 1980. The trial court held, *inter alia*, that the one year limitation became part of the contract and, since the law suit was brought more than one year after delivery, granted a summary judgment against Daitom. On appeal, the judgment was reversed and the case remanded to the trial court.] . . .

C. The Writings and the Contract

The trial court concluded that the parties' exchanged writings formed a contract. Thus, there was not a formal single document. Pennwalt's September 7, 1976 proposal constituted the offer and Daitom's October 5, 1976 purchase order constituted the acceptance.

It is essentially uncontested that Pennwalt's proposal constituted an offer. The proposal set forth in some detail the equipment to be sold to Daitom, the price, the terms of shipment, and specifically stated that the attached terms and conditions were an integral part of the proposal. One of those attached terms and conditions of sale limited the warranties to repair and replacement of defective parts and limited the period of one year from the date of delivery for any action for breach of warranty.[10]

---

[10] Paragraph 5 of the terms and conditions of sale stated in full (emphasis added):

    6. WARRANTIES:

The proposal was sent to Kintech and forwarded to Daitom with a recommendation to accept the proposal. Daitom sent the October 5, 1976 purchase order to Pennwalt. This purchase order constituted an acceptance of Pennwalt's offer and formed a binding contract for the sale only pursuant to 2-207(1), despite the statement of terms additional to or different from those in the offer.[11] But these terms were not without meaning or consequence. However, the acceptance was not expressly conditioned on Pennwalt accepting these additional or different terms.

---

a. Seller warrants that at the time of delivery of the property to the carrier, it will be, unless otherwise specified, new, free and clear of all lawful liens and security interests or other encumbrances unknown to Buyer. If, within a period of one year from the date of *such delivery* any parts of the property (except property specified to be used property or normal wear parts) fail because of material or workmanship which was defective at the time of such delivery, Seller will repair such parts, or furnish parts to replace them f.o.b. Seller's or its supplier's plant, provided such failure is due solely to such defective material or workmanship and is not contributed to by any other cause, such as improper care or unreasonable use, and provided such defects are brought to Seller's attention for verification when first discovered, and the parts alleged to be so defective are returned, if requested, to Seller's or its supplier's plant. *No action for breach of warranty shall be brought more than one year after the cause of action has accrued*

SELLER MAKES NO OTHER WARRANTY OF ANY KIND, EXPRESS OR IMPLIED, INCLUDING ANY WARRANTY OF FITNESS OF THE PROPERTY FOR ANY PARTICULAR PURPOSE EVEN IF THAT PURPOSE IS KNOWN TO SELLER.

In no event shall Seller be liable for consequential damage.

b. Because of varied interpretations of standards at the local level, Seller cannot warrant that the property meets the requirements of the Occupational Safety and Health Act.

[11] The principal additional or different terms referred to the reservation of warranties. Specifically:

(8) WARRANTY. The Seller warrants that the supplies covered by this purchase order will conform to the specifications, drawings, samples, or other descriptions furnished or specified by buyer, and will be fit and sufficient for the purpose intended, merchantable, of good material and workmanship, and free from defect. The warranties and remedies provided for in this paragraph . . . shall be in addition to those implied by or available at law and shall exist not withstanding [sic] the acceptance by Buyer of all or a part of this applies with respect to which such warranties and remedies are applicable.

There is a provision which Daitom contends made the acceptance expressly conditional on Pennwalt's accepting the additional or different terms which appeared in the pre-printed, standard "boilerplate" provisions on the back of the purchase order. It stated:

Acceptance. Immediate acceptance is required unless otherwise provided herein. It is understood and agreed that the written acceptance by Seller of this purchase order or the commencement of any work performance of any services hereunder by the Seller, (including the commencement of any work or the performance of any service with respect to samples), shall constitute acceptance by Seller of this purchase order and of all the terms and conditions of such acceptance is *expressly limited to such terms and conditions, unless each deviation is mutually recognized therefore in writing.* (Emphasis added.)

This language does not preclude the formation of a contract by the exchanged writings pursuant to § 2-207(1). Nor does it dictate the adoption of a conclusion holding that as a result the acceptance provided the applicable terms of the resulting contract. First, it is well established that a contract for the sale of goods may be made in any manner to show agreement, requiring merely that there be some objective manifestation of mutual assent, but that there must be. There is not a contract until it takes place. *See* U.C.C. § 2-204; . . . Here there is such an objective manifestation of agreement on essential terms of equipment specifications, price, and the terms of shipment and payment, all of which took place before the machinery was put to any test. The purchase order explicitly referred to and incorporated on its front Kintech's equipment specifications and Pennwalt's proposal. But we are unwilling to hold such a typewritten reference and incorporation by Daitom brings the matter to a close. The acceptance and warranty terms as provided for by the above excerpted acceptance clause, does manifest a willingness on all essential terms to accept the offer and form a contract. . . . This was, of course, before an attempt was made to use the equipment.

Second, the boilerplate provision does not directly address the instant case. The purchase order is drafted principally as an *offer* inviting acceptance. Although this court recognizes that the form may serve a dual condition depending on the circumstances, the imprecision of language that permits such service detracts from Daitom's argument of conditional acceptance.

Third, the courts are split on the application of § 2-207(1) and the meaning of "expressly made conditional on assent to the additional or different terms.". . . . *Roto-Lith Ltd. v. F.P. Bartlett & Co., Inc.,* 297 F.2d 497 (1st Cir. 1962) represents one extreme of the spectrum, that the offeree's response stating a term materially altering the contractual obligations solely to the disadvantage of the offeror constitutes a conditional acceptance. The other extreme of the spectrum is represented by *Dorton v. Collins & Aikman Corporation,* 453 F.2d 1161 (6th Cir. 1972), in which case the court held that the conditional nature of the acceptance should be so clearly expressed in a manner sufficient to notify the offeror that the offeree is unwilling to proceed with the transaction unless the additional or different terms are included in the contract. The middle of the spectrum providing that a response merely "predicating" acceptance on clarification, addition or modification is a conditional acceptance is represented by *Construction Aggregates Corp. v. Hewitt-Robins, Inc.,* 404 F.2d 505 (7th Cir. 1968), *cert. denied,* 395 U.S. 921 (1969).

The facts of this case, Daitom asserts, are not of a character that would suggest that there had been an unequivocal acceptance. The defendant-appellee was aware that the machinery had not even been tried. Once it was tried, it broke down in a very short time. It is hard to see a justifiable acceptance, Daitom asserts, when the buyer does not even know whether it works, and, in fact, learns after the fact, that it does not work. This fact alone renders the "contract" to be questionable.

The better view as to the meaning and application of "conditional acceptance," and the view most likely to be adopted by Pennsylvania, is the view in *Dorton* that the offeree must explicitly communicate his or her unwillingness to proceed with the transaction unless the additional or different terms in its response are accepted by the offeror. . . .

Having found an offer and an acceptance which was not made expressly conditional on assent to additional or different terms, we must now decide the effect of those additional or different terms on the resulting contract and what terms became part of it. The district court simply resolved this dispute by focusing solely on the period of limitations specified in Pennwalt's offer of September 7, 1976. Thus, the court held that while the offer explicitly specified a one-year period of limitations in accordance with § 2-725(1) allowing such a reduction, Daitom's acceptance of October 5, 1976 was silent as to the limitations period. Consequently, the court held that § 2-207(2) was inapplicable and the one-year limitations period controlled, effectively barring Daitom's action for breach of warranties.

While the district court's analysis undertook to resolve the issue without considering the question of the application of § 2-207(2) to additional or different terms, we cannot accept its approach or its conclusion. We are unable to ignore the plain implication of Daitom's reservation in its boilerplate warranties provision of all its rights and remedies available at law. Such an explicit reservation impliedly reserves the statutory period of limitations; without such a reservation, all other reservations of actions and remedies are without effect.

The statutory period of limitations under the U.C.C. is four years after the cause of action has accrued. UCC § 2-725(1). Were we to determine that this four-year period became a part of the contract rather than the shorter one-year period, Daitom's actions on breach of warranties were timely brought and summary judgment against Daitom was error.

We realize that our conclusion requires an inference to be drawn from a construction of Daitom's terms; however, such an inference and construction are consistent with the judicial reluctance to grant summary judgment where there is some reasonable doubt over the existence of a genuine material fact. . . . When taking into account the circumstances surrounding the application of the one-year limitations period, we have little hesitation in adopting the U.C.C.'s four-year limitations reservation, the application of which permits a trial on the merits. Thus, this court must recognize that certain terms in Daitom's acceptance differed from terms in Pennwalt's offer and decide which become part of the contract. The district court certainly erred in refusing to recognize such a conflict.

The difficulty in determining the effect of different terms in the acceptance is the imprecision of drafting evident in § 2-207. The language of the provision is silent on how different terms in the acceptance are to be treated once a contract is formed pursuant to § 2-207(1). That section provides that a contract may be formed by exchanged writings despite the existence of additional or different terms in the acceptance. Therefore, an offeree's response is treated as an acceptance while it may differ substantially from the offer. This section of the provision, then, reformed the mirror-image rule; that common law legal formality that prohibited the formation of a contract if the exchanged writings of offer and acceptance differed in any term.

Once a contract is recognized pursuant to § 2-207(1), § 2-207(2) provides the standard for determining if the additional terms stated in the acceptance become a part of the contract. Between merchants, such *additional* terms become part of the resulting contract *unless* 1) the offer expressly limited acceptance to its terms, 2) the additional terms materially alter the contract obligations, or 3) the offeror gives notice of his or her objection to the additional terms within a reasonable time. Should any one of these three possibilities occur, the *additional* terms are treated merely as proposals for incorporation in the contract and absent assent by the offeror the terms of the offer control. In any event, the existence of the additional terms does not prevent a contract from being formed.

Section 2-207(2) is silent on the treatment of terms stated in the acceptance that are *different,* rather than merely additional, from those stated in the offer. It is unclear whether "different" terms in the acceptance are intended to be included under the aegis of "additional" terms in § 2-207(2) and, therefore, fail to become part of the agreement if they materially alter the contract. Comment 3 suggests just such an inclusion.[12]   However, Comment 6 suggests that different terms in exchanged writings must be assumed to constitute mutual objections by each party to the other's conflicting terms and result in a mutual "knockout" of both parties' conflicting terms; the missing terms to be supplied by the U.C.C.'s "gap-filler" provisions.[13] At least one commentator, in support of this view, has suggested that the drafting history of the provision indicates that the word "different" was intentionally deleted from the final draft of § 2-207(2) to preclude its treatment under that subsection.[14] The plain language, comments, and drafting history of the provision, therefore, provide little helpful guidance in resolving the disagreement over the treatment of different terms pursuant to § 2-207.

Despite all this, the cases and commentators have suggested three possible approaches. The first of these is to treat "different" terms as included under the aegis of "additional" terms in § 2-207(2). Consequently, different terms in the

---

[12] Comment 3 states (emphasis added):
> Whether or not *additional or different* terms will become part of the agreement
> depends upon the provision of subsection (2).

It must be remembered that even official comments to enacted statutory text do not have the force of law and are only guidance in the interpretation of that text. *In re Bristol Associates, Inc.,* 505 F.2d 1056 (3d Cir. 1974) (while the comments to the Pennsylvania U.C.C. are not binding, the Pennsylvania Supreme Court gives substantial weight to the comments as evidencing application of the Code).

[13] Comment 6 states, in part:
> Where clauses on confirming forms sent by both parties conflict each party must be
> assumed to object to a clause of the other conflicting with one on the confirmation
> sent by himself . . . . The contract then consists of the terms expressly agreed to,
> terms on which the confirmations agree, and terms supplied by the Act, including
> subsection (2).

[14] *See* D.G. Baird & R. Weisberg, *Rules, Standards, and the Battle of the Forms: A Reassessment of § 2-207,* 68 VA. L. REV. 1217, 1240, n.61.

acceptance would never become part of the contract, because, by definition, they would materially alter the contract (*i.e.*, the offeror's terms). Several courts have adopted this approach. . . .

The second approach, which leads to the same result as the first, is that the offeror's terms control because the offeree's different terms merely fall out; § 2-207(2) cannot rescue the different terms since that subsection applies only to *additional* terms. Under this approach, Comment 6 (apparently supporting a mutual rather than a single term knockout) is not applicable because it refers only to conflicting terms in confirmation forms following *oral* agreement, not conflicting terms in the *writings* that form the agreement. This approach is supported by Professor Summers. J.J. WHITE & R.S. SUMMERS, UNIFORM COMMERCIAL CODE, § 1-2, at 29 (2d ed. 1980).

The third, and preferable approach, which is commonly called the "knock-out" rule, is that the conflicting terms cancel one another. Under this view the offeree's form is treated only as an acceptance of the terms in the offeror's form which did not conflict. The ultimate contract, then, includes those non-conflicting terms and any other terms supplied by the U.C.C., including terms incorporated by course of performance (§ 2-208), course of dealing (§ 1-205), usage of trade (§ 1-205), and other "gap fillers" or "off-the-rack" terms (*e.g.*, implied warranty of fitness for particular purpose, § 2-315). As stated previously, this approach finds some support in Comment 6. Professor White supports this approach as the most fair and consistent with the purposes of § 2-207. WHITE & SUMMERS, *supra*, at 29. Further, several courts have adopted or recognized the approach. . . .

We are of the opinion that this is the more reasonable approach, particularly when dealing with a case such as this where from the beginning the offeror's specified period of limitations would expire before the equipment was even installed. The approaches other than the "knock-out" approach would be inequitable and unjust because they invited the very kind of treatment which the defendant attempted to provide.

Thus, we are of the conclusion that if faced with this issue the Pennsylvania Supreme Court would adopt the "knock-out" rule and hold here that the conflicting terms in Pennwalt's offer and Daitom's acceptance regarding the period of limitations and applicable warranties cancel one another out. Consequently, the other provisions of the U.C.C. must be used to provide the missing terms.

This particular approach and result are supported persuasively by the underlying rationale and purpose behind the adoption of § 2-207. As stated previously, that provision was drafted to reform the infamous common law mirror-image rule and associated last-shot doctrine that enshrined the fortuitous positions of senders of forms and accorded undue advantages based on such fortuitous positions. WHITE & SUMMERS, *supra* at 25. To refuse to adopt the "knock-out" rule and instead adopt one of the remaining two approaches would serve to re-enshrine the undue advantages derived solely from the fortuitous positions of when a party sent a form. *Cf.*, 3 DUESENBERG & KING at 93 (1983 Supp.). This is because either approach other than the knock-out rule for different terms results in the offeror and his or her terms always prevailing solely because he or she sent the first form. Professor Summers argues that this advantage is not wholly unearned, because the offeree has an opportunity to review the offer, identify the conflicting terms and make his or her acceptance conditional. But this joinder misses the fundamental purpose of the U.C.C. in general and § 2-207 in particular, which is to preserve a contract and fill in any gaps if the parties intended to make a contract and there is a reasonable basis for giving an appropriate remedy. UCC §§ 2-204(3); 2-207(1); 2-207(3). Thus, this approach gives the offeree some protection. While it is laudible [sic] for business persons to read the fine print and boilerplate provisions in exchanged forms, there is nothing in § 2-207 mandating such careful consideration. The provision seems drafted with a recognition of the reality that merchants seldom review exchanged forms with the scrutiny of lawyers. The "knock-out" rule is therefore the best approach. Even if a term eliminated by operation of the "knock-out" rule is reintroduced by operation of the U.C.C.'s gap-filler provisions, such a result does not indicate a weakness of the approach. On the contrary, at least the reintroduced term has the merit of being a term that the U.C.C. draftpersons regarded as fair.

We now address the question of reverse and remand regarding Counts I and II. The result of this court's holding is that the district court erred in granting summary judgment against Daitom on Counts I and II of its complaint. Operation of the "knock-out" rule to conflicting terms results in the instant case in the conflicting terms in the offer and acceptance regarding the period of limitations and applicable warranties cancelling. In the absence of any evidence of course of performance, course of dealing, or usage of trade providing the missing terms, §§ 2-725(1), 2-313, 2-314, 2-315 may operate to supply a four-year period of limitations, an express warranty, an implied warranty of merchantability, and an implied warranty of fitness for a particular purpose, respectively. The ruling of the district court on Counts I and II does not invite this kind of a broad inquiry, and thus, we must recognize the superiority in terms of justice of the "knock-out" rule. Consequently, the ruling of the district court on Counts I and II must be reversed and the matter remanded for trial consistent with this court's ruling. . . .

BARRETT, CIRCUIT JUDGE, dissenting:

I respectfully dissent. Insofar as the issue of contract formation is concerned in this case, we are confronted with a "battle of the forms" case involving the interpretation and application of U.C.C. 2-207. I would affirm.

Pennwalt's proposal of September 7, 1976, was an "offer." It was submitted to Daitom in response to solicitations initiated by Daitom and it contained specific terms relating to price, delivery dates, etc., and its terms were held "open" for Daitom's acceptance within 30 days. In my view, Daitom accepted the offer with its purchase order. That order repeated the quantity, model number, and price for the items as those terms appeared in the Pennwalt proposal and, by reference, it incorporated four pages of specifications attached to Pennwalt's proposal or "offer." The purchase order did contain some different and additional language from that contained in Pennwalt's proposal. However, the Code has rejected the old mirror image rule. Thus, I agree with the district court's finding/ruling that a contract was formed in the circumstances described.

I also agree with the district court's conclusion that the terms of Pennwalt's proposal constituted the "terms of the contract." I do not agree, as Daitom argues, that its "acceptance" was made "conditional" upon Pennwalt's assent to the additional/different terms set forth in Daitom's purchase order. The court correctly found no such *express* condition in Daitom's acceptance.

The "knock-out" rule should not, in my view, be reached in this case. It can be applied only if, as Daitom argues and the majority agrees, the "conflicting terms" cancel each other out. The "knock-out" rule does have substantial support in the law, but I do not believe it is relevant in this case because the *only* conflicting terms relate to the *scope* of the warranty. In this case, it is not an important consideration because, pursuant to the express time limitations contained in Pennwalt's "offer," Daitom lost its right to assert any warranty claim. There was no term in Daitom's purchase order in conflict with the express one-year limitation within which to bring warranty actions. . . .

Questions

1. One source of the "knock-out rule" is section 2-207(3). Another is comment 6 to that section. Which of these did the court in *Daitom* rely upon? Does either apply according to its terms?

2. Do you agree with the *Daitom* court's decision to adopt the "knock-out rule"?

3. The other issue that the *Daitom* court addressed was when is a response that *purports* to be an acceptance "expressly made conditional on assent to the additional or different terms," so that it fails to qualify as an acceptance under section 2-207(1). Do you agree with the court's analysis of Daitom's responsive form language?

4. The two issues directly confronted by the court in *Daitom* are merely two of several that frequently arise in connection with section 2-207. Other recurring issues include: (i) how to distinguish additional terms from different terms; and (ii) if one or more of the parties is not a merchant, and thus additional terms in the acceptance are merely "proposals for addition to the contract," whether assent to the proposals can be manifested by the failure to object. The *Daitom* court implicitly dealt with the first of these two issues as it concluded that it was dealing with different terms. Do you agree with the court's conclusion on this point? What is the dissent's point regarding that issue? For a different view of the effect of a reservation of rights clause, *see Robert Bosch Corp. v. ASC Inc.*, 195 Fed. Appx. 503 (6th Cir. 2006).

The effect of the knock-out rule is often to leave the parties with whatever default term would exist under Article 2's gap filler rules. In other words, the parties' conflicting terms cancel each other out, and the contract is formed using whatever term Article 2 would supply when the parties' communications are silent on the subject involved. If one assumes that Article 2's gap fillers are fair terms, then perhaps the knock-out rule makes sense. However, consider the following scenario:

Illustration

Salvage Company acquires goods from Insurer. The goods had been stored in a warehouse that was flooded during a storm. Insurer had paid its client the replacement value of the goods and then sold the goods to Salvage Company for a small fraction of their original value. Salvage Company examined the goods and discarded the ones that were obviously defective but is unable to readily determine which of the remaining goods are merchantable and which are not. Salvage Company then sends an e-mail message to Wholesaler, offering to sell the goods without any warranty of merchantability or other warranty of quality. Wholesaler responds by sending Salvage Company a purchase order for the goods on Wholesaler's standard form. The form includes a provision that the seller warrants that the goods are merchantable. If the knock-out rule applies, Salvage Company will likely be making a warranty. *See* UCC § 2-314(1). Indeed, even if Salvage Company immediately reads Wholesaler's form, sees the problem, and calls Wholesaler to object, it is too late to change the terms of the contract (at least without Wholesaler's consent). The knock-out rule would have already bound Salvage Company to a term it expressly did not want.

Problem 2-5

A. Buyer, a consumer, telephones Seller to get a price quote and delivery date for organic apples for Buyer to use in making homemade applesauce. Buyer makes clear to Seller that Buyer is in the process of shopping for a supplier and will get back to the Seller if the Buyer is interested. After the telephone call, Seller faxes to Buyer an offer to sell 10 bushels of Crispy Pink apples for $10 per bushel, offer open until 5:00 p.m. that same day. Seller's fax contained an arbitration clause requiring binding arbitration of all disputes arising out of the agreement. Buyer sent Seller an e-mail message at 4:00 p.m. that same day stating that he would buy 10 bushels of Crispy Pink apples for $10 per bushel, delivery by Nov. 15. Is there an agreement? If so, on what terms?

B. After reading an advertisement, Buyer in Indiana telephones Seller in Illinois to order a sub-zero freezer designed for commercial use. The price is $9,200, which Buyer pays using a major credit card. Prior to shipment, Seller mails Buyer an acknowledgment of the transaction that properly describes the item and price. It also indicates that the transaction is subject to all of the terms printed on the back of the form. These terms include:
   (i) In the event of any problem with a shipment, customer must notify Seller in writing of such problem within 20 days of receipt or be barred from any remedy.

(ii) The contract is to be governed by the law of the State of Illinois.

(iii) Any dispute arising out of this transaction shall be subject to binding arbitration.

(iv) All goods will be shipped using Careful Carriers, Inc.

Prior to shipment, is there an agreement? If so, on what terms?

C. Buyer mails Seller a purchase order for 1,000 lbs. of green beans at $78¢/lb., delivery by November 15, payment within 30 days after delivery. The purchase order indicates that the transaction is subject to all of the terms printed on the back of the form. One of these terms says: "Buyer objects in advance to any additional or different terms on Seller's acknowledgment or confirmation." Seller responds with an acknowledgment of the order which correctly restates the quantity, price, and delivery terms but indicates that, on the date of delivery, interest will start accruing on the outstanding balance due. Prior to shipment, is there an agreement? If so, on what terms?

D. Buyer mails Seller a purchase order for 1,000 lbs. of honeydew melons at $1.28¢/lb., delivery by November 15, payment within 30 days after delivery. Seller responds with an acknowledgment of the order which correctly restates the quantity, price, and delivery terms, but indicates that all disputes arising out of the transaction will be subject to binding arbitration. In addition, the acknowledgment states the following: "This acknowledgment is expressly conditional on Buyer's assent to the terms hereof." Prior to shipment, is there an agreement? If so on what terms? If not, and an agreement is created by performance, is the arbitration clause part of the agreement?

E. Buyer mails Seller a purchase order for 1,000 gallons of vanilla ice cream at $1.85/gal., delivery by November 15, payment within 30 days after delivery. The purchase order contains the following: "This purchase order is expressly conditional on assent to the terms hereof. Buyer objects in advance to any different or additional terms in any acceptance." Seller responds with an acknowledgment of the order which correctly restates the quantity, price, and delivery terms, but indicates that all disputes arising out of the transaction will be subject to binding arbitration. One week later, Seller ships the goods and Buyer accepts them shortly after delivery. Is the arbitration clause part of the agreement?

F. Buyer telephones Seller to order 1,000 lbs. of jelly beans. During the conversation, which is very brief, they agree on a price and a delivery date. Later that day, Seller mails Buyer a written acknowledgment that states, among other things, that:
   (i) In the event of any problem with the shipment, customer must notify Seller in writing of such problem within 20 days of receipt or be barred from any remedy.
   (ii) The contract is to be governed by the law of the State of Illinois.
   (iii) Any dispute arising out of this transaction shall be subject to binding arbitration.

The next day, before receiving Seller's acknowledgment, Buyer sends Seller its own acknowledgment of the transaction. Among other things, Buyer's acknowledgment states that:
   (i) Seller will correct any problem with the shipment within 3 days of receiving notice thereof from Buyer, which notice may come within any reasonable time, regardless of whether Buyer still has possession of the goods.
   (ii) Any dispute arising out of this transaction shall be subject to binding arbitration.

Prior to shipment, is there a contract? If so on what terms?

G. Buyer, who operates a small business, sees an advertisement for personal computers made by Seller. Buyer writes to Seller stating the type of computer needed and the requisite components. Seller telephones Buyer and they agree on the computer and the price. Buyer gives Seller a credit card number and Seller charges that card for the price of the computer. Seller then ships the computer. In the box are two pages of standard terms, one of which commits the parties to arbitrate all disputes under ICC Rules in New York. The terms state in bold type: "Use of the computer will constitute an acceptance of these terms." Buyer uses the computer, which turns out to be unmerchantable. Buyer concedes that a contract was formed but argues that the arbitration clause was not part of the contract. What result?[15]

Problem 2-6

A. You represent Savanna Industries, a wholesaler of fine, colonial-style furniture to retailers throughout the country. Most of Savanna's customers telephone or fax in orders from Savanna's catalogue. Some of the faxed orders arrive on the customer's own purchase order form. Others are on the form that is included in Savanna's catalogue. Savanna is very proud of the quality of its furniture but over the years there have been a few, isolated problems. For these reasons, Savanna wants to be sure that all of its sales contracts: (i) include an agreement to arbitrate all disputes relating to the transaction; (ii) provide that the

---

[15] *See Stenzel v. Dell, Inc.*, 870 A.2d 133 (Me. 2005). Judge Easterbrook, concluded that even though the buyer paid for and the seller shipped the goods before the terms were disclosed, there was a "rolling contract" that was not concluded until the buyer used the goods and section 2-207 did not apply if only one party used a standard form. *ProCD, Inc. v. Zeidenberg*, 86 F.3d 1447 (7th Cir. 1996); *Hill v. Gateway 2000, Inc.*, 105 F.3d 1147 (7th Cir. 1997), *cert. denied*, 522 U.S. 808 (1997); *accord, Westendorf v. Gateway 2000, Inc.*, 2000 WL 307369 (Del. Ch. 2000), *aff'd*, 763 A.2d 92 (Del. 2000) (table). This analysis was rejected in *Klocek v. Gateway, Inc.*, 104 F. Supp. 2d 1332 (D. Kan. 2000), *dismissed for lack of subject matter jurisdiction*, 2000 WL 1372886 (D. Kan. 2000), *refusing to vacate first order*, 2001 WL 1568346 (D. Kan. 2001), in which the court held that the terms that came with the product were proposals for addition to the contract under section 2-207 and that the buyer did not expressly agree to that proposal. *But see Brower v. Gateway 2000, Inc.*, 676 N.Y.S.2d 569 (N.Y. Sup. Ct. App. Div. 1998), where the court refused to apply section 2-207 to a transaction where the contract was not formed until the 30-day period had expired but held that the arbitration clause, because of the prohibitive cost involved in the arbitration, was substantively unconscionable.

Of course, there are a legion of law review articles on this issue. *See, e.g.,* Ronald J. Mann & Travis Siebeneicher, *Just One Click, The Reality of Internet Retail Contracting*, 108 COLUM. L. REV. 984 (2008); Wayne R. Barnes, *Toward a Fairer Model of Consumer Assent to Standard Form Contracts: In Defense of Restatement Subsection 211(3)*, 82 WASH. L. REV. 227 (2007); Peter A. Alces, *Guerilla Terms*, 56 EMORY L.J. 1511 (2007); Robert A. Hillman, *Online Boilerplate: Would Mandatory Web Disclosure of E-Standard Terms Backfire?*, 104 MICH. L. REV. 837 (2006); Stephen E. Friedman, *Improving the Rolling Contract*, 56 AM. U. L. REV. 1 (2006).

buyer must notify Savanna in writing of any problem with the goods sold within four months of delivery or be barred from any remedy; and (iii) limit Savanna's liability for defective goods to refund of the purchase price (*i.e.*, disclaim responsibility for consequential damages). Draft Savanna's acknowledgment form so that these terms will be part of Savanna's sales contracts.

B. You represent Bountiful Merchandise, Corp., which owns department stores in several states. Bountiful purchases goods from many different suppliers. Most of Bountiful's purchases are made by completing one of Bountiful's own order forms and faxing the completed form to the seller. Bountiful insists that all its suppliers: (i) warrant the merchantability of their goods and be responsible for all consequential damages; (ii) agree that payment will be due, without interest, 90 days after delivery; and (iii) agree that if they sell the same goods to anyone else at a lower price within six months after the sale to Bountiful, they will retroactively lower the price charged to Bountiful to the lowest price charged to anyone else, and promptly rebate the difference. Draft Bountiful's order form so that these terms will be part of Bountiful's sales contracts.

C. Assume that Bountiful ordered goods from Savanna using the form you drafted in Part B. Savanna responded on the acknowledgment form you drafted in Part A.
    1. Before shipment, is there a contract? If so, what are its terms?
    2. How, if at all, would the analysis of Subpart 1 change if Savanna shipped the goods and Bountiful accepted and paid for them?

D. Based upon the above exercise, what methodology would you recommend to Bountiful to ensure that the terms it wanted were always a part of a contract, no matter how the contract was formed? Would you have a different methodology to recommend to Savanna to ensure that it would have the terms it wanted, no matter how the contract was formed?

The Article 2 revision struggled with the question of how to deal with the battle of the forms problem. Discussion of amended section 2-207 is in the Appendix. In essence, the issue is how to deal with the fact that businesses use standard forms to try to set terms of their contracts, in case something goes awry in a transaction. That being said, however, the vast majority of transactions are performed properly and nothing goes wrong. Thus, business people involved in the exchange of standard forms routinely pay no attention to the terms in the forms they give and receive. The only time the terms matter is if a dispute arises.[16] Given that operational construct, what legal principles should be used to determine whether a contract was formed from an exchange of forms? What legal principles should apply to determine the terms of such contracts?[17]

3. *Electronic Contracting and Assent*

An increasing percentage of sales contracting is conducted through electronic means. We do not mean merely through electronically transmitted communications, such as e-mail and fax. We mean also through computer-assisted technologies that obviate the need for a human representative of one or both of the parties involved. For example, one common practice with which you are no doubt familiar is for a customer to visit the website of the seller and order goods or services on line. In

---

[16] Section 2-207 results in significant amounts of litigation. *See, e.g., Foamade Indus. v. Visteon Corp.*, 2008 WL 582566 (Mich. Ct. App. 2008); *Tacoma Fixture Co. v. Rudd Co.*, 174 P.3d 721 (Wash. Ct. App.), *review denied*, 190 P.3d 55 (Wash. 2008); *Coosemans Specialties, Inc. v. Gargiulo*, 485 F.3d 701 (2d Cir. 2007); *E.C. Styberg Eng'g Co. v. Eaton Corp.*, 492 F.3d 912 (7th Cir. 2007); *Robert Bosch Corp. v. ASC Inc.*, 195 Fed. Appx. 503 (6th Cir. 2006); *Roanoke Cement Co., L.L.C. v. Falk Corp.*, 413 F.3d 431 (4th Cir. 2005); *Marvin Lumber and Cedar Co. v. PPG Industries, Inc.*, 401 F.3d 901 (8th Cir. 2005); *Standard Bent Glass Corp. v. Glassrobots Oy*, 333 F.3d 440 (3d Cir. 2003); *Polytop Corp. v. Chipsco, Inc.*, 826 A.2d 945 (R.I. 2003) (per curium); *Southern Illinois Riverboat Casino Cruises, Inc. v. Triangle Insulation and Sheet Metal Co.*, 302 F.3d 667 (7th Cir. 2002).

[17] Lawyers (and law professors) love this issue and have produce extensive law review articles on it. *See, e.g.,* Stephen W. Ranere, Note, *Charting a Course: How Courts Should Interpret Course of Dealing in a Battle-of-Forms Dispute*, 41 SUFFOLK U. L. REV. 671 (2008); Corneill A. Stephens, *Escape From the Battle of the Forms: Keep It Simple, Stupid*, 11 LEWIS & CLARK L. REV. 233 (2007); Colin P. Marks, *The Limits of Limiting Liability in the Battle of the Forms: U.C.C. Section 2-207 and the "Material Alteration" Inquiry*, 33 PEPPERDINE L. REV. 501 (2006); Omri Ben-Shahar, *An Ex-Ante View of the Battle of the Forms: Inducing Parties to Draft Reasonable Terms*, 25 INT'L REV. L. & ECON. 350 (2005).

such situations, no human representative of the seller participates in the contract-formation process

Typically, two different methods are used to manifest assent in such transactions. In so-called "click-wrap" agreements, the person using a computer to conduct a transaction (typically the buyer) uses a mouse to click an "I agree" button after the terms of the agreement are displayed. This form of agreement is commonly used in the downloading or installation of software but it could just as easily be used in a sale of goods or a lease of goods.[18] Another practice in the electronic environment is the use of so-called "browse-wrap" agreements. In this type of transaction, the user of the electronic interface may click on a button that says "place order," "confirm order," or "I agree," but the only terms of the agreement that are displayed are the description of the goods, the price, the quantity, and perhaps the shipping terms. The other terms are not displayed, but the website may provide a link to them or may simply display a notice that the transaction is governed by a set of terms and that using the website or engaging in some defined conduct will bind the user to the terms.[19]

At this point we are examining electronic contracting as it impacts the issue of assent to a bargain. We will consider some of the other issues in electronic contracting later in this Chapter.

---

[18] *See* Robert Lee Dickens, *Finding Common Ground in the World of Electronic Contracts: The Consistency of Legal Reasoning in Clickwrap Cases*, 11 MARQ. INTELL. PROP. L. REV. 379 (2007); Nancy S. Kim, *Clicking and Cringing*, 86 OR. L. REV. 797 (2007); Christina L. Kunz, *et al.*, *Click-Through Agreements: Strategies for Avoiding Disputes on Validity of Assent*, 57 BUS. LAW. 401 (2001). *See, e.g., Hotels.com, L.P. v. Canales*, 195 S.W.3d 147 (Tex. Ct. App. 2006).

[19] *See* Ian Rambarran & Robert Hunt, *Are Browse-Wrap Agreements All They Are Wrapped Up to Be?*, 9 TUL. J. TECH. & INTELL. PROP. 173 (2007); Mark A. Lemley, *Terms of Use*, 91 MINN. L. REV. 459 (2006); Christina L. Kunz, *et al.*, *Browse-Wrap Agreements: Validity of Implied Assent in Electronic Form Agreements*, 59 BUS. LAW. 279 (2003). *See, e.g., Southwest Airlines Co. v. BoardFirst, L.L.C.*, 2007 WL 4823761 (N.D. Tex. 2007).

For a discussion of other perspectives on electronic contracting, see Sylvia Mercado Kierkegaard, *E-contract Formation: U.S. and EU Perspectives*, 3 SHIDLER J. L. COM. & TECH. 12 (2007); Jane K. Winn & Brian H. Bix, *Diverging Perspectives on Electronic Contracting in the U.S. and EU*, 54 CLEV. ST. L. REV. 175 (2006).

Problem 2-7

Abel visits Retailer's website and decides to order a new toaster advertised for sale on the website. Abel clicks on the picture of the toaster and adds the toaster to his electronic shopping cart.

A. A screen pops up with the various terms including the following: "Any disputes concerning any product provided through this website must be resolved in binding arbitration." Two buttons are under the pop up screen one of which states "I agree" and the other of which states "I disagree." To actually complete the purchase, Abel must click on the "I agree" button. Clicking on the "I disagree" button removes the item from the electronic shopping cart. Abel clicks on "I agree" and completes ordering of the toaster. When the toaster arrives, it is a miserable failure at toasting anything. Is Abel bound by the arbitration clause?

B. Assume instead of the pop up screen as described above, when Abel clicks on the picture of the toaster to place the toaster in his electronic shopping cart, the screen changes to provide a hyperlink which states, "click here for terms of sale." Abel does not click on the hyperlink but rather completes his purchase of the toaster. If Abel had clicked on the hyperlink, Abel would have seen the same arbitration clause as stated above. When the toaster arrives, it is a miserable failure at toasting anything. Is Abel bound by the arbitration clause?

C. You have been asked to advise a retailer who is in the process of establishing a website on which customers may place their orders. What reasons, if any, are there for recommending a browse-wrap agreement rather than click-wrap agreement?

B.   Contract Formation in International Transactions

1.   CISG

The provisions for forming a contract governed by the CISG are found in Articles 14 through 24. These rules resemble the offer and acceptance rules of the common law more closely than they do the contract formation rules of Article 2. Article 14 defines an offer and requires that it be definite about the description of the goods, the quantity, and the price. Articles 15, 16, and 17 govern the effectiveness and revocation of offers. Articles 18, 20, 21, and 22 govern the manner and timing of acceptances.

Most notable is Article 19, which presents another approach to the battle of the forms.[20] To understand it, it is advisable to read its three sub-articles in order. Sub-article (1) adopts something very much like the common-law mirror image rule. A reply which purports to be an acceptance but which contains different or additional terms is really a rejection and counter-offer. Sub-article (2) cuts back on sub-article (1) by indicating that if the additional or different terms do not materially alter the terms of the offer, then the reply is an acceptance. The additional or different terms will become part of the contract unless the offeror promptly objects to them. Sub-article (3) significantly minimizes the scope of sub-article (2), however, by providing that virtually every conceivable term is in fact material.

To illustrate, assume that a buyer in California sends an offer in a record to a seller in Mexico City.[21] The seller responds with a record that purports to accept the offer but also contains a clause changing the delivery date. The seller ships later than the buyer expected but in accord with the seller's delivery date. The buyer accepts the goods and then uses them, even though it is very unhappy about the timing of the delivery. Under CISG Article 19, the seller's reply is a counter-offer

---

[20] *See* Henry D. Gabriel, *The Battle of the Forms: A Comparison of the United Nations Convention for the International Sale of Goods and the Uniform Commercial Code*, 49 BUS. LAW. 1053 (1994). For a survey of different countries' approaches to the battle of the forms issues concerning standard terms, *see* Kevin C. Stemp, *A Comparative Analysis of the "Battle of the Forms,"* 15 TRANSNATIONAL L. & CONTEMP. PROB. 243 (2005); James R. Maxeiner, *Standard-Terms Contracting in the Global Electronic Age: European Alternatives*, 28 YALE J. INT'L L. 109 (2003).

[21] Both the United States and Mexico have ratified the CISG.

because it contains an additional term (the delivery clause) that materially alters the offer. Buyer's conduct in accepting the goods indicates assent to the counter-offer, including the delivery clause. CISG Art. 18(3). In essence, the CISG adopts something like the last-shot rule that UCC section 2-207(1) sought to avoid. Under this construct, commercial parties under the CISG must read and object to terms in the forms or risk agreeing to them.

Problem 2-8

Revisit Problem 2-5. What would be the result in Parts B, C, and D if the transaction were governed by the CISG? What would be the result in each of those Parts if the transaction were governed by the CISG and the parties went ahead and performed (shipped and accepted the goods).[22]

2. *UNIDROIT Principles*

The UNIDROIT Principles of International Commercial Contracts are for international contracts what the Restatement (Second) of Contracts is for domestic transactions. They are not law, but they may provide persuasive guidance to courts and to parties. The UNIDROIT Principles on contract formation are closely analogous to the UCC Article 2 rules on contract formation. Offer and acceptance as well as the conduct of the parties may be sufficient to show agreement. UNIDROIT Art. 2.1.1. In addition, if the parties intend to agree, they may leave terms open yet still have a valid agreement. UNIDROIT Art. 2.1.14. The Principles contain a number of familiar offer and acceptance rules. UNIDROIT Arts. 2.1.2 through 2.1.13.

---

[22] *See Chateau des Charmes Wines Ltd. v. Sabate USA Inc.*, 328 F.3d 528 (9th Cir. 2003) (party who did not object to forum selection clause in other side's invoice sent after agreement formed did not agree to clause as the CISG requires agreement to terms and does not enforce unilateral attempts to modify terms).

Even if an arbitration clause is part of the parties' agreement under the CISG analysis, it still might not be enforceable. The United Nations Convention on the Recognition and Enforcement of Foreign Arbitral Awards (the New York Convention) requires an "agreement in writing" to arbitrate and then defines "agreement in writing" to "include an arbitral clause in a contract or an arbitration agreement, signed by the parties, or contained in an exchange of letters or telegrams." Art. II(2).

In a battle of the forms, a response that purports to be an acceptance but which contains non-material additional or different terms is treated as an acceptance. UNIDROIT Art. 2.1.11. The non-material terms become part of the agreement unless the offerer objects to the terms. *Id.* If the term is a standard term (whether material or non- material), the term is not effective if it is "not reasonably expected" by the other party or the other party has not "expressly accepted" it. UNIDROIT Art. 2.1.20. If the parties agree to terms and they also have standard terms that are "common in substance" the parties have a contract on those terms unless the other party indicates in advance or without undue delay that it does not intend to be bound to the contract. UNIDROIT Art. 2.1.22. Standard terms are "provisions which are prepared in advance for general and repeated use by one party and which are actually used without negotiation with the other party." UNIDROIT Art. 2.1.19.

SECTION 2.   BARRIERS TO ENFORCEABILITY

A. Statute of Frauds

1. *In General*

Some oral agreements are not enforceable because a statute of frauds requires that the agreement be evidenced by a signed writing to become a valid contract. Historically, the types of agreements covered by a statute of frauds include agreements to buy and sell real estate and agreements that cannot be performed within one year.[23] The Uniform Commercial Code has several provisions that could fairly be regarded as a statute of frauds,[24] including one applicable to the sale of goods. Read section 2-201.

The statute of frauds functions as a barrier to enforcement of an alleged agreement. If the plaintiff cannot prove compliance with the statute of frauds, the plaintiff's claim will fail. The typical lawsuit follows either of two patterns. After the plaintiff sues the defendant for breach of contract, the defendant either:

---

[23] *See* RESTATEMENT (SECOND) OF CONTRACTS § 110(1)(d), (e).

[24] *See* UCC §§ 5-104, 9-203(b)(3). Article 8 used to have a statute of frauds, *see* former § 8-319, but it was repealed as part of the 1994 revisions. *See* Art. 8 Prefatory Note IV.B.7. The pre-revision version of Article 1 also had a general statue of frauds for transactions in excess of $5,000, *see* former § 1-206, but that too was repealed in the revision process.

(i) submits a motion to dismiss, alleging that the plaintiff has not pled satisfaction of the statute of frauds; or

(ii) pleads the statute of frauds as an affirmative defense in its answer, and later moves for summary judgment on the basis that the plaintiff has not been able to produce a writing or other sufficient evidence to satisfy the statute of frauds.

Bear in mind that even if the plaintiff submits evidence that satisfies the statute of frauds, that does not mean that the plaintiff has proven that a contract exists. Satisfying the statute of frauds merely unlocks the door to the courthouse and allows the plaintiff the opportunity to prove the rest of its case. The plaintiff still has the burden of proving that the contract existed, what its terms were, and that the defendant breached it.

Two principal justifications have been asserted for the statute of frauds. First, the statute of frauds avoids fraudulent or perjured claims that an agreement was made. Second, the statute encourages the useful business habit of making a writing.[25] You should question these assertions. With respect to the first, it is worth noting that the CISG does not have a statute of frauds, *see* CISG Art. 11, and the UNIDROIT Principles do not require a writing of any sort, *see* UNIDROIT Art. 1.2. Indeed, England, which is where the statute of frauds originated, abandoned it more than a half-century ago. Moreover, while the statute of frauds may prevent one type of fraud – seeking judicial enforcement of an agreement that never existed – it would seem to increase the likelihood of another: denial of the existence of an agreement that was reached. The second justification presumes that encouraging individuals and businesses to memorialize their agreements is worth the added cost and that individuals and businesses will in fact modify their behavior because of the law. Both of these require some empirical research to confirm.

Problem 2-9

What does a plaintiff have to plead and prove to demonstrate compliance with section 2-201(1)? Based upon these requirements, what would you advise a client who is entering into transactions to do to ensure there is sufficient evidence to satisfy the statute of frauds?

---

[25] *See* Lawrence Vold, *The Application of the Statute of Frauds Under the Uniform Sales Act,* 15 MINN. L. REV. 391, 393–94 (1931); Jason S. Johnston, *The Statute of Frauds and Business Norms: A Testable Game-Theoretic Model*, 144 U. PA. L. REV. 1859 (1996).

2. The Exceptions

The general rule in section 2-201(1) is subject to four exceptions: one in subsection (2) and three in subsection (3). Subsection (2) is known as the "merchants must read their mail rule."[26] It provides that a merchant's receipt of a confirmation may be sufficient to satisfy the statute of frauds if the merchant fails to object in writing within ten days. Is it a good idea to limit this exception to communications "between merchants?"[27] Who qualifies as a merchant for the purposes of this rule? *See* UCC § 2-104 & cmt. 2.

Problem 2-10

A. The exception in section 2-201(2) applies only if the confirmation is "sufficient against the sender." What does that phrase mean and how does it limit the scope of subsection (2)? Construct a scenario in which the confirmation is sufficient against the sender and another in which the confirmation is not.

B. Silas runs a hardware store as a sole proprietor. Brittany is starting a landscaping business and needs to buy a large riding mower. On April 1, Brittany visited Silas's store and discussed purchasing a Jack Stallion 3000 riding mower for $3,700. The following day, Brittany sent an e-mail message to Silas, stating the following:

> Thanks for talking with me yesterday. This message is to confirm our agreement that I will be buying a Jack Stallion 3000 for $3,700, payment to be 90 days after delivery. I will come by on April 15 to pick up the mower. Thanks. – Brittany

Silas responded with the following message:

> I never agreed to payment in 90 days. I cannot possibly do business on such terms. I am happy to try to work something out with you or to arrange for alternative financing, but you'll have to come in to discuss it. – Silas.

---

[26] A point that is also borne out by UCC § 2-207(2).

[27] *See* Larry T. Garvin, *Small Business and the False Dichotomies of Contract Law*, 40 WAKE FOREST L. REV. 295 (2005).

If Brittany and Silas have no further discussions, and Brittany sues Silas for breach of contract, can Silas successfully raise the statute of frauds defense? If not, do they have a contract? What should Silas have done to preserve the statute of frauds defense?

CASAZZA V. KISER
313 F.3d 414 (8th Cir. 2002)

Bowman, Circuit Judge

This appeal arises from James Casazza's ill-fated effort to purchase a fifty-two-foot sailboat named the *"Andante"* from Joseph C. Kiser. Casazza sued Kiser seeking damages under the legal theories of breach of contract and promissory estoppel for Kiser's failure to sell him this boat. The District Court granted Kiser's motion to dismiss. We affirm.

I. Background

In late May 2001, Casazza read Kiser's listing of the *Andante* on an internet sales site. Shortly thereafter, Casazza contacted Kiser and expressed an interest in purchasing the boat. They agreed to meet during the weekend of June 2, 2001, in Ft. Lauderdale, Florida, where the *Andante* was located. Casazza first viewed the boat on June 2 and looked at it again with Kiser the following day. Casazza and Kiser met again on June 4, 2001, and, according to Casazza, negotiated an agreement for Casazza's purchase of the *Andante*. The details of this agreement were handwritten by each party on separate sheets of paper and at some point converted, presumably by Casazza, into a typewritten agreement (collectively, the "purchase terms"). That agreement provided for a sales price of $200,000 for the boat. The agreement further stated the sale was contingent on a marine survey, including a sea trial, satisfactory to Casazza. Among other provisions, the agreement also required payment by wire transfer and replacement of the mast step, and it detailed the logistics of transferring the boat from Florida to Virginia. Kiser never signed the agreement and the marine survey and sea trial did not take place.

During their meeting on June 4, Kiser gave Casazza a blank Coast Guard bill of sale to complete. The next day, Kiser and Casazza executed a software license transfer agreement for the boat's navigational software. This license agreement is the only document in the dispute signed by both parties and it does not refer to the *Andante*. Following these events, Casazza arranged for a marine survey, obtained an estimate for repair of the mast step, visited marinas, and tentatively reserved slip space for the *Andante* at a marina in Virginia. Things apparently went awry a week later, however, when Kiser informed Casazza that he would not sell him the boat. In response, Casazza initiated this suit and sought a temporary restraining order (TRO) to prevent Kiser from selling the *Andante* to someone else. While the application for the TRO was pending, but before Kiser had notice of it, Kiser sold the boat. Casazza amended his complaint and Kiser moved to dismiss the case on the basis of the statute of frauds. Casazza responded to Kiser's motion to dismiss and filed a Federal Rule of Civil Procedure 56(f) motion and affidavit requesting that the District Court's consideration of the motion to dismiss be delayed pending additional discovery.

On January 15, 2002, the District Court dismissed the action, concluding that additional discovery would not assist the court in the resolution of whether the statute of frauds applies to the dispute and that the defense barred Casazza's breach of contract and promissory estoppel claims. The District Court denied Casazza's motion for reconsideration. On appeal, Casazza argues the District Court erred in dismissing his claims.

II. Discussion

. . . We review de novo a district court's order granting a motion to dismiss, viewing the allegations in the complaint in the light most favorable to the plaintiff. . . . Like the District Court, we must accept the allegations of the complaint as true and dismiss the case only when "it appears beyond doubt that the plaintiff can prove no set of facts in support of his claim which would entitle him to relief." *Conley v. Gibson,* 355 U.S. 41, 45-46 (1957).

A. *The Statute of Frauds Defense*

Casazza contends the District Court erred when it dismissed his breach of contract claim, holding it was barred by the statute of frauds. Subject to certain limited exceptions, the statute of frauds renders unenforceable any unwritten contract for the sale of goods with a value over $500. . . . [Court applied Minnesota law – Eds.] Because Kiser raised the statute of frauds defense in his motion to dismiss, Casazza was required to affirmatively show the existence of an appropriate writing or an exception to this defense in order to avoid dismissal by the District Court. In this appeal, Casazza argues that the alleged contract was taken out of the statute of frauds by (1) the doctrine of part performance, (2) the existence of a sufficient writing, and (3) the possibility that Kiser may have a sufficient writing or that Kiser might admit a contract was formed between the parties had the District

Court granted Casazza's request for additional time for discovery. All these arguments are without merit.

(1) *Part Performance*

Under the part-performance exception to the statute of frauds, a writing is not required "with respect to goods for which payment has been made and accepted or which have been received and accepted." [§ 2-201(3)(c)]. Here, Casazza contends that his acceptance of the navigational software constitutes part performance of the parties' alleged agreement concerning the sale of the *Andante*. In support of this claim, Casazza relies on section [2-606(2)], which provides that "[a]cceptance of a part of any commercial unit is acceptance of that entire unit." According to Casazza, the navigational software is part of the *Andante*. Thus, Casazza argues, when he accepted this software, he accepted the *Andante*.

First, we question the applicability of section [2-606(2)] to the present dispute. The drafters of the commercial code designed this provision to limit a buyer's right of revocation of acceptance to whole units. As the Ninth Circuit observed of the uniform provision at issue here, "The commercial unit provision is included to protect *a seller* from having a buyer return *less* than a commercial unit. Return of less than a commercial unit would leave the seller with only components of a commercial unit, which would have severely reduced market value." *S & R Metals, Inc. v. C. Itoh & Co. (America),* 859 F.2d 814, 817 (9th Cir.1988) (first emphasis added) (citing *Abbett v. Thompson,* 263 N.E.2d 733, 735–36 (Inc. Ct. App. 1970) (holding buyer could not keep some parts of a car wash machine and revoke acceptance of the rest because the entire machine was a commercial unit and would have little value to the seller if incomplete)).

Second, even assuming section [2-606(2)] applies to the instant dispute, we conclude that under no circumstances could the software and the *Andante* be considered a single "commercial unit." Minnesota's Uniform Commercial Code states that:

> "Commercial unit" means such a unit of goods as by commercial usage is a single whole for purposes of sale and division of which materially impairs its character or value on the market or in use. A commercial unit may be a single article (as a machine) or a set of articles (as a suite of furniture or an assortment of sizes) or a quantity (as a bale, gross, or carload) or any other unit treated in use or in the relevant market as a single whole.

Minn.Stat. § 336.2-105(6) (2000). Viewing Casazza's allegations in the light most favorable to him, we are hard-pressed to see how the navigational software and the

Andante are a "single whole." Notably, Casazza concedes that the navigational software was purchased years after the *Andante* was built and that Kiser sold the boat to another party without it. Though Casazza distinguishes some cases cited in Kiser's brief, Casazza fails to cite a single case in support of his position that this Court should treat the *Andante* and the navigational software as a commercial unit, and our own research has not revealed any authority supporting this position. In short, we agree with the District Court that the doctrine of part performance cannot transmute Kiser's gift of the navigational software into a contract for the sale of the *Andante*.

(2) *Sufficient Writing*

Casazza also argues that the statute of frauds is inapplicable to this dispute because there is a sufficient writing showing the existence of a contract between the parties. The primary purpose of the writing requirement in the statute of frauds is to demonstrate that a contract for sale has indeed been made. *See* 1, JAMES J. WHITE & ROBERT S. SUMMERS, UNIFORM COMMERCIAL CODE § 2-4, at 63 (4th ed.1995). But the statute does not require one writing containing all the terms. *See Simplex Supplies, Inc. v. Abhe & Svoboda, Inc.,* 586 N.W.2d 797, 801 (Minn. Ct. App. 1998). Rather, "[s]everal papers may be taken together to make up the memorandum, providing they refer to one another, or are so connected together, by reference or by internal evidence, that parol testimony is not necessary to establish their connection with the contract." *Id.* (quoting *Olson v. Sharpless,* 55 N.W. 125, 126 (Minn. 1893)). In addition, "[t]he signature can be found on any document and may consist of 'any symbol executed or adopted by a party with present intention to authenticate a writing.'" *Id.* (quoting [§ 1-201(39)]). Casazza argues that the purchase terms, in particular the notes allegedly made by Kiser, and the executed software license transfer agreement constitute a sufficient writing. We disagree.

Casazza admits that he does not have a copy of a document that satisfies the statute of frauds. Casazza attempts to overcome this obstacle by arguing his pleadings reference the existence of a handwritten document allegedly prepared by Kiser, which – along with the executed software transfer agreement – constitute a sufficient writing. The typewritten agreement attached to Casazza's amended complaint is not signed by Kiser and there is no allegation that Kiser participated in its preparation. While Kiser did sign the software license transfer agreement, that document does not refer to any contemplated, proposed, or agreed contract for the sale of the *Andante*. We refuse to allow Casazza to proceed with his breach of contract claim on this basis because to do so would eviscerate the statute of frauds.

Casazza has failed to produce any document, or combination of documents, that satisfy the statute of frauds' writing requirement. Casazza's statements that a writing sufficient to satisfy the statute of frauds *may* exist is not enough to defeat Kiser's motion to dismiss.

(3) *Admissions Exception*

In a related argument, Casazza argues that the admissions exception to the statute of frauds applies to this dispute. *See* [§ 2-201(3)(b)]. That subsection provides that even when there is no signed writing sufficient to satisfy the writing requirement, the proponent of the exception can escape the requirements of the statute of frauds "if the party against whom enforcement is sought admits in pleading, testimony or otherwise in court that a contract for sale was made." *Id.* Here, Kiser has made no such admission. Nonetheless, Casazza argues that had the District Court granted his request for additional time for discovery pursuant to Fed. R. Civ. P. 56(f), Kiser might have made such an admission. Specifically, Casazza claims that Kiser may have a sufficient writing or that Kiser might admit a contract was formed between the parties if he were deposed. The District Court denied the request and found that resolution of whether the statute of frauds applies to the dispute did not require further factual development.

In light of our decision affirming the District Court's decision to dismiss Casazza's breach of contract claim, we need not reach the discovery issues raised in Casazza's Rule 56(f) petition. . . . The District Court held a hearing on the motion to dismiss on January 14, 2002. By that time – six months after the suit was filed – Casazza still had not produced any writing sufficient to satisfy the statute of frauds nor had he obtained an admission from Kiser that a contract existed. Given the period of time that elapsed and the conclusory nature of Casazza's request for a continuance, we find the District Court did not abuse its discretion by denying further discovery and ruling on the motion to dismiss. . . .

B. *Promissory Estoppel*

Casazza alternatively argues that even if the alleged contract fails to satisfy the statute of frauds, his case should be permitted to proceed because a statute of frauds defense is inapplicable to his promissory estoppel claim. The District Court rejected this argument, holding that Casazza's promissory estoppel claim rests on the same purported promise that forms the basis of his breach of contract claim and that to allow Casazza to pursue the promissory estoppel claim, despite the lack of a sufficient writing, "would negate the purpose of the statute of frauds." Memorandum and Order, January 15, 2002, at 5 n.1.

Promissory estoppel implies "a contract in law where none exists in fact." *Grouse v. Group Health Plan, Inc.,* 306 N.W.2d 114, 116 (Minn. 1981). "Under promissory estoppel, a promise which is expected to induce definite action by the promisee, and does induce the action, is binding if injustice can be avoided only by enforcing the promise." *Cohen v. Cowles Media Co.,* 479 N.W.2d 387, 391 (Minn. 1992).

In *Del Hayes & Sons, Inc. v. Mitchell,* 230 N.W.2d 588, 593-94 (Minn. 1975), the Minnesota Supreme Court identified three approaches courts have taken concerning the applicability of the statute of frauds defense to promissory estoppel claims. Under the first (or "RESTATEMENT") approach, "promissory estoppel will defeat the statute of frauds only when the promise relied upon is a promise to reduce the contract to writing." *Id.* The second approach described by the court, and adopted in numerous jurisdictions, rejects "the view that promissory estoppel can remove an oral contract from the statute of frauds." *Id.* at 594; *see also Lige Dickson Co. v. Union Oil Co.,* 635 P.2d 103, 107 (Wash. 1981) (holding "promissory estoppel cannot be used to overcome the statute of frauds in a case which involves the sale of goods"). According to the court, jurisdictions that have adopted this approach "do so because a promissory estoppel exception would likely render the statute of frauds nugatory." *Del Hayes,* 230 N.W.2d at 594; *see also McDabco, Inc. v. Chet Adams Co.,* 548 F. Supp. 456, 461 (D.S.C.1982) ("The [South Carolina] legislature has provided that the only exceptions to the requirements of a written contract of sale are provided in [section 2-201(2) and (3)]. Promissory estoppel is not included within these subsections."). The third and least restrictive approach described by the court states that an oral promise can satisfy the statute of frauds only "where the detrimental reliance is of such a character and magnitude that refusal to enforce the contract would permit one party to perpetrate a fraud." *Del Hayes,* 230 N.W.2d at 594. The court went on to note that "[a] mere refusal to perform an oral agreement, unaccompanied by unconscionable conduct, however, is not such a fraud as will justify disregarding the statute." *Id.; see also Resolution Trust Corp. v. Flanagan,* 821 F. Supp. 572, 574 (D. Minn.1993) ("under the doctrine of promissory estoppel, a party seeking to take an agreement out of the 'statute of frauds must demonstrate that application of the statute of frauds would protect, rather than prevent, the perpetration of a fraud' "). The *Del Hayes* court did not endorse any particular view and held that, under any approach, promissory estoppel was not available so as to remove the oral contract at issue in that case from the statute of frauds. *Del Hayes,* 230 N.W.2d at 594.

In this case, the District Court apparently adopted the second or "restrictive" approach, which prohibits Casazza from doing an end-run around the statute of frauds because his promissory estoppel claim is based on the very promise that the statute otherwise bars. We might be inclined to agree with Casazza that Minnesota does not endorse such a hard-nosed view. . . . Nonetheless, we affirm the District Court's dismissal of Casazza's promissory estoppel claim. Even if we assume Casazza is correct that Minnesota does not endorse the view that promissory estoppel can never overcome the statute of frauds defense in a case such as this, he fails to convince us that his claim could proceed under either of the remaining approaches discussed by the Minnesota Supreme Court in *Del Hayes.*

Casazza's promissory estoppel claim fails under the RESTATEMENT approach because he did not sufficiently allege that Kiser promised to reduce their oral agreement to writing. Casazza argues he made a sufficient allegation in his amended complaint, where he alleged that Kiser asked him to complete a blank Coast Guard bill of sale. In ruling on Casazza's motion for reconsideration, the District Court rejected this argument and held that "[e]ven a liberal reading of the Complaint . . . does not support the inclusion of such a claim." Order, February 7, 2002, at 2. Based on our own review of the amended complaint, we agree. The bill of sale is mentioned in only one line of Casazza's five-page amended complaint. Nowhere in this complaint does Casazza specifically allege that Kiser promised to reduce their oral agreement to writing. . . .

Casazza's promissory estoppel claim also fails under the so-called least restrictive approach. Under this approach, Casazza's promissory estoppel claim can only proceed "where the detrimental reliance is of such a character and magnitude that refusal to enforce the contract would permit one party to perpetrate a fraud." *Del Hayes,* 230 N.W.2d at 594. . . . Here, Casazza alleges that he and Kiser reached an agreement on the sale of the *Andante* and that he subsequently arranged for a survey, obtained an estimate for some repairs, visited marinas, and tentatively arranged slip space for the boat. Casazza also alleges that a week later, Kiser told him he was not going to sell him the boat. Nowhere in Casazza's amended complaint does he allege that Kiser did anything that would constitute a fraud. At most, Casazza alleges that Kiser broke their oral agreement after Casazza had expended some money and time in anticipation of buying the boat.

Casazza's allegations simply do not amount to detrimental reliance of the sort required to take this agreement out of the statute of frauds. *See Del Hayes,* 230

N.W.2d at 594 n.11 ("The fraud most commonly treated as taking an agreement out of the Statute of Frauds" occurs where "the other party has been induced to make expenditures or a change of situation . . . , *so that the refusal to complete the execution of the agreement is not merely a denial of rights which it was intended to confer, but the infliction of an unjust and unconscionable injury and loss.*" (quoting 3 WILLISTON, CONTRACTS (3d ed.) § 533A, p. 798) (emphasis added by *Del Hayes*)). Whatever we might think of Kiser's behavior, we find nothing in the pleadings to suggest that judicial refusal to enforce the oral agreement "would permit one party to perpetrate a fraud." *Id.* "[A] mere refusal to perform an oral agreement unaccompanied by unconscionable conduct . . . is not such a fraud as will justify disregarding the statute." *Id.* Casazza's promissory estoppel claim therefore must fail.

III. Conclusion

For the reasons stated, we affirm the order of the District Court dismissing Casazza's suit.

Notes

1. For a slightly different view on the amount of discovery a plaintiff may conduct before dismissing the complaint, see *DF Activities Corp. v. Brown*, 851 F.2d 920 (7th Cir 1988) (once defendant denies under oath the existence of the agreement, case should be dismissed).
2. For a different take on the use of promissory estoppel to circumvent the statute of frauds, see *B & W Glass, Inc. v. Weather Shield Mfg., Inc.*, 829 P.2d 809 (Wy. 1992) (promissory estoppel may justify enforcement of oral promise otherwise within the scope of UCC § 2-201).

Problem 2-11

What should Casazza have done in the interaction with Kiser to make sure that he would have been able to satisfy the statute of frauds? Would a confirming memorandum under section 2-201(2) have worked in this situation? Are Casazza and Kiser merchants? *See* UCC § 2-104.

Assume both parties are merchants and you are advising Casazza during the course of this interaction. What should Casazza have done? Now change sides and consider how Kiser should respond to the advice you gave Casazza.

Modifications to an existing agreement also may have to be in writing, either because the initial agreement requires modifications to be in writing or because the statute of frauds applies to the agreement as modified. *See* UCC § 2-209(2), (3). We will consider modifications further in Chapter Three.

Problem 2-12

BIM and Silicon Solutions allegedly entered an oral agreement for Silicon Solutions to produce and sell to BIM 50,000 integrated circuits for use in computers. The circuits were to conform to particular specifications furnished by BIM. BIM then issued purchase orders for 7,000 circuits. After manufacture and delivery, BIM accepted and paid for 4,000 circuits but rejected the remaining 3,000 on the basis of alleged quality problems. Silicon Solutions sued for damages caused by BIM's "wrongful" rejection of 3,000 circuits and for breach of contract for BIM's failure to order the remaining 43,000 circuits. BIM moved for a summary judgment on the basis of section 2-201. Silicon Solutions argued that the summary judgment should be denied because the statute of frauds was satisfied under section 2-201(3)(a) and (c). *See* UCC § 2-606 as to goods accepted.

Silicon Solutions cited *Impossible Electronic Techniques, Inc. v. Wackenhut Protective Systems, Inc.*, 669 F.2d 1026, 1036–37 (5th Cir. 1982), in which the court stated that the "statute exempts contracts involving 'specially manufactured' goods from the writing requirement because in these cases the very nature of the goods serves as a reliable indication that a contract was indeed formed." Further:

Where the seller has commenced or completed the manufacture of goods that conform to the special needs of a particular buyer and thereby are not suitable for sale to others, not only is the likelihood of a perjured claim of a contract diminished, but denying enforcement to such a contract would impose substantial hardship on the aggrieved party. . . . The unfairness is especially acute where . . . the seller has incurred substantial, unrecoverable expense in reliance on the oral promise of the buyer. . . . The crucial inquiry is whether the manufacturer could sell the goods in the ordinary course of his business to someone other than the original buyer. If with slight alterations the goods could be so sold, then they are not specially manufactured; if, however, essential changes are necessary to render the goods marketable by the seller to others, then the exception does apply.

How should the court rule?

3.   More on Electronic Contracting

Both the federal Electronic Signatures in Global and National Commerce Act ("E-Sign")[28] and the Uniform Electronic Transactions Act ("UETA")[29] potentially apply to transactions under Article 2. E-Sign's operative section, codified at 15 U.S.C. § 7001, does not apply if a state has enacted UETA.[30] Both E-Sign and UETA provide that signatures, contracts, or other records shall not be denied validity "solely" because they are in electronic form or that an electronic record was used in contract formation. Similarly, electronic records can satisfy the requirement of a writing that may be imposed under other law, such as by a statute of frauds. E-Sign § 7001(a); UETA § 7. No party is required to use electronic communications, and E-Sign incorporates some disclosure rules to use regarding electronic communications in transactions with consumers. E-Sign § 7001(b); UETA § 5. The United Nations Convention on the Use of Electronic Communications in International Contracts has provisions of similar import. Arts. 8 through 14. The United States has not yet ratified this Convention.[31]

---

[28] E-Sign is codified at 15 U.S.C. § 7001 *et seq.* Section 7003(a) does not exempt Article 2 transactions from its scope.

[29] UETA is in effect in 46 states and the District of Columbia. UETA section 3 does not exempt Article 2 transactions from its scope. In order for UETA to govern an Article 2 transaction, however, the parties have to agree to conduct the transaction electronically. UETA §§ 3 and 5(b).

[30] 15 U.S.C. § 7002.

[31] For a comparison, *see* Charles H. Martin, *The Electronic Contracts Convention, the CISG, and New Sources of E-commerce Law*, 16 TUL. J. INT'L & COMP. L. 467 (2008); Jennifer A.

The theory of these various promulgations is that electronic communication is a medium that may require some additional rules but does not require any change in the basic underlying legal principles of contract law. Hence their provisions are minimal and encourage electronic commerce, rather than impose an elaborate scheme of rules or directive.[32]

B. Unconscionability

Courts have always had the discretion to refuse to enforce an agreement. Sometimes they would declare an agreement void as against public policy.[33] Other times they would invalidate an agreement because it was unconscionable. That is, the agreement shocked the conscience of the court.[34] Article 2 codifies this rule in section 2-302. It authorizes a court to refuse to enforce an unconscionable agreement entirely or to excise the unconscionable provisions and enforce the remainder.

Unfortunately, nothing in the UCC purports to define the meaning and scope of the term "unconscionable." Still, there is some guidance. The UCC tells us that unconscionability is to be determined at the time of contracting, not at some later point when circumstances have changed. UCC § 2-302(1). In addition, it is a legal issue for the court, and thus not a factual one for the jury. *Id.* The comments then supply more help by identifying the underlying principle as "the prevention of oppression and unfair surprise." UCC § 2-302 cmt. 1.

Puplava, *Use and Enforceability of Electronic Contracting: The State of Uniform Legislation Attempting to Regulate E-commerce Transactions*, 16 MICH. ST. J. INT'L L. 153 (2007); Henry D. Gabriel, *United Nations Convention on the Use of Electronic Communications in International Contracts and Compatibility with the American Domestic Law of Electronic Commerce*, 7 LOY L. & TECH. ANN. 1 (2006–07); Charles H. Martin, *The UNCITRAL Electronic Contracts Convention: Will it Be Used or Avoided?*, 17 PACE INT'L L. REV. 261 (2005).

[32] *See* Ronald J. Mann & Travis Siebeneicher, *Just One Click, The Reality of Internet Retail Contracting*, 108 COLUM. L. REV. 984 (2008); John M. Norwood, *A Summary of Statutory and Case Law Associated with Contracting in the Electronic Universe*, 4 DEPAUL BUS. & COM. L.J. 415 (2006).

[33] *See* RESTATEMENT (SECOND) OF CONTRACTS §§ 178–96.

[34] *Compare* RESTATEMENT (SECOND) OF CONTRACTS § 208.

This comment has prompted courts and commentators[35] to suggest that there are two aspects to unconscionability: substantive unconscionability and procedural unconscionability. Substantive unconscionability (*i.e.,* "oppression") deals with the substantive terms of the contract, such as price, warranties, and limitations on remedy. Procedural unconscionability (*i.e.,* "unfair surprise") deals with the bargaining process and covers such things as lack of meaningful choice, deception, small print, and language barriers. Many courts require some aspect of both substantive and procedural unconscionability before they will give relief. Others are more lenient, and will permit an abundance of one to make up for a lack or minimal amount of the other.

Most of the successful claims of unconscionability arise in the consumer context. The early cases under Article 2 tended to involve sales of furniture or appliances at inflated prices to poorly educated or non-English speaking customers.[36] More recently, the cases tend to involve the enforceability of an arbitration clause in a consumer contract. The consumer's first attack on such a clause is usually to argue that the clause is not part of the agreement at all, relying on the contract formation rules of section 2-207. With some minor exceptions,[37] those arguments have not fared well.[38]

---

[35] Unconscionability is another area that is a favorite for law professors to write about. *See, e.g.,* Edith R. Warkentine, *Beyond Unconscionability: The Case for Using "Knowing Assent" as the Basis for Analyzing Unbargained-For Terms in Standard Form Contracts,* 31 SEATTLE UNIV. L. REV. 469 (2008); Wayne R. Barnes, *Toward a Fairer Model of Consumer Assent to Standard Form Contracts: In Defense of Restatement Subsection 211(3),* 82 WASH. L. REV. 227 (2007).

[36] *See, e.g., Morris v. Capitol Furniture & Appliance Co.,* 280 A.2d 775 (D.C. 1971); *Toker v. Westerman,* 274 A.2d 78 (N.J. Dist. Ct. 1970); *Toker v. Perl,* 247 A.2d 701 (N.J. Sup. Ct. 1968), *aff'd,* 260 A.2d 244 (N.J. Super. Ct. App. Div. 1970); *Frostifresh Corp. v. Reynoso,* 274 N.Y.S.2d 757 (N.Y. Dist. Ct. 1966), *rev'd only as to remedy,* 281 N.Y.S.2d 964 (N.Y. Sup. Ct. 1967); *Williams v. Walker-Thomas Furniture Co.,* 350 F.2d 445 (D.C. Cir. 1965).

[37] *E.g., Klocek v. Gateway, Inc.,* 104 F. Supp. 2d 1332 (D. Kan.), *dismissed for lack of subject matter jurisdiction,* 2000 WL 1372886 (D. Kan. 2000), *refusing to vacate first order,* 2001 WL 1568346 (D. Kan. 2001). *See also Rogers v. Dell Computer Corp.,* 138 P.3d 826 (Okla. 2005) (laying out the analysis but concluding that the record was not sufficiently complete to reach a determination).

[38] *E.g., Fiser v. Dell Computer Corp.,* 165 P.3d 328 (N.M. Ct. App. 2007), *rev'd on other grounds,* 188 P.3d 1215 (N.M. 2008); *M.A. Mortenson Co. v. Timberline Software Corp.,*

The consumer's second attack is to argue that the arbitration clause is unconscionable. All claims of unconscionability face an uphill battle. Courts generally are loathe to interfere with freedom of contract. Unconscionability claims against an arbitration clause face an even steeper incline, because the Federal Arbitration Act , 9 U.S.C. § 1, *et seq.*, codifies a strong national policy in favor of arbitrating private disputes. Nevertheless, there is a growing body of law that recognizes that – at least in consumer transactions – arbitration agreements can be unconscionable, particularly if they require arbitration in a remote location or require payment of a fee in excess of the amount of the underlying transaction.[39] While few of these cases have arisen under Article 2, some have.[40] Consider this recent example.

FISER V. DELL COMPUTER CORP.
188 P.3d 1215 (N.M. 2008)

Serna, Justice

We granted certiorari to review whether Defendant Dell Computer Corporation's Motion to Stay and Compel Arbitration pursuant to the Federal Arbitration Act was properly granted. We hold that, in the context of small consumer claims that would be prohibitively costly to bring on an individual basis,

---

998 P.2d 305 (Wash. 2000); *Hill v. Gateway 2000, Inc.*, 105 F.3d 1147 (7th Cir.), *cert. denied*, 522 U.S. 808 (1997).

[39] *See Ingle v. Circuit City Stores, Inc.*, 328 F.3d 1165 (9th Cir. 2003), *cert. denied*, 540 U.S. 1160 (2004) (arbitration clause in employment agreement unconscionable because of its one-way application, one-year limitations period, bar on class actions, and cost splitting provisions). *See also Ting v. AT&T*, 319 F.3d 1126 (9th Cir.(, *cert. denied*, 540 U.S. 811 (2003) (arbitration clause was unconscionable because it barred class actions, split costs inappropriately, and mandated that results be kept confidential); *Szetela v. Discover Bank*, 118 Cal. Rptr. 2d 862 (Cal. Ct. App. 2002), *cert. denied*, 537 U.S. 1226 (2003) (striking a ban on class actions from an arbitration clause). *But see Anders v. Hometown Mortgage Services, Inc.*, 346 F.3d 1024 (11th Cir. 2003) (limitations on remedies do not affect the enforceability of an arbitration agreement); *Rosen v. SCIL, LLC*, 799 N.E.2d 488 (Ill. Ct. App. 2003) (credit card arbitration agreement not unconscionable because it prohibited class actions).

[40] *See Brower v. Gateway 2000, Inc.*, 676 N.Y.S.2d 569 (N.Y. Sup. Ct. App. Div. 1998) (arbitration clause unconscionable because it made arbitration prohibitively expensive).

contractual prohibitions on class relief are contrary to New Mexico's fundamental public policy of encouraging the resolution of small consumer claims and are therefore unenforceable in this state. We reverse.

I. FACTUAL BACKGROUND AND PROCEEDINGS BELOW

Plaintiff Robert Fiser purchased a computer from Defendant via the company's website. He subsequently filed a putative class action lawsuit contending that Defendant systematically misrepresents the memory size of its computers. He alleges violations of the New Mexico Unfair Practices Act (UPA), the New Mexico False Advertising Act, the New Mexico Uniform Commercial Code (UCC), and common law concepts of breach of contract, breach of warranty, misrepresentation, violations of the covenants of good faith and fair dealing, bad faith, and unjust enrichment.

Central to the issue presented is the scant amount of damages alleged: Plaintiff estimates that Defendant's alleged misrepresentation results in a monetary loss to its customers of just ten to twenty dollars per computer.

Defendant filed a Motion to Stay and Compel Arbitration pursuant to the Federal Arbitration Act (FAA). *See* 9 U.S.C. §§ 3, 4 (2000). Defendant argued that, pursuant to the "terms and conditions" on its website at the time of the purchase, Plaintiff is required to individually arbitrate his claims and is precluded from proceeding on a classwide basis either in litigation or arbitration. The "terms and conditions" included an arbitration clause mandating that "any claim, dispute, or controversy . . . against Dell . . . [was subject to] binding arbitration administered by the National Arbitration Forum (NAF)." The terms also included a clause (hereinafter referred to as the class action ban) which directed that the arbitration was "limited solely to the dispute or controversy between [Plaintiff] and Dell."[41] Finally, the "terms and conditions" contained a choice-of-law provision declaring Texas law to be controlling. Although the parties disagree over whether Plaintiff assented to Defendant's "terms and conditions," we do not reach that issue. We assume without deciding, for the purpose of our analysis, that he assented to the terms.

---

[41] Although, in the past, the procedural rules of the NAF also did not allow for classwide arbitration, the rules have apparently been amended to provide for such a procedure since briefing was completed. *See* http://www.arb-forum.com/default.aspx and proceed through the links as follows: "programs and rules," "arbitration," "the code of procedure," "arbitration class procedures."

The district court agreed with Defendant that Plaintiff was bound by the arbitration provision and thus granted Defendant's motion. The Court of Appeals affirmed. Plaintiff petitioned for a writ of certiorari; both the New Mexico Attorney General and Public Justice filed amicus briefs in support of Plaintiff. Because we conclude that the class action ban is contrary to fundamental New Mexico public policy, we reverse.

II. DISCUSSION
A. *Application of Texas Law Would Violate New Mexico Public Policy*
1. New Mexico Respects Choice-of-Law Provisions Unless Application of the Chosen Law Would Contravene New Mexico Public Policy

The threshold question in determining the validity of the class action ban is which state's law must be applied to this potentially multi-state class action that was filed in New Mexico by a New Mexico resident against a defendant that maintains its principal place of business in Texas for damages relating to a contract that contains a choice-of-law clause directing that Texas law be applied.

New Mexico respects party autonomy; the law to be applied to a particular dispute may be chosen by the parties through a contractual choice-of-law provision. However, when application of the law chosen by the parties offends New Mexico public policy, our courts may decline to enforce the choice-of-law provision and apply New Mexico law instead. New Mexico courts will not give effect to another state's laws where those laws would "violate some fundamental principle of justice." *Reagan v. McGee Drilling Corp.*, 933 P.2d 867 (N.M. 1997).

Application of Texas law to the instant matter would likely require enforcing the class action ban. Unless enforcement of the class action ban would run afoul of fundamental New Mexico public policy, our conflict of law rules counsel respecting the choice-of-law provision and applying Texas law.

2. It is Fundamental New Mexico Policy that Consumers Have a Viable Mechanism for Dispute Resolution, No Matter the Size of the Claim

New Mexico policy strongly supports the resolution of consumer claims, regardless of the amount of damages alleged. That policy is demonstrated by several of our statutes. For example, the New Mexico legislature enacted the UPA, which is unequivocal: "[u]nfair or deceptive trade practices and unconscionable trade practices in the conduct of any trade or commerce are unlawful." Section 57-12-3. The UPA was clearly drafted to include a remedy for small claims: a party need not show any monetary damage to be entitled to an injunction, § 57-12-10(A), and "[a]ny person who suffers *any* loss of money . . . [may] recover actual damages or the sum of one hundred dollars ($100), whichever is greater." § 57-12-10(B) (emphasis added).

The fundamental New Mexico policy of providing consumers a mechanism for resolution is also seen in the False Advertising Act, which specifically empowers private individuals to bring rights of action in the name of the state and for "all others similarly situated." § 57-15-5.

Yet another example of New Mexico's fundamental public policy in ensuring that consumers have an opportunity to redress their harm is the Consumer Protection Division of the Attorney General's Office, which is charged with protecting New Mexico citizens from unfair and deceptive trade practices. In this effort, the Consumer Protection Division is authorized and funded to investigate suspicious business activities, informally resolve the complaints of dissatisfied consumers, educate citizens about their consumer rights, and file lawsuits on behalf of the public.

3. The Class Action Device is Critical to Enforcement of Consumer Rights in New Mexico

The opportunity to seek class relief is of particular importance to the enforcement of consumer rights because it provides a mechanism for the spreading of costs. The class action device allows claimants with individually small claims the opportunity for relief that would otherwise be economically infeasible because they may collectively share the otherwise prohibitive costs of bringing and maintaining the claim.

The opportunity for class relief and its importance to consumer rights is enshrined in the fundamental policy of New Mexico and evidenced by our statutory scheme. *See, e.g.,* Rule 1-023 NMRA (setting forth the rules of civil procedure governing class actions). Notably, the UPA specifically references class actions as a private remedy available under the act. § 57-12-10(E). Further, the New Mexico Uniform Arbitration Act declares that arbitration clauses that require consumers to decline participation in class actions are unenforceable and voidable. *See* NMSA 1978, §§ 44-7A-1(b)(4)(f), 44-7A-5 (2001). While this provision may be preempted by the FAA, *see Perry v. Thomas,* 482 U.S. 483, 492 n.9 (1987) ("A state-law principle that takes its meaning precisely from the fact that a contract to arbitrate is at issue does not comport with [the FAA].ates"), it is clear evidence of the fundamental New Mexico policy of allowing consumers a means to redress their injuries via the class action device.

In New Mexico, we recognize that the class action was devised for "vindication of the rights of groups of people who individually would be without effective strength to bring their opponents into court at all." *Romero v. Philip Morris, Inc.,* 109 P.3d 768 (N.M. 2005). A purpose of the class action is to conserve party resources. As the United States Supreme Court recognized,

> [t]he policy at the very core of the class action mechanism is to overcome the problem that small recoveries do not provide the incentive for any individual to bring a solo action prosecuting his or her rights. A class action solves this problem by aggregating the relatively paltry potential recoveries into something worth someone's (usually an attorney's) labor.

Amchem Prods., Inc. v. Windsor, 521 U.S. 591, 617 (1997). "Where it is not economically feasible to obtain relief within the traditional framework of a multiplicity of small individual suits for damages, aggrieved persons may be without any effective redress unless they may employ the class-action device." *Deposit Guar. Nat'l Bank, Jackson, Miss. v. Roper,* 445 U.S. 326, 339 (1980). The Federal Rules Advisory Committee recognized the critical nature of the class action to individuals with small claims when it directed that one of the grounds on which class certification may be appropriate is where "the amounts at stake for individuals [are] so small that separate suits would be impracticable." Fed. R. Civ. P. 23(b)(3), advisory committee note (1966 amendment).

Thus, beyond merely a procedural tool, the class action functions as a gatekeeper to relief when the cost of bringing a single claim is greater than the damages alleged. When viewed in this light, a contractual provision that purports to ban class actions for small claims implicates not just the opportunity for a class action but the more fundamental right to a meaningful remedy for one's claims. This Court has recognized that the right of access to the courts is part of the right to petition for redress of grievances guaranteed by both the United States and New Mexico constitutions. While the class action ban may or may not rise to the level of a constitutional violation, a prohibition on class relief where there is no meaningful alternative for redress of injury certainly does not provide for effective vindication of rights.

In view of the fact that Plaintiff's alleged damages are just ten to twenty dollars, by attempting to prevent him from seeking class relief, Defendant has essentially foreclosed the possibility that Plaintiff may obtain *any* relief. Thus, we conclude that Defendant's prohibition on class action relief, when applied to small claims plaintiffs, is contrary to New Mexico's fundamental public policy to provide a forum for relief for small consumer claims. The words of the California Supreme Court are apropos:

> By imposing this clause on its customers, [Defendant] has essentially granted itself a license to push the boundaries of good business practices to their furthest limits, fully aware that relatively few, if any, customers will seek legal remedies, and that any remedies obtained will only pertain to that single customer without collateral estoppel effect. The potential for millions of customers to be . . . without an effective method of redress cannot be ignored.

Discover Bank v. Super. Ct., 113 P.3d 1100, 1108 (Cal. 2005).

Defendant contends that Plaintiff has not met the evidentiary burden of proving that his damages are outweighed by the cost of bringing an individual claim. While we recognize that, in some cases, more extensive factfinding will be required, we emphasize that Plaintiff only alleges his damages to be between *ten and twenty dollars.* We do not find it necessary to engage in an exhaustive analysis regarding whether the economic and opportunity costs of bringing a ten to twenty dollar claim are prohibitive. In light of attorney's fees, the costs of gathering evidence and preparing the case, and the time spent educating himself on the issues and organizing and presenting the claim, the likelihood that Plaintiff's actual costs will exceed ten to twenty dollars is certain. The economic realities of the present case are clearly more tangible than the mere "risk" that Plaintiff will be faced with prohibitive costs. *Cf. Green Tree Fin. Corp.-Ala. v. Randolph,* 531 U.S. 79, 90–91 (2000) (holding that arbitration agreement's failure to address how parties would allocate arbitration costs does not render it per se unenforceable on the grounds that the claimant may be subjected to steep costs where claimant did not present evidence that she would be subjected to such high costs). Suffice it to say that "only a lunatic or a fanatic sues for [ten to twenty dollars.]" *Carnegie v. Household Int'l, Inc.,* 376 F.3d 656, 661 (7th Cir. 2004).

For all of the foregoing reasons, New Mexico's fundamental public policy requires that consumers with small claims have a mechanism for dispute resolution via the class action. Therefore, application of Texas law, that would allow the class action ban, is contrary to New Mexico public policy. Accordingly, we invoke the public policy exception and apply New Mexico law rather than Texas law to analyze the validity of the class action ban.

B.   *Under New Mexico Law, the Class Action Ban is Invalid Because It is Contrary to Public Policy and Therefore Unconscionable*

Plaintiff contends that the class action ban is unconscionable. This determination is a matter of law and is reviewed de novo. We agree.

The classic articulation of unconscionability is that it is comprised of two prongs: substantive unconscionability and procedural unconscionability. Substantive unconscionability relates to the content of the contract terms and whether they are illegal, contrary to public policy, or grossly unfair. *Padilla v. State Farm Mut. Auto. Ins. Co.,* 68 P.3d 901 (N.M. 2003); *Guthmann v. La Vida Llena,* 709 P.2d 675, 679 (N.M. 1985). Procedural unconscionability is determined by analyzing the circumstances surrounding the contract's formation, such as whether it was an adhesive contract and the relative bargaining power of the parties. *Guthmann,* 709 P.2d at 679. "The weight given to procedural and substantive considerations varies with the circumstances of each case." *Id.*

As set forth above, we concluded in the course of our conflict analysis that the class action ban violates New Mexico public policy. By preventing customers with small claims from attempting class relief and thereby circumscribing their only economically efficient means for redress, Defendant's class action ban exculpates the company from wrongdoing. "Denial of a class action in cases where it is appropriate may have the effect of allowing an unscrupulous wrongdoer to retain the benefits of its wrongful conduct." *Discover Bank,* 113 P.3d at 1106. On these facts, enforcing the class action ban would be tantamount to allowing Defendant to unilaterally exempt itself from New Mexico consumer protection laws. It is not hyperbole or exaggeration to say that it is a fundamental principle of justice in New Mexico that corporations may not tailor the laws that our legislature has enacted in order to shield themselves from the potential claims of consumers. Because it violates public policy by depriving small claims consumers of a meaningful remedy and exculpating Defendant from potential wrongdoing, the class action ban meets the test for substantive unconscionability.

In the instant case, the nature of the "terms and conditions" may or may not rise to the level of an adhesive or procedurally unconscionable contract. When a court makes an analysis into whether a particular contract is adhesive, it typically inquires into three factors: (1) whether it was prepared entirely by one party for the acceptance of the other; (2) whether the party proffering the contract enjoyed superior bargaining power because the weaker party could not avoid doing business under the particular terms; and [(3)] whether the contract was offered to the weaker party without an opportunity for bargaining on a take-it-or-leave-it basis.

Guthmann, 709 P.2d at 678. The Court of Appeals held that the terms did not constitute a contract of adhesion because there was no evidence that Plaintiff could not avoid doing business under the particular terms mandated by Defendant. While we agree that Defendant's "terms and conditions" may not rise to the level of an adhesive contract, we nevertheless conclude that the terms are unenforceable because there has been such an overwhelming showing of substantive unconscionability. For these reasons, the agreement is unconscionable under New Mexico law and will not be enforced in this state.[42]

C. Invalidation of the Arbitration Agreement and Embedded Exculpatory Class Action Ban is Not Preempted by the FAA

Having held that the class action ban is unenforceable in New Mexico, we turn to an examination of whether the FAA preempts our ruling. Congress enacted the FAA to counteract judicial hostility to arbitration. The Act provides that arbitration agreements "shall be valid, irrevocable, and enforceable, save upon such grounds that exist at law or in equity for the revocation of any contract." Section 2. While the FAA prevents "[s]tates from singling out arbitration provisions for suspect status," *Doctor's Assocs., Inc. v. Casarotto,* 517 U.S. 681, 687 (1996), it does not give arbitration provisions special protection either. It only requires that they be placed "upon the same footing as other contracts." *Scherk v. Alberto-Culver Co.,* 417 U.S. 506, 511 (1974). "Thus, generally applicable contract defenses, such as fraud, duress, or unconscionability, may be applied to invalidate arbitration agreements without contravening § 2." *Doctor's Assocs.,* 517 U.S. at 687. Because our invalidation of the ban on class relief rests on the doctrine of unconscionability, a doctrine that exists for the revocation of any contract, the FAA does not preempt our holding. Class action bans that effectively deny consumer plaintiffs relief are invalid in New Mexico, regardless of the contracts in which they are found.

D. The Class Action Ban is Not Severable

When a provision of a contract is determined to be unconscionable, we "may refuse to enforce the contract, or [we] may enforce the remainder of the contract

---

[42] We note that numerous other jurisdictions have also concluded that class action bans are unconscionable. *See, e.g., Shroyer v. New Cingular Wireless Servs., Inc.,* 498 F.3d 976, 984 (9th Cir. 2007); *Skirchak v. Dynamics Research Corp.,* 432 F. Supp. 2d 175, 180–81 (D. Mass. 2006); *Szetela v. Discover Bank,* 118 Cal. Rptr. 2d 862, 867 (Cal. Ct. App. 2002); *Kinkel v. Cingular Wireless, LLC,* 857 N.E.2d 250, 274–75 (Ill. 2006).

without the unconscionable clause, or [we] may so limit the application of any unconscionable clause as to avoid any unconscionable result." [§ 2-302]. Here, the class action ban is part of the arbitration provision and is central to the mechanism for resolving the dispute between the parties; therefore, it cannot be severed. We decline to enforce the arbitration provision.

III. CONCLUSION

Contractual prohibition of class relief, as applied to claims that would be economically inefficient to bring on an individual basis, is contrary to the fundamental public policy of New Mexico to provide a forum for the resolution of all consumer claims and is therefore unenforceable in this state. The arbitration provision is invalid and the Court of Appeals reversed. We remand for proceedings consistent with this opinion.

The CISG does not have any provisions that address the concept of unconscionability, perhaps because it does not apply to consumer transactions. *Cf.* CISG Art. 4 (disclaiming any concern with the "validity" of the contract or any of its provisions). The UNIDROIT Principles do not deal with invalidity arising from "immorality or illegality," UNIDROIT Art. 3.1, but do deal with issues of "gross disparity." UNIDROIT Art. 3.10.

Problem 2-13

In a contract for sale of a car from a car dealer, the document signed by the buyer provided that all disputes arising under the contract must be resolved in arbitration, with the arbitrator chosen by the seller. The clause also provided that the buyer would be responsible for half of the arbitrator's fee unless the seller won the dispute in which case, the buyer would be responsible for all fees. The buyer is college educated and read the document prior to signing it. The buyer did not like the clause and objected to it but the seller refused to sell the car to the buyer unless the buyer signed the document. The buyer really wanted the car and grudgingly signed the document. Predictably the car was a lemon and the buyer is consulting you regarding what to do now. In your research, you find that all car dealers in the area have the same clause in their sales contracts. Is the buyer stuck with the arbitration clause?

Problem 2-14

You represent an office supply store that purchased a high end printer for use in the store. The office supply store placed the order for the printer by telephone and the seller responded by promptly sending the office supply store an acknowledgment form. That form included a choice-of-forum clause that requires all litigation against the seller to be commenced in Illinois, where the seller's chief executive office is located. The office supply store is located in Florida and has never done business in Illinois. The printer broke down a few months after it was delivered and the seller refused to replace it. The office supply store, which had paid no attention to the acknowledgment form, then sued the seller in the state court in Florida. The seller moved to dismiss the case based upon the choice-of-forum clause. Is the choice-of-forum clause enforceable? What are the best arguments that it is not?

Problem 2-15

Sly Electronics's sales force consists largely of college students who sell stereo components out of their vans. The sales force is trained to make people believe – but without actually saying – that the goods are stolen. The gimmick is that customers (*i.e.,* "marks") will think they are getting a really good deal (a steal, so to speak), because they are buying stolen goods. In fact, the goods are not stolen and the sales force is properly licensed to sell goods on the street. Moreover, the deal is not very good at all. The typical markup is quite high. A component that Sly Electronics sells for $600 will typically cost it only $200 and retail for about $300. If a customer learns the truth after a purchase and sues to rescind the transaction, will the customer have a good claim of unconscionability? Why or why not? In analyzing this question, which comparison is the more appropriate consideration and why: (i) price to cost; or (ii) price to value?

CHAPTER THREE

TERMS OF THE CONTRACT – PART I

SECTION 1.   TERMS OF THE AGREEMENT

A. Usage of Trade, Course of Dealing, and Course of Performance

By now you know that there is a difference between the terms "agreement" and "contract." Review the definitions of those terms in section 1-201. Any analysis of the terms of a *contract* must begin with the terms of the parties' *agreement.*

The bargain that comprises the parties' agreement is based not merely on their exchange of promises or other communications. The agreement encompasses a much broader scope of relevant behavior. In addition to any statements made, the bargain can be derived from the particular parties' past, present, and future conduct, as well as the practices and usages of others engaging in the same trade or market. Read section 1-303.

In the UCC, course of performance, course of dealing, and usage of trade are concepts that encompass both the parties' behavior and the practices in a trade or market. Each of these concepts, which are defined in section 1-303(a)–(c), can be used to explain or cast meaning on the parties' express terms, or to otherwise supplement the parties' express terms. *See* UCC § 1-303(d).

A course of performance concerns how the parties to a particular transaction exercise the rights created or perform the duties imposed by their contract. It is a sequence of conduct by the parties to a particular transaction and can arise when the contract calls for the same act to be repeated multiple times. A course of performance often arises in an installment contract, but it is not limited to such transactions. *See* UCC § 2-612(1). A course of dealing is the conduct of these parties in prior dealings or transactions with one another. Usage of trade is how the members of the relevant industry or trade behave and informs the meaning they ascribe to particular terms. It is their set of standard practices and their lexicon for communicating with one another. And they follow these practices and use this lingo with such regularity that, unless expressly disclaimed, agreements among them can fairly be said to be based on the expectation such practices and meanings are part of their agreement.

There are three primary questions in thinking about course of performance, course of dealing, and usage of trade as part of the agreement and thus ultimately part of the contract of the parties. First, is there sufficient evidence to establish that a course of performance, course of dealing, or usage of trade exists? A party seeking to rely on such evidence generally has the burden to demonstrate the existence of the course of performance, course of dealing, or usage of trade.

Second, is evidence of a course of performance, course of dealing, or usage of trade admissible in a court proceeding concerning the transaction? This depends on two things. First, the party seeking to demonstrate the course of performance, course of dealing, or usage of trade must give advance notice to prevent unfair surprise. UCC § 1-303(g). In addition, the parol evidence rule in section 2-202 may, on some occasions, bar admission of the evidence. The parol evidence rule is discussed later in Chapter Five.

Third, whenever reasonably possible, evidence of course of performance, course of dealing, and usage of trade is to be construed as consistent with each other and with the parties' express terms. If it is not reasonable to construe them consistently,[1] the hierarchy set forth in section 1-303(e) controls: express terms govern, then course of performance, then course of dealing, and last, usage of trade.

Problem 3-1

You are a partner at a large law firm. One of the firm's clients is Orion Technologies, a company that manufactures and sells custom-designed robotics for use in extreme environments: space vehicles, deepwater research facilities, and subterranean excavations. Because its products are used in locations where they cannot readily be repaired, Orion has to be sure that its products will function properly.

Orion's long-time supplier of titanium rods has recently gone out of business. Its long-time supplier of resins and plastics has indicated that it will be raising prices by 20%. In response to these developments, Orion is negotiating with other companies to provide the needed materials. You will be asked to draft the supply contracts. Might there be any usages of trade that could be relevant to your task? If so, what might they be and how will you go about ascertaining what they are?

---

[1] *See Archer Daniels Midland Co. v. Brunswick County*, 129 Fed. Appx. 16 (4th Cir. 2005) (considering whether course of performance was consistent with or contradictory to the express terms of the agreement).

CISG and UNIDROIT Principles. The CISG also recognizes that agreements are made within the context of the parties' practices and usages in international trade, and that those practices and usages are part of the parties' agreement. CISG Art. 9. Interpreting the intent of the parties to an agreement also requires taking into account the parties' practices and usages in the trade. CISG Art. 8(3). The UNIDROIT Principles are similar. UNIDROIT Art. 1.9, Art. 4.3.

B. Good Faith

The UCC imposes a duty of good faith in the performance and enforcement of every transaction to which it applies. Read section 1-304. A similar duty exists in every contract. *See* RESTATEMENT (SECOND) OF CONTRACTS § 205. What does the obligation to act in good faith add to a party's contractual obligations? The answer to that requires a brief exploration of two things: (i) the scope of the good faith obligation; and (ii) the standard by which good faith is measured.

As to the scope of the good faith obligation, notice the language of section 1-304. It requires good faith in the "performance and enforcement" of a contract. The implications of this language are twofold. First, the duty of good faith does not arise until there is an underlying contract. That is, there must be a binding agreement between the parties. A corollary to this is that the obligation of good faith does not apply to pre-contract negotiations.[2] Second, the obligation of good faith is something that colors and illuminates contractual duties and rights, but it does not create an independent cause of action for breach. *See* UCC § 1-304 cmt.1. In this sense, the obligation is something like course of performance, course of dealing, and usage of trade. It is a lens through which to view and interpret the parties' agreement, but it does not and should not be used to contradict express terms.[3]

As to the standard for measuring good faith, that depends on two things: (i) whether the state has adopted the uniform version of revised Article 1; and (ii) whether the party is a merchant. Begin with Article 1. Under old Article 1, good faith meant merely "honesty in fact in the conduct or transaction concerned."

---

[2] *But see* UCC § 2-314 cmt. 3 (suggesting that the obligation of good faith requires a non-merchant to disclose – presumably before contracting – known but hidden defects in the goods).

[3] *See* PEB Commentary No. 10 (Feb. 10, 1994).

Former UCC § 1-201(19). This was a purely subjective standard. Revised Article 1 expands upon this standard by requiring "honesty in fact and the observance of reasonable commercial standards of fair dealing." UCC § 1-201(b)(20). This definition, which adds an objective element to good faith, was chosen in part because Article 2 had already had a similar definition of good faith for merchants. Read section 2-103(1)(b), which requires "honesty in fact and the observance of reasonable commercial standards of fair dealing in the trade." Note, the limitation to fair dealing "in the trade" was not incorporated in revised Article 1. Thus, the applicable standard depends on whether the state whose law governs has enacted revised Article 1 and, if so, whether the legislature adopted the heightened standard of good faith.[4]

	Standard from Old Article 1 Applies	Standard from Revised Article 1 Applies
Merchant	Honesty in fact and the observance of reasonable commercial standards of fair dealing in the trade.	Honesty in fact and the observance of reasonable commercial standards of fair dealing.
Non-merchant	Honesty in fact.	

As the comment to the revised definition in Article 1 makes clear, the requirement of "reasonable commercial standards of fair dealing" is not about commercial reasonableness, it is about "fair dealing." In other words, the duty of good faith is not a requirement to act non-negligently, it is a directive to act "fairly" in the transaction. *See* UCC § 1-201 cmt. 20.

So, what does good faith mean in the context of a particular transaction? In other words, how can one identify, based upon the standards noted above, whether a person has acted in good faith or bad faith? Does the concept merely limit the discretion that the contract purports to grant to one party, such as when a party has the discretion to fix the price in good faith under section 2-305? Consider the following case which arose in a context outside the UCC. To what extent do these

---

[4] Several states that have enacted revised Article 1 have not adopted the heightened standard of good faith.

ideas have force in the context of an Article 2 transaction?[5] Is Judge Posner talking about "honesty in fact" or the "observance of reasonable commercial standards of fair dealing" or about a different concept altogether?

MARKET STREET ASSOCIATES LTD. PARTNERSHIP V. FREY
941 F.2d 588 (7th Cir. 1991)

Posner, Circuit Judge

Market Street Associates Limited Partnership and its general partner appeal from a judgment for the defendants, General Electric Pension Trust and its trustees, entered upon cross-motions for summary judgment in a diversity suit that pivots on the doctrine of "good faith" performance of a contract. *Cf.* Robert Summers, *"Good Faith" in General Contract Law and the Sales Provisions of the Uniform Commercial Code*, 54 VA. L. REV. 195, 232–43 (1968). Wisconsin law applies – common law rather than Uniform Commercial Code, because the contract is for land rather than for goods, UCC § 2-102, and because it is a lease rather than a sale and Wisconsin has not adopted UCC art. 2A, which governs leases. . . .

In 1968, J.C. Penney Company, the retail chain, entered into a sale and leaseback arrangement with General Electric Pension Trust in order to finance Penney's growth. Under the arrangement Penney sold properties to the pension trust which the trust then leased back to Penney for a term of 25 years. Paragraph 34 of the lease entitles the lessee to "request Lessor [the pension trust] to finance the costs and expenses of construction of additional Improvements upon the Premises," provided the amount of the costs and expenses is at least $250,000. Upon receiving the request, the pension trust "agrees to give reasonable consideration to providing the financing of such additional Improvements and Lessor and Lessee shall negotiate in good faith concerning the construction of such Improvements and the financing by Lessor of such costs and expenses." Paragraph 34 goes on to provide that, should the negotiations fail, the lessee shall be entitled to repurchase the property at a price roughly equal to the price at which Penney sold it to the pension trust in the first place, plus 6 percent a year for each year since the

---

[5] *See, e.g.*, Harold Dubroff, *The Implied Covenant of Good Faith in Contract Interpretation and Gap-Filling: Reviling a Revered Relic*, 80 ST. JOHN'S L. REV. 559 (2006); Terri J. Dobbins, *Losing Faith: Extracting the Implied Covenant of Good Faith From (Some) Contracts*, 84 OR. L. REV. 227 (2005); James J. White, *Good Faith and the Cooperative Antagonist*, 54 SMU L. REV. 679 (2001).

original purchase. So if the average annual appreciation in the property exceeded 6 percent, a breakdown in negotiations over the financing of improvements would entitle Penney to buy back the property for less than its market value (assuming it had sold the property to the pension trust in the first place at its then market value).

One of these leases was for a shopping center in Milwaukee. In 1987 Penney assigned this lease to Market Street Associates, which the following year received an inquiry from a drugstore chain that wanted to open a store in the shopping center, provided (as is customary) that Market Street Associates built the store for it. Whether Market Street Associates was pessimistic about obtaining financing from the pension trust, still the lessor of the shopping center, or for other reasons, it initially sought financing for the project from other sources. But they were unwilling to lend the necessary funds without a mortgage on the shopping center, which Market Street Associates could not give because it was not the owner but only the lessee. It decided therefore to try to buy the property back from the pension trust. Market Street Associates' general partner, Orenstein, tried to call David Erb of the pension trust, who was responsible for the property in question. Erb did not return his calls, so Orenstein wrote him, expressing an interest in buying the property and asking him to "review your file on this matter and call me so that we can discuss it further." At first, Erb did not reply. Eventually Orenstein did reach Erb, who promised to review the file and get back to him. A few days later an associate of Erb called Orenstein and indicated an interest in selling the property for $3 million, which Orenstein considered much too high.

That was in June of 1988. On July 28, Market Street Associates wrote a letter to the pension trust formally requesting funding for $2 million in improvements to the shopping center. The letter made no reference to paragraph 34 of the lease; indeed, it did not mention the lease. The letter asked Erb to call Orenstein to discuss the matter. Erb, in what was becoming a habit of unresponsiveness, did not call. On August 16, Orenstein sent a second letter-certified mail, return receipt requested-again requesting financing and this time referring to the lease, though not expressly to paragraph 34. The heart of the letter is the following two sentences: "The purpose of this letter is to ask again that you advise us immediately if you are willing to provide the financing pursuant to the lease. If you are willing, we propose to enter into negotiation to amend the ground lease appropriately." The very next day, Market Street Associates received from Erb a letter, dated August 10, turning down the original request for financing on the ground that it did not "meet our current investment criteria": the pension trust was not interested in making loans for less than $7 million. On August 22, Orenstein replied to Erb by letter, noting that his letter of August 10 and Erb's letter of August 16 had evidently crossed in the mails, expressing disappointment at the turn-down, and stating that Market Street Associates would seek financing elsewhere. That was the last contact between the parties until September 27, when Orenstein sent Erb a letter stating that Market Street Associates was exercising the option granted it by paragraph 34 to purchase the property upon the terms specified in that paragraph in the event that negotiations over financing broke down.

The pension trust refused to sell, and this suit to compel specific performance followed. Apparently the price computed by the formula in paragraph 34 is only $1 million. The market value must be higher, or Market Street Associates wouldn't be trying to coerce conveyance at the paragraph 34 price; whether it is as high as $3 million, however, the record does not reveal.

The district judge granted summary judgment for the pension trust on two grounds that he believed to be separate although closely related. The first was that, by failing in its correspondence with the pension trust to mention paragraph 34 of the lease, Market Street Associates had prevented the negotiations over financing that are a condition precedent to the lessee's exercise of the purchase option from taking place. Second, this same failure violated the duty of good faith, which the common law of Wisconsin, as of other states, reads into every contract. . . . In support of both grounds the judge emphasized a statement by Orenstein in his deposition that it had occurred to him that Erb mightn't know about paragraph 34, though this was unlikely (Orenstein testified) because Erb or someone else at the pension trust would probably check the file and discover the paragraph and realize that if the trust refused to negotiate over the request for financing, Market Street Associates, as Penney's assignee, would be entitled to walk off with the property for (perhaps) a song. The judge inferred that Market Street Associates didn't want financing from the pension trust – that it just wanted an opportunity to buy the property at a bargain price and hoped that the pension trust wouldn't realize the implications of turning down the request for financing. Market Street Associates should, the judge opined, have advised the pension trust that it was requesting financing pursuant to paragraph 34, so that the trust would understand the penalty for refusing to negotiate.

We begin our analysis by setting to one side two extreme contentions by the parties. The pension trust argues that the option to purchase created by paragraph 34 cannot be exercised until negotiations over financing break down; there were no negotiations; therefore they did not break down; therefore Market Street Associates had no right to exercise the option. This argument misreads the contract. Although the option to purchase is indeed contingent, paragraph 34 requires the pension trust, upon demand by the lessee for the financing of improvements worth at least $250,000, "to give reasonable consideration to providing the financing." The lessor who fails to give reasonable consideration and thereby prevents the negotiations from taking place is breaking the contract; and a contracting party cannot be allowed to use his own breach to gain an advantage by impairing the rights that the contract confers on the other party. . . . Often, it is true, if one party breaks the contract, the other can walk away from it without liability, can in other words exercise self-help. . . . But he is not required to follow that course. He can stand on his contract rights.

But what exactly are those rights in this case? The contract entitles the lessee to reasonable consideration of its request for financing, and only if negotiations over the request fail is the lessee entitled to purchase the property at the price computed in accordance with paragraph 34. It might seem therefore that the proper legal remedy for a lessor's breach that consists of failure to give the lessee's request for financing reasonable consideration would not be an order that the lessor sell the property to the lessee at the paragraph 34 price, but an order that the lessor bargain with the lessee in good faith. But we do not understand the pension trust to be arguing that Market Street Associates is seeking the wrong remedy. We understand it to be arguing that Market Street Associates has no possible remedy. That is an untenable position.

Market Street Associates argues, with equal unreason as it seems to us, that it could not have broken the contract because paragraph 34 contains no express requirement that in requesting financing the lessee mention the lease or paragraph 34 or otherwise alert the lessor to the consequences of his failing to give reasonable consideration to granting the request. There is indeed no such requirement (all that the contract requires is a demand). But no one says there is. The pension trust's argument, which the district judge bought, is that either as a matter of simple contract interpretation or under the compulsion of the doctrine of good faith, a provision requiring Market Street Associates to remind the pension trust of paragraph 34 should be read into the lease.

It seems to us that these are one ground rather than two. A court has to have a reason to interpolate a clause into a contract. The only reason that has been suggested here is that it is necessary to prevent Market Street Associates from reaping a reward for what the pension trust believes to have been Market Street's bad faith. So we must consider the meaning of the contract duty of "good faith." The Wisconsin cases are cryptic as to its meaning though emphatic about its existence, so we must cast our net wider. We do so mindful of Learned Hand's warning, that "such words as 'fraud,' 'good faith,' 'whim,' 'caprice,' 'arbitrary action,' and 'legal fraud' . . . obscure the issue." *Thompson-Starrett Co. v. La Belle Iron Works,* 17 F.2d 536, 541 (2d Cir.1927). Indeed they do. . . . The particular confusion to which the vaguely moralistic overtones of "good faith" give rise is the belief that every contract establishes a fiduciary relationship. A fiduciary is required to treat his principal as if the principal were he, and therefore he may not take advantage of the principal's incapacity, ignorance, inexperience, or even naïveté. . . . If Market Street Associates were the fiduciary of General Electric Pension Trust, then (we may assume) it could not take advantage of Mr. Erb's apparent ignorance of paragraph 34, however exasperating Erb's failure to return Orenstein's phone calls was and however negligent Erb or his associates were in failing to read the lease before turning down Orenstein's request for financing.

But it is unlikely that Wisconsin wishes, in the name of good faith, to make every contract signatory his brother's keeper, especially when the brother is the immense and sophisticated General Electric Pension Trust, whose lofty indifference to small (= < $7 million) transactions is the signifier of its grandeur. In fact the law contemplates that people frequently will take advantage of the ignorance of those with whom they contract, without thereby incurring liability. . . . The duty of honesty, of good faith even expansively conceived, is not a duty of candor. You can make a binding contract to purchase something you know your seller undervalues. . . . That of course is a question about formation, not performance, and the particular duty of good faith under examination here relates to the latter rather than to the former. But even after you have signed a contract, you are not obliged to become an altruist toward the other party and relax the terms if he gets into trouble in performing his side of the bargain. . . . Otherwise mere difficulty of performance would excuse a contracting party-which it does not. . . .

But it is one thing to say that you can exploit your superior knowledge of the market – for if you cannot, you will not be able to recoup the investment you made in obtaining that knowledge – or that you are not required to spend money bailing out a contract partner who has gotten into trouble. It is another thing to say that you can take deliberate advantage of an oversight by your contract partner concerning his rights under the contract. Such taking advantage is not the exploitation of superior knowledge or the avoidance of unbargained-for expense; it is sharp dealing. Like theft, it has no social product, and also like theft it induces costly defensive expenditures, in the form of overelaborate disclaimers or investigations into the trustworthiness of a prospective contract partner, just as the prospect of theft induces expenditures on locks.

The form of sharp dealing that we are discussing might or might not be actionable as fraud or deceit. That is a question of tort law and there the rule is that if the information is readily available to both parties the failure of one to disclose it to the other, even if done in the knowledge that the other party is acting on mistaken premises, is not actionable. . . . Before the contract is signed, the parties confront each other with a natural wariness. Neither expects the other to be particularly forthcoming, and therefore there is no deception when one is not. Afterwards the situation is different. The parties are now in a cooperative relationship the costs of which will be considerably reduced by a measure of trust. So each lowers his guard a bit, and now silence is more apt to be deceptive.

Moreover, this is a contract case rather than a tort case, and conduct that might not rise to the level of fraud may nonetheless violate the duty of good faith in dealing with one's contractual partners and thereby give rise to a remedy under contract law. This duty is, as it were, halfway between a fiduciary duty (the duty of *utmost* good faith) and the duty merely to refrain from active fraud. Despite its moralistic overtones it is no more the injection of moral principles into contract law than the fiduciary concept itself is. . . . Summers, *supra,* at 204–07, 265–66. It would be quixotic as well as presumptuous for judges to undertake through contract law to raise the ethical standards of the nation's business people. The concept of the duty of good faith like the concept of fiduciary duty is a stab at approximating the terms the parties would have negotiated had they foreseen the circumstances that have given rise to their dispute. The parties want to minimize the costs of performance. To the extent that a doctrine of good faith designed to do this by reducing defensive expenditures is a reasonable measure to this end, interpolating it into the contract advances the parties' joint goal.

It is true that an essential function of contracts is to allocate risk, and would be defeated if courts treated the materializing of a bargained-over, allocated risk as a misfortune the burden of which is required to be shared between the parties (as it might be within a family, for example) rather than borne entirely by the party to whom the risk had been allocated by mutual agreement. But contracts do not just allocate risk. They also (or some of them) set in motion a cooperative enterprise, which may to some extent place one party at the other's mercy. "The parties to a contract are embarked on a cooperative venture, and a minimum of cooperativeness in the event unforeseen problems arise at the performance stage is required even if not an explicit duty of the contract." *AMPAT/Midwest, Inc. v. Illinois Tool Works,*

Inc., 896 F.2d 1035, 1041 (7th Cir. 1990). The office of the doctrine of good faith is to forbid the kinds of opportunistic behavior that a mutually dependent, cooperative relationship might enable in the absence of rule. " 'Good faith' is a compact reference to an implied undertaking not to take opportunistic advantage in a way that could not have been contemplated at the time of drafting, and which therefore was not resolved explicitly by the parties." *Kham & Nate's Shoes No. 2, Inc. v. First Bank*, 908 F.2d 1351, 1357 (7th Cir. 1990). The contractual duty of good faith is thus not some newfangled bit of welfare-state paternalism or the sediment of an altruistic strain in contract law, and we are therefore not surprised to find the essentials of the modern doctrine well established in nineteenth-century cases. . . .

The emphasis we are placing on postcontractual versus precontractual conduct helps explain the pattern that is observed when the duty of contractual good faith is considered in all its variety, encompassing not only good faith in the *performance* of a contract but also good faith in its *formation,* Summers, *supra,* at 220–32, and in its *enforcement. Harbor Ins. Co. v. Continental Bank Corp.,* 922 F.2d 357, 363 (7th Cir. 1990). The formation or negotiation stage is precontractual, and here the duty is minimized. It is greater not only at the performance but also at the enforcement stage, which is also postcontractual. "A party who hokes up a phony defense to the performance of his contractual duties and then when that defense fails (at some expense to the other party) tries on another defense for size can properly be said to be acting in bad faith." *Id.* . . . At the formation of the contract the parties are dealing in present realities; performance still lies in the future. As performance unfolds, circumstances change, often unforeseeably; the explicit terms of the contract become progressively less apt to the governance of the parties' relationship; and the role of implied conditions-and with it the scope and bite of the good-faith doctrine-grows.

We could of course do without the term "good faith," and maybe even without the doctrine. We could, as just suggested, speak instead of implied conditions necessitated by the unpredictability of the future at the time the contract was made. Suppose a party has promised work to the promisee's "satisfaction." As Learned Hand explained, "he may refuse to look at the work, or to exercise any real judgment on it, in which case he has prevented performance and excused the condition." *Thompson-Starrett Co. v. La Belle Iron Works*, 17 F.2d at 541. . . . That is, it was an implicit condition that the promisee examine the work to the extent necessary to determine whether it was satisfactory; otherwise the performing party would have been placing himself at the complete mercy of the promisee. The parties didn't write this condition into the contract either because they thought such behavior unlikely or failed to foresee it altogether. In just the same way – to switch to another familiar example of the operation of the duty of good faith – parties to a requirements contract surely do not intend that if the price of the product covered by the contract rises, the buyer shall be free to increase his "requirements" so that he can take advantage of the rise in the market price over the contract price to resell the product on the open market at a guaranteed profit. *Empire Gas Corp. v. American Bakeries Co.,* 840 F.2d 1333 (7th Cir. 1988). If they fail to insert an express condition to this effect, the court will read it in, confident that the parties would have inserted the condition if they had known what the future held. Of similar character is the implied condition that an exclusive dealer will use his best efforts to promote the supplier's goods, since otherwise the exclusive feature of the dealership contract would place the supplier at the dealer's mercy. *Wood v. Duff-Gordon,* 118 N.E. 214 (N.Y. 1917) (Cardozo, J.).

But whether we say that a contract shall be deemed to contain such implied conditions as are necessary to make sense of the contract, or that a contract obligates the parties to cooperate in its performance in "good faith" to the extent necessary to carry out the purposes of the contract, comes to much the same thing. They are different ways of formulating the overriding purpose of contract law, which is to give the parties what they would have stipulated for expressly if at the time of making the contract they had had complete knowledge of the future and the costs of negotiating and adding provisions to the contract had been zero.

The two formulations would have different meanings only if "good faith" were thought limited to "honesty in fact," an interpretation perhaps permitted but certainly not compelled by the Uniform Commercial Code, and anyway this is not a case governed by the UCC. We need not pursue this issue. The dispositive question in the present case is simply whether Market Street Associates tried to trick the pension trust and succeeded in doing so. If it did, this would be the type of opportunistic behavior in an ongoing contractual relationship that would violate the duty of good faith performance however the duty is formulated. There is much common sense in Judge Reynolds' conclusion that Market Street Associates did just that. The situation as he saw it was as follows. Market Street Associates didn't want financing from the pension trust (initially it had looked elsewhere, remember), and when it learned it couldn't get the financing without owning the property, it decided to try to buy the property. But the pension trust set a stiff price, so Orenstein decided to trick the pension trust into selling at the bargain price fixed in paragraph 34 by requesting financing and hoping that the pension trust would turn the request down without noticing the paragraph. His preliminary dealings with the pension trust made this hope a realistic one by revealing a sluggish and hidebound bureaucracy unlikely to have retained in its brontosaurus's memory, or to be able at short notice to retrieve, the details of a small lease made twenty years earlier. So by requesting financing without mentioning the lease Market Street Associates might well precipitate a refusal before the pension trust woke up to paragraph 34. It is true that Orenstein's second letter requested financing "pursuant to the lease." But when the next day he received a reply to his first letter indicating that the pension trust was indeed oblivious to paragraph 34, his response was to send a lulling letter designed to convince the pension trust that the matter was closed and could be forgotten. The stage was set for his thunderbolt: the notification the next month that Market Street Associates was taking up the option in paragraph 34. Only then did the pension trust look up the lease and discover that it had been had.

The only problem with this recital is that it construes the facts as favorably to the pension trust as the record will permit, and that of course is not the right standard for summary judgment. The facts must be construed as favorably to the nonmoving party, to Market Street Associates, as the record permits (that Market Street Associates filed its own motion for summary judgment is irrelevant, as we have seen). When that is done, a different picture emerges. On Market Street Associates' construal of the record, $3 million was a grossly excessive price for the property, and while $1 million might be a bargain it would not confer so great a windfall as to warrant an inference that if the pension trust had known about paragraph 34 it never would have turned down Market Street Associates' request for financing cold. And in fact the pension trust may have known about paragraph 34, and either it didn't care or it believed that unless the request mentioned that paragraph the pension trust would incur no liability by turning it down. Market Street Associates may have assumed and have been entitled to assume that in reviewing a request for financing from one of its lessees the pension trust would take the time to read the lease to see whether it bore on the request. Market Street Associates did not desire financing from the pension trust initially – that is undeniable – yet when it discovered that it could not get financing elsewhere unless it had the title to the property it may have realized that it would have to negotiate with the pension trust over financing before it could hope to buy the property at the price specified in the lease.

On this interpretation of the facts there was no bad faith on the part of Market Street Associates. It acted honestly, reasonably, without ulterior motive, in the face of circumstances as they actually and reasonably appeared to it. The fault was the pension trust's incredible inattention, which misled Market Street Associates into believing that the pension trust had no interest in financing the improvements regardless of the purchase option. We do not usually excuse contracting parties from failing to read and understand the contents of their contract; and in the end what this case comes down to – or so at least it can be strongly argued – is that an immensely sophisticated enterprise simply failed to read the contract. On the other hand, such enterprises make mistakes just like the rest of us, and deliberately to take advantage of your contracting partner's mistake during the performance stage (for we are not talking about taking advantage of superior knowledge at the formation stage) is a breach of good faith. To be able to correct your contract partner's mistake at zero cost to yourself, and decide not to do so, is a species of opportunistic behavior that the parties would have expressly forbidden in the contract had they foreseen it. The immensely long term of the lease amplified the possibility of errors but did not license either party to take advantage of them.

The district judge jumped the gun in choosing between these alternative characterizations. The essential issue bearing on Market Street Associates' good faith was Orenstein's state of mind, a type of inquiry that ordinarily cannot be concluded on summary judgment, and could not be here. If Orenstein believed that Erb knew or would surely find out about paragraph 34, it was not dishonest or opportunistic to fail to flag that paragraph, or even to fail to mention the lease, in his correspondence and (rare) conversations with Erb, especially given the uninterest in dealing with Market Street Associates that Erb fairly radiated. To decide what Orenstein believed, a trial is necessary. As for the pension trust's intimation that a bench trial (for remember that this is an equity case, since the only relief sought by the plaintiff is specific performance) will add no illumination beyond what the summary judgment proceeding has done, this overlooks the fact that at trial the judge will for the first time have a chance to see the witnesses whose depositions he has read, to hear their testimony elaborated, and to assess their believability.

The judgment is reversed and the case is remanded for further proceedings consistent with this opinion.

Problem 3-2

Strawberry Computer Co. manufactures and sells consumer electronic equipment. One of its biggest distributors is Better Buy, which sells the products of several manufacturers. Pursuant to a master agreement between the parties, Better Buy places orders on the 1st and 15th of each month, for delivery within 20 days. The contract calls for payment at "80% of Strawberry's suggested retail price on the day the order is accepted."

In July, Strawberry brought a new hand-held computer to the market with great fanfare. Customers lined up all night to buy them the next morning from the retailers who stocked them. Since then, sales have been brisk, but some consumers have complained that the device has inadequate memory. On October 12, Strawberry decided to lower the price of the new hand-held computer by 30% and to enhance its memory. Knowing of the contract with Better Buy, however, Strawberry made no announcement about these decisions. Instead, it waited until the 15th, when Better Buy placed an order for a large number of the hand-held computers. Strawberry immediately accepted the order and one hour later publicly announced the price decrease and memory enhancement. As a result, the computers that Better Buy agreed to purchase will be unmarketable except at a huge discount. Has Strawberry breached the duty of good faith?

C. Modification

1. Modification by Agreement

Contracting parties are, of course, free to modify their agreements or to waive their contractual rights. Indeed, course of performance itself can be viewed as a kind of implicit modification or waiver. Review UCC § 1-303(f). But course of performance is not the only source of modifications. The parties may expressly agree to modify the terms of their pre-existing agreement.

Traditionally, under the common law of contracts, agreements to modify a pre-existing contract were not enforceable unless supported by consideration. More modern authorities dispense with the requirement of consideration, and use some other principle to ensure a modicum of fairness. For example, under section 89 of the Restatement (Second) of Contracts, an agreement to modify is enforceable if "the modification is fair and equitable in view of circumstances not anticipated by the parties when the contract was made."

Article 2 is even more lenient. Read section 2-209(1) and comment 2. It uses "good faith," not consideration, as a policing mechanism to determine whether an agreement to modify should be enforced. Is that an adequate safeguard against extortion or economic duress? Consider the following case on whether a modification was sought and made in good faith.

ROTH STEEL PRODUCTS V. SHARON STEEL CORP.
705 F.2d 134 (6th Cir. 1983)

[In November, 1972, Sharon contracted to sell 200 tons of "hot rolled" steel per month to Roth through December, 1973. The price was $148 per ton. Sharon also "indicated" that it could sell "hot rolled" steel on an "open schedule" basis for $140 and discussed the "probability" that Sharon could sell 500 tons of "cold rolled" steel at prices varying with the type ordered. At that time, the steel industry was operating at 70% of capacity, steel prices were "highly competitive" and Sharon's quoted prices to Roth were "substantially lower" than Sharon's book price for steel. In early 1973, market conditions changed dramatically due to the development of an attractive export market and an increased domestic demand for steel. During 1973 and 1974, the steel industry operated at full capacity, steel prices rose and nearly every producer experienced substantial delays in filling orders. In March, 1973, Sharon notified all purchasers, including Roth, that it was discontinuing price concessions given in 1972.

After negotiations, the parties agreed that Roth would pay the agreed price until June 30, 1973 and a price somewhere between the agreed price and Sharon's published prices for the balance of 1973. Roth was initially reluctant to agree to this modification, but ultimately agreed "primarily because they were unable to purchase sufficient steel elsewhere to meet their production requirements." Sharon was supplying one-third of Roth's requirements and all other possible suppliers were "operating at full capacity and . . . were fully booked." The parties proceeded under this modification during the balance of 1973, although Sharon experienced difficulties in filling orders on time.

During 1974, the parties did business on an entirely different basis. Roth would order steel, Sharon would accept the order at the price "prevailing at the time of shipment." During 1974 and 1975, Sharon's deliveries were chronically late, thereby increasing the price to Roth in a rising market. Roth, however, acquiesced in this pattern because it believed Sharon's assurances that late deliveries resulted from shortages of raw materials and the need for equitable allocation among customers and because there was "no practical alternative source of supply." This acquiescence was jolted in May, 1974 when Roth learned that Sharon was allocating substantial quantities of rolled steel to one of Sharon's own subsidiaries for sale at premium prices. After several more months of desultory performance on both sides, Roth sued Sharon for breach of contract, with special emphasis upon the modified contract for 1973.   Sharon raised several defenses, including impracticability and, in the alternative, the agreed modification. The district court, after a long trial, held, *inter alia,* that Sharon was not excused from the 1973 contract on the grounds of impracticability and that the modification was unenforceable. A judgment for $555,968.46 was entered for Roth.

On appeal, the court of appeals affirmed the district court's decision on the impracticability, modification and other issues, but remanded the case for factual findings on whether Roth gave Sharon timely notice of breach.   On the impracticability defense under section 2-615(a), the court held that "Sharon's inability to perform was a result of its policy of accepting far more orders than it was capable of fulfilling, rather than a result of the existing shortage of raw materials." In refusing to enforce the modification of the 1973 contract, the court had this to say. – Eds.]

Celebrezze, Senior Circuit Judge

... C. In March, 1973, Sharon notified its customers that it intended to charge the maximum permissible price for all of its products; accordingly, all price concessions, including those made to the plaintiffs, were to be rescinded effective April 1, 1973. On March 23, 1973, Guerin [Roth's vice pres.] indicated to Metzger [Sharon's sales manager] that the plaintiffs considered the proposed price increase to be a breach of the November, 1972 contract. In an effort to resolve the dispute, Guerin met with representatives of Sharon on March 28, 1973 and asked Sharon to postpone any price increases until June or July, 1973. Several days later, Richard Mecaskey, Guerin's replacement, sent a letter to Sharon which indicated that the plaintiffs believed that the November, 1972 agreement was enforceable and that the plaintiffs were willing to negotiate a price modification if Sharon's cost increases warranted such an action. As a result of this letter, another meeting was held between Sharon and the plaintiffs. At this meeting, Walter Gregg, Sharon's vice-president and chairman of the board, agreed to continue charging the November, 1972 prices until June 30, 1973 and offered, for the remainder of 1973, to charge prices that were lower than Sharon's published prices but higher than the 1972 prices. Although the plaintiffs initially rejected the terms offered by Sharon for the second half of 1973, Mecaskey reluctantly agreed to Sharon's terms on June 29, 1973.

Before the district court, Sharon asserted that it properly increased prices because the parties had modified the November, 1973 contract to reflect changed market conditions. The district court, however, made several findings which, it believed, indicated that Sharon did not seek a modification to avoid a loss on the contract. The district court also found that the plaintiffs' inventories of rolled steel were "alarmingly deficient" at the time modification was sought and that Sharon had threatened to cease selling steel to the plaintiffs in the second-half of 1973 unless the plaintiffs agreed to the modification. Because Sharon had used its position as the plaintiffs' chief supplier to extract the price modification, the district court concluded that Sharon had acted in bad faith by seeking to modify the contract. In the alternative, the court concluded that the modification agreement was voidable because it was extracted by means of economic duress; the tight steel market prevented the plaintiffs from obtaining steel elsewhere at an affordable price and, consequently, the plaintiffs were forced to agree to the modification in order to assure a continued supply of steel. . . . Sharon challenges these conclusions on appeal.

The ability of a party to modify a contract which is subject to Article Two of the Uniform Commercial Code is broader than common law, primarily because the modification needs no consideration to be binding. [UCC § 2-209(1)]. A party's ability to modify an agreement is limited only by Article Two's general obligation of good faith. . . . In determining whether a particular modification was obtained in good faith, a court must make two distinct inquiries: whether the party's conduct is consistent with "reasonable commercial standards of fair dealing in the trade," . . . and whether the parties were in fact motivated to seek modification by an honest desire to compensate for commercial exigencies . . . [UCC § 2-103]. The first inquiry is relatively straightforward; the party asserting the modification must demonstrate that his decision to seek modification was the result of a factor, such as increased costs, which would cause an ordinary merchant to seek a modification of the contract. *See* Official Comment 2, [UCC § 2-209)] (reasonable commercial standards may require objective reason). The second inquiry, regarding the subjective honesty of the parties, is less clearly defined. Essentially, this inquiry requires the party asserting the modification to demonstrate that he was, in fact, motivated by a legitimate commercial reason and that such a reason is not offered merely as a pretext. . . . Moreover, the trier of fact must determine whether the means used to obtain the modification are an impermissible attempt to obtain a modification by extortion or overreaching. . . .

Sharon argues that its decision to seek a modification was consistent with reasonable commercial standards of fair dealing because market exigencies made further performance entail a substantial loss. The district court, however, made three findings which caused it to conclude that economic circumstances were not the reason that Sharon sought a modification: it found that Sharon was partially insulated from raw material price increases, that Sharon bargained for a contract with a slim profit margin and thus implicitly assumed the risk that performance might come to involve a loss, and that Sharon's overall profit in 1973 and its profit on the contract in the first quarter of 1973 were inconsistent with Sharon's position that the modification was sought to avoid a loss. Although all of these findings are marginally related to the question whether Sharon's conduct was consistent with reasonable commercial standards of fair dealing, we do not believe that they are sufficient to support a finding that Sharon did not observe reasonable commercial standards by seeking a modification. In our view, these findings do not support a conclusion that a reasonable merchant, in light of the circumstances, would not have sought a modification in order to avoid a loss. . . .

In the final analysis, the single most important consideration in determining whether the decision to seek a modification is justified in this context is whether, because of changes in the market or other unforeseeable conditions, performance of the contract has come to involve a loss. In this case, the district court found that Sharon suffered substantial losses by performing the contract *as modified.* . . . We are convinced that unforeseen economic exigencies existed which would prompt an ordinary merchant to seek a modification to avoid a loss on the contract; thus, we believe that the district court's findings to the contrary are clearly erroneous. . . .

The second part of the analysis, honesty in fact, is pivotal. The district court found that Sharon "threatened not to sell Roth and Toledo any steel if they refused to pay increased prices after July 1, 1973" and, consequently, that Sharon acted wrongfully. Sharon does not dispute the finding that it threatened to stop selling steel to the plaintiffs. Instead, it asserts that such a finding is merely evidence of bad faith and that it has rebutted any inference of bad faith based on that finding. We agree with this analysis; although coercive conduct is evidence that a modification of a contract is sought in bad faith, that prima facie showing may be effectively rebutted by the party seeking to enforce the modification. . . . Although we agree with Sharon's statement of principles, we do not agree that Sharon has rebutted the inference of bad faith that rises from its coercive conduct. Sharon asserts that its decision to unilaterally raise prices was based on language in the November 17, 1972 letter which allowed it to raise prices to the extent of any general industry-wide price increase. Because prices in the steel industry had increased, Sharon concludes that it was justified in raising its prices. Because it was justified in raising the contract price, the plaintiffs were bound by the terms of the contract to pay the increased prices. Consequently, any refusal by the plaintiffs to pay the price increase sought by Sharon must be viewed as a material breach of the November, 1972 contract which would excuse Sharon from any further performance. Thus, Sharon reasons that its refusal to perform absent a price increase was justified under the contract and consistent with good faith.

This argument fails in two respects. First, the contractual language on which Sharon relies only permits, at most, a price increase for cold rolled steel; thus, even if Sharon's position were supported by the evidence, Sharon would not have been justified in refusing to sell the plaintiff's hot rolled steel because of the plaintiffs' refusal to pay higher prices for the product. More importantly, however, the evidence does not indicate that Sharon ever offered this theory as a justification until this matter was tried. Sharon's representatives, in their testimony, did not attempt to justify Sharon's refusal to ship steel at 1972 prices in this fashion. Furthermore, none of the contemporaneous communications contain this justification for Sharon's action. In short, we can find no evidence in the record which indicates that Sharon offered this theory as a justification at the time the modification was sought. Consequently, we believe that the district court's conclusion that Sharon acted in bad faith by using coercive conduct to extract the price modification is not clearly erroneous. Therefore, we hold that Sharon's attempt to modify the November, 1972 contract, in order to compensate for increased costs which made performance come to involve a loss, is ineffective because Sharon did not act in a manner consistent with Article Two's requirement of honesty in fact when it refused to perform its remaining obligations under the contract at 1972 prices.[6] . . .

---

[6] The district court also found, as an alternative ground, that the modification was voidable because the plaintiffs agreed to the modification due to economic duress. *See, e.g., Oskey Gasoline & Oil Co. v. Continental Oil*, 534 F.2d 1281 (8th Cir.1976). Because we conclude that the modification was ineffective as a result of Sharon's bad faith, we do not reach the issue whether the contract modification was also voidable because of economic duress. We note, however, that proof that coercive means were used is necessary to establish that a contract is voidable because of economic duress. Normally, it cannot be used to void a contract modification which has been sought in good faith; if a contract modification has been found to be in good faith, then presumably no wrongful coercive means have been used to extract the modification.

2. Statute of Frauds

Even if the parties have agreed, in good faith, to modify their contract, in some circumstances that modification may not be enforceable due to the application of the statute of frauds. In fact, there are in essence two different statutes of fraud that can apply in such circumstances. First read section 2-209(3), review section 2-201 and the material in Chapter Two on the statute of frauds, and consider the following problem.

Problem 3-3

A. S and B enter into an oral agreement to sell 100 widgets for the total price of $400. Before any performance has occurred, the parties modify their agreement to double the quantity and the total price. Does the agreement have to meet the requirements of section 2-201 to be enforceable?

B. S and B enter into an agreement to sell 100 widgets for the total price of $1,000. There is a writing sufficient to satisfy section 2-201. Before performance, the parties agree to increase the quantity to 110 widgets, but with no change in price. Must the modification satisfy section 2-201 to be enforceable?

C. S and B enter into an agreement to sell 100 widgets for the total price of $1,000. There is a writing sufficient to satisfy section 2-201. Subsequently the parties agree to reduce the quantity to 90 widgets and to decrease the sale price to $900. Must the modification satisfy section 2-201 to be enforceable? *Compare Costco Wholesale Corp. v. World Wide Licensing Corp.*, 898 P.2d 347 (Wash. Ct. App. 1995) *with Zemco Manufacturing Inc. v. Navistar Int'l Transportation Corp.*, 186 F.3d 815 (7th Cir. 1999).

D. S and B enter into an agreement to sell 100 widgets for the total price of $1,000, delivery on June 1. There is a writing sufficient to satisfy section 2-201. Subsequently, the parties agree to change the delivery date to July 1. Must the modification satisfy section 2-201 to be enforceable?

Even if the agreement as modified satisfies the statute of frauds in section 2-201, perhaps because it is for a price of less that $500, it may still run afoul of a second sort of statute of fraud: one created by the initial agreement of the parties. Read section 2-209(2). This provision authorizes parties to a contract for sale to require that any modification to the agreement be in writing. This type of clause, which some refer to as a private statute of frauds, is more commonly known as a "no-oral modification" (NOM) clause. What is the purpose of the NOM clause? Why is there a "separate signing" requirement if a NOM clause is in a form supplied by a merchant to a non-merchant? Are there good reasons for not having a NOM clause in an agreement?

What happens if the parties' initial agreement has a NOM clause, the parties then orally agree to a modification, but the requirements of section 2-209(2) are not met? Does the agreed modification have any effect on the parties' rights and obligations? Unfortunately, the answer to this is complicated and involves the interaction of several related concepts: modification, waiver, and estoppel. Read section 2-209(4) and (5) and then consider the following illustration.

Illustration

S and B enter into a signed, written agreement for S to sell to B 1,000 widgets for $10,000, with delivery in four equal installments on four consecutive Mondays, beginning in one week. The agreement contains a clause providing that "no modification to this agreement will be binding unless made in writing and signed by both parties." Before the first delivery was due, S telephoned B and asked if the deliveries could be on Tuesday. B agreed. S delivered the first installment on the first Tuesday.

The agreement to modify the day for delivery was not in writing and, under the NOM clause and section 2-209(2), would be unenforceable. However, even though the modification is unenforceable, B may have waived the right to insist on delivery on Monday. To determine whether B has in fact made such a waiver, and if so, whether that waiver can be retracted, we need to analyze section 2-209(4) and (5).

Even a quick reading of section 2-209(4) should be enough to tell you that it does not actually say what qualifies as a waiver, merely that a failed modification can operate as one. Thus, we presumably need to consult the common law to determine whether B has made a waiver. The traditional definition of "waiver" is "the voluntary relinquishment of a known right." *See* RESTATEMENT (SECOND) OF

CONTRACTS § 84 cmt. b. B's actions appear to be voluntary and knowing, so in all likelihood B has waived the right to delivery on Monday.[7] In other words, B's agreement to modify, which may not be enforceable as a modification due to the no oral modification clause, nevertheless may act as a waiver of the right to claim that S has breached by the Tuesday delivery. However, absent either an enforceable agreement to modify or an express waiver, the mere act of accepting the one late delivery will not normally operate as a waiver of the right to complain about (or sue for breach because of) the late delivery. *See* UCC § 2-607(2), (3).

If B has waived its right to insist on Monday delivery, can B retract the waiver? Yes, but only by giving reasonable notification and only if S has not relied to its detriment so that such a retraction would be unjust. The application of this standard will likely produce a different result for the past delivery than for the future deliveries. B probably cannot retract the waiver for the first delivery for two reasons: (i) notification after the fact would probably not be reasonable; and (ii) S has relied on the waiver in such a way that retraction now would be unjust. However, B can probably retract the waiver with respect to future deliveries.[8]

Can S successfully argue that B's agreement to the first late delivery was not only an agreement to modify the delivery date for all four deliveries but in addition a waiver of the enforcement of the NOM clause? If S wins that argument, then B's agreement to modify the delivery dates for the future would be enforceable and B could not insist on the old delivery schedule absent S's agreement.[9]

Now try your hand at the following problem, which adds course of performance to the analysis.

---

[7] *See BMC Industries, Inc. v. Barth Indus., Inc.*,160 F.3d 1322 (11th Cir. 1998), *cert. denied*, 526 U.S. 1132 (1999). Another circuit insists that to have an enforceable waiver, there must be detrimental reliance on that waiver. *Wisconsin Knife Works v. National Metal Crafters*, 781 F.2d 1280 (7th Cir. 1986).

[8] B might not be able to retract the waiver even as to the future deliveries if S – after getting B's initial agreement to Tuesday delivery and before learning of the retraction – made arrangements for deliveries on Tuesdays and those arrangements would be difficult or expensive to change.

[9] *See Royster-Clark, Inc. v. Olsen's Mill, Inc.*, 714 N.W.2d 530 (Wis. 2006); *Honeywell Intern. Inc. v. Air Products & Chemical Co.*, 872 A.2d 944 (Del. 2005).

Problem 3-4

On March 15, S and B enter into a signed, written agreement for S to sell to B 10,000 widgets each month for the next twelve months. The agreement calls for delivery to B's premises by the 5th of each month, beginning in April. In April, S delivers the goods to a carrier on April 4, and the carrier delivers the widgets to B on April 7. B accepted the delivery without complaint.

A. Have the parties modified their agreement by their course of performance? *See* UCC § 2-208 cmt. 4. Has B waived its right to complain about the late delivery?

B. Subsequently, in both May and June, S delivered the widgets to the carrier before the 5th but the goods were not delivered to B until after the 5th. B did not complain about either delivery. Have the parties modified their agreement by their course of performance? May B notify S that all deliveries have to be at B's premises on time and that B will no longer accept late deliveries?

C. How, if at all, would your analysis change if the initial agreement provided that "no modification to this agreement will be binding unless made in writing and signed by both parties"?

CISG and UNIDROIT Principles. CISG Article 29 addresses modifications. Agreements to modify are enforceable. Although no general statute of frauds applies to modifications, CISG Art. 11, the parties may have a "no oral modification" clause. CISG Art. 29(2). The UNIDROIT Principles are similar, UNIDROIT Art. 2.1.18. Both the CISG and UNIDROIT Principles recognize the possibility of a party waiving the application of the NOM clause.

SECTION 2.   ADDING TO THE AGREEMENT: EXPRESS WARRANTIES

When the seller agrees to sell goods to the buyer, the parties' agreement will usually include terms – either expressly or implicitly through course of performance, course of dealing, or usage of trade – relevant to the nature and quality of the goods that the seller is to provide. These terms are called warranties. Most consumer think warranties are promises about how long the goods will last or will continue to function. While such promises are indeed warranties, the Article 2 concept of warranty is much broader and encompasses far more. Read section 2-313. Notice that each subsection and paragraph of this section contains both words of inclusion and words of exclusion or limitation. Let's parse it out. An express warranty can be created by any statement of fact or promise made by the seller to the buyer that relates to the good, UCC § 2-313(1)(a), or any description of the goods, UCC § 2-313(1)(b). Use of the words "warranty" or "guaranty" is not required. UCC § 2-313(2). Furnishing a sample or model also gives rise to an express warranty. UCC § 2-313(1)(c).

Let's pause for a moment, before looking at the limitations, to consider what this means. Consider a Seller who agrees to sell a "new brown horse" to Buyer for $3,000. That is a warranty. If, at the appointed place and time where the exchange is to occur, Seller tenders a child's 2-inch plastic horse, Seller will be in breach. The parties are free to make their own agreement, but "the probability is small that a real price is intended to be exchanged for a pseudo-obligation." UCC § 2-313 cmt. 4. Thus, Article 2 rejects, at least in part, the idea of "caveat emptor."

However, not every statement made during the contract formation process qualifies as a warranty. A statement purporting to be merely "the seller's opinion or commendation" does not create an express warranty. UCC § 2-313(2). Moreover, no express warranty is ever created unless the statement, promise, description, sample, or model is part of the "basis of the bargain." UCC § 2-313(1)(a), (b), (c). Accordingly, the first step in analyzing whether an express warranty claim has been created is to determine whether the language or actions of the seller is such as to rise to the level of a warranty. In other words, has the seller made an affirmation of fact or promise regarding the goods, supplied a description of the goods, or provided a sample or model of the goods, and is whatever the seller provided more than mere opinion or commendation? The second step is to determine whether the affirmation of fact, promise regarding the goods, description, sample or model is part of the "basis of the bargain."

Affirmation of fact or opinion. By far, most of the litigation regarding whether the seller has made an express warranty involves the distinction between an "affirmation of fact" and an "opinion." How do we know whether a statement is an affirmation of fact? One court described the distinction as follows:

> The decisive test for whether a given representation is a warranty or merely
> an expression of the seller's opinion is whether the seller asserts a fact of

which the buyer is ignorant or merely states an opinion or judgment on a matter of which the seller has no special knowledge and on which the buyer may be expected also to have an opinion and to exercise his judgment.[10]
Do you agree? Try the following problem. As you do so, identify the factors that are relevant in distinguishing fact from opinion.

Problem 3-5

In which, if any, of the following situations, has the seller made a statement that would qualify as an express warranty if the statement were part of the basis of the bargain?

A. A seller of women's clothing tells a customer that the dress the customer is trying on "looks good on you."

B. A seller of artwork tells a buyer that "it's a beautiful painting by a talented artist."

C. A seller of antiques describes a desk as a "Queen Anne," a vase as a "Ming," and a table as "antique."

D. A seller of sports memorabilia says that "this is the ball that Mike Lowell caught to win game four of the 2007 World Series."

E. A dealer in new cars stated to a buyer that a new car model was "the safest car in its class." *Cf. Gallagher v. WMK Inc.*, 2007 WL 4322531 (Ohio Ct. App. 2007).

F. A manufacturer of roofing shingles stated that the shingles had "improved waterproofing" and "longer life." *See Viking Yacht Co. v. Composites One LLC*, 496 F. Supp. 2d 462 (D. N.J. 2007).

G. A camera manufacturer advertised its new camera as providing "superior performance" and "professional quality" digital images. *See*

---

[10] *Royal Business Machines, Inc. v. Lorraine Corp.*, 633 F.2d 34, 41 (7th Cir. 1980).

National Mulch and Seed, Inc. v. Rexius Forest By-Products, Inc., 2007 WL 894833 (S.D. Ohio 2007).

H. A dealer in yachts stated to a buyer that a used boat was "seaworthy." *See Keith v. Buchanan*, 220 Cal. Rptr. 392 (Cal. Ct. App. 1985).

I. A dealer of thoroughbred race horses stated in negotiations with a potential buyer that a particular horse was "sound." *See Sessa v. Riegle*, 427 F. Supp. 760 (E.D. Pa. 1977), *aff'd* 568 F.2d 770 (3d Cir. 1978); *see also Simpson v. Widger*, 709 A.2d 1366, 1371 (N.J. Super. A.D. 1998) (discussing the meaning of the phrase "sound horse").

Now that you have worked on Problem 3-5, do you think the distinction between fact and opinion is a sound basis for drawing a line between what qualifies as an express warranty and what does not? Is it easy for buyers to distinguish between them?[11]

Basis of the bargain. We now turn to the second limitation on what qualifies as an express warranty: the requirement that the affirmation of fact, promise, description, sample or model must be part of the "basis of the bargain." At first blush, this may seem like an innocuous or even obvious requirement. Yet bear in mind that no other express terms must meet this test to become part of the parties' agreement. For example, if the seller stated during negotiations it would deliver the goods at a specified time and place, we would not inquire whether the statement is a "basis of the bargain" to determine if it was an enforceable promise. So why should affirmations of fact, promises related to the goods, descriptions of the goods, or a sample or model of the goods, be subject to this test? Does this test make any sense if the seller's representation regarding the quality of the goods is contained in the purchase agreement documentation? For example, if the seller states in the purchase agreement document that the good has a precise capability (such as 100 RPM, or a top speed of 50 MPH), should the buyer have to engage in further proof to demonstrate that this representation was part of the basis of the bargain?

---

[11] *See* David A. Hoffman, *The Best Puffery Article Ever*, 91 IOWA L. REV 1395, 1435 (2006) ("Jurists and regulatory authorities routinely assume that buyers of goods, services and securities ignore puffing statements. This . . . is simply untrue. Marketing scholars have demonstrated that puffing statements are believed on their own terms, and lead some individuals to further imply facts about the puffed speech that are untrue.").

What does the phrase "basis of the bargain" mean? Must the buyer demonstrate reliance on the seller's representation in order to prove the seller made an express warranty? Comment 3 to section 2-313 suggests not but courts do not all agree.

> There is a clear split of authority among the jurisdictions as to whether a buyer must show reliance on a statement or representation for it to be considered part of the "basis of the bargain." Some jurisdictions require a strict showing of reliance. Other jurisdictions have no reliance requirement. And still other jurisdictions have applied a rebuttable presumption of reliance.[12]

Related to this is whether statements made or received after the offer and acceptance process – or even after the parties have tendered their performance – can be part of the "basis of the bargain." Given that no consideration is needed to modify a sale-of-goods contract, *see* UCC § 2-209, do the assertions made on documents inside the package of prepackaged products constitute express warranties? It is hard to deny that such statements could and should give rise to liability; indeed, cases hold that assertions in operating manuals for automobiles and the like that are never read by the buyer prior to the purchase may constitute express warranties.[13]

If the bargain can include things seen or heard after the agreement is formed, then what about advertisements published by the seller but never seen by the buyer? Perhaps never seen by any resident of the particular buyer's state? For example, would an assertion by a manufacturer about product quality made in the interior of China, only in Chinese, and seen only by Chinese citizens constitute an express warranty that is part of the basis of the bargain for a buyer in New Jersey? If reliance means anything, that case is hard to swallow, but where then does one draw the line between the case of the manual or package insert and the case of the advertising published in a distant land and never seen? Of course, one can say that the purchaser of a product expects to get some instructions and statements within the box and that the buyer of a GM pickup truck expects the same. In that sense there might possibly be "reliance." Is that a satisfactory distinction?

Now consider the following case. Should it matter that the buyer knew that the seller's representation was unlikely to be true? What does this case add to your

---

[12] *Cole v. General Motors Corp.*, 484 F.3d 717, 726 (5th Cir. 2007).

[13] *See, e.g., Forbes v. General Motors Corp.*, 935 So.2d 869 (Miss. 2006) (statement in owner's manual); *Rite Aid Corp. v. Levy-Gray*, 894 A.2d 563 (Md. 2006) (pharmacy package insert). *Compare Jarrett v. Duro-Med Indus.*, 2008 WL 89932 (E.D. Ky. 2008).

understanding of the requirements for an express warranty, more specifically, the requirement that the seller's representation be part of the basis of the bargain?

ROGATH V. SIEBENMANN
129 F.3d 261 (2d Cir. 1997)

McLaughlin, Circuit Judge

BACKGROUND

This case revolves around a painting, entitled "Self Portrait," supposedly painted in 1972 by a well-known English artist, Francis Bacon.

In July 1993, defendant Werner Siebenmann sold the Painting to plaintiff David Rogath for $570,000. In the Bill of Sale, Siebenmann described the provenance of the Painting and warranted that he was the sole owner of the Painting, that it was authentic, and that he was not aware of any challenge to its authenticity.

Problems arose three months later when Rogath sold the Painting to Acquavella Contemporary Art, Inc., in New York, for $950,000. Acquavella learned of a challenge to the Painting's authenticity and, on November 1, 1993, requested that Rogath refund the $950,000 and take back the Painting. Rogath did so, and then sued Siebenmann in the Southern District of New York (Batts, J.) for breach of contract, breach of warranty and fraud.

Rogath moved for partial summary judgment on the breach of warranty claims, and the district court granted his motion. *See Rogath v. Siebenmann*, 941 F. Supp. 416, 422-24 (S.D.N.Y. 1996). The court concluded that (1) Siebenmann was unsure of the provenance of the Painting when he sold it to Rogath; (2) he was not the sole owner of the Painting; and (3) when he sold the Painting to Rogath he already knew of a challenge to the Painting's authenticity by the Marlborough Fine Art Gallery in London. *See id.* The court awarded Rogath $950,000 in damages, the price at which he had sold it to Acquavella. *See id.* at 424-25. The court dismissed, *sua sponte*, Rogath's remaining claims for fraud and breach of contract "in light of the full recovery on the warranties granted herein." *Id.* at 425. Finally, a few days later, the court denied Rogath's motion to attach the money that Siebenmann had remaining from the proceeds of the initial sale to Rogath.

Siebenmann appeals the grant of partial summary judgment. Rogath cross-appeals the denial of his motion for attachment and the dismissal of his fraud and breach of contract claims.

DISCUSSION

Siebenmann concedes that his promises and representations set forth in the Bill of Sale constitute warranties under New York law. He claims, however, that Rogath was fully aware when he bought the Painting that questions of authenticity and provenance had already been raised regarding the Painting. He maintains that, under New York law, Rogath therefore cannot rest claims for breach of warranty on the representations made in the Bill of Sale.

We review *de novo* the district court's disposition of Rogath's motion for partial summary judgment. . . . The parties agree that New York law applies.

A. Breach of Warranty under New York Law

The Bill of Sale provides:

> In order to induce David Rogath to make the purchase, Seller . . . make[s] the following warranties, representations and covenants to and with the Buyer.
>
> 1. That the Seller is the sole and absolute owner of the painting and has full right and authority to sell and transfer same; having acquired title as described in a copy of the Statement of Provenance signed by Seller annexed hereto and incorporated herein; [and] that the Seller has no knowledge of any challenge to Seller's title and authenticity of the Painting. . . .

Because the Bill of Sale was a contract for the sale of goods, Rogath's breach of warranty claims are governed by Article Two of the Uniform Commercial Code ("UCC"). . . . Section 2-313 of the UCC provides that "[a]ny description of the goods which is made part of the basis of the bargain creates an express warranty that the goods shall conform to the description." N.Y.U.C.C. § 2-313(1)(b) (McKinney 1993).

Whether the "basis of the bargain" requirement implies that the buyer must rely on the seller's statements to recover and what the nature of that reliance requirement is are unsettled questions. . . . Not surprisingly, this same confusion haunted the New York courts for a time. . . .

Some courts reasoned that the buyer must have relied upon the accuracy of the seller's affirmations or promises in order to recover . . . .

Other courts paid lip service to a "reliance" requirement, but found that the requirement was met if the buyer relied on the seller's promise as part of "the basis of the bargain" in entering into the contract; the buyer need not show that he relied on the truthfulness of the warranties. . . .

Finally, some courts reasoned that there is a "reliance" requirement only when there is a dispute as to whether a warranty was in fact given by the seller. These courts concluded that no reliance of any kind is required "where the existence of an express warranty in a contract is conceded by both parties." . . . In these cases, the buyer need establish only a breach of the warranty.

In 1990 New York's Court of Appeals dispelled much of the confusion when it squarely adopted the "basis of the bargain" description of the reliance required to recover for breach of an express warranty. In *CBS Inc. v. Ziff-Davis Publishing Co.*, 553 N.E.2d 997 (N.Y. 1990), the court concluded that "[t]his view of 'reliance' – i.e., as requiring no more than reliance on the express warranty as being a part of the bargain between the parties – reflects the prevailing perception of an action for breach of express warranty as one that is no longer grounded in tort, but essentially in contract." *Id.* at 1001. The court reasoned that "[t]he critical question is not whether the buyer believed in the truth of the warranted information . . . but whether [he] believed [he] was purchasing the [seller's] promise [as to its truth]." *Id.* at 1000–01 (quotations omitted and some insertions altered).

CBS was not decided on the basis of the UCC, probably because the sale of the magazine business at issue did not constitute the sale of goods. . . . Nevertheless, the court relied heavily on UCC authorities, *see CBS*, 553 N.E.2d at 1000–01, expressly noting that "analogy to the Uniform Commercial Code is 'instructive'." *Id.* at 1002 n.4.

In 1992, in a case also involving the sale of a business, we followed the New York Court of Appeals and delineated fine factual distinctions in the law of warranties: a court must evaluate both the extent and the source of the buyer's knowledge about the truth of what the seller is warranting. "Where a buyer closes on a contract in the full knowledge and acceptance of facts *disclosed by the seller* which would constitute a breach of warranty under the terms of the contract, the buyer should be foreclosed from later asserting the breach. In that situation, unless the buyer expressly preserves his rights under the warranties . . ., we think the buyer has waived the breach." *Galli v. Metz*, 973 F.2d 145, 151 (2d Cir. 1992) (emphasis added) . . . . The buyer may preserve his rights by expressly stating that disputes regarding the accuracy of the seller's warranties are unresolved, and that by signing the agreement the buyer does not waive any rights to enforce the terms of the agreement. *See Galli*, 973 F.2d at 150.

On the other hand, if the seller is not the source of the buyer's knowledge, *e.g.*, if it is merely "common knowledge" that the facts warranted are false, or the buyer has been informed of the falsity of the facts by some third party, the buyer may prevail in his claim for breach of warranty. In these cases, it is not unrealistic to assume that the buyer purchased the seller's warranty "as insurance against any future claims," and that is why he insisted on the inclusion of the warranties in the bill of sale. *Galli*, 973 F.2d at 151 . . . .

In short, where the seller discloses up front the inaccuracy of certain of his warranties, it cannot be said that the buyer – absent the express preservation of his rights – believed he was purchasing the seller's promise as to the truth of the warranties. Accordingly, what the buyer knew and, most importantly, whether he got that knowledge from the seller are the critical questions. *See Galli*, 973 F.2d at 151; *Chateaugay*, 155 B.R. at 650–51.

1. What Siebenmann Knew

Here, as the district court pointed out, Siebenmann, the seller, produced no evidence to contradict Rogath's evidence that Siebenmann knew of the cloud that hung over the Painting's authenticity before he sold it to Rogath. Siebenmann admits that he was told that the Marlborough Gallery was troubled by certain peculiarities of the Painting – including shiny black paint (as opposed to the matte black that Bacon apparently preferred) and the use of pink paint (which Bacon evidently did not use) – that suggested that Bacon was not the painter.

Siebenmann also admits that Julian Barran, a London art dealer, had earlier refused to buy the Painting because of doubts harbored by the Marlborough Gallery. Moreover, there was uncontroverted evidence that, on a prior occasion, Siebenmann's attempted sale of the Painting to a client of Robert Peter Miller, the owner of an art gallery in New York, was aborted when (1) Miller learned that the Marlborough had concerns about the Painting's authenticity, and (2) David Sylvester, a British art critic, advised Miller not to proceed with the purchase because of the Marlborough objection and because Sylvester himself was not sure of the authenticity of the Painting.

Finally, Siebenmann does not deny that in June 1993 he received a fax from Anita Goldstein, an art dealer in Zurich, Switzerland, stating that "everybody is afraid of the authenticity" of the Painting.

2. What Siebenmann Told Rogath: Reasonable Inferences

In an affidavit in opposition to Rogath's motion for partial summary judgment, Siebenmann stated that "I spoke directly with David Rogath about the controversy created by the Marlborough Gallery towards this painting." He also said that, in a phone conversation with Rogath on July 13, 1993, "I specifically mentioned

Marlborough Gallery and the 'problems' or the 'controversy' that it had produced for this painting. . . . Mr. Rogath brushed aside the Marlborough Gallery controversy. He told me he had experienced difficulties with this particular gallery in the past and did not consider them to be especially reputable." In his deposition, Siebenmann added that he told Rogath on the phone "that I had problems with the Marlborough Gallery."

Siebenmann also filed an affidavit from Ronald Alley, the curator of the Tate Gallery in London, England, and the author of a survey of Bacon's work as well as several other writings about Bacon. Alley stated:

> I was phoned by Mr David Rogath, hitherto unknown to me, who said that he was thinking of buying the painting and asked whether it was correct that I had seen it and thought it to be authentic. My reply, to the best of my recollection, can be summarized as follows: "It is a picture which did not pass through Marlborough Fine Art and is said to have a provenance which sounds quite plausible but is more or less impossible to check. Both Ms Beston of Marlborough Fine Art and David Sylvester say they don't think it is by Bacon, but Sylvester knows it only from a photograph. I flew to Geneva for the day to look at it in a warehouse and felt convinced it was genuine."

For his part, Rogath denied that he was aware of any challenges to the authenticity or provenance of the Painting before entering into the Bill of Sale. He stated in his affidavit:

> During our telephone conversation, Mr. Siebenmann did not tell me that the Marlborough Gallery had "questioned" or "reserved judgment" about the Painting, or had caused any "problems" or "controversy" concerning the Painting. He said nothing at all like that during the conversation. Neither did Mr. Alley, in our subsequent conversation, refer to any such matters. He certainly did not tell me that Ms. Beston and Mr. Sylvester "don't think it is by Bacon." In fact, I spoke with Mr. Alley after the inauthenticity of the Painting had become known to me. . . . Had either Mr. Siebenmann or Mr. Alley hinted to me that the Painting was of questioned authenticity, it would have been a "red flag" for me, as I had no desire to spend some $600,000 dollars to purchase a painting the authenticity of which was in dispute. . . .

Here, the Bill of Sale states that the warranties induced Rogath to buy the Painting, but Rogath did not "expressly preserve his rights" under the Bill of Sale, as required by *Galli*. . . . Accordingly, exactly what Siebenmann told Rogath is clearly crucial. . . . On the other hand, what Alley may have told Rogath about the authenticity and provenance of the Painting is immaterial. . . . Only if the seller, Siebenmann himself, informed Rogath of doubts about the provenance or challenges to authenticity will Rogath be deemed to have waived any claims for breach of warranty arising from the written representations appearing in the Bill of Sale. . . .

As Rogath emphasizes, Siebenmann nowhere specifically alleges that he informed Rogath of his doubts about the authenticity and provenance of the Painting. He merely alluded to the "controversy" or "problems" with the Marlborough Gallery. Still, Siebenmann's testimony, however ambiguous, may justify the inference that Rogath knew more than he now claims to have known when he entered into the Bill of Sale.

At the very least, there is indisputable ambiguity in the affidavits about the pivotal exchange between Rogath and Siebenmann. We are satisfied that genuine issues of fact persist. In this posture, we must draw all reasonable inferences in Siebenmann's favor. . . . Accordingly, as regards the Marlborough challenge, summary judgment on Rogath's claims for breach of the warranties of provenance and no challenges to authenticity is inappropriate. . . .

3. What Sylvester Said

Sylvester's doubts about the Painting also cannot justify summary judgment for Rogath, but for different reasons. Siebenmann was aware that "Sylvester advised Miller not to proceed with the purchase of the Painting because of the 'Marlborough objection and that he wasn't sure himself of the authenticity of the painting.'" Siebenmann did not claim to have disclosed to Rogath Sylvester's statement. Indeed, in his affidavit opposing Rogath's summary judgment motion, Siebenmann stated that he did not consider Sylvester's doubts to be a challenge. Siebenmann's nondisclosure could constitute a breach of warranty-but only if Sylvester's statement was a "challenge" to authenticity. We conclude that the question of whether Sylvester's statement constituted a challenge poses factual issues for trial.

A contractual term is ambiguous where it may be ascribed "conflicting reasonable interpretations." *Mellon Bank, N.A. v. United Bank Corp. of N.Y.*, 31 F.3d 113, 116 (2d Cir. 1994). "As a general matter, we have held that when a contract is ambiguous, its interpretation becomes a question of fact and summary judgment is inappropriate." *Id.*

Although the parties apparently agree as to what Sylvester said, reasonable minds could differ as to whether what he said constituted a challenge apart from the Marlborough challenge. Sylvester's recommendation that the buyer not proceed "because of the Marlborough objection" could reasonably be interpreted as merely advice to heed the Marlborough challenge. Further, a rational juror could interpret the statement that "[Sylvester] wasn't sure" as evincing an ambivalence on the part of Sylvester that did not rise to the level of a challenge, especially given that Sylvester himself had not seen the Painting, but only photographs of it.

In this context, moreover, the term may well be a specialized one. It is hardly clear as a matter of law that "challenge" includes every mention by one person of the fact that a challenge has been made by another person (or, for example, that it would include Anita Goldstein's statement that "everybody is afraid of the authenticity" of the Painting). Nor is it clear as a matter of law whether the term "challenge" would include an expression of uncertainty by someone who had never seen the painting in question. If Siebenmann proffers art-industry or other evidence as to the meaning of this ambiguous contract term, its meaning will be a question for the jury at trial. . . .

CONCLUSION

The order granting Rogath's motion for partial summary judgment is vacated, and the case is remanded to the district court for disposition not inconsistent with this opinion.

Problem 3-6

Buyer needed a high-speed printer for use in Buyer's offices. In discussions with Seller's sales representative, Buyer received assurances that its X3000 printer could print 35 black-and-white pages per minute and 20 color pages per minute. The sales representative also assured Buyer that Buyer would be very happy with the printer. Buyer also picked up the sales brochure for the X3000, which stated that the X3000 had a "60,000 pages per month duty cycle." Buyer purchased the printer. Inside the box containing the printer was an owner's manual which contained the following language: "Seller warrants that the printer will be free of defects in material and workmanship for one year from date of delivery." Which, if any, of the statements made by the sales representative, in the brochure, and in the owner's manual constitute an express warranty?

Privity. Many courts have held that a lack of privity is not a bar to recovery on an express warranty.[14] In other words, if a manufacturer or other remote seller makes a representation that otherwise meets the test of section 2-313, the fact that the buyer suing on the express warranty was not in privity with (did not buy the goods from) the remote seller did not preclude the suit. The rationale for this is very simple:

> To hold otherwise could allow unscrupulous manufacturers who make public representations about their product's performance to remain insulated from express-warranty liability if consumers did not purchase the product directly from them.[15]

See also UCC § 2-318. We will return to the question of privity in Chapter Seven, when we discuss buyer's remedies, and in Chapter Eight, when we discuss the relationship of Article 2 to other law.

CISG. Article 30 of CISG states that the seller "must deliver the goods . . . as required by the contract and this Convention." Article 35(1) then provides that the seller "must deliver goods which are the . . . quality and description required by the contract and which are contained or packaged in the manner required by the contract." Unless the parties have agreed otherwise, the goods do not conform to the contract unless they "possess the qualities of goods which the seller has held out to the buyer as a sample or model" and "are contained or packaged in the manner usual for such goods or, where there is not such manner, in a manner adequate to preserve and protect the goods." CISG Art. 35(2)(c)-(d). Note that neither the phrase "express warranty" nor "basis of the bargain" is used and the "sample or model" issue is treated as a "gap filler."

The key question is what does the contract require. The answer is easy when the description of the goods and representations and promises dealing with the quality of the goods are contained in a writing assented to by both parties. But suppose that the core description or that representations about the goods made to

---

[14] *See e.g., Tex Enterprises, Inc. v. Brockway Standard, Inc.*, 66 P.3d 625 (Wash. 2003) (distinguishing express warranty from implied warranty regarding relaxation of privity requirement). *See* Harry M. Flechtner, *Enforcing Manufacturers' Warranties, "Pass Through" Warranties, and the Like: Can the Buyer Get a Refund?* 50 RUTGERS L. REV. 397 (1998); Curtis R. Reitz, *Manufacturers' Warranties of Consumer Goods*, 75 WASH. U. L.Q. 357 (1997); Donald F. Clifford, *Express Warranty Liability of Remote Sellers: One Purchase, Two Relationships*, 75 WASH. U. L.Q. 413 (1997).

[15] *U.S. Tire-Tech, Inc. v. Boeran, B.V.*, 110 S.W.3d 194, 198 (Tex. Ct. App. 2003).

the buyer during negotiations or after the contract is formed do not appear in the written contract. Presumably, the buyer must prove that the description or affirmations are part of the contract and that the goods failed to conform. In this process, there is considerable latitude for extrinsic evidence to be admitted. *See* CISG Art. 8, 9, 11, and 12.[16]

UNIDROIT Principles. Because the Principles are not directed solely to the provision of goods, its default rules on the quality of performance are somewhat difficult to apply. A party may have an obligation to achieve a particular result (as opposed to a "best efforts" standard. To determine if a party has that obligation, the contract must be interpreted. Factors in that interpretation include the way the obligation is expressed, the price or other terms, the degree of risk involved in achieving that result, and the ability of the other party to influence that performance. UNIDROIT Arts. 5.1.4, 5.1.5. If the quality of performance is not fixed or determined by the contract terms, a party is bound to render a performance "of a quality that is reasonable and not less than average in the circumstances." UNIDROIT Art. 5.1.6.

SECTION 3.   ADDING TO THE AGREEMENT: GAP FILLERS

A. Overview

When most sales agreements are made, the parties have not discussed all of the terms of their deal. This is certainly true for most informal transactions but it is also true for some formal, negotiated deals. Think about the last time you ordered goods over the phone or on the internet. In all likelihood, you and the seller agreed on the nature and quantity of the goods involved, the price, and the method of payment. But did you discuss who would bear the risk of loss if the goods were damaged or destroyed en route? Did you detail what your rights would be if the goods were not delivered on time or were defective?

Because it would be too burdensome for the parties – and to commerce generally – to require contracting parties to reach express agreement on all the terms that could be relevant to a transaction, the law allows them to omit some or even many terms from their *agreement* (which includes usage of trade, course of

---

[16] *See also* Andrew J. Kennedy, *Recent Developments: Nonconforming Goods Under the CISG–What's A Buyer to Do?*, 16 DICK. J. INT'L L. 319 (1998).

performance, and course of dealing). The law then supplies the missing terms into their *contract*. These supplied terms – known as gap fillers – can include such minor matters as risk of loss and method of payment, but can also include more significant terms, such as the price and warranties. Even most remedies for breach can be thought of as gap fillers because the parties are free by agreement to change them.

Before exploring the gap fillers in detail and considering whether there is a common policy underlying them, it is necessary to understand that there are two conditions to having an enforceable contract. Read section 2-204(3). It allows the parties to make an enforceable agreement – *i.e.,* a contract – if they have "intended to make a contract" and there is a "reasonably certain basis for giving an appropriate remedy." Gap fillers can play a role in the analysis of both of these conditions.

If there are unresolved material terms, and one of the parties is resisting enforcement of the bargain, the court must decide whether the parties intended to make a bargain that the legal system should enforce. In line with basic contract principles, the parties' intent to enter into an enforceable agreement must be manifested objectively in some manner. What factors are relevant to this determination of intent? Section 2-204(1) indicates that the parties' conduct can be relevant. Presumably, the relative completeness of the agreement is also relevant. In other words, the more terms they have discussed and agreed to – or which can be implied into their agreement by applicable course of performance, course of dealing, or usage of trade – the more likely it is that they intend to be bound. After all, parties often intend to be bound by their agreements even though they still need and expect to work out a few details later. If the parties have left matters to be specified later, those specifications must generally be made in good faith. UCC § 2-311(1). Conversely, the fewer terms they have resolved, the more likely it is that they are still in the midst of negotiations and do not yet intend to have a contract. That said, sometimes the parties may have omitted a single term because they have not yet been able to agree on it and they expect not to be bound until they do. Similarly, sometimes when parties have resolved only a few terms they nevertheless expect to be bound and expect the unresolved matters will be resolved later or supplied by gap fillers. Even a sketchy agreement can be filled in and made complete. Thus, the parties' intent to be bound will often have to be judged from something other the presence or absence of some terms.

If the parties did intend to enter into an enforceable bargain, the next question is whether there is a "reasonably certain basis for giving an appropriate remedy."

Because we have not yet studied the remedies built into Article 2, consider the following very brief summary of the remedies for breach.

In a sale of goods contract, the basic obligation of the seller is to deliver goods that conform to the contract requirements and the basic obligation of the buyer is to accept those goods and pay for them. UCC § 2-301. If the buyer breaches the contract by failing to pay as agreed when goods are delivered to and accepted by the buyer, the seller's damage remedy is to recover the price of the goods. UCC § 2-709. If the buyer breaches the contract by refusing conforming goods, the seller is damaged if the price of the goods in the marketplace is less than the contract price that the buyer agreed to pay. UCC § 2-708. Conversely, if the seller breaches the contract by tendering nonconforming goods and the buyer rejects those goods, the buyer is damaged if the market price for conforming goods is higher than the price that the buyer agreed to pay for the goods. UCC § 2-713. If the seller breaches by tendering nonconforming goods and the buyer accepts those goods, the buyer is damaged by the difference in value of the goods which the buyer got and the goods the buyer contracted for. UCC § 2-714.

From this very brief summary, it is clear that to have a "reasonable basis" for determining a remedy, the terms addressing price, quantity, quality, and delivery are very important. The gap fillers in Article 2 address all of these issues. They can be, and often are, used to help determine what the duties of each party are, whether there is a breach, and if there is a breach, how to measure damages. Thus the Article 2 gap fillers permit parties who intend to contract to leave terms open or indefinite with the security that some standard will be available to create an enforceable contract because there is a "reasonably certain basis for giving an appropriate remedy." *See* UCC § 2-204(3).

As we study the gap fillers in this Chapter and the next, consider how the ability to have an enforceable agreement prior to nailing down every term, and the presence of the Article 2 gap fillers, effects the negotiation of the sales contract.[17] Does the policy choice to have statutory gap fillers influence what clauses are drafted as part of the written documentation of the contract? Does it influence the scope of the negotiations? Does it foster an undue amount of disputes as courts wrestle with "incomplete" agreements? If you were revising the law, would you make different choices about how to deal with the problem of incomplete agreements? What are the gap fillers? Here is an incomplete list.

---

[17] *See, e.g.*, Scott Baker & Kimberly D. Krawiec, *Incomplete Contracts in a Complete Contract World*, 33 FLA. ST. U. L. REV. 725 (2006).

Warranties	§ 2-312 (warranty of title)
	§ 2-313 (express warranties)[18]
	§ 2-314 (implied warranty of merchantability)
	§ 2-315 (implied warranty of fitness)
Quantity and price of the goods	§ 2-305 (open price term)
	§ 2-306 (output and requirements contracts)
Payment	§ 2-304 (price payable in money)
	§ 2-310 (time for payment)
	§ 2-507(1) (condition to duty to tender payment)
	§ 2-511(2), (3) (manner of tendering payment)
	§ 2-512 (payment before inspection)
Manner and time of the seller's duty to tender the goods	§ 2-307 (delivery in a single lot)
	§ 2-308 (place of delivery)
	§ 2-309 (time of delivery)
	§ 2-503 (manner of delivery)
	§ 2-504 (duties in a shipment contract)
	§ 2-511(1) (condition to duty to tender)
Buyer's inspection, acceptance, and rejection of the goods	§ 2-513 (buyer's right to inspect goods)
	§ 2-601 (buyer's rights on improper tender)
	§ 2-602 (manner and effect of rejection)
	§ 2-606 (acceptance of goods)
	§ 2-607 (effect of acceptance of goods)
	§ 2-612(2) (rejection in installment contracts)
Risk of loss	§ 2-509 (risk of loss generally)
	§ 2-510 (risk of loss after breach)
Other	§ 2-311 (obligations in making specifications)
	§ 2-508 (seller's right to cure)
	§ 2-603 (buyer's duties as to rejected goods)
	§ 2-604 (buyer's rights to rejected goods)
	§ 2-608 (revocation of acceptance)

Based upon what we have looked at so far, the sequence of analytical steps in determining the terms of a sale of goods transaction should be as follows. First, determine whether the parties have reached an agreement. To do this, consult the rules on contract formation discussed in Chapter Two. Then identify the express

---

[18] Express warranties themselves are not gap fillers, but the rules in section 2-313 on how express warranties are formed could, presumably, be changed by agreement. Thus, the rule on how express warranties are created are themselves a sort of gap filler.

terms of their agreement and ask whether the parties have intended to contract. *See* UCC § 2-204. In looking at that question, the completeness of the agreement is relevant but not determinative. Next, identify the remaining terms of the parties' agreement by considering any applicable course of dealing, course of performance, or usage of trade. Then, consider whether there are any gaps. If there are, and if filling in those gaps is not precluded by the parties' agreement as previously determined, look to the provisions of Article 2 to fill them. Finally, determine if there is an appropriate basis for providing an appropriate remedy for breach of contract. Test your understanding of these analytical steps by considering the following problem.

Problem 3-7

A. Seller agreed in a record signed by both parties to sell one skid loader to Buyer for $20,000. Nothing was stated in the record concerning delivery of the skid loader. Buyer insisted Seller deliver the skid loader to Buyer's place of business and Seller insisted that Buyer come pick it up. Buyer refused to pick up the skid loader or to pay any amount of the purchase price until Seller delivered the skid loader. Seller sued Buyer for breach of contract.
  1. Is this an enforceable contract?
  2. If so, has anyone breached the contract?

B. Brad and Stephanie, who are both merchants, agree during a telephone conversation to buy and sell, respectively, $1,000 worth of widgets. Brad sends a written confirmation stating, "Enjoyed doing business with you. Look forward to receiving 50 widgets for a price of $1,000." On the same day, Stephanie sends Brad a written confirmation stating, "Thanks for the order. Will promptly ship 40 widgets for total price of $1,000." The confirmations cross in the mail. Prior to any further action by either party, do the parties have a contract?

C. Would it make a difference in Part A above, if Buyer had purchased several pieces of construction equipment in the past year from Seller and in each of those previous purchases, Seller had delivered the equipment to Buyer?

The policies underlying gap fillers. Once the UCC drafters made the policy decision that agreements with open terms could be treated as enforceable contracts, and that missing terms could be supplied by law, the drafters had to determine the content of the gap fillers. Should the gap fillers be the terms that are the most fair? The most economically efficient? The most common? The ones most consistent with the parties' likely expectations? Should the rules strive for neutrality between sellers and buyers or favor one over the other? Should the rules be the same for both consumer and commercial transactions? Should agreements for long-term relationships be treated the same as single, isolated transactions? Perhaps the rules should be ones that the parties would not likely agree to, so as to encourage them to reach an express agreement, or designed to force one party to reveal critical information to the other. Consider these different objectives as we study the gap fillers in more detail. Do you see a common underlying policy? If so, do you agree with it?

CISG and UNIDROIT Principles. The CISG contains several provisions detailing the obligations of the seller and the buyer in a contract for a sale of goods, and which can be thought of as gap fillers. In terms of the seller's delivery obligation, Article 31 states where the seller must deliver, Article 33 provides when the seller must deliver, and Article 35 addresses the quality of the goods the seller must deliver. In terms of the buyer's obligation to take the goods and pay the price, Article 55 addresses open price contracts, Article 57 states the place of payment, Articles 58 and 59 address when the buyer must pay, and Article 60 addresses the obligation to take delivery of the goods.

The UNIDROIT Principles also contain several general statements regarding the obligations of the contracting parties. The Principles recognize the ability to contract with open terms. Art. 4.8. The Principles address the price term in Article 5.1.7 and the payment obligation in Article 6.1.7. The Principles also address performance obligations in Articles 6.1.1 through 6.1.6.

B. Examining Particular Gap Filler Provisions: Warranties

1. *Implied Warranty of Merchantability*

Article 2 provides that, unless properly disclaimed,[19] some sellers make an "implied" warranty that goods are merchantable. Read section 2-314. Understanding this section requires analysis of two basic issues. First, which sellers make the implied warranty of merchantability? In other words, under what circumstances does the warranty arise? Second, what does it mean to promise that the goods are "merchantable"?

As to the first issue, note that only sellers who are merchants make the implied warranty of merchantability. Although a non-merchant seller can, of course, expressly warrant that the goods are merchantable, *see* UCC § 2-314 cmt. 4, only merchant sellers make the warranty as an implied warranty. However, not even all merchants make the implied warranty of merchantability; the warranty arises only if the seller is a "merchant with respect to goods of that kind." As to what this limitation means, see UCC §§ 2-104 cmt. 2; 2-314 cmt. 3.

Problem 3-8

Which, if any, of the following sellers make the implied warranty of merchantability?

A. Artisan makes stained glass baubles to be hung in windows and sells the baubles at the local, semi-annual crafts fair. If Artisan has a full-time job as an accountant, is that relevant to the analysis?

B. Best Car Rental, which is in the business of renting cars on a daily and weekly basis, sells the oldest cars in its rental fleet every four months.

C. Caterer, who regularly provides and cooks food for, and serves the food at, wedding receptions.

D. Directed Decorating, Inc. is in the business of finding antiques for decorating expensive hotel lobbies. When it locates items that it thinks

---

[19] *See* UCC § 2-316. Disclaimers of implied warranties are considered in Chapter Five.

are suitable for a client, it puts the client in touch with the seller and receives a finding fee from the client.

As to the second issue – what does "merchantable" mean? – see UCC § 2-314(2). The most important paragraph is (2)(c), which requires the goods be fit for their ordinary purpose. In other words, a washing machine must wash clothes, presumably without tearing them to shreds. A clothes dryer must dry without incinerating the clothes or setting the buyer's house on fire. If this seems obvious, bear in mind that it represents a huge change from old common law, under which the buyer received no more than what the seller expressly promised. Courts examine the "fit for the ordinary purpose" aspect of merchantability from the perspective of the reasonable expectation of the average purchaser or user as to how the good will perform when put to its ordinary use.[20]

The remaining standards in subsection (2), while perhaps less important, can still be significant. Consider section 2-314(2)(f), which requires that the goods conform to promises and affirmations of fact on the container or label. How does that comport with the requirement for express warranties that they be part of the basis of the bargain? Consider also the requirement in section 2-314(2)(b) that fungible goods be of "fair average quality." Does that mean that half of all fungible goods – all of them below average quality – breach the warranty of merchantability? Note that section 2-314(2)(b) – along with paragraph (a) – is keyed to the contract description of the goods. Thus, analysis of what this warranty covers must begin with an identification of the contract description of the goods.

Now consider the requirement in section 2-314(2)(a) that the goods pass without objection in the trade. Without any proof of what the relevant trade standards are, a claim for breach under this provision may fail. Similarly, if a product is new and no average or usual standards have arisen for assessing performance or quality, this aspect of merchantability may not help the buyer.

Nothing in the text of section 2-314 limits the warranty of merchantability to new goods. Accordingly, the warranty is made even for used goods, as long as the

---

[20] *See Moss v. Batesville Casket Co.*, 935 So.2d 393, 401–02 (Miss. 2006) (plaintiffs failed to establish how long they would expect wooden casket to preserve remains, breach of implied warranty of merchantability claim fails). *See also Koken v. Black & Veatch Const., Inc.*, 426 F.3d 39, 51–52 (1st Cir. 2005); *Mitchell v. BBB Services Co.*, 582 S.E.2d 470 (Ga. Ct. App. 2003); *Castro v. QVC Network, Inc.*, 139 F.3d 114 (2d Cir. 1998); *Jackson v. Nestle-Beich, Inc.*, 589 N.E.2d 547 (Ill. 1992).

seller is a merchant with respect to goods of that kind and the seller has not successfully disclaimed the warranty. However, the scope and meaning of the warranty is significantly reduced for used goods. Read comment 3 to section 2-314. As one court stated:

> [The] ordinary buyer in a normal commercial transaction has a right to expect that the goods . . . will not turn out to be completely worthless. The purchaser cannot be expected to purchase goods offered by a merchant for sale and use and then find the goods are suitable only for the junk pile. On the other hand, a buyer who has purchased goods without obtaining an express warranty as to their quality and condition cannot reasonably expect that those goods will be the finest of all possible goods of that kind. Protection of the buyer under the uniform commercial code lies between these two extremes. If an item is used or is second hand, surely less can be expected in the way of quality than if the item is purchased new. . . . The buyer's knowledge that the goods are used, the extent of their prior use, and whether the goods are significantly discounted may help determine what standards of quality should apply to the transaction.[21]

To what extent should the buyer's misuse of the good impact the analysis of whether the good is merchantable? Given the focus on the buyer's expectations regarding the goods in defining merchantability, what uses should the seller reasonably expect the buyer to have for the goods? For example, should the seller of a hair dryer anticipate that buyers may use the hair dryer in a high humidity environment (*i.e.*, the bathroom after a shower)? Would a hair dryer that shorts out in that circumstance be merchantable? In many states, the buyer's misuse of the product will mean that the product did not breach the implied warranty of merchantability or may reduce the damages that the buyer may recover if part of the damages are attributable to the misuse of the product.[22]

Problem 3-9

In which, if any, of the following scenarios has the implied warranty of merchantability been breached?

---

[21] *International Petroleum Services, Inc. v. S & N Well Service, Inc.*, 639 P.2d 29, 32, 34 (Kan. 1982).

[22] *See Gillespie v. Sears, Roebuck & Co.*, 386 F.3d 21 (1st Cir. 2004) (seller was entitled to an unreasonable use instruction when buyer operated table saw without the safety guards).

A. Aparicio purchased a new lawn mower from Dealer on May 1. On each of the next three weekends, Aparicio successfully used the mower to cut the grass at Aparicio's home. The fourth time Aparicio attempted to use the mower, the ignition malfunctioned so the motor would not start. *See* UCC § 2-725(2). *See also Gillespie v. Sears, Roebuck & Co.*, 386 F.3d 21 (1st Cir. 2004).

B. Boggs was served a salmon fillet at the local restaurant, Fish 'N Chips. While eating the salmon, Boggs choked on a bone and had to have the bone surgically extracted from Bogg's throat at the local hospital. *See Webster v. Blue Ship Tea Room, Inc.*, 198 N.E.2d 309 (Mass. 1964). *Compare Mexicali Rose v. Superior Ct.*, 822 P.2d 1292 (Cal. 1992); *Schafer v. JLC Food Systems, Inc.*, 695 N.W.2d 570 (Minn. 2005).

C. Conigliaro, a professional weaver, purchased five lots of yarn from Stannick Looms, Inc. The yarn was all supposed to be Magenta No. 02. When it was delivered, there were noticeable variations in color although each was labeled Magenta No. 02. Conigliaro objected and Stannick stated that the difference in color was due to natural differences in the yarn composition and how each lot of yarn had taken the dye. Stannick maintains that the color variations are permissible variations that are normal for each dye lot.

D. DiMaggio purchased a new car from Dealer for $30,000. The car complied with all government required product safety equipment but was rated low by national consumer reporting firms for front impact safety due to compartment invasion at high speed impact. DiMaggio was severely injured in a high velocity, head-on collision because the engine was pushed 12 inches into the passenger compartment.

E. Eckersley, a photographer, purchased an expensive new digital camera on line from 34th Street Camera, a retailer. When the camera arrived, Eckersley removed the camera from its box and noticed that the serial number on the camera was preceded by the letters "UK." Eckersley telephoned the manufacturer and learned that: (i) the camera was intended for distribution in Europe; (ii) although the manufacturer expressly warranted all cameras of the same model that were intended for distribution in the U.S., the manufacturer made no warranty for the camera Eckersley had purchased; and (iii) the manufacturer would not permit any of its authorized repair facilities to fix the camera if indeed it ever did malfunction.

F. Foxx purchased a used six-year-old pickup truck from Dealer for $5,000. The truck had been driven 80,000 "tough" miles without any serious mechanical problems. The day after the sale, the engine failed. Assume that the $5,000 purchase price was at the low end of the "blue book" range for this model truck but that such a truck with this kind of engine problem has a fair market value of $750.

G. Garciaparra purchased a two-year old used car from Dealer. A few weeks later, the car's entire electrical system shorted out, requiring extensive and expensive repair efforts.   During the repairs, Garciaparra's mechanic discovered and informed Garciaparra that the car has extensive water damage that must have resulted from a flood or hurricane. Does it matter to the analysis if Dealer was aware at the time of sale that the car had been salvaged from a storm?

H. Hoyt purchased a box of gloves from Home Improvement Supplier that indicated that the gloves were "latex free." The box was mislabeled and the gloves contained latex. Hoyt suffered a severe allergic reaction. Does Hoyt have a cause of action against Supplier?

What is the rationale for imposing this implied warranty on some merchant sellers but not others? Does that rationale help determine the meaning of "merchantable" goods? In an influential article,[23] William L. Prosser, suggested three overlapping justifications for the implied warranty of merchantability. The first was that the seller had made a "misrepresentation of fact" upon which the

---

[23] *See* William L. Prosser, *The Implied Warranty of Merchantable Quality*, 27 MINN. L. REV. 117, 122 (1943). There is close relationship between the idea of unmerchantable and the concept of product defect in tort law for purposes of strict liability under RESTATEMENT (SECOND) OF TORTS § 402A. *See Castro v. QVC Network, Inc.*, 139 F.3d 114 (2d Cir. 1998). We will consider the relationship between products liability as a matter of tort law and implied warranty of merchantability liability in Chapter Eight.

buyer had relied. For Prosser, this was "obviously" a tort theory. The second was that the warranty "has in fact been agreed upon by the parties as an unexpressed term of the contract for sale." The warranty was inferred from language, conduct, circumstances and was "pure" contract. The third was that the warranty was "imposed by law" as a matter of policy. The loss from "defective" goods should be placed upon the seller "because he is best able to bear it and distribute it to the public, and because it is considered that the buyer is entitled to protection at the seller's expense." For the third justification, Prosser had in mind cases where defective food caused personal injuries to buyers and consumers.

Privity. Whether a person not in privity with the seller may recover for breach of the implied warranty of merchantability is a hotly debated issue as to which the states have varying answers.[24] *See* UCC § 2-318. We will return to the question of privity in Chapter Seven, when we discuss buyer's remedies, and in Chapter Eight, when we discuss the relationship of Article 2 to other law.

CISG. Article 35(2)(a), (c), and (d) are the counterparts to UCC § 2-314.

2. Implied Warranty of Fitness for Particular Purpose

Read section 2-315. Packed in only a few lines of text are four requirements for this implied warranty to arise:
1. The seller must have reason to know of the buyer's particular purpose;
2. The buyer must have a particular purpose;[25]
3. The seller must have reason to know that the buyer is relying on the seller's skill or judgment to select or supply suitable goods; and
4. The buyer must in fact rely on the seller's skill or judgment.[26]

Notice what is not a requirement. The seller need not be a merchant with respect to the goods of that kind, or even a merchant at all. That said, the third and fourth

---

[24] *Compare Blanco v. Baxter Healthcare Corp.*, 70 Cal. Rptr. 3d 566 (Cal. Ct. App. 2008) (privity required) *with Gonzalez v. Pepsico, Inc.*, 489 F. Supp. 2d 1233 (D. Kan. 2007) (privity not required in consumer transaction based upon interpretation of state statute other than the UCC as overriding the UCC requirement of privity).

[25] Section 2-315 does not actually say this, but it can be inferred from the first clause.

[26] Section 2-315 does not actually say this either, but again it can be inferred from what is said. The point is also made in the last sentence of comment 1 and by numerous courts. *E.g., Leal v. Holtvogt*, 702 N.E.2d 1246, 1256 (Ohio Ct. App. 1998)

requirements are unlikely to be satisfied if the seller is not a merchant. Notice what else is not required. Nothing in the statute indicates that the buyer's reliance has to be reasonable. Of course, in situations in which it would be wholly unreasonable for the buyer to rely on the seller, the seller may have no reason to know that the buyer is in fact relying, and the warranty will still not arise.

The warranty of fitness arises only if the buyer has a particular purpose. What distinguishes a "particular purpose" from an ordinary purpose? Consider the following case excerpt.

> Ingram's purpose for the goods it purchased from Pott was to use them to carry heavy petroleum products on the Mississippi and its tributaries and to heat those products to facilitate their discharge in cold climates. Pott characterizes the goods at issue as heating-coil-equipped tank barges, and argues that carrying and heating heavy petroleum products is the customary use of such products. Pott maintains that Ingram's use of the barges and the heating coils is not unique or peculiar to Ingram's business, since others use heating-coil-equipped tank barges in precisely the same manner; Pott itself had constructed over thirty such barges for use in the same manner before it built these four for Ingram.
>
> Ingram, however, rejoins that Pott errs in suggesting that its use of the goods must be unique to fall within the fitness-for-a-particular-purpose warranty, arguing instead that the question is one of degree. According to Ingram, the proper characterization of the goods here is tank barges, rather than heating-coil-equipped tank barges. Tank barges, Ingram continues, are used to carry a multitude of cargoes, including a variety of chemicals, molasses, and oils and fuel oils of many kinds. The barges here were equipped with steam coils to enable Ingram to carry a particular kind of cargo – cargo that sometimes requires heating to aid discharge. Further, neither Pott nor Ingram deals solely or predominantly in barges that have steam coils; Pott builds and Ingram operates all sorts of barges. In these circumstances, Ingram concludes, the particular-purpose requirement is met.
>
> We agree with Ingram that its use of the goods need not be one-of-a-kind to meet the requirements of [§ 2-315]. It is doubtful that even the Comment's example of using a shoe to climb mountains would qualify as a unique use of the shoe. Instead, as we read Comment 2, the key inquiry is not whether anyone else can be found who puts the goods to the same use, but whether the buyer's use is sufficiently different from the

customary use of the goods to make it not an ordinary use of the goods; that a buyer's use is not entirely idiosyncratic does not mean that it is ordinary. . . . Therefore, that others put tank barges to the same use as Ingram does not preclude finding that a warranty of fitness exists.

Whether Ingram's purpose diverges sufficiently from the customary purposes of other buyers to be considered particular turns to a great extent on whether one accepts Pott's characterization of the goods as heating-coil-equipped tank barges, or instead accepts Ingram's portrayal of them as tank barges, which have been equipped with heating coils to serve a particular purpose. And this in turn hinges upon how the factual context in which Ingram and Pott struck their bargain is interpreted. To return to the Comment's shoe illustration, is this case more like one in which a buyer goes to a general shoe store and buys a pair of shoes for mountain climbing, or one in which a buyer goes to a mountain-climbing gear store to buy shoes for this purpose? This is, ultimately, a question of fact. . . . Here, since Ingram operates and Pott builds barges for a variety of uses, we are unable to conclude that the District Court was clearly erroneous in finding that an implied warranty of fitness for a particular purpose arose.[27]

What other issues do you see in applying the implied warranty of fitness for a particular purpose? Is it good policy to make the seller liable for this implied warranty? What is the difference between this warranty and the implied warranty of merchantability or an express warranty?

Privity. Because of the reliance requirement that is part of the implied warranty of fitness for particular purpose, liability under this warranty is usually restricted to the seller from whom the buyer purchased the goods. There may be some circumstances, however, where the buyer can demonstrate reliance on a manufacturer's specific assurances to the buyer regarding a product. Should the buyer be able to recover from the manufacturer based upon this implied warranty?[28] We will return to the question of privity in Chapter Seven, when we discuss buyer's remedies, and in Chapter Eight, when we discuss the relationship of Article 2 to other law.

CISG. Article 35(2)(b) is the counterpart to UCC § 2-315.

---

[27] *Ingram River Equip., Inc. v. Pott Indus., Inc.*, 816 F.2d 1231, 1233–35 (8th Cir. 1987).

[28] *See Duall Bldg. Restoration, Inc. v. 1143 East Jersey Ave., Associates, Inc.*, 652 A.2d 1225 (N.J. Super. Ct. A.D. 1995).

Problem 3-10

A. Construct a scenario in which the seller would be making an implied warranty of fitness for particular purpose. If it helps, think of a situation that might arise in a hardware or auto parts store.

B. Buyer purchased a new car from Dealer for $30,000. The car complied with all government required product safety equipment but was rated low by national consumer reporting firms for front impact safety due to compartment invasion at high speed impact. When Buyer visited with the Dealer's sales person regarding the Buyer's need for a car, Buyer told the sales person that Buyer needed a car that was very safe. Buyer explained that she would be commuting on two-lane, winding mountain roads, and needed something that Buyer could rely on to keep her safe in the event of a serious collision. Dealer's sales person recommended the car that Buyer purchased. Buyer was severely injured in a high velocity, head-on collision because the engine was pushed 12 inches into the passenger compartment. Buyer sued Dealer for breach of the implied warranty of fitness for particular purpose. What result?

3. *Warranties of Title and Noninfringement*

The previous three warranties have all been concerned with the quality of the goods that are the subject of the sales contract. The warranties of title and noninfringement, on the other hand, are concerned with whether someone – other than the buyer or seller – will be able to interfere with the buyer's use or possession of the goods, or will put the buyer to the time and trouble of defending the buyer's right to use and possess the goods. Read section 2-312. Subsection (1) provides for the warranty of title; subsection (3) provides for the warranty of noninfringement.[29]

As you dissect these statutory provisions, consider the following basic questions about these two warranties. First, what kind of sellers make these warranties? Second, under what circumstances is the warranty made? Third, what is the content

---

[29] Section 2-312(2) governs the ability to disclaim the warranty of title and is discussed in Chapter Five.

of the warranty? More specifically, what is "good title"? What is the difference between "good title" and "rightful transfer"? Consideration of these questions requires an excursion into the concept of title, both under Article 2 and the common law.

Title. Title can be defined as the right of ownership, or at least as evidence of the right of ownership (nominal ownership). Article 2 has relatively few provisions on "title" to goods. Indeed, the drafters consciously chose to de-emphasize the role of title in sales-of-goods transactions. This point is made expressly in section 2-401, which states that "[e]ach provision of this Article with regard to the rights, obligations and remedies of the seller, the buyer, purchasers or other third parties applies irrespective of title to the goods except where the provision refers to such title." In spite of this attempt to de-emphasize title as a concept to be used to resolve disputes between the seller and the buyer, the definition of a "sale" under Article 2 is the "passing of title from the seller to the buyer for a price." *See* UCC § 2-106(1). And, we have seen, many of the provisions of Article 2 depend upon there being a "sale" transaction.

The rules about title in section 2-401 may be relevant in resolving a wide variety of controversies that are beyond the scope of Article 2, *e.g.*, the right of the buyer's creditors to levy on goods still in the seller's possession, the coverage of an insurance policy, the applicability of a state sales tax, the criminal responsibility of a person accused of larceny, or whether property becomes part of the buyer's estate in a bankruptcy.[30] However, for issues within the scope of Article 2, title is relevant only if the applicable provisions expressly refer to title. The most important of these are sections 2-403 and 2-312.

Rights of a transferee. Read section 2-403. The first sentence of subsection (1) specifies the basic rule applicable to almost any transfer of property: a purchaser takes the rights that the transferor had or had power to transfer. The second and third sentences expand on that general rule by indicating when a transferor has the power to transfer more rights than the transferor owns. In other words, in the circumstances described in the statute, a purchaser is able to obtain greater rights than its transferor had. These circumstances all involve situations when the transferor has "voidable title" (as opposed to void title or no title). A transferor with voidable title can transfer good title to a good faith purchaser for value. Read

---

[30] *See Iker v. Estate of Jones*, 863 N.E.2d 666 (Ohio Ct. App. 2006); *Concord General Mut Ins. Co. v. Sumner*, 762 A.2d 849 (Vt. 2000). We will consider property issues in Chapter Ten.

the definitions of "purchase," "purchaser," and "good faith" in UCC § 1-201. Notice that a good faith purchaser for value acquires good title from a transferor with voidable title only if the purchaser takes delivery of the goods under a "transaction of purchase."

A classic example of "voidable" title at common law arises when a seller of goods, induced by a fraudulent representation by the buyer, delivers the goods to the buyer under a contract for sale. In that case, the buyer's title to the goods is "voidable" in the sense that the seller can go to court to rescind the transaction and get the goods back. However, the buyer is nevertheless able to transfer good title to a good faith purchaser for value. After such a transfer, the original seller no longer can reclaim the goods.

The case of *Johnson & Johnson Products, Inc. v. Dal International Trading Co.,*[31] illustrates these principles. In that case, the seller misrepresented to its supplier that the goods supplied would be distributed only in Poland. In fact, the seller distributed the goods through various intermediaries in the so-called "gray market" to buyers in the United States. When the supplier sought an injunction against further sales in the United States, one of the buyers claimed the seller had had voidable title and that the buyer was a "good faith purchaser for value" under section 2-403(1). The court agreed, holding that the buyer had no reason to suspect that there was fraud (even though it had reason to believe it had purchased "gray" goods) and, therefore, there was no duty to investigate or inquire as to whether there might have been a misrepresentation. In short, the buyer was "honest in fact" because it did not "subjectively" suspect that the title was flawed and proceeded with the purchase "despite his or her suspicions."

The classic instance of "void" title occurs when a thief steals goods from the rightful owner. This act involves no voluntary transfer of possession. A buyer of the goods from the thief – or any person to whom the thief has delivered the goods – gets no protection under section 2-403.

Entrustment. Section 2-403 has another provision that expands on the general rule that a transferee receives only those rights that the transferor has or has power to convey. Read sections 2-403(2), (3), and 1-201(b)(9) on the definition of "buyer in ordinary course of business."[32] These provisions allow a merchant to whom

---

[31] 798 F.2d 100 (3d Cir. 1986).

[32] For an example of an analysis of the requirements of entrustment, merchant status, and qualification as a buyer in ordinary course of business, *see Lindholm v. Brant*, 925 A.2d 1048 (Conn. 2007).

goods have been entrusted to transfer good title to a buyer in ordinary course of business. A classic example of the entrustment provisions occurs when the owner of a piece of jewelry in need of repair delivers it to jeweler who both repairs and sells goods of that kind. If the jeweler sells and delivers the item to a buyer in ordinary course of business, that buyer will acquire all the owner's rights in the item. As one court put it:

> The entrustment provision of the UCC is designed to enhance the reliability of commercial sales by merchants who deal in the kind of goods sold. . . . It shifts the risk of resale to the one who leaves his property with the merchant. . . . When a person knowingly delivers his property into the possession of a merchant dealing in goods of that kind, that person assumes the risk of the merchant's acting unscrupulously by selling the property to an innocent purchaser. The entrustment provision places the loss upon the party who vested the merchant with the ability to transfer the property with apparent good title.[33]

Colorable claims against the title. Return now to the text of section 2-312(1). The seller warrants that the title the buyer is receiving is "good." What if the title is "good" but the circumstances are such that there are colorable claims regarding whether the title is good? Consider the words of the South Dakota Supreme Court:

> Comment 1 to UCC § 2-312 states a buyer is entitled to "receive a good, clear title transferred . . . in a rightful manner so [the buyer] will not be exposed to a lawsuit in order to protect it." A split of authority persists on the scope of § 2-312. Decker relies on those cases which hold that a breach of warranty of title occurs only when an outstanding superior title exists.[34] Other courts hold that under § 2-312 mere initiation of a colorable challenge, one which is not spurious, regardless of the outcome, is sufficient to violate the warranty of title. . . . We find the latter to be the better rule. . . . Purchasers should not be required to enter into a contest on the validity of ownership over [the goods they purchased].[35]

---

[33] *DeWeldon, Ltd. v. McKean*, 125 F.3d 24, 27–28 (1st Cir. 1997).

[34] Indeed, the UCC drafters flatly stated "The warranty of quiet possession is abolished." UCC § 2-312 cmt. 1. Yet the same comment states, "Disturbance of quiet possession, although not mentioned specifically, is one way, among many, in which the breach of the warranty of title may be established."

[35] *Colton v. Decker*, 540 N.W.2d 172, 175–76 (S.D. 1995). This case involved a car which

Cases on the warranty of noninfringement are of similar import. They typically arise when some third party claims that the goods sold to the buyer infringe on the third party's copyright, patent or trademark. However, the third party need not have a valid claim of infringement for the seller to have breached the warranty. As one court put it recently:

> A third party's claim of infringement . . . must cast a "substantial shadow" on the buyer's ability to make use of the goods in question, in order to constitute a breach of the warranty against infringement. . . . [T]his does not mean that [the buyer] would have to actually prove the validity of the infringement claim to succeed on this warranty argument, only that . . . the infringement claim is of a substantial nature that is reasonably likely to subject the buyer to litigation, and has a significant and adverse effect on the buyer's ability to make use of the goods in question.[36]

More recently, another court stated an even more lenient test:

> [T]he section 2-312(3) warranty covers a broad scope of infringement claims and is not limited to claims that ultimately will prove successful in litigation. . . . [It] applies to all claims of infringement that have any significant and adverse effect on the buyer's ability to make use of the purchased goods, excepting only frivolous claims that are completely devoid of merit.[37]

Problem 3-11

What factors might be relevant to whether a purchaser is acting in good faith for the purposes of section 2-403? *See Tempur-Pedic International, Inc. v. Waste to Charity, Inc.*, 483 F. Supp. 2d 766 (W.D. Ark. 2007).

---

was also subject to a certificate of title. In many states, a certificate of title will not be conclusive proof of ownership. The precise effect of certificate of title laws on the question of ownership of motor vehicles is beyond the scope of these materials.

[36] *Sun Coast Merchandise Corp. v. Myron Corp.*, 922 A.2d 782, 796–97 (N.J. Super. Ct. App. Div. 2007).

[37] *Pacific Sunwear of Cal., Inc. v. Olaes Enters., Inc.*, 84 Cal. Rptr. 3d 182, 193 (Cal. Ct. App. 2008).

Problem 3-12

In which, if any, of the following scenarios has the seller breached the warranty of title?

A. Seller, who had stolen a diamond necklace, sold it to Buyer who knew nothing of the theft.   Does it matter whether Seller is a merchant?[SRt]What if Seller is homeless person in tattered clothing?

B. Seller purchased a used diamond necklace from Thackery, and a few days later sold and delivered the necklace to Buyer. Shortly thereafter, Seller and Buyer learn that Thackery had stolen the necklace from Owner.

C. Seller, who had acquired a diamond necklace by paying for it with a check that was later dishonored, sold and delivered the necklace to Buyer.

D. Seller, who had borrowed a diamond necklace from Friend to wear at a party, sold and delivered the necklace to Buyer.

E. Seller, a jeweler who had received a diamond necklace from Owner to repair and clean it, sold and delivered the necklace to Buyer.

F. Seller, a jeweler, contracted to sell a diamond necklace to Buyer, who made a down payment and promised to pay the remainder of the purchase price rest the following day. Buyer agreed to allow Seller to retain possession until Buyer paid the price in full. Later that day, Seller sold and delivered the same necklace to Purchaser. If Seller has breached the warranty of title, in which of the two transactions did that breach occur?

Privity. Generally, the buyer's remedy for breach of the warranty of title and the warranty of noninfringement is against the seller in privity of contract with the buyer. We will return to the question of privity in Chapter Seven, when we discuss buyer's remedies, and in Chapter Eight, when we discuss the relationship of Article 2 to other law.

CISG. Article 4(b) of the CISG provides that, except as otherwise expressly provided, the Convention, "is not concerned with . . . the effect which the contract may have on the property in the goods sold." In other words, the CISG says nothing about how a stranger to the contract may enforce its claim to the goods, whether by recovery of the goods or conversion. Similarly, it says nothing about whether or how the sales contract affects the third party's rights. In short, the CISG has no analog to the rules in section 2-401 on when good title can be transferred by a seller who does not have good title. For this reason, the provisions of the UCC may govern claims to the goods located in a U.S. jurisdiction.[38]

However, the CISG does have rules similar to the warranties of title and noninfringement. Specifically, Article 41, which deals with title or a security interest, is the counterpart to section 2-312(1) and Article 42, which deals with intellectual property, is the counterpart to section 2-312(3). Collectively, they provide that the seller, with certain limitations, must deliver goods which are free from third-party claims. Failure to do so is a breach of contract for which the buyer may pursue appropriate remedies. CISG Art. 45.

UNIDROIT Principles. The Principles do not specifically address title or infringement issues. However, to the extent the seller has promised to "sell" goods to the buyer, the provisions regarding the parties' performance obligations could perhaps be interpreted to provide for some type of warranty for the buyer. *See* UNIDROIT Arts. 5.1.1 through 5.1.6.

---

[38] *See Usinor Industeel v. Leeco Steel Products Inc.*, 209 F. Supp. 2d 880 (N.D. Ill. 2002) (because the CISG does not cover the property rights aspects of the contract for sale, the provisions of the Illinois Commercial Code governed the seller's property claim to the goods located in Illinois).

CHAPTER FOUR

TERMS OF THE CONTRACT – PART II

This Chapter continues the discussion of gap fillers that began in Chapter Three, Section 3. It focuses on the gap filler rules regarding quantity, price, delivery, and payment. Remember, to the extent the parties' agreement already addresses these items, the gap fillers in Article 2 do not override that agreement.

SECTION 1. QUANTITY

Quantity is the single term least susceptible to being supplied by a gap filler. Virtually no principle that the drafters might have chosen to base the gap filler rules on would yield an obvious answer. Beyond that, if the statute of frauds applies to a sale-of-goods transaction, quantity is the one essential term that the writing must contain. *See* UCC § 2-201. However, there are two situations in which a quantity term can be implied: (i) when the parties agree to buy and sell all or some fixed percentage of the seller's output; and (2) when the parties agree to buy and sell all or a fixed percentage of the buyer's requirements. Read section 2-306(1).[1]

There are several things worth noting about this provision. First, it is more a rule on how to interpret an output or requirements term that the parties have agreed to than a true gap filler. It never implies an output or requirements term when the parties have not agreed to one.

Second, some courts have been concerned with whether an output or requirements term is enforceable if it is not an "exclusive" arrangement to get "all" output or requirements from the counter party. The concern is that if the buyer does not commit to buy "all" its requirements from the seller, or the seller does not commit to sell "all" of its output to the buyer, there may really be no enforceable commitment (mutuality of obligation), and the agreement may amount to little more than the option of one party. However, as long as the agreement calls for a quantity measured by output or requirements, the lack of exclusivity should not matter.

---

[1] A commitment to supply output or to buy requirements is a quantity term which, because it can be interpreted and limited under section 2-306(1), satisfies the statute of frauds. *See PMC Corp. v. Houston Wire & Cable Co.*, 797 A.2d 125, 128–31 (N.H. 2002).

Third, when do the requirements or output "occur in good faith"? Does that allow the buyer to have no requirements or the seller to have no output? As one court put it, the

> seller assumes the risk of all good faith variations in the buyer's requirements even to the extent of a determination to liquidate or discontinue the business. . . . The rule is based on a reliance on the self-interest of the buyer, who ordinarily will seek to have the largest possible requirements. Protection against abuse is afforded by penetrating through any device by which the requirement is siphoned off in some other form to the detriment of the seller. The requirement of good faith is the means by which this is enforced and self-interest in its undistorted form is maintained as the standard.[2]

What, then, is bad faith in this setting? What if the decision is simply to make more profit on an alternative segment of its business and thus limit losses on the line subject to the output or requirements term? The comments suggest that a buyer's decision to shut down based on a lack of orders is fine, but a similar decision made to "curtail losses" would not be. Can such a line really be drawn? Would not the amount of the projected loss from continued performance be relevant to the good faith question?

Fourth, does the "unreasonably disproportionate" language mean that a buyer or seller who goes out of business and thus ceases to have requirements or output will be in breach? Several courts have held that the answer is no, but that is not a universal approach.[3]

Fifth, how is the "unreasonably disproportionate" standard to be applied when there is no shut down? Consider one court's view:

---

[2] *HML Corp. v. General Foods Corp.*, 365 F.2d 77, 81 (3d Cir. 1966) (burden on seller to prove bad faith in the buyer's requirements).

[3] *See Empire Gas Corp. v. American Bakeries Co.*, 840 F.2d 1333 (7th Cir. 1988); *Brewster of Lynchburg, Inc. v. Dial Corp.*, 33 F.3d 355 (4th Cir. 1994); *Wiseco, Inc. v. Johnson Controls, Inc.*, 155 Fed. Appx. 815 (6th Cir. 2005). *But see Simcala, Inc. v. American Coal Trade, Inc.*, 821 So. 2d 197 (Ala. 2001) (holding both tests apply so that a buyer may be in breach if the requirements are unreasonably disproportionate to stated estimates even if the decrease is in good faith). For an example of a court holding that a decrease in seller's output is governed only by the good faith test and not by the unreasonably disproportionate test, *see Waste Stream Environmental, Inc. v. Lynn Water and Sewer Commission*, 2003 WL 917086 (Super. Ct. Mass. 2003).

Obviously this language [unreasonably disproportionate – ed.] is not the equivalent of "lack of good faith"– it is an elementary rule of construction that effect must be given, if possible, to every word, clause and sentence of a statute. . . . The phrase is keyed to stated estimates or, if there be none, to "normal or otherwise comparable prior" requirements. While "reasonable elasticity" is contemplated by the section (*see* Official Comment, par. 2 to UCC § 2-306), an agreed estimate shows a clear limit on the intended elasticity, similar to that found in a contract containing minimum and maximum requirements (*see* Official Comment, par. 2 to UCC § 2-306). The estimate "is to be regarded as a center around which the parties intend the variation to occur" (*supra*).

The limitation imposed by the term "unreasonably disproportionate" represents a departure from prior case law, wherein estimates were generally treated as having been made simply for the convenience of the parties and of no operative significance. . . . It is salutary in that it insures that the expectations of the parties will be more fully realized in spite of unexpected and fortuitous market conditions. . . . Thus, even where one party acts with complete good faith, the section limits the other party's risk in accordance with the reasonable expectations of the parties.

It would be unwise to attempt to define the phrase "unreasonably disproportionate" in terms of rigid quantities. In order that the limitation contemplated by the section take effect, it is not enough that a demand for requirements be disproportionate to the stated estimate; it must be *unreasonably* so in view of the expectation of the parties. A number of factors should be taken into account in the event a buyer's requirements greatly exceed the contract estimate. These include the following: (1) the amount by which the requirements exceed the contract estimate; (2) whether the seller had any reasonable basis on which to forecast or anticipate the requested increase . . . ; (3) the amount, if any, by which the market price of the goods in question exceeded the contract price; (4) whether such an increase in market price was itself fortuitous; and (5) the reason for the increase in requirements.[4]

In that case, the court held that the buyer's doubling of its requirements was unreasonably disproportionate to stated estimates. Of particular relevance to that

---

[4] *Orange & Rockland Utilities, Inc. v. Amerada Hess Corp.*, 397 N.Y.S.2d 814, 818–19 (N.Y. App. Div. 1977).

conclusion was that the buyer was demanding more oil in order to sell the increased quantity in the market for the increased price, whereas the buyer's estimates had been based upon its plans to burn oil to produce electricity for its customer base.

Problem 4-1

Seller, a wholesale dealer in plywood, and Buyer, a producer of pine veneer, entered into a five-year, written agreement under which Buyer agreed to purchase 50,000 square feet of plywood per year at $1.00 per square foot. The agreement, dated July 1, 2005, included terms on the time and method of shipment and payment.

A. On July 1, 2008, the market price of plywood had climbed to $4.00 per square foot. The increase was due, primarily, to sharpened demand for forest products. Seller wants to get out of the contract with Buyer in order to resell all of its plywood in the market at the higher price. Buyer has purchased the entire 50,000 square feet of plywood each year at the price of $1.00 per square foot. Does Seller have any argument?

B. Assume the same facts except that Buyer agreed to purchase its annual "requirements" of plywood from Seller at $1.00 per square foot. The contract did not explicitly say "all of our requirements exclusively from Seller." Furthermore, the contract did not provide for estimates of quantity or maximum-minimum quantities which Buyer could not exceed. Buyer's annual requirements for the first three years were 25,000, 32,500 and 35,000 square feet. During the fourth year, with the market price at $4.50 per square foot, Buyer requested a total of 60,000 square feet, the capacity of its production facility. Seller objected. Does Seller have any basis for resisting Buyer's demand?

C. Assume the same facts as B above except that in the fourth year, Buyer requested a total of 5,000 square feet of plywood due to an economic depression in the local building market, which dropped the demand for pine veneer. Seller objected. What arguments do you make on behalf of Seller?

SECTION 2.   PRICE

What if the parties do not have an express term setting the price of the goods and the relevant usage of trade, course of performance, or course of dealing do not help determine the price?   In many cases, the absence of an agreed-upon price would suggest that the parties did not yet finish making their bargain.   However, if the parties so intend, they may form a contract with an open or indefinite price, provided "there is a reasonably certain basis for giving an appropriate remedy." *See* UCC §§ 2-204(3), 2-305(1).   If, on the other hand, the parties did not intend to be bound in the absence of fixing a price, there is no contract and each party is entitled to restitution to the extent it has performed.   UCC § 2-305(4).

Section 2-305 addresses, and thereby implicitly authorizes, four different types of agreement on price:

  (i)   the agreement is silent on price;
  (ii) the price is to be agreed upon later by the parties;
  (iii) the price is to be fixed in reference to some market or other standard set by a third party; and
  (iv) the price is to be set by one of the parties.

The first three of these are covered by subsection (1).   If the agreement is silent, the price is to be agreed upon later but if the parties fail to agree, or the mechanism for setting the price fails for a reason not the fault of either party, then the contract price is a "reasonable price at the time for delivery."

The third method is also governed, in part, by section 2-305(3).   If the mechanism for setting the price fails through the fault of one of the parties, then the other party may either set a reasonable price or cancel the contract.

The final method – one party may set the price – is governed by section 2-305(2).   That subsection uses the good faith concept to limit the price fixer's discretion.   How much discretion does a party have to fix a price that is not a reasonable market price?[5]   Consider the following case.

---

[5] *See TCP Indus., Inc. v. Uniroyal, Inc.*, 661 F.2d 542 (6th Cir. 1981) (setting prices for a chemical within a range of market prices on both the spot and long term market was good faith); *Au Rustproofing Center, Inc. v. Gulf Oil Corp.*, 755 F.2d 1231 (6th Cir. 1985) (need not be the market price to be setting the price in good faith); *Havird Oil Co. v. Marathon Oil Co.*, 149 F.3d 283 (4th Cir. 1998) (good faith price fixed where seller charged all its customers a non-discriminatory wholesale price which was competitive with other wholesalers and conduct followed "reasonable commercial standards of fair dealing in the trade").

MATHIS V. EXXON CORP.
302 F.3d 448 (5th Cir. 2002)

Jerry E. Smith, Circuit Judge

This is a breach of contract suit brought by fifty-four gasoline station franchisees against Exxon Corporation ("Exxon") for violating the Texas analogue of the Uniform Commercial Code's open price provision. We affirm.

I.

Exxon markets its commercial gas bound for retailers primarily through three arrangements: franchisee contracts, jobber contracts, and company operated retail stores ("CORS"). A franchisee rents Exxon-branded gas stations and enters into a sales contract for the purchase of Exxon-brand gas. The contract sets the monthly quantity of gas the franchisee must purchase and allows Exxon to set the price he must pay. The franchisee pays the dealer tank wagon price ("DTW") and takes delivery of the gas at his station.

A jobber contract requires the purchaser to pay the "rack price," which usually is lower than the price charged to franchisees. There is no sale of gas to CORS by Exxon, because the stores are owned by Exxon and staffed by its employees. Instead, an intra-company accounting is recorded that is equivalent to the price charged franchisees in the same price zone.

All the plaintiff franchisees operate stations in the greater Houston, Texas, and Corpus Christi, Texas, areas. The genesis of the dispute is the allegation that Exxon has violated the law and its contracts with these franchisees for the purpose of converting their stores to CORS by driving the franchisees out of business.

Since 1994, franchisees have been barred from purchasing their gas from jobbers, so all their purchases have been governed by the terms of the Retail Motor Fuel Store Sales Agreement, under which the "DEALER agrees to buy and receive directly from EXXON all of the EXXON-branded gasoline bought by DEALER, and at least seventy-five percent (75%) of the volume shown in [a specified schedule]. . . . DEALER will pay EXXON for delivered products at EXXON's price in effect at the time of the loading of the delivery vehicle."

This "price in effect," also known as the dealer tank wagon price ("DTW"), forms the heart of the present dispute. Exxon claims this arrangement is the industry standard and that almost all franchisor-franchisee sales of gasoline are governed by a similar price term. Plaintiffs respond that the DTW price charged under this clause is "consistently higher" than the rack price paid by jobbers plus transportation costs.

The franchisees originally filed Sherman Act, Clayton, Act, and Petroleum Marketing Practices Act ("PMPA") claims against Exxon in addition to the breach of contract claim. The antitrust claims were abandoned, and the district court granted Exxon a judgment as a matter of law ("j.m.l.") on the PMPA claims. The court retained jurisdiction over the purely state law causes of action that had been supplemental to the federal claims.

Trial proceeded solely on the Texas breach of contract action, with only six plaintiffs testifying. The thrust of their testimony was that Exxon had set the DTW price at an uncompetitive level to drive them out of business (so as to replace their stores with CORS). Some of the plaintiffs testified that their franchises were unprofitable; they presented documents and witnesses to show that Exxon intended that result to drive them out of business.

The franchisees also submitted a market study showing that 62% of the franchisees in Corpus Christi were selling gas below the DTW price. The franchisees supported their theory of the case by calling Barry Pulliam as an expert witness on the economics of the gasoline market in Houston and Corpus Christi. Pulliam concluded that Exxon's DTW price was not commercially reasonable from an economic perspective because it was a price that, over time, put the purchaser at a competitive disadvantage. Pulliam noted that "commercial reasonableness" is a legal term, and he was not there to define it for the jury.

Pulliam's conclusion rested on two main facts. First, he showed that 75% of the franchisee's competitors were able to purchase gasoline at a lower price. Second, he calculated a commercially reasonable DTW price by adding normal distribution charges to the average rack price of gasoline charged by Exxon and its competitors. He concluded that Exxon's DTW price exceeded the sum of these other prices by four or more cents per gallon.

Exxon countered with Michael Keeley, who testified that Exxon's DTW price was commercially reasonable because it reflected the company's investment in land, the store, transportation, and managers. Keeley explained that Exxon recovers these costs through rent and the sale of gas.

The jury awarded $5,723,657 – exactly 60% of the overcharge calculated by Pulliam. . . . [Exxon appealed on three grounds, only one of which is reproduced here. – Eds.]

II.

Exxon contends that because it charged its franchisees a DTW price comparable to that charged by its competitors, the breach of contract claim is precluded as a matter of law. . . . The question is whether there was evidence permitting the jury to conclude that Exxon breached a term of the franchise agreement.

III.

Texas law, which tracks the Uniform Commercial Code, implies a good faith component in any contract with an open price term. Specifically,

[t]he parties if they so intend can conclude a contract for sale even though the price is not settled. In such a case the price is a reasonable price at the time of delivery . . . A price to be fixed by the seller or by the buyer means a price for him to fix in good faith.

[§ 2-305]. The parties agree that the franchise agreement term governing the purchase of gasoline is an open price term.

The meaning of "good faith" is further defined in several other sections of the code. The definitions section explains good faith as "honesty in fact in the conduct or transaction concerned." [§ 1-201(19)]. Wherever the term "good faith" is used throughout the code, it means "as least what is here stated." [§ 1-201(19) cmt. 19].

Additional meaning to the term may be added within a given article. *Id.* Section [2-103], regarding merchants, further explains the term: " 'Good faith' in the case of a merchant means honesty in fact and the observance of reasonable commercial standards of fair dealing in the trade." Finally, "[g]ood faith includes the observance of reasonable commercial standards of fair dealing in the trade if the party is a merchant. [§ 2-103]. But, in the normal case a 'posted price,' 'price in effect,' 'market price,' or the like satisfies the good faith requirement." [§ 2-305 cmt. 3].

The key disagreement is over what constitutes a breach of the duty of good faith. Exxon contends it has satisfied that duty because it has charged the plaintiffs a DTW price within the range of its competitors' DTW prices, thereby satisfying the "commercial reasonableness" meaning of good faith. Plaintiffs respond that good faith encompasses both objective and subjective duties. Even if Exxon is right, and its prices are within the range of its competitors', the argument runs, a subjective intent to drive the franchisees out of business would abridge the good faith duty of the open price term.

The pivotal provision is comment 3 to [§ 2-305]. Some of the language of comment 3 and [§ 2-103] leaves the meaning of good faith for open price terms in doubt. Comment 3 mentions that good faith "includes" commercial reasonableness, but notes that certain established prices satisfy the good faith requirement. Section [2-103] defines good faith with the subjective "honesty in fact" test. Thus, plaintiffs argue that an open price set according to a fixed schedule is set in good faith only if there is no improper motive animating the price-setter. Exxon replies that comment 3 speaks directly to prices set by a fixed schedule and consecrates them as in good faith per se.

In the absence of comment 3, there is no doubt Exxon would be subject to both the subjective "honesty in fact" good faith of [§ 1-201(19)] and the objective "commercial reasonableness" good faith of [§ 2-103]. The difficult question is whether comment 3 creates an exception to the normal principles of good faith governing the sale of goods.

No court in this circuit, and no Texas state court, has squarely addressed this question. Fortunately, because the Texas open price provision replicates that of the UCC, we can seek guidance from other courts.

To decide whether comment 3 creates an exception, we turn first to the text of the comment and the related sections of the Texas version of the UCC. In full, comment 3 reads,

> Subsection (2), dealing with the situation where the price is to be fixed by one party rejects the uncommercial idea that an agreement that the seller may fix the price means that he may fix any price he may wish by the express qualification that the price so fixed must be fixed in good faith. Good faith includes observance of reasonable commercial standards of fair dealing in the trade if the party is a merchant. (Section 2-103). But in the normal case a "posted price" or a future seller's or buyer's "given price," "price in effect," "market price," or the like satisfies the good faith requirement.

[§ 2-305 cmt. 3].

The bare text offers little to resolve the question. First, the comment notes that good faith "includes" reasonable commercial standards. This implies that the good faith required of a merchant setting an open price term encompasses both objective and subjective elements. The comment also creates a good faith safe harbor for such merchants when they use various sorts of fixed prices. But this safe harbor is applicable only in the "normal case." This suggests the safe harbor is not absolute, but it does nothing to define what takes a case out of the safe harbor.

As we will explain, we conclude that the "normal case" of comment 3 is coextensive with a merchant's residual "honesty in fact" duty embodied in

[§§ 1-201(19) and 2-103]. Thus, the comment embraces both the objective (commercial reasonableness) and subjective (honesty in fact) senses of good faith; objective good faith is satisfied by a "price in effect" as long as there is honesty in fact (a "normal case"). This conclusion finds support in three sources: the structure of the UCC, its legislative history, and the caselaw.

Reading comment 3 to embody two different meanings of "good faith" tracks the general structure of the UCC. Courts and commentators have recognized that the meaning of "good faith" is not uniform throughout the code. The cases and commentary treat the "good faith" found in article 1 as subjective and the good faith found only in article 2 as objective. Thus, there is nothing inconsistent in comment 3's using "good faith" in both the objective and the subjective senses.

The history of comment 3 bolsters this conclusion. Some drafters of the UCC worried that for the "great many industries where sales are not made at fixed prices," such as the steel industry, where "practically every contract" is made at "the seller's price in effect," if § 2-305 "is to apply . . . it means that in every case the seller is going to be in a lawsuit . . . or he could be, because there isn't any outside standard at all." *Proceedings of Enlarged Editorial Bd. Of Am. Law Inst.* (Sunday Morning Session, Jan. 28, 1951) (statement of Bernard Broeker). The drafters considered wholly exempting such contracts from § 2-305, or stating that for a price in effect, the only test is whether the merchant engaged in price discrimination. One drafter explained that the steel industry wanted to make "clear that we do not have to establish that we are fixing reasonable prices, because that gets you into the rate of return of profit, whether you are using borrowed money, and all those questions." *Id.*

The committee responded to these worries with the current comment 3: "[I]n the normal case a 'posted price' or a future seller's or buyer's 'given price,' 'price in effect,' 'market price,' or the like satisfies the good faith requirement." The drafter's solution was to avoid objective good faith challenges to prices set by reference to some "price in effect," while preserving challenges to discriminatory pricing. *See Hearing Before the Enlarged Editorial Board January* 27–29, 1951, VI BUSINESS LAWYER 164, 186 (1951) (explaining this intent). Nothing in the proceedings leading to the addition of comment 3 suggests that the overall subjective good faith duty of §§ 1-201 and 2-103 was to be supplanted; the evidence is quite to the contrary.

The drafters ultimately rejected two suggested addendums to § 2-305:

An agreement to the effect that the price shall be or be adjusted to, or be based upon, or determined by reference to the seller's going price, price in effect, regular price, market price, established price, or the like, at the time of the agreement or at any earlier or later time, is not an agreement to which this subsection is applicable. . . . An agreement such as this is an agreement under which the seller or the buyer does not have any burden of showing anything other than that he has not singled out the particular other party for discrimination.

Proceedings of Enlarged Editorial Bd. (statement of Bernard Broeker). Both of these recommendations are more sweeping than is the language ultimately adopted. The first would have omitted any mention of the good faith duty for open price provisions; the second would have limited the duty of the price-setter to that of avoiding discrimination.

The existing comment, however, avoids challenges to prices set according to an open price term unless that challenge is outside the normal type of case. Although price discrimination was the type of aberrant case on the minds of the drafters, price discrimination is merely a subset of what constitutes such an aberrant case. Any lack of subjective, honesty-in-fact good faith is abnormal; price discrimination is only the most obvious way a price-setter acts in bad faith – by treating similarly-situated buyers differently.

The caselaw supports this interpretation of comment 3. Courts that have addressed the normalcy question have consistently held that a lack of subjective good faith takes a challenge outside the bounds of what is normal.[6]

Like the plaintiffs in *Nanakuli, Allapattah,* and *Wayman,* the franchisees here are alleging a breach of good faith grounded not in Exxon's failure to price in accord with an established schedule, but in its failure to set the price in good faith. Suits recognizing such a cause of action are rare, and with good reason: We would

---

[6] *See, e.g., Nanakuli Paving & Rock Co. v. Shell Oil Co.,* 664 F.2d 772, 806 (9th Cir.1981) (stating that "the dispute here was not over the amount of the increase – that is, the price that the seller fixed – but over the manner in which that increase was put into effect"); *Allapattah v. Exxon Corp.,* 61 F. Supp. 2d 1308, 1322 (S.D. Fla.1999) ("Because the parties' dispute is not over the actual amount of the purchase price Exxon charged for its wholesale gasoline to its dealers, but rather over the manner in which the wholesale price was calculated without considering the double charge for credit card processing, the instant action is not the 'normal' case."); *cf. Wayman v. Amoco Oil Co.,* 923 F. Supp. 1322, 1349 (D. Kan.1996), *aff'd,* 145 F.3d 1347 (10th Cir.1998) ("[T]his court believes the present case is a normal case. If there was evidence that Amoco had, for example, engaged in discriminatory pricing or tried to run plaintiffs out of business, then the court's decision might be different.").

be ill-advised to consider a case to be outside the norm based only on an allegation of improper motive by the party setting the price.

Plaintiffs produced enough evidence to escape comment 3's "normal case" limitation. They showed, for example, that Exxon planned to replace a number of its franchises with CORS, that the DTW price was higher than the sum of the rack price and transportation, that Exxon prevented the franchisees from purchasing gas from jobbers after 1994, and that a number of franchisees were unprofitable or non-competitive.[7]

For example, one Exxon document stated that the company's "Marketing Strategy for 1992-1997 is to reduce Dealer stores (est. 30%)." Another document set forth Exxon's plans to reduce dealer stations in Houston from 95 to 45, and to increase CORS from 83 to 150, between 1997 and 2003. James Carter, the Regional Director of the Exxon/Mobil Fuels Marketing Company, testified that Exxon made more of a profit from a CORS than from an independent lessee store. These plans and observations were validated by the fact that the number of dealer stations steadily declined.

An exhibit called the "Houston Screening Study" evaluated the strategy of "surplusing" (i.e., eliminating) 21 of 37 locations inside the Highway 610 loop. Of the 93 lessee-dealer stations, 69 would be done away with, but 73 of the 91 CORS would be kept.

Further indication of plans to shift from dealer-lessees to CORS is shown by Exxon's dissatisfaction with outlets featuring service bays. Exxon documents showed that service bays – generally associated with lessee-dealer locations – were becoming less profitable, while stations with convenience stores – generally associated with CORS – were the wave of the future. A document entitled "Retail Store Chain Outlook" revealed Exxon's plan to reduce stations with service bays from 2,506 to 190 from 1991 to 2005. That document included a plan to "[e]xpand CORS to improve profitability and to compete efficiently with private brands/distributors" and "[e]mphasize CORS operations in markets with high level of rack to retail competition."

---

[7] This case is distinguishable from *Meyer v. Amerada Hess*, 541 F. Supp. 321 (D.N.J.1982), in which the court found "no evidence" of dishonesty in the setting of a DTW price. In Meyer, though, the only evidence tending to show bad faith was the retailer's unprofitability. *Id.* at 331. Significantly, other retailers were profiting, and the plaintiff retailer was being charged rent below the economic value of the property. *Id.* at 332.

Exxon's answer on appeal is that these documents "say nothing about using pricing to accomplish a 'plan' to eliminate dealers." Although that is so, there was sufficient evidence on this issue to go to the jury, which was free to, and apparently did, draw the inference connecting pricing to the elimination of dealer-lessees. The consequence of the jury's decision is that this case exceeds the "normal case" limit of [§ 2-305 comment 3].

We still, however, must examine the content of the duty of subjective good faith. Although no Texas or Fifth Circuit case has squarely addressed the meaning of the good faith clause of [§ 2-305], Texas courts repeatedly have held that the "honesty in fact" definition of good faith found in [§ 1-201(19)] is tied to the actual belief of the participant in the transaction. Thus, the same version of the facts accepted by the jury – that Exxon intended to drive the franchisees out of business – that takes this case out of the "normal" set of cases for purposes of comment 3 also satisfies the criteria for bad faith.[8]

Exxon's bad faith, in this regard, is shown by the record. Facing the competition of self-service stations that were either selling food and other goods or had bare pumps with no overhead costs incurred in servicing vehicles, Exxon decided years ago that retail marketing through franchise dealers was becoming economically unsound. Although Exxon decided to move to CORS in Houston and jobbers in Corpus Christi, this decision was not communicated to its franchisees. Because of profit from their other sales, CORS could, and did, sell gas for less than the franchise dealers paid to Exxon for their gas. And the jobbers delivered Exxon gas to their dealers for less than Exxon franchisees were required to pay for their delivered gas, but Exxon prohibited its franchisees from buying at this lower price from the jobbers.

The loss of competitive position and profit to plaintiff franchisees was inevitable and foreseeable to Exxon. Although Exxon witnesses denied receiving complaints, its dealers testified that they had complained often and for years, without success, until the very eve of trial.

---

[8] *See also Allapattah*, 61 F. Supp. 2d at 1322 (explaining that "a merchant [who] acts in a manner intended to drive a franchisee out of business" violates the duty of good faith found in the UCC). Similarly, one court has recognized that a "predatory intent" to "set the prices with the intent to drive [franchisees] out of business and take over the stations" is a claim cognizable under the good faith provisions of the UCC. *E.S. Bills, Inc. v. Tzucanow*, 700 P.2d 1280, 1283–84 (Cal. Ct. App. 1985).

Accordingly, the jury's finding that Exxon breached its duty of good faith in setting the DTW price it charged the plaintiffs is not without foundation in the law or the evidence. As we have recounted, plaintiffs offered ample evidence tending to prove their version of price-setting. Accordingly, there is no error in the refusal to grant Exxon j.m.l. on the breach of contract claim. . . . Affirmed.

The *Mathis* reasoning was rejected in a remarkably similar case in Texas state court.[9] In that case, the court ruled that the wholesaler's price, which was on the high end – but nevertheless within – the range of prices charged by other wholesalers and which was applied on a non-discriminatory basis was fixed in good faith. The franchisees claimed that the wholesaler was trying to put them out of business, but there was no evidence on that point comparable to the evidence presented in *Mathis*. The *Mathis* interpretation of good faith was also rejected by the Sixth Circuit, which ruled that both prongs of good faith – "honesty in fact" and "reasonable commercial standards of fair dealing" have an objective meaning.[10] More recently, the First Circuit approved of the approach in *Mathis*.[11] In doings so, the court noted if the seller's obligation in fixing the contract price was merely to set a nondiscriminatory price, then section 2-305(2) would have been phrased in those terms, rather than in reference to good faith.

Problem 4-2

A. On February 1, Seller agreed in a writing signed by both Seller and Buyer to sell 1,000 sacks of Delaware Cobbler potatoes to Buyer, delivery at Buyer's plant by March 15, at a price "to be agreed at delivery." The market price on February 1 was $7 per sack. On March 15, Seller tendered delivery of the goods and requested the Buyer agree to a price of $15 per sack. The market price on March 15 was $12 and rising. Buyer rejected the tender and proposed price and obtained other potatoes for $13 per sack. In subsequent litigation, Buyer claimed that

---

[9] *Shell Oil Co. v. HRN, Inc.*, 144 S.W.3d 429 (Tex. 2004).

[10] *Tom-Lin Enterprises, Inc. v. Sunoco, Inc.*, 349 F.3d 277 (6th Cir. 2003)

[11] *Marcoux v. Shell Oil Products Co.*, 524 F.3d 33 (1st Cir. 2008), *petition for cert. filed*, 77 U.S.L.W. 3106, 3209 (Aug. 21 & Sept. 19, 2008).

Seller breached the contract. Seller argued that there was no contract. Who should prevail?

B. On February 1, Seller agreed in a writing signed by both Seller and Buyer to sell 1,000 sacks of Delaware Cobbler potatoes to Buyer, delivery at Buyer's plant by March 15, at "the price on the Chicago commodities board of trade on March 15." The market price on February 1 was $7 per sack. On March 15, Seller tendered delivery of the goods. On March 14, the Chicago commodities board of trade had been shut down by the government agency regulating the board due to widespread fraud in trading on the board. On March 13, this type of potato was trading for $12 per sack. Seller demanded that price. Buyer rejected the tender and proposed price and obtained other potatoes for $11 per sack. In subsequent litigation, Seller claimed that Buyer breached the contract. Buyer argued that there was no contract. Who should prevail?

C. On February 1, Seller agreed in a writing signed by both Seller and Buyer to sell 1,000 sacks of Delaware Cobbler potatoes to Buyer, delivery at Buyer's plant by March 15, at a price "to be set by an independent third party agreed to by Buyer and Seller." The market price on February 1 was $7 per sack. On March 15, Seller tendered delivery of the goods. Buyer refused to agree to any third party that Seller suggested and refused to designate any third party. On March 15, the market price of potatoes was $13 per sack. Buyer refused the potatoes. Seller sued Buyer for breach of contract. What result?

SECTION 3.   DELIVERY AND PAYMENT

Article 2 contains several gap filler rules concerning the timing and manner of delivery of the goods and the timing and manner of payment. These terms often will be supplanted by the express or implied terms of the parties' agreement. However, in many transactions, some or all of these gap fillers will apply because the agreement is silent on these points.

Let's start by reviewing section 2-301. That section tells us that the seller's general obligation is to deliver goods that conform to the contract and that the buyer's general obligation is to accept and pay for those goods. What it does not tell us is how those obligations are to be fulfilled or who is to tender first.

Read sections 2-507(1) and 2-511(1). The first of these provisions makes the seller's tender of the goods a condition to the buyer's obligation to accept and pay for them. The second makes the buyer's tender of payment a condition to the seller's obligation to tender the goods. Does this make sense? Yes. These are concurrent conditions. Collectively they mean that, in the absence of agreement to the contrary, the parties are to tender simultaneously. If either fails to tender at the appropriate time and place, the other party is excused from further performance. In the unlikely event that both parties fail to tender, then neither condition is met, with the result that neither party has breached the contract. In essence, by their mutual lack of performance, the parties have implicitly agreed to terminate their contract.

In most situations, however, either the parties expressly agree that one of them will tender performance first or such agreement is implicit in their course of performance, course of dealing, or in usage of trade. Although a dispute about tender can arise if the buyer is to perform first, most disputes about tender arise in the context of agreements when the seller is to tender before the buyer. In any event, the sequence does not significantly alter the parties' rights and responsibilities, so for purposes of continuing discussion, we will assume that the parties have agreed that seller is to tender the goods before the buyer is obligated to tender payment.

The three preliminary questions regarding the seller's tender are what, where, and when. As to what, read sections 2-106(2), 2-601, and 2-307. The first two of these provisions require the seller to tender conforming goods. In other words, the goods must conform to the contract description. The third of these provisions requires the seller to tender goods in one lot. *Cf.* UCC § 2-612(1).

As to where must the seller tender, read, section 2-308. In general, it requires the seller to tender at the seller's place of business or, if the seller has none, at the seller's residence. Why do you think the drafters chose to make tender presumptively due at the seller's place of business or residence rather than at the buyer's place of business or residence? As to when, read section 2-309(1). It requires tender within a reasonable time. That is, of course, an extremely fact-specific determination.[12]

---

[12] *See Marjam Supply Co. v. BCT Walls & Ceilings, Inc.*, 2003 WL 21497515 (E.D. Pa. 2003) (factors that determine reasonable time for delivery include the nature of the goods,

The remaining aspects of the seller's duty to tender the goods vary depending on how the seller is to fulfill that obligation. Specifically, Article 2 has rules for three different scenarios: (i) the seller is to tender the goods directly to the buyer; (ii) the seller is authorized or has agreed to ship the goods to the buyer using a carrier; and (iii) the goods are in the possession of a bailee and are be tendered without being moved.

In each of these three scenarios, the primary questions are as follows. First, what must the seller do to fulfill the duty to tender the goods? Second, to what extent may the buyer inspect the goods prior to deciding whether to accept or reject them? Third, when is the buyer's obligation to tender the price due? Intertwined with these issues is the question of when the risk of loss passes. That is, at what point does the responsibility for any casualty to the goods pass from the seller to the buyer? We now explore these questions for each of the three scenarios in turn.

A. Seller's Direct Tender of the Goods

1. Tender of Delivery

Assume that the seller is to directly tender the goods to the buyer, rather than through an intermediary such as a carrier or a bailee of the goods. Read section 2-503(1), which sets forth the seller's basic tender obligations (for the present ignore subsections (2) through (5) of section 2-503). This provision uses quite a few vague and undefined terms, with the result that numerous issues can arise regarding the propriety of any particular tender of delivery. What does it mean to "put and hold" the goods? What notification is "reasonably necessary" to enable the buyer to take delivery? What is a "reasonable hour" and how long is "reasonably necessary to enable the buyer to take possession"? Consider also section 2-311 as it relates to the seller's tender obligation. Given all these vague standards, does section 2-503(1) accomplish anything? Does it help parties identify what their obligations are in advance or, if the parties cannot work out their differences, does it merely give a jury the license to find either party in breach? Consider the next problem. As you do so, remember that all of these provisions are

---

the purpose that the goods will be used for, the extent of the seller's knowledge of the buyer's intentions, transportation conditions, and the nature of the market).

subject to variation if the parties have otherwise agreed through express terms, course of performance, course of dealing or usage of trade.

Problem 4-3

A. Seller agreed to tender 100 bushels of wheat to Buyer for $4 per bushel. In each scenario described below, determine whether Seller has complied with its tender obligation. If you are unsure, identify what you need to know to be able to come to a conclusion on that issue.

1. Seller called Buyer and told it the wheat was ready to be picked up. When Buyer arrived that afternoon, Seller only had 95 bushels available and the auger usually used to load the wheat into trucks was broken down.

2. Seller called Buyer and told it the wheat was ready to be picked up. When Buyer arrived that afternoon, Buyer tested the wheat Seller had available and it was clearly moldy.

3. Seller called Buyer and told it the wheat was ready to be picked up, and told Buyer that someone better get there in 2 hours or Seller was going to sell the wheat to someone else.

4. Seller called Buyer and told it the wheat was ready to be picked up and Buyer protested that this delivery time was not convenient for Buyer and that Buyer could not take delivery for two months.

5. Seller called Buyer and told it the wheat was ready to be picked up at Seller's warehouse 300 miles away from both Buyer's and Seller's location.

6. Seller called Buyer and told it the wheat was ready to be picked up. When Buyer arrived that afternoon, Buyer did not have a truck capable of holding 100 bushels of wheat and wanted to take half that afternoon and half the next afternoon.

7. Buyer and Seller had agreed that Seller would deliver the wheat to Buyer's farm on April 3. On April 3, Seller drove onto Buyer's farm with the truckload of wheat in one of Seller's own trucks. Buyer did not have its storage facility cleaned out and asked Seller to come back the next day. *See* UCC § 2-311(3).

B. Go back in time and draft a term that would define the seller's tender of delivery obligation in the above scenario variations. What difficulties do you have in drafting that tender of delivery term?

2. Buyer's Inspection

Once the seller tenders goods, the buyer must either accept or reject the goods. Before deciding whether to accept or reject the goods, the buyer will often want to inspect them to determine if they in fact conform to the contract's requirements. Read section 2-513(1). It gives the buyer the right to inspect the goods at a reasonable time and place and in a reasonable manner,[13] unless the parties have specified the timing, place, and method of inspection. This right to inspect precedes the buyer's obligation to accept and pay for conforming goods, and therefore protects the buyer from accepting or paying for nonconforming goods.

Two words of caution here. First do not confuse acceptance and rejection of *the goods* with acceptance and rejection of *an offer*. Acceptance and rejection of an offer relates to contract formation and was discussed in Chapter Two. Acceptance and rejection of the goods relates to contract performance and is discussed here. Second, do not equate taking *possession* of the goods with *acceptance* of the goods. One of the ways a buyer may inspect goods is to take possession and test the goods for a reasonable period of time to determine if they conform to the contract. Indeed, if the goods are supposed to meet specified performance or purity standards, there may be no ready means to inspect without first taking possession. In such situations, taking possession of the goods is not, by itself, sufficient to constitute acceptance of them.

Either before or upon expiration of the buyer's inspection rights, the buyer must either accept or reject the goods. The buyer cannot do both,[14] and because failure to seasonably reject constitutes acceptance,[15] the buyer cannot do neither. However,

---

[13] *See HCI Chemicals (USA), Inc. v. Henkel KGaA*, 966 F.2d 1018 (5th Cir. 1992) (holding that the place for inspection specified in UCC § 2-513(1) was not displaced by agreement).

[14] *See* UCC §§ 2-602(2)(a) (rejection makes any exercise of ownership of the goods by the buyer wrongful against the seller); 2-607(2) (acceptance precludes rejection).

[15] *See* UCC § 2-606(1)(b) (failure to reject constitutes acceptance).

the buyer may be permitted to accept some goods and reject others.[16] If the buyer accepts the goods, three principal consequences ensue. First, the buyer is precluded from rejecting the goods. UCC. § 2-607(2). Second, the buyer becomes obligated to pay the contract price. UCC § 2-607(1). Third, if there is a problem with the goods, the buyer will have the burden of proving that the goods fail to conform to the contract in order to be entitled to any remedy. UCC § 2-607(4). Even if the goods or tender fail to conform to the contract requirements, the buyer has only a small window of opportunity to revoke that acceptance and force the goods back on the seller. UCC § 2-608.

If the buyer rejects the goods, the buyer may not exercise ownership over them and, if the buyer has possession of them, the buyer must hold them for the seller. UCC § 2-602(2).

The buyer's *decision* to accept or reject the goods is separate and distinct from the buyer's *right* to accept or reject the goods. If the goods conform to the contract, the buyer has no right to reject the goods. If the buyer nevertheless does reject them, the buyer will be in breach and the seller will have a cause of action. UCC § 2-703. However, if the goods fail in any respect to conform to the contract requirements, the seller will have breached the contract. *See* UCC §§ 2-301, 2-711. The buyer in that circumstance generally has the right to either accept or reject the goods. *See* UCC § 2-601.[17] If the buyer accepts, the buyer will become obligated to pay the contract price but may be entitled to recover damages caused by the nonconformity. UCC §§ 2-607(1), (2), (3), 2-714. If the buyer rejects the goods in a timely manner, the buyer may recover other damages for the seller's breach. UCC § 2-711.

In Chapter Seven, we will explore in more detail the interplay among rejection, acceptance, and revocation of acceptance. For now, focus on the interplay between the buyer's right to inspect the goods and the choice to accept or reject the goods. The buyer has an incentive to inspect the goods to avoid accepting goods that do not conform to the contract requirements. Remember, once the buyer accepts the goods, the buyer is obligated to pay the contract price even if the goods do not conform to the contract. In addition to not wanting to pay for non-conforming goods, the buyer may wish to avoid costly unloading and storage of the goods. Remember also that the length of the inspection period is not limitless. This point

---

[16] *See* UCC § 2-601(c).

[17] The rules are slightly different in installment contracts. *See* UCC § 2-612(2).

is contained both in section 2-513 itself and in section 2-606(1)(b), which provides that the buyer is deemed to have accepted the goods if the buyer fails to reject them after having had a reasonable opportunity to inspect. Thus, the buyer can effectively lose the right to inspect by waiting too long to exercise that right.

What if the buyer has agreed to pay the contract price before the goods are available for inspection? The buyer has a right to inspect before payment *or* acceptance. UCC § 2-513(1). Thus, even if the buyer has agreed to pay prior to *inspection*, the buyer still has the right to inspect the goods prior to *acceptance* of the goods. UCC § 2-512(2). Occasionally, the buyer will argue that even though it has agreed to pay before inspection, the nonconformity of the goods should excuse the buyer from paying before inspection. Section 2-512(1) addresses that circumstance.

3. Buyer's Payment

If the parties have so agreed, the seller may extend credit to the buyer to allow the buyer to pay later. However, a credit sale is not presumed. Therefore, the buyer generally is obligated to pay in full upon acceptance of the goods. UCC §§ 2-607(1), 2-310(a) cmt. 1. If either party has the right to have delivery occur in lots, then the seller may demand payment for each lot delivered if the price can be properly apportioned. UCC § 2-307.

The buyer may pay in money or by any other manner, UCC §§ 2-511(2), 2-304, unless the parties have agreed to a particular payment mechanism.

Problem 4-4

Seller agreed to tender 100 bushels of wheat to Buyer for $4 per bushel. Seller informed Buyer that the wheat was ready for delivery. Seller loaded the wheat in Seller's own truck and drove the load to Buyer's facility.

A. Seller insisted Buyer hand over the contract price before it would unload the wheat. Buyer protested that it had a right to inspect the wheat before having to give Seller the $400. What would you advise Seller to do?

B. Buyer insisted that Seller should unload the wheat and Buyer would send a sample of the load to a testing facility to test for contamination. If the test came back clean, Buyer would pay the $400 contract price. Seller protested when it found out the testing process takes two weeks. What would you advise Buyer to do?

C. You represent Buyer at the inception of the relationship between Buyer and Seller. Draft an inspection term to propose to Seller. If you represented Seller, would you agree to the term as drafted? What modifications would you make? What inspection term would you suggest that Seller include in the standard sales agreement that it proposes to all of its buyers?

Problem 4-5

A. In a writing signed by both parties, John has agreed to sell his entire collection of novels to Alice for $5,000. His entire basement is filled with these books, enough books to fill three medium size rental trucks. John is insisting that Alice come get all the books at one time, but has not agreed to any particular date when Alice is available. Alice wants John to deliver the books to her house on two different Saturdays and wants to pay for the books only after John has delivered them all and she has determined that all of them are in satisfactory condition. She wants to give him $4,000 of the purchase price in cash and the other $1,000 in the form of a used computer and printer. John does not want the computer, but wants $5,000 in cash. The signed writing did not contain any terms that addressed the time or manner of delivery or the time or manner of payment. Both parties are contending that the other has breached the contract. What result?

B. You represent one of the parties. Redraft the writing between the parties to avoid the problems you encountered in Part A.

4. Risk of Loss

Risk of loss refers to which party will suffer the loss of any casualty to the goods. In other words, assume that at some point after the contract is formed but before performance is completed, the goods are damaged or destroyed. That casualty may be the result of weather, vandalism, theft, fire, or any other similar event. Regardless of the nature of the event, the fact remains that the parties were – collectively – wealthier before the casualty than after. One of them (or their insurers) will have to suffer the loss. Put another way, before the transaction they – collectively – had both the goods and the contract price for them. After the casualty, they had only the contract price. The one who does not get the money will have the risk of loss.

Risk of loss is related to contract performance and breach. If the seller has the risk of loss and the goods are damaged or destroyed, the seller has to bear the financial loss. In addition, if the seller fails to tender conforming goods to the buyer, the seller may also be liable for breach.[18] Similarly, if the buyer bears the risk of loss and the goods are lost or damaged, the buyer will often be liable for the price of the goods, UCC § 2-709(1), and will not be able to recover against the seller because of the casualty to the goods.

So at what point in a sale-of-goods transaction does the risk of loss pass from the seller to the buyer? First, remember that the parties are free to reach agreement on this point; the rules in Article 2 are merely gap fillers in the event the parties' agreement is silent on risk of loss. *See* UCC § 2-509(4). Second, under Article 2, the passage of the risk of loss from the seller to the buyer does not depend upon passage of title to the goods.[19] Instead, allocation of the risk of loss depends on the manner in which the seller is to tender delivery and whether the seller has made a conforming tender.[20] There are three principles underlying the rules on risk of loss.

---

[18] *Cf.* UCC §§ 2-613, 2-615 (which occasionally excuse the seller from further performance if the goods or the seller's ability to provide them is damaged or destroyed).

[19] *See* UCC § 2-401. There is more than a passing similarity among sections 2-503, 2-509, and 2-401. Title may be relevant to other issues, such as liability for taxes or for criminal acts regarding property. It may also determine who has rights under insurance policies. *See* Jeanne L. Schroeder, *Death and Transfiguration: The Myth that the U.C.C. Killed "Property,"* 69 TEMP. L. REV. 1281 (1996); *P & O Nedlloyd, Ltd. v. Sanderson Farms, Inc.,* 462 F.3d 1015 (8th Cir. 2006).

[20] *See* Robert L. Flores, *Risk of Loss in Sales: A Missing Chapter in the History of the*

First, the party who controls the goods, and is thus in the best position to avoid the loss, should bear the risk. *See* UCC § 2-509 cmt. 3. Second, the party most likely to have insurance protection under the circumstances should bear the risk. *Id.* Third, the party in breach should bear the risk of loss. *Compare* UCC § 2-509 *with* § 2-510.

Read sections 2-509 and 2-510. Absent an agreement otherwise and absent breach, if the tender of delivery is not being made through an intermediary such as a carrier or bailee, the relevant rule is in UCC § 2-509(3). That section provides two different rules based upon whether the seller is a merchant. If the seller is not a merchant, the risk of loss will pass to the buyer upon tender of delivery of conforming goods. If the seller is a merchant, the risk of loss will pass to the buyer upon the buyer's receipt of conforming goods. Section 2-103 contains a definition of receipt. *See* UCC §§ 2-104 (defining "merchant"), 2-106 (regarding the meaning of conformity).

Problem 4-6

Seller agreed to tender 100 bushels of wheat to Buyer for $4 per bushel. Seller informed Buyer that the wheat was ready for delivery.

A. Seller loaded the wheat in Seller's own truck. During the drive to Buyer's facility, the truck caught fire and all the wheat was destroyed. Who had the risk of loss? Does it matter whether Seller is a merchant?

B. After Seller informed Buyer that the wheat was ready to be picked up but before Buyer could arrive to get the wheat, Seller's storage facility burned to the ground, destroying the wheat that Seller intended for Buyer. Who had the risk of loss? Does it matter whether Seller is a merchant?

C. After Seller informed Buyer that the wheat was ready to be picked up, Buyer asked Seller to leave the wheat in big bins on Seller's dock and

U.C.C.: Through Llewellyn to Williston and A Bit Beyond, 27 PAC. L.J. 161 (1996); Margaret Howard, *Allocation of Risk of Loss Under the UCC: A Transactional Evaluation of Sections 2-509 and 2-510*, 15 UCC L.J. 334 (1983); Note, *Risk of Loss in Commercial Transactions: Efficiency Thrown Into the Breach*, 65 VA. L. REV. 557 (1979).

Buyer would pick up the wheat after hours. Seller did so, leaving the wheat in unlocked bins on Seller's loading dock. Before Buyer arrived, vandals poured paint on the wheat contained in the bins. Who had the risk of loss? *See McKenzie v. Olmstead*, 587 N.W.2d 863 (Minn. Ct. App. 1999).

D. Seller loaded the wheat in Seller's own truck and dropped the wheat at Buyer's storage facility after hours. The wheat was in unlocked bins. Buyer did not know that the wheat had been delivered. During the night, vandals poured paint over the wheat in the bins. Who had the risk of loss? *See In re Thomas*, 182 B.R. 347 (Bankr. S.D. Fla. 1995).

E. Buyer tendered a personal check to Seller. Seller is still in possession of the wheat in unlocked bins on Seller's property. Before the check cleared, vandals poured paint on the wheat. Who had the risk of loss? *See Capshaw v. Hickman*, 880 N.E.2d 118 (Ohio Ct. App. 2007).

B. Seller's Tender of the Goods through Shipping the Goods

Now consider a situation in which the seller has agreed to tender the goods before buyer must tender payment and has agreed to ship the goods to the buyer. If the seller uses its own vehicles or transportation device to deliver the goods to the buyer, the tender of delivery rules and risk of loss rules we have discussed above will control. However, if a seller ships goods to the buyer using a carrier, such as a railroad or trucking company, different tender of delivery rules apply.

When the seller uses a carrier to ship the goods to the buyer, the seller will agree with the carrier to a contract that instructs the carrier to deliver the goods to the buyer at a designated address. That contract with the carrier will also set the price of shipment and contain any special instructions needed to safely transport the goods. However, this contract between the seller and the carrier is separate and distinct from the contract between the seller and the buyer for the sale of the goods. Moreover, it is the seller's contract with the buyer that determines what responsibilities the seller has with respect to tender. For this purpose, sales contracts that call for shipping the goods using a carrier come in two varieties: "shipment" contracts and "destination" contracts.

1.   Tender of Delivery and Risk of Loss in a Shipment Contract

Read comment 5 to section 2-503. The presumption is that when the seller agrees to deliver goods by shipping them using a carrier, the seller is agreeing to a "shipment contract." In a shipment contract, the seller's tender obligation is governed by sections 2-503(2) and 2-504. *See also* UCC § 2-311. Under those provisions, tender of the goods occurs when the seller delivers the goods to the carrier, makes a reasonable contract with the carrier to transport the goods, and informs the buyer of the shipment. As a result, the seller has no responsibility for the condition of the goods after that point. If the goods are damaged or destroyed during transit, the seller will have already fully performed. Section 2-509(1)(a) makes that clear by putting on the buyer the risk of loss of or damage to the goods during transit. The effect of this is that the buyer will be liable to the seller for the buyer's performance under the sales contract if the goods are lost or damaged during transit. This liability will either be for the price of the goods, UCC § 2-709(1)(a), or damages for breach of contract, UCC § 2-703. Of course, if the goods are lost or damaged in transit in a shipment contract, the buyer may have claims for the loss or damage to the goods against the carrier, or as against the parties that caused the loss or damage to the goods under other law.[21] *See* UCC § 2-722.

If the buyer has insured the goods, the insurance company will indemnify the buyer to the extent obligated under the policy and, through equitable or contractual subrogation, assert any claims that the buyer might have against persons who caused the loss, or any claims against the carrier. Notice however, that section 2-504 does not require that the seller insure the goods. The buyer is the one that must either

---

[21] The carrier generally has the obligation to take reasonable care of the goods. UCC § 7-309. The liability of carriers is determined under federal and state legislation and international treaties that, in turn, depend upon the type of carrier and the scope of its operation. The liability of domestic overland carriers in interstate commerce, *i.e.*, railroads and truckers, is regulated by federal law and the liability of intrastate domestic carriers is regulated by state law, including section 7-309. *See* James C. Hardman, *Legal, Practical, and Economic Aspects of Third Party Motor Carrier Services: An Overview*, 34 TRANS. L.J. 237 (2007); Michael E. Crowley, *The Limited Scope of the Cargo Liability Regime Covering Carriage of Goods by Sea: The Multimodal Problem*, 79 TUL. L. REV. 1461 (2005); Paul Stephen Dempsey, *Transportation: A Legal History*, 30 TRANS. L.J. 235 (2003).

insure against or personally suffer any loss of the goods in a shipment contract.[22]
One of the functions of the notice requirement in section 2-504 is to allow the buyer
to obtain insurance for the goods if the buyer does not already have insurance that
covers the goods while in transit.

2.   *Tender of Delivery and Risk of Loss in a Destination Contract*

If the contract is a destination contract, the seller's obligation is to tender
conforming goods to the buyer (not merely to the carrier). In other words, tender
occurs after transportation of the goods, not before. UCC § 2-503(3). Section
2-509(1)(b) then governs the risk of loss in a destination contract. Under that
provision, the seller has the risk of loss during transit and the risk of loss passes to
the buyer only upon the tender of goods by the carrier to the buyer. Thus, as
between the seller and the buyer, the seller has taken the responsibility for the
condition of the goods in transit. *See* UCC § 2-311(3). If goods are lost or damaged
in transit, the seller will have breached the sales contract because conforming goods
were not tendered at the conclusion of the transit. UCC § 2-711. The seller will
have the right to pursue the carrier or third parties for the loss or damage to the
goods under other principles of law. *See* UCC § 2-722. If the seller insured the
goods, the insurance company will indemnify the seller and, in all probability, assert
any claims the seller may have against third parties through subrogation.

3.   *Shipment or Destination Contract*

How do you distinguish a shipment contract from a destination contract? Both
are likely to specify the location to which the goods must be shipped. Thus,

---

[22] The buyer may have an insurable interest in the goods even though the buyer is not the
owner of the goods, or in possession of the goods. UCC § 2-501. For the scope of insurable
interest in property insurance cases, *see* John M. Stockton, *An Analysis of Insurable Interest
Under Article Two of the Uniform Commercial Code,* 17 VAND. L. REV. 815 (1964). *See
also* Robert S. Pinzur, *Insurable Interest: A Search for Consistency*, 46 INS. COUNSEL J. 109
(1979). For an example of a court using Article 2 to determine if a seller retained an
insurable interest after tender of the goods to a buyer who had prepaid in full, *see Spirit of
Excellence, Ltd. v. Intercargo Ins. Co.*, 777 N.E.2d 660 (Ill. Ct. App. 2002).

specifying a destination for the goods does not mean the seller has agreed to a destination contract. The key inquiry is whether the seller agreed to take responsibility for the goods during shipment. If not, then the contract is a shipment contract. If the seller has agreed to take that responsibility for the goods during shipment, then the contract is a destination contract.

One of the primary mechanisms for deciding to what the buyer and seller have agreed is the use of customary shipping terms, such as "F.O.B." (free on board) or "C.I.F." (cost, insurance and freight). *See* UCC §§ 2-319 through 2-324. In the absence of such terms, the assumption is that the sales contract is a "shipment" contract. Accordingly, clear evidence will be needed to show that the buyer and seller have agreed to a "destination" contract. Thus, whether the parties have agreed to a shipment or a destination contract is primarily a matter of interpreting the sales agreement, including the meaning of any shipping terms the parties have used.[23]

Problem 4-7

Seller in South Dakota contracted to manufacture and sell to Buyer in New York custom window wall panels to be used in a building that Buyer was constructing. The agreement provided that "all windows are to be shipped properly crated/packaged/boxed for cross-country motor freight transit and delivered to" the construction site in New York. Seller delivered the windows to Carrier, made a contract with Carrier to deliver the goods to Buyer at the construction site, and notified Buyer of the shipment. The goods were severely damaged during transit.

A. If the windows were properly packaged, who bears the risk of loss?

B. How, if at all, would the analysis change if the agreement had provided that "all windows are to be shipped properly crated/packaged/boxed for

---

[23] *See Wilson v. Brawn of California, Inc.*, 33 Cal. Rptr. 3d 769 (Cal. Ct. App. 2005) (consumer mail order was a shipment contract); Ademuni-Odeke, *Insurance of F.O.B. Contracts in Anglo-American and Common Law Jurisdictions Revisited: The Wider Picture*, 31 TUL. MAR. L.J. 425 (2007); Daniel E. Murray, *Risk of Loss of Goods in Transit: A Comparison of the 1990 Incoterms with Terms from Other Voices*, 23 U. MIAMI INTER-AM. L. REV. 93 (1991).

cross-country motor freight transit and delivered at" the construction site in New York? *See Windows, Inc. v. Jordan Panel Systems Corp.,* 177 F.3d 114 (2d Cir. 1999).

C. Assume the windows were improperly packaged.
    1. Who would bear the risk of loss if the damage was caused by the improper packaging?
    2. Who would bear the risk of loss if the damage was fully attributable to Carrier's negligence?

4. Buyer's Right to Inspect

How does shipment of the goods affect the buyer's right to inspect? Reread section 2-513. Unless the buyer and seller have agreed to alter the buyer's inspection rights, the buyer has the right to inspect goods before the buyer is obligated to pay for the goods or accept them. In both shipment contracts and destination contracts, such inspection may be at any reasonable time and place, and thus can occur at the beginning of shipment (before or when the seller delivers the goods to the carrier) or the place of delivery. The buyer may hire a third party to accomplish that inspection.

However, the timing of inspection does not affect the buyer's right to reject. If the goods in a shipment contract are not conforming when they arrive, the buyer will have a right to reject (and the seller will have the risk of loss) only if the goods also were not conforming at the time they were delivered to the carrier or if the tender to the carrier was otherwise defective. If the nonconformity is something that might have occurred in transit, it may be difficult for the buyer to prove that the goods were nonconforming before the carrier started to transport them. Thus, the buyer has some incentive to inspect the goods at the starting point to determine if the goods conform to the contract when tendered to the carrier. Of course, inspection at that point is often not practical.

The same point applies to the risk of loss. The timing of the inspection does not affect when the risk of loss passes. In a shipment contact, the risk of loss will have passed to the buyer if the goods conformed to the contract when the goods were placed in the possession of the carrier. If the goods were not conforming when tendered to the carrier, the risk of loss will not have passed. UCC § 2-510. However, if the goods were completely destroyed during transit, the buyer may not be able to show that the tender was nonconforming, and thus may end up bearing the risk of loss.

Because the risk of loss in a destination contract passes upon tender of conforming goods at the destination, the buyer usually has little incentive to inspect the goods when they are delivered to the carrier and will usually wait to inspect them at the destination.

5. *Payment Against Documents of Title and the Effect on Buyer's Right to Inspect*

In both shipment and destination contracts, when goods are shipped by carrier, the carrier will usually issue a form of a document of title known as a bill of lading.[24] Read the definition of document of title and bill of lading in section 1-201. A carrier is a type of bailee, someone who takes possession, but not ownership, of the goods in order to do something with the goods that the bailor wants done with them, in this case transport the goods. A bill of lading issued by the carrier functions both as a receipt for the goods and as the contract for carriage of the goods. The carrier will then insist that the bill of lading be presented to it wherever the goods are to be offloaded in order to make sure that the carrier is releasing the goods to the right person.

In either a shipment or destination contract, the seller's tender obligation therefore includes tendering to the buyer all documents of title that are either required under the sales contact or are otherwise necessary for the buyer to obtain possession of the goods. UCC §§ 2-503(3), (5), 2-504(b). Thus, in shipment and destinations contracts, the seller must tender both the *conforming goods to the carrier* and the *required document of title to the buyer*.

If the buyer has not agreed with the seller to pay upon presentation of the documents to the buyer, the seller may simply send the bill of lading to the buyer or if an electronic bill of lading is used, enable the buyer to obtain control of the bill

---

[24] Rights and obligations arising out of a document of title and the bailment relationship are governed, in part, by UCC Article 7. Documents of title come in two flavors, negotiable and non-negotiable. UCC § 7-104. If the bill of lading is negotiable, it also serves as evidence of good title to the goods. UCC § 7-502. The carrier's responsibility during transit is governed by Article 7 (*see* UCC § 7-309 prescribing the duty of care) and applicable federal law. *See Paper Magic Group, Inc. v. J.B. Hunt Transport, Inc.*, 318 F.3d 458 (3d Cir. 2003).

of lading. UCC § 7-106. The buyer will then be able to use the bill of lading to obtain the goods from the carrier. Once the buyer obtains access to the goods, the buyer will be able to inspect the goods and decide whether to accept and pay for them.

If the buyer has agreed with the seller to pay upon presentation of documents of title, the buyer has waived its right to inspect the goods prior to payment and must pay upon presentation of the documents. UCC §§ 2-310(b), (c), 2-513(3). The buyer may inspect the *documents* and reject the documents if the *documents* do not comply with the sales contract terms. If the buyer does pay upon tender of the documents, the buyer will no longer have a right to assert defects in the documents that are apparent on the face of the *documents*. UCC § 2-605(2). However, the buyer still retains its right to inspect the *goods* prior to acceptance, UCC § 2-513(1), and payment for the goods is not acceptance of the goods. UCC § 2-512(2). In other words, payment by the buyer upon tender of the documents of title does not waive any nonconformity with respect to the goods or impair the buyer's right to reject the goods. UCC §§ 2-601, 2-612.

Thus, if the buyer has agreed to pay upon tender of documents, the seller will typically place the goods with the carrier, obtain the necessary documents from the carrier, and then send the documents to the seller's agent at the location where the carrier is to release the goods to the buyer. The seller's agent will present the documents to the buyer and obtain the buyer's payment. The buyer will then take the documents to the carrier, obtain the goods, inspect them, and decide whether to accept or reject the goods.

How can you tell if the buyer has agreed to pay upon tender of the document of title? Merely because a document of title is used to facilitate transportation does not mean that the buyer has agreed with the seller to pay against documents. Rather, such agreement is generally reflected in the meaning of the shipping term it has agreed to with the seller. For example, if the buyer and seller have agreed to a "C.I.F." or "C & F" shipment term, the presumption is that the buyer has agreed to pay upon tender of the required documents of title. UCC § 2-320(4).[25]

---

[25] If the buyer has agreed to pay only after the goods have arrived, inspection is allowed prior to the buyer being obligated to pay. UCC §§ 2-321(3), 2-513(3), 2-310.

6. *Shipment under Reservation*

One more Code section needs to be considered before trying your hand at some problems. When the seller is authorized to ship goods to the buyer, the seller may ship the goods under reservation. UCC § 2-310(b). Shipment under reservation is a method for the seller to reserve a security interest in the goods in order to make sure the goods are not released to the buyer until the buyer has paid for the goods. To ship the goods under reservation, the seller will obtain the documents of title from the carrier as set forth in section 2-505(1). Mere shipment under reservation does not undermine the buyer's right to inspect the goods before payment. UCC § 2-310(b). Rather, the buyer will often be able to have access to the goods to inspect them, although the carrier is not authorized to release the goods to the buyer until the buyer pays for the goods.

The seller's shipment under reservation, which serves to ensure the buyer pays upon receipt of the goods, is compatible with the default rule in Article 2 that payment is due upon the buyer's receipt of the goods. UCC § 2-310. A corollary to this is that if the seller has agreed to sell the goods on credit to the buyer, that is, if the buyer is obligated to pay sometime after receipt of the goods, the seller would be in breach of the sales contract if the seller shipped the goods under reservation.[26]

Problem 4-8

Seller contracted with Buyer to ship a carload of factory equipment from Chicago to Phoenix, F.O.B. Chicago. The contract price was $10,000, to be paid by a cashier's check. Nothing was said about when payment was to be made. Seller shipped the goods on October 1, with delivery expected on October 5. Carrier issued a negotiable bill of lading "to the order of Seller" and delivered it to Seller. That afternoon Seller sent the bill of lading to an agent in Phoenix. The bill of lading arrived on October 2 and on October 3, while the goods where still en route from Chicago, the agent

---

[26] Even if the seller breaches the contract for sale with the buyer by shipping under reservation when it had no right to do so, the buyer's rights in regard to the goods or the rights under a negotiable document of title are not impaired. UCC § 2-505(2). In addition, if the seller was not entitled to ship under reservation because it had agreed that the buyer could pay after receipt of the goods, the seller would have made an improper contract for transportation under section 2-504.

tendered the bill of lading to Buyer and demanded payment. Buyer refused to pay, arguing there was no duty to pay until the goods were tendered. Is Buyer correct?

Problem 4-9

Seller and Buyer agreed to a shipment contract. Seller then contracted with B & O Railroad to ship the goods to Buyer. Seller neglected to inform B & O that the goods needed to be securely tied down to avoid any shifting in transit. Even minor shifting had the potential to damage sensitive components installed inside the goods. B & O secured the goods in the usual manner which allowed some shifting of contents during shipment. When the goods arrived, the Buyer inspected them and determined that some of them were not functioning properly.

A. Assuming that Buyer could prove the failure to function properly was caused by the load shifts during transit, does Buyer have a good argument that Seller breached its tender obligation?

B. Who had the risk of loss for the damage during shipment?

Problem 4-10

Seller, in California, received a written order for lumber sent by Buyer from its place of business in Portland, Oregon. The order provided in part:

> To Seller:
> Ship to Buyer, Council Bluffs, Iowa Rate 1.20 (show on bill of lading) Routing SP UP (via Colby, Kansas) Shipment One week Terms: Regular 2% ADF 10 days Please Show Buyer as Shipper * * * Thoroughly Air Dried White Fir–WCLA Rules No. 15 Constr. & Btr., Allow. 25% standard ALS S4S EE DET–Clean Bright Stock one (1) Carload.

Two days later, Seller loaded a railroad car provided by the carrier with conforming lumber and sealed the door. Later that day, Seller prepared an invoice for Buyer as follows:

> Shipped to Buyer Council Bluffs, Iowa * * * F.O.B. delivered $1.20 rate. * * * 31,152' White Fir, A.D. 2 × 4 STD. & BTR. S4S at $84.00 Per M–$2,616.77.

Seller also prepared a non-negotiable bill of lading naming Buyer as both Consignor and Consignee and presented it to an agent of the railroad. The agent signed the bill of lading and Seller immediately mailed the bill and the invoice to Buyer.

Before the bill and invoice were received and before Carrier picked up the loaded car, fire broke out without the fault of Seller and the goods were destroyed. Buyer argued that the risk of loss had not passed before the fire. More specifically, Buyer argued that the term "F.O.B. delivered" in context meant that Seller had agreed to deliver the goods "at a particular destination" and that risk of loss would not pass until the goods were "duly tendered" at that destination. *See* UCC § 2-509(1)(b). Is that argument correct?

7. *Documentary Draft Transactions*

In any transaction in which the seller has procured documents of title from the carrier, the seller must somehow get the documents to the buyer to enable the buyer to retrieve the goods from the carrier. One way to do this is simply to send the documents to the buyer or the buyer's agent. However, if the buyer has agreed to pay against the documents, the seller will not want to release the documents to the buyer without getting the payment.

Instead of sending the documents to an agent located in the buyer's area, the seller may use the banking system as a method of getting the documents of title to the buyer when the buyer has agreed to pay against documents. When using the banking system to present the documents to the buyer, the seller will often use a draft payable to the order of the seller, drawn on the buyer, and signed by the seller. UCC § 3-104. Thus the seller is the payee, the buyer is the drawee, and the seller is the drawer. The seller will give that draft and accompanying documents of title to the seller's bank. The seller's bank will forward the draft and documents through the banking system to the buyer's bank. UCC § 4-501. When the draft and the documents arrive at the buyer's bank, the buyer's bank will present the draft and the documents to the buyer. UCC § 4-503.

Upon release of the documents of title to the buyer,[27] the buyer may obtain the goods from the carrier. If the buyer fails to pay or accept the draft as required, the buyer's bank (known as the 'presenting bank') has some ability to deal with the goods because the bank is not supposed to release the goods to the buyer. UCC §§ 4-503, 4-504. The presenting bank will seek instructions from its transferor, which request will be communicated back to the seller. UCC § 4-501. The seller will send instructions as to what it wants the presenting bank to do with the goods.

If the seller uses the documentary draft mechanism and the buyer has not agreed to pay against documents, the seller has breached its contract with the buyer by impairing the buyer's right to inspect the goods prior to payment.[28]

C. Seller's Tender of Goods in Possession of a Bailee When the Goods are to Be Delivered Without Being Moved

1. *Tender of Delivery*

Let us assume that the goods that are the subject of the contract for sale are stored in a warehouse operated by someone other than the seller. This may occur, for example, when a farmer wishes to sell grain stored in a silo operated by a cooperative. The seller and buyer agree that the seller will give the buyer access to

---

[27] If the draft is payable within the three days after presentment, the bank will release the documents to the buyer only upon payment. UCC §§ 4-503, 2-514. If the draft is payable more than three days after presentment to the buyer, the bank will insist on the buyer's "acceptance" of the draft in order to release the documents to the buyer. UCC §§ 4-503, 2-514. Acceptance of a draft is the drawee's (in this case the buyer's) signed engagement to pay that the buyer/drawee writes on the draft when the draft is presented to the buyer/drawee. UCC § 3-409. The buyer's "acceptance" of the draft obligates the buyer to pay according to the terms of the draft as accepted when the draft is later presented for payment. UCC § 3-413.

[28] A variation on this basic transaction is the seller's sale of the draft and the documents to a bank for a discounted amount. The bank would have a security interest in the draft and the documents. UCC § 4-210. In addition, the bank is an Article 2 financing agency, section 2-104(2), and has rights as to the goods as specified in sections 2-506 and 2-707. For an excellent discussion of the documentary draft transaction in greater detail, *see* E. Allan Farnsworth, *Documentary Drafts Under the Uniform Commercial Code*, 22 BUS. LAW. 479 (1967).

the goods which will remain in the warehouse until the buyer needs them. A warehouse is a type of bailee. A warehouse, when it takes goods for storage, may issue a warehouse receipt for the goods. A warehouse receipt, like a bill of lading, is a type of document of title. Read the definition of warehouse receipt in section 1-201.[29]

The seller's obligation to tender delivery may be satisfied in several ways, if the parties have not otherwise agreed. If the warehouse has issued a negotiable warehouse receipt, the seller's tender is complete upon the tender of that document to the buyer. UCC § 2-503(4)(a). That is because any warehouse that has issued a negotiable warehouse receipt covering goods will not release the goods to anyone other than the person presenting the warehouse receipt. UCC §§ 7-403(c), 7-502. Alternatively, if the warehouse has not issued a negotiable document of title, the seller may fulfill its tender obligation by obtaining an acknowledgment from the warehouse that the buyer has the right to possess the goods. UCC § 2-503(4)(a).

There are two other ways in which a seller may be able to tender the goods: (i) delivering to the buyer a nonnegotiable warehouse receipt issued by the warehouse; or (ii) giving the buyer a written direction to the warehouse to deliver the goods to the buyer (this document is known as a delivery order). UCC § 2-503(4)(b). However, both of these methods of tender fail if the buyer seasonably objects (unless the buyer has agreed otherwise). Moreover, if the bailee does not honor the nonnegotiable warehouse receipt or the delivery order, the seller's tender is similarly defeated.

2. Buyer's Inspection Right

Unless agreed otherwise, the buyer has the right to inspect the goods prior to payment or acceptance. UCC § 2-513(1). Thus, upon the seller's tender as described above, the buyer has a reasonable opportunity to inspect the goods stored in the warehouse and decide whether to accept or reject the goods. After that inspection, if the buyer does not reject the goods, the buyer will have to pay for them.

As with sales contracts involving shipment of the goods, the buyer may have agreed in this situation to pay upon tender of the documents of title. If so, the

---

[29] Just as we saw with bills of lading, a warehouse receipt may be either negotiable or non-negotiable. UCC § 7-104.

consequences are the same as those discussed previously with respect to inspection after payment. However, just as when goods are shipped, merely because a document of title, such as a warehouse receipt, is issued does not mean that the buyer has agreed to pay upon tender of that document.

3.   *Risk of Loss*

Under section 2-509(2), the risk of loss will pass to the buyer if the goods are in the hands of a bailee and the parties agree the goods are to be delivered without being moved.[30] There is a symmetry between sections 2-509(2) and 2-503(4). Thus if tender of delivery takes place through tender of a negotiable document of title, the risk of loss moves from the seller to the buyer at that time. UCC § 2-509(2)(a). If the tender of delivery is made by the bailee acknowledging that the buyer is entitled to possession of the goods, risk of loss passes to the buyer at that point. UCC § 2-509(2)(b).[31] If the seller tenders a nonnegotiable document or a delivery order, the risk of loss passes to the buyer after the buyer has had a reasonable time to present the document or delivery order to the bailee. UCC §§ 2-509(2)(c), 2-503(4)(b).

Even though the goods are in the possession of a bailee at the time of contracting, the parties may agree that the bailee is to ship or deliver the goods to the buyer (thus moving the goods in the delivery process) rather than simply acknowledge that the buyer is entitled to possession. If so, risk of loss is governed by the normal rules applicable to shipment or delivery contracts, rather than under section 2-509(2).[32]

Problem 4-11

Seller, an appliance manufacturer, contracted to sell 200 ovens to Buyer, an appliance retailer. Buyer did not have sufficient capacity to store the ovens at Buyer's premises, so Seller and Buyer agreed that the ovens

---

[30] The warehouse has the obligation to take reasonable care of the goods. UCC § 7-204.

[31] *See Jason's Foods, Inc. v. Peter Eckrich & Sons, Inc.*, 774 F.2d 214 (7th Cir. 1985) (the bailee's acknowledgment must be to the buyer).

[32] *Commonwealth Petroleum Co. v. Petrosol Int'l, Inc.*, 901 F.2d 1314 (6th Cir. 1990).

would remain in the warehouse run by Bonded Storage, Inc. Delivery was due on April 5 and on that day Seller offered to indorse a negotiable warehouse receipt covering 200 ovens to Buyer if Buyer would pay the purchase price in full. Buyer refused because it wanted to pay for the ovens as it took each one out of storage after it was sold to a customer. Has Seller complied with its tender obligations? Does Buyer have a right to pay as it has asserted?

Problem 4-12

Red Feather, a fine filly, won her first race. Owner shipped her back to the stable by common carrier, taking a non-negotiable bill of lading naming Owner as the consignee. While the horse was in transit, Owner sold Red Feather to Buyer for $10,000. Owner accepted a check for $10,000, handed Buyer the non-negotiable bill of lading and stated "she's all yours." Two hours later, Red Feather was killed in an accident while still in the carrier's possession. Who had the risk of loss?

D. Delivery, Inspection, and Payment Under International Law

1. CISG

The seller's general duties to deliver the goods and hand over the documents are particularized in Articles 31 through 34 and are largely similar to the rules under the UCC. Article 31 deals with the place of delivery in cases where the seller is not "bound to deliver the goods at any other particular place." If the contract does not involve carriage of the goods, the place of delivery is the seller's place of business or the more specific location where the parties knew the goods were or would be manufactured. Art.31(b), (c). *Compare* UCC § 2-308. Article 34 governs the seller's obligation to deliver documents. The time for delivery is the time specified in or implied by the contract, if any, otherwise within a reasonable time. Art. 33.

If the contract involves carriage of the goods, the seller must hand over the goods "to the first carrier for transmission to the buyer." Art. 31(a). For example, if a seller in Chicago has agreed to transport the goods to a buyer in Paris (and there is no other delivery term), the first carrier might be a train from Chicago to New York, even though the goods will then be delivered to a vessel for shipment. Article

32 states what the seller's other obligations are when goods are handed over to the first carrier. Note that the seller has a limited duty to notify the buyer, Art. 32(1), and has no duty to arrange for the carriage of the goods or to obtain insurance on their carriage unless required by the contract. Art. 32(2)-(3). Please read these sections and compare them to UCC § 2-504.

Under Article 53, the "buyer must pay the price for the goods and take delivery of them as required by the contract and this Convention." In the absence of contrary agreement, the place for payment is the seller's place of business or where the documents are handed over. Art. 57. The time for payment is the time of the seller's tender. *See* Art. 58. The buyer has a right to inspect the goods "within as short a period as is practicable under the circumstances," Art. 38(a), and is not bound to pay until he has had an opportunity to examine the goods, unless the procedures for payment in the agreement are inconsistent with the right to examine. Art. 58(3).

If the contract involves "carriage of the goods, the seller may dispatch the goods on terms whereby the goods, or documents controlling their disposition, will not be handed over to the buyer except against payment of the price." Art. 58(2). *Compare* UCC § 2-310(b) (regarding the seller's shipment under reservation). No agreement by the buyer is required. The usual practice is that, unless otherwise agreed, the buyer must pay against documents of title even though the goods are still in the middle of the ocean. While the buyer must wait until the goods arrive to inspect, the buyer can discount the documents of title or use them as collateral to obtain a loan if the delay puts the buyer under a financial strain.

2.   *UNIDROIT Principles*

Because the Principles are not focused solely on the sale of goods but instead may be used in a wide variety of contract types, the provisions do not directly address delivery and inspection of the goods. Rather the Principles focus on a more generalized statement of performance obligations in Articles 6.1.1 (time for performance), 6.1.2 (performance at one time or in installments), 6.1.3 (partial performance), 6.1.4 (order of performance), 6.1.5 (early performance), and 6.1.6 (place of performance). The Principles address payment in Articles 6.1.7 (payment by check or other instrument), 6.1.8 (payment by funds transfer), and 6.1.9 and 6.1.10 (payment by currency).

CHAPTER FIVE

TERMS OF THE CONTRACT – PART III

SECTION 1.   AGREEMENT TO OVERRIDE GAP FILLER PROVISIONS

A. Principles of UCC Article 1

As we learned in Chapters Three and Four, Article 2 contains a large number of gap fillers. If the parties' agreement – that is, their bargain in fact as supplemented by usage of trade, course of performance, and course of dealing – covers a particular term, there is no "gap" to fill. It is only when those sources of "agreement" do not address a particular term that resort to the Code's gap fillers is necessary to flush out the parties' contract. This point, which to some extent is implicit in the distinction between the defined terms "agreement" and "contract," is also borne out by section 1-302. Read section 1-302.

In general, parties are free to vary the effect of the Article 2 rules that apply to their contract. However, as section 1-302 indicates, there are two limitations on this freedom. First, the obligations of good faith, diligence, and reasonableness cannot be disclaimed, although the parties may determine standards for the fulfillment of those obligations, as long as those standards are not manifestly unreasonable. UCC § 1-302(b). Second, some provisions of Article 2 cannot be varied by agreement. The language of section 1-302(a) suggests that all such exceptions are expressly identified in the Code. However, this point is belied by comment 1, which indicates that the exceptions "vary in explicitness" and suggests that the statute of frauds in section 2-201 is not variable even though nothing in that provision so states. No doubt there are other provisions that are also not variable. As to what they are, that is an open question. One thing we do know is that, pursuant to section 1-302(c), we cannot infer that a provision is invariable merely because it fails to state that it can be varied.[1]

This discussion raises a related question. Can parties to a contract for the sale of goods opt out of application of usage of trade, course of dealing, and course of performance as part of their agreement? Why might parties want to do so?

---

[1] For a humorous dissertation on this issue, *see* Scott J. Burnham, *Is Article 2 Regulatory or Facilitatory? A Socratic Dialogue*, 68 OHIO ST. L.J. 57 (2007). *See also* Sarah Howard Jenkins, *Contracting Out of Article 2: Minimizing the Obligation of Performance & Liability for Breach*, 40 LOY. L.A. L. REV. 401 (2006).

Problem 5-1

A. Review the gap filler provisions studied in Chapters Three and Four and identify the rules that impose an obligation of good faith, diligence, reasonableness or care.

    1. If your last name begins with a letter from A to M, identify for each of those rules what standard a buyer would want to specify to measure the performance of that duty. Be prepared to explain why the standard you have identified is not "manifestly unreasonable."

    2. If your last name begins with a letter from N to Z, identify for each of those rules what standard a seller would want to specify to measure the performance of that duty. Be prepared to explain why the standard you have identified is not "manifestly unreasonable."

B. Identify each Article 2 provision studied so far (other than section 2-201) that you think is not variable by agreement of the parties and explain why you think the provision is not variable by agreement.

B. Warranty Disclaimers

In Chapter Three we explored express warranties, the warranty of merchantability, the warranty of fitness for particular purpose, and the warranty of title. Often, sellers wish to escape liability for breach of these warranties. One way to do that is to limit the seller's responsibility for damages (*i.e.*, to reduce the seller's exposure for breach). Remedy limitations are addressed in subsection C below. Another way for a seller to limit its exposure is to entirely disclaim one or all of the warranties (*i.e.*, to prevent certain problems with the goods from being a breach at all). Read section 2-316, which applies to express warranties, the implied warranty of merchantability, and the implied warranty of fitness for particular purpose. Now read section 2-312(2), which applies to the warranty of title. No explicit provision governs disclaimers of the warranty of noninfringement.

Express warranties. First consider section 2-316(1). It provides that words or conduct relevant to the creation of express warranty are, to the extent possible, to be read consistently with words purporting to negate or limit express warranties. Often, however, it is not possible to read the terms consistently. For example, suppose that Seller sends Buyer a sample of the goods along with a proposed written agreement that expressly states: "Seller makes no express warranties." Buyer signs the written agreement after inspecting the sample. If the sample truly is part of the basis of the bargain – and it might not be given the language in the written agreement – then it would be virtually impossible to harmonize the conduct relevant to the creation of the warranty with the words purporting to negate it. In such a case, section 2-316(1) provides that the attempted disclaimer fails. The reason for this is expressed in comment 1 to section 2-313: " 'Express' warranties rest on 'dickered' aspects of the individual bargain, and go so clearly to the essence of that bargain that words of disclaimer in a form are repugnant to the basic dickered terms."

Because of this, it is almost a contradiction in terms for the seller to disclaim an express warranty. The seller can avoid an express warranty by not making it, but it is virtually impossible to disclaim one that has been made. Virtually impossible, but not completely impossible. The seller may be able to use the parol evidence rule to exclude evidence of an alleged express warranty. The parol evidence rule is discussed below in Section 2 of this Chapter.

Implied warranty of merchantability and implied warranty of fitness for particular purpose. One of the rationales underlying the implied warranty of merchantability as a gap filler is to give effect to the likely and reasonable expectations of the parties. Buyers of new goods from a merchant generally expect that the goods are fit for their ordinary purpose, that is, that the goods work. Admittedly, expectations might be different if the law were different. However, even if the legal rule were *caveat emptor*, it is likely that most buyers would expect merchant sellers to repair or replace defective goods or refund the price paid. Given that the implied warranty of fitness for particular purpose arises only when the buyer relies on the seller's skills or judgment, it is likely that giving efficacy to the parties' reasonable expectations is one of the rationales underlying this implied warranty too.

Nevertheless, because these warranties are merely gap fillers, not mandatory contract terms, it is possible for the parties by their agreement to exclude or disclaim them. That then raises the question of what the law should require for a disclaimer to be effective. Must the effort to disclaim be something that is likely to change the buyer's expectations? If a disclaimer is buried in fine print and expressed in dense legalese will it nevertheless be effective? Should it be? Read section 2-316(2) and (3). *See also* UCC § 1-201(b)(10) (defining "conspicuous"). Now try the following problems.

Problem 5-2

A. Identify all the methods for disclaiming the implied warranty of merchantability.

B. Silicon Solutions, Inc. manufactures and sells HDTVs. Last month, some of its televisions were damaged when the warehouse in which they had been stored was flooded during a storm. Silicon Solutions unpacked and examined the televisions and discarded those that were obviously damaged. However, it was unable to rule out the possibility that the remainder might have less visible damage. Silicon Solutions repackaged the remaining televisions and then offered to sell them to Retailer. In which, if any, of the following scenarios will the implied warranty of merchantability be disclaimed?
   1. The purchase agreement that both Retailer and Silicon Solutions signed contained the following language just above the signature lines in bold type: "There are no warranties, express or implied, included as a part of this transaction."
   2. The purchase agreement that both Retailer and Silicon Solutions signed contained the following language just above the signature lines in the same font as the remainder of the document: "The goods are sold as is."

C. Construct a scenario in which the implied warranty of merchantability would be disclaimed under section 2-316(3)(b).

Problem 5-3

Identify all the methods for disclaiming the implied warranty of fitness for particular purpose.

Compliance with the rules of section 2-316 is always necessary – but not always sufficient – to disclaim the implied warranties of merchantability and fitness for particular purpose. Even if a disclaimer complies with section 2-316, the disclaimer may still be unconscionable under section 2-302, and therefore unenforceable.[2] In addition, sometimes law outside Article 2 may invalidate an attempted disclaimer.[3]

Problem 5-4

Butler, an experienced commercial fisherman, purchased from Dealer a new diesel engine for Butler's fishing boat. In the discussions prior to the sale, Dealer and Butler discussed the power that Butler needed for the fishing boat. Based on Dealer's recommendation, Butler purchased the Powertrane 1000, which Dealer then installed on Butler's boat. Over the next four months, a number of mechanical problems arose, including the emission of excessive quantities of heavy black smoke. Dealer was unable to correct the problems and the engine was removed from the boat. Butler thinks that the engine did not function properly because it lacked the power to propel the fishing boat. Butler's expert will testify that the engine was unmerchantable due to the recurring mechanical problems.

When Butler took delivery of the engine, Butler signed Dealer's standard form purchase order. The front of the purchase order contained a number of terms and conditions. In the center of the front, this statement appeared:

> BOTH THIS ORDER AND ITS ACCEPTANCE ARE SUBJECT TO TERMS AND CONDITIONS STATED IN THIS ORDER.

On the reverse side of the order at the top of the page, the following words appeared: TERMS AND CONDITIONS. Under that caption were eleven numbered paragraphs, one of which contained a disclaimer in the following form:

> THE SELLER HEREBY DISCLAIMS AND EXCLUDES ALL IMPLIED WARRANTIES, INCLUDING THE IMPLIED WARRANTY OF MERCHANTABILITY.

Butler did not read and was not asked to read anything on the back of the purchase order.

---

[2] *See Hutton v. Deere & Co.*, 210 F.3d 389 (10th Cir. 2000) (concluding on facts that disclaimer of implied warranties was not unconscionable).

[3] *See* Donald F. Clifford, Jr., *Non-UCC Statutory Provisions Affecting Warranty Disclaimers and Remedies in Sales of Goods*, 71 N.C. L. REV. 1011 (1993).

A. Butler sued Dealer for damages resulting from breach of an implied warranty of merchantability and breach of the implied warranty of fitness for particular purpose. Dealer defended on the ground that it did not make or had successfully disclaimed both warranties under section 2-316(2). What result?

B. How, if at all, would the analysis change if Butler were not a commercial fisherman but instead purchased the engine for use on Butler's pleasure boat?

C. How, if at all, would the analysis change if Dealer were not a merchant?

Warranty of title. The warranty of title is not designated as an "implied" warranty, and thus cannot be disclaimed pursuant to the rules of § 2-316(3). *See* UCC § 2-312 cmt. 6. However, it is possible to disclaim the warranty of title. Read section 2-312(2).

Problem 5-5

A. Under what circumstances, if any, would a buyer be likely to agree to a disclaimer of the warranty of title?

B. Section 2-312 indicates that the warranty of title can be disclaimed by language or circumstances. Construct a scenario in which the parties say nothing about the warranty of title but, because of the specific circumstances, the warranty would nevertheless be disclaimed.

CISG and UNIDROIT Principles. The CISG does not have a comparable section on disclaiming warranties. Rather, Article 35(3) limits the seller's liability under that Article if the buyer "knew or could not have been unaware" of the nonconformity at the time of contract formation. The UNIDROIT Principles do not have any specific provisions on disclaimers of warranty.

C. Remedy Limitations

Most merchant sellers are willing to stand behind the quality of the goods they sell. For many of them, market pressures and concern for business reputation almost require that they agree either to replace defective goods or refund the purchase price. Merchants who refuse to do so might benefit in the short run, but over time are apt to find themselves with few customers. Thus, few merchant sellers of new goods try to disclaim the warranty of merchantability.

What merchants as a rule do not want, however, is unlimited damages for any defective goods they sell. A seller of stereo components may be quite willing to replace a receiver that short circuits the day after the sale, but will not want to pay for the house that burned to the ground because of that defect. A seller of lawnmowers might be willing to replace a mower if the blades fly off during first use, but would rather not pay damages for the buyer's arm that got severed in the process. In short, most sellers are willing to accept some responsibility for their wares, but not unlimited responsibility. They do not want to be on the hook for damages that exceed – by several orders of magnitude – the price of or profit margin on the goods they sell.

Article 2 allows the parties to limit or alter the remedies that would normally be applicable for breach. In other words, the normal rules on remedy are a bit like gap-filler rules, which the parties are free to alter by agreement. However, just as there are hurdles a seller must jump over to disclaim the implied warranty of merchantability, the implied warranty of fitness, or the warranty of title, there are restrictions on the parties' ability to limit remedies. Before we turn our attention to these limitations, it is important to have a basic understanding of the remedies that Article 2 provides. We will explore remedies more in depth in Chapters Seven (buyer's remedies) and Nine (seller's remedies), so the following explanation is merely a synopsis of the basic remedy rules and is intended to provide a context for the rules on how parties may limit their remedies.

Traditional remedies. The buyer's and seller's remedies in Article 2 are consistent with the approach typically available for breach of contract in that they attempt to protect the aggrieved party's expectation interest.[4] Keep in mind that there are two things always in play when a seller or buyer breaches the sales

---

[4] We will consider remedies under the CISG and the UNIDROIT Principles in Chapter Seven on buyer's remedies and in Chapter Nine on seller's remedies.

contract: (1) what happens to the goods; and (2) how should the aggrieved party's damages be calculated.

Seller's breach and buyer's remedies. The buyer's remedies depend on the nature of the seller's breach and who has the goods. If the seller breaches by repudiating its obligations or by simply failing to tender the goods, the buyer has the right to cancel the deal, recover the price that has been paid, and recover damages. Those damages will be based on either the difference between the contract price and the market price of the goods or, if the buyer purchases substitute goods from another source, the difference between the contract price and the price of the substitute goods. In addition, the buyer is entitled to consequential and incidental damages. *See* UCC §§ 2-711, 2-712, 2-713, 2-715. Alternatively, in some limited circumstances the buyer has the right to ask a court to require the seller to tender the goods. If the buyer is successful in that effort, the buyer will be liable for the price of the goods. *See* UCC §§ 2-502, 2-716, 2-709.

If the seller makes a nonconforming tender – such as if the goods themselves are nonconforming or tender is untimely – the buyer must decide whether to accept or reject the goods. If the buyer properly rejects the goods, the buyer may cancel the deal, recover the price that has been paid, and recover damages in the same manner as if the seller had repudiated or otherwise failed to make a tender of the goods. *See* UCC §§ 2-711, 2-601, 2-612. If the buyer accepts the goods, the buyer will be obligated to pay the contract price. However, the buyer will be entitled to damages arising from the nonconformity. Most commonly, these damages are the difference between the value of the goods accepted and the value of the conforming goods, plus consequential and incidental damages. *See* UCC §§ 2-607, 2-709, 2-714, 2-715.

In some limited circumstances, a buyer who has accepted nonconforming goods may revoke its acceptance. Such a revocation of acceptance is generally treated like a rejection of the goods. As a result, the buyer may cancel the deal, recover the price that has been paid, and recover damages based upon the difference between the contract price and the price of replacement goods or the market price of the goods, plus consequential and incidental damages. *See* UCC §§ 2-608, 2-711, 2-712, 2-713, 2-715.

Buyer's breach and seller's remedies. The seller's remedies for the buyer's breach also depend on who has the goods. If the buyer repudiates its obligations under the contract before the seller has delivered the goods, the seller may stop or withhold delivery of the goods, cancel the deal, and recover damages. Those damages will be measured in one of three ways: (i) the difference between the resale price and the contract price; (ii) the difference between the market price and the contract price; or (iii) the lost profit on the transaction. *See* UCC § 2-702(1), 2-703, 2-705, 2-706, 2-708. The seller is also entitled to incidental damages. UCC § 2-710. If the buyer has prepaid some or all of the price, the buyer has the right to restitution of that amount, subject to an offset of the seller's damages. UCC § 2-718(2).

In some cases, the buyer may make an effective rejection of the goods even though the seller's tender conformed to the contract requirements. In other words, the buyer's rejection is wrongful but effective, with the result that the seller gets the goods back. In such a case, the seller will have the same three possible damage remedies identified above.

If the buyer has accepted the goods, the buyer is obligated for the contract price of the goods plus any incidental damages the seller has suffered. UCC §§ 2-709, 2-710. In other words, a buyer who breaches by failing to pay is obligated for the price. However, in some limited circumstances, as an alternative to seeking a judgment for the price, the seller may be able to reclaim the goods from the buyer. UCC §§ 2-507, 2-712(2).

Rules on limiting remedies. We now examine the rules on how parties may limit the remedies that would otherwise be available. Read sections 2-718(1) and 2-719. These provisions provide two different methods for a party to limit liability for breach: (i) to liquidate damages; and (ii) to limit the type of remedies available. Before proceeding to analyze each of these rules, bear in mind that both types of limitations come into play only if a party is in breach. A warranty disclaimer, on the other hand, changes the seller's duty as to the goods so that a defect in quality or title might not become a breach at all. Thus, do not confuse the rules discussed above on disclaimer of warranty with the rules discussed below on limiting remedies.

1. Liquidated Damages

A liquidated damages clause is a term in the parties' agreement that mandates that damages for breach be computed in a manner different from the normal measures of damages that would otherwise apply. As a term of the parties' agreement, a liquidated damages clause is subject to the restrictions on enforceability that apply to all aspects of the agreement. Thus, for example, it must not be unconscionable. In addition, section 2-718(1) lists several other factors that affect the validity of a liquidated damages clause. Why are these factors important? What is the purpose of subjecting these terms to judicial scrutiny? Read section 1-305. Does that help provide an answer to these questions?

Problem 5-6

Butterfield Co., a baker, planned to expand its capacity by 30%. Accordingly, on March 1, it ordered a custom-made oven from Sure Fire, a manufacturer, to be delivered not later than September 1. Butterfield informed Sure Fire of its planned expansion and stated that "time was of the essence." Butterfield had developed a new bread for hotels and restaurants and wanted to be in production for the fall convention season. Sure Fire and Butterfield negotiated over how to deal with the risk of delay in delivery.

After discussing Butterfield's current profit margin and the probabilities that an expansion would be profitable, Sure Fire agreed, in a clause labeled "Liquidated Damages," to pay Butterfield $1,000 for every day of a non-excusable delay in delivery. Sure Fire did not deliver the oven until October 1. Butterfield claimed liquidated damages in the amount of $30,000. Sure Fire, however, can establish that the convention business during September was very slow and that, at best, Butterfield would have made only $2,500 in net profits if the oven had been delivered on time. Is the agreed damage clause enforceable under section 2-718?

2. *Limited Remedies*

In contrast to liquidated damage clauses, which tend to specify a dollar amount of damages or a formula for computing them, limitations on remedy tend to eliminate an entire category of damages or other type of remedy that would otherwise be available. For example, the agreement may specify that neither party will be entitled to consequential damages or that the buyer's only remedy for nonconforming goods will be repair or replacement of the goods. Because such a clause is a term of the parties' agreement, it is subject to all the normal tests of enforceability. In addition, Article 2 contains further qualifications on the enforceability of remedy limitations. Read section 2-719. Subsection (1) allows parties to agree to add to or reduce the types of remedies normally available. It also allows them to change the way in which damages are to be computed. Such contractual rules are presumed to be optional unless the agreement expressly makes them exclusive. UCC § 2-719(1)(b).

Subsections (2) and (3) then contain two important limitations on the freedom granted in subsection (1). Subsection (2) provides that if a limited remedy "fails of its essential purpose," then the normal statutory remedies become available. When does a limited remedy fail of its essential purpose? The classic case is when a seller limits remedy for breach to repair or replacement of defective parts and the entire good is destroyed because of a single defective part. At that point, replacing the one defective part would not be of much use to the buyer.

Problem 5-7

Construct another scenario in which a limited remedy fails of its essential purpose.

Subsection (3) allows the parties to limit or exclude consequential damages. However, a limitation on consequential damages is prima facie unconscionable with respect to personal injury resulting from defective consumer goods. Of course, the "prima facie" language merely creates a presumption of unconscionability, one that the seller can rebut.[5]

Problem 5-8

Construct a scenario in which an exclusion of consequential damages, including damages for personal injury, from defective consumer goods would not be unconscionable.

It is not uncommon for sellers to incorporate into their standard agreements two different remedy limitations: one that limits remedy to repair or replacement of defective goods and another that disclaims responsibility for consequential damages (other than damages for personal injury). In such situations, what happens if the

---

[5] Remember from our study of unconscionability in Chapter Two that a court can refuse to enforce any particular term based upon that principle, even if it does not refuse to enforce the entire agreement. Section 2-719(3) merely provides a presumption of unconscionability for a particular term.

limitation of remedy to repair or replacement fails of its essential purpose? Does the exclusion of consequential damages also fail? Consider the following case.

RAZOR V. HYUNDAI MOTOR AMERICA
854 N.E.2d 607 (Ill. 2006), *cert. denied*, 549 U.S. 1181 (2007)

Justice Freeman delivered the judgment of the court, with opinion:

[Plaintiff purchased a new Hyundai Sonata . In connection with the purchase, the manufacturer provided a written promise to "[r]epair or replace[] any component originally manufactured or installed by Hyundai Motor Company or Hyundai Motor America (HMA) that is found to be defective in material or workmanship under normal use and maintenance, except any item specifically referred to in the section 'What is Not Covered.' " However, the manufacturer also disclaimed responsibility for incidental and consequential damages. The car malfunctioned and, despite numerous repair efforts, could not be fixed. Plaintiff sued and the jury awarded her $5,000 for the diminished value of the car and $3,500 for aggravation, inconvenience, and lost use. – Eds.]

ANALYSIS
. . .

I. Enforceability of Hyundai's Disclaimer of Incidental/Consequential Damages

The main issue before this court is the enforceability of Hyundai's disclaimer of incidental and consequential damages. Hyundai argues that the disclaimer is independent of the limited remedy, and the disclaimer may stand even if its limited remedy failed of its essential purpose. Hyundai contends that the disclaimer may be overridden only if it is itself unconscionable, a standard which Hyundai argues has not been met in the instant case. Plaintiff responds that the disclaimer should fall with the limited warranty, and contends that even if this court finds them to be severable, the disclaimer in this case was unconscionable.

A. *"Independent" vs. "Dependent" Approach to*
Provisions Limiting Remedy and Excluding Consequential Damages

. . . . [T]o determine the enforceability of a consequential damages disclaimer in a limited warranty, we look to state law. In Illinois, the sale of goods is governed by article 2 of the Uniform Commercial Code (UCC). Central to this case is section 2-719 of the UCC. . . .

In this case, Hyundai's limited warranty contained both a limitation of remedy and an exclusion of consequential damages. The warranty expressly limited the buyer's remedies to repair and replacement of nonconforming parts, as permitted under section 2-719(1)(a). However, the warranty additionally provided that incidental or consequential damages were "not covered," as permitted under section 2-719(3).

Plaintiff claimed-and the jury found-that the Hyundai limited remedy had failed of its essential purpose because of the persistence of the no-start problem with plaintiff's car. Hyundai does not question this factual determination in this appeal. Thus, according to section 2-719(2) of the UCC, plaintiff was entitled to remedy "as provided in this Act.". . . This does not end the inquiry insofar as consequential damages are concerned, however. Subsection (3) of section 2-719 is part of "this Act" – *i.e.,* the UCC-and subsection (3) permits a seller to limit or exclude consequential damages unless to do so would be unconscionable. It still must be determined, therefore, whether a limited remedy failing of its essential purpose defeats a disclaimer of consequential damages.

There are two main schools of thought on the issue. Some courts and commentators conclude that a limited remedy failing of its essential purpose operates to destroy any limitation or exclusion of consequential damages in the same contract. This approach is known as the "dependent" approach, because the enforceability of the consequential damages exclusion depends on the survival of the limitation of remedy.

Our appellate court issued one of the seminal cases for the dependent approach, *Adams v. J.I. Case Co.,* 261 N.E.2d 1 (Ill. Ct. App. 1970). There, the plaintiff purchased a tractor, pursuant to a purchase agreement which limited his remedy to repair and replacement and also disclaimed consequential damages. The tractor had severe mechanical problems and was in a repair shop for over a year. Plaintiff filed suit, seeking consequential damages for the business he claimed to have lost because defendants were "wilfully dilatory or careless and negligent in making good their warranty." The court concluded:

> The limitations of remedy and of liability are not separable from the obligations of the warranty. Repudiation of the obligations of the warranty destroys its benefits. The complaint alleges facts that would constitute a repudiation by the defendants of their obligations under the warranty, that repudiation consisting of their wilful failure or their careless and negligent compliance. It should be obvious that they cannot at once repudiate their obligation under their warranty and assert its provisions beneficial to them.

Adams, 261 N.E.2d 1.

In defense of the dependent approach, the United States District Court for the Northern District of Illinois has reasoned:

> [P]laintiff also was entitled to assume that defendants would not be unreasonable or wilfully dilatory in making good their warranty in the event of defects in the machinery and equipment. It is the specific breach of the warranty to repair that plaintiff alleges caused the bulk of its damages. This Court would be in an untenable position if it allowed the defendant to shelter itself behind one segment of the warranty when it has allegedly repudiated and ignored its very limited obligations under another segment of the same warranty, which alleged repudiation has caused the very need for relief which the defendant is attempting to avoid.

Jones & McKnight Corp. v. Birdsboro Corp., 320 F. Supp. 39, 43–44 (N.D. Ill. 1970) (applying Illinois law). . . .

Plaintiff suggests that the dependent approach is followed by a majority of jurisdictions to consider the issue. While this may have been true 15 to 20 years ago[6] (see D. Goetz, *Special Project: Article Two Warranties in Commercial Transactions: An Update,* 72 CORNELL L. REV. 1159, 1307 (1987) ("A majority of cases have answered correctly that the failure of an exclusive remedy voids the consequential damages exclusion clause")), it is no longer the case. Rather, the majority of jurisdictions now follow the other of the two main approaches, the "independent" approach. 1 E. FARNSWORTH, FARNSWORTH ON CONTRACTS § 4.28(a), at 605–06 (3d ed. 2004) ("some courts have gone so far as to hold that if UCC 2-719(2) applies, related limitations on remedies should all fall like a house of cards, so that a provision barring recovery of consequential damages would also be invalidated. However, most courts have rejected this view"). This school of thought holds that a limitation of consequential damages must be judged on its own merits and enforced unless unconscionable, regardless of whether the contract also contains a limitation of remedy which has failed of its essential purpose.

---

[6] We note that all of the law review articles and all but one of the non-Illinois court decisions plaintiff cites were decided in 1990 or before. The sole post-1990 foreign authority plaintiff cites, *Bishop Logging Co. v. John Deere Industrial Equipment Co.,* 455 S.E.2d 183 (S.C. 1995), did not follow the dependent approach, but rather the "case-by-case" approach. *Bishop Logging,* 455 S.E.2d at 191-93.

A representative case adopting the independent approach is *Chatlos Systems v. National Cash Register Corp.,* 635 F.2d 1081 (3d Cir. 1980) (applying New Jersey law). There, the court rejected the dependent approach, holding:

> [T]he better reasoned approach is to treat the consequential damage disclaimer as an independent provision, valid unless unconscionable. This poses no logical difficulties. A contract may well contain no limitation on breach of warranty damages but specifically exclude consequential damages. Conversely, it is quite conceivable that some limitation might be placed on a breach of warranty award, but consequential damages would expressly be permitted.
>
> The limited remedy of repair and a consequential damages exclusion are two discrete ways of attempting to limit recovery for breach of warranty. The [UCC], moreover, tests each by a different standard. The former survives unless it fails of its essential purpose, while the latter is valid unless it is unconscionable. We therefore see no reason to hold, as a general proposition, that the failure of the limited remedy provided in the contract, without more, invalidates a wholly distinct term in the agreement excluding consequential damages. The two are not mutually exclusive.

Chatlos Systems, 635 F.2d at 1086. . . .

A third approach, "applied relatively infrequently," is the "case by case" approach. D. Hagen, Note, *Sections 2-719(2) & 2-719(3) of the Uniform Commercial Code: The Limited Warranty Package & Consequential Damages,* 31 VAL. U. L. REV. 111, 131 (1996). Under this approach, "[a]n analysis to determine whether consequential damages are warranted must carefully examine the individual factual situation including the type of goods involved, the parties and the precise nature and purpose of the contract." *AES Technology Systems, Inc. v. Coherent Radiation,* 583 F.2d 933, 941 (7th Cir. 1978).

Neither of the parties to this appeal argues in favor of the case-by-case approach, which has been criticized as "not supported by the [UCC] or its official comments." 31 VAL. U.L. REV. at 132. The authorities espousing it have sometimes confused it with the "independent" approach (see, *e.g., Smith v. Navistar International Transportation Corp.,* 957 F.2d 1439, 1443–44 (7th Cir. 1992)) (erroneously stating that *Chatlos Systems* had adopted the case-by-case approach). Moreover, although one of the factors cited in favor of the case-by-case approach is that it "allows some measure of certainty" (*Smith,* 957 F.2d at 1444), it has been observed that it in fact "provides *less* predictability than the dependent or independent approaches." (Emphasis added.) 31 VAL. U.L. REV. at 131.

Additionally, notwithstanding that the case-by-case approach might appear to tread a middle ground between the dependent approach (which is generally more favorable for buyers) and the independent approach (which is generally more favorable for sellers), this is not necessarily so. In *AES Technology*, where the case-by-case approach originated, the contract at issue contained no disclaimer or limitation of consequential damages, only a limitation of remedy. The court affirmed the trial court's conclusion that the limited remedy had failed of its essential purpose. *AES Technology*, 583 F.2d at 940. However, the court inferred a consequential damage disclaimer from the limitation of remedy (*AES Technology*, 583 F.2d at 941 n. 9) and proceeded to enforce that inferred disclaimer against the buyer even though the limited remedy had failed of its essential purpose, because "the express provisions of the contract and the factual background" indicated that the parties intended for the buyer to "bear the risk of the project"(*AES Technology*, 583 F.2d at 941). The court inferred a consequential damages disclaimer where none existed, struck the language from which the disclaimer was inferred, then enforced the disclaimer against the buyer anyway, based on the court's understanding of "the factual background." This result could not have been reached under either the dependent or independent approach, and we find the analysis difficult to reconcile with the UCC itself.

We find the case-by-case approach injects uncertainty into the UCC, an area of the law in which uniformity and certainty are highly valued. [Citing former UCC § 1-102(2)(c)] . . . It leads to results which are difficult to reconcile with the provisions of the UCC, and has been criticized as having no basis in the UCC or its comments. 31 VAL. U.L. REV. at 132. We decline to adopt it.

Rather, we agree with the reasoning in *Chatlos Systems*, and adopt the independent approach. The independent approach is more in line with the UCC and with contract law in general. Nothing in the text or the official comments to section 2-719 indicates that where a contract contains both a limitation of remedy and an exclusion of consequential damages, the latter shares the fate of the former. To the contrary, as noted in *Chatlos Systems*, the different standards for evaluating the two provisions-"failure of essential purpose" versus "unconscionability"-strongly suggest their independence. *See also* 1 WHITE AND SUMMERS' UNIFORM COMMERCIAL CODE § 12-10(c), at 668 (4th ed. 1995) (endorsing the independent approach as most in accord with considerations of freedom of contract).

When a contract contains a limitation of remedy but that remedy fails of its essential purpose, it is as if that limitation of remedy does not exist for purposes of the damages to which a plaintiff is entitled for breach of warranty. . . . When a contract contains a consequential damages exclusion but no limitation of remedy, it is incontrovertible that the exclusion is to be enforced unless unconscionable. . . . Why, then, would a limitation of remedy failing of its essential purpose destroy a consequential damages exclusion in the same contract? We see no valid reason to so hold.

Indeed, the dependent approach operates to nullify all consequential damage exclusions in contracts which also contain limitations of remedy. For if the limited remedy fails of its essential purpose, the consequential damages exclusion would also automatically fall – regardless of whether it is unconscionable – and if the limitation of remedy does not fail of its essential purpose, the buyer would not be entitled to consequential damages in any event; he would be entitled only to the specified limited remedy.

The two provisions – limitation of remedy and exclusion of consequential damages – can be visualized as two concentric layers of protection for a seller. What a seller would most prefer, if something goes wrong with a product, is simply to repair or replace it, nothing more. This "repair or replacement" remedy is an outer wall, a first defense. If that wall is breached, because the limited remedy has failed of its essential purpose, the seller still would prefer at least not to be liable for potentially unlimited consequential damages, and so he builds a second inner rampart as a fallback position. That inner wall is higher, and more difficult to scale – it falls only if unconscionable.

The independent approach has not been immune to criticism, of course. The Eighth Circuit has rejected the independent approach under Minnesota law, based on the concern that "a buyer when entering into a contract does not anticipate that the sole remedy available will be rendered a nullity, thus causing additional damages." *Soo Line R.R. Co. v. Fruehauf Corp.*, 547 F.2d 1365, 1373 (8th Cir. 1977) (applying Minnesota law). Additionally, one commentator has chastised the independent approach for "rel[ying] on imprecise assumptions about the parties' intent and an unpersuasive interpretation of section 2-719." K. Murtagh, Note, *UCC Section 2-719: Limited Remedies and Consequential Damage Exclusions*, 74 CORNELL L. REV. 359, 362 (1989) (concluding that independent approach is "inherently weak"). This article suggests that by engaging in "literal construction of the parties' contract," the independent approach "encourages overly formalistic drafting," which "unfairly favors the party who can afford sophisticated bargaining techniques to ensure the use of his contract terms." 74 CORNELL L. REV. at 363. The article also contends that it is erroneous to conclude that the parties intend to shift the risk of consequential loss to the buyer, because "[t]he language structure itself does not indicate that the parties even considered the possibility of the ineffective limited remedy." 74 CORNELL L. REV. at 364. *Adams* and *Jones & McKnight,* two of the earliest cases adopting the dependent approach, implicitly concluded that the independent approach was simply unfair to the buyer. See *Adams,* 261 N.E.2d 1; *Jones & McKnight,* 320 F. Supp. at 43-44.

We recognize these objections to the independent approach, but do not find them compelling. The reasoning in *Adams* and *Jones & McKnight,* for example, is based on the seller's failure to perform being willful. This incorporates considerations of bad faith on the part of the seller. As we discuss below, the seller's bad faith is a possible basis for finding enforcement of a limitation of consequential damages to be unconscionable. However, the dependent approach strips away limitations of consequential damages whenever a limited remedy fails of its essential purpose, without regard to the good or bad faith of the seller, which we believe goes too far.

The objections to the independent approach in *Soo Line* and the law review article noted above are similarly unpersuasive. Both argue that the independent approach is unfair because the buyer may not intend to renounce consequential damages when the limited remedy has failed of its essential purpose. *Soo Line,* 547 F.2d at 1373; 74 CORNELL L. REV. at 364. But this seems to ignore the plain language of the contract in a fundamental way – for if the buyer does not intend to renounce consequential damages when the limited remedy has failed, in what context *could* the disclaimer of consequential damages operate? As noted above, we believe this is a fundamental defect in the dependent approach, that it renders the disclaimer of consequential damages an utter nullity. If a limited remedy has *not* failed of its essential purpose, that is of course the buyer's only remedy, by definition – this is what it means to have a limited remedy. So in this circumstance a disclaimer of limited damages would be of no effect because it would be redundant. If, as the above critics argue, the disclaimer of limited damages ought not to be enforced when the limited remedy *has* failed of its essential purpose, the language would never have any effect. Moreover, to the extent that the independent approach encourages parties to pay attention in the drafting process (see 74 Cornell L.Rev. at 363), we see this as a point in favor of the independent approach, rather than the contrary. . . .

Moreover, we disagree with the reasoning, although not necessarily the result, in *Adams.* There, in refusing to enforce the consequential damages limitation, our appellate court focused on the allegedly tortious nature of defendants' conduct which caused the limited remedy to fail of its essential purpose. The court concluded that defendants were entitled to none of the protections included in the contract because they had "repudiat[ed] . . . their obligations under the warranty." This implies that the sellers' alleged bad faith in repudiating their obligations under the warranty played a part in the analysis – but the dependent approach does not take the seller's good or bad faith into account. Under the dependent approach, the seller is stripped of the protection of a consequential damages disclaimer once a limited remedy has failed of its essential purpose, *regardless* of the seller's good or bad faith.

A seller's deliberate or negligent failure to supply a limited remedy can be taken into consideration in determining whether enforcement of a consequential damages waiver is unconscionable. The unconscionability determination is not restricted to the facts and circumstances in existence at the time the contract was entered into. . . . Indeed, section 2-719(3) itself expressly provides that matters which become known only subsequent to the drafting of the contract – *i.e.,* the type of injuries suffered as a result of breach – are relevant to the unconscionability calculus. . . . As many of the authorities favoring the dependent approach have noted, there is rarely any basis for concluding that when the parties entered into their contract, the buyer intended to assume the risk of the seller's willful or negligent default on his only obligation for breach of warranty. It may well be that in a case such as *Adams,* where the defendant is alleged to have acted in bad faith, the correct result would be to declare a consequential damages exclusion unenforceable. . . . Accordingly, we believe that a plaintiff must be allowed to point to a defendant's conduct, or any other circumstance which he believes would make enforcement of a consequential damages exclusion unconscionable. But the plain language of the UCC indicates that this step, of evaluating whether the exclusion is unconscionable, must be taken before a contractual consequential damages exclusion may be done away with. . . .

We conclude that the independent approach is the better-reasoned and more in accordance with the plain language of the UCC. This conclusion is buttressed by the fact that a majority of jurisdictions to consider the issue have adopted the independent approach. Illinois generally follows the majority interpretation of UCC provisions, in order to serve the underlying UCC policy of " 'mak[ing] uniform the law among the various jurisdictions.' " *Connick v. Suzuki Motor Co.,* 675 N.E.2d 584 (Ill. 1996), quoting [§ 1-102(2)(c)]. Contractual limitations or exclusions of consequential damages will be upheld unless to do so would be unconscionable, regardless of whether the contract also contains a limited remedy which fails of its essential purpose.

B. *Unconscionability*

Accordingly, the mere fact that the jury found the limited remedy to have failed of its essential purpose does not destroy the provision in the warranty excluding consequential damages. However, this does not mean that the exclusion of consequential damages will necessarily be upheld. Rather, that provision must be judged on its own merits to determine whether its enforcement would be unconscionable. . . .

A determination of whether a contractual clause is unconscionable is a matter of law, to be decided by the court. . . . Unconscionability can be either "procedural" or "substantive" or a combination of both. . . . Procedural unconscionability refers to a situation where a term is so difficult to find, read, or understand that the plaintiff cannot fairly be said to have been aware he was agreeing to it, and also takes into account a lack of bargaining power. . . . Substantive unconscionability refers to those terms which are inordinately one-sided in one party's favor.

Hyundai argues that plaintiff introduced no evidence to support the trial court's determination that the consequential damages exclusion was unconscionable. We disagree. The record reveals a number of facts which tend to support a finding of unconscionability. The warranty was entirely preprinted. Plaintiff – a consumer – had no hand in its drafting, and no bargaining power at all with respect to its terms. Moreover, the clause in question is intended to limit the drafter's liability. Each of these facts leads this court to disfavor the clause. . . . However, we need not – and we do not – hold that these general circumstances alone or in combination render the clause unconscionable.

An additional fact particular to this case tips the balance in plaintiff's favor. That is the lack of evidence that the warranty, which contained the disclaimer of consequential damages, had been made available to the plaintiff at or before the time she signed the sale contract. The warranty and its consequential damages exclusion were contained in the owner's manual, which was placed in the glove compartment of the car, where it was unavailable to the consumer until after she took delivery. No portion of the sale contract contained in the record before us even mentions the warranty. Moreover, plaintiff testified without contradiction that she never saw any part of the written warranty, much less the disclaimer of consequential damages, until she looked in her owner's manual after she had signed the contract and driven the car off the lot. Thus, *on this record,* we must conclude that the warranty information, including the disclaimer of consequential damages, was not made available to the plaintiff at or before the time she signed the purchase contract.

In its petition for rehearing, Hyundai argues that the disclaimer is not procedurally unconscionable because it was written in capital letters in "plain, simple, understandable language, not legalese," that was "easy to see and easy to read." These aspects of the disclaimer are irrelevant, however, in the case of a limitation of liability withheld from the buyer until after the purchase contract has been signed. It simply does not matter how large the type was or how clearly the disclaimer was expressed if the consumer did not have the opportunity to *see* the language before entering into the contract to purchase the car. . . . As previously noted, procedural unconscionability refers to a situation where a term is so difficult to find, read, or understand that the plaintiff cannot fairly be said to have been aware he was agreeing to it. Surely, whatever other context there might be in which a contractual provision would be found to be procedurally unconscionable, that label must apply to a situation such as the case at bar where plaintiff has testified that she never saw the clause; nor is there any basis for concluding that plaintiff *could* have seen the clause, before entering into the sale contract. "[A] limitation of liability given to the buyer after he makes the contract is ineffective." *Frank's Maintenance,* 408 N.E.2d 403. . . .

II. Warranty Damages

. . . . Because the limited remedy failed of its essential purpose, plaintiff was entitled to pursue the other remedies afforded by the UCC. . . . Under the UCC, "The measure of damages for breach of warranty is the difference at the time and place of acceptance between the value of the goods accepted and the value they would have had if they had been as warranted, unless special circumstances show proximate damages of a different amount." [UCC § 2-714(2)] . . . . [The court remanded for a new trial on the damages question, as the trial court erred in excluding plaintiff's testimony regarding the car's value.–ed.]

CONCLUSION

For the reasons given above, the judgment of the appellate court is affirmed in part and reversed in part, and the judgment of the circuit court is also affirmed in part and reversed in part. We remand for a new trial on the issue of warranty damages. . . .

Justice McMORROW, dissenting from denial of rehearing

I initially joined the majority opinion in this case. I remain in agreement with the majority in its adoption of the independent approach in analyzing limitations of remedy and disclaimers of consequential damages. However, in light of arguments regarding unconscionability that were raised in Hyundai's petition for rehearing, as well as subsequent changes made by the court to its opinion, I believe that rehearing should be allowed. . . . [Discussion of the Magnuson Moss Act and regulations are omitted.]

I note, in addition, that there are difficulties with the majority's unconscionability holding even when considered solely as a matter of state contract law, without reference to the federal regulations. In finding Hyundai's consequential damages disclaimer unconscionable, the majority concludes that this exclusion is void and unenforceable as a matter of public policy. The clear implication of such a holding is that Hyundai did something wrong, such as hiding the exclusion "in a maze of fine print." *Frank's Maintenance & Engineering, Inc. v. C.A. Roberts Co.,* 408 N.E.2d 403 (Ill. Ct. App. 1980). However, in the case at bar Hyundai committed no such infraction. Instead, Hyundai's transgression was that it failed to make the warranty "available to the plaintiff at or before the time she signed the sale contract." 854 N.E.2d at 623. This raises the question of how Hyundai could have avoided this transgression and ensured that the warranty was conveyed to plaintiff. The majority insists that the inclusion of the warranty in the purchase contract is not the only way in which "plaintiff could . . . have received the warranty." There are other possibilities, the majority asserts, but these possibilities are not identified. 854 N.E.2d at 623–24.

If the warranty must be made available to the consumer at or before the time the purchase contract is signed, and if, as the majority concludes, the warrantor may not rely on the seller to meet this responsibility, then there is, in my view, only one possible way in which the warrantor could satisfy this obligation. The warrantor must have a representative physically present on the seller's premises to make sure that the warranty is conveyed to the consumer, thereby ensuring the warranty's enforceability. A moment's reflection reveals the unreasonableness of such a requirement. Under the majority's holding, which is not limited to automobile manufacturers, any manufacturer who warrants a product sold at a retail outlet would need to hire representatives for each of the many such outlets that sold the manufacturer's products. This is an impossible burden to place on the manufacturer. It is unreasonable for the majority to hold Hyundai responsible for failing to do something that cannot realistically be achieved.

There is another way in which the majority's decision here is objectionable. The majority reasons that, because Hyundai's consequential damages disclaimer was not provided to plaintiff at or before the time she signed the purchase contract, this exclusion was not part of the agreement and is void and unenforceable. However, according to the record evidence cited by the majority, it was the entire warranty, and not just the consequential damages exclusion, that was unavailable to plaintiff at the time she signed the contract. As the majority asserts:

> [P]laintiff testified without contradiction that she never saw any part of the written warranty, much less the disclaimer of consequential damages, until she looked in her owner's manual after she had signed the contract and driven the car off the lot. Thus, *on this record,* we must conclude that the warranty information, including the disclaimer of consequential damages, was not made available to the plaintiff at or before the time she signed the purchase contract. (Emphasis in original.)

854 N.E.2d at 623.

Under the majority's reasoning, if the consequential damages exclusion is void because it was not made available to plaintiff and was not part of the agreement entered into by plaintiff, the same is also true of the warranty as a whole. It follows that, if the warranty itself is void, *i.e.,* not part of the agreement, plaintiff should not be able to bring suit against Hyundai under the warranty. Nevertheless, in the case at bar, the majority holds, *sua sponte,* that Hyundai's exclusion is void because it was not conveyed to plaintiff. The majority does not, however, reach the same conclusion regarding the warranty as a whole. This is inconsistent.

The majority's holding regarding Hyundai's consequential damages disclaimer is objectionable for yet another reason. In my view, the majority's decision on this issue is detrimental to consumers. By holding that Hyundai's consequential damages exclusion is unenforceable because Hyundai failed to do something that it could not realistically accomplish, the majority is discouraging manufacturers from offering written warranties at all. While a manufacturer's decision to provide such warranties undoubtedly is influenced by competitive pressures, the benefits of offering a warranty will be considerably diminished if the manufacturer has no control over the scope of the warranty offered. Under the majority's holding, the ability of a manufacturer to control this scope through exclusions such as a disclaimer of consequential damages is severely constrained, if not eliminated. Faced with such a prospect, a manufacturer might very well conclude that it is no longer cost effective to offer a written warranty. Such a result would indeed be anticonsumer. . . .

Because of my disagreement with the majority on these points, I respectfully dissent from the modification of the opinion upon denial of rehearing. It is my belief that this court could benefit from briefing on these matters. I note, too, that this court allows successive petitions for rehearing where a majority opinion has been modified upon denial of rehearing. In light of the extensive modifications made by the majority here, I suggest the filing of such a petition. For the foregoing reasons, I vote to grant Hyundai's petition for rehearing.

Problem 5-9

Given the different standards applicable to liquidated damages clauses and limitations on remedy, it is important to distinguish between them. What is the difference, given that each may place a cap on damages?

CISG and UNIDROIT Principles. CISG Article 6 allows the parties to alter the effect of any of the CISG provisions. It does not specifically address limited remedies or liquidated damages terms. The UNIDROIT Principles allow for a specified sum of money as damages regardless of actual harm suffered. That agreed sum can be reduced if it is "grossly excessive" in relation to the harm suffered. UNIDROIT Art. 7.4.13. The Principles also allow for a limited remedy to be provided if such a remedy is not "grossly unfair" in light of the contract purposes. UNIDROIT Art. 7.1.6.

SECTION 2.   PROVING THE TERMS OF THE CONTRACT: THE PAROL EVIDENCE RULE

Suppose the parties have reached an agreement that is enforceable as a contract under Article 2. Some or all of the terms of the agreement are contained in a writing that is signed by both parties. After performance commences, a dispute erupts over the obligations under the contract. The dispute may involve the meaning of the terms included in the writing. Alternatively, the dispute may involve a term that one party alleges that both sides had agreed to but which is not included in the writing. In either case, there is an honest disagreement. What evidence is admissible to determine meaning of terms in the writing? What evidence is admissible with respect to alleged terms that are not included in the writing? The place to start the analysis is with section 2-202, Article 2's version of the parol evidence rule.[7] Review as well the material in Chapter Three regarding usage of trade, course of dealing, and course of performance. UCC § 1-303.

The parol evidence rule operates as a gate keeper that determines what evidence the finder of fact may consider in deciding to what terms the parties have agreed. In general, it restricts the parties' ability to introduce evidence that would contradict a writing that memorializes their agreement. Do not confuse the parol evidence rule with the statute of frauds, which we studied in Chapter Two. Although both serve the same general goal (encouraging written terms) – the statute of frauds may require a writing for an agreement to be enforceable and the parol evidence rule gives primacy to certain writings by not allowing the parties to contradict them – they have very different scopes. Indeed, it would be the extremely unusual case that presented problems under both rules. Statute of frauds problems tend to arise only when there is no signed writing; parol evidence rule questions arise only when there is a writing adopted by both parties. Moreover, the two rules have different effects. If the parties' agreement does not satisfy the statute of frauds, the agreement is unenforceable. If the parol evidence rule excludes evidence of some alleged terms, the remainder of the agreement is still enforceable, only the excluded terms are affected.

The first question to ask in any dispute about the parol evidence rule is whether the rule applies at all. Read section 2-202. For the rule to apply, the parties must have a writing "intended by the parties as a final expression of their agreement with respect to such terms as are included therein." This requirement of a final written expression is often phrased as a question whether the parties have intended to at least partially "integrate" their agreement into the writing. *Cf.* RESTATEMENT (SECOND) OF CONTRACTS § 210. Intent to partially integrate terms of the agreement into a writing means that the parties intended that, as to the terms discussed in the writing, the writing's terms are final.   This partial integration should be distinguished from what is referred to as a "full integration." A full integration means that the parties intended not only that the writing be final as to what the writing addresses, but also that the writing is complete: that all the terms agreed to were expressed in the writing. Thus in a fully integrated writing, the terms stated

---

[7] Even though these materials will refer to a "writing," electronic records may also be the subject of a parol evidence rule dispute. *See* Electronic Signatures in Global and National Commerce Act (E-Sign), 15 U.S.C. § 7001; Uniform Electronic Transactions Act (UETA) § 7.

in the writing are the final, complete, and exclusive statement of the terms in the record. Put another way, a fully integrated writing expresses the entire agreement.

Even when the parol evidence rule applies – either because a writing is a final written expression of the parties' agreement or because a writing purports to express the entire agreement – evidence of allegedly supplementary or contradictory terms might be excluded from the jury. However, whether proffered evidence will be excluded depends on several factors:

(i)   whether the writing is a complete and exclusive statement of the parties' agreement (*i.e.,* the entire agreement or fully integrated) or merely a final written expression (*i.e.* partially integrated);

(ii) whether the proffered terms are oral, written or implicit terms based on course of performance, course of dealing, or usage of trade;

(iii) whether the proffered terms supplement or contradict the writing; and

(iv) whether the proffered terms (oral or written) arose prior to the writing or contemporaneously with it.

Problem 5-10

Complete the following chart by noting whether the evidence described would be admissible in the situation described. For example, is evidence of prior, oral supplementary terms admissible when there is a final, written expression of the parties' agreement, but that writing does not purport to contain the entire agreement? Is it admissible if the writing represents the parties' entire agreement (*i.e.,* if the writing is a complete and exclusive statement of the terms)?

Terms Sought to Be Admitted			Final Written Expression	Entire Agreement
Supplementary	Oral	Prior		
		Contemporaneous		
	Written	Prior		
		Contemporaneous		
	Usage of Trade, Course of Dealing & Performance			
Contradictory	Oral	Prior		
		Contemporaneous		
	Written	Prior		
		Contemporaneous		
	Usage of Trade, Course of Dealing & Performance			

As difficult as it may be to isolate and chart out the various rules in section 2-202, it is far more difficult to apply them. These difficulties usually fall into any of three recurring problems.

First, how is the court to distinguish among non-final writings, writings intended as a final expression of the parties' agreement, and writings intended as a complete and exclusive statement of the terms? If you think about it, how can any writing qualify as a complete and exclusive statement if there are indeed prior or contemporaneous agreements? The existence of parol evidence would seem to contradict the very idea that the writing contains the entire agreement of the parties.

Predictably there are differing views on how courts are to go about classifying the writing before them. One approach is to look at the "four corners" of the writing and from that writing and that writing alone determine whether the writing is complete. A merger clause – that is, a clause that expressly states that the parties' negotiations are merged into the writing and that the writing is a complete and exclusive statement of the parties' agreement – is highly probative, albeit not conclusive, on this point. Another approach is to consider the parol evidence itself to determine whether the writing is complete. One suspects that courts following the latter approach may reach a conclusion on the scope of the writing on whether they believe the parol evidence.

The second problem concerns how to distinguish parol evidence that supplements the writing from parol evidence that contradicts it.[8] Various tests have been proposed, including the following:

(i)   parol evidence is inconsistent if it directly contradicts or negates a term in the writing;

(ii) parol evidence is inconsistent if there is the absence of reasonable harmony between the proffered term and the term in the writing;

(iii) the parol evidence is inconsistent if the proffered term is one that the parties would certainly have included in the writing if they had in fact agreed to it; and

(iv) the parol evidence is supplementary if the proffered term is one that might have naturally been omitted from the writing.[9]

The third problem concerns evidence offered to "explain" the terms expressed in the writing. *See* UCC § 2-202. Must the term in the writing be ambiguous in order for explanatory evidence to be admissible? The official comments reject a threshold requirement of ambiguity for the admission of evidence concerning course of performance, course of dealing, and usage of trade. *See* UCC § 2-202 cmt. 1(c). However, that comment does not speak to other types of explanatory evidence and whether it is admissible if the writing is not ambiguous. Here again, approaches differ. Some courts will admit the evidence only if they first conclude the writing is ambiguous. Others follow a more liberal approach and allow in any relevant evidence to explain terms in the writing, including evidence of prior negotiations and agreements. *See* RESTATEMENT (SECOND) OF CONTRACTS § 214.

---

[8] Indeed if there is a merger clause, would not all evidence of prior additional terms be contradictory?

[9] The first two tests are articulated in *Alaska Northern Development, Inc. v. Alyeska Pipeline Service Co.*, 666 P.2d 33 (Alaska 1983), *cert. denied*, 464 U.S. 1041 (1984). The third test comes from the comment to section 2-202. The fourth test is from section 216 of the Restatement (Second) of Contracts.

There are four remaining things about the parol evidence rule to keep in mind. First, the parol evidence rule never bars evidence of subsequent terms. In other words, if one party alleges that the parties, after adopting a final written expression of their agreement, agreed to a new or different term, the parol evidence rule will never keep out evidence of that alleged agreement. However, we have already seen that the parties may, in their written agreement, require that future amendments be in writing. *See* UCC § 2-209(2).

Second, the parol evidence rule does not bar evidence of fraud or mistake, even if that evidence comes from the time period prior to execution of the record.[10]

Third, getting past the parol evidence rules does not mean that the allegedly supplementary or contradictory term will become part of the parties' contract. It merely means that the jury or other fact finder will receive the evidence. If the fact finder does not believe the evidence or is swayed by contrary evidence, the party offering the evidence may still ultimately fail in its efforts. In short, the parol evidence rule is merely a gatehouse to the fact finder, and getting past the gate does not prove the point, it merely enables arguments to be made.

Finally, assuming the evidence is admissible, how is it proven? Trade usage and other context evidence are facts to be established by the moving party. *See* UCC § 1-303. Because these facts are normally not presumed to exist, the moving party has the "burden of establishing" them, *i.e.*, that party must persuade the "trier of fact that the existence of the fact is more probable than its nonexistence." UCC § 1-201(b)(8). The moving party, therefore, has both the burden of production and the burden of persuasion.

As you ponder the parol evidence rule and attempt to solve the problems below, consider what purposes the rule serves. Why should terms in a writing be accorded more respect than terms not in a writing? If you were drafting a written agreement for the parties to sign, what would you put in the document in order to exclude the types of evidence that may otherwise be used to explain, supplement, or contradict terms in that document?

---

[10] *See, e.g.,* David Frisch & John D. Wladis, *U.C.C. Survey: General Provisions, Sales, Bulk Transfers, and Documents of Title*, 47 BUS. LAW. 1517, 1520–21 (1992); RESTATEMENT (SECOND) OF CONTRACTS § 214.

Problem 5-11

Fiber Industries sold fiber to carpet manufacturers for use in making carpets. Salem Carpet bought trademark fiber from Fiber Industries on an order-by-order basis. There were no written documents other than the individual purchase orders and acknowledgment forms. Both Salem's purchase order form and Fiber Industries' acknowledgment form contained "merger" clauses, which provided that the form "contains all the terms and conditions of the purchase agreement and shall constitute the complete and exclusive agreement between Seller and Purchaser." In August, Fiber Industries announced that it was withdrawing from the carpet industry, but that it would supply all customers in an "orderly fashion" until the phase-out was complete. Salem accepted a final order of fiber at a contract price of $407,128.40, but refused to pay the full amount because of losses suffered as a result of Fiber Industries' withdrawal from the market. Salem claimed that there was a "customary practice" in the carpet industry obligating Fiber Industries to fill all orders made by Salem during the projected market life of any carpet style which utilized fiber manufactured by Fiber Industries. Salem was prepared to establish a usage that the "carpet manufacturer will continue to make its branded fiber available for the useful life of the carpet style or for sufficient time to allow the carpet manufacturer to produce and sell sufficient carpet to recoup the large start-up expenses incurred in introducing and marketing a new line of branded carpet."

A. Assume that both contract forms were silent on the issue. Assume, further, that the usage could be established. Should the court admit evidence of the usage?

B. Assume that instead of establishing that evidence under the rubric of "usage of trade," Salem wanted to introduce evidence to the same effect based upon the discussions of the parties that occurred before Salem ordered the fiber. Again assume that both contract forms were silent on the issue. Should that evidence be admitted?

C. Assume that Salem's purchase order provided that the seller of goods that are supplied pursuant to the purchase order promises to "support the integration of all materials supplied to the buyer into the carpet manufactured by the buyer." Assume that under the analysis pursuant to section 2-207, that term in the purchase order was part of the parties' agreement.   Salem argues that the usage of trade evidence will demonstrate what was meant by that term.

1.   Assuming the usage of trade is established, should evidence of that usage be admitted?

2.   Assume that instead of establishing that evidence under the rubric of "usage of trade," Salem wanted to introduce evidence to the same effect based upon the discussions of the parties that occurred before Salem ordered the fiber. Should that evidence be admitted?

Problem 5-12

Lomborg, a boat dealer, advertised a 42 foot Pearson sailing sloop for sale. The boat was manufactured in 1960 and had a wooden hull. Fisk, an experienced sailor, had never purchased a sloop with a wooden hull. Without the assistance of a third party, Fisk examined the boat carefully and could find nothing wrong. Fisk questioned Lomborg who, at various times stated:

"This beauty was her owner's pride and joy";

"It's in great shape";

"The boat is sound";

"It rides the waves like a dream";

"The wood is solid throughout"; and

"We will replace any dry rot free of charge."

After hearing all of these statements, Fisk agreed to buy the sloop for $50,000.   Fisk purchased the boat for personal use. At the time of contracting, Fisk signed a writing prepared by Lomborg which, on the front, provided in part as follows:

> WARRANTIES. Buyer is buying the goods AS IS WHERE IS and no representations or statements have been made by seller except as herein stated, so that no warranty, express or implied, arises apart from this writing.

Fisk took delivery of the boat, paid the purchase price and went for a long, wet sail. The boat appeared to leak at the stern. Fisk hired an expert to inspect the area and that expert found extensive dry rot, which had clearly been there at the time of the sale. The estimated cost to repair the boat was $15,000.

A. Fisk claimed damages for breach of warranty. Lomborg argued that all warranties, express or implied, had been disclaimed. Is Lomborg correct? Review section 2-316.

B. Should it matter when the disclaimers were delivered to Fisk? Suppose the writing with the disclaimers was delivered to Fisk after Fisk signed a purchase agreement to buy the boat?

CISG and UNIDROIT Principles. Article 11 of the CISG provides that no writing is required for an enforceable contract. Article 8 allows "all relevant circumstances" to be used to determine the intent of the parties. Article 9 allows for reliance on usage of trade and practices the parties have established between themselves. Thus, the CISG does not provide a screen for the admissibility of evidence that is comparable to the parol evidence rule. The UNIDROIT Principles are of similar effect, relying on interpretation based upon all relevant circumstances. UNIDROIT Arts. 4.1 through 4.7. However, if the document has a merger clause indicating that the document contains the complete agreement of the parties, the terms in that document cannot be contradicted or supplemented by evidence or prior statements or agreements. Those prior statements or agreements may, however, by used to explain the terms of the document. UNIDROIT Art. 2.1.17.

CHAPTER SIX

PERFORMANCE ISSUES

In this Chapter, we consider four matters relevant to the parties' obligations to perform: (i) assignment of contract rights and delegation of contract duties; (ii) a party's authority to terminate a contract for a reason other than breach; (iii) what recourse a party has when it becomes insecure about whether the other will perform and the effect of a repudiation; and (iv) excuse. There is no theme connecting these different concepts and rules, but all are worth studying before we move on to the next Chapter, where we begin in earnest to study breach and its effects.

SECTION 1.   ASSIGNMENT AND DELEGATION

Often one or both parties to a sales contract wish to transfer its contractual rights or obligations to someone else. When that is the case, any one or more of several questions may arise. For example, may the seller delegate its obligation to deliver conforming goods to another person? If the seller does delegate performance, must the buyer accept performance from that new person? May the seller assign to another person the seller's right to the payment due from the buyer? If so, does the buyer have to pay that other person? Similarly, may the buyer assign to another person the buyer's right to receive the goods, and if so, must the seller tender performance to that assignee? May the buyer delegate to someone else its obligation to pay for the goods, and if it does, will the seller have any recourse against the buyer if the delegatee does not pay?

The Article 2 provision on assignment and delegation, section 2-210, builds upon the common-law principles in this area. Unfortunately, in many first-year courses on contracts, assignment and delegation principles are not covered. Thus, for many students, this will be new material and for others it will be a summary review of these principles.

The first place to start is to get the terminology straight. Rights are *assigned*, duties are *delegated*. Thus, for example, the seller in an Article 2 contract has the obligation to deliver conforming goods in accordance with the contract terms and the right to receive payment in accordance with the contract terms. If the seller and a third person agree that the third person will tender the conforming goods to the buyer, the seller has *delegated* its obligation to perform. If, in contrast, the seller transfers the right to payment under the contract to a third person, the seller will have *assigned* its right. Similarly, a buyer may assign its right to receive goods or delegate its obligation to pay for them.

It is of course possible to assign rights and delegate duties to the same person, but that is not necessary. A buyer or seller may assign rights without delegating duties, or may delegate duties without assigning rights. Similarly, a buyer or seller may delegate duties to one person and assign rights to another.

How is an assignment of rights or a delegation of duties effectuated? Generally an assignment requires an agreement between the assignor and the assignee. Similarly, a delegation requires an agreement between the delegator and the delegatee. RESTATEMENT (SECOND) OF CONTRACTS §§ 327, 328.

The most interesting questions are: (i) whether the counter-party to the contract must agree to the other party's assignment or delegation to the third person, (ii) whether a contractual prohibition on assignment or delegation is effective; and (iii) what effect a delegation or assignment has on the parties to the contract.

Let's start with delegation. Read section 2-210(1), (6). It provides that parties are free – absent agreement to the contrary – to delegate their contractual duties. There is an exception, however, if the other party has a substantial interest in having the original promisor perform. Given the nature of the parties' primary duties – the seller to tender conforming goods and the buyer to pay for them – the buyer is far more likely than the seller to have a substantial interest in having its contracting party, rather than a delegatee, perform. Do you see why?

The rules regarding assignments are similar. Read section 2-210(2) and (3). Absent agreement to the contrary, each party is free to assign its right to receive performance from the other, and such an assignment does not generally require the consent of the person that is to render the performance. Thus, in a very typical case, the seller in an Article 2 transaction assigns to a third party its rights to receive payment from the buyer. The buyer in such a case generally has no ground for objection because the duty to pay is not affected much by the identity of the payee. In fact, many sellers regularly assign their rights to receive payment from buyers as a way of obtaining the funds needed to finance the seller's business.[1] Because of

---

[1] This assignment is in fact an Article 9 transaction in which the assignment of the seller's right to receive payment (generally an account, in Article 9 terminology) is the creation of a security interest in that right to payment. The Article 9 rules on assignment of rights to payment are contained in sections 9-403 through 9-409 and generally have the same thrust as stated in section 2-210(3). The creation of a security interest in the right to payment that is generated out of an Article 2 sales contract is governed by Article 9.

the need to permit such free transfers of payment rights, even if the agreement between the buyer and seller purports to prohibit the seller from assigning its right to payment, the seller will nevertheless be permitted to do so, and making such an assignment will not constitute a breach of the contract with the buyer. *See* UCC §§ 2-210(3), 9-406(d).

Assignment is prohibited, even in the absence of a clause prohibiting assignment, if it would materially change the duty of the other party, materially change its duty, or materially increase the risk that it will not receive the return performance. UCC § 2-210(2). This limitation is most likely to apply to an effort of the buyer to assign its rights.

Problem 6-1

Fill out the chart below to show whether the assignment or delegation is allowed and, if permitted only in limited circumstances, what the applicable standard is.

	Assignment		Delegation	
	By Buyer	By Seller	By Buyer	By Seller
No Contractual Prohibition				
Contractual Prohibition				

In general, whenever one party assigns rights to a third party, the assignee steps into the shoes of the assignor and has the same rights as the assignor. To illustrate, assume a seller assigns its right to receive payment from the buyer. Once the buyer is notified of the assignment and instructed to pay the assignee, the buyer generally may discharge its obligation to pay only by rendering its performance (payment) to the assignee. RESTATEMENT (SECOND) OF CONTRACTS § 338; UCC § 9-406(a). However, absent an agreement by the buyer to the contrary, the buyer will retain the ability to assert against the assignee the same defenses to payment that the buyer could have asserted against the assignor/seller. *See* RESTATEMENT (SECOND) OF CONTRACTS §§ 336, 337; UCC §§ 9-403, 9-404.

The effect of a delegation is a bit different. A delegation of duties does impose the duty to perform on the delegatee. However, it does not normally relieve the delegating party of the obligation to perform. Thus, for example, if the seller delegates its duty to tender conforming goods to a third party, the third party becomes obligated to perform and seller remains responsible for any unexcused failure of that third party to perform.[2] Similarly, if the buyer delegates the duty to pay, and the delegatee does not pay in accordance with the contract terms, the seller will be permitted to seek relief against both the buyer and the delegatee (but will be limited to a single satisfaction).[3]

Problem 6-2

Seller agreed to sell specially manufactured goods to Buyer in return for a price. Seller and Buyer negotiated extensively over the specifications for the goods and one of the terms is that Buyer must approve the prototype that Seller will create before creating a full production run. Buyer is obligated to pay Seller for production of the prototype, if the prototype is satisfactory to Buyer.

A. Seller assigned the contract to Manufacturer, who accepted the assignment. Manufacturer has created the prototype. While there does not appear to be anything wrong with the prototype, Buyer does not want to deal with Manufacturer, preferring to deal with Seller. Does Buyer have to accept the prototype from Manufacturer? Does Buyer have to pay Manufacturer? How, if at all, would the analysis change if the contract between Seller and Buyer prohibited assignment?

---

[2] The seller would, however, be discharged of this responsibility if the buyer had agreed to a novation; that is, if the buyer had agreed to accept the third party's performance and to discharge the seller of the duty. *See* RESTATEMENT (SECOND) OF CONTRACTS § 318(3) & cmt. d.

[3] For the relationship between delegation of duties and suretyship principles, *see* Gary L. Monserud, *The Privileges of Suretyship for Delegating Parties Under UCC Section 2-210 in Light of the New Restatement of Suretyship*, 37 WM. & MARY L. REV. 1307 (1996).

B. Buyer assigned the contract to Best Company, which accepted the assignment. Seller created the prototype but does not want to deal with Best Company. What would you tell Seller? Would it matter if the contract between Seller and Buyer prohibited all contract assignments?

CISG and UNIDROIT Principles. The CISG does not address issues of assignment of rights and delegation of duties. Chapter 9 of the UNIDROIT Principles contains numerous rules regarding assignment and delegation. These principles mirror the common-law approach described above with one notable exception. The baseline presumption is that the counter-party must consent to the assignment. UNIDROIT Art. 9.3.3. That basic presumption is subject to an exception if it is an assignment of the right to payment of a monetary obligation which may be assigned even though there is a term in the parties' agreement prohibiting assignment. UNIDROIT Art. 9.1.9. Such an assignment in contravention of an anti-assignment term is effective, although it is a breach of the contract between the assignor and the counter-party.

SECTION 2.   TERMINATION OF A CONTRACT

Article 2 uses two different terms to refer to the premature ending of a contract for the sale of goods: cancellation and termination. Cancellation is a right that an aggrieved buyer or seller has upon the other's breach. *See* UCC §§ 2-106(4), 2-703(f), 2-711(1). Termination, in contrast, refers to putting an end to a contract for a reason other than breach. Read section 2-106(3). The effect of termination is to discharge all executory (*i.e.* unperformed) obligations of the parties without further liability. However, rights and remedies are preserved to the extent they accrue from obligations due before the termination becomes effective. UCC § 2-106(3).

Typically, termination is something that occurs when the contract calls for the seller to provide goods to the buyer over an extended period of time. For example, the contract may call for the seller to provide either a stated quantity of goods each month or all of the buyer's requirements. The agreement may say nothing about termination, may identify a specific termination date, or may provide for termination upon the occurrence of a particular event or upon notification by either party of a decision to terminate.

If the agreement provides for termination upon a stated time or event, then that provision will govern termination, subject to the usual exceptions for lack of mutual assent, unconscionability, modification, and the like. If the agreement does not provide for termination upon an agreed time or event, then either party may terminate by giving reasonable notification to the other. *See* UCC § 2-309(2), (3). As to how far in advance a notification must be given to be "reasonable," consult section 1-205 on reasonable time. One test that courts have used is whether the notification was given in sufficient time for the recipient to obtain substitute arrangements or performance.[4]

The right to terminate is, of course, subject to the duty of good faith, UCC § 1-304, but that does not mean that the terminating party needs a good reason to terminate the contract. Consider the following discussion of good faith in *Santa Fe Custom Shutters & Doors, Inc. v. Home Depot U.S.A., Inc.*, 113 P.3d 347, 358–60 (N.M. Ct. App.), *cert. denied*, 113 P.3d 345 (N.M. 2005), in which a shutter manufacturer sued a retailer for terminating their contract after the manufacturer, in reliance on their contract, spent considerable sums to expand production:

> SFCS argues that notwithstanding the at-will nature of its business relationship with Home Depot, we should treat Home Depot's exercise of its right to terminate its relationship with SFCS as a breach of the duty of good faith. SFCS argues that unless we apply the duty of good faith to limit Home Depot's right to terminate,
>
> > [Home Depot] would be free to (a) entice, through misrepresentation, a company like [SFCS] to enter into a contractual relationship of indefinite duration requiring enormous up-front investments and debt, (b) promise a partnership likely to produce substantial profits, (c) fail to keep binding promises to professionally market the company's product, and (d) before the anticipated profits could be realized, terminate the arrangement in breach of any notion of good faith and fair dealing.
>
> We agree with SFCS that the implied duty of good faith applies in the context of a termination of a contract of indefinite duration. That does not mean, however, that the general duty of good faith overrides the right to terminate "at any time" specifically conferred by [UCC § 2-309(2)].
>
> There can be no question that the broad terms of UCC § 1-203 [rev. UCC § 1-304] [recognizing an implied duty of good faith]

---

[4] *See Coburn Supply Co. v. Kohler Co.*, 342 F.3d 372 (5th Cir. 2003).

mandate that the limitation of good faith apply to all actions taken under the authority of the Code. This, however, does not answer the question of what is meant by "good faith" in the context of a notice to terminate an indefinite duration contract. The very absence of any predicate that must be established as a condition precedent to terminating the contract emphasizes the absence of any significance to the good faith concept in this particular situation.

RONALD A. ANDERSON, ANDERSON ON THE UNIFORM COMMERCIAL CODE § 2-309:49 (3d ed. 1997 rev.). Other leading commentators agree: "We do not believe that ideas of good faith should be used to deprive a terminating party of the rights it would otherwise have under 2-309(2)." 1 JAMES J. WHITE & ROBERT S. SUMMERS, UNIFORM COMMERCIAL CODE 140 (4th ed. 1995). We agree with Home Depot that "[t]he essence of the at-will doctrine is the right of either party to cease doing business without liability for *future* profits the other party hopes it will earn if the relationship continues." (Emphasis added.)

The implied duty of good faith does not confer on a district court "a roving commission to do whatever its wishes in the name of fairness." *Cf. United Props. Ltd. v. Walgreen Props., Inc.,* 82 P.3d 535 (N.M. 2003) (discussing limitations on the authority of a district court exercising equity jurisdiction to relieve a party from the consequences of its failure to exercise an option in accordance with the terms of a lease). If SFCS desired the security of a contract binding Home Depot to a business relationship lasting a specific term of years, it was free to bargain for such a term. In the absence of such a term, Home Depot had the right to terminate its contractual relationship with SFCS "at any time," under [UCC § 309(2)], and this was so without regard to whether the contract had been in effect for a reasonable time when Home Depot terminated the contract. ANDERSON, *supra* at § 2-309:36. The district court concluded that SFCS was entitled to damages for lost profits calculated over a five-year period beginning January 1, 2000. In view of Home Depot's right to terminate its contracts with SFCS at any time, which there is no dispute Home Depot exercised on March 20, and July 17, 2000, the district court's use of the five-year period in calculating benefit-of-the-bargain damages was error.

Our decision does not inexorably lead to the hyperbolically dire consequences predicted by SFCS for several reasons. First, we see no reason for precluding a party who has been fraudulently induced to enter into a contract from electing to recover costs incurred in preparing to perform the contract as an alternative to seeking damages for the loss of the benefit of the bargain. *See* E. ALLAN FARNSWORTH, CONTRACTS § 12.16 (3d ed.1999) (discussing reliance interest as an alternative measure of damages for breach of contract); RESTATEMENT (SECOND) OF TORTS § 549(1)(b) (1977) (recognizing that victim of fraud may recover pecuniary loss suffered as the result of reliance upon the misrepresentation). SFCS could have sought recovery of damages measured by its "enormous" up-front investment; instead, SFCS elected to pursue damages measured by the benefit of the bargain. Second, if the breaching party's representations in fact are binding promises, those promises may be enforced under established principles of contract law. Under our holding, SFCS is entitled to damages based upon profits that would have accrued if Home Depot had professionally marketed SFCS's products and services over the period *prior to* termination. SFCS may also be entitled to *post*-termination damages if the district court determines on remand that Home Depot failed to provide reasonable notification of its decision to terminate its business relations with SFCS and SFCS suffered damages due to the lack of reasonable notification.

Based upon the reasoning of the New Mexico Court of Appeals, what does exercising the right in good faith to terminate a contract mean?

CISG and UNIDROIT Principles. CISG Article 29 provides that a contract may be terminated by agreement and if the contract provides that a termination must be in writing, such a term is enforceable unless a party has waived its right to insist on the writing and the other party has relied on that waiver. The CISG does not seem to address the same issue that section 2-309 addresses, that is the ability to give a notice of termination when the contract does not address the ability to terminate a contract of indefinite duration. The UNIDROIT Principles simply state that either party may end a contract of indefinite duration upon giving notice to the other party a "reasonable time in advance." UNIDROIT Art. 5.1.8.

SECTION 3.   INSECURITY AND REPUDIATION

A. Insecurity and Adequate Assurance

Once a buyer and seller enter into a contract for the sale of goods, either or both of the parties may become uneasy about the ability of the other party to perform. The reasons why a party may become worried that the other party may not perform are as varied as the types of goods and relationships that are the subject matter of "transactions in goods." For example, a defect in a specially manufactured prototype might lead the buyer to question the seller's ability to tender conforming goods. A shortage of needed raw materials may lead the buyer to question the seller's ability to tender any goods at all. A rail strike might imperil the seller's ability to deliver the goods on time. On the other side, news reports that the buyer is experiencing financial difficulty may give the seller concern about the buyer's ability to pay. A decision by the buyer to discontinue certain lines of business may cause the seller to question whether the buyer still wants and will accept the goods called for under the contract. Complaints by the buyer about minor problems with a prototype may give the seller reservations about whether the buyer is seeking an excuse to not perform.[5] What may a party do when it has grounds to question the other party's ability or willingness to perform?

Read section 2-609. It allows a party with reasonable grounds for insecurity to demand adequate assurance of future performance, and to suspend its own performance until it receives such assurances. The first question that must be considered is when does a party have reasonable grounds for insecurity? Notice that a party's reasons will be tested by an objective, not subjective, standard and if the transaction is between merchants, commercial standards apply to determine reasonable grounds for insecurity. UCC § 2-609(2).

Some circumstances are easy to deal with because Article 2 provides a statutory basis for finding the grounds for insecurity to be reasonable. For example, section 2-210(6) expressly provides that delegation of duties provides reasonable grounds

---

[5] *See Brisbin v. Superior Valve Co.*, 398 F.3d 279 (3d Cir. 2005) (buyer's failure to respond timely to seller, not providing results of tests of prototypes, and engaging in "stalling" behavior gave seller reasonable grounds for insecurity regarding buyer's commitment to performing the contract); *Rad Concepts, Inc. v. Wilks Precision Instrument Co.*, 891 A.2d 1148 (Md. Ct. App. 2006) (buyer's failure to pay under one contract gave seller reasonable grounds for insecurity related to another contract).

for insecurity. In addition, if a seller discovers its buyer to be insolvent, the seller has the right to withhold delivery of the goods and insist on a cash payment. UCC § 2-702(1). In other circumstances, the reasonableness of any insecurity will be a question of fact, the resolution of which can be difficult to predict.

If a party has reasonable grounds for insecurity, it may make a written demand of the other for adequate assurance. The concerned party may then suspend its own performance while it awaits the reassurance. If the other party does not respond appropriately, the concerned party may treat that failure as a repudiation, cancel the contract, and pursue remedies for breach. *See* UCC §§ 2-610, 2-703(f), 2-711(1).

The more difficult questions are: (i) for what should the concerned party ask? and (ii) what response would be adequate? Is the concerned party entitled to request that the other party agree to additional obligations that are not part of the contract? Is a response that simply acknowledges the contract and pledges future performance sufficient? There is much uncertainty in this process. That uncertainty is exacerbated by the fact that the concerned party may make a demand for assurance when it in fact does not have reasonable grounds for insecurity or may demand more assurance than it is entitled to receive. Such action in and of itself could give the other party reasonable grounds for insecurity or even constitute a repudiation of the concerned party's obligation under the contract.[6]

TOP OF IOWA COOPERATIVE V. SIME FARMS, INC.
608 N.W.2d 454 (Iowa 2000)

Ternus, Justice

The appellee, Top of Iowa Cooperative, sued the appellant, Sime Farms, Inc., for damages arising out of Sime Farms' failure to deliver corn under four hedge-to-arrive (HTA) contracts. Sime Farms claimed that the contracts were illegal and that, in any event, the Coop had repudiated the contract by making an

---

[6] For good background discussion, *see* Lawrence B. Wardrop, Jr., *Prospective Inability in the Law of Contracts,* 20 MINN. L. REV. 380 (1936); Alan G. Dowling, Note, *A Right to Adequate Assurance of Performance in All Transactions: UCC § 2-609 Beyond Sales of Goods,* 48 S. CAL. L. REV. 1358 (1975). *See also,* R. J. Robertson, Jr., *The Right to Demand Adequate Assurance of Due Performance: Uniform Commercial Code Section 2-609 and Restatement (Second) of Contracts Section 251,* 38 DRAKE L. REV. 305 (1988–89); Larry T. Garvin, *Adequate Assurance of Performance: Of Risk, Duress, and Cognition,* 69 U. COLO. L. REV. 71 (1998).

unreasonable demand for assurances. A jury found in favor of the Coop and awarded damages against Sime Farms. We affirm.

I. *Background Facts and Proceedings*

A. *Hedge-to-arrive contracts.* Before we discuss the particular facts of this case, it is helpful to briefly review the nature of HTA contracts. "[I]n a basic HTA contract, a farmer and grain elevator enter into a contract that contemplates delivery of a specified quantity of grain at a fixed point in time in the future." *Andersons, Inc. v. Horton Farms, Inc.,* 166 F.3d 308, 319 (6th Cir.1998). In a typical HTA contract, the elevator sets the price it is willing to pay based on the open market price on the Chicago Board of Trade (CBOT) for the delivery period, minus what is known as the basis.[7] (The basis is simply the elevator's cost of doing business, such as transportation costs, storage, labor, and utilities, plus a profit.) Upon entering into an HTA contract, the elevator hedges its purchase by simultaneously selling a futures contract on the CBOT, thereby protecting itself from any change in the cash price of corn at the date of delivery.

Although the transaction up to this point is relatively straightforward, there are several complicating factors. First, grain elevators must conduct their trading on the CBOT through licensed brokers. When the price of corn on the futures market rises, the contract with the broker typically requires the elevator to pay what is known as "margin money" – the difference between the original futures contract price and the current futures price – in order to maintain its futures position.[8] The elevator recovers the margin money when it sells the corn delivered by the farmer

---

[7] In the Midwest, the market price for grain such as corn is set on the open market established by the CBOT. During trading hours on the CBOT, contracts are bought and sold for the future delivery of corn in the months of December, March, May, July, and September. Contracts bought and sold on the CBOT are known as "futures contracts." The price established by the CBOT for the buying and selling of grain is widely disseminated to the public.

[8] The requirement of margin payments arises from the nature of futures contracts. One court has explained these contracts in the following manner:

> Parties who enter futures contracts do not agree to pay the price that prevails when they buy the contracts; they agree to pay the price that prevails when the contracts expire (or the positions are closed by offsetting transactions). A contract for September corn, entered into in March, will fluctuate in price until September, when its final price is determined by the price of the cash commodity at the delivery point.

Nagel v. ADM Investor Servs., Inc., 65 F. Supp. 2d 740, 753 (N.D. Ill. 1999).

at a higher cash price.[9] Of course, if the farmer does not deliver, the elevator has no grain to sell, and it cannot recover its margin. Thus, the elevator's hedged position remains risk-free only so long as the farmer can be counted upon to deliver the grain specified under the contract.

In addition, HTA contracts prevalent in the 1990's had two features that distinguished them from traditional grain contracts where the parties agreed on a fixed price for a specified future delivery date. In HTA contracts, the basis was not set at the time of contracting. Rather, the farmer was allowed to choose when to set the basis, provided it was done within the time period specified in the contract. This contract term introduced an element of speculation into the contract, because an elevator's basis generally fluctuated. Consequently, a farmer who delayed setting the basis was open to the risk that the elevator's basis would increase, thereby lowering the price the farmer would receive for his grain.

The second element of risk in HTA contracts is introduced when the farmer is allowed to postpone delivery to a later date. This practice is known as rolling. When the price of grain rises by or near the time set for delivery, the farmer may prefer to sell his grain on the current cash market for a higher price rather than deliver the grain to the elevator for the contract price. Under these circumstances, the parties may agree to modify the contract by delaying, or rolling, the delivery date to a date in the future. To preserve its hedged position, the elevator buys back, at the current price, the futures contract it had previously sold on the CBOT and enters into another futures contract to sell grain on the new delivery date.

The complicating factor in rolling is that the price of corn for the new date of delivery generally is not the same as the current price for the old delivery date. This difference is called the spread. If the new price is higher, the spread is positive and

---

[9] An example will illustrate how hedging works and how it protects the elevator from any price risk. We will make the following assumptions. The Coop contracts to purchase 20,000 bushels of corn from Sime Farms for a December 1995 delivery date. The CBOT price for December 1995 corn is $2.49 at the time of contracting, so Sime Farms is entitled to receive $2.49 minus the basis upon delivery. The Coop hedges this transaction by selling a futures contract on the CBOT at the same price of $2.49. In the months leading to December 1995, the price of December corn rises to $3.00. As the price rises, the broker requires the Coop to pay a total of $ .51 (margin money) to preserve its futures position. Sime Farms delivers the corn in December 1995, as agreed. The Coop pays Sime Farms $2.49 less the basis, which the Coop retains. As noted, the price of December corn is $3.00. The Coop then sells the delivered corn for $3.00, thereby netting $.51 and recovering its margin money. Thus, both parties end up with the proceeds they bargained for in the original contract.

will result in a gain or carry. If the new price is lower, however, it will result in a loss or inverse. This gain or loss is fixed at the time of the roll and is added to or deducted from the new contract price under the rolled HTA contract. Thus, when the farmer decides to roll, he can determine at that time whether he will incur a gain or loss. The problematic risk arises when the farmer rolls to a month when he will not have grain on hand to deliver. He has then exposed himself to an additional, unknown risk because he will have to roll again before he will be able to make the agreed-upon delivery. If the market deteriorates and the price of corn falls, the farmer may ultimately be required to deliver grain at a significant loss.

Unfortunately, this predicament is precisely the situation that faced Sime Farms in the summer of 1996, which brings us to the facts of this case. . . .

B. *Factual background.* Top of Iowa Cooperative is a farmer-owned cooperative that operates in several locations, including Lake Mills, Iowa. Prior to January 1995, the Lake Mills location was owned and operated as the Farmers Coop Elevator Company of Lake Mills. Sime Farms, Inc. is an Iowa corporation wholly owned by Mark Sime. As its name suggests, its business is farming. Sime Farms is a member of the Coop, and for many years prior to the time in question, did nearly all of its grain and agronomy business with the Coop's predecessor, Farmers Coop Elevator Company. (In the remainder of this opinion, we refer to both entities as the Coop.)

In the fall of 1994 and the spring of 1995, Sime Farms entered into three HTA contracts with the Coop. These contracts called for the delivery of a total of 40,000 bushels of corn in December 1995. This grain represented Sime Farms' entire annual corn production. One month before delivery was due under these contracts, Sime Farms contracted to sell an additional 20,000 bushels of corn for delivery in May 1996. The Coop hedged each contract by selling futures contracts on the CBOT for corresponding delivery dates.

In November 1995, Sime Farms rolled its December 1995 delivery dates to March 1996. Although the HTA contracts did not specifically address the ability of Sime Farms to roll, the contracts contemplated this possibility by providing for a fee of one cent per bushel for each roll. Handwritten modifications were made on the contracts indicating the new delivery dates. The contract price was also adjusted to reflect the spread between the current December 1995 futures price and the March 1996 futures price. This adjustment was a positive six cents, a seven-cent carry minus the one-cent roll fee. Sime Farms then sold its 1995 crop on the cash market at a price significantly higher than the December 1995 futures price it had contracted to receive under the original HTA contracts.

Although the roll to March 1996 resulted in a gain or carry, the parties were aware at the time of this roll that a roll to July 1996 or December 1996 would result in a significant inverse, or loss. The parties also knew that Sime Farms would have to roll again into at least December 1996 because it had no grain to deliver until it harvested its 1996 crop.

In February 1996, the contracts were rolled to May 1996. This roll resulted in a gain of slightly less than three cents per bushel, which was added to the contract price. In April 1996, all four contracts were rolled to July 1996. This roll resulted in a thirteen-cent-per-bushel loss or inverse, and so this amount was deducted from the price the Coop agreed to pay Sime Farms for July delivery. By late April 1996, the inverse between July 1996 and December 1996 was around $1.30 per bushel. Because Sime Farms had no corn to deliver in July 1996, it was faced with the prospect of rolling into December 1996 at a significant loss, or breaching its contracts with the Coop. If Sime Farms breached the contracts, the Coop would have to repurchase the offsetting futures it held on the CBOT, resulting in a loss of the margin money it had paid.

By May 1996, the Coop was becoming increasingly concerned about farmers' abilities and willingness to perform on the outstanding HTA contracts. The Coop's manager, Paul Nesler, spoke with Mark Sime at least once in May regarding the inverse situation and the effect of rolling into December. Sime told Nesler that he would get back to the Coop about what he planned to do, but he never did. The Coop's concerns were heightened even further when, that same month, the Iowa Attorney General's office announced that some of the HTA contracts might be "illegal."

On June 6, 1996, the Coop sent a letter to Sime Farms and similarly-situated producers in which the Coop stated that "[i]n response to recent market and non-market developments," the Coop wanted to confirm that its customers holding HTA contracts were capable of and intended to perform. The Coop stated it would consider compliance with the following two conditions as adequate assurance of Sime Farms' ability and willingness to perform:

(1) payment in full of all commissions and margins previously paid by the Coop, or a binding letter of credit obligating an institutional lender to pay such commissions and margins; and

(2) the return of a signed copy of the Coop's letter agreeing to delivery of the agreed-upon quantity of grain on or before the delivery dates set forth in the contracts.

Finally, the Coop stated that a failure to provide the requested assurances would constitute a repudiation of the contract.

The next day Mark Sime came to the Coop to discuss the letter. Nesler informed Sime that Sime Farms could roll its contracts to December 1996 and would not be required to reimburse the Coop for the margin calls already paid. Nesler also told Sime that the Coop would consider a buy-out of the contracts by Sime Farms over a period of time at a low interest rate. Nesler called Sime a few days later to find out what Sime wanted to do. Sime told Nesler that the Coop would be receiving a letter from Sime Farms' lawyer.

The Coop did in fact receive a letter from Sime Farms' attorney later that day. In this letter Sime Farms took the position that the Coop's demand for assurances was an attempt to change the terms of the HTA contracts and that the Coop had no grounds to do so. Sime Farms also asserted the illegality of the contracts under the Commodity Exchange Act, 7 U.S.C. §§ 1-25. Sime Farms' attorney closed his letter by informing the Coop that Sime Farms did "not intend to deliver at a price which includes the losses your elevator agreed to assume in the contract relating to unfavorable margins." Upon receipt of this letter, the Coop terminated the futures positions it held in reliance on the Sime Farms HTA contracts. Sime Farms did not deliver grain under any of the contracts. This lawsuit followed.

C. *Course of the litigation.* The Coop claimed in this lawsuit that Sime Farms breached its contracts with the Coop by failing to give adequate assurances upon the Coop's reasonable demand for such assurances. *See* [§ 2-609] (providing that party's failure to provide adequate assurance after a justified demand is a repudiation of the contract). Sime Farms asserted several counterclaims, including a request for a declaratory judgment that the contracts were illegal and unenforceable under the Commodity Exchange Act. Sime Farms also claimed as an affirmative defense that the Coop breached the contracts by making an unwarranted and unreasonable demand for assurances. . . . [At trial, the trial court held the HTA contracts were not illegal and the jury found for the Coop on the breach of contract claim. – Eds.]

II. *Issues on Appeal*

Sime Farms . . . claims that the Coop, as a matter of law, did not have reasonable grounds to be insecure concerning Sime Farms' performance of the contracts . . . [and] that the Coop's demand for assurances amounted to a repudiation as a matter of law, thereby excusing Sime Farms from performing. . . .

IV. *Was The Trial Court Correct in Ruling That the Coop had Generated a Jury Question on the Issue of Whether the Coop had Reasonable Grounds for Insecurity?*

A. *Statement of issue.* One basis for the Coop's breach of contract claim was that Sime Farms failed to provide reasonable assurances upon the Coop's demand for such assurances. This claim arises from article 2 of the Iowa Uniform Commercial Code, which governs the sale of grain in Iowa. . . . Under the U.C.C., a party to a contract who has reasonable grounds to believe that the other party will be unwilling or unable to perform his contractual obligations may require the party to provide adequate assurances of performance.

Sime Farms sought a directed verdict on the basis that the Coop lacked reasonable grounds for insecurity as a matter of law and, therefore, had no right to make a demand for assurances. The trial court held that the Coop had generated a jury question on the issue of reasonable grounds for insecurity and, accordingly, denied Sime Farms' motion. This ruling is assigned as error on appeal. . . .

C. *Applicable legal principles.* Section [2-609] of the Iowa U.C.C. provides in relevant part:

1. A contract for sale imposes an obligation on each party that the other's expectation of receiving due performance will not be impaired. When reasonable grounds for insecurity arise with respect to the performance of either party the other may in writing demand adequate assurance of due performance and until that party receives such assurance may if commercially reasonable suspend any performance for which that party has not already received the agreed return.

2. Between merchants the reasonableness of grounds for insecurity and the adequacy of any assurance offered shall be determined according to commercial standards.

Because the reasonableness of a party's insecurity is determined by commercial standards, there must be an objective factual basis for the insecurity, rather than a purely subjective fear that the party will not perform. *See* R.J. Robertson, Jr., *The Right to Demand Adequate Assurance of Due Performance: Uniform Commercial*

Code Section 2-609 and Restatement (Second) of Contracts Section 251, 38 DRAKE L. REV. 305, 322 (1988-89).

> Generally, the existence of grounds for insecurity is a question of fact: Whether a party has reasonable grounds for insecurity depends upon many factors including the [party's] exact words or actions, the course of dealing or performance between the particular parties and the nature of the industry. What constitutes reasonable grounds for insecurity in one case might not in another. Consequently, the trier of fact must normally answer whether grounds for insecurity exist.

1 JAMES J. WHITE & ROBERT S. SUMMERS, UNIFORM COMMERCIAL CODE § 6-2, at 286 (4th ed.1995) [hereinafter WHITE & SUMMERS] . . . . Nevertheless, occasions do arise where the undisputed facts establish that insecurity or the lack of insecurity existed as a matter of law. . . .

D. *Discussion.* The Coop's letter to Sime Farms reveals two grounds for insecurity: (1) the inverse in the market; and (2) statements in the press with respect to the unenforceability of HTA contracts. Because neither ground relates specifically to Sime Farms, Sime Farms asserts these facts do not provide reasonable grounds for the Coop to be concerned about Sime Farms' performance.

> "Clearly, the drafters of the Code did not intend that one party to a contract can go about demanding security for performance of the other whenever he gets nervous about a contract. Some reason for the demand for assurances must precede the demand."

Robertson, 38 DRAKE L. REV. at 323 (quoting *Cole v. Melvin,* 441 F. Supp. 193, 203 (D.S.D. 1977)). In many cases, the grounds for insecurity are specifically tied to the party or the contract. *See, e.g., AMF, Inc.,* 536 F.2d at 1170 (holding that where prototype had never performed satisfactorily and evidence existed that seller was not actively working on project, buyer had reasonable grounds for insecurity); *Scott v. Crown,* 765 P.2d 1043, 1046 (Colo. Ct. App. 1988) (finding fact that investigator told seller of active complaints against buyer and that buyer failed to make personal contact after seller refused to load wheat constituted grounds for insecurity). On the other hand, "[a] ground for insecurity need not arise from or be directly related to the contract in question." U.C.C. § 2-609 official cmt. 3.

> The grounds for insecurity need not arise from circumstances directly related to the parties or the contract itself. Thus, where the market price of a commodity is rising, the buyer may be justified in seeking assurances of

performance from the seller *even though the seller did nothing to cause buyer's insecurity.*

WHITE & SUMMERS § 6-2, at 288 (emphasis added). Furthermore, in *Diskmakers, Inc. v. DeWitt Equipment Corp.,* 555 F.2d 1177 (3d Cir.1977), the Third Circuit Court of Appeals stated:

> "As between merchants, the test for determining when reasonable grounds for insecurity arise and what will constitute an adequate assurance of future performance is a commercial criterion. *Any facts which should indicate to a reasonable merchant that the promised performance might not be forthcoming when due should be considered reasonable grounds for insecurity . . . ."*

555 F.2d at 1180 (quoting N.J. Stat. Ann. § 12A:2-609 study cmt. 1 (1962)) (emphasis added).

We think the market conditions existing in June 1996, combined with the widely-publicized statements that HTA contracts were illegal and unenforceable, are facts that would support a jury finding that the Coop had a reasonable basis to be concerned that Sime Farms may not perform under its contracts. The inverse in the market unquestionably made delivery under the contracts an unprofitable venture for Sime Farms. Although the Coop agreed in the contracts to pay all margins and commissions, both parties understood that any inverse would be deducted from the contract price if Sime Farms chose to roll the contracts. Consequently, if a future roll became necessary, the ultimate risk of an inverse market rested with the producer, not the Coop. That was precisely the situation here; another roll was inevitable because Sime Farms had no grain to deliver under the July contracts. Consequently, it would eventually have to roll at least to December 1996, at which time the inverse would reduce its price per bushel to a level at which it would not even recover its costs of production. Clearly, a producer in these circumstances would have every incentive to claim that the contracts were illegal and unenforceable, as the Iowa Attorney General's office had opined.

In addition, the jury was entitled to consider the market factors in the context of the relationship between the Coop and Sime Farms. *See* WHITE & SUMMERS § 6-2, at 286 ("Whether a party has reasonable grounds for insecurity depends upon many factors including the [party's] exact words or actions, the course of dealing or performance between the particular parties and the nature of the industry."); *see also Johnson v. Land O'Lakes,* 181 F.R.D. 388, 395 (N.D. Iowa 1998) (stating that "evidence of the context in which the demand is made is certainly relevant and admissible"). The Coop's local manager, Paul Nesler, spoke with Mark Sime in

May to determine what Sime Farms intended to do about its July contracts. Sime was clearly aware of the inverse in the market and his need to roll the contracts to December; yet he did not contact the Coop to take any steps to work out a plan.

Sime Farms places great reliance on the testimony of Nesler, who when asked, "Did you ever believe that he [Sime] wouldn't deliver before June 6, 1996?" responded, "No, I thought Mark would probably deliver." Sime Farms claims that this testimony establishes as a matter of law that the Coop was never insecure about Sime Farms' performance. Although Nesler signed the demand for assurances on behalf of the Coop, he testified he did not draft it. The jury could certainly have concluded that Nesler's personal feelings did not reflect the Coop's belief as to Sime Farms' likely performance. Moreover, Nesler stated several times in his testimony that he was concerned that Sime had not come to the Coop with a plan, especially in view of Nesler's request that he do so. The jury was entitled to consider Nesler's testimony in its entirety and, in doing so, could discount some testimony and give more credit to other testimony. The weight to be given Nesler's testimony was for the jury to determine.

We hold there was sufficient evidence to generate a jury question on whether the Coop had an objectively reasonable basis for insecurity. Therefore, the trial court did not err in refusing to grant Sime Farms' motion for directed verdict on this basis.

V. *Was the Coop's Demand for Assurances Unreasonable as a Matter of Law?*

A. *Issue and scope of review.* Sime Farms claimed at trial that the Coop's demand for assurances was unreasonable as a matter of law and, as a result, constituted a repudiation of the contract. It claims that the trial court erred in failing to grant its motion for directed verdict on this issue. We apply the same scope of review as set out in the preceding division of this opinion.

B. *Applicable law.* Sime Farms' repudiation argument rests on its contention that the Coop's demand for assurances imposed conditions that went beyond the contract and that the Coop's performance was contingent upon acquiescence to these conditions. Sime Farms contends such a demand constitutes an anticipatory repudiation.

We disagree with Sime Farms' contention. The mere fact that the assurances demanded by the Coop necessitated action beyond that required by the contract does not render the demand unreasonable as a matter of law. As noted by a leading treatise on the Uniform Commercial Code,

[a]ll demands for adequate assurance call for more than was originally promised under the contract, and that is precisely what 2-609 authorizes. If, for example, it was appropriate to sell on open credit at the outset of a contract but subsequent events cause insecurity, 2-609 calls for modification of the contract to provide greater security to the seller than the seller could have demanded, absent such insecurity. Thus it is the very purpose of 2-609 to authorize one party to insist upon more than the contract gives.

WHITE & SUMMERS § 6-2, at 288; *see also* U.C.C. § 2-610 official cmt. 2 ("[A] demand by one or both parties for more than the contract calls for in the way of counter-performance is not in itself a repudiation."); Robertson, 38 DRAKE L.REV. at 341 (noting that an insecure promisee can demand assurance in the nature of additional performances not required by the underlying contract, provided there are reasonable grounds for insecurity). . . .

In summary, the mere fact that the Coop demanded performance beyond that required by the contract did not transform its demand into a repudiation as a matter of law. Therefore, the trial court did not err in submitting the question of the reasonableness of the Coop's demands to the jury. . . . Affirmed.

Compare the court's decision in *Top of Iowa Cooperative, supra,* with the following excerpt from a concurring opinion in *Pittsburgh-Des Moines Steel Co. v. Brookhaven Manor Water Co.,* 532 F.2d 572, 583–84 (7th Cir. 1976):

Although I agree with the result reached in the majority opinion, I differ with the reasoning. Reasonable men could certainly conclude that PDM had legitimate grounds to question Brookhaven's ability to pay for the water tank. When the contract was signed, the parties understood that Brookhaven would obtain a loan to help pay for the project. When the loan failed to materialize, a prudent businessman would have "reasonable grounds for insecurity." I disagree that there must be a fundamental change in the financial position of the buyer before the seller can invoke the protection of UCC § 2-609. Rather, I believe that the Section was designed to cover instances where an underlying condition of the contract, even if not expressly incorporated into the written document, fails to occur. *See* Comment 3 to UCC § 2-609. Whether, in a specific case, the breach of the condition gives a party "reasonable grounds for insecurity" is a question of fact for the jury.

UCC § 2-609, however, does not give the alarmed party a right to redraft the contract. Whether the party invoking that provision is merely requesting an assurance that performance will be forthcoming or whether he is attempting to alter the contract is a mixed question of law and fact, depending in part upon the court's interpretation of the obligations imposed on the parties. In this case, PDM would have been assured only if significant changes in the contract were made, either by receiving Betke's personal guarantee, by attaining escrow financing or by purchasing an interest in Brookhaven. The district court could probably conclude as a matter of law that these requests by PDM demanded more than a commercially "adequate assurance of due performance."

Problem 6-3

Seller agreed to manufacture special equipment for Buyer on credit. Delivery was to be in installments, with payment for each installment within 15 days of delivery. Seller commenced performance but, before any deliveries were made, Seller began to hear unfavorable comments about Buyer's credit. After a quick check, the following facts emerged: (1) Dun & Bradstreet had recently reduced Buyer's credit rating; (2) Buyer's working capital was fully stretched out and some suppliers were experiencing delays in payment; (3) Buyer had recently changed banks, and the "word" was out that Buyer's financial condition was "extended" and that care should be exercised before extending any credit; and (4) Buyer's overall financial condition had worsened since the date of the contract.

A. You represent Seller. On the day before the first delivery was due, Seller called you for a conference. With the credit information on the table, Seller stated that unless you could persuade it otherwise, it would refuse to deliver the goods unless Buyer paid cash. What would you recommend? *See* UCC §§ 1-201(b)(23), 2-702(1), 2-609. Does Seller have reasonable grounds to believe that Buyer is insolvent?

B. Assume you persuade Seller to exercise caution and talk to Buyer before taking action. Seller, therefore, gives Buyer a written demand for "adequate assurance" by asking for a letter of credit, and temporarily suspends the first delivery. UCC § 2-609(1). Buyer, in response, establishes solvency and claims that the current situation is "temporary" and refuses to provide a letter of credit as that was not the originally agreed payment mechanism. Buyer, however, states that long-term viability depends upon getting prompt delivery of the equipment, which is needed in the business, on credit. If there are delays, no assurances can be given. Has Seller demanded more than adequate assurance? Does Buyer's response constitute "adequate assurance" of due performance?

Problem 6-4

Seller agreed to manufacture special equipment for Buyer on credit. Delivery was to be in installments with payment for each installment 15 days after delivery. About one month before Seller was due to deliver the first installment, Buyer began to hear unfavorable things about Seller's financial condition: (1) Dun & Bradstreet had recently reduced Seller's credit rating; (2) Seller's working capital was fully stretched out and some suppliers were experiencing delays in payment; (3) Seller had recently changed banks, and the "word" was out that Seller's financial condition was "extended" and that care should be exercised before extending any credit; and (4) Seller's overall financial condition had worsened since the date of the contract.

Does Buyer have reasonable grounds for insecurity? If so, what assurances would you suggest Buyer request?

Problem 6-5

Big Discount Corp. is a major retailer with stores throughout the United States. It is the largest retailer of discount consumer products and has such market power that it can command heavy discounts from its suppliers. Big Discount has a reputation for paying its suppliers late and for insisting they accept return of unsold merchandise. Most suppliers put up with this because they fear losing Big Discount as a customer, which would precipitate a significant decline in their sales volume. Big Discount requires all its suppliers to agree to a standard set of contract terms. As general counsel for Big Discount, you are considering adding the following two clauses to all future sales contracts:

> Under no circumstances shall Supplier be entitled to demand adequate assurance of future performance or to suspend its performance pending receipt from Big Discount of assurances of future performance.
>
> Big Discount may, whenever it desires, demand from Supplier adequate assurance of Supplier's future performance. Such a demand may include whatever assurances of Supplier's performance that Big Discount deems appropriate. Upon such a demand, Big Discount may suspend its own performance until it receives from Supplier the assurances demanded.

Would these clauses be enforceable? Why or why not?

B. Repudiation

We now come to the concept of repudiation. Repudiation is not the failure to tender performance when due. Failing to perform a contract obligation by the required time is a breach of contract, but it is not a repudiation. A party repudiates a contract obligation when, *before* performance is due, that party signals to the other that it will not perform as required. That signaling may either be an outright statement such as "I will not perform" or it might be more implicit, such as by taking actions that indicate that the promised performance will not be forthcoming.

The materials above should make it clear that if a party reasonably demands assurances of future performance under section 2-609, it may treat the other party's refusal to adequately respond as a repudiation. Repudiation may also come from the demand for assurances itself, if that demand is unjustified or otherwise unreasonable.[10] Less clear is whether repudiation can arise from circumstances other than the conduct or communications of a party. For example, suppose the buyer learns that the seller's only manufacturing facility was destroyed in a storm. Would that constitute a repudiation by the seller? Read comment 1 to section 2-610.

When faced with a repudiation, what options does the other party to the contract have? The traditional answer was that the non-repudiating party had to continue its own performance because the repudiating party could always change its mind and

---

[10] *See, e.g., Carnes Co. v. Stone Creek Mechanical Inc.*, 412 F.3d 845 (7th Cir. 2005) (party refusing to perform until other party covered costs it was not obligated to absorb was a repudiation); *Thunder Basin Coal Co. v. Southwestern Public Service Co.*, 104 F.3d 1205 (10th Cir. 1997) (buyer repudiated when it stated it would perform only in accord with its own interpretation of the contract).

tender performance when its performance was due. The more modern approach is contained in section 2-610. Under that approach, if there is a repudiation *and* the loss of the repudiated performance "substantially impairs" the value of the contract to the other party, the non-repudiating party may suspend its own performance and either await performance by the repudiating party or resort to remedies for breach. We will study those remedies in Chapters Seven and Nine. If the non-repudiating party chooses to wait, the repudiating party may retract its repudiation. *See* UCC §§ 2-610(a), 2-611.

Although these rules are relatively clear in the abstract, they are quite murky in their application. Consider the uncertainty attendant in the parties' interaction. If a party thinks the other side has repudiated, suspends its own performance, and resorts to remedies for breach, a court might later determine that the other party did not in fact repudiate. As a result, the party that suspended its performance may have itself, by that act, breached the contract. The whole process of demanding adequate assurances or declaring that the other side has repudiated is a bit like a game of chicken. Whoever blinks first loses. If you can bluff or bully the other side into accepting your position, then you win. But if you can't, you risk being declared in breach and incurring all the liabilities therefor. A lawyer faced with a call from a client in this situation is wise to be cautious. Consider the following problem. In doing so, note that the first step in determining whether there is reasonable grounds for insecurity or a repudiation, is to determine what each parties' contract obligations are.

Problem 6-6

Buyer contracted with the Ace Supply Co. for Ace to furnish at a fixed price a large quantity of specially tooled valves for use in an improved line of equipment. Ace agreed to deliver the valves in six equal installments at three month intervals. Buyer stated that the installments were geared to a long range production schedule and a projected increase in demand for the equipment. Buyer furnished design drawings to assist Ace in "tooling up," gave Ace six months of lead time, and advanced 25% of the contract price. Two weeks before the first installment was due, Buyer appeared in your office with the following email from Ace:

> As suggested in our telephone conversation of last week, our engineers have determined that the design drawings which you furnished us were incomplete to produce the valves that you need, based upon the prototype we have developed from the drawings. As determined in discussions between your engineers and ours, we have revised the drawings but now must retool our original model valve at considerable additional expense and some delay. Due to this delay, we will not be able to deliver the first installment as originally scheduled. We expect that you will cover the extra expenses we will incur. We anticipate catching up by the time the second installment is due.

Buyer disputes that its drawings were in error and wants to end the contract and recover the 25% advance. Upon close questioning, you discover the following: (1) the delay in delivery will "wreak havoc" with Buyer's production schedule and existing contractual commitments; (2) if the contract were canceled, Buyer would purchase half of the quantity of valves called for in the contract from another manufacturer who guaranteed full performance in four months; (3) Buyer's estimated demand for the valves was about 50% too high; and (4) in Buyer's judgment, Ace would "probably" meet the next installment and make up the late deliveries. What is your advice?

CISG and UNIDROIT Principles. Under the CISG Article 71, a party may suspend performance if it is apparent that the other party will not perform a substantial part of that party's contract obligation. That suspension includes withholding delivery of the goods. The party suspending performance must give notice that it is suspending performance and must continue performance if the other party provides adequate assurance of performance. This suspension with notice process does not apply if it appears that the other party will commit a "fundamental breach" of the contract. In that case, the aggrieved party may declare the contract avoided. CISG Art. 72. In that circumstance, if time permits and if the other party has not affirmatively declared it will not perform, the aggrieved party must give notice and allow the other party to provide adequate assurance of performance. A breach is fundamental when "it results in such detriment to the other party as substantially to deprive him of what he is entitled to expect under the contract, unless the party in breach did not foresee and a reasonable person of the same kind in the same circumstances would not have foreseen such a result." CISG Art. 25.

The UNIDROIT Principles are similar. If it is clear that there will be a "fundamental non-performance" the aggrieved party may put an end to the contract or may demand adequate assurance and withhold its own performance. Failure to provide adequate assurance also gives the aggrieved party the ability to put an end to the contract. UNIDROIT Arts. 7.3.3 and 7.3.4.

SECTION 4.   EXCUSE FROM PERFORMANCE

As the time for the parties to perform their respective contract obligations draws nigh, one or both of them may encounter circumstances that make performance impracticable or more difficult than anticipated. When a party encounters difficulty in performance, it may seek a modification of its contractual obligation. If the parties agree to a modification, then the party that encountered difficulty will not be seeking an excuse from its contact obligations. But if there is no agreed modification, a party that encounters such a problem may seek to be excused from performing its contract obligation because of it. Article 2 has several provisions that address this situation: sections 2-613 through 2-616. Before analyzing those sections, however, one fundamental point needs to be made.

Contracts are risk allocation devices. The seller and buyer agree that the seller will provide goods pursuant to the contract requirements and the buyer agrees to accept and pay for those conforming goods. UCC § 2-301. By engaging in those mutual promises, the buyer has, to some degree, accepted the risk that it may not need or want the goods. The seller, in turn, has accepted the risk that it may not be able to provide the goods on time or at all. The parties may have contemplated some of the risks that might interfere with those respective performances and included a term in their agreement that excuses one or both parties from certain specified risks. For example, the parties may have agreed that either party may be excused if a fire, flood or war, prevents that party from performing. Such a term is commonly called a "force majeure" clause.

The most interesting and difficult issues arise when the parties did not include a force majeure clause in their agreement or the problem that developed is outside the scope of whatever such clause their agreement does contain. Might a party in such a case still be excused from performing? How is a court to determine whether excusing performance would be consistent with the allocation of risks in the contract or contrary to it?

To illustrate with a simple example, assume Seller has agreed to sell a car to Buyer for a set price. The day before the scheduled delivery date, and before the risk of loss has passed to the buyer,[11] the nearby river floods, the car is engulfed in water, it floats down the river, and is totally destroyed. Seller asks Buyer to forget the whole deal because Seller can no longer tender the car. Buyer refuses, arguing that Seller had the risk that the car would be damaged or destroyed prior to delivery and demands that Seller either provide a substantially similar car for the original contract price or pay Buyer damages for breach. If Seller is excused from performance, Seller will still suffer the loss of the value of the car (at least if it was not fully insured) but Buyer will not be entitled to recover damages for breach of contract. If Seller is not excused from performance, Seller will have to pay damages to Buyer in addition to suffering the loss of the value of the car. Such damages would typically be measured by the difference between the value of the car promised and the contract price. *See* UCC § 2-713(1). The excuse doctrine allocates the loss from the car's destruction to either Seller or Buyer, but does not prevent the destruction of the car.

With this background in mind, turn your attention to the relevant UCC provisions. The four sections deal with at least four different types of problems:

Problem	UCC Section(s)
Destruction of identified goods	§ 2-613
Obstruction of delivery method	§ 2-614(1)
Obstruction of payment method	§ 2-614(2)
Damage to production facilities or other interference with tender	§ 2-615 (seller's rights) § 2-616 (buyer's rights)

Section 2-613 deals with the destruction of goods identified to the contract when it was made and is premised upon the common-law doctrine of impossibility of performance.[12] A classic example would be the car scenario discussed on the previous page: a used car dealer contracts to sell a particular car to a buyer and, before delivery, the car is destroyed through no fault of the seller.

Section 2-614 does two things. First, under certain circumstances it excuses one party from using the delivery or payment mechanisms called for in the contract.

---

[11] *See* section 2-509, discussed in Chapter Four.

[12] *Cf.* RESTATEMENT (SECOND) OF CONTRACTS § 263. The Restatement uses the term "impracticability" rather than "impossibility." *See id.* at Ch. 11, Reporter's Note.

Second, it then requires that the excused party use and the counter-party accept commercially reasonable substitutes.

Section 2-615 is the most difficult of the excuse rules to understand and apply. It rests on a concept called "impracticability,"[13] and excuses performance when the impracticability results from the occurrence of a contingency "the non-occurrence of which was a basic assumption on which the contract was made." Not every difficulty that arises makes performance impractical. For example, events giving rise to excuse under section 2-613 (casualty to identified goods) are not covered by section 2-615. *See* UCC § 2-615 cmt. 1. In addition, the official comments attempt to distinguish between market events – such as increases in the cost of raw materials – which do not give rise to excuse, and capacity events – such as a shutdown of major sources of supply – which do. *See* UCC § 2-615 cmt. 4.

A seller asserting excuse under section 2-615 must seasonably notify the buyer, and if its capacity to perform has been diminished but not destroyed, allocate its ability to perform among its customers in a reasonable manner. UCC § 2-615(b), (c). The buyer generally has the option, however, to terminate the contract rather than to accept less than full performance. UCC § 2-616.

One other point is worth noting. All of these provisions are subject to contrary agreement. In other words, the parties may, in their agreement, expressly provide either for no excuse under any circumstances or for excuse on a more lenient standard. Section 2-615 makes this point expressly but even the other provisions are subject to variation by agreement. *See* UCC § 1-302.

Before you tackle the problems that follow, consider the following explanation of the principles of excuse from *Speciality Tires of America, Inc. v. The CIT Group/Equipment Financing, Inc.*, 82 F. Supp. 2d 434, 437–40 (W.D. Pa. 2000).

> In the overwhelming majority of circumstances, contractual promises are to be performed, not avoided: *pacta sunt servanda*, or, as the Seventh Circuit loosely translated it, "a deal's a deal." *Waukesha Foundry, Inc. v. Industrial Engineering, Inc.*, 91 F.3d 1002, 1010 (7th Cir. 1996). This is an eminently sound doctrine, because typically
>
>> a court cannot improve matters by intervention after the fact. It can only destabilize the institution of contract, increase risk, and make parties worse off. . . . Parties to contracts are entitled to seek, and retain, personal advantage; striving for that advantage is the source of much economic progress. Contract law does not require

---

[13] *Cf.* RESTATEMENT (SECOND) OF CONTRACTS § 261.

parties to be fair, or kind, or reasonable, or to share gains or losses equally.

Industrial Representatives, Inc. v. CP Clare Corp., 74 F.3d 128, 131–32 (7th Cir. 1996). Promisors are free to assume risks, even huge ones, and promisees are entitled to rely on those voluntary assumptions. JOHN D. CALAMARI & JOSEPH M. PERILLO, THE LAW OF CONTRACTS § 13.16, at 522 (4th ed. 1998). Futures contracts, as just one example, are so aleatory that risk-bearing is their sole purpose, yet they are fully enforceable.

Even so, courts have recognized, in an evolving line of cases from the common law down to the present, that there are limited instances in which unexpectedly and radically changed conditions render the judicial enforcement of certain promises of little or no utility. This has come to be known, for our purposes, as the doctrines of impossibility and impracticability. Because of the unexpected nature of such occurrences, litigated cases usually involve, not interpretation of a contractual term, but the judicial filling of a lacuna in the parties agreement. Such "gap-filling," however, must be understood for what it is: a court-ordered, as opposed to bargained-for, allocation of risk between the parties. As such, it must be applied sparingly.

Traditionally, there were three kinds of supervening events that would provide a legally cognizable excuse for failing to perform: death of the promisor (if the performance was personal), illegality of the performance, and destruction of the subject matter; beyond that the doctrine has grown to recognize that

> relief is most justified if unexpected events inflict a loss on one party and provide a windfall gain for the other or where the excuse would save one party from an unexpected loss while leaving the other party in a position no worse than it would have without the contract.

CALAMARI & PERILLO, *supra* § 13.1, at 496. Thus, the Second Restatement of Contracts expresses the doctrine of impracticability this way:

> Where, after a contract is made, a party's performance is made impracticable without his fault by the occurrence of an event the non-occurrence of which was a basic assumption on which the contract was made, his duty to render that performance is discharged, unless the language or the circumstances indicate the contrary.

RESTATEMENT (SECOND) OF CONTRACTS § 261 (1981). Article 2 of the U.C.C., which applies to the sale of goods presented by the case *sub judice*, puts it similarly:

> Delay in delivery or non-delivery in whole or in part by a seller . . . is not a breach of his duty under a contract for sale if performance as agreed has been made impracticable by the occurrence of a contingency the non-occurrence of which was a basic assumption on which the contract was made. . . .

U.C.C. § 2-615(1).

The principal inquiry in an impracticability analysis, then, is whether there was a contingency the non-occurrence of which was a basic assumption underlying the contract. It is often said that this question turns on whether the contingency was "foreseeable," on the rationale that if it was, the promisor could have sought to negotiate explicit contractual protection. This, however, is an incomplete and sometimes misleading test. Anyone can foresee, in some general sense, a whole variety of potential calamities, but that does not mean that he or she will deem them worth bargaining over. *See* CALAMARI & PERILLO, *supra* § 13.18, at 526; JOHN E. MURRAY, MURRAY ON CONTRACTS, § 112, at 641 (3d ed. 1990) ("If 'foreseeable' is equated with 'conceivable', nothing is unforeseeable"). The risk may be too remote, the party may not have sufficient bargaining power, or neither party may have any superior ability to avoid the harm. As my late colleague Judge Teitelbaum recited two decades ago in a famous case of impracticability:

> Foreseeability or even recognition of a risk does not necessarily prove its allocation. Parties to a contract are not always able to provide for all the possibilities of which they are aware, sometimes because they cannot agree, often because they are too busy. Moreover, that some abnormal risk was contemplated is probative but does not necessarily establish an allocation of the risk of the contingency which actually occurs.

Aluminum Co. of Am. v. Essex Group, Inc., 499 F. Supp. 53, 76 (W.D. Pa. 1980) (applying Indiana law) (quoting *Transatlantic Financing Corp. v. United States,* 363 F.2d 312 (D.C. Cir. 1966)). So, while the risk of an unforeseeable event can safely be deemed not to have been assumed by the promisor, the converse is not necessarily true. *See* RESTATEMENT

(SECOND) OF CONTRACTS § 261 cmt. c. Properly seen, then, foreseeability, while perhaps the most important factor,

> is at best one fact to be considered in resolving first how likely the occurrence of the event in question was and, second, whether its occurrence, based on past experience, was of such reasonable likelihood that the obligor should not merely foresee the risk but, because of the degree of its likelihood, the obligor should have guarded against it or provided for non-liability against the risk.

Wolf Trap, 817 F.2d at 1102–03.[14]

It is also commonly said that the standard of impossibility is objective rather than subjective – that the question is whether the thing can be done, not whether the promisor can do it. This too is more truism than test, although Pennsylvania courts have couched their decisions in this rhetoric. Indeed, the FIRST RESTATEMENT took such an approach, but the SECOND simply applies "the rationale . . . that a party generally assumes the risk of his own inability to perform his duty." . . . This holds particularly when the duty is merely to pay money . . . . It is therefore "preferable to say that such ['subjective'] risks as these are generally considered to be sufficiently within the control of one party that they are assumed by that party." 2 E. ALLAN FARNSWORTH, FARNSWORTH ON CONTRACTS § 9.6, at 619-20 (2d ed. 1998). It is, of course, essential that the impossibility asserted by the promisor as a defense not have been caused by the promisor. *Id.* § 9.6, at 613–14.

Generally speaking, while loss, destruction or a major price increase of fungible goods will not excuse the seller's duty to perform, the rule is different when the goods are unique, have been identified to the contract or are to be produced from a specific, agreed-upon source. In such a case, the nonexistence or unavailability of a specific thing will establish a defense of impracticability. Thus, § 263 of the Second Restatement recites:

> If the existence of a specific thing is necessary for the performance of a duty, its failure to come into existence, destruction, or such deterioration as makes performance impracticable is an event the

---

[14] Another respected text defines the unforeseeable as "an event so unlikely to occur that reasonable parties see no need explicitly to allocate the risk of its occurrence, although the impact it might have would be of such magnitude that the parties would have negotiated over it, had the event been more likely." CALAMARI & PERILLO, *supra*, § 13.18, at 526.

non-occurrence of which was a basic assumption on which the contract was made.

Problem 6-7

Seller, an art dealer, owned an etching by Picasso. Buyer, a collector, examined it at Seller's gallery and, after negotiations, Seller agreed to sell it to Buyer for $75,000. Under the written contract for sale, Buyer was to return with a cashier's check the next day and pick up the etching. Buyer returned check in hand but, alas, the Picasso was destroyed by fire during the night.

A. What are the rights and duties of the parties? *See* UCC §§ 2-613, 2-509. Would it matter what caused the fire? Suppose the fire was caused by a neglected coffee pot, a short in the wiring, or a lightening strike? *See* UCC § 2-613 & cmt. 1.

B. Suppose, instead, that the Picasso, unknown to Seller, had been stolen and was replevied from Seller by the true owner prior to Buyer's return rather than destroyed by fire? Any difference in analysis?

C. Assume that Seller had agreed to sell to Buyer print #10 from a series. After the agreement was made, print #10 was damaged by water. Seller has in its possession print #12, undamaged, from the same series. Is Seller excused from delivery?

D. In any case in which Seller would be able to be excused under section 2-613, what are Buyer's options?

Problem 6-8

Can UCC § 2-613 apply to fungible goods? If so, construct a scenario in which the seller of fungible goods would be excused from performance because of a casualty to the goods.

Problem 6-9

Supersonic Motors, Inc. manufactures rotor blades for jet engines. Its customers include several domestic defense contractors who manufacture aircraft for the U.S. military and several makers of civilian aircraft. On October 1, Supersonic agreed in writing to sell 60,000 rotor blades to Bingo Aircraft, a Seattle-based manufacturer of aircraft. The agreement calls for delivery of 5,000 rotor blades on the first day of each of the next twelve months.

A. In which, if any, of the following scenarios, would Supersonic be excused from performing in whole or in part?

   1. Because of an economic boom in China and several developing countries, and the concomitant increase in the demand for industrial metals, the price of the aluminum and titanium that Supersonic needs to manufacture rotor blades has tripled since it entered into the agreement with Bingo. Performance under the contract with Bingo would now cause Supersonic to lose money.

   2. Because of a strike by the Industrial Metal Workers of the World, Supersonic cannot get from any supplier the metal it needs to manufacture the rotor blades. No one knows how long the strike will last.

   3. Because of a strike by Supersonic's employees, Supersonic cannot manufacture the rotor blades called for under the contract with Bingo. No one knows how long the strike will last.

   4. Because of a strike by the nation's rail workers, Bingo cannot ship the rotor blades to Bingo by rail, as was anticipated. Shipment by truck would be possible but far more expensive and would significantly increase the chance of damage to the rotor blades during transit. No one knows how long the rail strike will last.

   5. Because of a fire at Supersonic's only manufacturing plant, Supersonic cannot manufacture the rotor blades on time and it anticipates at least a four-month delay in its ability to deliver the goods.

B. On October 15, a freak meteor storm severely damages Supersonic's only manufacturing plant. It will take about ten months to repair the facility and

resume normal production. Supersonic's warehouse of rotor blades was
also damaged but 60,000 rotor blades of the type called for by the contract
with Bingo were undamaged. Supersonic also has a contract to sell
120,000 rotor blades to BusAir. Supersonic now has to determine how to
allocate the undamaged rotor blades between Bingo and BusAir?

1. Would it be permissible to sell all 60,000 to Bingo and none to
   BusAir, on the ground that this would at least make one customer
   happy?
2. Would it be permissible to sell all of the rotor blades to BusAir if
   BusAir is a regular customer and Bingo is not?
3. Would it be permissible to sell all of the rotor blades to whichever
   customer is willing to pay the most?
4. Would it be permissible to favor a customer that needs the rotor
   blades to manufacture military aircraft over a customer that needs
   the rotor blades to manufacture civilian aircraft?

Buyer's excuse. Neither section 2-613 nor 2-615 purport to excuse the buyer
from performing; both provide relief only for sellers. Does that mean the buyer is
never excused from performance based on unforeseen events? Consider Judge
Posner's words:

> Since impossibility and related doctrines are devices for shifting risk in
> accordance with the parties' presumed intentions, which are to minimize
> the costs of contract performance, one of which is the disutility created by
> risk, they have no place when the contract explicitly assigns a particular
> risk to one party or the other. As we have already noted, a fixed-price
> contract is an explicit assignment of the risk of market price increases to the
> seller and the risk of market price decreases to the buyer, and the
> assignment of the latter risk to the buyer is even clearer where, as in this
> case, the contract places a floor under price but allows for escalation. If,
> as is also the case here, the buyer forecasts the market incorrectly and
> therefore finds himself locked into a disadvantageous contract, he has only
> himself to blame and so cannot shift the risk back to the buyer by invoking
> impossibility or related doctrines. . . . Since "the very purpose of a fixed
> price agreement is to place the risk of increased costs on the promisor (and

the risk of decreased costs on the promisee)," the fact that costs decrease steeply . . . cannot allow the buyer to walk away from the contract.[15]

Does Judge Posner's view hold force when the buyer is seeking to be excused because of a significant change in the market due to an event such as widespread flooding, acts of terrorism, war, or a change in government regulation? Suppose a new government regulation mandates that users of natural gas implement costly environmental controls and, because of that, the buyer cannot use as much natural gas as the contract calls for.[16] What if the buyer's whole purpose for the goods has been frustrated? Does the common-law doctrine of frustration of purpose remain available to help the buyer? *See* UCC §§ 1-103(b), 2-615 cmt. 9 ("the reason of the present section may well apply and entitle the buyer to the exemption").[17] Consider the following two problems.

Problem 6-10

Plumber and Supplier are both located in Microville, a small town that recently announced plans to build a sewer system to replace existing septic tanks. After Microville informed Plumber that Plumber was the low bidder on the sewer system installation contract, Plumber contracted to buy from Supplier 12,000 tube fittings. These fittings are used to connect residential plumbing to a central sewer system; they have no other use. Microville then decided that the sewer system was too expensive and would not be built.

A. Is Plumber entitled to any relief from the contract with Supplier?

B. The agreement between Plumber and Supplier provided that Plumber would pay for the tube fittings through a funds transfer from Plumber's bank, Great Northern Bank. Yesterday, Great Northern Bank was

---

[15] *Northern Indiana Public Service Co. v. Carbon County Coal Company*, 799 F.2d 265, 278 (7th Cir. 1986).

[16] *See International Minerals & Chemical Corp. v. Llano, Inc.*, 770 F.2d 879 (10th Cir.), *cert. denied*, 475 U.S. 1015 (1986) (excusing the buyer from taking all the gas contracted for). *Compare* RESTATEMENT (SECOND) OF CONTRACTS § 264.

[17] *Compare* RESTATEMENT (SECOND) OF CONTRACTS § 265.

taken over by federal regulators and Plumber's deposit account was frozen. Supplier is ready to deliver the fittings and Plumber has asserted it is excused from performing the contract with Supplier. Is Plumber correct?

Problem 6-11

Trucking Services, Inc. has a fleet of semi-trailer trucks engaged in hauling goods across the country. In 2006, Trucking Services entered into a five-year contract with Oil Supply Co. for diesel fuel at a fixed price of $2.50 per gallon for the first year. The agreement calls for the price in subsequent years to be computed each December 1 based upon the wholesale price charged by Exxon Corp. at a refinery in Mississippi, plus 5 cents.

On December 1, 2006, the fuel for the second year was re-priced at $2.60 per gallon. On December 1, 2007, the fuel was re-priced for the third year at $3.40 per gallon. During the first six months of 2008, the wholesale price in the market went to $4.50 per gallon due to political unrest in the Middle East, insurgent activity in Africa, and storms in the Gulf of Mexico that reduced the production capacity of several hundred drilling platforms and oil refineries.

Exxon Corp. has refused to honor its long-term contract to sell diesel fuel to Oil Supply Co., which similarly called for a fixed price subject to annual re-pricing based on the wholesale price charged by Exxon Corp. at a refinery in Mississippi. As a result, instead of making 5¢ per gallon on its contract with Trucking Services, Oil Supply Co. is losing more than $1 per gallon (because it must buy at the wholesale market price and then sell at the substantially lower contract price), and is facing severe financial distress. Oil Supply Co. wants to renegotiate its deal with Trucking Services but Trucking Services has refused. You represent Oil Supply Co.

A. What advice would you give?

B. If you could redraft the agreement between Oil Supply Co. and Trucking Services, what would you provide in that agreement?

C. If you could redraft the agreement between Oil Supply Co. and Exxon, what would you provide in that agreement?

CISG and UNIDROIT Principles.[18] CISG Article 79 addresses excuse from performance. A party may be excused if it proves that the "failure was due to an impediment beyond his control and that he could not reasonably be expected to have taken the impediment into account" at the time the contract was formed, or that could not be avoided, or overcome. The party seeking excuse under this provision must give timely notice to the other party.

The UNIDROIT Principles have a provision that is very similar to CISG Art. 79. UNIDROIT Art. 7.1.7. In addition, the Principles address "hardship where the occurrence of events fundamentally alters the equilibrium of the contract either because the cost of a party's performance has increased or because the value of the performance a party receives has diminished" and those events were not reasonably foreseeable and were beyond the control of the parties. UNIDROIT Art. 6.2.2. In the case of hardship, a party may request renegotiation from the other party and if unable to reach agreement, may go to court for a readjustment of the benefits and burdens of the contract. UNIDROIT Art. 6.2.3.

---

[18] For a discussion of excuse in the international arena, *see* Carla Spivack, *Of Shrinking Sweatsuits and Poison Vine Wax: A Comparison of Basis for Excuse Under U.C.C. § 2-615 and CISG Article 79*, 27 U. PA. J. INT'L ECON. L. 757 (2006); Francesco G. Mazzotta, *Why Do Some American Courts Fail to Get it Right?*, 3 LOY. U. CHI. INT'L L. REV. 85 (2005); Catherine Kessedjian, *Competing Approaches to Force Majeure and Hardship*, 25 INT'L REV. L. & ECON. 415 (2005).

CHAPTER SEVEN

BUYER'S REMEDIES FOR SELLER'S BREACH

SECTION 1. OVERVIEW

This Chapter addressed the various ways in which a seller may breach a contract for the sale of goods and the remedies the buyer has for that breach under Article 2. The next Chapter explores the buyer's rights and remedies under other law. Chapter Nine then considers the ways in which the buyer may breach and the seller's concomitant remedies for those breaches.

Determining breach. The place to start in determining whether the seller has breached is to identify the terms of the contract. In an Article 2 contract, the basic obligation of the seller is to deliver goods that conform to the contract requirements. UCC § 2-301. Obviously, everything that we have studied up to this point in time is important in determining whether the seller has complied with that obligation. The parties' agreement – including both express terms and terms implied through course of performance, course of dealing, and usage of trade – along with the Article 2 gap fillers, determine the seller's obligations on such matters as the type, quantity, and quality of the goods, the time for delivery, and the method of delivery. All of these items comprise the contract obligation.

Even after the terms are identified, it may not be entirely clear which party has breached. This is true for several reasons. First, many of the parties' obligations are couched in terms of reasonable behavior,[1] and parties may disagree over what is reasonable. Second, other obligations may be based on similarly vague or indefinite standards that are difficult to apply.[2] Third, the parties may slide into a

---

[1] *See, e.g.,* UCC §§ 2-306(1) (requiring that a quantity demanded in a requirements or output contract not be unreasonably disproportionate to a stated estimate or normal needs or output); 2-309(1) (requiring the seller to ship or deliver within a reasonable time); 2-503(1) (requiring that the seller's tender of the goods be at a reasonable hour, be held open for a reasonable time, and be accompanied by a notification reasonably necessary to enable the buyer to take delivery); 2-504(a) (requiring a seller to make a reasonable contract for the shipment of goods); 2-513(1) and 2-606(1)(b) (collectively giving the buyer a reasonable time to inspect the goods).

[2] *See, e.g.,* § 2-314(2) (requiring that goods, to be merchantable, pass without objection in the trade, be of fair average quality, be fit for their ordinary purpose, and be adequately contained, packaged, and labeled).

dispute in such a way that it is unclear who was the first to act improperly. For example, and as discussed in Chapter Six, consider a scenario in which a buyer asks for adequate assurances, the seller does not respond, and then the buyer refuses to go forward with the deal. The seller's failure to provide assurances might constitute a breach through repudiation. However, if the buyer was not entitled to request assurances, perhaps because the buyer had no reasonable grounds for insecurity, the seller's failure to respond would not be a repudiation and the buyer's later refusal to go forward would constitute a breach. Only after determining which party has breached the contract can one determine what remedies for that breach are available to the aggrieved party.

Finally, even if it is clear which party failed to perform, that failure may have been excused. For example, and as we also saw in Chapter Six, a seller who fails to tender the goods may be excused if the goods were destroyed through no fault of the seller. The buyer in that case will neither get the goods nor have a cause of action for breach.

It is also worth remembering that, even if you are certain that the seller breached, the parties may have limited the remedies available for that breach. As discussed in Chapter Five, the parties are generally free to limit or exclude the remedies normally available for breach through well-drafted disclaimers or liquidated damages clauses. So, in this Chapter, we will assume that the parties have an agreement that is enforceable (*i.e.,* a contract) under Article 2 (see Chapter Two), the seller has breached one or more obligations in the contract (see Chapters Three and Four), the buyer's remedies for breach have not been limited (see Chapter Five), and the seller's breach is not excused (see Chapter Six).

Typical seller's breaches and buyer's responses. There are several different ways in which a seller can breach a sales contract, and the remedies available to the buyer depend on the nature of the seller's breach. First, the seller may simply fail to tender any goods at all. This may occur if, prior to the time for tender, the seller repudiated the contract. Alternatively, the seller may fail to provide the goods without previously informing the buyer that no goods will be forthcoming. In each of these circumstances, the buyer has two basic remedy options: (i) seek specific performance – that is, use court processes to attempt to force the contracted goods out of the seller and recover damages from the seller for the delay; or (ii) cancel the contract and seek monetary damages from the seller measured either by the cost of a replacement transaction or by the market price of the goods. We will study these options in Section 2 of this Chapter.

Second, the seller may breach by making an improper tender. This could be as simple as tendering the goods after the time for doing so has expired or by tendering goods that are defective or otherwise fail to meet the contract requirements. In such cases, the buyer again has two basic choices: (i) reject the goods, cancel the contract with the seller, and seek monetary damages for the breach measured either by the cost of a replacement transaction or the market price of the goods; or (ii) accept the goods and seek damages measured by the reduction in value attributable to the nonconformity. Sometimes, the nonconformity is not apparent when the goods are tendered and the buyer accepts the goods unaware of the problem and therefore unaware of the right to reject them. For example, there might be microscopic cracks in metal girders that render them unfit for their ordinary purpose. Other goods may lack the tensile strength, elasticity, colorfastness, or viscosity specified in the contract. In some of these circumstances, the buyer who has accepted the goods may be able to revoke acceptance of the goods. That is, the buyer may be able to return the goods to the seller and seek damages as if the buyer had rejected the goods initially. We will study the buyer's rejection, acceptance, and revocation of acceptance remedies in Section 3 of this Chapter.

Finally, the seller may tender the goods and fail to perform installation services, or repair services as specified in the parties' agreement, or may perform those ancillary services in an unsatisfactory manner. The buyer's typical option in these cases is to recover damages for the harm caused by that breach. Article 2 does not contain any specific remedy provisions regarding remedies for breach of the seller's obligation to provide ancillary services, but does not preclude application of common-law concepts regarding damage remedies. UCC § 1-103.

All of the buyer's remedial options are grounded in the traditional principle of contract law of protecting the buyer's expectation interest. That is, all are designed to put the aggrieved buyer in the position it would have been in if the contract had been performed. UCC § 1-305. Given that perspective, and the common-law view that a contract breach is not a moral wrong, punitive damages are not generally available for breach of a sales contract. *See* UCC § 1-305 (prohibiting punitive damages except where specifically allowed).[3]

---

[3] The common law of contracts does allow for punitive damages if there is an independent tort and some sort of wilfulness or malice. *See* RESTATEMENT (SECOND) OF CONTRACTS § 355; *McIntosh v. Magna Systems, Inc.*, 539 F. Supp. 1185 (N.D. Ill. 1982). Given that the usual breaches of sales contracts do not involve malice and the parties' obligation of "good faith" is not an independent obligation, UCC § 1-304, punitive damages are generally not available in Article 2 cases.

Although the buyer's remedies under Article 2 are designed to protect the buyer's expectancy, Article 2 does not simply codify that principle. Instead, it contains several specific rules, each applicable to one or more of the situations described above. The starting point for analyzing these statutory provisions is section 2-711, which provides an *incomplete* list of options. The other relevant provisions are sections 2-502, 2-712, 2-713, 2-714, 2-715, 2-716, and 2-717.

After discussing these remedies for the seller's breach, this Chapter then explores three additional topics. Section 4 addresses the effect of the seller's breach on the risk of loss for the goods. Section 5 address how the statute of limitations affects the buyer's ability to pursue remedies for the seller's breach. Section 6 then considers the buyer's remedies under Article 2 against a remote seller of the goods.

SECTION 2.   SELLER'S REPUDIATION OR FAILURE TO TENDER GOODS

Assume the seller has repudiated its contract obligations or failed to tender the goods at the time required by the contract. Section 2-711 provides the buyer with two basic options: (i) attempt to recover the goods from the seller or (ii) cancel the contract with the seller and seek damages for the seller's breach. We first consider the ability of the buyer to obtain the goods from the seller and then consider the buyer's right to cancel the contract and sue the seller for damages.

A.   Buyer's Ability to Obtain the Goods from the Seller

Article 2 gives an aggrieved buyer the right to force the seller to tender the goods in several limited circumstances. Read sections 2-716 and 2-502. These two sections cover three basic situations:

§ 2-716(1)	Specific Performance
§ 2-716(3)	Replevin of Identified Goods
§ 2-502	Recovery by a Pre-paying Buyer

To use one of these remedies, the buyer must obtain a court order. None of these remedies allows the buyer to engage in "self-help" behavior to get the goods from the seller.

First consider the remedy of specific performance. Under general contract law, specific performance – that is, a court order requiring the breaching party to perform its contract obligations – is not the usual remedy. The customary remedy is an award of monetary damages. An order for specific performance, which is a type of injunction, requires the requesting party to demonstrate that it is entitled to such equitable relief. That generally requires proof that an award of monetary damages would be inadequate, that the specific performance order would not be unduly difficult for the court to enforce or supervise, and that the order would not cause undue hardship or be unfair under the circumstances. The decision whether to award specific performance is within the discretion of the court.[4]

Article 2 builds upon this common-law foundation and slightly broadens the grounds for granting specific performance of a sales contract. Read section 2-716(1) and (2). There are two things worth noting about these provisions. First, subsection (1) provides that specific performance "may" be decreed. It does not purport to mandate specific performance in any instance.[5] Thus, the common-law limitations on specific performance presumably remain relevant.

Second, subsection (1) refers to two different circumstances when specific performance may be appropriate: (i) when the goods are unique; and (ii) other proper circumstances. The reason why specific performance may be available to contracts involving unique goods is easy to appreciate. In such cases, the buyer has no other source for the goods. Thus, if the Smithsonian were to contract to sell the Hope Diamond or the *Spirit of St. Louis* to another museum, that other museum would likely have a good claim to specific performance in the event the Smithsonian failed or refused to perform.[6]

---

[4] *See* RESTATEMENT (SECOND) OF CONTRACTS §§ 357–69; Steven Shavell, *Specific Performance versus Damages for Breach of Contract; An Economic Analysis*, 84 TEX. L. REV. 831 (2006); Melvin A. Eisenberg, *Actual and Virtual Specific Performance, The Theory of Efficient Breach, and the Indifference Principle in Contract Law*, 93 CAL. L. REV. 975 (2005).

[5] *See also* UCC § 2-716 cmt. 1 (similarly indicating that the remedy remains within "the court's sound discretion").

[6] *See* RESTATEMENT (SECOND) OF CONTRACTS § 360, cmt. c.

Problem 7-1

Construct a scenario in which the goods contracted for are not unique but a decree of specific performance would nevertheless be appropriate.

Problem 7-2

You represent the buyer in a proposed sale of goods transaction. Although the goods involved are not unique, the buyer is adamant about avoiding the hassle, delay, and expense associated with finding another source of supply in the event the seller chooses not to perform. If you include a clause in the written agreement purporting to make an award of specific performance available in the event of the seller's breach, will such a clause be enforceable? Why or why not?

As an alternative to specific performance, the buyer could assert a right to replevy identified goods. Read section 2-716(3). Because replevin is a legal right, not an equitable remedy, it is not subject to judicial discretion or to the other limitations on the award of specific performance. A court will order replevin if the buyer proves that it has a right to possession of the goods that is superior to the rights of the seller.[7] Section 2-716(3) provides two grounds for assertion of that superior right to possession: (i) the buyer is unable to effect cover for goods – that is, the buyer cannot find substitute goods elsewhere; or (ii) the seller has shipped the goods under reservation, thereby in effect retaining a security interest in the goods to secure the buyer's obligation to pay the purchase price,[8] and the buyer has tendered the amount due. Both of these grounds require that the goods be identified to the contract.

Now read section 2-502, which allows a buyer who has prepaid in whole or part for the goods identified to the contract to assert a right to recover the goods. This right also applies to two different circumstances: (i) when the goods are purchased for personal, family, or household purposes; or (ii) when the seller becomes insolvent within ten days after receipt of the first payment.

---

[7] State procedural statutes may have other requirements for ordering replevin such as posting a bond, if the replevin order is obtained before a final trial on the merits of the dispute between the buyer and the seller.

[8] *See* UCC § 2-505.

Unlike the specific performance remedy, both the right of replevin in section 2-716(3) and the right to recover goods in section 2-502 require that the goods be identified to the contract for sale. Read section 2-501 on how the goods become identified to the contract for sale. Identification is the moment when the buyer begins to acquire property rights in specific goods (in addition to contract rights against the seller) and it typically occurs when the seller indicates which goods will be used to fulfill its obligations under this particular contract with this particular buyer.

It is important to emphasize, absent the buyer's successful exercise of a right to obtain the goods pursuant to sections 2-502 or 2-716, or the buyer obtaining an Article 9 security interest in the goods to secure the seller's obligation to deliver them to the buyer,[9] the buyer has no other right to force the goods out of the seller's hands. Thus, merely prepaying for the goods gives a buyer no right to extract the goods from the seller.

A buyer who obtains a court order requiring the seller to tender the goods is liable to pay the seller the unpaid portion of the contract price. That point is made expressly in section 2-502(1) but is no doubt also true with respect to situations covered by section 2-716. *See* UCC §§ 2-607, 2-709. Does such a buyer have a damage remedy for the harm caused by the delay in delivery? *See* UCC §§ 2-715, 1-103, 1-305. *Compare* UCC §§ 2-712(2), 2-713(1), 2-714(3).

Problem 7-3

A. Buyer contracted to purchase Seller's car for $5,000. At the time for delivery, Seller refused to deliver the car. In which of the scenarios depicted in the chart that follows, if any, will Buyer be able to obtain the car?

---

[9] In that circumstance, Article 9 governs the buyer's right to recover the goods from the seller. *See generally* UCC § 9-609 (allowing self help repossession for the secured party (the buyer) in the event of the debtor's (the seller) default, as long as such repossession can be conducted without a breach of the peace); Thomas H. Jackson & Anthony T. Kronman, *A Plea for the Financing Buyer*, 85 YALE L.J. 1 (1975).

	Buyer made a $1,000 down payment	Buyer made no down payment
Buyer wants the car for family purposes		
Buyer wants the car for business purposes		

B. Seller contracted to manufacture and sell to Buyer award plaques for Buyer's top producing sales representatives. Buyer planned to present the plaques at a special ceremony at Buyer's annual shareholders meeting. One week before the delivery date under the contract, and before any plaques had been manufactured, Seller repudiated the contract.

  1. Will Buyer be able to obtain the plaques from Seller?

  2. How, if at all, would the analysis change if Seller had started to manufacture the plaques but repudiated the contract before it completed the manufacturing process?

C. On June 1, Steel Supplier contracted to sell to Builder 6,000 steel beams for use in one of Builder's construction projects. Although Builder did not know it, on that date Steel Supplier was insolvent. The contract called for Builder to make an initial $100,000 payment on June 15. The balance of the purchase price was due upon delivery, which was slated for July 1. Builder made the first payment on June 15. The following day, Steel Supplier segregated 6,000 steel beams from the remainder of its industry and marked them for shipment to Builder. Two days later, Steel Supplier informed Builder that it was insolvent and repudiated the contract. Is Builder entitled to recover the steel beams from Steel Supplier?

CISG and UNIDROIT Principles. CISG Article 46 allows a buyer to obtain specific performance of the seller's obligations unless the buyer has resorted to an inconsistent remedy. In some circumstances the buyer may be able to compel the seller to deliver substitute goods or to repair defective goods. CISG Article 28, however, allows a court to refuse to order specific performance, even if the buyer would be entitled to it under Article 46, if the domestic law of that court would not allow for specific performance in that circumstance.[10]

Under the UNIDROIT Principles, Article 7.2.2 allows for specific performance of non-monetary obligations subject to certain exceptions. Specific performance will not be required if performance is impossible, unduly burdensome, or uniquely personal. The requesting party may also not obtain specific performance if it could obtain substitute performance elsewhere or has unreasonably delayed the request for specific performance.

B. Buyer's Right to Cancel the Contract and Obtain Damages

If either the buyer is not entitled to get the goods from the seller who fails to deliver, or the buyer chooses not to try, the buyer may cancel the contract and seek monetary damages from the seller. UCC § 2-711(1).

Buyer's cancellation of the contract. When a buyer justifiably cancels a contract, the buyer's duty to perform under the contract is discharged but the buyer nevertheless retains its rights to obtain damages for the seller's breach. Cancellation in effect means that the buyer no longer expects the seller to perform and that the buyer will not be rendering any more performance. Read section 2-106(3) and (4). Article 2 does not prescribe any procedure for cancelling a contract and does not require that the buyer notify the seller that the contract has been cancelled. Indeed, the buyer should be careful in communicating with the seller; any notification of cancellation should not impair or discharge its right to obtain damages. *See* UCC § 1-306.

Damages. As noted above, the buyer's damage remedies are based upon the expectation principle; they seek to place the buyer in the position the buyer would have been in if the seller had fully performed. UCC § 1-305. When the seller has not delivered the goods, the buyer is entitled to a return of any price that has been paid. UCC § 2-711(1). In addition to recovering the price that has been pre-paid, the buyer has two different options for measuring its expectation interest. First, the buyer may obtain substitute goods from someone else – that is, "cover" – and obtain damages from the seller measured by "the difference between the cost of cover and

---

[10] Harry M. Flechtner, *Buyers' Remedies in General and Buyers' Performance-Oriented Remedies*, 25 J.L. & COM. 339 (2005); Steven Walt, *For Specific Performance Under the United Nations Sales Convention*, 26 TEX. INT'L L.J. 211 (1991).

the contract price." UCC § 2-712(2). Let's pause for a moment. Consider which of the following two computations that phrase contemplates:

$$\text{damages} = \text{cost of cover} - \text{contract price}$$
$$\text{damages} = \text{contract price} - \text{cost of cover}$$

Even a moment's reflection should tell you that the buyer is damaged by the seller's non-delivery only if the cost of cover exceeds the contract price (so that the buyer paid more to acquire the goods from someone else than the buyer would have paid under the contract if the seller had performed). If the cost of cover was less than the contract price, the buyer is not damaged by – and in fact benefitted from – the seller's breach. Thus, the statutory formula is the first one listed above, not the second.

Alternatively, the aggrieved buyer may recover the difference between the market price and the contract price of the goods. UCC § 2-713. Consider which of the following is the proper expression of that formula:

$$\text{damages} = \text{market price} - \text{contract price}$$
$$\text{damages} = \text{contract price} - \text{market price}$$

In both cases – cover damages and market damages – the buyer may also recover incidental and consequential damages. UCC § 2-715. To illustrate the relationship between the specific damage remedies in Article 2 and the expectation principle, consider this example.

Example

State Street Motors contracts to sell a new car to Buyer for $40,000. Buyer pays $1,000 down and promises to pay the $39,000 balance upon delivery, which is slated to occur in two weeks (when State Street Motors expects to obtain the car from the manufacturer).

On the date for delivery, State Street Motors refuses to sell the car to Buyer. Perhaps State Street Motors was unable to obtain the car from the manufacturer, but the reason is not material. The point is, State Street Motors breaches by failing to tender performance. Buyer cancels the contract and State Street Motors becomes obligated to return the $1,000 down payment to Buyer. UCC § 2-711(1).

If, as is likely, the market price for such cars is fairly stable and, as is also likely, the $40,000 contract price was the car's fair market value – *i.e.*, was at the market price – Buyer is unlikely to have any damages. Buyer can probably find another seller willing to sell an identical car for $40,000. Whether Buyer chooses to purchase a car from another seller or not will make no difference. In either case, Buyer will have no other remedy (save perhaps a few incidental or consequential damages). The same would be true if the market price at the time for delivery were less than $40,000. Not only would Buyer have no additional damages, but Buyer would actually be better off because of the breach by State Street Motors: Buyer will have been excused from paying more for the car than it is worth.

If, on the other hand, the market price of the car at the time for delivery is $42,000 – which may be the case if the market price had risen after the original contract was formed or if the contract price had been below market at the time the parties reached their agreement – then Buyer will have two options. If Buyer purchases an identical car from another seller for $42,000, Buyer can recover the $2,000 difference between the original contract price and the cost of cover from State Street Motors. UCC § 2-712 (cover price minus contract price). After doing so, Buyer will be in the same economic situation as if the transaction with State Street Motors had been performed: Buyer will have a car and will have paid a net amount of $40,000 ($1,000 down payment + $42,000 cover price – return of $1,000 down payment – $2,000 in cover damages).

If Buyer does not purchase a substitute car, Buyer's expectation damages will be the same, but will be based on the market price of the car rather than the cost of cover. UCC § 2-713(1) (market price – contract price).

As you can see by this example, the remedial formulas are based upon the assumption that the cover price or the market price represents the value of the goods and that the aggrieved buyer has been damaged if it does not receive the full value of the goods to the extent that value exceeds the contract price for the goods.

Damages based on the cover price. An aggrieved buyer is not required to cover but often has both business and legal incentives to do so. From a business perspective, the buyer may need the goods for use in manufacturing or to otherwise maintain its operations. From a legal perspective, the buyer's ability to recover consequential damages depends upon whether the buyer has engaged in reasonable efforts to mitigate the harm caused by the breach. UCC § 2-715(2). For example, if failure to receive the goods will significantly disrupt the buyer's manufacturing or other operations such as by causing delay, obtaining substitute goods is often one relatively easy way to mitigate that type of consequential harm.[11]

In order to qualify as a cover transaction for purposes of section 2-712, the cover transaction must be made in good faith and without unreasonable delay. UCC § 2-712(1). These limitations are important to prevent the buyer from playing the market at the seller's expense. For example, if the market price for the goods fluctuates, the buyer – even one who needs the goods and knows it will eventually cover – might wait before entering into a cover transaction. If the market price goes down, the buyer pays less for the substitute goods and pockets the difference. If the market price rises, the buyer spends more but then seeks to treat the added cost as cover damages. The requirements that cover be effected in good faith and without unreasonable delay insulate the seller from this risk.

The good faith requirement may also help reduce the buyer's incentive to not seek the best price it could get for the cover transaction. Generally if someone else is paying the bill, there might be little incentive to obtain the goods at a reasonable price. The issue is whether the seller should be forced to pay a higher damage amount because the buyer did not take appropriate action under the circumstances to find the best price for the goods. While the price the buyer pays for the cover goods need not be the lowest possible price, the good faith limitation on recovering cover based damages helps to contain the buyer's discretion regarding the price it pays for the substitute goods.

Another limitation on cover damages is that the goods purchased must be a reasonable substitute for the goods due from the breaching seller. UCC § 2-712(1). This prevents the buyer from using the fortuity of the seller's breach to "upgrade" the quality of the goods. In other words, if the buyer purchases substitute goods that are of a higher quality than the goods contracted for, the buyer may not be entitled to cover damages.[12] While some difference in quality between the contracted for goods and the cover goods is tolerable, the seller should not have to pay for a significant upgrade in the quality.

Other issues occasionally arise in connection with cover. One such issue is whether the cover transaction can be with the breaching seller. For example,

---

[11] Remember that if there is serious disruption to the buyer's operation, the buyer may want to consider making the case for specific performance or replevin under section 2-716.

[12] *See TVI, Inc. v. Infosoft Technologies, Inc.*, 2008 WL 239784 (E.D. Mo. 2008); *Hessler v. Crystal Lake Chrysler-Plymouth, Inc.*, 788 N.E.2d 405 (Ill. Ct. App. 2003); *Ctkovic v. Boch, Inc.*, 2003 WL 139779 (Mass. App. Div. 2003).

assume that the seller repudiates the contract but then offers to supply the same goods for a higher price. If the buyer accepts that substitute transaction, has the buyer covered so that the higher price sets its damages? If so, how is that situation to be distinguished from a mere modification to the original transaction? If the buyer refuses to buy the goods at the higher price, has the buyer acted unreasonably so that it has failed to mitigate its consequential damages?[13] Another recurring issue is whether the buyer "covers" by creating the goods internally instead of buying them from a third party. In that situation, how would the cost of cover be computed?[14]

Damages based on the market price. Compared to the many questions involved in determining if the cover price is appropriate to use in the buyer's damage calculation, the market price calculation seems relatively simple. If the buyer has not covered – and only if the buyer has not covered[15]– the buyer may seek damages based on the market price for the goods. That market price is based on the price at the time the buyer learned of the breach, UCC § 2-713(1), and at the place of tender, UCC § 2-713(2). Obviously, the place for tender will be determined from the agreement of the parties, as supplemented by the Code's gap fillers.

The time the buyer learned of the breach is somewhat more troublesome. Section 2-723 provides a special rule on the time for measuring market damages if trial on the issue occurs before the scheduled time for performance. This can occur if the contract for sale was a long-term supply contract. Outside the context of a long-term supply contract, however, the Code does not give much guidance on how to determine when the buyer learned of the breach. A reccurring situation, giving rise to conflicting judicial decisions, involves a seller who has repudiated a contract. In such situations, the buyer has the right to wait a commercially reasonable time for the seller to perform or the buyer may immediately resort to remedies for breach. Review section 2-610. Should these options influence the determination of when the buyer learned of the breach?[16] If the market price fluctuates between the time

---

[13] *See Kelsey-Hayes Co. v. Galtaco Redlaw Castings Corp.*, 749 F. Supp. 794 (E.D. Mich. 1990).

[14] *See Dura-Wood Treating Co. v. Century Forest Indus., Inc.*, 675 F.2d 745 (5th Cir.), *cert. denied*, 459 U.S. 865 (1982).

[15] *See* UCC § 2-713 cmt. 5.

[16] *Compare Hess Energy, Inc. v. Lightning Oil Co.*, 338 F.3d 357 (4th Cir. 2003) (date of

the seller repudiates and a commercially reasonable time after repudiation, at which time should the market price be measured? Should the answer depend upon whether the buyer is actually awaiting the seller's performance? Another issue about when the buyer learned of the seller's breach can arise in a shipment contract. In some cases, the buyer may not learn of the breach until the goods fail to arrive at the destination, even though the seller breached days before by failing to tender the goods to the carrier. On which of those dates should the market price be measured?

How is market price proven? Read sections 2-723 and 2-724.

Expenses saved. The damage formulas based on the cover price and the market price both require that expenses saved as a consequence of the breach be deducted from the sum that the buyer is otherwise entitled to recover from the seller. This deduction is necessary to ensure that the damages awarded are limited to the amount necessary to protect the buyer's expectancy. To illustrate this principle, assume a seller agreed to sell equipment worth $100,000 to a buyer. The buyer expected to expend $1,000 to make modifications to its facilities to install the goods and, absent the sales contract, would have no need to make the modifications. The seller repudiates before the buyer makes any expenditures for the modifications. The buyer then decides either not to cover or to purchase substitute goods that do not necessitate the modifications. The buyer has saved $1,000 in expenses that should be deducted from the cover price-contract price or market price-contract price differential.

Buyer's incidental and consequential damages. Both section 2-712 (cover damages) and section 2-713 (market damages) also give the aggrieved buyer the right to recover incidental and consequential damages. Section 2-715 then defines what qualifies as incidental and consequential damages. Consequential losses are harms that the buyer suffers because the seller has not provided the goods. For example, assume the buyer has contracted to purchase a crank shaft to replace the broken one it uses in its mill. A failure to get the new crank shaft may result in a significant loss in business while the mill is shut down. Such lost profits may be recoverable. Under the common law, there are four principal limitations of the availability of an award for consequential damages:

(i) the damages must actually be caused by the breach;

---

tender under the contract) *with Cosden Oil & Chemical Co. v. Karl O. Helm Aktiengesellschaft*, 736 F.2d 1064 (5th Cir. 1984) (commercially reasonable time after the repudiation).

(ii) the consequential damages must arise from circumstances that the breaching party had reason to know about at the time the contract was formed;

(iii) the consequential damages must not have been readily avoidable by appropriate mitigating actions; and

(iv) the aggrieved party must prove the consequential damages with reasonable certainty.[17]

Section 2-715 expressly incorporates the first three of these limitations. No doubt the fourth also applies as a supplemental rule of law. *See* UCC §§ 1-103(b); 2-715 cmt. 4.

Incidental damages are a category of damages created by the drafters of Article 2. Under the common law, the types of damages comprising incidental damages would be subsumed within the category of consequential damages. Article 2 treats incidental damages separately because they are the sort of damages that arise naturally from the seller's breach and thus do not need to be subject to the common law's limiting principle of foreseeability. Rather, to recover incidental damages, the aggrieved party needs only to show that the incidental damages were caused by the breach and were reasonably incurred expenses. UCC § 2-715(1). Incidental damages that arise when the seller does not deliver the goods include the expenses associated with effecting cover, other than the cost of the cover goods. These may include, for example, the cost of long distance phone calls made to identify a willing seller of a suitable substitute goods.

Now use these principles to determine how buyer's damages should be measured in the following problems.

Problem 7-4

State Street Motors contracts to sell a new car to Buyer for $40,000. The car is to have power windows, heated seats, and an enhanced stereo package. Buyer pays $1,000 down and promises to pay the $39,000 balance upon delivery, which is slated to occur in two weeks (when State Street Motors expects to obtain the car from the manufacturer).

On the date for delivery, State Street Motors refuses to sell the car to Buyer because State Street Motors was unable to obtain the car with the

---

[17] *See* RESTATEMENT (SECOND) OF CONTRACTS §§ 347, 350–352. *See also* George S. Geis, *Empirically Assessing Hadley v. Baxendale*, 32 FLA. ST. U. L. REV. 897 (2005).

specified options from the manufacturer. Buyer cancels the contract and then purchases from a different seller a car of the same make and model. Buyer pays $42,000 for the substitute car, which also comes with a moon roof and air conditioning but lacks the enhanced stereo system. The enhanced stereo system is an option that retails for $500. What is the measure of Buyer's damages under section 2-712? What other facts might affect the analysis of this question?

Problem 7-5

On June 1, Blue Sky Airlines contracts to purchase 200,000 gallons of jet fuel from Supersonic Aviation at a price of $5 per gallon for delivery to Blue Sky's facilities in Chicago on July 1. On June 15, Supersonic Aviation repudiates the contract. Blue Sky Airlines makes the following purchases:

- 100,000 gallons of jet fuel on June 16 for $5.20 per gallon;
- 200,000 gallons of jet fuel on June 21 for $5.40 per gallon; and
- 200,000 gallons of jet fuel on June 28 for $5.60 per gallon.

A. If all of the June purchases are for delivery to Blue Sky's facilities in Chicago, what is the proper measure of Blue Sky's damages under section 2-712?

B. How, if at all, would that analysis change if the June 16th purchase called for delivery to Blue Sky's facilities in Atlanta?

Problem 7-6

Manufacturer, located in Phoenix, agreed to sell ten wooden desks to Buyer, located in Seattle. Each desk was a standard unit ordered from Manufacturer's catalog, priced at $500 per desk, for a total purchase price of $5,000. Buyer made a down payment of $100 and agreed to pay the rest 30 days after the Buyer received the desks in Seattle. The parties agreed to ship the goods F.O.B. Phoenix on June 1. The parties agreed that Manufacturer would use Excellent Cargo Haulers, Inc. to transport the goods. The cost of shipping the desks was approximately $50 per desk.

On May 20, Manufacturer notified Buyer that it would not be able to supply the desks ordered as it had discontinued its production of that model, and offered to sell a different model for $800 per desk. Buyer sent the following response:

> Due to your inability to supply the desks contracted for, please cancel our order and refund our down payment of $100 plus interest.

Buyer then purchased ten desks from Office Supply Co. located in Seattle for $6,000 with no charge for delivery to Buyer's office. The desks are bigger and contain more storage space than the desks Buyer had ordered from Manufacturer, but are made of metal instead of wood. Buyer spent approximately one week searching for desks that would work in its office space, and made numerous phone calls to find a supplier that could deliver the desks to Buyer on short notice. Even so, Office Supply was not able to deliver the desks to Buyer until June 15, delaying Buyer's office expansion by several weeks. Buyer estimates that it incurred losses as it had to pay employees who could not work and it lost sales due to the inability of its employees to do their jobs.

A. What are Buyer's remedies against Manufacturer?

B. What if Buyer was able to purchase ten desks from Office Supply Co. for $4,000? How does that change the analysis?

C. What if Buyer does not buy any desks at all and forgoes the planned office expansion due to a downturn in the economy? How does that change the analysis?

Problem 7-7

On April 1, Bride, who is planning a massive wedding reception on Long Island, contracts to purchase 5,000 lbs of live lobsters for $50,000 from Seafarer, a resident of Maine. The contract calls for delivery, F.O.B. Bar Harbor, Maine, on July 1. The cost of shipping the live lobsters from Bar Harbor to Long Island is $2,000. On June 1, Seafarer telephones Bride and repudiates the contract. Bride is unable to find sufficient lobsters elsewhere and ends up purchasing roast beef on June 15, which she then serves at the reception. If the market price of lobsters is as indicated on the following chart, what is the proper measure of Bride's damages? *See* UCC § 2-610.

	April 1	June 1	June 15	July 1
Bar Harbor	$10/lb.	$12/lb.	$13/lb.	$14/lb.
Long Island	$11/lb.	$13/lb.	$14/lb.	$15/lb.

Problem 7-8

Sand & Stone Supply Co. contracts to sell to Builder all the gravel Builder needs for road construction over a 10-year period. The price for the gravel is adjusted yearly based upon published averages. In the fifth year of performance, Sand & Stone repudiates the contract. Builder sues for damages a year later.

A. If the case comes up for trial the following year (*i.e.*, in year seven of the contract), what is the time for measuring market price?

B. If the case comes up for trial four years after the buyer filed the lawsuit (*i.e.*, after the contract would have expired on its own), what is the time for measuring market damages?

The damages formulas in sections 2-712 and 2-713 probably do a good job of protecting the aggrieved buyer's expectancy interests in most situations. However, it is impossible for one or two relatively simple statutory formulas to account for all the situations that may arise. As a result, the statutory formulas on occasion seem to yield a result inconsistent with the general rule of section 1-305(a) that the aggrieved party be put in the same position as if the contract had been fully performed.[18] What should happen then? Consider the following problems.

---

[18] Actually, the principle expressed in section 1-305(a) is that the aggrieved party be put in "as good a position" as if the contract had been performed.

Problem 7-9

On March 1, Builder contracted to construct an office building for Developer. Under the terms of that contract, Builder is to acquire the necessary materials and Developer will recompense Builder at cost plus 10%. On April 1, Builder and Steel Supplier agree that Steel Supplier will sell Builder 500 steel girders of specified dimensions and hardness for a price of $70,000. Delivery is to occur by June 1. In May, Steel Supplier informs Builder that it will not be able to deliver the goods on time. Builder purchases the needed girders from a substitute seller who, because of the need for quick delivery, charges Builder $90,000. What is the proper measure of Builder's damages for Steel Supplier's breach? *See KGM Harvesting Co. v. Fresh Network*, 42 Cal. Rptr. 2d 286 (Cal. Ct. App. 1995).

Problem 7-10

Butane is in the business of buying and selling heating oil. Butane buys in bulk from large refineries in the Gulf Coast and sells quantities to distributors and retailers in the Midwest. On August 1, Butane contracts to purchase 100,000 gallons of heating oil from Supplier in New Orleans for $2.50 per gallon. The contract calls for delivery F.O.B. New Orleans on November 1. The cost of transporting the heating oil to Butane's facilities in St. Louis is expected to be $5,000.

On August 3, Butane contracts to sell 100,000 gallons to Customer. That contract states a price of $2.70 per gallon and calls for delivery on November 10, F.O.B. Butane's place of business in St. Louis. The cost of transporting the fuel to Customer is expected to be $500.

In October, the market price of heating oil skyrockets to $4.50 in New Orleans and $4.70 in St. Louis, and Supplier repudiates the contract with Butane. Butane is unable to procure heating oil from another source in time to make delivery to Customer, and so Butane reluctantly repudiates that contract.

A. Assuming Customer will hold Butane responsible for all of Customer's damages, what is the proper measure of Butane's damages against Supplier? *Compare H-W-H Cattle Co. v. Schroeder*, 767 F.2d 437 (8th

Cir. 1985); *Allied Canners & Packing, Inc. v. Victor Packing Co.*, 209
Cal. Rptr. 60 (Cal. Ct. App. 1984), *with TexPar Energy, Inc. v. Murphy
Oil USA, Inc.*, 45 F.3d 1111 (7th Cir. 1995); *Tongish v. Thomas*, 840
P.2d 471 (Kan. 1992).

B. Assuming Customer waives all its claims for breach against Butane,
    what is the proper measure of Butane's damages against Supplier?

C. How, if at all, would the analysis change if Butane planned to burn the
    heating oil it purchased from Supplier for its own heating needs?

**Buyer's damages for seller's repudiation or nondelivery under CISG and
UNIDROIT Principles.** CISG Article 75 allows the buyer's damages to be
measured using the price of substitute goods and Article 76 allows the buyer's
damages to be measured using the "current" price of the goods, a reference to the
market price. The buyer's ability to use either provision to measure its damages
depends upon the buyer's ability to avoid the contract for fundamental breach. A
fundamental breach can occur when the seller repudiates its obligations under the
contract or when the seller fails to deliver any goods. CISG Arts. 25, 49, and 72.
To avoid the contract for fundamental breach, the buyer must give notice of that fact
to the seller. CISG Art. 26. The buyer may also be entitled to consequential
damages, CISG Art. 74, subject to reduction if the buyer fails to engage in
appropriate mitigation efforts, CISG Art. 77.

The UNIDROIT Principles are similar. An aggrieved party that has terminated
a contract may measure its damages using a replacement cost, UNIDROIT Art.
7.4.5, or by a current price, UNIDROIT Art. 7.4.6. The UNIDROIT Principles also
allow for recovery of consequential damages proven with sufficient certainty and
foreseeability and subject to a mitigation principle. UNIDROIT Principles Arts.
7.4.2 through 7.4.4 and 7.4.8.

SECTION 3. SELLER'S TENDER FAILS TO CONFORM TO THE
CONTRACT REQUIREMENTS

After any tender of goods by the seller, the buyer must either accept or reject
the goods. The buyer's decision to accept or reject the goods will significantly
affect each party's rights from that point forward. For example, if the buyer accepts

the goods, the buyer becomes obligated to pay the contract price. UCC § 2-607(1). This is so even if the goods or the seller's tender did not conform to the contract requirements. However, acceptance of the goods does not deprive the buyer of all remedies for breach. The buyer may still maintain an action for damages for any problem with the goods or the tender, UCC § 2-714, and may, in some situations, even be entitled to revoke its acceptance, UCC § 2-608, and recover damages for the seller's breach based upon a cover price or market price measurement, UCC §§ 2-712, 2-713, 2-715.

In contrast, if the buyer rejects the goods after a nonconforming tender, the buyer generally does not become obligated to pay for the goods. In addition, the buyer has an action for breach of contract based upon the cover price or market price measurement. UCC §§ 2-712, 2-713, 2-715. However, in some circumstances, the seller may have a right to circumvent the buyer's cause of action by curing the problem with the goods or the tender. UCC § 2-508.

The remainder of this section discusses when the buyer has the right to reject, what the buyer must do to reject, the effect of rejection or acceptance, and how the decision to accept or reject the goods following a nonconforming tender determines the buyer's subsequent remedial options.[19] Before considering those questions, it is important to have a proper understanding of the meaning of rejection of the goods. Rejection of the goods is the buyer's determination to refuse the seller's tender of the goods. It is not a rescission or repudiation of the contract; it is merely a refusal of the seller's tender of performance.

A. Acceptance or Rejection of the Goods

Analysis of the buyer's acceptance or rejection of the goods involves two separate inquiries: (i) does the buyer have the right to reject the goods; and (ii) has the buyer actually and effectively rejected the goods.

---

[19] In Chapter Nine, we will discuss the buyer's breach by wrongfully rejecting the goods and what effect that the buyer's decision to reject or accept the goods has on the seller's remedies for the buyer's breach.

1. Buyer's Right to Reject

Analysis of the buyer's right to reject the goods begins with section 2-601, which states that the buyer may reject if "the goods or the tender of delivery fail in any respect to conform to the contract." Read the definition of "conforming" in section 2-106(2). This is known as the "perfect tender rule," and it places a rather high burden on the seller given that little in this world is perfect. However, the perfect tender rule is subject to two important limitations.

First, as expressly noted in section 2-601 and as discussed in Chapter Five, the parties may have agreed to limit the remedies available for a breach. *See* UCC §§ 2-718, 2-719. For example, the parties' agreement may limit the buyer's right to reject the goods to situations involving major defects, rather than cosmetic problems. Alternatively, the agreement may provide that the buyer's exclusive remedy for a tender of nonconforming goods is recovery of liquidated damages. Such a provision would appear to preclude the buyer's ability to reject the goods for a nonconformity. On the other hand, the buyer's right to reject nonconforming goods is such an integral part of the structure of Article 2, courts may be reluctant to interpret such a clause as truly negating the buyer's right to reject and instead restrict the clause to accepted goods. More important, usage of trade, course of dealing, and course of performance – which are components of the parties' agreement – may circumscribe the buyer's right to reject goods for minor defects. Perhaps the general obligation of good faith imposed by section 1-304 does so as well.[20]

The second limitation on the buyer's right to reject arises in installment contracts. *Compare* UCC §§ 2-601 *with* 2-612. An installment contract is one which calls for delivery of the goods in separate lots, with acceptance after each delivery. UCC §§ 2-612(1), 2-307.[21] In such a contract, the buyer's remedies are limited in two ways. First, the buyer's right to reject an individual installment of goods is limited to instances in which the nonconformity of that installment substantially impairs the value of that installment and cannot be cured.[22] If the

---

[20] *See* William H. Lawrence, *Appropriate Standards for a Buyer's Refusal to Keep Goods Tendered by a Seller*, 35 WM. & MARY L. REV. 1635 (1994).

[21] The mere fact that the buyer has agreed to *pay* in installments does not make the arrangement an installment contract.

[22] If the nonconformity as to the installment is a defect in the required documents, the

problem does not substantially impair the value of the installment to the buyer or if the seller gives adequate assurance that it plans to cure the nonconformity and the buyer is not entitled to cancel the entire contract, the buyer must accept that installment. UCC § 2-612(2). Second, the buyer is entitled to cancel an installment contract only if the nonconformity as to one or more installments substantially impairs the entire value of the entire contract. UCC § 2-612(3).

Nothing in the Code defines or explains "substantial impairment." Some courts have analogized the standard to the concept of "material breach" under the common law, which is similarly vague and often difficult to apply.[23] What is clear is that substantial impairment is to be judged not in the abstract, but in reference to the normal and specifically known purposes of the contract. UCC § 2-612 cmt. 4. Thus, a brief delay that would not normally provide grounds for rejecting an installment might nevertheless qualify as substantial impairment if the seller is aware that it will cause significant problems for the buyer.

One possible reason underlying this more restrictive rule on rejection of goods in installment contracts may be a desire to preserve the parties' relationship. The theory is that, unlike in a one-shot transaction, the parties in an installment contract have more at stake in continued cooperation and the law should recognize and

---

substantial impairment rule does not seem to apply. The buyer may reject the goods due to that nonconformity in the required documents.

[23] *E.g., Midwest Mobile Diagnostic Imaging, L.L.C. v. Dynamics Corp. of America*, 965 F. Supp. 1003 (W.D. Mich 1997), *aff'd*, 165 F.3d 27 (6th Cir. 1998). *See also* RESTATEMENT (SECOND) OF CONTRACTS § 241, indicating that the following factors are to be considered in determining whether a breach is material:

(a) the extent to which the injured party will be deprived of the benefit which he reasonably expected;

(b) the extent to which the injured party can be adequately compensated for the part of that benefit of which he will be deprived;

(c) the extent to which the party failing to perform or to offer to perform will suffer forfeiture;

(d) the likelihood that the party failing to perform or to offer to perform will cure his failure, taking account of all the circumstances including any reasonable assurances; [and]

(e) the extent to which the behavior of the party failing to perform or to offer to perform comports with standards of good faith and fair dealing.

respect this different. Do you agree? Is the underlying assumption correct?[24] Even if it is, might it not counsel in favor of expanding the seller's right to cure following rejection, rather than limiting the buyer's right to reject in the first instance?

In both installment contracts and non-installment contracts, a buyer who has the right to reject the goods need not choose the same action with respect to all the goods. Instead, the buyer may accept some of the goods and reject others, so long as the buyer accepts complete commercial units. *See* UCC § 2-601(c). Thus a buyer of three computers could accept two and reject one but a buyer of shoes could not accept the left and reject the right and a car buyer could not accept the chassis and reject the motor. *See* UCC § 2-105(6) (defining "commercial unit").

Problem 7-11

Sterling, Inc. is a vegetable distributor and Bluto Foods Co. is a manufacturer of canned soups. On April 1, the parties entered into a written contract for the sale of 1,000 bushels of "Early Girl" tomatoes at $40.00 per bushel, to be shipped F.O.B. Sterling's place of business on or before July 15. The goods were to be delivered in a single lot and Bluto was to make payment 30 days after the goods were received. Nothing was said in the agreement about rejection.

A. Assuming there is no evidence regarding the impact upon the value of the bargain, in which of the following independent scenarios could Bluto properly reject all of the tomatoes?
   1. A timely tender of 990 bushels of tomatoes.
   2. A timely tender of 1,000 bushels of tomatoes, ten bushels of which contained a variety other than "Early Girl."
   3. A tender of 1,000 bushels of "Early Girl" tomatoes that had been shipped on July 16.
   4. A tender of 1,000 bushels of "Early Girl" tomatoes that were shipped on July 14 but, because of an erroneous delivery

---

[24] "[T]ransactors do not necessarily want the relationship-preserving norms they follow in performing contracts and cooperatively resolving disputes among themselves to be used by third-party neutrals to decide cases when they are in an end-game situation." Lisa Bernstein, *Merchant Law in a Merchant Court: Rethinking the Code's Search for Immanent Business Norms*, 144 U. PA. L. REV. 1765, 1770 (1996).

instruction by Sterling, transit took four more days than normal. UCC § 2-504.

B. Assume Sterling tendered 1,000 bushels but 50 of them were rotten.
    1. May Bluto accept the 950 bushels of good tomatoes and reject the 50 bushels of rotten tomatoes?
    2. May Bluto accept 500 bushels of the good tomatoes and reject the remainder?

C. Suppose Sterling agreed to ship 100 bushels by July 15, and 100 bushels each week for the next 9 weeks.
    1. May Bluto reject the entire first shipment if it was ten bushels short? What if ten bushels had rotten tomatoes? What if the entire shipment were sent one day late?
    2. Assume that in the first shipment, 10 bushels were missing. Sterling shipped the 10 bushels along with the second shipment, but the second shipment (110 bushels) had five bushels that were rotten. The third shipment arrived five days late and the fourth shipment contained 200 bushels (which overwhelmed Bluto's capacity for properly dealing with the tomatoes). The fifth shipment contained 100 bushels and was on time, but 10 bushels contained a variety of tomatoes other than "Early Girl." May Bluto reject the fifth shipment and cancel the contract?

Problem 7-12

You represent Sterling, Inc., a vegetable distributor negotiating a contract to sell 1,000 bushels of "Early Girl" tomatoes to Bluto Foods Co., a manufacturer of canned soups. The contract will call for the tomatoes to be shipped in a single lot. What sort of clause would you draft to limit or eliminate the buyer's rejection right?

2. Making the Rejection Effective

Acceptance and rejection of the goods are contrary actions. As noted in the discussion of the buyer's inspection rights in Chapter Four, the buyer cannot do both and the buyer cannot do neither. Perhaps because of that, Article 2 does not state what a buyer must do to reject the goods; it merely states what is not an effective rejection, *see* UCC § 2-602(1), and identifies the acts that qualify as acceptance. *See* UCC § 2-606. A buyer who wants to reject the goods must avoid doing anything that qualifies as an acceptance of them. Thus, for example, the buyer wishing to reject the goods must not inform the seller that the buyer will take or retain the goods despite their nonconformity, and must not do any act inconsistent with the seller's ownership of the goods. UCC § 2-606(1)(a), (c). Of course, merely taking possession of the goods does not, by itself, necessarily qualify as acceptance because that act is often merely a prelude to inspecting the goods.

However, doing nothing will not be effective as a rejection. A buyer who fails to make an effective rejection after the opportunity to inspect has expired is deemed to have accepted the goods and thus will be liable for the price of the goods, even though the buyer may also have a claim for breach of contract against the seller if the goods or tender were nonconforming to the contract requirements. UCC § 2-606(1)(b), 2-607(1), (2). Therefore, the buyer needs to reject within a reasonable time and must seasonably notify the seller of the rejection. UCC §§ 2-602(1), 1-205, 1-202. A failure to provide this notification in a timely manner renders the attempted rejection ineffective; that is the buyer will be deemed to have accepted the goods.

The timing of the buyer's notification to the seller of rejection is connected to the length of time that is necessary for a reasonable inspection of the goods as allowed under section 2-513. Under that section, the buyer has a reasonable time for inspection of the goods prior to acceptance. The amount of time that is reasonable will undoubtedly depend upon many factors, including the complexity of the goods.

Problem 7-13

A buyer can give or fail to give the section 2-602(1) notification in two different situations: when the buyer has a right to reject the goods and when the buyer does not have the right to reject the goods. As a result, there are four possible situations:
- (i)   a right to reject coupled with a timely notification;
- (ii) a right to reject coupled with an untimely notification;
- (iii) no right to reject coupled with a timely notification; and
- (iv) no right to reject coupled with an untimely notification.

Using the matrix below, and the Code sections cited above, determine for each of these situations: (i) whether the buyer has accepted the goods; and (ii) which party has breached the contract.

	Timely Notification of Rejection	Untimely Notification of Rejection
Right to Reject		
No Right to Reject		

Article 2 does not specify what the buyer's notification of rejection must include. No doubt the buyer must make clear in some manner that the buyer will not take or keep the goods. Therefore, the buyer need not specify the basis for rejection. In other words, the buyer need not – to have an effective rejection – detail the defects with the goods or nonconformity with the tender. Nevertheless, the buyer does have an incentive to include that information. Read section 2-605(1). This provision precludes the buyer from relying on an unstated defect to justify the buyer's rejection of the goods in certain circumstances. When this rule applies, the buyer's rejection of the goods will still be *effective*, but may no longer be *rightful*. If the buyer cannot rely on the unstated problem to justify the rejection, and if there are no other problems that justify the rejection, this section may make the rejection wrongful. Put simply, it can convert a breach by the seller (tendering nonconforming goods) into a breach by the buyer (failing to accept).

Problem 7-14

Review the matrix in problem 7-13. How, if at all, do the requirements placed on the buyer in section 2-605(1) affect the answer to the two questions posed? In other words, if the buyer fails to inform the seller of a problem with the goods in a situation in which the buyer had a right to reject and gave timely notification of rejection (the upper left box), what result will follow?

Problem 7-15

Your client is Bulk Movers, Inc., a commercial trucking company. It is negotiating to purchase five trucks from Semi-Tough Motors, Inc., a retailer, with one truck to be delivered on the first day of each of the next five months. When trucks are delivered, Bulk Movers wants to be able to drive the trucks and put them through a rigorous mechanical examination. Draft language to propose to Semi-Tough that would preserve Bulk Movers' right to reject any truck that does not conform to the contract requirements after the mechanical examination.

B. Effect of Rejection

Assume the buyer has rightfully and effectively notified the seller that it is rejecting the goods. The seller will typically respond in any one of three ways. First, the seller may want to try and fix the nonconformities and thus offer a cure to the buyer. Second, the seller may decide to simply take the goods back and refund whatever portion of the purchase price the buyer has already paid. Third, the seller may resist the buyer's efforts to reject and refuse to take the goods back. In each of these cases, the buyer may seek an award of damages based upon the seller's breach. In this section, we explore these three topics: the seller's right to cure, the buyer's actions with respect to the rejected goods, and the buyer's right to damages.

1. *The Seller's Right to Cure*

Upon learning of the buyer's rejection, the seller will often wish to cure the nonconformity. Sometimes the seller wants to do this for legal reasons: to avoid or reduce liability to the buyer for breach. More commonly, the seller wants to do this for business or ethical reasons: to salvage the transaction (and any profit associated with it), to have satisfied customers, and to fulfill its promises. Assuming the parties' agreement does not expand or limit the seller's right to cure,[25] section 2-508

---

[25] *See Mercury Marine v. Clear River Constr. Co.*, 839 So. 2d 508 (Miss. 2003) (limitation of remedy clauses may preclude buyer's ability to reject the goods and require the buyer to

governs the seller's ability to force a cure on the buyer. Notice, that nothing in that section requires the seller to cure the problem. Section 2-508 gives the seller a right but does not impose a duty. Notice also that nothing in that section, or Article 2, allows the buyer to require the seller to cure the breach.[26] Section 2-508 is a one-way provision, it gives the seller a right to cure if it chooses to do so, it does not give the buyer a right to force the seller to cure.

Problem 7-16

You represent the buyer who is negotiating the purchase of some custom-built manufacturing equipment. You are contemplating proposing a clause that would give the buyer the right to insist that the seller cure defects with the goods. What benefit, if any, would such a clause have?

Section 2-508 does not give the seller a right to cure all the time. Instead that right to cure is limited to two situations: (i) when the time for the seller's performance has not expired; and (ii) when the seller had reasonable grounds to believe that the goods would be acceptable. The first of these is fairly easy to understand, but also fairly limited. If the contract calls for delivery by June 1 and the seller tenders nonconforming goods on May 17, the seller will have two weeks to cure the breach by tendering conforming goods. The second situation is less obvious.

Problem 7-17

Construct a scenario in which a seller who tendered nonconforming goods would have a right to cure because the seller had reasonable grounds for believing the tender would be acceptable. If possible, keep your scenario simple, one that involves a sale of household goods to a consumer.

Section 2-508 does not specify what qualifies as a cure. Presumably, it is something that negates the effect of the breach and puts the buyer in the position as

---

accept the seller's proffered cure).

[26] Although if the seller's breach consists of not repairing defective goods, the buyer may be able to get an award of specific performance. *See* UCC § 2-716.

if the seller had performed properly. What this means in any particular case will depend on the precise nature of the seller's breach.

For example, assume the seller has provided goods that fail to conform to the contract. To cure the breach, the seller will have to provide the buyer with conforming goods. In some circumstances that may mean that the seller can repair the goods; in other circumstances it may mean that the seller must provide replacement goods. If the repaired or replacement goods, as the case may be, do not then conform to the contract requirements, the seller will of course not have cured the breach.

But what if the seller's breach is a late delivery of conforming goods? Is it possible for the seller to cure that breach? Unless the seller can reverse time, the answer is no, that breach cannot be cured. Of course, even though late delivery may not be cured, the buyer may waive the breach or agree to some discount against the price or other compensation for the late delivery. While not a "cure" of the breach, the buyer's agreement to such compensation for the late delivery would constitute a settlement of the buyer's claim for breach of contract against the seller.

What is the consequence of the buyer refusing a cure that the seller has a right to provide and has attempted to provide? Has the buyer breached the contract?

Now try your hand at a few more problems.

Problem 7-18

Barbara purchased a car from State Street Motors. In each of the following independent scenarios, determine whether State Street Motors has offered to cure the breach.

A. While driving the car home from the showroom, the rear-view mirror fell off the windshield. State Street Motors offered to re-attach the mirror at no charge to Barbara.

B. The first time Barbara attempted to start the car after she got it home, the starter would not engage.
   1. State Street Motors offered to replace the starter the next day with a new part provided by the manufacturer at no charge to Barbara.
   2. State Street Motors offered to replace the starter with a new part provided by the manufacturer at no charge to Barbara. State Street Motors did not have a new starter on hand and it estimated that it

would take three business days to receive one, unless Barbara were willing to pay the cost of express shipping. *See Travelers Indem. Co. v. Maho Machine Tool Corp.*, 952 F.2d 26 (2d Cir. 1991).

C. While driving the car home from the showroom, the entire exhaust system fell off. State Street Motors offered to replace the exhaust system with parts salvaged from other cars in its inventory. *Compare Bowen v. Foust*, 925 S.W.2d 211 (Mo. Ct. App. 1996); *Zabriskie Chevrolet, Inc. v. Smith*, 240 A.2d 195 (N.J. Super. Ct. 1968), *with Wilson v. Scampoli*, 228 A.2d 848 (D.C. 1967).

D. On the drive home from the showroom, the car stalled when Barbara stopped at a red light and would not restart. State Street Motors towed the car to its repair shop and replaced the battery. The car seemed to be running fine and Barbara drove it home. The next day, the car started but several electrical systems in the car went haywire; the horn would not stop sounding, the lights were blinking on and off, and the radio would not work. Barbara could not drive it given the problems the car was having. State Street Motors towed the car to the dealership and replaced several electrical components. Two days later, the check engine light on the dash board came on. Barbara brought the car back in, State Street Motors inspected it, and then assured her that the problems was due to an electrical malfunction in the dashboard (*i.e.,* there was nothing in fact wrong with the engine). State Street Motors offered to repair the car at no cost to Barbara. Barbara objected and told State Street Motors that she did not want the car any more. Instead, she wanted a new, trouble free car. State Street Motors refused to take the car back.

Problem 7-19

Buyer contracts to purchase bolts for its assembly process from Seller. Because there is limited storage space at Buyer's facility, and Buyer can store only a few days worth of bolts there, Seller has agreed to deliver the bolts "just in time" for use in the Buyer's process. Under the terms of the agreement, deliveries are scheduled for the beginning of the day every Tuesday and Friday for the next three months.

A. Due to a mix up at the Seller's shipping department, the bolts due to Buyer's plant on Friday were not delivered on Friday. Buyer called Seller and Seller promised that the bolts would be there no later than the following Monday afternoon. Buyer protests because, under current production rates, Buyer will not have enough bolts to get through the entire day on Monday. Seller says it will try and get the bolts there more quickly but cannot promise that the bolts will be there before the end of the day on Monday. What are Buyer's options at this point? What are the risks of each course of action? What should Buyer do to preserve the most flexibility in making arguments later on if Buyer sues Seller for breach of contract? Does section 2-508 apply to this situation?

B. Seller delivered a shipment of bolts to Buyer on Tuesday morning. Buyer tested a sampling of the bolts and notified Seller early that afternoon that Buyer was rejecting the bolts because they failed the testing process. Seller promises to send a new shipment of bolts that should arrive by Wednesday morning. Does Buyer have to accept that offer to cure? UCC §§ 2-508, 2-612.

C. Over the course of the first two months of the contract period, Seller's deliveries of bolts were often late and the bolts were of a poor (nonconforming) quality. Seller has consistently sent replacement bolts when Buyer has complained but Buyer's production process has been interrupted on several occasions. Buyer has called you because the bolts Seller delivered today were not of the required quality. When Buyer called Seller to reject the installment, Seller again promised to send new bolts by the next morning. Buyer is fed up and wants to find a new supplier. If Buyer refuses to allow Seller to send replacement bolts and cancels the contract, will Buyer have breached? UCC §§ 2-508, 2-612.

D. Buyer is negotiating with a new supplier for bolts. In light of the past experience with Seller, Buyer wants you to draft a clause that will allow the Buyer to demand a cure when it wants to, refuse a cure it does not want, and get out of the deal if it thinks the supplier is not performing adequately. Draft language to accomplish that goal.

2.   Care of the Rejected Goods

In some cases, such as when the buyer is to pick up the goods at the seller's location, the buyer may reject the goods before any transfer of possession occurs. In such a case, the buyer will have no duty to care for the rejected goods. Similarly, if the seller is to deliver the goods to the buyer, on rare occasions it may be so obvious that the goods or tender are nonconforming that the buyer rejects the goods before they are offloaded and the buyer never takes possession of them. More commonly, though, the buyer takes delivery of the goods from the seller or a carrier before discovering the nonconformity and only later – after inspecting the goods – does the buyer reject them.

What does the buyer do with the rejected goods in its possession? The buyer is in essence a bailee, holding possession of goods that belong to another. *See* UCC § 2-401(4). Not surprisingly, Article 2 requires that a buyer in possession of the rejected goods take reasonable care of the goods for the time necessary to allow the seller to retrieve the goods. UCC § 2-602(2)(b). A merchant buyer may have further duties, including an obligation to comply with the seller's instructions regarding the goods and a duty to sell goods that are perishable or declining rapidly in value. UCC § 2-603.

The buyer may also have rights in the rejected goods. In particular, if the buyer has paid part of the price or has incurred expenses in dealing with the goods, the buyer will have a security interest – in other words, a lien – in the goods to secure those amounts. Read section 2-711(3). *See also* UCC § 9-110. The buyer may refuse to return the goods until the seller refunds the price paid and compensates the buyer for the expenses incurred. If the seller fails to do so, the buyer may sell the goods using the sale process found in section 2-706 (which will be discussed in Chapter Nine) and credit amounts received against the seller's obligations. In addition, if the seller fails instruct the buyer what to do with the goods, the buyer may sell the goods and remit the proceeds of the sale to the seller, minus the expenses of storage and conducting the sale. Read section 2-604.

A buyer who uses rejected goods, other than pursuant to its rights or duties outlined above, runs the risk that it will be deemed to have accepted the goods. *See* UCC § 2-606 cmt. 4. In other words, if the buyer's post-rejection use of the goods is inconsistent with the seller's ownership of the goods or otherwise wrongful as to the seller, the seller may treat the buyer's post-rejection actions as an acceptance of the goods (making the buyer liable for the price, UCC § 2-607(1)) or bring a claim for conversion (making the buyer liable for the value of the goods under tort law). *See* UCC § 2-602(2)(a).

One obvious implication of this rule is that the buyer should normally refrain from subjecting rejected goods to a manufacturing process. For example, a buyer of plastic resin that uses the resin to make injection moldings will likely be deemed to have accepted the resin despite any previous communications to the contrary.

Nevertheless, this rule can present a problem for the buyer. In some unusual situations, the buyer cannot realistically avoid using the goods despite having rejected them. Consider the case of a buyer who purchases new wall-to-wall carpeting, which the seller installs in the buyer's living room on a Friday afternoon. Within moments after the installer leaves, the buyer notices a noxious odor emanating from the carpet. The buyer calls the seller, unequivocally rejects the goods, and demands that they be removed. The seller promises to have the carpet taken out on Monday morning. Over the weekend, may the buyer walk on the carpet or must the buyer stay out of the living room to avoid accepting the goods?

There can be little doubt that this carpet purchaser will have a license to make limited use of the carpet over the weekend. But what if the buyer's use of the goods is avoidable but undertaken in an effort to minimize consequential damages? The paradigm case is a consumer who has purchased a car or mobile home, rightfully and effectively rejected that good, but needs to continue using it for transportation or living space because the seller refuses to allow the buyer to return the goods. The evolving majority view is that if the buyer's use is reasonable and necessary under the circumstances, that use is neither an acceptance nor a conversion of the rejected goods.[27] As one court noted:

> The reasonableness of the buyer's use of a defective good is a question of
> fact for the jury that is to be based on the facts and circumstances of each

---

[27] *Romy v. Picker Int'l, Inc.*, 1992 WL 70403 (E.D. Pa. 1992), *aff'd*, 986 F.2d 1409 (3d Cir. 1993) (use of MRI machine by doctor after revocation was reasonable and part of the duty to mitigate damages); *North River Homes, Inc. v. Bosarge*, 594 So. 2d 1153 (Miss. 1992) (use of mobile home for 12 months after revocation justified by seller's assurances of cure and buyer's financial inability to move); *Braden v. Stem*, 571 So. 2d 1116 (Ala. 1990) (buyer's use of used car for seven months after revocation justified because buyer needed the car to transport a child); *Cuesta v. Classic Wheels, Inc.*, 818 A.2d 448 (N.J. Super. Ct. App. Div. 2003) (use of the car for two years after attempted revocation could be reasonable, remanded for determination). *See* John R. Bates, *Continued Use of Goods After Rejection or Revocation of Acceptance: The UCC Rule Revealed, Reviewed, and Revised*, 25 RUTGERS L.J. 1 (1993).

case. Several factors that the jury may consider include the seller's instructions to the buyer after revocation of acceptance; the degree of economic and other hardship that the buyer would suffer if he discontinued using the defective good; the reasonableness of the buyer's use after revocation as a method of mitigating damages; the degree of prejudice to the seller; and whether the seller acted in bad faith.[28]

Problem 7-20

Bancroft purchased a new laptop computer over the internet from Silicon Systems, the manufacturer. Bancroft purchased the laptop for use on business when traveling and to replace an aging desktop computer that Bancroft used at home. When the laptop arrived, Bancroft noticed immediately that the screen was scratched. Nevertheless, Bancroft installed several software applications onto the laptop. Although the computer seemed to be operating properly, Bancroft called Silicon Systems to complain about the scratched screen and reject the computer. The customer service representative instructed Bancroft to return the laptop and promised to send a replacement after Silicon Systems received the damaged laptop. Bancroft objected to the delay, noting that this would take several days. Bancroft was scheduled to leave on a business trip in two days and needed a laptop to make a presentation. The customer service representative politely but firmly insisted that Silicon Systems would not send a replacement until it received the original back. The representative also indicated that if Bancroft used the original laptop on that trip or otherwise failed to send it back within 24 hours, Silicon Systems would have no way of knowing whether the laptop was damaged before or after Bancroft received it, and would therefore not take it back. Left with no alternative Bancroft took the laptop on the business trip and used it for the scheduled presentation. Has Bancroft accepted the laptop?

Notice that the captions of sections 2-602 and 2-603 refer to "rightfully rejected" goods and that section 2-711(3) applies only after a rightful rejection. Read section 1-107 regarding the effect of captions. Certainly, the buyer who has wrongfully but effectively rejected the goods should take reasonable care of the

---

[28] *Johannsen v. Minnesota Valley Ford Tractor Co.*, 304 N.W.2d 654, 658 (Minn. 1981).

goods. After all, the buyer's effective rejection means that the buyer has not accepted the goods and the goods are thus the seller's property. *See* UCC § 2-401(4). However, that buyer is probably not protected by the provisions of sections 2-602, 2-603, 2-604 or 2-711. Therefore, if a buyer in that situation sells the goods, such action would probably be inconsistent with the seller's ownership interest and thus an acceptance. UCC § 2-606.

3. *Rejection and the Right to Damages*

If a seller makes a nonconforming tender, so that the buyer has a right to reject the goods, the seller will have breached the contract. The buyer's rejection of the goods effectively forces the seller to take the goods back. The buyer will then have a right to damages for the seller's breach and is in basically the same position as if the seller never delivered the goods. To the extent the buyer has paid any part of the price, the buyer is entitled to a return of the price paid, which the buyer may recover by foreclosing on its security interest in the rejected goods. The buyer is also entitled to an award of damages based either on a cover transaction or the market price. *See* UCC § 2-711. These cover or market price based damages are not part of the amount that can be collected by foreclosing on the security interest. *See* UCC § 2-711(3). In addition to cover or market price based damages, the buyer may also recover incidental and consequential damages. UCC § 2-715. Some of the likely incidental damages are included within the amount that is secured by the buyer's security interest in the goods. *Compare* UCC § 2-711(3) *with* § 2-715(1). The remaining incidental damages and the consequential damages are not recoverable through foreclosure of the security interest. The issues regarding proving cover or market price based damages, incidental, and consequential damages are the same as discussed previously.

C. Acceptance and the Effect of Acceptance

As we have learned so far, the buyer accepts the goods by signifying to the seller that the buyer is accepting, by failing to effectively reject the goods after the time for inspection expires, or by dealing with the goods in a manner inconsistent with the seller's ownership. UCC § 2-606(1). Remember, it is not always clear when the time for inspection expires, so it is not always clear whether the buyer who has said nothing to the seller has in fact accepted the goods.

There are several important consequences to the buyer's acceptance of the goods:

(i) the buyer is precluded from rejecting the goods, UCC § 2-607(2);

(ii) the buyer becomes obligated to pay the contract price, UCC § 2-607(1), although if the seller's tender is in fact nonconforming, the buyer will still be entitled to various remedies, UCC §§ 2-714, 2-715;

(iii) the buyer must notify the seller of any breach within a reasonable time or will be barred from any remedy, UCC § 2-607(3)(a);

(iv) the buyer assumes the burden of proof on any claim of breach with respect to the accepted goods, UCC § 2-607(4);[29] and

(v) in a non-installment contract, the buyer loses the right to cancel the contract, *compare* UCC § 2-711(1) *with* § 2-714, a point which can be important if the market price of the goods has declined since the contract was formed and the buyer would now like to put that loss on the seller.

1. Notice of Breach

The buyer's acceptance of the goods is **not** a waiver of its right to pursue claims for the seller's nonconforming performance. Instead, the buyer retains the right to sue for damages provided the buyer gives reasonable notification of the breach to the seller. UCC § 2-607(3)(a).

This notification requirement raises two issues. First, what is a "reasonable time" within which the buyer must notify the seller of the problem? *See* UCC §§ 1-205, 1-202. Second, what must the notification say? Read comment 4 to

---

[29] If the buyer rejects the goods, the burden of proof would rest on whoever becomes the plaintiff in the resulting lawsuit. If the buyer is the plaintiff, suing the seller for cover or for damages based on market price, the buyer would have the normal plaintiff's burden of proof to establish the elements of its case, one of which is that the seller breached the contract. If the seller is the plaintiff and is suing the buyer for breach of contract, alleging a wrongful rejection of the goods, the seller would have the burden of proof that the buyer breached the contract. That is, the seller would have to show that the goods were conforming and that the buyer therefore had no right to reject the goods.

section 2-607.[30] Both of these issues are informed by the purpose of the notice requirement and by the harsh result of the buyer's failure to comply: the loss of all remedies.

What are the purposes of requiring the buyer to notify the seller of the breach with respect to accepted goods? A leading case has suggested that notification serves at least the following four purposes:

(1) to prevent surprise and allow the seller the opportunity to make recommendations on how to cure the nonconformance;

(2) to permit the seller the fair opportunity to investigate and prepare for litigation; . . .

(3) to open the way for normal settlement of claims through negotiation . . . [; and]

(4) to protect the seller from stale claims and provide certainty in contractual arrangements.[31]

Another reason is to permit the seller to preserve its rights against its own supplier, which might be particularly important if the statute of limitations were about to expire on the seller's claim against its supplier.[32]

Notice that the first reason identified above referred to giving the seller the opportunity to make recommendations on how to cure, not to facilitate the seller's right to cure. Other courts have expressly suggested that notification protects the seller's right to cure,[33] but is that really correct? Review section 2-508 on when the seller has a right to cure.

Given the draconian effect of an untimely or inadequate notification, courts are fairly lenient. Nevertheless, most agree that some sort of pre-litigation notification is required. In other words, filing a complaint does not satisfy the requirement of section 2-607.

---

[30] This rule should not be confused with section 2-605, which provides that the buyer's failure to particularize operates as a waiver of unstated defects. The rule of section 2-605 applies only to *rejected* goods; the notification requirement of section 2-607(3)(a) applies only to *accepted* goods.

[31] *Aqualon Co. v. Mac Equipment, Inc.*, 149 F.3d 262, 269 (4th Cir. 1998)

[32] *See Hebron v. American Isuzu Motors, Inc.*, 60 F.3d 1095, 1098–99 (4th Cir. 1995) (indicating that notification served the important function of "minimizing prejudice to the seller from the passage of time").

[33] *Id.* at 1099.

Problem 7-21

Baker makes bread for sale to markets and restaurants within a 30-mile radius. One April 1, one of Baker's automated baking machines broke down and Baker was unable to fix it. Before the end of the day, Baker ordered the necessary replacement parts from Supplier, explaining that they were needed to get the machine operating and that, without the machine, Baker had to reduce capacity and pay employees overtime wages to generate even that lower level of production. Supplier promised to deliver the replacement parts by April 4. It is now April 5 and Supplier has not yet delivered the goods. The delay is costing Baker substantial amounts of money. What notification of the breach, if any, must Baker provide to Supplier?

As with many of Article 2's rules on default, the parties may vary the effect of the notification requirement of section 2-607(3)(a) by specifying what would be a reasonable time. *See* UCC §§ 1-205(b), 1-302. Presumably, they could even dispense with the notification requirement entirely.

Problem 7-22

You are drafting a form that the seller of high-end kitchen appliances (*e.g.,* large stoves and sub-zero refrigerators) will use when it sells them to consumers and restaurants. The seller wants to make an express warranty that the goods are free from defects in materials and workmanship at the time of the sale. Draft a clause that details when the buyer must notify the seller of any breach with respect to any goods received. Do you need to worry about whether the clause you draft is unconscionable? *See* UCC §§ 2-302, 2-719. *Compare* UCC § 1-302(b).

2. Damages

Assuming the buyer has given the seller adequate and timely notification of breach, the buyer will have a claim for damages against the seller for the nonconforming tender of goods that the buyer has accepted. Read sections 2-714 and 2-715. To understand those remedies, consider the situation the buyer is in.

The buyer has either accepted goods that fail to conform to the contract or has accepted conforming goods that were tendered in a nonconforming manner. As a result, the buyer is liable to the seller for the contract price of the accepted goods, even if those goods are defective or otherwise do not conform to the contract. UCC §§ 2-607(1), 2-709(1). The buyer, however, has not received the full benefit of the bargain it made with the seller. Section 2-714 is designed to compensate the buyer for its failure to receive the seller's promised performance. It does this by protecting the buyer's expectation interest in three distinct ways.

Subsection (1) covers a nonconforming tender. For example, it applies if a seller has delivered conforming goods late or has delivered less than the full quantity of goods called for in the contract. In such a case, the buyer is entitled to recover damages for the losses caused by the defect in the seller's performance. Subsection (2) applies to breach of warranty cases. It provides for damages based on the difference in value between the goods as delivered and the goods as promised. Subsection (3) authorizes the measures of recovery in subsections (1) and (2) to be supplemented by an award of incidental and consequential damages. *See* UCC § 2-715. If the buyer notifies the seller, the buyer may deduct its section 2-714 damages from any portion of the purchase price that the buyer still owes under the contract. UCC § 2-717.

Now try to apply these rules to a few problems. In doing so, remember the expectation principle discussed in connection with the buyer's other remedies. Consider whether the buyer's lost expectancy in a breach of warranty case is better measured by the cost of replacement or the cost of repair. Contemplate what might qualify as the "special circumstances" to which section 2-714(2) refers.

Problem 7-23

Blaisdell Soup, Inc. contracted on May 1 to purchase 10,000 bushels of # 1 grade tomatoes for $10 per bushel from Sun Farms, Inc. The market price at the time the contract was entered into was $8 per bushel.

A. On August 10, the time for delivery, Sun Farms tendered 10,000 bushels of # 2 grade tomatoes. Caught at the end of the season and unable to get the higher grade of tomatoes elsewhere, Blaisdell Soup accepted the tomatoes. Grade #2 tomatoes at that time had a market price at $7 per bushel. The market price of # 1 grade tomatoes was $9 per bushel. Sun Farms claims the contract price of $100,000. What damages may Blaisdell Soup deduct from the price under section 2-714(2)?

B. How, if at all, would the answer to Part A change if, at the time of acceptance, the market price of # 1 tomatoes had risen in value to $12 per bushel and # 2 tomatoes were worth $9 per bushel?

C. On August 10, the time for delivery, Sun Farms tendered 10,000 bushels of what appeared to be # 1 grade tomatoes, which Blaisdell Soup accepted. Upon unpacking the crates, however, Blaisdell Soup discovered that the entire lot was decaying. Blaisdell Soup salvaged the lot for $1,000 and purchased replacement tomatoes from another grower for $13 per bushel. What is the proper measure of Blaisdell Soup's damages?

D. On August 10, the time for delivery, Sun Farms tendered 6,000 bushels of #2 tomatoes instead of the 10,000 #1 grade tomatoes contracted for. Blaisdell Soup accepted the tomatoes and resold them for $7 per bushel. Blaisdell Soup then purchased 10,000 bushels of #1 tomatoes from another supplier for $11 per bushel. How should damages be measured?

E. How, if at all, would the answer to Part D change if Blaisdell Soup did not purchase any replacement tomatoes?

Problem 7-24

Seller agreed to manufacture, sell, and deliver 500 railroad cars to Railroad for the approximate price of $10 million ($20,000 per car). After delivery and acceptance of the goods, Railroad discovered cracks in the structure and weld of many cars. Seller refused to repair, claiming it had no responsibility for the alleged defects, and Railroad implemented its own program of repair at a total cost of $5 million ($10,000 per car). Railroad brought suit under section 2-714(2) and alleged: (1) the value of each car as warranted was $20,000; (2) the cost to repair each car was $10,000; and (3) the value of the car as repaired was $19,000. Therefore, the "difference in value" under section 2-714(2) is $11,000 per car, the cost to repair plus the difference in value between the car as warranted and the car as repaired.

A. Is Railroad correct? What arguments should Seller make in defense? Does it make any difference if the cars were worth $15,000 as delivered?

B. Suppose Railroad spent $10,000 per car to repair and the value of each car as repaired was $22,000. How much should Railroad recover?

As in the case of non-delivery, the buyer's right to an award of consequential damages is limited in four ways. The buyer must prove that the breach actually caused the loss, the loss was foreseeable, the loss could not have been reasonably prevented, and the type and amount of the loss is reasonably certain. Even with these limitations, a buyer's incidental and consequential damages can far exceed the contract price.

Problem 7-25

Silicon Solutions, Inc., which manufactures circuit boards for use in personal computers, contracted to sell 10,000 circuit boards to Baseline Computers Corp. over the course of one year for $50 per board. The circuit boards were to be manufactured according to specifications that Silicon Solutions and Baseline Computers agreed to at the beginning of the contract period. After Silicon Solutions had supplied 4,000 circuit boards to Baseline, and Baseline had installed those boards into computers that had been sold to customers, Baseline started to receive numerous customer complaints regarding the performance of the computers with the Silicon Solutions circuit boards. After a month-long investigation, and after Baseline had received and installed another 1,000 Silicon Solutions circuit boards, Baseline determined that Silicon Solutions had not manufactured the boards according to the required specifications.

Baseline stopped accepting Silicon Solutions circuit boards and cancelled the contract. Baseline then purchased 5,000 replacement boards from Awesome Manufacturers, Inc. for $60 per board. Baseline installed replacement boards in the 1,000 computers with Silicon Solutions boards that it still owned. It also has pledged to repair at no charge to its customers the 4,000 computers that it sold with Silicon Solutions boards. To date, 1,000 computers have been returned for repair and the average cost of shipping – which Baseline has paid – has been $25 per computer. Each computer takes two hours to repair and reprogram. Baseline Computers bills its technician's time at $50 per hour. Silicon Solutions does not want its defective circuit boards back and it costs Baseline Computers 20 cents per board to dispose of them in an environmentally safe manner.

A.   If Baseline has already paid for the 5,000 boards received from Silicon Solutions and given proper notification of the breach, how much in damages is Baseline entitled to recover from Silicon Solutions?

B.   Because of these events, Silicon Solutions is considering including in its future agreements with its customers and Baseline is considering including in its future agreements with its suppliers a clause that clearly allocates the risk of defective component parts.
   1.   If your last name begins with a letter from A to M, draft such a clause on behalf of Silicon Solutions.
   2.   If your last name begins with a letter from N to Z, draft such a clause on behalf of Baseline.

D. Revocation of Acceptance of the Goods

A buyer who accepts goods may no longer reject the goods. UCC § 2-607(2). However, under section 2-608, a buyer is entitled to revoke acceptance in the following, limited circumstances:
   (A) a nonconformity "substantially impairs" the value of the goods to the buyer;
   (B) there has been no substantial change in the condition of the goods other than one caused by the nonconformity; and
   (C) at least one of the following:
      (i)   the buyer had a reasonable assumption that the nonconformity would be cured but it has not been cured;
      (ii) the nonconformity was difficult to discover and that difficulty induced the buyer to accept the goods; or

(iii) the seller assured the buyer that the goods were conforming and those assurances induced the buyer to accept the goods without discovery of the nonconformity.

Right to revoke acceptance. As you can see, this right to revoke acceptance is a fairly restricted one. Whereas a buyer may generally reject goods for any nonconformity, a buyer may revoke acceptance of the goods only if their nonconformity substantially impairs their value. We have encountered a "substantial impairment" standard before, when we considered rejection of goods in installment contracts. However, the language of the two provisions is slightly different. The standard for revocation of acceptance requires that the nonconformity substantially impair the value of the goods "to him," meaning to the buyer. UCC § 2-608(1). Those words are noticeably absent from the rule on rejection of goods in an installment contract. *Cf.* UCC § 2-612(2), (3). Query if this difference in language has any impact on how the standard is to be applied.

Notice of revocation. As we saw with rejection, the buyer must notify the seller of the intention to revoke acceptance within a reasonable time after the ground for revocation was or should have been discovered. A revocation is not effective until such notification is sent. UCC §§ 2-608(2), 1-202(d). However, the time period for giving notice of revocation of acceptance is apparently longer than the period for giving notification of rejection. *See* UCC § 2-608 cmt. 4. Moreover, no specific content of the notification is required. *See* UCC § 2-608 cmt. 5. In other words, the standards applicable to notification following an initial rejection do not apply. *Cf.* UCC §§ 2-605, 2-607(3)(a).

Suppose the buyer has no right to revoke acceptance under the standard in section 2-608 but nonetheless gives a timely notification of revocation that contains all the required content. Is this treated as a wrongful but effective revocation, with the same consequences as a wrongful but effective rejection? No. There is no such thing as a wrongful but effective revocation. A buyer can successfully revoke acceptance of the goods only when the buyer both has the right to revoke and gives effective notification of revocation. If the attempted revocation is either not justifiable or is justifiable but the buyer fails to give an effective notification, the buyer will not have undone the acceptance of the goods. *See* UCC § 2-709 cmt. 5.

Effect of a justifiable and effective revocation. Revocation of acceptance of the goods is not a cancellation or termination of the contract or rescission of the contract. UCC § 2-608 cmt. 1. It is merely undoing the acceptance of the goods that have been tendered. The buyer will still be entitled to expectation-based damages using either the cover price or market price measurement, plus incidental and consequential damages.

Care of goods after revocation. A buyer who justifiably and effectively revokes acceptance of the goods is treated exactly as if the buyer had rejected the goods. Thus, the buyer is not liable for the purchase price, may cancel the contract, and may seek damages measured in the same way as if the seller had repudiated or not delivered. UCC § 2-711(1). The buyer also has all the rights and duties with respect to goods in its possession as a buyer who rejects, including the right to a security interest in the goods to cover the price paid and any incidental damages incurred. UCC §§ 2-711(3), 2-602(2), 2-603, 2-604.

Revocation and the right to cure. One issue of some controversy is whether the seller has a right to cure following revocation.[34] A simple syllogism suggests that the seller does: (i) the buyer has the same rights and duties regarding the goods as if the buyer had rejected them, UCC § 2-608(3); (ii) the seller often has a right to cure after rejection, *see* UCC § 2-508, and thus (iii) the seller may have a right to cure following revocation. However, to the extent that the buyer revokes under section 2-608(1)(a) – having accepted on the reasonable belief the cure would be forthcoming and after waiting a reasonable time, the nonconformity remains uncured – it makes no sense to give the seller yet more time to cure. A revocation of acceptance under section 2-608(1)(b) may, however, give rise to a right to cure.[35]

Problem 7-26

In which, if any, of the following scenarios will the buyer have a right to revoke acceptance of the goods? Assume in each case that the seller has made an implied warranty of merchantability that has not been disclaimed.

A. Armani purchased 100 bolts of Egyptian cotton fabric to make shirts. After using about 45 bolts to make shirts, Armani discovered that the shirts permanently discolored when pressed, making the shirts unfit for sale and the remaining fabric unsuitable for use.

---

[34] *See* Howard Foss, *The Seller's Right to Cure When the Buyer Revokes Acceptance: Erase the Line in the Sand*, 16 S. ILL. U. L.J. 1 (1991).

[35] *Cf. Lile v. Kiesel*, 871 N.E.2d 995 (Ind. Ct. App. 2007) (no right to cure following revocation).

B. Biker purchased a new motorcycle for personal use. Two weeks after accepting the motorcycle, a crack in the fuel line caused gasoline to escape and ignite. The entire bike was engulfed in flames. The bike was destroyed and Biker was seriously injured.

C. Cantankerous purchased a new mobile home for personal use. Several weeks after accepting delivery, and after the first hard rain, Cantankerous noticed a leak in the roof. The seller promptly repaired the leak but a few weeks later a new leak developed in a different location.
    1. Although the seller attempted to repair the second leak, it reappeared after the next rain.
    2. After again attempting to repair the second leak, it reappeared for the third time following another rain.
    3. The seller concludes that the only way to permanently repair the leak is to remove the roof (a process that involves sawing it off), install new flashing, and then reattach the roof. Seller is willing to do this at no charge but Cantankerous does not want a mobile home with a roof that has been sawn off and reattached.

D. Dartmouth ordered 500 green 3-ring binders from an office supply store. Dartmouth planned to distribute the binders at a conference it was putting on for potential customers. When the binders arrived, Dartmouth inspected them and noticed that they were assorted colors, not all green. This rendered the binders unsuitable for Dartmouth's purpose, so Dartmouth contacted the supply store, which promised to send replacements immediately. No replacements ever arrived.

Problem 7-27

On February 1, Sterling Inc. contracted to manufacture and sell to Ballistics, Inc. a new machine capable of manufacturing 50 bullets per minute. The price was $500,000, of which 25% was to be paid at the time of contracting with the balance due 30 days after delivery. Ballistics made the down payment. Under the agreement, Sterling was to deliver, install, and test the machine by June 1.

On June 1, Sterling delivered and installed the machine and gave it a two-hour test run. Ballistics' purchasing officer, who was present, was impressed and saw no apparent problems, but said that she would like "a little more time to see how it works." By June 14, Ballistics' personnel had noticed a problem in production rate and by June 21 it was clear that the machine, even though operating smoothly, was producing only 40 bullets per minute. Ballistics' engineers searched for the problem but could not find it. Ballistics continued to use the machine throughout this period, but the purchasing officer was already looking for a different manufacturer.

On July 1, Sterling telephoned to inquire how things were going and to request payment of the balance of the price. Ballistics, for the first time, informed Sterling that the machine was not producing bullets at the required rate. The same day, Ballistics faxed a notice to Sterling stating, in essence, that: (1) the machine's production did not conform to the contract; (2) Ballistics would not pay the price; and (3) Sterling should pick up the machine immediately.

On July 5, Sterling's engineers appeared at Ballistics' plant and asked to inspect the machine. By July 7, Sterling's engineers conceded that there was a problem with the machine that existed at the time it was installed. Sterling offered to repair the machine at its cost and stated that when repaired the machine would be "good as new." Ballistics declined the offer, stating that Sterling had no right to "cure" the defect and that Ballistics would not pay the balance of the price unless Sterling delivered a new machine. Sterling refused, stating that repair was its best offer.

On July 10, Ballistics contracted with Epoch Manufacturing for a similar machine. The price was $750,000 and delivery was promised for September 1. Ballistics continued to use Sterling's machine until September 1, when Epoch's machine was delivered and installed. Epoch's machine works perfectly. Sterling refused to pick up its machine or to give directions to Ballistics for disposition. The machine is now stored in a separate building on Ballistics' property.

Sterling is threatening to sue Ballistics for the price of the machine. Ballistics, in turn, wants its down payment back along with cover damages. How should a court resolve this situation?

Problem 7-28

You are a district court judge. The following case has just been tried in a bench trial. The following are the facts you have heard.

Standard Plywood, Inc., a lumber wholesaler located in Billings, Montana, and Bargain Village, Inc., a lumber yard located in Minneapolis, Minnesota, signed a written document that provided as follows:

> Standard Plywood will deliver to Bargain Village, Inc., FOB Billings, 50 pallets of plywood sheets 50" by 65" on November 1. Price is $100 per pallet. Shipment will be by rail or truck at discretion of seller.

On October 30, Standard Plywood delivered to Burlington Northern Railyard in Billings, 45 pallets of plywood sheets measuring 50" by 65" for shipment to Bargain Village in Minneapolis. Standard Plywood obtained a non-negotiable bill of lading from Burlington Northern naming itself as consignee and sent the document to Bargain Village by Federal Express on November 1. Bargain Village received the non-negotiable bill of lading on November 2.

On November 5, Burlington Northern notified Bargain Village that 45 pallets were available for pickup. Bargain Village went to the railyard and wanted to inspect the plywood before loading it on its trucks. Burlington Northern called Standard Plywood to see if inspection should be allowed. Standard Plywood replied that Bargain Village was not entitled to inspect the goods as it had not paid for them. Bargain Village argued with Standard Plywood but to no avail. Bargain Village then loaded the 45 pallets unopened and transported them to its place of business.

Upon opening the pallets on November 6, Bargain Village discovered the pallets contained 90 sheets of plywood per pallet. Bargain Village telephoned Standard Plywood to complain that the shipment did not contain 50 pallets and that each of the 45 pallets delivered was short 10 sheets. Standard Plywood replied that, as far as it knew, in the wholesale trade each pallet always has 90 sheets, not 100. Bargain Village maintained at trial that it had never heard of such a thing, each pallet it had purchased from other wholesalers always contained 100 sheets.

On November 30, Bargain Village sent Standard Plywood a fax stating that it rejected the plywood "due to the shortage in delivery" and requested that Standard Plywood send instructions as to what to do with the plywood. Standard Plywood faxed a reply stating that Bargain Village had no right to reject or revoke, that it would not take the plywood back, and demanded the price for 45 pallets of plywood. Bargain Village stored the plywood from the 45 pallets in its warehouse for a month and then sold the plywood for $80 per pallet in December. Standard Plywood sued Bargain Village for the price of the plywood (45 pallets times $100 per pallet). Bargain Village denied liability for the price and counterclaimed for damages for breach of contract.

Write the opinion deciding the case.

E. Nonconforming Tender Under the CISG and UNIDROIT

CISG. The buyer's remedies for the seller's breach of a contract governed by the CISG are somewhat different than those of a buyer under an Article 2 contract. The seller has the general duty to deliver the goods required by the contract. Art. 30. That duty includes the obligation to provide goods that conform to the contract requirements. Art. 36. Once the goods are tendered, the buyer has the obligation – not merely a right, but an obligation – to examine them. Art. 38. If the seller delivers nonconforming goods, the buyer must give notice of the nature of the nonconformity within a reasonable time after the buyer discovered or should have discovered the nonconformity, as long as that time period is not longer than two years (or the time period of an explicit guarantee). Art. 39. Failure to give notice as required precludes the buyer from being able to rely on the nonconformity to show a breach by the seller. However, this bar on remedies is subject to two exceptions: (i) if the seller was aware or should have been aware of the lack of conformity and failed to tell the buyer, Art. 40; or (ii) if the buyer had a reasonable excuse for failing to give notice, Art. 44.

The buyer has several remedial options when the seller delivers nonconforming goods. First, the buyer may require the seller to tender a conforming performance, if that is reasonable under the circumstances. That conforming performance may be by either substitute goods or repair. The buyer is entitled to request substitute goods only if the original tender was a fundamental breach, Art. 46, and only if the buyer can return the originally delivered goods, Art. 82. The buyer may allow the seller additional time for tendering that conforming performance and, unless the seller notifies the buyer that it will not perform within that time period, the buyer may not exercise any other remedies for breach while awaiting performance. The buyer, however, does not waive its rights to damages for delay. Art. 47. The seller may also insist on providing a cure, and if reasonable under the circumstances, the buyer will be required to accept that cure. Art. 48.

Second, if the seller does not cure, then the buyer may reduce the price owed for the goods based upon the value of the goods actually delivered. Art. 50. If the buyer refuses a cure that the seller is entitled to make under Article 48, the buyer cannot reduce the price owed.

Third, the buyer may be able to declare the contract avoided if the seller has either committed a fundamental breach (Art. 25) or failed to deliver the goods and refuses or fails to deliver the goods within a further set time period. Arts. 49, 51(2). The buyer has to act within a reasonable time to declare the contract avoided. Art. 49. In an installment contract, the buyer may declare the contract avoided if the failure of the seller to perform is a fundamental breach of the entire contract. Art. 73. If the contract is avoided, the buyer may recover damages based upon a reasonable replacement transaction, Art. 75, or based upon the market price, Art. 76. Damages include liability for consequential losses, Art. 74, unless the buyer failed to give reasonable notice of the nonconformity. Art. 44. The buyer has to take reasonable action to mitigate damages. Art. 77.

Avoidance of the contract releases the parties from future obligations but preserves the aggrieved party's right for damages. Avoidance of the contract also entitles each party to restitution of the benefit transferred to the other side. Art. 81. Subject to some specific exceptions, a buyer may not declare the contract avoided if it is unable to make restitution of any goods delivered. Art. 82. The buyer who has declared the contract avoided must preserve the goods delivered. Art. 86. The buyer may store them and recover the expense of doing so, Art. 87, and in some circumstances sell the goods for the benefit of the seller. Art. 88.

Thus the ability of the buyer to force the goods back onto the seller is determined by whether the buyer may avoid the contract for fundamental breach. Fundamental breach is most closely related to the concept of substantial impairment, not perfect tender. Art. 25.

UNIDROIT Principles. As discussed earlier, the UNIDROIT Principles were drafted for use in many different types of international contracts, not just contracts for the sale of goods. Thus there are no specific provisions on rejection, acceptance, or revocation of acceptance of the goods. The focus is more broadly on an aggrieved party's rights when the other side tenders a nonconforming performance. Having said that, the concepts in the UNIDROIT Principles are similar to the concepts in the CISG.

The aggrieved party may require the nonperforming party's performance in some circumstances, Art. 7.2.2, including the right to require repair or replacement of the defective performance, Art. 7.2.3. The nonperforming party may, in some circumstances, insist on curing the initially tendered nonconforming performance. Art. 7.1.4. The aggrieved party may also be entitled to terminate the contract if the nonperforming party's failure to perform is a fundamental non-performance, Art. 7.3.1, as long as the aggrieved party gives timely notice of that termination. Art. 7.3.2. Termination relieves both parties of future obligations to perform but preserves the aggrieved party's right to remedies for the other side's nonperformance. Art. 7.3.5. Upon termination, each side must make restitution of the performance received. Art. 7.3.6. In this circumstance, the aggrieved party would then be able to seek damages for the failure to obtain the contracted for performance based either on a replacement transaction or on proof of the current price for the performance, Art. 7.4.5, Art. 7.4.6, as well as damages for further harm. All damages must be certain, foreseeable, and appropriately mitigated. Art. 7.4.1 through Art. 7.4.4, Art. 7.4.8. If the aggrieved party does not terminate the contract, then it would be able to recover for the harm caused by the failure to receive a fully conforming performance, as long as those damages are certain, foreseeable, and appropriately mitigated. Art. 7.4.1 through Art. 7.4.4, Art. 7.4.8. The aggrieved party would be able to set off those damages against any amounts owed under the contract to the other party. Art. 8.1.

SECTION 4.   SELLER'S BREACH AND THE RISK OF LOSS FOR THE GOODS

As we learned in Chapter Four, until the seller tenders or delivers the goods, the seller generally has the risk of loss for those goods. Section 2-509 provides the point at which the risk of loss passes to the buyer when the goods and the tender are conforming to the contract. However, if the goods or the tender do not conform to the contract such that the buyer has a right to reject the goods, section 2-510(1) provides that the risk of loss remains with the seller.

Problem 7-29

Sterling, Inc. is a vegetable distributor and Bluto Foods Co. is a manufacturer of canned soups. On April 1, the parties entered into a written contract for the sale of 1,000 bushels of "Early Girl" tomatoes at $40.00 per bushel, to be shipped F.O.B. Sterling's place of business on or before July 15 and delivered in "green" condition, a term having definite meaning in the trade. The goods were to be delivered in a single lot and Bluto was to make payment 30 days after the goods were received. Nothing was said in the agreement about rejection.

Sterling arranged for Carrier to transport the tomatoes from the fields where they were grown to Bluto's manufacturing facility. However, Sterling neglected to arrange for transport in refrigerated cars, so by the time the tomatoes arrived at Bluto's facility, the tomatoes were overripe, rotting, and definitely not in "green" condition.

A. If the tomatoes were in "green" condition when delivered to Carrier, who would have the risk of loss for these tomatoes? UCC §§ 2-601, 2-503, 2-504, 2-509, 2-510. Advise Bluto about what to do now.

B. If the tomatoes were not in "green" condition when delivered to Carrier, who would have the risk of loss for these tomatoes?

C. How, if at all, would the analysis change if the contract between Sterling and Bluto stated that shipment was "F.O.B. Bluto's facility"?

D. Assume that Sterling arranged for Carrier to refrigerate the tomatoes during transport, but Sterling did not give notice to Bluto that the tomatoes had been shipped. Carrier's boxcar containing the tomatoes had an equipment failure and the tomatoes were not refrigerated during the entire time of transport. The tomatoes arrived in rotten condition. Who has the risk of loss for the tomatoes? Who has an action against Carrier for the damage to the tomatoes? UCC §§ 7-309, 2-722.

Even if the goods or the tender are nonconforming, and the buyer has the right to reject the goods, if the buyer nevertheless accepts the goods, the buyer will have thereby assumed the risk of loss for the goods. UCC § 2-510(1).

If the buyer rightfully revokes acceptance of the goods, often the buyer will still have possession of the goods even though title to the goods re-vests in the seller. UCC § 2-401(4). Nothing in Article 2 explicitly provides whether the risk of loss remains with the buyer or passes back to the seller. However, section 2-510(2) does indicate that the buyer may treat the risk of loss as having remained with the seller from the beginning "to the extent of any deficiency in [the buyer's] effective insurance coverage." Thus, apparently, the risk of loss remains with the revoking buyer who has insurance but passes back to the seller to the extent the buyer is uninsured or underinsured. Whether the buyer's insurance covers the goods in the buyer's possession after revocation of acceptance is a matter left to the insurance contract and insurance law; Article 2 does not speak to it. The revoking buyer does have an insurable interest in the goods, UCC § 2-501, but that does not mean the buyer's insurance policy will in fact cover those goods.

What if the revoking buyer fails to take reasonable care of the goods and that failure is the cause of the loss that ensues? Although the seller might have the risk of loss to the extent of any deficiency in the buyer's insurance coverage, the buyer would have a duty to care for the goods, UCC §§ 2-603, 2-608(3), and thus should be accountable for damages stemming from the buyer's failure to take reasonable care of the goods.

CISG and UNIDROIT Principles. Under the CISG, the risk of loss for the goods passes to the buyer when the goods are given to the first carrier unless the parties agree that the risk will pass to a particular carrier at a particular place. In order for that main rule to operate, the goods must be identified to the contract with the buyer. Art. 67. If the goods are already in transit when the contract is formed, the risk passes to the buyer at the time the contract is formed unless the seller knows at that time that the goods have already been lost or damaged. Art. 68. If the goods are not being shipped, then the risk passes to the buyer when the goods are tendered to the buyer for delivery. Art. 69. If the goods are lost or damaged after the risk has passed to the buyer, the buyer is obligated to pay for the goods, unless the loss or damage is due to the seller's actions or omissions. Art. 66. If the seller commits a fundamental breach of contract, the passage of the risk of loss is unaffected, but the buyer has all of its remedies for breach of contract. Art. 70. The buyer will be excused from making restitution of the goods, if the contract is avoided for fundamental breach, if the loss or damage to the goods was not the buyer's fault. Art. 82. The UNIDROIT Principles do not address risk of loss.

SECTION 5.   STATUTE OF LIMITATIONS

A buyer seeking to recover damages from a seller for breach of contract must bring its cause of action within the time period prescribed by the applicable statute of limitations. The statute of limitations for claims under Article 2 is four years, although the parties are free to reduce that time to one year. UCC § 2-725(1).

Even with a clear limitations period, there are two recurring issues under most statutes of limitations. First, when does the cause of action accrue? Second, is there anything that might stop or toll the running of the limitations period? Read section 2-725. As you can see, section 2-725(2) provides that a claim for breach of warranty normally accrues when the seller tenders delivery. This is true even if the buyer is then unaware of the problem. However, there is an exception if the warranty "explicitly extends to future performance of the goods" and "discovery of the breach must await the time of such performance," in which case the cause of action accrues when the buyer discovers or should have discovered the breach with respect to the future performance.

Thus, for example, a seller who simply warrants that the goods are merchantable will not have to deal with a suit commenced more than four years after the goods are tendered. Any breach of that warranty occurs upon tender. But what if the seller warrants that "the goods will function properly for one year"? Is that a promise of future performance such that a cause of action breach might not accrue until some time later? How should a seller's unfulfilled promise to repair or replace defective goods be treated? Is it even a breach of warranty claim at all? These are, by far, the most commonly litigated issues under section 2-725.[36] Consider the following recent case.

MYDLACH V. DAIMLERCHRYSLER CORP.
875 N.E.2d 1047 (Ill. 2007)

Justice Fitzgerald delivered the judgment of the court, with opinion:

Plaintiff, Lucy Mydlach, filed a three-count complaint in the circuit court of Cook County against defendant, DaimlerChrysler Corporation, alleging claims under the Magnuson-Moss Warranty-Federal Trade Commission Improvement Act (Magnuson-Moss Act or Act) (15 U.S.C. § 2301 *et seq.* (1994)). The circuit court granted defendant's motion for summary judgment, holding that the claims were time-barred under the four-year statute of limitations contained in section 2-725 of the Uniform Commercial Code. The appellate court affirmed in part and reversed in part. For the reasons discussed below, we affirm in part and reverse in part the

---

[36] Larry T. Garvin, *Uncertainty and Error in the Law of Sales: The Article Two Statute of Limitations*, 83 B.U. L. REV. 345 (2003).

judgment of the appellate court and remand the matter to the circuit court for further proceedings.

BACKGROUND

On June 20, 1998, plaintiff purchased a used 1996 Dodge Neon, manufactured by defendant, from McGrath Buick-Nissan (McGrath) in Elgin, Illinois. The vehicle was originally put into service on June 24, 1996, with a three-year/36,000-mile limited warranty. The warranty provided, in relevant part, as follows:

The "**Basic Warranty**" begins on your vehicle's **Warranty Start Date** which is the **earlier** of (1) the date you take delivery of your new vehicle, **OR** (2) the date the vehicle was first put into service * * *.

The "Basic Warranty" covers the cost of all parts and labor needed to repair any item on your vehicle (except as noted below) that's defective in material, workmanship, or factory preparation. You pay nothing for these repairs.

The "**Basic Warranty**" covers every Chrysler supplied part of your vehicle, **EXCEPT** its tires and cellular telephone. * * *

* * *

These warranty repairs or adjustments (parts and labor) will be made by your dealer at no charge using new or remanufactured parts.

* * *

The "**Basic Warranty**" lasts for 36 months from the vehicle's Warranty Start Date **OR** for 36,000 miles on the odometer, whichever occurs first.

(Emphasis in original.)

At the time of plaintiff's purchase in 1998, the car's mileage was 26,296. Thus, the warranty had approximately one year or 10,000 miles remaining.

Beginning July 7, 1998, plaintiff brought the car to McGrath and another authorized dealership several times for a variety of problems, including a recurring fluid leak. Plaintiff claimed that the dealerships' repair attempts were unsuccessful and, as a result, she could not use the vehicle as intended. Plaintiff ultimately filed suit against defendant on May 16, 2001, seeking legal and equitable relief, as well as attorney fees and costs, under the Magnuson-Moss Act. Plaintiff alleged breach of written warranty (count I), breach of the implied warranty of merchantability (count II), and revocation of acceptance (count III).

The case initially proceeded to arbitration, where a decision was entered in favor of defendant. Plaintiff rejected the arbitrators' decision and the case was returned to the trial court. After further discovery, defendant filed a motion for summary judgment. Defendant argued that counts I and II of plaintiff's complaint were subject to the four-year statute of limitations found in section 2-725 of the UCC and that, as provided by section 2-725(2), the statute of limitations commenced upon "tender of delivery" of the vehicle to its original purchaser in June 1996. Thus, according to defendant, plaintiff's suit, filed in May 2001, was outside the four-year limitations period. With respect to count III, defendant argued that plaintiff was not entitled to seek revocation of acceptance because no privity existed between plaintiff and defendant, and because plaintiff could not prove the underlying breach of implied warranty claim.

Plaintiff responded that her claims were not time-barred because the "tender of delivery" referenced in the UCC was the tender of delivery to her, and not to the original purchaser. Plaintiff also argued that a lack of privity is not a bar to a claim for revocation of acceptance against a manufacturer who is also a warrantor.

Relying on *Nowalski v. Ford Motor Co.,* 781 N.E.2d 578 (Ill. Ct. App. 2002), the trial court agreed with defendant that plaintiff's claims were time-barred and granted defendant's motion for summary judgment on all three counts. The trial court denied plaintiff's motion for reconsideration, and plaintiff appealed.

The appellate court reversed the trial court's grant of summary judgment on counts I and III, and affirmed the grant of summary judgment on count II. As to the limitations issue, the appellate court followed *Cosman v. Ford Motor Co.,* 674 N.E.2d 61 (Ill. Ct. App. 1996), rather than *Nowalski,* and held that:

> plaintiff's right to bring a breach of written warranty action based on the promise to repair accrued when defendant allegedly failed to successfully repair her car after a reasonable number of attempts and that the four-year statute of limitations did not begin to run until that time.

The appellate court also held that plaintiff could properly pursue revocation of acceptance as an equitable remedy under the Magnuson-Moss Act if her breach of warranty claim was successful.

We allowed defendant's petition for leave to appeal. Because plaintiff does not seek cross-relief as to count II of her complaint, the only counts before this court are counts I and III.

ANALYSIS

[The Court's discussion of the Magnuson-Moss Act is omitted. The Court found that the manufacturer's warranty was a Magnuson-Moss warranty and concluded that the statute of limitations in Article 2 should apply to the Magnuson-

Moss warranty claim. We will consider the Magnuson-Moss Act in Chapter Eight.
– Eds.].

Preliminarily, we note that the future-performance exception to the four-year
limitations period, set forth in [UCC § 2-725(2)], is not at issue in this case. As will
be discussed in greater detail below, a repair or replacement warranty like the one
issued by defendant here "has nothing to do with the inherent quality of the goods
or their future performance." *Cosman,* 674 N.E.2d at 68. *See also* C. Reitz,
Manufacturers' Warranties of Consumer Goods, 75 WASH. U. L.Q. 357, 364 n. 24
(1997) ("Promises to repair or replace refer to future performance of sellers, not to
future performance of goods"); L. Lawrence, *Lawrence's Anderson on the Uniform
Commercial Code* § 2-625:129, at 332 (3d ed.2001) (discussing difference between
a warranty of future performance and a covenant to repair or replace). Accordingly,
we turn our attention to the balance of the statute and the parties' arguments relative
thereto.

Defendant argues that section 2-725 should be applied as written. Thus,
because the statute provides that a "breach of warranty occurs when tender of
delivery is made," and tender of delivery of the Dodge Neon was first made in June
1996, plaintiff's suit, filed in May 2001, was untimely. *See Nowalski,* 781 N.E.2d
at 584 (holding that cause of action for breach of three-year/36,000-mile limited
warranty accrued when the vehicle was delivered and not when defendant failed to
successfully repair the vehicle). Plaintiff argues that a repair warranty cannot be
breached until the manufacturer fails to repair the vehicle after a reasonable
opportunity to do so, and that the appellate court did not err in finding her complaint
was timely filed. *See Cosman,* 674 N.E.2d at 68 (holding that breach of six-
year/60,000-mile limited power-train warranty "cannot occur until Ford refuses or
fails to repair the powertrain if and when it breaks").[37]

We begin our analysis by turning to the language of article 2 of the UCC.
Section 2-725(2) plainly states that "[a] breach of warranty occurs when tender of
delivery is made." The *Nowalski* opinion, on which defendant relies, concluded that
once article 2 of the UCC is chosen as the analogous state statute from which to

---

[37] The same divergence of opinion on the limitations issue that is exemplified by *Nowalski*
and *Cosman* exists among our sister states. *See generally* L. Garvin, *Uncertainty and Error
in the Law of Sales: The Article Two Statute of Limitations,* 83 B.U.L. REV. 345, 377–81
(2003) (discussing the split among state courts in their approach to repair or replacement
promises).

borrow the statute of limitations, the analysis begins and ends with the "tender of delivery" language quoted above. *Nowalski,* 781 N.E.2d at 584. We disagree. . . .

Although the parties agree that defendant's warranty is a "written warranty" under the Magnuson-Moss Act, they disagree as to whether the warranty is an "express warranty" under the UCC. Defendant argues that the repair warranty qualifies as an express warranty and that plaintiff's claim is therefore governed by the tender-of-delivery rule in section 2-725(2). Plaintiff argues that it does not qualify as an express warranty and that her claim is not subject to the tender-of-delivery rule.

Section 2-313 of the UCC explains how express warranties are created. . . . The UCC makes plain that an express warranty is related to the quality or description of the goods. . . .

In other words, an express warranty, for purposes of the UCC, obligates the seller to deliver goods that conform to the affirmation, promise, description, sample or model. If a seller delivers conforming goods, the warranty is satisfied. If the seller delivers nonconforming goods, the warranty is breached at that time. Even if the buyer is unaware that the goods, as delivered, do not conform to the seller's affirmation, promise, description, sample or model, the warranty has been breached. Under this scenario, the statutory pronouncement that "[a] breach of warranty occurs when tender of delivery is made" makes perfect sense, and the four-year limitations period commences at that time. . . .

The warranty in the present case, however, is not related to the quality or description of the goods at tender. It does not warrant that the vehicle will conform to some affirmation, promise, description, sample or model. Rather, the warranty promises only that the manufacturer will repair or replace defective parts during the warranty period. As defendant made clear in its brief before this court:

> DaimlerChrysler's limited warranty was not a promise that the vehicle would be defect free and in the event of a breach of warranty, Plaintiff would be limited to repair or replacement of the vehicle. Rather, DaimlerChrysler's limited warranty promised to cover the cost to repair or replace defective parts in the automobile for the time period covering 36 months or 36 thousand miles.

Although defendant's warranty qualifies as a "written warranty" under the [Magnuson-Moss] Act, it is not an "express warranty" under the UCC, and is thus not the type of warranty that can be breached on "tender of delivery". . . . Accordingly, we reject defendant's argument that the four-year limitations period for breach of the repair warranty commenced upon delivery of the Dodge Neon in 1996, and we overrule the *Nowalski* opinion on which defendant relies.

Our conclusion that the repair warranty is not a UCC express warranty, and thus not subject to the tender-of-delivery rule set forth in the second sentence of section 2-725(2), does not render section 2-725(2) irrelevant for purposes of determining when the limitations period began on plaintiff's claim under the Magnuson-Moss Act. The first sentence of section 2-725(2) remains applicable. The first sentence states: "[a] cause of action accrues *when the breach occurs,* regardless of the aggrieved party's lack of knowledge of the breach." (Emphasis added.) . . . . Although the UCC does not expressly state when the breach of a repair promise occurs, we may refer to the law that exists outside of the UCC. *See* [UCC § 1-103] ("Unless displaced by the particular provisions of this Act, the principles of law and equity shall supplement its provisions").

Generally, "[w]hen performance of a duty under a contract is due any non-performance is a breach." RESTATEMENT (SECOND) OF CONTRACTS § 235, at 211 (1979). Performance under a vehicle manufacturer's promise to repair or replace defective parts is due not at tender of delivery, but only when, and if, a covered defect arises and repairs are required. In that event, if the promised repairs are refused or unsuccessful, the repair warranty is breached and the cause of action accrues, triggering the four-year limitations period. . . . This is the approach advocated by some commentators. For example, in his discussion of the appropriate treatment of a manufacturer's express warranty to repair or replace defective parts, Professor Lawrence states:

> The sounder approach is to recognize that the failure to repair or replace is merely a breach of contract and not a breach of warranty, and therefore no cause of action arises until the seller has refused to repair or replace the goods. This is because until the seller has failed or refused to make the repairs or provide a replacement, the buyer, not being entitled to such a remedy, has no right to commence an action for damages. As a result, the action is timely if brought within four years of the seller's failure or refusal.

L. LAWRENCE, LAWRENCE'S ANDERSON ON THE UNIFORM COMMERCIAL CODE § 2-725:101, at 303 (3d ed.2001).

The correctness of this approach is manifest when we consider consumer claims for breach of repair warranties that run for periods longer than the three years/36,000 miles at issue here. For example, consider the case of a consumer who purchases a vehicle carrying a five-year/50,000-mile repair warranty. If the four-year limitations period commences at "tender of delivery," the limitations period for a breach of the repair promise occurring in year five will expire before the breach even occurs, thus rendering the repair warranty unenforceable during its final year. Statutes of limitations, however, are intended "to prevent stale claims, not to preclude claims before they are ripe for adjudication." *Guzman v. C.R. Epperson Construction, Inc.,* 752 N.E.2d 1069 (2001). Even a four-year warranty could be rendered unenforceable if breach of the repair promise occurred near the end of the warranty period. In that case, the buyer would have only the briefest of periods in which to file suit.

Defendant argues that concerns about the enforceability of longer-term repair warranties are inapplicable to the facts of this case and without merit. We disagree. Although the repair warranty at issue here ran for three years, our holding in this case will apply equally to longer-term warranties. Such warranties are common in the automobile industry. Adoption of defendant's position would be an invitation to manufacturers and sellers of automobiles, as well as other goods, to engage in misleading marketing. That is, a manufacturer or seller could use the marketing advantage of a longer repair warranty, yet escape the accompanying obligations of that warranty by pleading the statute of limitations in defense. Such a result is contrary to the very purpose of the Magnuson-Moss Act: "to improve the adequacy of information available to consumers" and "prevent deception." 15 U.S.C. § 2302(a) (1994).

Defendant also argues that unless the tender-of-delivery rule in section 2-725 is given effect, the limitations period for breach of limited warranty actions will be "limitless" and "uncertain." This argument is without merit. Because the promise to repair or replace defective parts is only good during the warranty period, the latest a breach of warranty can occur is at the very end of that period. Accordingly, the statute of limitations will expire, at the latest, four years after the warranty period has run. If breach of a repair warranty occurs earlier in the warranty period, the limitations period for that breach will expire sooner, but in no event will the warrantor's exposure extend beyond the warranty period, plus four years. Thus, contrary to defendant's argument, commencing the four-year limitations period from the date the warrantor fails or refuses to repair the vehicle does not result in a limitless limitations period.

We recognize, of course, that a fact question may arise as to the date on which a repair warranty was breached which, in turn, would create some uncertainty as to when the four-year limitations period should commence. Fact questions of this nature, however, frequently arise in cases where the statute of limitations has been pled in defense. Resolution of this type of uncertainty is a classic function of the trier of fact. . . . We therefore reject defendant's argument that commencing the limitations period when the warrantor fails or refuses to repair the defect – rather than at tender of delivery – will create unacceptable uncertainty in the limitations period.

Turning to the facts of this case, the record indicates that plaintiff brought her vehicle to McGrath and another authorized dealer on several occasions beginning in July 1998. At that point, assuming the alleged defects were covered defects, defendant was obligated (through its authorized dealer) to make good on its repair promise. Plaintiff's lawsuit, filed in May 2001, is therefore timely. Accordingly, we affirm that portion of the judgment of the appellate court which reversed the grant of summary judgment in favor of defendant as to count I of the complaint. . . .

[The court's discussion concerning the ability to revoke acceptance against a remote seller is omitted. The Court held that such revocation is not permitted. – Eds.]

CONCLUSION

For the reasons discussed above, we affirm the judgment of the appellate court reversing the trial court's grant of summary judgment in favor of defendant as to count I of the complaint, and reverse the judgment of the appellate court reversing the trial court's grant of summary judgment in favor of defendant as to count III of the complaint. We remand this matter to the trial court for further proceedings.

Problem 7-30

On June 1, 2006, Bristol Manufacturers contracted to purchase factory equipment from Sunshine Fabricators for delivery and installation no later than June 25. Sunshine warranted that the goods were free from defects and would function according to promised specifications for a period of one year from the date of delivery. The equipment was delivered on June 25, but the installation was not completed until July 1. On April 1, 2007, Bristol notified Sunshine that the machine had stopped working. Several days later, Sunshine technicians arrived at Bristol's plant and attempted to fix the problem. After three weeks of effort, the equipment still did not work. The technicians left the premises on April 26, 2007 insisting that they would return to repair the machine. They never did and in August 2007, Bristol notified Sunshine that it considered Sunshine to have breached the contract. In an effort to keep its business functioning, Bristol removed the equipment from the floor, put it in storage, and then installed replacement equipment acquired from a different seller. In October 2010, Bristol consults you, its attorney, about the matter. Does Bristol have a valid claim for breach of contract? If so, has the statute of limitations run on Bristol's claims for breach of contract? Why or why not?

CISG and UNIDROIT Principles. The CISG does not have any limitations period, but the United States has ratified the Convention on the Limitations Period in the International Sale of Goods. In general, the limitations period is four years from accrual of the cause of action, with the cause of action accruing when the breach occurred, subject to several specific rules on when the breach occurs. Arts. 8 through 12. For example, a claim for nonconformity of the goods accrues when the goods are handed over to the buyer unless the seller has made a specific undertaking regarding the goods for a period of time. Arts. 10 and 11. There are also several provisions on "tolling" the limitations period. Arts. 12 through 21.

The UNIDROIT Principles contain several provisions addressing limitations on bringing the action with a general three year time period from the time the obligee knows of the facts giving rise to the claim. Art. 10.2. The Principles also contain several tolling rules. Arts. 10.4 through 10.8.

SECTION 6.   PRIVITY ISSUES

The discussion of buyer's remedies has addressed what the buyer may do when it is faced with a breach by its seller. In many cases, however, the buyer is not pursuing a remedy against its seller, rather, the buyer is pursuing a remedy against a remote seller, such as a manufacturer. To facilitate a discussion of the Article 2 remedies that a buyer may have against a remote seller, consider the following scenario:

Manufacturer
    | – April 1
Distributer
    | – June 1
Retailer
    | – August 1
Buyer

Buyer purchased a new microwave oven from Retailer on August 1. The microwave was made by Manufacturer, who had sold it to Distributor, who in turn had sold it to Retailer. When Buyer first plugs the microwave into an electrical outlet and attempts to use it to cook some food, the microwave turns on (*i.e.*, the interior lights go on and the plate in the center rotates) but the food does not cook. Retailer has gone out of business and Buyer has no information about or ability to identify Distributor. So, Buyer seeks recourse against Manufacturer.

Buyer's rights against Manufacturer are complicated by a series of issues and questions. These include:

1. Did Manufacturer make any warranties or promises to Buyer about the goods? In dealing with this question, consider what evidence might be used to show that Manufacturer made an express warranty under section 2-313.[38] Consider also whether section 2-314 creates an implied warranty from Manufacturer to Buyer that the goods will be merchantable.[39]

2. Did Manufacturer make any express or implied warranties to Distributor or Retailer that may be extended to Buyer for harm of this type? Read section 2-318. Section 2-318 is based upon the concept of third-party beneficiary rights under a contract.

3. Assuming a source of warranty liability does exist, so that Buyer has a viable cause of action against Manufacturer, to what remedies is Buyer entitled? For example, may Buyer reject or revoke acceptance of the microwave and obtain from Manufacturer a refund of the price?[40] UCC §§ 2-601, 2-608, 2-711. If so, would the refund amount be the price that Buyer paid to Retailer or the presumably lower price that Distributor paid to Manufacturer? If Buyer does return the microwave to Manufacturer, may Buyer also obtain market damages under section 2-713 or cover damages under section 2-712? If Buyer does not return the microwave, may Buyer obtain an award of damages against Manufacturer under section 2-714? If so, must Buyer give notification of the breach to Manufacturer or would notification to Retailer satisfy the obligation under section 2-607?[41] By when must such notification be given? Would Buyer be

---

[38] *See In re McDonalds French Fries Litigation*, 503 F. Supp. 2d 953 (N.D. Ill. 2007).

[39] *See Curl v. Volkswagen of Am. Inc.*, 871 N.E.2d 1141 (Ohio 2007).

[40] *See Mydlach v. DaimlerChrysler Corp., supra.*

[41] *See In re Bausch & Lomb Inc. Contact Lens Solutions Products Liability Litigation*, 2008

entitled to an award of incidental and consequential damages against Manufacturer? UCC § 2-715. If so, must the consequential harm have been foreseeable by Manufacturer or would be it sufficient if Retailer has reason to know of the harm at the time of the sale to Buyer?

4. When does the statute of limitations period start to run on the breach of warranty claim against Manufacturer, when Manufacturer tendered delivery to Distributor or when Retailer tendered delivery to Buyer?[42]

These questions should illustrate the difficulty of applying a statutory regime based upon privity considerations to a non-privity relationship.

Now consider the following case, which deals primarily with whether the implied warranty of merchantability extends to a remote buyer down the chain of title.

HYUNDAI MOTOR AMERICA, INC. V. GOODIN
822 N.E.2d 947 (Ind. 2005)

Boehm, Justice

We hold that a consumer may sue a manufacturer for economic loss based on breach of the implied warranty of merchantability even if the consumer purchased the product from an intermediary in the distribution chain. There is no requirement of "vertical" privity for such a claim.

Facts and Procedural Background

On November 18, 2000, Sandra Goodin test drove a Hyundai Sonata at AutoChoice Hyundai in Evansville, Indiana. The car was represented as new and showed nineteen miles on the odometer. Goodin testified that when she applied the brakes in the course of the test drive she experienced a "shimmy, shake, pulsating type feel." The AutoChoice salesperson told her that this was caused by flat spots on the tires from extended inactivity and offered to have the tires rotated and inspected. After this explanation, Goodin purchased the Sonata for $22,710.00.

The manufacturer, Hyundai, provided three limited warranties: 1 year/12,000 miles on "wear items;" 5 years/60,000 miles "bumper to bumper;" and 10 years/100,000 miles on the powertrain. Hyundai concedes that brake rotors, brake

---

WL 2308759 (D.S.C. 2008).

[42] *See Mydlach v. DaimlerChrysler Corp., supra.*

calipers, and brake caliper slides were subject to the 5 year/60,000 mile warranty covering "[r]epair or replacement of any component originally manufactured or installed by [Hyundai] that is found to be defective in material or workmanship under normal use and maintenance." To claim under this warranty, a vehicle must be serviced by an authorized Hyundai dealer who is then reimbursed by Hyundai for any necessary parts or labor.

Three days after the car was purchased, Goodin's husband, Steven Hicks, took it back to AutoChoice for the promised tire work. Goodin testified that she continued to feel the shimmy but did nothing further for a month. On December 22, she took the car to a different Hyundai dealer, Bales Auto Mall, in Jeffersonville, Indiana, for an unrelated problem and also made an appointment six days later for Bales to inspect the brakes. Bales serviced the brake rotors for warping, but on May 1, 2001, Goodin returned to Bales complaining that the vehicle continued to vibrate when the brakes were applied. Bales found the rotors to be out of tolerance and machined them. Eighteen days later Goodin again returned to Bales, reporting that she still felt vibrations and for the first time also heard a "popping" noise. Goodin told the service advisor at Bales that she thought there may be a problem with the suspension, and Bales changed and lubed the strut assembly. Eleven days later Goodin once more brought the car to Bales reporting continued shimmy and also a "bed spring type" noise originating from the brakes. The Bales mechanic was unable to duplicate the brake problem, but balanced and rotated the tires as Goodin had requested. One week later Goodin returned to Bales where she and Jerry Hawes, Bales's Service Manager, test drove the Sonata. The brake problem did not occur during the test drive, but Hawes identified a noise from the direction of the left front tire and repaired the rubber mounting bracket.

Goodin told Hawes that the brake problem had occurred about seventy percent of the time. The problem was worse when it was wet or cool, was consistently occurring when she drove down a steep hill near her home, and was less frequent when a passenger's weight was added. Goodin made arrangements to leave the car with Hawes at Bales, but, according to Hawes, over a several day period he could not duplicate the symptoms Goodin reported.

On August 24, 2001, Goodin took her car back to her original dealer, AutoChoice, reporting that the brakes "squeak and grind when applied." Goodin left the car with AutoChoice where the left front rotor was machined and loose bolts on the front upper control arm were tightened. Goodin testified that after this five-day procedure the brakes began to make the same noises and vibrations even before she arrived home.

In October 2001 Goodin hired an attorney who faxed a letter to Hyundai Motor America giving notice of her complaint and requesting a refund of the purchase price. On November 13, 2001, Goodin filed a complaint against Hyundai Motor America, Inc. alleging claims under the Magnuson-Moss Warranty Act, 15 U.S.C. §§ 2301-2312, for breach of express warranty, breach of implied warranty, and revocation of acceptance. On April 23, 2002, in anticipation of litigation, Goodin hired William Jones to inspect her car. Jones noted that the odometer read 57,918 miles and the car was still under warranty. Jones drove the car approximately five miles and found "severe brake pulsation on normal stops" which "was worse on high speed stops." Although he did not remove the tires to inspect the brake rotors, Jones opined that the rotors were warped and defective or there was "a root cause that has not been discovered and corrected by the repair facilities." His ultimate conclusion was that the "vehicle was defective and unmerchantable at the time of manufacture and unfit for operation on public roadways." Three weeks later, after the 5 year/60,000 mile warranty had expired, Goodin's husband, Hicks, replaced the rotors with new rotors from a NAPA distributor. After this repair, according to Hicks, the pulsation went from "very bad" to "mild" and "less frequent."

Steven Heiss, District Parts and Service Manager for Hyundai Motor America served as the liaison between Hyundai and the dealers and provided warranty training. If a dealer is not performing repairs correctly, Hyundai, through its liaisons, addresses the problem. Heiss inspected Goodin's Sonata on October 21, 2002. At that point the Sonata had been driven 77,600 miles. He testified that during his twenty-three mile test drive he neither heard the noise described by Goodin nor felt any vibration from the brakes. However, Heiss did hear a "droning noise" which he later concluded was due to a failed left rear wheel bearing. He regarded this as a serious problem and not one caused by abuse or misuse of the vehicle. The wheel bearing would have been covered by the 5 year/60,000 mile warranty. Before his inspection, Heiss had been told that the rotors had been changed by Hicks five months earlier, and when Heiss measured the rotors he found that they were out of standard. Heiss testified a miscast from the factory was one of a number of possible reasons for damaged rotors.

At the conclusion of a two day trial, the jury was instructed on all claims. Over defendants' objection, the instructions on implied warranties made no reference to a privity requirement. The jury returned a verdict for Hyundai on Goodin's breach of express warranty claim, but found in favor of Goodin on her claim for breach of implied warranty of merchantability. Damages of $3,000.00 were assessed . . . .

Hyundai orally moved to set aside the verdict as contrary to law on the ground that Goodin purchased the car from AutoChoice and therefore did not enjoy vertical privity with Hyundai. The court initially denied that motion, but the following day set aside the verdict, holding lack of privity between Goodin and Hyundai precluded a cause of action for breach of implied warranty. Goodin then moved to reinstate the verdict, and, after briefing and oral argument, the trial court granted that motion on the ground that Hyundai was estopped from asserting lack of privity.

Hyundai appealed, asserting: (1) it was not estopped from asserting a defense of lack of privity; and (2) lack of vertical privity barred Goodin's recovery for breach of implied warranty of merchantability. The Court of Appeals agreed on both points, holding that Hyundai was not estopped from asserting that privity was an element of Goodin's prima facia case, and, because privity was lacking, Goodin did not prove her case. . . . The Court of Appeals was "not unsympathetic" to Goodin's claims but regarded itself as bound by a footnote in *Martin Rispens & Son v. Hall Farms, Inc.,* 621 N.E.2d 1078, 1084 n.2 (Ind.1993), where this Court stated: "In Indiana, privity between the seller and the buyer is required to maintain a cause of action on the implied warranties of merchantability." *Id.* at 784. We granted transfer.

Vertical Privity

. . .

C. *Origins of Privity*

Indiana has adopted the Uniform Commercial Code, notably its provision that: "A warranty that the goods shall be merchantable is implied in a contract for their sale if the seller is a merchant with respect to goods of that kind." Ind. Code § 26-1-2-314(1)(2004). Hyundai asserts, and the Court of Appeals found, Indiana law requires vertical privity between manufacturer and consumer when economic damages are sought. Goodin argues that traditional privity of contract between the consumer and manufacturer is not required for a claim against a manufacturer for breach of the implied warranty of merchantability. . . .

Privity originated as a doctrine limiting tort relief for breach of warranties. The lack of privity defense was first recognized in *Winterbottom v. Wright,* 152 Eng. Rep. 402 (Ex. 1842). In that case, the court sustained a demurrer to a suit by an injured coachman for breach of warranty by a third party who contracted with the owner to maintain the coach. In this century, however, *MacPherson v. Buick Motor Co.,* 111 N.E. 1050 (N.Y. 1916), and *Henningsen v. Bloomfield Motors, Inc.,* 161 A.2d 69 (N.J. 1960), established that lack of privity between an automobile manufacturer and a consumer would not preclude the consumer's action for personal injuries and property damage caused by the negligent manufacture of an automobile. "Vertical" privity typically becomes an issue when a purchaser files a breach of warranty action against a vendor in the purchaser's distribution chain who is not the purchaser's immediate seller. Simply put, vertical privity exists only between immediate links in a distribution chain. *Rheem Mfg. Co. v. Phelps Heating & Air Conditioning, Inc.,* 714 N.E.2d 1218, 1228 n.8 (Ind. Ct. App. 1999). A buyer in the same chain who did not purchase directly from a seller is "remote" as to that seller. *Id.* "Horizontal" privity, in contrast, refers to claims by nonpurchasers, typically someone who did not purchase the product but who was injured while using it. Goodin purchased her car from a dealership and is thus remote from the manufacturer and lacks "vertical" privity with Hyundai.

"Although warranty liability originated as a tort doctrine, it was assimilated by the law of contracts and ultimately became part of the law of sales." 2 Hawkland, UCC Series, § 2-318:1 at 771 (2001). But "privity is more than an accident of history. It permitted manufacturers and distributors to control in some measure their risks of doing business." Richard W. Duesenberg, *The Manufacturer's Last Stand: The Disclaimer,* 20 Bus. Law 159, 161 (1964). Because vertical privity involves a claim by a purchaser who voluntarily acquired the goods, it enjoys a stronger claim to justification on the basis of freedom of contract or consensual relationship. It nevertheless has come under criticism in recent years, and this is the first opportunity for this Court to give full consideration to this issue.

D. *Indiana Case Law*

Although this Court did not address the issue, even before the Products Liability Act, both the Court of Appeals and federal courts applying Indiana law held that a claimant was not required to prove privity to succeed in a personal injury action in tort based on breach of implied warranties. Three federal court decisions drew on these decisions to conclude that privity of contract is not required in Indiana to maintain a cause of action for personal injury based on breach of an implied warranty.

However, several Court of Appeals decisions subsequently held that recovery of economic loss for alleged failure of the expected benefit of the bargain based on breach of implied warranty under the UCC required a buyer to be in privity of contract with the seller.

This Court has mentioned the common law privity requirement in the context of actions sounding in contract only once, and that in a footnote. *Martin Rispens*

& Son v. Hall Farms, Inc., 621 N.E.2d 1078 (Ind.1993), addressed negligence and express and implied warranty claims by a farmer against both the direct seller and the grower of seed that allegedly damaged the farmer's crops. The footnote cited to the UCC and two Court of Appeals decisions and other courts have taken the footnote as settled Indiana law on this issue. As the Court of Appeals put it in its decision in this case:

> [T]he [footnote] indicates our supreme court's unequivocal acceptance that privity between a consumer and a manufacturer is required in order to maintain a cause of action for breach of an implied warranty of merchantability. . . . Any change in the law removing the privity requirement in implied warranty actions should be left to that court. . . . To the extent Goodin argues that this result is inequitable, we are not entirely unsympathetic. Whether the cons of the vertical privity rule outweigh the pros is something for either our supreme court or the General Assembly to address.

In *Martin Rispens,* the implied warranty claims were rejected based on an effective disclaimer of implied warranty, under Indiana Code section 26-1-2-316(2) which permits parties to agree to exclude or modify implied warranties if done in a particular manner. The farmer did not present privity as an issue on transfer to this Court and neither party briefed it. It was not necessary to the decision. Accordingly, the language in *Martin Rispens,* though often cited, is dicta and we accept the invitation from the Court of Appeal to reconsider it.

Indiana law, as developed in the Court of Appeals, has already eroded the privity requirement to some degree. In *Thompson Farms, Inc. v. Corno Feed Products, Inc.,* 366 N.E.2d 3 (Ind. App. 1977), the Court of Appeals permitted the plaintiff to recover on an implied warranty where it was shown that the contractual arrangements between the manufacturer and the dealer who sold to the plaintiff created an agency relationship; and the manufacturer's agents participated significantly in the sale both through advertising and personal contact with the buyer. Under those circumstances the Court of Appeals held that the manufacturer was a "seller" within the meaning of Indiana Code section 26-1-2-314. *Richards v. Goerg Boat & Motors, Inc.,* 384 N.E.2d 1084 (Ind. App. 1979), involved a defective boat sold by a dealer where the manufacturer's agents also engaged in personal contact with the buyer by giving demonstrations and attempting to adjust the loss after the sale. The Court of Appeals then, following *Thompson Farms, Inc.,* held that the participation in the sale by the manufacturer was sufficient to bring it into the transaction as a seller within the requirements of Indiana Code section

26-1-2-314. However, if the plaintiff could not show perfect vertical privity or an exception to the rule, then the plaintiff could not prove the claim. *Candlelight Homes, Inc. v. Zornes*, 414 N.E.2d 980, 982 (Ind. Ct. App. 1981).

E. *Statutory Developments in Indiana*

The Product Liability Act, Indiana Code § 34-20-2-1 *et seq.* (1999), does not require a personal injury plaintiff to prove vertical privity in order to assert a products liability claim against the manufacturer. Even before the Product Liability Act in 1978, the requirement of privity of contract in warranty actions in Indiana began to erode in 1963 with the passage of the Uniform Commercial Code under section 2-318:

> A seller's warranty whether express or implied extends to any natural person who is in the family or household of his buyer or who is a guest in his home if it is reasonable to expect that such person may use, consume or be affected by the goods and who is injured in person by breach of the warranty. A seller may not exclude or limit the operation of this section.

I.C. § 26-1-2-318. Section 2-318 was taken verbatim from the UCC as originally prepared by the Uniform Code Committee Draftsmen in 1952. It eliminated "horizontal" privity as a requirement for warranty actions. However, that version of 2-318 took no position on the requirement of vertical privity.

The purpose of the original version of section 2-318, which remains unchanged in Indiana today, was to give standing to certain non-privity plaintiffs to sue as third-party beneficiaries of the warranties that a buyer received under a sales contract. That version of section 2-318 provided only that the benefit of a warranty automatically extended to the buyer's family, household, and houseguests. It was intended to, and did, accomplish its goal of "freeing any such beneficiaries from any technical rules as to [horizontal] privity." U.C.C. § 2-318 cmt. 2. Some states refused to enact this version of section 2-318, and others adopted nonuniform versions of the statute. In 1966, in response to this proliferation of deviant versions of a purportedly uniform code, the drafters proposed three alternative versions of section 2-318. Only California, Louisiana, and Texas have failed to adopt one of these three versions of section 2-318.

The majority of states, including Indiana, retained or adopted the 1952 version of section 2-318, which now appears in the Uniform Commercial Code as "Alternative A." Alternative B provides that "any natural person who may reasonably be expected to use, consume or be affected by the goods and who is injured in person by breach of warranty" may institute a breach of warranty action against the seller. U.C.C. § 2-318 cmt. 3. Alternative B expands the class of potential plaintiffs beyond family, household, and guests, and also implicitly abolishes the requirement of vertical privity because the seller's warranty is not limited to "his buyer" and persons closely associated with that buyer. Alternative B is applicable only to claims for personal injury.

> Because Alternatives A and B of 2-318 are limited to cases where the plaintiff is "injured in person," they do not *authorize* recovery for such loss. But neither do they *bar* a non-privity plaintiff from recovery against such a remote manufacturer for direct economic loss. Thus, Alternatives A and B of 2-318 do not prevent a court from abolishing the *vertical* privity requirement even when a non-privity buyer seeks recovery for direct economic loss.

1 James J. White & Robert S. Summers, Uniform Commercial Code 593 (4th ed.1995) (emphasis in original).

Alternative C is the most expansive in eliminating the lack-of-privity defense. It provides that: "A seller's warranty whether express or implied extends to any person who may reasonably be expected to use, consume or be affected by the goods and who is injured by breach of the warranty." Alternative C expands the class of plaintiffs to include other nonpurchasers such as the buyer's employees and invitees, and bystanders. Alternative C also eliminates the vertical privity requirement, but is not restricted to "personal" injury. Because Alternative C refers simply to "injury," plaintiffs sustaining only property damage or economic loss in some states have been held to have standing to sue under this language. This is consistent with the stated objective of the drafters that the third alternative follow "the trend of modern decisions as indicated by Restatement of Torts 2d § 402A (Tentative Draft No. 10, 1965) in extending the rule beyond injuries to the person." *Hawkland, supra,* at 770.

The commentaries to the UCC were careful to explain that these alternatives were not to be taken as excluding the development of the common law on the issue of vertical privity:

> [Alternative A] expressly includes as beneficiaries within its provisions the family, household and guests of the purchaser. Beyond this, the section in this form is neutral and is not intended to enlarge or restrict the developing case law on whether the seller's warranties, given to his buyer who resells, extend to other persons in the distributive chain.

U.C.C. § 2-318, cmt. n. 3.

F. *Privity as an Obsolete Requirement as Applied to Consumer Goods*

There is a split of authority in other jurisdictions with similar or identical versions of section 2-318 on the availability of implied warranty claims by remote purchasers, particularly if only economic loss is claimed, as in the present case. Courts of other jurisdictions that have retained or adopted Alternative A note that the statute speaks only to horizontal privity, and is silent as to vertical privity. *See, e.g., Morrow v. New Moon Homes, Inc.*, 548 P.2d 279, 287 (Alaska 1976); *Kassab v. Central Soya*, 432 Pa. 217, 246 A.2d 848, 855 (1968), *overruled on other grounds, AM/PM Franchise Ass'n v. Atlantic Richfield Co.*, 526 Pa. 110, 584 A.2d 915, 926 (1990). As the Pennsylvania Supreme Court put it: "Merely to *read* the language [of § 2-318] is to demonstrate that the code simply fails to treat this problem.... There thus is nothing to prevent this court from joining in the growing number of jurisdictions which, although bound by the code, have nevertheless abolished vertical privity in breach of warranty cases." *Kassab v. Central Soya*, 246 A.2d 848, 856 (Pa. 1968) (emphasis in original), *overruled on other grounds, AM/PM Franchise Ass'n v. Atlantic Richfield Co.*, 584 A.2d 915, 926 (Pa. 1990). Indiana has not legislated on this issue since 1966 when the UCC adopted these three alternatives. More recently, the "Buyback Vehicle Disclosure" statute eliminated the lack-of-privity defense for actions under that section. *See* I.C. § 24-5-13.5-13(c) (1995). In short, the General Assembly in keeping Alternative A left to this Court the issue of to what extent vertical privity of contract will be required.[43]

---

[43] Several jurisdictions that have adopted Alternative A have abolished privity. *See Morrow v. New Moon Homes*, 548 P.2d 279, 291–92 (Alaska 1976); *Manheim v. Ford Motor Co.*, 201 So. 2d 440 (Fla.1967); *Groppel Co., Inc. v. U.S. Gypsum Co.*, 616 S.W.2d 49, 58 (Mo. Ct. App.1981) (abolishing vertical privity and extending implied warranty to remote purchasers even when only economic loss is claimed); *Peterson v. N. Am. Plant Breeders*, 354 N.W.2d 625, 631 (Neb. 1984); *Hiles Co. v. Johnston Pump Co.*, 560 P.2d 154, 157 (Nev. 1977); *Spring Motors Distrib., Inc. v. Ford Motor Co.*, 489 A.2d 660, 676 (N.J. 1985); *Old Albany Estates Ltd. v. Highland Carpet Mills, Inc.*, 604 P.2d 849, 852 (Okla.1979); *Spagnol Enters., Inc. v. Digital Equipment Corp.*, 568 A.2d 948, 952 (Pa. Super. 1989); *Dawson v. Canteen Corp.*, 212 S.E.2d 82, 82–83 (W. Va. 1975).

Others have retained the common law privity rule. *See Flory v. Silvercrest Indus.*, 633 P.2d 383, 388 (Ariz. 1981); *Ramerth v. Hart*, 983 P.2d 848, 852 (Idaho 1999) (upheld vertical privity requirement but left open the possibility of a different conclusion if the combination of the privity requirement and the economic loss rule proved unjust); *Presnell Constr. Managers, Inc. v. EH Constr., LLC*, 134 S.W.3d 575, 579 (Ky. 2004); *Energy*

Courts that have abolished vertical privity have cited a variety of reasons. Principal among these is the view that, in today's economy, manufactured products typically reach the consuming public through one or more intermediaries. As a result, any loss from an unmerchantable product is likely to be identified only after the product is attempted to be used or consumed. Others have cited the concern that privity encourages thinly capitalized manufacturers by insulating them from responsibility for inferior products. Yet others have focused on the point that if implied warranties are effective against remote sellers it produces a chain of lawsuits or crossclaims against those up the distribution chain. And some focus on the reality in today's world that manufacturers focus on the consumer in communications promoting the product.

Finally, some jurisdictions have abolished privity in warranty actions where only economic losses were sought based on the notion that there is "no reason to distinguish between recovery for personal and property injury, on the one hand, and economic loss on the other." *Hiles Co. v. Johnston Pump Co.,* 560 P.2d 154, 157 (Nev. 1977). A variance on this theme is the view that abolishing privity "simply recognizes that economic loss is potentially devastating to the buyer of an unmerchantable product and that it is unjust to preclude any recovery from the manufacturer for such loss because of a lack of privity, when the slightest physical injury can give rise to strict liability under the same circumstances." *Groppel Co., Inc. v. U.S. Gypsum Co.,* 616 S.W.2d 49, 59 (Mo. Ct. App. 1981). One court preserving the privity requirement expressed the view that "there may be cases where the plaintiff may be unfairly prejudiced by the operation of the economic loss rule in combination with the privity requirement." *Ramerth v. Hart,* 983 P.2d 848, 852 (Idaho 1999).

In Indiana, the economic loss rule applies to bar recovery in tort "where a negligence claim is based upon the failure of a product to perform as expected and the plaintiff suffers only economic damages." *Martin Rispens,* 621 N.E.2d at 1089. Possibly because of the economic loss rule, Goodin did not raise a negligence claim here. Furthermore, at oral argument Goodin's attorney pointed to the warranty disclaimer in the Buyer's Order as a bar to Goodin's ability to sue her direct seller,

---

Investors Fund, L.P. v. Metric Constructors, Inc., 525 S.E.2d 441, 446 (N.C. 2000); *Hupp Corp. v. Metered Washer Serv.,* 472 P.2d 816 (Or. 1970); *Messer Griesheim Indus. v. Cryotech of Kingsport, Inc.,* 131 S.W.3d 457, 463 (Tenn. Ct. App. 2003); *City of La Crosse v. Schubert, Schroeder & Associates, Inc.,* 240 N.W.2d 124, 126 (Wis. 1976), *overruled on other grounds, Daanen & Janssen v. Cedarapids, Inc.,* N.W.2d 842 (Wis. 1998).

AutoChoice, which could then have sued Hyundai for reimbursement. This disclaimer, Goodin contends, precluded a chain of claims ultimately reaching the manufacturer. Therefore, Goodin claims that if this Court does not abolish the vertical privity requirement she will be left without a remedy for Hyundai's breach of its implied warranty of merchantability, and Hyundai's implied warranty becomes nonexistent in practical terms.

The basis for the privity requirement in a contract claim is essentially the idea that the parties to a sale of goods are free to bargain for themselves and thus allocation of risk of failure of a product is best left to the private sector. Otherwise stated, the law should not impose a contract the parties do not wish to make. The Court of Appeals summarized this view well:

> Generally privity extends to the parties to the contract of sale. It relates to the bargained for expectations of the buyer and seller. Accordingly, when the cause of action arises out of economic loss related to the loss of the bargain or profits and consequential damages related thereto, the bargained for expectations of buyer and seller are relevant and privity between them is still required.

> Implied warranties of merchantability and fitness for a particular use, as they relate to economic loss from the bargain, cannot then ordinarily be sustained between the buyer and a remote manufacturer.

Richards, 384 N.E.2d at 1092. We think that this rationale has eroded to the point of invisibility as applied to many types of consumer goods in today's economy. The UCC recognizes an implied warranty of merchantability if "goods" are sold to "consumers" by one who ordinarily deals in this product. Warranties are often explicitly promoted as marketing tools, as was true in this case of the Hyundai warranties. Consumer expectations are framed by these legal developments to the point where technically advanced consumer goods are virtually always sold under express warranties, which, as a matter of federal law run to the consumer without regard to privity. 15 U.S.C. § 2310. . . . Given this framework, we think ordinary consumers are entitled to, and do, expect that a consumer product sold under a warranty is merchantable, at least at the modest level of merchantability set by UCC section 2-314, where hazards common to the type of product do not render the product unfit for normal use.

Even if one party to the contract – the manufacturer – intends to extend an implied warranty only to the immediate purchaser, in a consumer setting, doing away with the privity requirement for a product subject to the Magnuson-Moss Warranty Act, rather than rewriting the deal, simply gives the consumer the contract the consumer expected. The manufacturer, on the other hand is encouraged to build quality into its products. To the extent there is a cost of adding uniform or standard quality in all products, the risk of a lemon is passed to all buyers in the form of pricing and not randomly distributed among those unfortunate enough to have acquired one of the lemons. Moreover, elimination of privity requirement gives consumers such as Goodin the value of their expected bargain, but will rarely do more than duplicate the Products Liability Act as to other consequential damages. The remedy for breach of implied warranty of merchantability is in most cases, including this one, the difference between "the value of the goods accepted and the value they would have had if they had been as warranted." I.C. § 26-1-2-714(2). This gives the buyer the benefit of the bargain. In most cases, however, if any additional damages are available under the UCC as the result of abolishing privity, Indiana law would award the same damages under the Products Liability Act as personal injury or damage to "other property" from a "defective" product. *Gunkel v. Renovations, Inc.,* 822 N.E.2d 150 (Ind. 2005).

For the reasons given above we conclude that Indiana law does not require vertical privity between a consumer and a manufacturer as a condition to a claim by the consumer against the manufacturer for breach of the manufacturer's implied warranty of merchantability.

We will return to privity issues when we consider the liability of a seller under other law in the next Chapter. For now, try your hand at the following problems.

Problem 7-31

Manufacturer makes photocopiers for business use. Manufacturer is very proud of its products and expressly warrants on its order acknowledgment forms that the copiers will not break down for three years from the date of purchase. Manufacturer sold a copier to Distributor on June 1, 2008.

Distributor sells business machines made by several different companies, including Manufacturer. Because Distributor does not make anything on its own, and therefore has no control over the quality of the products it sells, Distributor expressly and effectively disclaims all express and implied warranties in its sales agreements. Distributor advises its customers to seek recourse against the maker of any malfunctioning product Distributor has sold. Among other things, this protects Distributor if one of its suppliers makes a defective product and then goes out of business, leaving Distributor on the hook for any warranty liability. On December 1, 2008, Distributor sold the copier it purchased from Manufacturer to Retailer.

Retailer sells business machines, including photocopiers, in a single metropolitan area. Retailer expressly warrants that all products it sells will not break down for one year from the date of purchase. Retailer sold the copier it obtained from Distributor to Buyer on April 1, 2009.

A. Against whom, if anyone, will Buyer have a cause of action if the jurisdiction in which all the sales occurred has abolished the need for vertical privity and the copier malfunctions on:
   1. November 1, 2009?
   2. November 1, 2010?
   3. November 1, 2011?

B. How, if at all, would the analysis of Part A change if the jurisdiction in which all the sales occurred has not abolished the need for vertical privity?

C. Buyer is a corporation and uses the machine to set up a home office for a senior vice president. It put the copier in the vice president's home. The copier malfunctioned on November 1, 2009 by short circuiting in a manner that started a fire and destroyed the vice president's home. Fortunately, no one was injured. If the jurisdiction in which all the parties are located has abolished the need for vertical privity and has enacted one of the standard alternatives in section 2-318, against whom, if anyone, does the vice president have a cause of action? Give a separate analysis for each of the alternatives A through C in section 2-318.

CISG and UNIDROIT Principles. The CISG and the UNIDROIT Principles do not address remedies for entities that are not in privity of contract.

CHAPTER EIGHT

BUYER'S REMEDIES UNDER OTHER LAW

SECTION 1. OVERVIEW

Modern contract law – including Article 2 of the Uniform Commercial Code – is grounded in the principle of freedom of contract. In that sense, it is premised on a centuries-old model of contracting in which the parties are located near each other and freely negotiate the terms of every deal. Under that premise, everyone is free to contract or to refrain from contracting except on the terms they desire. Although modern law in some ways has recognized how antiquated these premises are,[1] freedom of contract remains a fundamental underlying premise.

In the modern age, most contracting is done through the use of standardized forms in either print or electronic format. As a result, many buyers – most notably consumers – are unable to effectuate any changes to the standard terms presented by prospective sellers. Rather the seller presents terms on a take-it-or-leave-it basis. In addition, many sellers of similar types of products have similar terms, so that the ability of a buyer to shop for more favorable terms is non-existent. Even if sellers of a product do offer different terms, most buyers lack the time, incentive, and awareness to shop around for the best terms. They tend to focus on price, convenience, and the business reputation of the seller, not on the terms of the sale.

In this environment, sellers have every economic incentive to attempt to limit liability to the lowest level possible in the event the goods fail to function properly, even if the seller otherwise offers good customer service. In other words, the seller may choose to do more than its contracts require, but would prefer to have the option to base its decision on business considerations, not on legal requirements.

To illustrate this point, consider this scenario. Buyer purchases a computer to use in its business. Because of a defect in the computer's hard drive, Buyer loses all of its customer data and eventually Buyer's business fails. The computer seller may not have warranted the hard drive against defects because it adequately disclaimed all warranties under Article 2. Perhaps more likely, it warranted the hard drive against defects but limited remedies to a refund or replacement of the hard drive, and adequately excluded liability for all consequential losses. The seller may, either as a matter of customer service or pursuant to its warranty, replace Buyer's hard drive. But in no event will the seller be liable for the damages caused

---

[1] *See, e.g.*, UCC § 2-207.

by the loss of the customer data and the eventual failure of Buyer's business. That is the point of the seller either disclaiming all warranties or excluding liability for consequential harm. If Buyer attempts to recover that type of loss from the seller, the seller will pull out the documentation in which the warranty disclaimer or the limitation on recovery of consequential damage is maintained, and inform Buyer that the seller is not liable for that type of harm.

We have already seen three ways in which Article 2 provides some modicum of protection for buyers:

(i) limitations on the process a seller may use to disclaim the implied warranty of merchantability, UCC § 2-316;

(ii) restoration of Article 2's default rules on remedies if a limited remedy fails of its essential purpose, UCC § 2-719(2); and

(iii) an invitation to courts to police bargains they find to be unconscionable, UCC §§ 2-302, 2-719(3).

Whether these protections are adequate for buyers is highly questionable. The broadest of the three – unconscionability – typically requires both procedural and substantive problems with the bargain before relief will be available, and therefore requires an individualized determination of the facts of the case. The other protections require litigation to determine if the seller has properly disclaimed the warranty or provided an adequate limited remedy. Litigation is an expensive proposition.

Another possible way to protect buyers would be to mandate a certain set of minimum terms or ban certain abusive terms. The European Union has decided to use this method to protect buyers.[2] That approach would be problematic in the United States, however, because it directly contradicts the deeply ingrained freedom of contract principle. Moreover, there would be great difficulty in getting the relevant players to agree on the terms that should be mandated or prohibited.

---

[2] *See* European Union, Council Directive 93/13/EEC of 5 April 1993 on unfair terms in consumer contracts; Jennifer S. Martin, *An Emerging Worldwide Standard for Protections of Consumers in the Sale of Goods: Did We Miss an Opportunity with Revised UCC Article 2?*, 41 TEX. INT'L L.J. 223 (2006); Larry Bates, *Administrative Regulation of Terms in Form Contracts: a Comparative Analysis of Consumer Protection*, 16 EMORY INT'L L. REV. 1 (2002); Linda J. Rusch, *The Relevance of Evolving Domestic and International Law on Contracts in the Classroom: Assumptions About Assent*, 72 TUL. L. REV. 2043, 2073–75 (1998).

Nevertheless, a hodgepodge of federal and state statutes, along with some common-law tort developments, provide some protections to buyers in particular circumstances. In this Chapter, we examine a sampling of these additional buyer protections, with the caveat that any particular state may have different protections for buyers and careful research is required whenever one is trying to determine if the buyer has any remedies in addition to those available under UCC Article 2.[3]

SECTION 2.   MAGNUSON-MOSS WARRANTY ACT

The Magnuson-Moss Warranty Act (MMWA)[4] is a federal law adopted in 1975 that governs written warranties of consumer products. It was enacted to make such warranties more understandable and to ensure that they provide certain minimum rights. It is essentially a kind of truth-in-labeling law for written warranties of consumer products. All such warranties must be clearly designated as either a "full warranty" or a "limited warranty" and must clearly identify how long they last (*e.g.*, three months; lifetime). MMWA § 103. There are important rules on both types of warranty. Some of these rules are in the Act itself, *see* MMWA §§ 104, 108, others are contained in regulations promulgated by the Federal Trade Commission.[5] You should be sure to consult both the Act itself and the regulations issued under it when presented with any issue or problem to which the Act might apply.

The Magnuson-Moss Act does not require sellers or manufacturers of goods to make a warranty. It merely regulates the warranties they do make. Moreover, the Act does not displace what we have learned about warranties under UCC Article 2.

---

[3] Congress has regulated a variety of specific products, such as cigarettes and medical devices. When Congress regulates a product, and that product causes harm, courts must confront the degree to which the federal scheme preempts state law, such as Article 2 or common-law tort actions. Because each federal scheme is different, the degree of preemption, if any, may be different. *See Altria Group, Inc. v. Good*, 129 S. Ct. 538 (U.S. 2008) (fraud claim under Maine Unfair Trade Practices Act not preempted by the Federal Cigarette Labeling and Advertising Act).

[4] It is codified in the United States Code at 15 U.S.C. §§ 2301–12. The text references the provisions by the section numbers in the bill, instead of the United States Code section numbers.

[5] The Federal Trade Commission Rules are in 16 C.F.R. pts. 700–03.

Instead, the Act gives additional rights to a buyer whenever the Act applies.[6] *See* MMWA § 111(b). Indeed, anyone who makes a warranty governed by the Act is prohibited from disclaiming any implied warranty that would arise under Article 2. *See* MMWA §§ 104(a)(2), 108.

The key benefit of the Act is that if a warrantor violates its obligations under the Act, the injured "consumer" is entitled to recover the reasonable attorney's fees incurred in any successful enforcement action. MMWA § 110(d). This effectively allows buyers – when the Act applies – to convert state-law implied warranty claims into federal claims which give rise to recovery of attorney's fees. This right is critical because it gives injured consumers the ability to prosecute a claim that would otherwise be too small to justify the expense involved. Accordingly, this right to attorney's fees is liberally enforced, even when the amount at stake is small in comparison:

> In rendering its opinion, the district court commented favorably on the professional standing of plaintiff's trial counsel and found the skill, time, and labor involved reasonable. The court further stated that the fee of $125 an hour requested by plaintiff's counsel was reasonable. Thus, the only justifications for limiting plaintiff's fees to approximately fifteen percent of the amount requested are the result obtained and the low value of the case. We conclude that the district court abused its discretion in failing to consider the remedial nature of the acts involved.

> In consumer protection as this, the monetary value of the case is typically low. If courts focus only on the dollar value and the result of the case when awarding attorney fees, the remedial purposes of the statutes in question will be thwarted. Simply put, if attorney fee awards in these cases do not provide a reasonable return, it will be economically impossible for attorneys to represent their clients. Thus, practically speaking, the door to the courtroom will be closed to all but those with either potentially substantial damages, or those with sufficient economic resources to afford the litigation expenses involved. Such a situation would indeed be ironic: it is but precisely those with ordinary consumer complaints and those who

---

[6] If there is a direct conflict between the requirements of the federal act and applicable state law, then the federal act would control pursuant to the federal supremacy clause in the Constitution. *See* U.S. Const. Art. IV.

cannot afford their attorney fees for whom these remedial acts are intended.[7]

A more detailed exploration of the Magnuson-Moss Act must begin with its scope. Unfortunately, the Act does not have a single provision that identifies the situations to which it applies. Therefore, one must peruse the operative sections of the act, identify the key words, and then review the statutory definitions of those terms to ascertain the scope of the Act.

Problem 8-1

A. Make a list of the terms you think are important in defining the scope of the Magnuson-Moss Act and read the definitions of those terms in MMWA § 101. Draft a succinct and accurate statement of the scope of the Magnuson-Moss Act.

B. To which, if any, of the following transactions might the Magnuson-Moss Act apply? What additional facts do you need to know to determine whether the Act in fact applies to these transactions?
  1. The purchase of a motor home for use by an individual as a recreational vehicle.
  2. The purchase of a motor home by ABX News for use by one of its crews to travel from place to place in gathering news stories.
  3. The lease of a motor home by an individual to use on a month-long vacation touring the southwest.[8]

Once you decide that the Magnuson-Moss Act applies to a transaction, the next step is to determine what impact, if any, it has.[9] The key to this is the distinction

---

[7] *Jordan v. Transnational Motors, Inc.*, 537 N.W.2d 471, 473–74 (Mich. Ct. App. 1995).

[8] *Compare Parrot v. DaimlerChrysler Corp.*, 130 P.3d 530 (Ariz. 2006) (lessee is not a "consumer" under the Magnuson-Moss Act); *DiCintio v. DaimlerChrysler Corp.*, 768 N.E.2d 1121 (N.Y. 2002) (same), *with American Honda Motor Co. v. Cerasani*, 955 So. 2d 543 (Fla. 2007) (lessee is a "consumer" under the Magnuson-Moss Act); *Peterson v. Volkswagen of Am., Inc.*, 697 N.W.2d 61 (Wis. 2005) (same).

[9] The Magnuson-Moss Act is a consumer protection law and thus, as with most laws of that type, disclosure of information is important. Section 102 of the Act requires the "warrantor" to make the "written warranty" available in readily understandable language. When must that

between a full warranty and a limited warranty. Read MMWA §§ 104, 108. Notice that a warranty designated as a "full warranty" will be deemed to meet the standards applicable to such warranties even if the text of the writing does not purport to do so. MMWA § 104(e).

Most warrantors, if they make a written warranty under the Act, do not make a full warranty. Rather, they make a limited warranty. Do you see why?

Problem 8-2

A. Find a written warranty provided to you in connection with the purchase of a consumer good. Is it designated a "full" or a "limited" warranty? Does it comply with the Magnuson-Moss Act requirements?

B. List all of the differences between a "written warranty" under the Magnuson-Moss Act and an "express warranty" under UCC section 2-313.

C. Identify how, if at all, the implied warranty of merchantability may be disclaimed or limited by:
   1. A supplier making a Magnuson-Moss Act full warranty.
   2. A supplier making a Magnuson-Moss Act limited warranty.

D. Identify how, if at all, a clause excluding the buyer's ability to recover consequential damages is affected if the supplier makes a full or limited warranty under the Magnuson-Moss Act.

One of the key benefits of the Magnuson-Moss Act is that it eliminates the need for vertical privity with respect to a claim under a written warranty. It does this in two ways. First, the "warrantor" under the Act need not be the seller; it could be the manufacturer. *See* MMWA § 101(4), (5). Second, the "consumer" entitled to enforce the written warranty includes "any person to whom such product is transferred." MMWA § 101(3). This ensures, among other things, that someone who receives a warranted consumer product as a gift can benefit from the written

---

disclosure be made? *See* 16 C.F.R. pt. 702. In your shopping for consumer products, have you ever seen the MMWA disclosure of a "written warranty" as contemplated in the FTC regulation?

warranties that accompany the product.[10] Note, if "transferred" refers not only to transfers of ownership but also to transfers of possession, then this rule might also solve many horizontal privity problems as well.

Less clear is whether the Act abrogates the privity requirement for actions based on the implied warranty of merchantability or the implied warranty of fitness for particular purpose. Courts are divided on whether a manufacturer who makes a written warranty covered by the Act can be directly liable to the consumer on an implied warranty if the applicable state law requires vertical privity.[11] Similarly, it remains unclear whether a consumer enforcing remedies under the Magnuson-Moss Act are entitled to revoke acceptance against a remote seller even if that remedy is not available under Article 2.[12]

Problem 8-3

A. A trucking company occasionally sells its used trucks to independent buyers when it buys new trucks to replace its aging fleet. In making these sales, the trucking company gives a 30-day limited warranty against defects in the engine. It also disclaims all implied warranties in a manner that satisfies the tests of UCC section 2-316. A buyer of one of the used trucks complained that the truck it bought was not merchantable because the chassis had cracks in it. Assuming the truck sold was indeed not merchantable, is the trucking company liable for that breach of warranty?

B. Manufacturer sold a new truck to Truck Dealer. In that transaction, Manufacturer disclaimed all implied warranties pursuant to the rules

---

[10] These principles also apply to service contracts covered by the Act.

[11] *Compare Voelker v. Porsche Cars N. Am., Inc.*, 353 F.3d 516 (7th Cir. 2003) (state law privity rules still apply for actions on implied warranties); *Rentas v. DaimlerChrysler Corp.*, 936 So. 2d 747 (Fla. Ct. App. 2006) (privity required to bring action for breach of implied warranty), *with Rothe v. Maloney Cadillac, Inc.*, 518 N.E.2d 1028 (Ill. 1988) (privity not required to assert implied warranty of merchantability claim against remoteseller who had made a written warranty).

[12] *See Mydlach v. DaimlerChrysler Corp.*, 875 N.E.2d 1047 (Ill. 2007) (revocation of acceptance not available against remote seller); *Gochey v. Bomardier, Inc.*, 572 A.2d 921 (Vt. 1990) (revocation of acceptance allowed against manufacturer).

in UCC section 2-316. Manufacturer did, however, provide a written limited warranty, to be given to any buyer of the vehicle from Truck Dealer. That warranty promised to repair any defects in material or workmanship in the truck's engine appearing during the first 100,000 miles or three years, whichever came first. When Buyer purchased the vehicle from Truck Dealer, Truck Dealer provided the written warranty to Buyer. Does Buyer get an implied warranty of merchantability from the manufacturer?

Another possible benefit of the Magnuson-Moss Act – one that has engendered considerable debate – may be a prohibition on subjecting warranty claims to binding arbitration. The Magnuson-Moss Act expressly permits a consumer's claim to be subject to informal settlement procedures. *See* MMWA § 110(a)(3). Submission to these procedures can be a *precondition* to bringing suit in court, but courts disagree on whether the procedures can serve as a *substitute for* judicial action.[13]

Problem 8-4

Standard Luxury Vehicles, Inc., an authorized dealer of Wanderer Motor Homes, sold a Wanderer Luxury II motor home to Bridget for $80,000. In the discussion prior to the sale, Standard's owner told Bridget that the motor home was an energy efficient model and should get at least 15 miles per gallon in a normal mix of city and highway driving. Bridget was intending to take the motor home across the United States, stopping to golf at every public course Bridget could find as research for a book on public golf courses. Standard knew what Bridget intended since she told Standard's owner in the course of looking at various models of motor

---

[13] Amy J. Schmitz, *Curing Consumer Warranty Woes Through Regulated Arbitration*, 23 OHIO ST. J. ON DISP. RESOL. 627 (2008); *Koons Ford of Baltimore, Inc. v. Lobach*, 919 A.2d 722 (Md. 2007) (arbitration clause in warranty is not enforceable); *Davis v. Southern Energy Homes, Inc.*, 305 F.3d 1268 (11th Cir. 2002), *cert. denied*, 538 U.S. 945 (2003) (arbitration clause in warranty is enforceable).

Even if the Magnuson-Moss Act renders the arbitration clause unenforceable, that effect may be limited to claims arising under the written warranty. Plaintiffs who are suing solely on implied warranties and using the Magnuson-Moss Act as a vehicle for attorney's fees may still be bound to arbitrate.

homes. The document that Bridget signed when she agreed to buy the motor home provided the following:

> The Wanderer Luxury II motor home is warranted by the manufacturer to be free of defects in materials or workmanship at the time of delivery. Buyer's sole remedy is that an authorized dealer will repair or replace any defective parts for 1 year from the date of delivery. DEALER AND MANUFACTURER MAKE NO OTHER WARRANTIES, EXPRESS OR IMPLIED, INCLUDING THE WARRANTY OF MERCHANTABILITY AND FITNESS FOR A PARTICULAR PURPOSE. Dealer or Manufacturer are not liable for any consequential or incidental damages. This writing is the complete, exclusive and final statement of all terms of the sale.

Bridget took delivery of the motor home on March 1, 2007. On March 5, 2007, Bridget returned the motor home to the dealership due to whistling sounds in the windows. Standard resealed the windows and Bridget took the motor home back on March 10, 2007. From April through November, Bridget returned the motor home to Standard four separate times to fix various items such as a leak in the roof, a malfunctioning refrigerator, a cracked sewage hose, and an overheating engine. Bridget's trouble with the motor home continued throughout the winter (December through February) including a propane leak in the stove resulting in a short hospital stay for Bridget and her spouse due to gas inhalation and a leaky shower stall resulting in ruined carpeting. Each time Bridget took the motor home to Standard, the problem was successfully repaired. However, each time, Bridget had to drive from wherever she was on her golf odyssey to Standard's dealership. As a result, Bridget only got to play about half of the golf courses she had planned on, resulting in a delay in her book project.

On March 1, 2008, Bridget drove the motor home to Standard's location and told Standard that she was returning the motor home due to the many problems that she had experienced, including the fact that, over the course of the year, the motor home averaged only 10 miles per gallon. Bridget demanded return of her purchase price. Standard refused to take the motor home back and told Bridget the one-year warranty period was up and she was on her own with the motor home. The manufacturer did not respond to Bridget's complaint. Advise Bridget. Include in your analysis all parties' likely arguments.

SECTION 3.   UNFAIR AND DECEPTIVE PRACTICES

Federal law prohibits unfair and deceptive acts and practices in commercial activity. The relevant statutory provisions are amazing for their brevity:

15 U.S.C. § 45(a)

Declaration of unlawfulness; power to prohibit unfair practices . . .

(1) Unfair methods of competition in or affecting commerce, and unfair or deceptive acts or practices in or affecting commerce, are hereby declared unlawful.

(2) The [Federal Trade] Commission is hereby empowered and directed to prevent persons, partnerships, or corporations, . . . from using unfair methods of competition in or affecting commerce and unfair or deceptive acts or practices in or affecting commerce.

The Federal Trade Commission has issued a variety of regulations pursuant to the authority granted to it in the act. Three of these regulations merit our attention.

First, the FTC has a rule regarding a "cooling off" period for sales made at a location other than the seller's place of business. 16 C.F.R. pt. 429. The basic import of this regulation is that it is an unfair and deceptive practice to use high pressure sales tactics in the buyer's home. To guard against that practice, in certain defined situations, the buyer is given a three-day right to cancel the sale and the seller is required to inform the buyer of that right. 16 C.F.R. § 429.1. Although the transactions to which the regulation applies are often referred to as in-home sales, they need not actually occur in the buyer's home. The regulation also applies to sales made in temporary locations, such as convention centers and fairgrounds. 16 C.F.R. § 429.0.

Second, the FTC has issued a rule that in a mail order or telephone sale, the seller must be able to ship the merchandise to the buyer within the time the seller represents, or the buyer is entitled to cancel the order. 16 C.F.R. pt. 435. This guards against an unfair trade practice of getting advance payment for an item and then delaying fulfilment of the order unreasonably. Third, the FTC has issued a regulation regarding accurate disclosure of any warranty offered in the sale of a used vehicle and accurate representation of the mechanical condition of the used vehicle. 16 C.F.R. pt. 455. This rule guards against the unfair trade practice of misrepresenting the warranties offered and the state of the used vehicle. These are just three examples of the types of actions that the FTC has determined to be unfair and deceptive trade practices.

The FTC enforces the act and the regulations issued under it by bringing enforcement actions against sellers.[14] Most courts hold that the buyer does not have a private right of action under the act and regulations. However, many states have similar statutes prohibiting unfair and deceptive trade practices. While these statutes often empower a state official, such as the attorney general, to enforce the law, many also provide for a private cause of action. *See, e.g.*, Wash. Rev. Code ch. 19.86. These state acts can reach a substantial amount of unscrupulous behavior, including bait-and-switch tactics, advertising great deals and then not having a reasonable number of the goods on hand for sale, and all the conduct prohibited by the FTC regulations. The buyer's ability to recover against the seller for unfair and deceptive trade practices is thus usually under the state analogs to the federal act and regulations.[15]

The FTC has engaged in enforcement action regarding other aspects of seller behavior, including protecting the customers' data from piracy, and prohibiting false and misleading information to consumers regarding the advertising for products.[16] A seller engaging in selling goods needs to be thoroughly aware of the prohibitions regarding unfair and deceptive trade practices that operate at both the state and federal level. Conversely, a buyer who is stuck with a malfunctioning or disappointing product should determine whether there is a means of recovery using the prohibitions on unfair and deceptive trade practices.

SECTION 4.   LEMON-LAWS

Most states have enacted laws that protect consumer buyers of new vehicles. The basic approach of these laws is to give the dealer or manufacturer a specified

---

[14] For an interesting decision in which the FTC found violations of the Magnuson-Moss Act to be an unfair trade practice, *see In the Matter of Gateway 2000, Inc.*, 126 F.T.C. 888 (1998).

[15] Mark E. Budnitz, *The Federalization and Privatization of Public Consumer Protection Law in the United States: Their Effect on Litigation and Enforcement*, 24 GA. ST. U. L. REV. 663 (2008).

[16] *See, e.g.*, Stephen F. Ambrose, Jr., *et al.*, *Survey of Significant Consumer Privacy Litigation in the United States in 2007*, 63 BUS. LAW. 653 (2008); Jean Noonan and Michael Goodman, *Third-Party Liability for Federal Law Violations in Direct-to-Consumer Marketing: Telemarketing, Fax, and E-mail*, 63 BUS. LAW. 585 (2008).

time in which to repair defects or nonconformities covered by a warranty. If the vehicle is not repaired within that time or after a certain number of attempts, the buyer is entitled to a replacement vehicle or a refund of the purchase price. That is the general approach, but of course the laws vary in the details. For example, some may apply only to sales of vehicles while others also cover extended leases. Some may protect only consumer buyers while others protect all buyers. Some may impose liability on the seller, some on the manufacturer, and some on both. And some may give relief only if the problems substantially impair the value of the vehicle while others are not so limited.

Moreover, the time for repair will vary from state to state, as will the process the buyer must follow to seek redress under the act and the applicable limitations period. Other variations involve the remedies available, in particular whether the buyer is entitled to incidental, consequential, or punitive damages and whether the seller is entitled to any offset for the buyer's use of the vehicle.[17] Note also, if the buyer traded in a used vehicle, the seller may have already resold it before the buyer seeks to rescind purchase of the new, defective vehicle. In such a case, it will be impossible to return the used car to the buyer. Accordingly, even though the parties may have negotiated a net deal, the price stated for each vehicle in the contract will be very important in determining the amount of restitution to which the buyer is entitled.

Consider the following case exploring the application of Oregon's lemon law.

LILES V. DAMON CORP., 198 P.3d 926 (2008)

Durham, J.

Plaintiffs brought this action under ORS 646A.400 to ORS 646A.418, commonly known as Oregon's Lemon Law, seeking replacement of a motor home that they had purchased. The issue on review concerns the proper interpretation of ORS 646A.402, which we quote below in full. Under that statute, a statutory remedy is "available to a consumer" if, among other things, the manufacturer of a

---

[17] *See* Annotation, *Validity, Construction and Effect of State Motor Vehicle Warranty Legislation (Lemon Laws)*, 88 A.L.R. 5th 301 (2001); Phillip R. Nowicki, *State Lemon Law Coverage Terms: Dissecting the Differences*, 11 LOY. CONSUMER L. REP. 39 (1999); Joan Vogel, *Squeezing Consumers: Lemon Laws, Consumer Warranties, and a Proposal for Reform*, 1985 ARIZ. ST. L. J. 589.

motor vehicle has received "direct written notification" from the consumer and "has had an opportunity to correct the alleged defect." ORS 646A.402(3).

After a trial, the trial court found that plaintiffs had satisfied the statutory requirements and granted relief. Specifically, the court rejected defendant's contention that ORS 646A.402(3) obligated plaintiffs to afford defendant the opportunity to correct the alleged defect *after* sending written notification to defendant and *before filing* their action. In its judgment, the court made the following finding of fact:

> The Court finds that the manufacturer did receive adequate written
> notification of these defects from the Plaintiffs and that the manufacturer
> also had ample opportunity to correct the defects.

On appeal, the Court of Appeals reversed. The Court of Appeals concluded that the conditions in the statute applied in sequence: that is, the delivery of the consumer's "direct written notification" of the defect must occur before the manufacturer has any "opportunity to correct" the defect under the statute. Moreover, the court determined that each statutory condition "must be met before seeking a remedy under the Lemon Law[,]" meaning that plaintiffs had to satisfy each condition *before filing* their action. According to the Court of Appeals, plaintiffs had satisfied the written notice requirement but, after doing so, had not provided defendant an opportunity to correct the alleged defect before filing their action. This court granted review to determine whether the Court of Appeals had correctly construed the requirements in Oregon's Lemon Law.

We view the evidence in the light most favorable to plaintiffs, who prevailed at trial. On December 30, 2002, plaintiffs purchased a motor home from a dealer in Sandy, Oregon. Defendant manufactured the motor home. According to the trial court's finding, plaintiffs

> began contacting the factory representatives by phone in April of 2003
> regarding the water leak problems they were experiencing with the unit.
> They contacted the factory representative about the many problems with the
> motor home numerous times between April 2003 and December 2003. The
> Plaintiffs also presented numerous times between April 2003 and
> December 2003. The Plaintiffs also presented numerous repair orders from
> the selling dealer representing many unsuccessful attempts to repair the
> water leaks in this unit during that same period [of] time.

The vehicle dealer performed most of the unsuccessful attempts to repair the leaks. However, the trial court found that, on one occasion, defendant directed plaintiffs to submit the vehicle for repair at a different repair shop. That attempted repair occurred on December 9, 2003, but it, too, was unsuccessful. According to the trial court, that attempted repair "was specifically authorized by the manufacturer as their attempt to cure the defect[ ]" and "was an opportunity to correct the defect before the lawsuit was filed even though written notice wasn't given."

On December 23, 2003, an attorney representing plaintiffs sent a letter to defendant under Oregon's Lemon Law. The letter described the water leak problems and plaintiffs' unsuccessful efforts to resolve them through multiple repair efforts and through several discussions with defendant's representatives, including its president and "the field person for Damon in charge of repairs." The letter requested the replacement remedy under the Lemon Law, ORS 646A.404(1)(a), which we quote below. . . . Defendant received the letter described above on December 29, 2003. Plaintiffs filed their action the next day, December 30, 2003. In January 2004, plaintiffs informed defendant that it could have access to the vehicle, but defendant took no further action to assess or repair the rainwater leaks. The case was tried to the court sitting without a jury on February 24, 2005, and the court entered judgment for plaintiffs on June 7, 2005. As noted, the Court of Appeals reversed, and we allowed plaintiffs' petition for review.

This case requires the interpretation of several statutory provisions in Oregon's Lemon Law. We begin with the text and context of the statutes and endeavor to give meaning to all parts of those statutes.

ORS 646A.402 provides:

The remedy under the provisions of ORS 646A.400 to 646A.418 is available to a consumer if:

(1) A new motor vehicle does not conform to applicable manufacturer's express warranties;

(2) The consumer reports each nonconformity to the manufacturer, its agent or its authorized dealer, for the purpose of repair or correction, during the period of one year following the date of original delivery of the motor vehicle to the consumer or during the period ending on the date on which the mileage on the motor vehicle reaches 12,000 miles, whichever period ends earlier; and

(3) The manufacturer has received direct written notification from or on behalf of the consumer and has had an opportunity to correct the alleged defect. "Notification" under this subsection includes, but is not limited to, a request by the consumer for an informal dispute settlement procedure under ORS 646A.408.

ORS 646A.404(1) describes the remedy that is available to a consumer:

If the manufacturer or its agents or authorized dealers are unable to conform the motor vehicle to any applicable manufacturer's express warranty by repairing or correcting any defect or condition that substantially impairs the use, market value or safety of the motor vehicle to the consumer after a reasonable number of attempts, the manufacturer shall:

(a) Replace the motor vehicle with a new motor vehicle; or

(b) Accept return of the vehicle from the consumer and refund to the consumer the full purchase or lease price paid, including taxes, license and registration fees and any similar collateral charges excluding interest, less a reasonable allowance for the consumer's use of the vehicle.

ORS 646A.406 creates a presumption, potentially usable during litigation, about whether the vehicle manufacturer or dealer has undertaken a "reasonable number of attempts" to conform the vehicle to applicable manufacturer's express warranties. That statute provides, in part:

(1) It shall be presumed that a reasonable number of attempts have been undertaken to conform a motor vehicle to the applicable manufacturer's express warranties if, during the period of one year following the date of original delivery of the motor vehicle to a consumer or during the period ending on the date on which the mileage on the motor vehicle reaches 12,000 miles, whichever period ends earlier:

(a) The same nonconformity has been subject to repair or correction four or more times by the manufacturer or its agent or authorized dealer, but such nonconformity continues to exist; or

(b) The vehicle is out of service by reason of repair or correction for a cumulative total of 30 or more business days.

(2) A repair or correction for purposes of subsection (1) of this section includes a repair that must take place after the expiration of the earlier of either period.

. . .

(4) In no event shall the presumption described in subsection (1) of this section apply against a manufacturer unless the manufacturer has received prior direct written notification from or on behalf of the consumer and has had an opportunity to cure the defect alleged.

ORS 646A.412(1) describes additional remedies available to a consumer in a successful action under the statute "against a manufacturer...." ORS 646A.414(1) confirms that the statute does not create an action against a vehicle dealer.

Several features of the statutory text are noteworthy. The statutory remedy is "available to a consumer" under ORS 646.402 only if the consumer communicates certain information to others. First, under ORS 646A.402(2), the consumer must "report[ ]" the defects to "the manufacturer, its agent or its authorized dealer, for the purpose of repair or correction" within the timeframe that the subsection describes. The statute does not require that communication to be in writing. Second, the consumer or someone acting on the consumer's behalf must give the manufacturer "direct written notification." The statute does not describe the information that the consumer's written notice must contain beyond confirming that a consumer's request for an informal dispute settlement procedure under ORS 646A.408 constitutes notification. There is no dispute here that plaintiffs satisfied both of the statutory notice requirements described above.

The issue presented is whether defendant "has had an opportunity to correct the alleged defect" under ORS 646A.402(3). As noted, defendant contends that the opportunity for correction must occur *after* it receives the consumer's written notification under ORS 646A.402(3) but also *before* the consumer files an action. Defendant asserts that plaintiffs afforded it no opportunity to correct the defect under the statute because only one day elapsed between its receipt of plaintiffs' attorney's letter on December 29, 2003, and the filing of the action on December 30, 2003.

Defendant's contention that a single day did not afford a reasonable opportunity to correct the vehicle's defects fails because it proceeds from an erroneous construction of ORS 646A.402(3). Notably, the statute does not state that the consumer's written notification and the manufacturer's opportunity for correction are *prefiling* requirements – that is, required procedural steps that must occur before the filing of the action. Rather, ORS 646A.402 states that those requirements are conditions that must exist if the statutory remedy is to be "available to a consumer[.]"

That distinctive terminology refers to conditions that the court must assess when it exercises its authority to grant or deny the requested remedy; it does not create a prefiling requirement. When the legislature has created prefiling procedural requirements in other contexts, it has used terms that unmistakably convey that intent. . . . ORS 646A.402(3) lacks any counterpart to the substantive terms of those prefiling requirements. . . .

The "opportunity to correct" requirement in ORS 646.402(3) assures the manufacturer that it will have a chance to repair or correct the nonconformity of which the consumer complains before the court determines the availability of the statutory remedies to the consumer. The statute affords at least two opportunities to the consumer to identify the nonconformity for that purpose: (1) the report to the manufacturer, its agent or its authorized dealer under ORS 646A.402(2), and (2) the written notification under ORS 646.402(3). As noted, the first of those methods may be accomplished orally, in writing, or a combination of both.

It is significant that ORS 646A.402(3) does not require the consumer's "direct written notification" to include any specific contents, such as a particular description of the vehicle's defects. The written notification under subsection (3) may consist of as simple a message as a request for an informal dispute settlement procedure that might not include any "allegations" of a vehicle's defects.

The terms of ORS 646A.402, viewed in their entirety, indicate that, when the court determines whether a statutory remedy is available to the consumer, the consumer must have (1) reported the vehicle's defect to the manufacturer, its agent, or authorized dealer in a timely manner; and (2) given a direct written notification to the manufacturer. In addition, the manufacturer must have had an opportunity to correct *that* defect, not some different defect. The ordinary meaning of the word "alleged" in ORS 646A.402(3) does not confine the manufacturer's opportunity to repair solely to a defect that the consumer has described in the written notification.

Finally, the legislature's intent becomes clear when we contrast the wording of ORS 646A.402(3) with that of ORS 646A.406(4), quoted above. In the latter statute, the legislature has assured manufacturers that the described presumption in favor of the consumer will not apply against them "unless the manufacturer has received *prior* direct written notification from or on behalf of the consumer and has had an opportunity to cure the defect alleged." (Emphasis added.) The term "prior" in that context confirms that, for purposes of applying the presumption, the consumer notification must precede the manufacturer's opportunity to cure the defect.

The legislature did not include the word "prior" in ORS 646A.402(3) and, if possible, we must accord legal meaning to that omission. That task is not difficult in this case. In ORS 646A.406(4), the legislature determined that a manufacturer should be protected from the operation of the evidentiary presumption unless it had engaged in specific conduct: failing to use an opportunity to cure the vehicle defect *after* receiving direct written notification from the consumer. By contrast, under ORS 646A.402(3), the written notification is a condition regarding the availability of the statutory remedy and it serves to ensure that the manufacturer is aware of the consumer's dispute, but it need not necessarily precede the manufacturer's opportunity to correct in order for the statutory remedy to be available.

We can discern the legislature's intent from an examination of the statutory text in context. In doing so, we have given effect to every part of the pertinent statutes, including the legislature's omission of the word "prior" in ORS 646A.402(3), as noted above. Because the legislature's intent is clear from our inquiry into text and context, further inquiry is unnecessary.

In this case, before the trial court adjudicated the availability of the statutory remedy to plaintiffs under ORS 646A.402, defendant had an opportunity to correct the defect that was the subject of plaintiffs' action. On December 9, 2003, plaintiffs, acting on defendant's instructions, submitted their vehicle for repair at a facility selected by defendant. That attempted repair was unavailing. A separate opportunity to repair occurred when plaintiffs made the vehicle available to defendant in January 2004, after plaintiffs filed this action. Defendant took no action in response to that opportunity to repair the vehicle. The filing of the action did not cut off defendant's opportunity to correct the defects in plaintiffs' vehicle. We are satisfied that defendant had an ample opportunity to cure the vehicle's alleged defects before the trial court determined that the statutory remedy was available to plaintiffs under ORS 646.402.

The decision of the Court of Appeals is reversed. The judgment of the circuit court is affirmed.

SECTION 5.   LIABILITY USING TORT LAW PRINCIPLES

As we learned in studying warranties under UCC Article 2, the implied warranty of merchantability requires that the goods sold be, among other things, fit for their ordinary purpose. UCC § 2-314(2)(c). This protects the buyer's likely expectations in the bargain and was an erosion of the doctrine of *caveat emptor*.[18]

---

[18] Warranty disputes involving claims protecting this economic bargain arose between sellers and buyers who were in privity of contract. In the early Seventeenth Century, however, these claims were asserted in tort as an action on the case. The buyer had to establish the elements of deceit, *i.e.*, that the seller made an express representation about the nature of the goods knowing it to be false. By 1790, the action of deceit, with its requirements of scienter by the

However, the implied warranty of merchantability is not made by all sellers. Non-merchants and merchants not in the business of selling goods of that kind do not make the warranty. Moreover, because the warranty is a creature of contract, even merchants who normally would make the warranty may disclaim it pursuant to the rules of section 2-316. Indeed, merchants can disclaim all warranty liability.

So, consider the case of a merchant seller who has not made a written warranty covered by the Magnuson-Moss Act, not made any express warranties under section 2-313, and has properly disclaimed all implied warranties under section 2-316. Yet the goods sold malfunction and cause harm. Is there any basis for holding the seller liable for that harm? This is where tort law comes into play, in particular, the law of products liability.

Section 402A of the Restatement (Second) of Torts, which was intended to summarize the developing case law in this area, establishes the standard for imposing strict liability – as opposed to liability arising from negligence – of a merchant seller.[19] It provides:

---

representor and reliance by the representee, had developed into a separate writ or action. At about the same time, the English courts first permitted an express warranty claim to be brought in assumpsit, the action in which most contract claims were pursued. By 1802, scienter was no longer a requirement in assumpsit for breach of an express warranty, but other limiting formalities, *i.e.*, that the representation must be an express term of the contract and intended by the seller to be a warranty, still remained. This early interaction between representations of quality made in exchange transactions and the tort forms of action led Dean Prosser to conclude that warranty was a "freak hybrid born of the illicit intercourse of tort and contract." William L. Prosser, *The Assault Upon the Citadel (Strict Liability to the Consumer),* 69 YALE L.J. 1099, 1126 (1960). During the Nineteenth Century, warranty theory developed into the tripartite form which we know today: an express warranty, an implied warranty of fitness for particular purpose, and an implied warranty of merchantability (fitness for "ordinary" purposes).

[19] For a discussion of the principles of tort products liability and the history of its evolution *see* David G. Owen, *The Evolution of Products Liability Law,* 26 REV. LITIG. 955 (2007); Linda J. Rusch, *Products Liability Trapped By History: Our Choice of Rules Rules Our Choices,* 76 TEMPLE L. REV. 739 (2003); Marshall S. Shapo, *Products at the Millennium: Traversing a Transverse Section,* 53 S.C. L. REV. 1031 (2002); James J. White, *Reverberations from the Collision of Tort and Warranty,* 53 S.C. L. REV. 1067 (2002); Frances E. Zollers, *et al., Looking Backward, Looking Forward: Reflections on Twenty Years of Product Liability Reform,* 50 SYRACUSE L. REV. 1019 (2000); William K. Jones, *Product Defects Causing Commercial Loss: The Ascendancy of Contract over Tort,* 44 U.

(1) One who sells any product in a defective condition unreasonably dangerous to the user or consumer or to his property is subject to liability for physical harm thereby caused to the ultimate user or consumer, or to his property, if

(a) the seller is engaged in the business of selling such a product, and

(b) it is expected to and does reach the user or consumer without substantial change in the condition in which it is sold.

(2) The rule stated in Subsection (1) applies although

(a) the seller has exercised all possible care in the preparation and sale of his product, and

(b) the user or consumer has not bought the product from or entered into any contractual relation with the seller.

Note that section 402A deals only with personal injury and damage to property other than the goods sold. It does not apply if the only harm is to the defective goods themselves.

Section 402A and the cases under it raise a number of interesting issues that are typically explored in law school courses on torts or products liability. We concentrate on only two of them. First, whether there is any meaningful difference between whether a product is defective under section 402A and whether it is unmerchantable under UCC section 2-314. Second, whether and to what extent the damages available in a strict products liability action differ from those available for breach of the implied warranty of merchantability.

Apart from strict liability under section 402A, many states recognize a tort cause of action for misrepresentation.[20] This cause of action generally requires a material misrepresentation of fact on which the plaintiff justifiably and

---

MIAMI L. REV. 731 (1990); Richard E. Speidel, *Warranty Theory, Economic Loss, and the Privity Requirement: Once More Into the Void,* 67 B.U. L. REV. 9 (1987); David A. Rice, *Product Quality Laws and the Economics of Federalism,* 65 B.U. L. REV. 1 (1985); Ingrid M. Hillinger, *The Merchant of Section 2-314: Who Needs Him?,* 34 HASTINGS L.J. 747 (1983); Herbert D. Titus, *Restatement (Second) of Torts Section 402A and the Uniform Commercial Code,* 22 STAN. L. REV. 713 (1970); William L. Prosser, *The Implied Warranty of Merchantable Quality,* 27 MINN. L. REV. 117 (1943); Karl N. Llewellyn, *On Warranty of Quality and Society,* 36 COLUM. L. REV. 699 (1936); Walton H. Hamilton, *The Ancient Maxim Caveat Emptor,* 40 YALE L.J. 1133 (1931); Samuel Williston, *Representation and Warranty in Sales–Heilbut v. Buckleton,* 27 HARV. L. REV. 1 (1913); Emlin McClain, *Implied Warranties in Sales,* 7 HARV. L. REV. 213 (1903).

[20] *See* RESTATEMENT (SECOND) OF TORTS § 525 (fraudulent misrepresentation causing pecuniary loss); § 552 (negligent misrepresentation causing pecuniary loss); RESTATEMENT (THIRD) OF TORTS § 9 (liability for misrepresentation causing harm to person or property).

detrimentally relies. Such claims often bear a striking similarity to claims from breach of an express warranty, and we explore the relationship between misrepresentation and express warranty in the last part of this section.

A. Product Defect Defined

The key requirement of the implied warranty of merchantability is that the goods sold be fit for their ordinary purpose. Accordingly, any good that is not fit for its ordinary purpose will breach that warranty – in other words, it will be defective. A slightly different standard applies to determine whether a product is defective for the purpose of strict liability in tort. Consider the following case.

CASTRO V. QVC NETWORK, INC.
139 F.3d 114 (2d Cir. 1998)

Calabresi, Circuit Judge

In this diversity products liability action, plaintiffs-appellants alleged, in separate causes of action for strict liability and for breach of warranty, that defendants-appellees manufactured and sold a defective roasting pan that injured one of the appellants. The United States District Court for the Eastern District of New York (Leonard D. Wexler, *Judge*) rejected appellants' request to charge the jury separately on each cause of action and, instead, instructed the jury only on the strict liability charge. The jury found for appellees and the court denied appellants' motion for a new trial. This appeal followed. We hold that, under New York law, the jury should have been instructed separately on each charge, and, accordingly, reverse and remand for a new trial on the breach of warranty claim.

I. BACKGROUND

In early November 1993, appellee QVC Network, Inc. ("QVC"), operator of a cable television home-shopping channel, advertised, as part of a one-day Thanksgiving promotion, the "T-Fal Jumbo Resistal Roaster." The roaster, manufactured by U.S.A. T-Fal Corp. ("T-Fal"), was described as suitable for, among other things, cooking a twenty-five pound turkey.[21] Appellant Loyda Castro

---

[21] At the time that QVC and T-Fal agreed to conduct the Thanksgiving promotion, T-Fal did not have in its product line a pan large enough to roast a turkey. T-Fal therefore asked its

bought the roasting pan by mail and used it to prepare a twenty-pound turkey on Thanksgiving Day, 1993.

Mrs. Castro was injured when she attempted to remove the turkey and roasting pan from the oven. Using insulated mittens, she gripped the pan's handles with the first two fingers on each hand (the maximum grip allowed by the small size of the handles) and took the pan out of the oven. As the turkey tipped toward her, she lost control of the pan, spilling the hot drippings and fat that had accumulated in it during the cooking and basting process. As a result, she suffered second and third degree burns to her foot and ankle, which, over time, has led to scarring, intermittent paresthesia, and ankle swelling.

It is uncontested that in their complaint appellants alleged that the pan was defective and that its defects gave rise to separate causes of action for strict liability and for breach of warranty. Moreover, in the pre-charge conference, appellants' counsel repeatedly requested separate jury charges on strict liability and for breach of warranty. The district court, nevertheless, denied the request for a separate charge on breach of warranty. Judge Wexler stated that "you can't collect twice for the same thing," and deemed the warranty charge unnecessary and "duplicative." The court, therefore, only gave the jury the New York pattern strict products liability charge.

The jury returned a verdict for appellees QVC and T-Fal. . . . Appellants subsequently moved, pursuant to Federal Rule of Civil Procedure 59, that the jury verdict be set aside and a new trial be ordered for various reasons including that the court had failed to charge the jury on appellants' claim for breach of warranty. . . . [T]he district court denied appellants' Rule 59 motion, reasoning that the breach of warranty and strict products liability claims were "virtually the same." This appeal followed.

------

parent company, located in France, to provide a suitable roasting pan as soon as possible. The parent provided a pan (designed originally without handles and for other purposes). To this pan two small handles were added so that it could be used to roast a turkey. T-Fal shipped the pan to QVC in time for the early November campaign.

II. DISCUSSION

. . .

A. Two Definitions of "Defective" Product Design

Products liability law has long been bedeviled by the search for an appropriate definition of "defective" product design.[22] Over the years, both in the cases and in the literature, two approaches have come to predominate. The first is the risk/utility theory, which focuses on whether the benefits of a product outweigh the dangers of its design.[23] The second is the consumer expectations theory, which focuses on what a buyer/user of a product would properly expect that the product would be suited for.[24]

Not all states accept both of these approaches. Some define design defect only according to the risk/utility approach. . . . Others define design defect solely in terms of the consumer expectations theory. . . . [25]

One of the first states to accept both approaches was California, which in *Barker v. Lull Engineering Co.,* 573 P.2d 443 (Cal. 1978), held that "a product may be found defective in design, so as to subject a manufacturer to strict liability for resulting injuries, under either of two alternative tests" – consumer expectations and

---

[22] *See generally* W. Page Keeton, *The Meaning of Defect in Products Liability Law,* 45 MO. L.REV. 579 (1980); W. Page Keeton, *Product Liability and the Meaning of Defect,* 5 ST. MARY'S L.J. 30 (1973); Guido Calabresi & Jon T. Hirschoff, *Toward a Test for Strict Liability in Torts,* 81 YALE L.J. 1055 (1972).

[23] According to the New York Court of Appeals, the risk/utility calculus, which requires "a weighing of the product's benefits against its risks," *Denny v. Ford Motor Co.,* 662 N.E.2d 730, 735 (N.Y. 1995), is " 'functionally synonymous'" with traditional negligence analysis, *id.* Despite the fact that there are some significant differences, the risk/utility calculus is in many ways similar to the Learned Hand negligence test.

[24] The New York Court of Appeals explains that "the UCC's concept of a 'defective' product requires an inquiry only into whether the product in question was 'fit for the ordinary purposes for which such goods are used.' " *Denny,* 662 N.E.2d at 736 (quoting U.C.C. § 2-314(2)(c)). Thus, the breach of warranty cause of action "is one involving true 'strict' liability, since recovery may be had upon a showing that the product was not minimally safe for its expected purpose." *Id.* Some scholars have characterized this inquiry as centering on whether the manufacturer or the user is in a better position to decide about safety. *See* Calabresi & Hirschoff, *supra* note [19], at 1060.

[25] Still others apply a "modified consumer expectations test" that incorporates risk/utility factors into the consumer expectations analysis. . . .

risk/utility. *Id.* at 455.[26] Several states have followed suit and have adopted both theories.

.... Prior to the recent case of *Denny v. Ford Motor Co.,* 662 N.E.2d 730 (N.Y. 1995), it was not clear whether New York recognized both tests. In *Denny,* the plaintiff was injured when her Ford Bronco II sports utility vehicle rolled over when she slammed on the brakes to avoid hitting a deer in the vehicle's path. The plaintiff asserted claims for strict products liability and for breach of implied warranty, and the district judge – over the objection of defendant Ford – submitted both causes of action to the jury. The jury ruled in favor of Ford on the strict liability claim, but found for the plaintiff on the implied warranty claim. On appeal, Ford argued that the jury's verdicts on the strict products liability claim and the breach of warranty claim were inconsistent because the causes of action were identical.

This court certified the *Denny* case to the New York Court of Appeals to answer the following questions: (1) "whether, under New York law, the strict products liability and implied warranty claims are identical"; and (2) "whether, if the claims are different, the strict products liability claim is broader than the implied warranty claim and encompasses the latter."

In response to the certified questions, the Court of Appeals held that in a products liability case a cause of action for strict liability is not identical to a claim for breach of warranty.... Moreover, the court held that a strict liability claim is not per se broader than a breach of warranty claim such that the former encompasses the latter.... Thus, while claims of strict products liability and breach of warranty are often used interchangeably, under New York law the two causes of action are definitively different. The imposition of strict liability for an alleged design "defect" is determined by a risk-utility standard, ... The notion of

---

[26] The court stated:

> First, a product may be found defective in design if the plaintiff establishes that the product failed to perform as safely as an ordinary customer would expect when used in an intended or reasonably foreseeable manner. Second, a product may alternatively be found defective in design if the plaintiff demonstrates that the product's design proximately caused his injury and the defendant fails to establish, in light of the relevant factors, that, on balance, the benefits of the challenged design outweigh the risk of danger inherent in such design.

Barker, 573 P.2d at 455–56. Placement of the burden of proving the product's risks and utility on the manufacturer is not, however, a necessary part of the risk/utility test....

"defect" in a U.C.C.-based breach of warranty claim focuses, instead, on consumer expectations. . . .

B. *When Should a Jury be Charged on Both Strict Liability and Warranty Causes of Action?*

Since *Denny,* then, it has been settled that the risk/utility and consumer expectations theories of design defect can, in New York, be the bases of distinct causes of action: one for strict products liability and one for breach of warranty. This fact, however, does not settle the question of when a jury must be charged separately on each cause of action and when, instead, the two causes are, on the facts of the specific case, sufficiently similar to each other so that one charge to the jury is enough.

While eminent jurists have at times been troubled by this issue,[27] the New York Court of Appeals in *Denny* was quite clear on when the two causes of action might meld and when, instead, they are to be treated as separate. It did this by adding its own twist to the distinction – namely, what can aptly be called the "dual purpose" requirement. . . . Thus in *Denny,* the Court of Appeals pointed out that the fact that a product's overall benefits might outweigh its overall risks does not preclude the possibility that consumers may have been misled into using the product in a context in which it was dangerously unsafe. . . . And this, the New York court emphasized, could be so even though the benefits in other uses might make the product sufficiently reasonable so that it passed the risk/utility test.

---

[27] Thus Justice Traynor in the early and seminal California strict products liability case, *Greenman v. Yuba Power Products,* 377 P.2d 897 (Cal. 1963), did not make a clear distinction between them. *See id.* at 901 ("[I]t should not be controlling [for purposes of establishing a manufacturer's liability] whether plaintiff selected the [product] because of the statements in the brochure, or because of the [product's] own appearance of excellence that belied the defect lurking beneath the surface, or because he merely assumed that it would safely do the jobs it was built to do."). And likewise, Judge Eschbach in *Sills v. Massey-Ferguson, Inc.,* 296 F. Supp. 776 (N.D. Ind. 1969), stated that although they represented different causes of action, in the case before him, he could not distinguish between them, and then added that "[w]hile this court is unwilling to hold that there is *never* a significant difference between the two theories, it is plain that the outcome of the vast majority of cases is not affected by this fine legal distinction." *Id.* at 779.

In *Denny,* the Ford Bronco II was not designed as a conventional passenger automobile. Instead, it was designed as an off-road, dual purpose vehicle.[28] But in its marketing of the Bronco II, Ford stressed its suitability for commuting and for suburban and city driving. . . . Under the circumstances, the Court of Appeals explained that a rational factfinder could conclude that the Bronco's utility as an off-road vehicle outweighed the risk of injury resulting from roll-over accidents (thus passing the risk/utility test), but at the same time find that the vehicle was not safe for the "ordinary purpose" of daily driving for which it was also marketed and sold (thus flunking the consumer expectations test). . . .

That is precisely the situation before us. The jury had before it evidence that the product was designed, marketed, and sold as a multiple-use product. The pan was originally manufactured and sold in France as an all-purpose cooking dish without handles. And at trial, the jury saw a videotape of a QVC representative demonstrating to the television audience that the pan, in addition to serving as a suitable roaster for a twenty-five pound turkey, could also be used to cook casseroles, cutlets, cookies, and other low-volume foods.[29] The court charged the jury that "[a] product is defective if it is not reasonably safe[,] [t]hat is, if the product is so likely to be harmful to persons that a reasonable person who had actual knowledge of its potential for producing injury would conclude that it should not have been marketed in that condition." And, so instructed, the jury presumably found that the pan, because it had many advantages in a variety of uses, did not fail the risk/utility test.

But it was also the case that the pan was advertised as suitable for a particular use – cooking a twenty-five pound turkey. Indeed, T-Fal added handles to the pan in order to fill QVC's request for a roasting pan that it could use in its Thanksgiving

---

[28] Indeed, as Ford argued, the design features that appellant complained of – high center of gravity, narrow track width, short wheel base, and a specially tailored suspension system--were important to preserve the vehicle's utility for off-road use. . . . But, it was these same design features that made the vehicle susceptible to rollover accidents during evasive maneuvers on paved roads. . . .

[29] Appellants also introduced into evidence a "sell sheet" prepared by T-Fal, which described for the QVC salespersons the uses and characteristics of the product, including not only cooking a twenty-five pound turkey, but also an extensive list of several low-volume foods, such as cake, lasagna, and stuffed potatoes. While the "sell-sheet" was an internal document, and therefore, could not have influenced consumer expectations, it does shed light on the meaning of the videotaped commercial.

promotion. The product was, therefore, sold as appropriately used for roasting a twenty-five pound turkey. And it was in that use that allegedly the product failed and injured the appellant.

In such circumstances, New York law is clear that a general charge on strict products liability based on the risk/utility approach does not suffice. The jury could have found that the roasting pan's overall utility for cooking low-volume foods outweighed the risk of injury when cooking heavier foods, but that the product was nonetheless unsafe for the purpose for which it was marketed and sold – roasting a twenty-five pound turkey – and, as such, was defective under the consumer expectations test. That being so, the appellants were entitled to a separate breach of warranty charge.[30]

III. CONCLUSION

In light of the evidence presented by appellants of the multi-purpose nature of the product at issue, the district court, applying New York law, should have granted appellants' request for a separate jury charge on the breach of warranty claim in addition to the charge on the strict liability claim. Accordingly, we reverse the order of the district court denying the motion for a new trial, and remand the case for a new trial on the breach of warranty claim, consistent with this opinion.

———————

Section 2 of the Restatement (Third) of Torts defines a product defect as follows:

A product is defective when, at the time of sale or distribution, it contains a manufacturing defect, is defective in design, or is defective because of inadequate instructions or warnings. A product:

———————

[30] Appellees argue that "[t]he roaster had only a single purpose which was to be a vessel for cooking." But that misses the point of the dual purpose test. Indeed, the same argument could have been made in the *Denny* case: that the Ford Bronco II had a single purpose, namely driving. What characterizes both of these cases, however, is that there was evidence before the jury of the "dual purposes" to which the products could be put. As the Court of Appeals stated in *Denny,* it is "the nature of the proof and the way in which the fact issues [are] litigated [that] demonstrate[ ] how the two causes of action can diverge." . . . In the instant case, given the evidence before the jury of the pan's dual purposes, the failure to charge the jury on breach of warranty could not be harmless error.

(a) contains a manufacturing defect when the product departs from its intended design even though all possible care was exercised in the preparation and marketing of the product;

(b) is defective in design when the foreseeable risks of harm posed by the product could have been reduced or avoided by the adoption of a reasonable alternative design by the seller or other distributor, or a predecessor in the commercial chain of distribution, and the omission of the alternative design renders the product not reasonably safe;

(c) is defective because of inadequate instructions or warnings when the foreseeable risks of harm posed by the product could have been reduced or avoided by the provision of reasonable instructions or warnings by the seller or other distributor, or a predecessor in the commercial chain of distribution, and the omission of the instructions or warnings renders the product not reasonably safe.

This definition was very controversial in the development of the Restatement (Third) of Torts.[31] It also presents an obvious potential overlap with the failure of goods to be fit for their ordinary purpose.[32] Do you agree with how the court in *Castro* dealt with that potential overlap? Should there be different tests for a design defect under tort law and unmerchantable goods under contract law?[33]

---

[31] *See e.g.,* James A. Henderson, Jr. & Aaron D. Twerski, *Achieving Consensus on Defective Product Design*, 83 CORNELL L. REV. 867 (1998); John F. Vargo, *The Emperor's New Clothes: The American Law Institute Adorns a "New Cloth" for Section 402A Products Liability Design Defects - A Survey of the States Reveals a Different Weave*, 26 U. MEM. L. REV. 493 (1996); Marshall S. Shapo, *In Search of the Law of Products Liability: The ALI Restatement Project*, 48 VAND. L. REV. 631 (1995); Thomas C. Galligan, *Contortions Along the Boundary Between Contracts and Torts*, 69 TUL. L. REV. 457 (1994). For a brief historical view by the co-reporters of the development of the new Restatement, *see* James A. Henderson, Jr. & Aaron D. Twerski, *What Europe, Japan and Other Countries, Jr. Can Learn from the New American Restatement of Products Liability*, 34 TEX. INT'L L.J. 1 (1999).

[32] *See* Aaron D. Twerski, *Chasing the Illusory Pot of Gold at the End of the Rainbow: Negligence and Strict Liability in Design Defect Litigation*, 90 MARQ. L. REV. 7 (2006) (discussion of the Restatement Third as in essence a negligence standard); Ellen Wertheimer, *The Biter Bit Unknowable Dangers, The Third Restatement, and the Reinstatement of Liability Without Fault*, 70 BROOK. L. REV. 889 (2005) (discussing evolution of the design defect concept); James A Henderson, Jr. & Aaron D. Twerski, *A Fictional Tale of Unintended Consequences: A Response to Professor Wertheimer*, 70 BROOK. L. REV. 939 (2005).

[33] The Restatement (Third) approach in comment n to § 2 provides:

Problem 8-5

The New York Court of Appeals in *Denny v. Ford Motor Co.*, 662 N.E.2d 730 (N.Y. 1995) ruled that: (1) a cause of action for strict liability is not identical to a claim for breach of warranty; and (2) a strict liability claim is not necessarily broader than a breach of warranty claim such that the former encompasses the latter. Relying on that, the Second Circuit in *Castro* ruled that a claim for breach of the implied warranty of merchantability might exist even though the jury had concluded that there was no viable strict products liability claim. However, is the inverse situation possible? Can a strict products liability claim exist even though there is no actionable claim for breach of the implied warranty of merchantability? Construct a scenario in which the warranty of merchantability is made but not breached and yet a strict liability claim would exist under the standard set forth in section 402A of the Restatement (Second) of Torts.

B. The Economic Loss Rule as a Limit on Tort Liability

Suppose a seller sells an unmerchantable generator to a homeowner. The generator explodes, destroying itself, causing personal injury to the homeowner, and burning down the homeowner's garage where the generator was installed. The homeowner has suffered harm due to the loss of value of the generator itself, recoverable under UCC section 2-714 and consequential losses due to the personal injury and damage to other property, recoverable under UCC section 2-715. Suppose, further, that the homeowner would be foreclosed from recovery by one or more limitations upon warranty liability found in the UCC, *e.g.*, failure to give notice of the breach, lack of contractual privity, an enforceable consequential

---

This Restatement contemplates that a well coordinated body of law governing liability for harm to persons or property arising out of the sale of defective products requires a consistent definition of defect, and that the definition properly should come from tort law, whether the claim carries a tort label or one of implied warranty of merchantability.

See also David G. Owen, *Proof of Product Defect*, 93 KY. L. J. 1 (2004–05) (discussing the factors and evidence relevant to proving product defect).

damage exclusion, a disclaimer of warranty liability, or expiration of the statute of limitations. If the homeowner pursues a claim in strict products liability in tort, most courts would apply some version of the economic loss rule to limit the damages available. Reread Restatement (Second) of Torts section 402A. Under this rule, a tort recovery would be restricted to the damages for personal injury and the damages for losses to property other than the generator that was the subject of the sales contract.[34] Consider the following discussion of the economic loss rule and its rationale.[35]

LOCKHEED MARTIN CORP. v. RFI SUPPLY, INC.
440 F.3d 549 (1st Cir. 2006)

Torruella, Circuit Judge

This case involves three parties: Plaintiff Lockheed Martin Corporation ("Lockheed"), Defendant Rantec Power Systems, Inc. ("Rantec"), and Third-Party Defendants Factory Mutual Research Corporation ("FMRC") and Factory Mutual Insurance Corporation (collectively, the "FM Entities"). Lockheed appeals the district court's grant of Rantec's motion for summary judgment against Lockheed. . . . We affirm . . . .

---

[34] Ralph C. Anzivino, *The Economic Loss Doctrine: Distinguishing Economic Loss From Non-Economic Loss*, 91 MARQ. L. REV. 1081 (2008); David Gruning, *Pure Economic Loss in American Tort Law: An Unstable Consensus*, 54 AM. J. COMP. L. 187 (2006); Anita Bernstein, *Keep It Simple: An Explanation of the Rule of No Recovery for Pure Economic Loss*, 48 ARIZ. L. REV. 773 (2006); Linda J. Rusch, *Products Liability Trapped by History: Our Choice of Rules Rules Our Choices*, 76 TEMP. L. REV. 739 (2003); Eileen Silverstein, *On Recovery in Tort for Pure Economic Loss*, 32 U. MICH. J. L. REFORM 403 (1999); Richard C. Ausness, *Replacing Strict Liability with a Contract-Based Products Liability Regime*, 71 TEMP. L. REV. 171 (1998).

[35] Should the rationale of this case apply to contracts that are not governed by Article 2? *See Paramount Aviation Corp. v. Agusta*, 288 F.3d 67 (3d Cir. 2002) (holding that in a contract for services, the economic loss rule does not apply); *Quest Diagnostics, Inc. v. MCI Worldcom, Inc.*, 656 N.W.2d 858 (Mich. Ct. App.), *appeal denied*, 671 N.W.2d 886 (Mich. 2003) (economic loss doctrine does not bar recovery when person suffers economic harm and not in a contractual relationship with the plaintiff).

I. *Factual Background and Procedural History*

   A. Lockheed and Rantec

Lockheed is an advanced technology company incorporated in Maryland that also has its principal place of business in Maryland. Rantec is a Delaware corporation with its principal place of business in Missouri. Rantec designs and constructs anechoic chambers.[36] On April 15, 1992, Lockheed and Rantec entered into a written contract in which Rantec agreed to design and construct an anechoic chamber at a Lockheed facility in Merrimack, New Hampshire. As part of the contract, Rantec was required to "design, fabricate, and install a fire detection and sprinkler system" in the chamber. The contract contained a warranty clause providing that "[a]ll equipment and workmanship shall be guaranteed to be free from defects by [Rantec] for a period of one (1) year after final acceptance, unless a different warranty is specified." Rantec completed construction of the chamber in late 1992, and final acceptance occurred in 1993.

The fire detection system consisted of, *inter alia,* smoke detectors, fire alarms, valves, telescoping sprinkler assemblies ("TSAs"), and sprinkler heads. The TSAs were retracted above and outside the chamber and were designed to extend into the chamber when the detection system identified smoke or fire but not immediately release water. Once the temperature exceeded a certain level, a fusible link incorporated in the sprinkler head would melt and water would be released into the chamber.

The present case stems from two incidents involving flooding of Lockheed anechoic chambers. In December 1996, an anechoic chamber at a Lockheed facility in California suffered water damage when three of the TSAs broke and water flooded the chamber. On March 27, 1997, the sprinkler system at the anechoic chamber in New Hampshire malfunctioned. The fire suppression system activated due to a defect in an electronic panel sold and installed by another contractor not party to this suit. The TSAs extended and some of the sprinkler heads broke and released a large amount of water into the chamber. The foam and sub-flooring of the chamber suffered $400,000 of damage. According to Lockheed, also damaged by the flood were a pedestal and positioning system costing over $160,000. These items were not provided under the contract with Rantec. Lockheed did not include these items in its complaint and did not amend its complaint to add these items.

---

[36] An anechoic chamber is a steel shielded room padded with foam material to absorb light and sound. These chambers are used by Lockheed to test antenna signals for aerospace and military applications.

On December 20, 1999, Lockheed brought suit against Rantec . . . alleging claims stemming from the incidents in California and New Hampshire. . . . Lockheed raised the following claims regarding the New Hampshire events: (1) negligence, (2) strict liability, and (3) implied warranties.

B. Rantec and the FM Entities

FMRC performs testing, issues product standards, and publishes a directory of "FM Approved" products for use in fire suppression systems. Rantec's claims against the FM Entities stemmed from FMRC's approval of Rantec's TSAs on the condition that they be equipped with certain sprinkler heads-the sprinkler heads that broke when the TSAs extended into Lockheed's anechoic chamber. After Lockheed sued Rantec, Rantec moved to add the FM Entities as Third-Party Defendants. . . .

C. Proceedings Below

. . . [T]he district court granted Rantec's motion for summary judgment against Lockheed . . .[and] found that the economic loss doctrine barred Lockheed's tort claims and that the implied warranties' claims were barred by the statute of limitations. . . .

II. *Discussion*

. . .

B. Lockheed's Tort Claims

The parties agree that New Hampshire law governs this case. The district court found that, under New Hampshire law, Lockheed's tort claims were barred by what is known as the economic loss rule. Under the economic loss rule, a party generally may not recover in tort for "economic loss." We begin by discussing how the New Hampshire courts have defined "economic loss" and applied the economic loss rule.

The New Hampshire Supreme Court has defined "economic loss" as "the diminution in the value of a product because it is inferior in quality," *Ellis v. Robert C. Morris, Inc.,* 513 A.2d 951, 954 (N.H. 1986), *overruled on other grounds by Lempke v. Dagenais,* 547 A.2d 290, 297–98 (N.H. 1988), and "that loss resulting from the failure of the product to perform to the level expected by the buyer[, which] is commonly measured by the cost of repairing or replacing the product," *Lempke,* 547 A.2d at 296. The New Hampshire Supreme Court has also stated that "[w]hen a defective product accidentally causes harm to persons or property, the resulting harm is treated as personal injury or property damage. But when damage occurs to the inferior product itself . . . the harm is characterized as economic loss."

Ellis, 513 A.2d at 954. The New Hampshire Supreme Court has also noted that "[i]t is clear that the majority of courts do not allow economic loss recovery in tort, but that economic loss is recoverable in contract," *Lempke,* 547 A.2d at 296, and that a party usually may not recover damages for economic loss via a tort claim. . . . . The district court found that the flooding was caused by a malfunction of the anechoic chamber and that the only thing damaged was the chamber itself. The district court therefore concluded that Lockheed suffered only economic loss and could not recover on its negligence or strict liability claims.

Lockheed argues that, under New Hampshire law, the economic loss rule does not bar tort actions where a defect "actually poses an affirmative risk of harm to persons or property." Lockheed would have us look to how the damage occurred and, if we find that the defect or accident posed an affirmative risk to persons or property, find that its tort claims are not barred by the economic loss rule.[37] However, we see nothing in the New Hampshire cases dealing with economic loss indicating that, when determining whether or not loss is economic, the New Hampshire courts would inquire into the risk posed by an accident or defect in a product. Instead, the New Hampshire cases are clear that when a product harms only itself, the loss is economic and may not be recovered in tort. For example, in a recent New Hampshire Supreme Court case, the court stated that "[w]hen a defective product accidentally causes harm to persons or property [*other than the defective product itself*], the resulting harm is treated as personal injury or property damage." *Kelleher v. Lumber,* 891 A.2d 477, 494 (2005) (quoting *Ellis,* 513 A.2d at 954) (alteration in original) (emphasis added). The court went out of its way to add the phrase "other than the defective product itself," which was not present in *Ellis.* The implication of this statement is that, when a defective product accidentally causes harm to itself, that harm is *not* treated as personal injury or property damage but is instead treated as economic loss, which is not recoverable in tort. The New Hampshire Supreme Court has therefore clearly rejected the logic behind Lockheed's argument.

---

[37] In making this argument, Lockheed states that its view is consistent with "that of the overwhelming majority of courts around the country." We disagree. As the United States Supreme Court noted in *East River Steamship Corp. v. Transamerica Delaval, Inc.,* 476 U.S. 858 (1986), the majority of courts have held that a party may not recover in tort when a product's malfunction damages only the product itself, regardless of the manner in which the damage occurred or the risk posed by the defect.

We also think that this approach comports with the policies behind several fundamental tenets of contract and tort law. Lockheed argues that the purpose of the economic loss doctrine is to distinguish between a product that fails to perform as promised and a product whose defect poses an actual risk of injury or damage, and that the dividing line between tort and contract should not hinge on the fortuity of what happened to be damaged. To our knowledge, the New Hampshire courts have not explicitly addressed these arguments. However, the United States Supreme Court has done so in *East River S.S. Corp. v. Transamerica Delaval, Inc.,* 476 U.S. 858 (1986). In *East River,* an admiralty case, the Court discussed the merits of the majority view of the economic loss doctrine – that damage to a product caused by that product is economic loss and not recoverable in tort – as well as the view argued by Lockheed-that the economic loss doctrine should turn on the affirmative risk posed by the defective product. In rejecting the position advocated by Lockheed, the Court stated that such a position, "which essentially turn[s] on the degree of risk, [is] too indeterminate to enable manufacturers easily to structure their business behavior." *Id.* at 870. The Court also stated that

> [t]he distinction that the law has drawn between tort recovery for physical injuries and warranty recovery for economic loss is not arbitrary and does not rest on the "luck" of one plaintiff in having an accident causing physical injury. The distinction rests, rather, on an understanding of the nature of the responsibility a manufacturer must undertake in distributing his products. When a product injures only itself the reasons for imposing tort duty are weak and those for leaving the party to its contractual remedies are strong.

Id. at 871. As the Court noted, "[e]ven when the harm to the product itself occurs through an abrupt, accident-like event, the resulting loss due to repair costs, decreased value, and lost profits is essentially the failure of the purchaser to receive the benefit of its bargain-traditionally the core concern of contract law."[38] *Id.* at 870.

---

[38] Lockheed admits that if there had been a fire in the chamber but the sprinkler system failed to extinguish it, or if the sprinkler system had interfered with the chamber's ability to send or receive signals, then it would likely be barred by the economic loss doctrine because these situations would have involved a failure of the chamber to perform. Lockheed attempts to distinguish these situations from the flooding of the chamber, arguing that the flooding had nothing to do with the chamber's ability to perform. However, we see no difference between the situations. Part of the chamber's ability to perform was the fire suppression system's ability to extend the TSAs into the chamber if there was a fire but not release water until a

Further, Lockheed's position would eviscerate the line between tort and contract and would allow tort, in many ways, to swallow up contract law. As the Supreme Court noted in East River, "[p]roducts liability grew out of a public policy judgment that people need more protection from dangerous products than is afforded by the law of warranty. It is clear, however, that if this development were allowed to progress too far, contract law would drown in a sea of tort." *Id.* at 866. Lockheed's view would lead to just that result. It would allow any party who suffered damage as a result of a product's malfunction to bring a tort claim by asserting that the malfunction occurred in a way that might have harmed another person or property, regardless of whether any other person or property was actually harmed. We think the better approach is to look at what in fact happened, not what could have happened.

In sum, it is clear from the New Hampshire cases, especially *Kelleher,* the New Hampshire Supreme Court's most recent case regarding the economic loss rule, that New Hampshire has adopted the majority view of the economic loss rule which the Supreme Court discussed in *East River.* Therefore, if the flooding caused by the allegedly defective sprinkler systems damaged only the product itself, then the economic loss rule prohibits Lockheed from recovery on its tort claims.

We turn now to address whether the flooding damaged only the product itself. Lockheed makes two arguments regarding this issue. First, it argues that the fire suppression system and the anechoic chamber were different products, and that the defect in the fire suppression therefore damaged another product – the anechoic chamber. However, as Rantec points out, the parties' contract for the anechoic chamber included the fire suppression system as a component part of the chamber, not a separate product. As part of the contract, the parties included a document entitled "Tapered Anechoic Chamber, Compact Range Chamber Technical Specification." Paragraph 1.0 of this document, entitled "Introduction," stated that "[t]his document provides specification information for a tapered anechoic chamber. . . ." Paragraph 2.0, entitled "Tapered Anechoic Chamber and Control

---

certain temperature was reached. Here, there were two failures to perform: (1) the sprinklers descended into the chamber when there was not a fire, and (2) the sprinklers released water into the chamber even though there was no fire. This latter occurrence was, in many ways, a failure of the sprinkler system to perform one of its most basic functions-to not release water into the chamber simply because the TSAs had been deployed. We therefore reject Lockheed's attempts to distinguish the present situation from other situations where it admits that there would be a failure of performance.

Room," stated that "[t]he specification is for a tapered anechoic chamber to be used as a general purpose facility for RCS test and antenna pattern measurements. . . . The contractor will design, fabricate, and test the chamber, including all HVAC, fire detection and suppression" utilities. From these provisions, it is clear that the fire suppression system was a component part of the anechoic chamber according to the technical specifications for the chamber agreed upon by the parties. The anechoic chamber and fire suppression system are therefore properly regarded as a single unit. As the Supreme Court noted in *East River,* "[s]ince all but the very simplest of machines have component parts, [a contrary] holding would require a finding of property damage in virtually every case where a product damages itself." 476 U.S. at 867.

Lockheed's second argument is that there were in fact other items in the chamber when it was flooded: a pedestal and positioning system. However, as Rantec points out, Lockheed never mentioned these items in its complaint and never amended its complaint to include these items. Lockheed attempts to get around this issue by arguing that, under the Federal Rules of Civil Procedure's notice pleading standard, it was not required to itemize its damages in the complaint. Lockheed also argues that the complaint, fairly read, gave notice to Rantec that these other items were in the chamber. We disagree for several reasons. First, while the Federal Rules of Civil Procedure require only notice pleading, there is nothing in the complaint that would put Rantec on notice that Lockheed was claiming anything other than damage to the chamber itself. A review of the complaint reveals no mention of other items in the chamber. Instead, the complaint repeats several times that "plaintiff's anechoic chambers were doused with water and severely damaged." Lockheed also specified that the "anechoic foam and sub-flooring in the chamber" was damaged. Nothing in the complaint provides the slightest indication that there were other items in the chamber or that Lockheed suffered damage to anything other than the chamber itself. We see no reason to allow Lockheed to claim damage to other items when it never bothered to mention or even hint toward damage to anything beyond the anechoic chamber itself in the complaint. . . . Because Lockheed failed to give any indication in its complaint that it was alleging damage to anything other than the anechoic chamber, we will not consider alleged damage to the pedestal and positioning system in this appeal.

C. Lockheed's Implied Warranties Claims

Lockheed also brought claims for breach of implied warranties under New Hampshire's Uniform Commercial Code ("UCC").[39] The district court assumed, *arguendo,* that the contract was governed by the UCC. The court then found that the UCC's statute of limitations – codified as N.H. Rev. Stat. § 382-A:2-725 ("Section 2-725") – applied to Lockheed's claims. Section 2-725 provides for a four-year statute of limitations commencing at the time the cause of action accrues. . . . The district court found that Lockheed accepted the chamber in 1993 and did not file its complaint until 1999. The court therefore found that Lockheed's claims were barred by the statute of limitations. The court, moreover, found no reason for equitable tolling.

On appeal, Lockheed makes two arguments. First, it argues that the statute of limitations in Section 2-725 does not apply to its case. Alternatively, it argues that equitable tolling applies. . . . This is a case of a party who received a product that malfunctioned several years after purchase. Such cases occur all the time, and we see no reason to apply the rarely used doctrine of equitable tolling to Lockheed's case. We therefore find that Lockheed's implied warranties' claims are barred by the four-year statute of limitations period in Section 2-725.

III. *Conclusion*

For the foregoing reasons, we affirm the district court's grant of summary judgment in favor of Rantec as to Lockheed's claims. . . .

––––––––––––––––

In *Jimenez v. The Superior Court of San Diego County*, 58 P.3d 450 (Cal. 2002) the defendants manufactured windows which were installed by others in mass-produced homes. The defendants did not own or control the homes under construction. The windows were defective with the result that physical damage to other parts of the homes occurred. The court in a long opinion with a strong dissent held: (i) the manufacturer was strictly liable in tort to the purchaser of the homes for harm resulting from the defects; and (ii) strict liability extended to physical damage to other parts of the houses in which the windows were installed. In rejecting an argument that recovery was barred by the economic loss rule, the court held that the "economic loss rule allows a plaintiff to recover in strict products

––––––––––––––––––––––––––––

[39] Lockheed could not bring any express warranty claims because the warranty in the contract was for one year and had long expired.

liability in tort when a product defect causes damage to 'other property' that is property other than the product itself," *id.* at 483, and that the damaged homes were property other than the defective windows.

In concurring, Judge Kennard suggested that the economic loss doctrine would bar recovery in tort for damage to property in which a defective product was installed only if the installed component had lost its separate identity (the component became part of the whole). According to Judge Kennard, the windows were "not so integrated into houses as to lose their separate identity." *Id.* at 487. Thus, damage to other parts of the house was not damage to the product itself.

In dissent, Judge Brown argued that the economic loss doctrine should apply under what he called a "product sold" test:

> Here plaintiff bought their homes as single integrated products complete with windows and other constituent parts one would expect in a home. They allege the windows were defective and caused damage to the other parts of their homes, but plaintiffs suffered no personal injury from these defects, nor was any property, other than the homes themselves, damaged. In other words, the product they bought – their homes – did not meet the quality standard they expected at the time of purchase. In those circumstances, the economic loss rule limits their recovery to the bargain. If for some reason, such as a limited warranty, they find their contractual remedies inadequate, that fact is a function of their bargain with the other; it is not a loss the general public should have to subsidize.

Id. at 496. Which is the better view and why?

CISG. Article 5 provides that the Convention "does not apply to the liability of the seller for death or personal injury caused by the goods to any person." Thus, the classic personal injury products liability case – whether brought against the seller or anyone else – would be governed by other law. Property damage, including economic loss to the goods sold, are recoverable under Article 74, which states that damages for "breach of contract by one party consist of a sum equal to the loss, including loss of profit, suffered by the other party as a consequence of the breach." But even if there is a breach of contract through the tender of non-conforming goods under Article 35, the CISG appears to be limited to direct contractual relations between the seller and the buyer. *See* CISG Art. 1(1), which states that the CISG "applies to contract of sale of goods between parties whose places of business are in different states" and Article 35(1) which states that the seller must deliver goods that are of the quality and description "required by the contract." The CISG is silent on whether parties other than the buyer's immediate seller may be liable for damages resulting from their manufacture or sale of defective products.

UNIDROIT Principles. The Principles have no specific provisions regarding liability for personal injury. The aggrieved party is entitled to full compensation for harm suffered as a result of breach of contract, including physical suffering. UNIDROIT Art. 7.4.2. The Principles apply to the parties to the contract and to intended beneficiaries of the contract, UNIDROIT Art. 5.2.1 through 5.2.6, but do not speak to the issues of liability to other persons who may not fall into that category.

C. Misrepresentation

As noted at the beginning of this section, the relationship between the tort of misrepresentation and the law of express warranty is an uncertain one. The question is basically whether the buyer may recover in tort against a seller for misrepresentation when the buyer may not be able to recover against the seller for breach of an express warranty, typically because the warranty action is barred by the statute of limitations, UCC § 2-725, or the requirement of timely notice of breach of warranty in the case of accepted goods, UCC § 2-607. The buyer may also be seeking tort recovery because the seller has adequately disclaimed liability for consequential damages in the sales contract. UCC § 2-719.

A cause of action for misrepresentation generally requires a material misrepresentation of fact on which the plaintiff justifiably and detrimentally relies. The evidence needed to prove such reliance is often the same evidence that would be necessary to show that a statement was part of the basis of the parties' bargain, and thus qualifies as an express warranty. Accordingly, there would appear to be substantial overlap between a claim for misrepresentation and a claim for breach of an express warranty.

On the other hand, while an action for breach of an express warranty requires no showing of evil intent, an action for misrepresentation typically requires negligence, recklessness, or actual fraud by the seller who made the misrepresentation. Moreover, a successful plaintiff on a misrepresentation cause of action is generally entitled to reliance damages, as opposed to compensation based on lost expectancy.

Given these similarities and differences, one question courts must often confront is whether the cause of action for misrepresentation is barred if the buyer seeks to recover only for the economic losses it has suffered due to the misrepresentation.[40] In other words, if the buyer is not seeking damages for personal injury or for losses to other property, but is instead seeking to recover only for the loss in the value of the sold item and consequential harm (including reliance costs and lost profits), the claim is arguably one which should be subject to the terms of their negotiated relationship – *i.e.,* to their contract – and not left to the law of tort. On the other hand, at a certain level, a seller should not be able to engage in knowing fraudulent misrepresentations and then be able to disclaim its liability for the resulting harm. Consider the discussion of these issues in the following case.

CERABIO LLC v. WRIGHT MEDICAL TECHNOLOGY, INC.
410 F.3d 981 (7th Cir. 2005)

Rovner, Circuit Judge

In this contract dispute, CERAbio, LLC and its sole member, Phillips Plastics Corporation (collectively "CERAbio"), claims that it delivered all of the assets of the corporation, including its technological know-how, to Wright Medical Technology, Inc. (Wright), but that Wright failed to pay the remaining half of the agreed-upon sales price. Wright countered that not only was the technological knowledge provided by CERAbio worthless and that it therefore had not performed its end of the deal, but that CERAbio had also committed fraud and had been negligent both in the formation and performance of the contract. Upon CERAbio's motion, the district court granted summary judgment on Wright's tort counter claims. At trial, the jury ruled in favor of CERAbio on the contract claims. On appeal, Wright challenges the district court's ruling on summary judgment . . . .

I.

Wright designs, manufactures, and sells medical devices and products, including bone replacement products known as biologics, frequently used during implantation surgery to replace lost bone and provide a framework for new bone growth. In the late 1990's, CERAbio developed a bone replacement product made from tricalcium phosphate ("TCP"). The Food and Drug Administration approved

---

[40] Steven C. Tourek, *et al., Bucking the "Trend": The Uniform Commercial Code, The Economic Loss Doctrine, and Common Law Causes of Action for Fraud and Misrepresentation,* 84 IOWA L. REV. 875 (1999).

the new product, Apatight, for use in humans as a bone void filler. CERAbio obtained patents for the Apatight production process and material.

In early 2001, Wright representatives learned about Apatight at a trade conference. CERAbio was strictly a research and development company which did not manufacture or sell Apatight or other products commercially. Wright markets and sells biologics worldwide and was looking to expand its product offerings in the bone replacement market, so a match seemed ideal. CERAbio negotiated with Wright to provide Apatight to Wright which Wright would then market and sell. Eventually, the negotiations evolved and Wright decided to purchase substantially all of CERAbio's assets, including all patents and know-how.

Prior to entering into the Agreement, CERAbio informed Wright that it had an established and repeatable process for producing Apatight and that all of the raw materials necessary were commercially available. Under the terms of the August 5, 2002 Agreement between the parties ("Agreement"), Wright agreed to pay $3 million for the CERAbio assets with $1.5 million payable upon closing and a second installment of $1.5 million due no later than three days after Wright verified that it was able to produce Apatight ("Verification"). The contract defined the parameters of Verification and required that CERAbio transfer assets to Wright, that it train Wright's employees, and that Wright produce three test lots of Apatight using the specific work instructions supplied by CERAbio. Wright had sixty days to attempt to produce the three test lots of Apatight in its Memphis facility using commercially reasonable efforts. If it failed to do so, under the Agreement, CERAbio would have the opportunity to access Wright's manufacturing equipment and cooperate with Wright to produce the three Apatight test lots again, using commercially reasonable efforts.

After the closing, Wright attempted to buy TCP powder, one of the key raw materials needed to manufacture Apatight, but found that it was no longer available. Plasma Biotal, the manufacturer of the necessary TCP powder, had started making a new TCP powder with a different particle size – one that would not work properly utilizing the Apatight manufacturing instructions. Plasma Biotal still had a limited supply of the original powder, but it had become contaminated. Wright and CERAbio dispute when CERAbio became aware that the powder was unavailable and the role that the unavailability of the powder played in the ability to seal the deal. From this point forward, the statements of facts in the two briefs begin to read like two unrelated novels. When the facts are digested, however, it appears that the parties do not wholly dispute the course of events, but instead dispute where the blame lies.

According to the appellant Wright, CERAbio knew prior to closing on the Agreement that the TCP powder was unavailable, but nevertheless represented to Wright that all of the materials necessary to produce Apatight were generally commercially available. To support this claim, Wright points to the deposition of CERAbio's senior product development engineer, Dr. Ying Ko, who testified that CERAbio knew prior to closing that the TCP powder was no longer available. CERAbio does not necessarily disagree that it knew of the availability problem, it focuses instead on the fact that it was possible to work around the problem and to produce Apatight without the original TCP powder. And so while it may have known that one form of the powder was unavailable, CERAbio says, it thought that other powders were available and acceptable alternatives. It thus counters Dr. Ko's testimony by pointing to evidence that Plasma Biotal had assured Dr. Ko that it could produce an "original style" powder. It further implies also that even if CERAbio did know that the powder was unavailable, the Agreement between the two parties put the onus on Wright to engage in due diligence in order to verify the availability of all necessary materials. Finally, it claims that Wright itself was aware of the powder unavailability problem prior to the closing. CERAbio's spin, in a nutshell, is that the unavailability of the TCP powder was not CERAbio's fault and that with some revisions to the work instructions Apatight could be produced using the new powder, but that Wright never gave CERAbio the chance. It also argues that Wright eventually found a manufacturer who could make a "look-alike" powder but decided instead to shut CERAbio out of the process, produce the virtually identical ceramic bone replacement, Cellplex, on its own, and claim it as its own new creation to avoid paying the remainder of the $1.5 million fee and royalties.[41]

Wright, of course, has a different story to tell. Shortly after closing, CERAbio informed Wright that the instructions had to be changed due to the unavailability of the TCP powder – a problem that CERAbio claimed not to have known about prior to closing on the Agreement. Wright claims that, based on these representations, it consented to oral modifications of the Agreement – permitting CERAbio to make changes to the work instructions and to attempt twelve "pre-verification" production runs over the course of several months. Wright points to evidence that CERAbio did, in fact, know about the availability problem prior to

---

[41] Under the Agreement Wright was to pay 7.5% royalties on products primarily derived from CERAbio technology and 3% on products incorporating the transferred technology in part.

closing and argues that had it known that CERAbio had hidden its knowledge of the unavailability, it never would have agreed to the modification.

In the meantime, in light of the powder unavailability, efforts to resolve the problem proceeded on two fronts. Plasma Biotal tried to replicate the old powder it had been producing originally, and CERAbio employees were working at Wright from late August 2002, to early November 2002, to see if they could alter the work instructions to come up with a process for manufacturing Apatight using the new powder. These attempts were called "pre-verification" efforts since the formal Verification process described in the Agreement could not begin without the old powder or an appropriate substitute. Both parties agree that no successful test lots were produced during this time. CERAbio claims that Verification failed because Wright threw CERAbio's scientists out just as they were on the cusp of success. It did so, says CERAbio, because Wright had independently learned that Plasma Biotal had developed a new "look-a-like" powder that would work in the process and it wanted to proceed to develop the TCP bone replacement product on its own to avoid paying royalties. CERAbio claims that had it known about the existence of the new powder, it could have completed the Verification process in two or three weeks.

Wright, on the other hand, claims that after two or three months of unsuccessful tries (the exact amount of time is the subject of some debate, but not relevant for these purposes), it became clear to Wright that the effort was fruitless. On November 8, 2002, Wright notified CERAbio that it considered CERAbio to be in breach of the Agreement, and proceeded with its own efforts to produce a bone replacement product.

Both parties agree that Wright eventually succeeded in creating a marketable bone replacement product called Cellplex. Wright, of course, argues that it created Cellplex using a completely different process than the one invented by CERAbio. CERAbio claims that the process for manufacturing Cellplex differs only slightly from the process CERAbio developed to manufacture Apatight and then sold to Wright, and that the two end products are virtually identical.

CERAbio sued Wright for the second $1.5 million installment it believes Wright owes under the Agreement. Wright countered with its own contract claim alleging that CERAbio failed to provide its end of the bargain under the terms of the Agreement and therefore was not entitled to the final payment. In addition, Wright claimed that CERAbio's misrepresentations caused Wright to incur unplanned expenses in excess of $500,000, direct damages of over $880,000, and lost profits as of the time of trial of over $6.7 million.

Wright also counter-sued claiming fraudulent inducement of the contract, fraud in the performance of the contract, pre-contract negligent representation, and negligent misrepresentation in the performance of the contract. The district court judge granted summary judgment for CERAbio on all of Wright's tort claims. . . .

On appeal, Wright challenges the district court's [summary judgment on the tort claims]. . . .

II.

. . . . CERAbio moved the district court for summary judgment on all of the defendant's counter claims other than its claim for breach of contract, namely Wright's counterclaims for pre-contract fraudulent inducement and negligent misrepresentation, and post-contract fraudulent and negligent misrepresentation in the performance of the contract. [The court determined that Wisconsin law applied to this issue. –ed.]

. . . . The district court concluded that each of Wright's four tort-based counterclaims was barred by the economic loss doctrine. The economic loss doctrine seeks to preserve the distinction between contract and tort law and to prevent parties from eschewing agreed-upon contract remedies and seeking broader remedies under tort theory than the contract would have permitted. *Ins. Co. of N. Am. v. Cease Elec. Inc.,* 688 N.W.2d 462, 467 (Wis. 2004). "Economic loss" for purposes of the doctrine is "the loss in a product's value which occurs because the product is inferior in quality and does not work for the purposes for which it was manufactured and sold." *Id.* The economic loss doctrine "forbids commercial contracting parties (as distinct from consumers, and other individuals not engaged in business) to escalate their contract dispute into a charge of tortious misrepresentation if they could easily have protected themselves from the misrepresentation of which they now complain." *All-Tech Telecom, Inc. v. Amway Corp.,* 174 F.3d 862, 866 (7th Cir. 1999) (applying Wisconsin law). In short, parties cannot use tort principles to circumvent the terms of an agreement. . . . doctrine's purpose is to "maintain the fundamental distinction between tort law and contract law; protect commercial parties' freedom to allocate economic risk by contract; and encourage the party best situated to assess the risk of economic loss, the commercial purchaser, to assume, allocate, or insure against that risk." *Digicorp, Inc. v. Ameritech Corp.,* 662 N.W.2d 652, 659 (Wis. 2003).

Recently (since the parties briefed the issue on appeal), the Wisconsin Supreme Court has held that the economic loss doctrine does not apply to claims for the negligent provision of services. *Cease Elec.,* 688 N.W.2d at 472. Wright claims that the contract between itself and CERAbio centered on the provision of services, that is, the installation of equipment, training, and achievement of Verification. CERAbio, on the other hand, maintains that the Asset Purchase Agreement is a contract for the sale of all assets of a business, not a service contract like the one in *Cease Electric*. We agree with CERAbio that the service contract exception should not apply. Our review of the Asset Purchase Agreement confirms that it was indeed a contract for the sale of all of the assets of CERAbio. The fact that some of the assets included technological knowledge and skills that had to be transferred from CERAbio's employees to Wright's employees does not alter the fundamental nature of the contract as one for the sale of goods. Moreover, the policy considerations that prompted the Wisconsin Supreme Court to exempt service contracts from the economic loss doctrine are simply not at play here. Most service contracts, the Wisconsin Supreme Court reasoned (like those to mow the lawn or unclog a drain), are oral and informal and parties rarely hire attorneys to allocate risks and limit remedies. *Cease Elec.*, 688 N.W.2d at 470–71. In many service contracts, furthermore, the information disparities between the parties make it unlikely that each party can negotiate the terms with the same level of bargaining power. *Id.* at 471. None of these policy considerations apply in this case. Wright and CERAbio, both well-represented, sophisticated business parties, drafted complex, detailed agreements which could and indeed did allocate risks and assign remedies. We conclude, therefore, that the economic loss doctrine applies.

The question then becomes whether there are any exceptions to the economic loss doctrine that might keep Wright's tort claims alive. The district court correctly discerned that Wisconsin recognizes a fraud in the inducement exception to the economic loss doctrine. The court below, however, incorrectly stated that the Wisconsin Supreme Court had expressly adopted a narrow exception akin to the one announced in a Michigan case – *Huron Tool and Eng'g Co. v. Precision Consulting Servs., Inc.,* 532 N.W.2d 541 (Mich. Ct. App. 1995). That very narrow exception limits fraud in the inducement claims to situations where the claimed fraud is extraneous to, rather than interwoven with the contract, that is, where the fraud concerns those matters that were not expressly or impliedly addressed in the contract. *Digicorp,* 662 N.W.2d at 662. *Digicorp,* however, did not so hold. Although four justices of the five-member court recognized some form of a fraud in the inducement exception to the economic loss doctrine, only two justices announced their recognition of a narrow *Huron-Tool*-like exception. *Id.* at 662. Two justices dissented announcing that they would have upheld the previous broad exception set forth in *Douglas-Hanson Co. v. BF Goodrich Co.,* 598 N.W.2d 262

(Wis. Ct. App. 1999), *aff'd*, 607 N.W.2d 621 (Wis. 2000), allowing a plaintiff to make a claim for intentional misrepresentation when the misrepresentation fraudulently induces a plaintiff to enter into a contract. *Digicorp*, 662 N.W.2d at 670. A third justice concluded in a dissent that any fraud in the inducement exception was unnecessary. *Id.* at 667. In short, a majority (three) of the justices overruled the broad exception announced in *Douglas-Hanson*, but a separate, but different three-member majority rejected the narrow *Huron Tool* exception. *See Tietsworth v. Harley Davidson, Inc.*, 677 N.W.2d 233, 243–44 (Wis. 2004). The most we can discern from *Digicorp*, therefore, is that the fraud in the inducement exception to the economic loss doctrine is more narrow than that announced in *Douglas-Hanson* and that it does not apply when the fraud pertains to the character and quality of the goods that are the subject matter of the contract. *Id.* at 244.[42]

This is enough information, however, for us to conclude that the fraud in the inducement exception should not apply to the specific facts of this case. Recall that the purpose of the fraud in the inducement exception is to address the "special situation where parties to a contract appear to negotiate freely – which normally would constitute grounds for invoking the economic loss doctrine – but where in fact the ability of one party to negotiate fair terms and make an informed decision is undermined by the other party's fraudulent behavior." *Digicorp*, 662 N.W.2d at 662 (quoting *Huron Tool*, 532 N.W.2d at 545). It does not address the situation where "the only misrepresentation by the dishonest party concerns the quality or character of the goods sold, [as] the other party is still free to negotiate warranty and other terms to account for possible defects in the goods." *Id.* Tort remedies are inappropriate where commercial contracting parties could have easily protected themselves from the misrepresentation of which they now complain. *All-Tech*

---

[42] Like Wisconsin, Delaware and Tennessee also limit the fraud in the inducement exception to matters not expressly addressed in the contract. *See Trinity Indus., Inc. v. McKinnon Bridge Co., Inc.*, 77 S.W.3d 159, 172 (Tenn. Ct. App. 2001) ("Courts should be particularly skeptical of business plaintiffs who-having negotiated an elaborate contract or having signed a form when they wish they had not-claim to have a right in tort whether the tort theory is negligent misrepresentation, strict tort, or negligence."); *Christiana Marine Serv. Corp. v. Texaco Fuel and Marine Mktg., Inc.*, 2002 WL 1335360, *5 (Del. Super. Ct. 2002) ("The economic loss doctrine . . . forbids plaintiffs from recovering in tort for losses suffered that are solely economic in nature . . . . While initially a doctrine related to product liability actions, the courts have expanded the doctrine's application beyond its original scope to any kind of dispute arising from a commercial transaction where the alleged damages do no harm to a person or to property other than the bargained for item."). . . .

Telecom, 174 F.3d at 866. In this case, the parties to the contract were two sophisticated and well-represented business entities. The crux of their agreement centered around the sale and purchase of the assets of CERAbio's business – primarily a process for producing Apatight. Wright's primary concern should have been, and indeed was, whether it was purchasing a process that could be replicated by Wright. Of course, if it could not, Wright would be paying $3 million dollars for a product with no value to it. Wright was free to, and in fact did, negotiate warranty and other terms to account for the possibility that the process could not be replicated. Wright's remedies, therefore must be limited to contract claims.

As we have cautioned before, we do not mean to imply that the tort of misrepresentation is abolished in all cases in which the plaintiff and defendant are commercial entities with a pre-existing contractual relationship. *Id.* at 866. The fraud in the inducement exception to the economic loss doctrine, however, does not apply in this particular case where two sophisticated commercial entities created contractual remedies to address the concern that the product Wright was purchasing from CERAbio might not result in the desired outcome either because the process was not repeatable or because the starting materials were not available. The alleged fraud in this case pertains to the character and quality of the product that is the subject matter of the contract. *See Tietsworth,* 677 N.W.2d at 244. "Misrepresentations such as these, that ultimately concern the quality of the product sold, are properly remedied through claims for breach of warranty." *Cooper Power Sys., Inc. v. Union Carbide Chems. & Plastics Co., Inc.,* 123 F.3d 675, 682 (7th Cir. 1997).

Whether or not the process was repeatable was addressed contractually by the complex process set forth in the contract for Verification. The agreement between the parties was contingent upon Wright producing three test lots meeting the specifications outlined in the Agreement. Of course, if the starting materials were not available, Verification could not be achieved. The Agreement addressed the availability of starting materials in another manner as well. The disclaimer of warranty provision contained in the Non-Disclosure Agreement specified that CERAbio provided all information to Wright on an "as is" basis and that CERAbio:

> makes no warranty, either express or implied, concerning the Information, including, without limitation, its accuracy, completeness, or to the non-infringement of intellectual property rights or other rights of third persons or Discloser. Recipient assumes all risk in, and Discloser will not be liable for any damages arising out of, use of information including, without limitation, business decisions made or inferences drawn by

Recipient in reliance on the Information or the fact of the disclosure of the Information.

. . . This type of disclaimer is referred to as a non-reliance clause. Furthermore, the integration clause in the asset purchase agreement incorporates this non-disclosure agreement and likewise allocates to Wright the risk that the information provided by CERAbio might be incomplete or incorrect. This clause states:

> This Agreement, including schedules and exhibits referred to herein, and the NDA [Non-Disclosure Agreement] embody the entire agreement and understanding of the parties hereto . . . . There are no restrictions, promises, representations, warranties, covenants or undertakings of Seller contained in any material made available to Buyer pursuant to the terms of the NDA, or the correspondence between Seller and Buyer.

. . . . These provisions allocated to Wright the risk that the information provided by CERAbio might be incomplete or incorrect. Wright assured CERAbio in writing that it would not rely on information provided by CERAbio. Not only does this non-reliance clause verify that the alleged fraud was interwoven with the parties' contractual agreement, and thus barred by the economic loss doctrine, it also confirms the district court's finding that Wright could not have reasonably relied on CERAbio's oral representation as to the viability of the process or the availability of starting materials.

Wright challenges the proposition that commercial parties can never demonstrate reasonable reliance on misrepresentation in the face of a non-reliance clause. For this portion of the dispute, we must consider the force and effect of a clause in the contract – the non-reliance clause – which the parties agreed to construe in accordance with Delaware law. Although the Delaware Supreme Court has offered no definitive conclusion, recent opinions of the Delaware chancery courts have repeatedly concluded that "sophisticated parties to negotiated commercial contracts may not reasonably rely on information that they contractually agreed did not form a part of the basis for their decision to contract." *H-M Wexford LLC v. Encorp, Inc.,* 832 A.2d 129, 142 (Del. Ch. 2003). . . .

Wright lashes at this windmill of Delaware authority by arguing that none of the cases established a *per se* rule that commercial parties can never demonstrate reasonable reliance on misrepresentations in the face of a purported non-reliance clause. Wright claims instead that those courts made fact-specific determinations about whether plaintiffs could have reasonably relied upon the defendants' misrepresentations. This may, in fact, be the case, but it does not get Wright anywhere. The relevant facts in *Great Lakes* have a familiar ring. The case involved "two highly sophisticated parties, assisted by industry consultants and experienced legal counsel, [who] entered into carefully negotiated disclaimer language after months of extensive due diligence . . . [and who] explicitly allocated their risks and obligations in the Purchase Agreement." *Id.* at 555. Noting the carefully negotiated and crafted nature of the agreements, the *Great Lakes* court concluded that "to allow [the buyer] to assert, under the rubric of, claims that are explicitly precluded by contract, would defeat the reasonable commercial expectations of the contracting parties and eviscerate the utility of written contractual agreements." *Id.* at 556. The same is true here.

This philosophy is not unique to the Delaware courts. This court and others have held that a written anti-reliance clause in a stock purchase agreement precludes any claim of deceit by prior representations. *Rissman v. Rissman,* 213 F.3d 381, 383 (7th Cir. 2000). In *Rissman* we pointed out that a non-reliance clause is part of the negotiated bargain. *Id.* at 384. CERAbio could have assumed the risk of claims based on oral statements it made, but it likely would have increased the purchase price accordingly. *Rissman,* 213 F.3d at 388. . . . Even were we to take a less absolute, case-by-case assessment of the validity of the non-reliance clause (as urged by the concurrence in *Rissman*), our conclusion would not differ. In this case the parties were sophisticated commercial entities assisted by counsel and the facts surrounding the materiality and intentionality of the misrepresentation are highly contested. *See Rissman,* 213 F.3d at 388 (Rovner, J., concurring) (considering factors that might be relevant in determining whether an investor's reliance on prior statements was reasonable despite the existence of a non-reliance clause). We are not unsympathetic to the notion that Wright was purchasing a secret process and therefore in all likelihood it could not investigate independently whether the starting materials were commercially available, but "[c]ontractual language serves its function only if enforced consistently," *id.* at 385, and parties to contracts are best served by rulings enforcing the express terms of agreements into which they enter.

Wright and CERAbio bargained for the allocation of risks contained in the Agreement and Wright accepted the risk that it might receive faulty oral information from CERAbio. The district court correctly concluded, therefore, that Wright's counterclaim for fraudulent inducement could not stand.

Wright's other counterclaims allege negligent misrepresentation in the formation of the contract, negligent misrepresentation in the performance of the contract, and fraud in the performance. Any economic loss caused by these acts, however, is best addressed through the contractual remedies to which the parties agreed.

For example, Wright claims that CERAbio negligently misrepresented information that induced Wright to enter into the Agreement. Although the Wisconsin Supreme Court has not yet specifically addressed the economic loss doctrine in this context, the appellate courts have laid the ground work. . . . It is no stretch to assume that the Wisconsin Supreme Court would follow suit. In describing the policy reasons surrounding the economic loss doctrine, that court has followed a path that protects commercial parties' freedom to allocate economic risk and encourages the party best situated to assess the risk of economic loss, and to assume, allocate, or insure against that risk. . . . For the same reasons, we conclude that the district court was correct in determining that the economic loss doctrine would preclude Wright's claims that CERAbio negligently or fraudulently misrepresented information during the performance of the contract to convince the defendant that verification had occurred. These are simple contract claims disguised in tort claim clothing. If CERAbio breached its duties to perform its tasks during Verification, Wright's remedy lies in contract.

Wright argues that Tennessee law applies to its post-contract fraud claims. But under Tennessee law, like Wisconsin law, we see no support for allowing Wright to wrap its contract claims in tort language. In *Ritter v. Custom Chemicides, Inc.,* 912 S.W.2d 128, 133 (Tenn. 1996), the Tennessee Supreme Court made clear that it was joining the economic loss doctrine bandwagon noting that negligence theory was an inappropriate method to resolve injuries causing economic loss (in the *Ritter* case, from product liability). *Id.* "When a product does not perform as expected," the *Ritter* court went on to explain, "the buyer's remedy should be governed by the rules of contract, which traditionally protect expectation interests." *Id.* This conclusion followed logically from a much earlier Tennessee Supreme Court decision ruling that a cause of action for breach of contract – even negligent or fraudulent – remains in contract rather than tort. *Mid-South Milling Co. v. Loret Farms, Inc.,* 521 S.W.2d 586, 588 (Tenn. 1975). The Tennessee appellate court has applied *Ritter* and *Mid-South Milling* to a contract for the sale of goods, holding that "[i]n a contract for the sale of goods where the only damages alleged come under the heading of economic losses, the rights and obligations of the buyer and seller are governed exclusively by contract." *Trinity Indus., Inc. v. McKinnon Bridge Co., Inc.,* 77 S.W.3d 159, 171 (Tenn. Ct. App.2001). The *Trinity Indus.* court noted the breadth of the economic loss doctrine in Tennessee stating, "[c]ourts should be particularly skeptical of business plaintiffs who-having negotiated an elaborate contract . . . claim to have a right in tort whether the tort theory is negligent misrepresentation, strict tort, or negligence." *Id.* at 172.

For these reasons we uphold the district court's ruling granting summary judgment to CERAbio on Wright's counter claims sounding in tort. . . .

Now read UCC section 2-721 and the following provisions of the Restatement (Second) of Torts.

Section 525

One who fraudulently makes a misrepresentation of fact, opinion, intention or law for the purpose of inducing another to act or to refrain from action in reliance upon it, is subject to liability to the other in deceit for pecuniary loss caused to him by his justifiable reliance upon the misrepresentation.

Section 552

(1) One who, in the course of his business, profession or employment, or in any other transaction in which he has a pecuniary interest, supplies false information for the guidance of others in their business transactions, is subject to liability for pecuniary loss caused to them by their justifiable reliance upon the information, if he fails to exercise reasonable care or competence in obtaining or communicating the information.

(2) Except as stated in Subsection (3), the liability stated in Subsection (1) is limited to loss suffered

(a) by the person or one of a limited group of persons for whose benefit and guidance he intends to supply the information or knows that the recipient intends to supply it; and

(b) through reliance upon it in a transaction that he intends the information to influence or knows that the recipient so intends or in a substantially similar transaction.

(3) The liability of one who is under a public duty to give the information extends to loss suffered by any of the class of persons for whose benefit the duty is created, in any of the transactions in which it is intended to protect them.

How should the idea of misrepresentation in tort be reconciled with the idea of breach of express warranty in contract?

Problem 8-6

Return to Problem 8-4. Assume that Standard intentionally misled Bridget regarding the mileage that the motor home would obtain. Should Bridget have any tort remedy for that misrepresentation?

CHAPTER NINE

SELLER'S REMEDIES FOR BUYER'S BREACH

SECTION 1. OVERVIEW

This Chapter addresses the various ways in which a buyer may breach a contract for the sale of goods and the remedies available to the seller for the buyer's breach.

Determining breach. In an Article 2 contract, the basic obligation of the buyer is to accept and pay for goods that conform to the contract requirements. UCC § 2-301. Much of what we studied in Chapters Two through Six regarding the terms of the contract is relevant in determining whether a breach has occurred and, if so, by whom. For example, if the seller tendered the goods, a review of the contract terms is necessary to determine whether the goods are in fact conforming. If the goods do conform to the contract requirements, the buyer will have an obligation to accept and pay for them and the buyer will be in breach by refusing to accept or failing to pay. If the goods tendered are nonconforming, it will be the seller who is in breach.

Similarly, if the seller refused to tender the goods, it will be necessary to determine whether that refusal was justified, perhaps because the seller reasonably demanded assurances of future performance and the buyer did not respond. If the seller's refusal to tender performance was not justified, the seller will be in breach. If it was justified, the buyer will have breached and the seller will be entitled to seek redress. In short, just as we saw in the discussion of buyer's remedies, it is critical to evaluate the parties' behavior in sequence and in reference to the terms of the contract.

Entitlement to remedies. Even if the buyer has breached the contract, that breach may in some rare circumstances be excused (Chapter Four), with the effect that the seller will not be entitled to pursue remedies for breach. Even if the buyer's breach is not excused, the contract may restrict the seller's remedies for breach pursuant to a liquidated damages clause or some other limitation (Chapter Three). For purposes of this Chapter, we will assume that the parties have an enforceable Article 2 contract, that the buyer has breached one or more contract obligations, that breach is not excused, and that the seller's remedies have not been limited.

Typical breaches and remedies. The remedies available to an aggrieved seller are catalogued, albeit incompletely, in section 2-703. Read that provision. Did you notice what is conspicuously missing? If you did not, read it again. There is no conjunction connecting the various subsections; there is neither an "and" nor an "or." Thus, the section lists the various remedies but does not indicate which may be used together and which are mutually exclusive alternatives. *See* UCC § 2-703 cmt. 1.

The answer to that problem lies in part in section 1-305, which as we learned in Chapter Seven states that UCC remedies should put the non-breaching party in a position as if the contract had been fully performed. In short, the UCC adopts the traditional, common-law principle that the aggrieved party is entitled to expectation damages. Of course, that principle by itself does not say much about when each of the listed remedies is available and when it is not. We need something more.

We also learned in Chapter Seven that the remedies available to the buyer for the seller's breach depend on two principal things: (i) the nature of the breach; and (ii) who has the goods. Those the two factors are also critical in determining the remedies available to the seller following the buyer's breach.

Let us start by considering what happens if the buyer has accepted the goods, that is, the buyer has the goods and breached the contract by failing to pay the price when due. This is probably the most common way buyers breach contracts for the sale of goods. In such a case, the buyer is liable for the price, plus incidental damages. The result of that remedy is the buyer ends up with the goods and the seller ends up with the contract price. The parties' expectations are therefore realized, assuming the buyer in fact pays the judgment. In some limited cases the seller may be entitled instead to reclaim the goods from the buyer. This remedy restores the parties to their pre-contract position, and is thus a restitutionary remedy, not an expectancy measure of recovery. Both of these remedies are discussed in Section 2 of this Chapter.

The buyer may also breach by: (i) repudiating its obligation to pay for or accept the goods, (ii) failing to make a payment when due (even if it does not repudiate its obligations), (iii) wrongfully but effectively rejecting the goods, (iv) wrongfully refusing to allow the seller to cure when the seller has a right to cure, or (v) wrongfully attempting to revoke acceptance of the goods. If the seller still has the goods or they are in transit, the seller may be allowed to withhold or stop delivery of the goods and to recover damages for the buyer's breach of contract. If the goods have been delivered to the buyer, the buyer's wrongful refusal to keep them may mean that the goods end up back in the seller's possession. In either case, when the seller has the goods, the seller's damages will be measured in one of three alternative ways: (i) the difference between the contract price and the resale price of the goods; (ii) the difference between the contract price and the market price of the goods; or (iii) the lost profit on the breached transaction. In addition to recovery based upon one of these measurements, the seller is also entitled to incidental, but not consequential, damages. All of these measures are designed to give the seller the benefit of the bargain. The seller may also be entitled to cancel the contract. In some extremely limited circumstances, the seller may be entitled to the price of the goods even though the buyer has not accepted or kept the goods. These remedies will be discussed in Section 3 of this Chapter.

After discussing the seller's remedies for the buyer's breach, this Chapter focuses on two related matters. Section 4 discusses the effect of the buyer's breach on the risk of loss and Section 5 discusses the effect of the statute of limitations on the seller's remedies.

SECTION 2.   SELLER'S REMEDIES WHEN THE BUYER HAS THE GOODS

A buyer who has accepted the goods becomes obligated to pay the purchase price. *See* UCC § 2-301. Accordingly, Article 2 has a very clear remedy for a seller when the buyer has accepted the goods but has breached by refusing to pay: the seller is entitled to recover the contract price of the goods plus incidental damages. Read UCC § 2-709. This measure of damages protects the seller's expectancy. Of course, as we have already seen, the buyer may still be entitled to an offset to the extent that the accepted goods are nonconforming, and the seller has therefore breached an express or implied warranty. UCC §§ 2-714, 2-717.

Example

Bacchanalian Catering, Inc. contracted to purchase from Specialty Displays a large, custom-manufactured sign depicting the company's logo: the Roman god Bacchus. Under the terms of the contract, the purchase price was $6,400, the seller was to deliver by July 1, and the buyer was to pay within 30 days after delivery. Specialty Displays delivered the sign on June 30. Bacchanalian Catering accepted the sign before noticing that the logo was not colored precisely as the contract required. When Specialty Displays refused to cure the defects, Bacchanalian Catering spent $1,300 changing the company's logo on brochures and stationery to match the logo on the sign. Despite the nonconformity of the sign's color, Bacchanalian

Catering is liable for the $6,400 price. However, that obligation may be offset by the damages caused by the breach, measured by any difference in value between the goods as promised and the goods as delivered, together with incidental and consequential damages. UCC § 2-714. Assuming the sign is worth $6,400 despite the improper coloration, Bacchanalian Catering would still be permitted to deduct the $1,300 spent on new brochures and stationery, provided those expenses are recoverable consequential damages under section 2-715. UCC § 2-717.

The seller's right to the price when the buyer accepts the goods is a useful remedy only if the buyer has the ability to pay. In many cases, a more effective remedy – albeit one that does not protect the seller's expectancy – would be to get the goods back. Most laypersons and some merchant sellers are surprised to learn, however, that an unpaid seller does not normally have the right to return of the goods. There are, however, two main exceptions to this general rule.

First, the seller may have a *contractual* right to get the goods. Such a right is created when the buyer grants a security interest in the purchased goods to secure the buyer's obligation to pay the purchase price. A security interest is a consensual lien on personal property – the analog to a mortgage on real property – and is governed by UCC Article 9. Any seller with concern about the buyer's ability to pay the purchase price should take a security interest in the goods to secure that payment obligation. If the buyer then fails to make payment when due, the seller would be entitled either to peaceably repossess the goods or to obtain a writ of replevin instructing the sheriff to seize the goods and return them to the seller. *See* UCC § 9-609. The necessary language in the parties' agreement for the seller to have a security interest can be very short and simple. A single sentence "seller retains a security interest in the goods sold to secure the buyer's obligations under this agreement" would suffice. So too would a phrase that the seller "retains title" to the goods sold, because the UCC treats such a clause as one that merely creates a security interest. That language does not actually prevent title from passing to the buyer once the goods have been delivered to the buyer. UCC §§ 1-201(b)(35), 2-401(1).

The second way in which the seller may be able to recover the goods is through a *legal* right called "reclamation."[1] Reclamation is available in two very limited

---

[1] Even though the right of reclamation is not expressly limited to the situation where the buyer has accepted the goods, in practical effect, that is the only time that it matters. If the

circumstances. In the first situation, the buyer has tendered payment, but the payment mechanism has failed. The classic example of this occurs when the buyer tenders a check that is later dishonored when the seller submits it for collection. Section 2-507 gives the seller the right to reclaim the goods within a reasonable time after the payment mechanism fails, provided the sale was a "cash sale," that is, provided the buyer was supposed to make payment on delivery. If the buyer purchased on credit (delivery now, payment later) and the buyer's subsequent check for the purchase price bounces, the seller does not have a right to reclaim under section 2-507.

The other situation giving rise to a right of reclamation occurs when the seller has agreed to sell the goods on credit and shortly after delivery discovers that the buyer is insolvent. UCC § 2-702(2). *See also* UCC § 1-201(b)(23) (defining "insolvency"). The seller may reclaim the goods by making a demand on the buyer within ten days of the buyer's receipt of the goods. The ten-day time period does not apply if the buyer has made a "misrepresentation of solvency" in writing within three months before the goods were delivered.[2]

A seller who successfully reclaims the goods from the buyer under section 2-702(2) is precluded from all other remedies, including apparently incidental damages. UCC § 2-702(3). There is no similar limitation following reclamation under section 2-507. Is this distinction justifiable? Why should the seller who reclaims under section 2-702 not be entitled to expectation damages? Perhaps the principle underlying section 2-702(2) is that the buyer has engaged in fraudulent behavior by taking the goods when it is insolvent and thus the seller is entitled to rescind the contract for sale as a remedy for that fraud. With a rescission of the contract and recovery of the goods, the seller is no longer entitled to expectation-based damages for breach of the contract.[3] Perhaps another point worth noting is

---

buyer has effectively rejected the goods, the seller has a right to take the goods back because of the rejection, not based upon any right of reclamation. If the buyer has not effectively rejected the goods, the buyer will have accepted the goods. UCC § 2-606.

[2] The additional time to reclaim if the buyer has made a written misrepresentation of solvency may be limited if the buyer seeks bankruptcy protection. *See* 11 U.S.C. § 546(c).

Both of these reclamation rights operate only against the buyer. In Chapter Ten, we will consider whether those rights are effective against creditors of the breaching buyer or people who purchase the goods from the breaching buyer.

[3] *See* Larry T. Garvin, *Credit, Information, and Trust in the Law of Sales: The Credit Seller's Right of Reclamation*, 44 UCLA L. REV. 247 (1996).

that if the buyer truly is insolvent, the buyer's unsecured creditors (those without any liens to secure the obligation that buyer owes them) are unlikely to be fully paid the debts due them. By allowing the seller to reclaim the goods, the seller is to some extent already being made whole, and thereby favored over those other creditors of the buyer. To entitle the seller to more would be unfair to those other creditors.

Because the sellers' reclamation rights are quite limited, sellers – particularly those who sell on credit – should consider taking a security interest in the goods sold to better protect their right to payment.

CISG and UNIDROIT Principles. Neither the CISG nor the UNIDROIT Principles use the acceptance or rejection concept to control the remedies that the aggrieved seller may recover. Under the CISG, the aggrieved seller has two basic options if the buyer has the goods. First, Article 62 allows the aggrieved seller to require the buyer to pay the price. Alternatively, Article 81 entitles the seller to avoid the contract, recover the goods from the buyer (the seller must also make restitution to the buyer), and seek damages. Both remedies are subject to the limitation in Article 28 that allows a court to refuse to order a remedy if the court's local law would permit such a refusal.

The UNIDROIT Principles are similar. The aggrieved seller may require the buyer to pay the price. Art. 7.2.1. Alternatively, the aggrieved seller could terminate the contract for fundamental nonperformance, Art. 7.3.1, which allows each party to make a claim for restitution of what they have provided under the contract. Art. 7.3.6. The aggrieved seller would still be able to recover damages for the buyer's breach. Arts. 7.3.5, 7.4.1. through 7.4.8.

SECTION 3.   SELLER'S REMEDIES WHEN THE SELLER HAS THE GOODS

There are several ways in which a seller may end up with the goods after the buyer breaches. For example, a buyer may breach by repudiating its obligation to perform or by failing to make a required payment before tender of delivery. In such cases, the seller's first remedial option is to withhold or stop delivery of the goods to the buyer. UCC § 2-703(a), (b). Alternatively, a buyer may refuse to accept goods that conform to the contract or unjustifiably attempt to revoke acceptance, thereby leaving the goods with or returning the goods to the seller. Whatever the nature of the buyer's breach, the seller who has the goods may also wish to recover damages. This section first addresses the seller's ability to withhold or stop delivery of the goods and then discusses the seller's four alternative measures of damages.

A. Seller's Ability to Withhold or Stop Delivery

The provisions allowing the seller to withhold or stop delivery are found in UCC §§ 2-703(a), (b), 2-702(1) and 2-705.[4] Collectively, these provisions allow the seller to keep the goods from the buyer if the buyer has repudiated, failed to make payment, or is insolvent.[5] However, the seller's authority is limited in several ways. To understand the limits it is important first to understand the terminology used in these provisions. Withholding delivery refers to situations in which the seller has the goods. Stopping delivery refers to situations in which a carrier or other bailee has the goods. The second important thing to understand is the scope of these different provisions, which is illustrated by the following chart:

	Withhold Delivery	Stop Delivery
For Buyer's Breach	§ 2-703(a)	§§ 2-703(b), 2-705
For Buyer's Insolvency	§ 2-702(1)	§§ 2-702(1), 2-705

By and large, the seller's right to withhold delivery after the buyer's repudiation or breach is unlimited. However, the seller's right to stop delivery is more restricted. That is because of the burden it imposes on carriers. *See* UCC § 2-705 cmt. 1. Moreover, even if the seller has a right to stop delivery to the buyer, that does not mean that a carrier must follow the seller's instructions. *See* § 2-705(3).

---

[4] A related right is found in section 2-505 regarding the seller's ability to ship under reservation, which in essence allows the seller to claim a security interest in the goods and withhold the goods from the buyer until the buyer pays the price. Review the material in Chapter Four on shipment under reservation.

The seller may have rights to withhold or stop delivery under other law, such as UCC Article 9, if the seller has taken a security interest in the goods and the buyer's actions are a default under the security agreement. The rights of a seller as a secured party under Article 9 are beyond the scope of these materials.

[5] Determining insolvency is not an easy matter. Read section 1-201(b)(23).

Thus, when goods are with a carrier, the first question to consider is whether the seller has a right as against the buyer to stop delivery. The second question is whether the seller may require the carrier to stop delivery and return the goods. The third question is what liability will the seller have to the carrier or the carrier have to the buyer if the carrier follows the seller's instructions and stops delivery of the goods. Read UCC §§ 2-703(a), (b), and 2-705 and try the following problem.

Problem 9-1

Seattle Gems, Inc., a gem wholesaler, contracted to sell diamonds to Bellevue Jewelry, Inc., F.O.B. Seattle Gems' place of business. Upon notification of shipment, Bellevue Jewelry was to make a funds transfer to Seattle Gems' bank account. Seattle Gems shipped the diamonds to Bellevue Jewelry using Federated Carriers. Federated issued a negotiable bill of lading naming Seattle Gems as consignee. Bellevue Jewelry failed to make the funds transfer after Seattle Gems notified Bellevue Jewelry the goods had been shipped. Seattle Gems contacted Federated and instructed Federated not to deliver the package to Bellevue Jewelry, but to hold it until Seattle Gems otherwise notified Federated.

A. Did Seattle Gems act rightfully in ordering Federated to hold the package? What difference, if any, would it make if Seattle Gems had reliable information that Bellevue Jewelry had defaulted on its obligations to its primary lender?

B. Does Federated have to obey Seattle Gems' instructions? What risk is Federated taking if it delivers the goods contrary to Seattle Gems' instruction?

C. How does your analysis change if Federated issued a nonnegotiable bill of lading?

CISG and UNIDROIT Principles. Under the CISG, the seller may prevent delivery of the goods to the buyer if it becomes clear that the buyer will not substantially perform its obligations because of a deficiency in the buyer's ability to perform, the buyer's conduct in performing or preparing to perform, or creditworthiness. That right to withhold delivery applies even if the seller has already placed the goods in transit. The seller must notify the buyer so as to give the buyer an opportunity to provide adequate assurance that the buyer will perform. Art. 71. If the buyer has repudiated or failed to render pre-delivery performance such that the buyer has committed a fundamental breach, the seller may declare the contract avoided and thus would not be obligated to deliver the goods. Arts. 72, 81.

The UNIDROIT Principles allow the seller to withhold its performance if the buyer has not performed as required by the contract. Art. 7.1.3.

B.   Seller's Right to Cancel the Contract

In a non-installment contract, whenever the buyer breaches a contract for the sale of goods, the seller may cancel the contract and seek damages for the buyer's breach. UCC § 2-703(f). Review section 2-106(3) and (4) on the distinction between termination and cancellation. As we have already seen, cancellation allows the aggrieved party – in this case, the seller – to end the contract as a remedy for the buyer's breach. No notification is required and it means that the seller neither expects the buyer to perform in the future nor plans to tender performance of its own remaining contract obligations. Cancellation does not waive the seller's right to seek damages for breach from the buyer, either as to the buyer's past performance or as to the buyer's future performance.

The seller's right to cancel is limited in installment contracts. *See* UCC §§ 2-612(3), 2-703. The buyer's breach with respect to one or more installments gives the seller the right to cancel the whole contract – and thereby terminate the obligation to tender further installments – only if that breach is a "substantial impair[ment] of the value of the whole contract." Of course, even if the buyer's breach does not impair the value of the whole contract for the seller, it nevertheless gives the seller a right to demand adequate assurance of future performance, UCC § 2-612 cmt. 6, and to suspend its own performance until the buyer provides such assurances. UCC § 2-609(1).

Problem 9-2

Burgess Heating, Inc. agreed to buy 500 stoves from Sizzle Stoves for $200 per stove. The parties agreed that Sizzle would deliver the stoves in two installments (approximately 15 days apart), with 20% paid upon delivery of the first installment and the remaining amount paid in 30 days.

Sizzle delivered 250 stoves to Burgess. Burgess gave Sizzle a check for $20,000. That check was dishonored. Burgess has accepted the delivered stoves and is expecting delivery of the remaining stoves. The remaining 250 stoves are sitting in Sizzle's warehouse. Sizzle has consulted you regarding its options against Burgess. Advise Sizzle.

CISG. If a buyer commits a fundamental breach, *see* Art. 25, the seller may avoid the contract. If the seller elects to avoid the contract, the seller generally must notify the buyer unless the breach is the buyer's repudiation of its obligation. Art. 72. In an installment contract, if it appears that the buyer has breached its obligations as to one or more installments such that the seller has grounds to conclude that the buyer's performance as to the future installments would be a fundamental breach, the seller may avoid the contract. Art. 73. The effect of the avoidance is to effectively cancel the contract leaving the seller's ability to pursue damages intact. Art. 81.

UNIDROIT Principles. The seller may terminate the contract if the buyer's failure to perform is a fundamental non-performance. Arts. 7.3.1, 7.3.3. The seller must give notice of the termination to the buyer. Art. 7.3.2. Termination does not affect the seller's rights to damages for the buyer's breach. Art. 7.3.5.

C. Seller's Damages

The seller has the following four, general options for computing damages when the buyer breaches by refusing to accept (*i.e.,* wrongfully rejecting) or to keep possession (*i.e.,* wrongfully attempting to revoke acceptance) of the goods:

(i)   Resell the goods and recover the difference between the resale price of the goods and the contract price, UCC § 2-706;

(ii) Recover the difference between the market price of the goods and the contract price, UCC § 2-708(1);

(iii) If the previous two measures would be inadequate, recover the lost profit on the transaction, UCC § 2-708(2); and

(iv) If the goods are not readily marketable to anyone else, recover the contract price, UCC § 2-709.

All four measures expressly authorize the seller to also recover incidental damages. They also have something else in common: all are designed to protect the seller's expectancy in one way or another. They are all therefore consistent with the principle, expressed in section 1-305, of putting the aggrieved seller in the position as if the breaching buyer had fully performed its contractual obligations. To demonstrate this point, and the relationship among the four alternatives, consider the following example:

Example

Dealer contracts to sell a lithograph to Buyer for $10,000. Buyer is required to pay $2,000 one week before delivery and the remaining $8,000 at delivery. If all goes according to plan, on the date of delivery, Dealer will have $10,000 and Buyer will have the lithograph. Of course, the lithograph may be worth more or less than $10,000 at the time of contracting, and may be worth the same or a different amount at the time of delivery.

Now assume that Buyer fails to pay the $2,000 down payment and therefore has breached the contract. Dealer cancels the contract and refuses to deliver the lithograph to Buyer. Thus Dealer has the lithograph instead of the $10,000 that Buyer promised to pay.

If the lithograph were really worth only $9,000, Dealer could presumably sell it for that amount and then recover the $1,000 difference between the contract price and the resale price from Buyer under section 2-706. That would leave Dealer with $10,000 ($9,000 from the resale purchaser and $1,000 in damages from Buyer) and no lithograph, which is exactly what Dealer expected to have. Alternatively, Dealer could keep the lithograph and recover the $1,000 (the contract price minus the lithograph's market price value) from Buyer under section 2-708(1). Dealer would therefore have a $9,000 lithograph and a $1,000 recovery, and thus a total equal to what Dealer expected to have.[6] As this scenario suggests, normally there should not be much difference between the market price and

---

[6] Although resale damages may seem like a more pure measure of lost expectancy than market damages do (because the seller expected to part with the goods and does indeed part with them following a resale but may still have them when using market damages), it is worth noting that market damages are the more traditional remedy. Moreover, market damages can be analogized to the seller reselling to itself at the market price.

the resale price of the goods, and thus not much difference between recovery under section 2-706 and section 2-708(1).[7]

If the lithograph were worth $11,000, neither section 2-706 nor 2-708(1) would yield any recovery from Buyer. That is because Dealer has *apparently* not been harmed by Buyer's breach. Quite the opposite, Buyer's breach appears to have left Dealer with a lithograph worth $11,000 instead of the $10,000 Dealer expected to have. However, sometimes Dealer's true injury is not apparent.

Consider what happens if Dealer resells the lithograph to another buyer for $10,000. Dealer now has the money and not the lithograph. This appears to be what Dealer expected to have if Buyer had performed. Do not overlook the significance of this. If the original contract price was for the fair market value of the goods, which is most often the case, and the market price has not changed from the time the contract was formed to the time the seller was supposed to tender the goods, which is also likely, a seller is likely to have little or no damages if the buyer reneges on the deal. But what if there were many copies of the lithograph, and Dealer could have sold one to Buyer, one to the resale purchaser, and still fill all the other orders that might come in? On such facts, Buyer's breach will have caused Dealer to lose volume. Put another way, the resale was not really enabled by or in substitution for Buyer's breach. Dealer would have made two sales had Buyer not breached, but because Buyer breached Dealer made only one; Dealer has lost a sale. On these facts, Dealer may be entitled to recover the profit Dealer failed to realize on the sale to Buyer. UCC § 2-708(2). This lost-profit measure of recovery compensates Dealer's expectation interest on the breached contract.

Now consider what happens if Dealer is unable to resell the lithograph at all because there is no market for it (perhaps it is a portrait of Buyer that no one else would want). In that circumstance, Dealer is stuck with goods worth $0 instead of the $10,000 Dealer expected to have. Dealer will therefore be entitled to recover the contract price from Buyer. UCC § 2-709. Of course, to prevent overcompensation, if Dealer gets the price from Buyer, Dealer will have to hold the lithograph for Buyer.

---

[7] What situation would likely lead to a significant difference between the resale price of the goods and the market price of the goods?

With this simple example in mind, we now examine each of these remedial formulas in more detail.   We will first study the three alternative damage measurements – damages based upon resale price, market price, or lost profit – followed by a brief look at the seller's ability to recover the price. We will then examine the seller's claim for incidental damages. Finally, we will examine how these remedies work when the buyer has prepaid in whole or part for the goods.

1. Damages Based upon Resale of the Goods

No seller is required to resell the goods in order to set its damages. However, there are often both legal and business reasons for the seller to do so. The legal reason is that market damages may be difficult to prove, particularly if the goods are unusual or unique. As a result, the resale price may be easier to determine than the market price. The business reason is that sellers typically do not want to keep the goods. If the seller is a merchant engaged in the business of selling goods of that kind, the seller will want to get rid of this excess inventory. Even if the seller was making an isolated sale, say perhaps of used equipment, the seller may want to get rid of the goods to free up space for something else. Put simply, sellers generally do not want to retain goods they have already contracted to sell. However, reselling the goods does not automatically mean that the resale price will be used to calculate the seller's damages. For the seller to be able to recover resale damages, the resale must satisfy several requirements. Read section 2-706.

For a resale to be proper under section 2-706, "every aspect of the sale . . . must be commercially reasonable." UCC § 2-706(2). In addition, if the resale will be a public sale – that is, an auction – the seller must generally provide the breaching buyer with reasonable notification of the time and place of the resale and make the goods available for reasonable inspection by prospective bidders.   UCC § 2-706(4)(b), (c). If, as is more common, the resale will be a private sale – that is, anything other than an auction – the seller must normally give the breaching buyer reasonable notification of its intention to resell. UCC § 2-706(3). As you can see, the reference to reasonableness makes each of these requirements somewhat vague, with the result that the seller can rarely be certain that a planned resale will in fact be proper.[8]

---

[8] Article 9 of the UCC imposes many of the same standards on a secured party who wants to dispose of the collateral. *See* UCC §§ 9-610, 9-611. Thus, judicial decisions under

Assuming that the seller's resale does satisfy with the requirements of section 2-706, the measure of the seller's damages are:

Contract price
− Resale price
+ Incidental damages
− Expenses saved

= Damages

Problem 9-3

A. You represent a merchant that buys, repairs, and sells used photocopy machines. The merchant wants to know what it must do when reselling goods following a buyer's breach of a sales contract to preserve its ability to use the resale price as the basis for computing its damages against the breaching buyer. Write a manual for the seller explaining what the seller should and should not do when reselling goods after a contract is breached.

B. Supersonic Aviation, located in Cincinnati, Ohio, agreed to sell Blue Sky Airlines, located in Florida, 100,000 gallons of jet fuel at $5.00 per gallon. The contract provided for shipment of the fuel to Blue Sky, F.O.B. Miami, FL. The cost of shipping the fuel would have been 10¢ per gallon. After the market price for jet fuel fell, Blue Sky repudiated the deal. Supersonic Aviation then resold the fuel in a transaction complying with section 2-706 to Federated Shipping, located in Cleveland, for $4.50 per gallon, F.O.B. Cincinnati. The cost of shipping the fuel to Cleveland was 2¢ per gallon. What are Supersonic Aviation's damages?

Sometimes, particularly if the contract calls for the sale of fungible goods, the goods will not be identified at the time the contract is made. They may even not be

---

Article 9 may be useful in analyzing whether a seller has complied with the requirements of section 2-706. Since 2001, Article 9 has contained some statutory safe harbors for the application of its analogous rules. *See* UCC §§ 9-612, 9-613, 9-614. It is less clear whether these safe harbor rules would be relevant to an Article 2 resale.

identified at the time the buyer breaches if the breach is by repudiation. In such cases, the seller may use section 2-704 in conjunction with section 2-706. Read section 2-704. Section 2-704(1) allows the seller to identify goods to the breached contract. The seller can then resell these goods pursuant to section 2-706.

Sometimes, the seller has begun, but not completed, manufacturing the goods when the buyer breaches. Section 2-704 gives the seller two options in such cases: (i) resell the goods in their unfinished state and recover damages based upon that resale; or (ii) resell the goods after finishing them. However, the seller must exercise reasonable commercial judgment to mitigate damages in deciding which option to follow.

Problem 9-4

Bacchanalian Catering, Inc. contracted to purchase from Specialty Displays a large, custom-manufactured sign depicting the company's logo: the Roman god Bacchus. Under the terms of the contract, the purchase price was $6,400, the seller was to deliver by July 1, and the buyer was to pay within 30 days after delivery. In mid-June, after concluding that its logo was alienating some potential customers, Bacchanalian Catering decided it no longer wanted the sign and so informed Specialty Displays.

At that point, Specialty Displays had expended about $4,000 of the $4,800 it had expected to incur in performing under the contract and had nearly completed manufacturing the sign. The sign was not readily marketable to anyone else in its unfinished state. However, it could be disassembled and some of its parts salvaged for other uses. The salvage value would be about $100 more than the cost of disassembly. Alternatively, Specialty Displays could spend another $2,000 to modify the sign so that it might appeal to other buyers. The president of Specialty Displays estimates that there is a 50% chance that it could sell the modified sign to another buyer for $5,000. What should Specialty Displays do?

2. Damages Based upon Market Price of the Goods

Just as an aggrieved buyer is permitted to use the market price of the goods to set its damages against a breaching seller, an aggrieved seller may use the market price of the goods to set its damages against a breaching buyer. Read section

2-708(1). The formula for measuring market damages is much the same as the formula for computing resale damages:

$$
\begin{array}{r}
\text{Unpaid contract price} \\
- \text{Market price} \\
+ \text{Incidental damages} \\
- \text{Expenses saved} \\
\hline
= \text{Damages}
\end{array}
$$

Notice that, unlike in the measure of resale damages in section 2-706, the word "unpaid" modifies the phrase "contract price" in the first line. Later in this section, we will consider whether a buyer who has pre-paid in whole or part gets a credit for the price paid against the damages owed. For now, you should ignore the word "unpaid." If that causes you concern, if you are reticent to disregard the clear text of the Code, bear in mind that it is very difficult to draft a statutory measure of damages that works for all situations, and thus it is advisable to view all the formulas in the damages rules of Article 2 more as strongly worded suggestions than as statutory mandates. The goal, as expressed in section 1-305, is to provide the aggrieved party with a recovery based on its lost expectancy. If a damage formula fails to do that in some cases, it is generally a good idea to stick with the guiding principle and depart from the formula. We will see this again when we cover the measure of damages for lost profits. Thus, the general measure of the seller's market damages is really:

$$
\begin{array}{r}
\text{Contract price} \\
- \text{Market price} \\
+ \text{Incidental damages} \\
- \text{Expenses saved} \\
\hline
= \text{Damages}
\end{array}
$$

Notice that the market price is to be determined at the time and place the seller was to tender the goods. As discussed in Chapter Four, the time and place for tender must be determined from the parties' contract: that is, from the parties' agreement as supplemented, to the extent necessary, by Article 2's gap fillers.

Query, though, whether it makes sense to calculate market damages based on the market price at the time the goods were to be tendered if the buyer repudiated before then. Recall that under section 2-610 the seller as the aggrieved party may either await performance for a commercially reasonable time or immediately resort to remedies for breach. If the seller elects to treat the buyer's repudiation as an immediate breach, why should the computation of the damage amount have to wait for some later time?

One of the difficulties in applying section 2-708(1) is the difficulty in proving what the market price is at the relevant time and place. Sections 2-723 and 2-724 provide some guidance on this point, and the latter is particularly helpful if the goods are fungible commodities subject to widely distributed price quotations. However, proving the market price of unique goods can be very difficult. Even for goods such as used cars and rare coins, which may be the subject of standard price quotations, value may vary significantly with condition.

Another issue lurking in section 2-708(1) is whether market damages are or should be available if the seller has resold the goods. Certainly the aggrieved seller cannot obtain damages under both section 2-706 and 2-708(1). Even though the roadmap of damages in section 2-703 does not expressly preclude the use of both provisions simultaneously, using them together would clearly overcompensate the seller and violate the principle of section 1-305. However, may the seller resell and still collect market damages under section 2-708(1)? Read section 2-706 cmt. 2.[9] Would the resale price that the seller obtained be good evidence of the market price for the goods?

Remembering the expectation principle for damages, consider why there might be a difference between the resale price and the market price. If the cause of the difference is market fluctuation based upon the difference in time between when the goods were sold and when the market price is measured, who should bear the risk of that market fluctuation? If the cause of the difference is the seller's negotiating skill in making the deal with the second buyer, does that help you decide which measurement is the better measure of the seller's expectancy interest? What if the seller obtains recovery from the buyer based upon market damages, and then subsequently resells the goods for a price that is higher than the market price that was the basis of the damages against the buyer? Should the seller have to reduce the judgment amount by the amount of the difference between the resale price and the market price? Should the timing of the resale transaction matter to the way in which the seller's expectancy interest is measured?

---

[9] Remember, as discussed in Chapter Seven, if the buyer engages in a cover transaction within the meaning of section 2-712, the buyer is precluded from recovering damages based upon the market price.

Problem 9-5

Supersonic Aviation, located in Cincinnati, Ohio, agreed to sell Blue Sky Airlines, located in Florida, 100,000 gallons of jet fuel at $5.00 per gallon. The contract provided for shipment of the fuel to Blue Sky, F.O.B. Miami, FL, with shipment to be made no later than February 25, and delivery at the destination by March 1. The cost of shipping the fuel would have been 10¢ per gallon. Blue Sky repudiated the deal on February 15, after the market price for jet fuel fell to $4.00 per gallon. Thereafter, the market price started to rise again. On February 25, the market price of jet fuel was $4.25 per gallon; on March 1, the market price of jet fuel was $4.50 per gallon. On March 7, Supersonic Aviation resold the fuel to Federated Shipping, located in Cleveland, for $4.75 per gallon, F.O.B. Cincinnati. Supersonic Aviation's cost of storing the fuel from February 25 to March 7 was $1,000.

A. If Supersonic Aviation notified Blue Sky on February 17 of its intent to resell the fuel, what are Supersonic Aviation's damages?

B. If Supersonic Aviation never notified Blue Sky of its intent to resell the fuel, what are Supersonic Aviation's damages?

There is one exception to the rule that the market price is measured at the time of the tender of the goods. Section 2-723 provides that if the buyer has repudiated and the case comes to trial before the time for performance (the seller's tender of the goods) was due, the time for measuring the market price is when the seller learned of the buyer's repudiation.

Problem 9-6

Supersonic Aviation, located in Cincinnati, Ohio, agreed to sell Blue Sky Airlines, located in Florida, 10,000 gallons of jet fuel at $5.00 per gallon for 10 years. The contract provided for shipment of the fuel to Blue Sky, FOB Miami, FL, with shipment to be no later than February 25 of each year, and delivery at the destination by March 1. The cost of shipping the fuel was 10¢ per gallon. Blue Sky repudiated the deal in the sixth year, when similar jet fuel was selling for $4.00 per gallon. Blue Sky does not take delivery in years seven, eight, or nine of the contract. The case comes up for trial in August of the ninth year of the contract. Supersonic Aviation submits proof that the market price of jet fuel is currently $4.50 per gallon. It also submits evidence that the market price was $4.10 in year seven, $4.20 in year eight, and $4.40 in year nine.

A. What amount or amounts should be used to compute market damages?

B. What amount or amounts should be used to compute market damages if the case came to trial in year eleven (that is, after the ten-year term of the contract would have run) and the market price in year ten was $5.50 per gallon?

3. *The Lost Profit Measurement*

The lost profit measurement appears to be a remedy of last resort. Section 2-708(2) provides that the lost profit measurement is available only if market damages are "inadequate to put the seller in as good a position as performance would have done." While the section does not explicitly provide that lost profits are available if resale damages under section 2-706 would also be inadequate, that is probably an implicit requirement.

Neither section 2-708 nor the comments to it identify the circumstances when damages measured by the market price (or resale price) would be inadequate to protect the seller's expectation interest. The one generally accepted circumstance – but perhaps not the only one – is when the seller is a "lost volume" seller. But it is not enough that the seller merely have lost volume by the buyer's breach. Consider one court's description of when a seller is a lost volume seller:

> We agree . . . that, under some circumstances, the measure of damages provided under 2-708(1) will not put a reselling seller in as good a position as it would have been in had the buyer performed because the breach resulted in the seller losing sales volume. However, we disagree with the definition of "lost volume seller" adopted by other courts. Courts awarding lost profits to a lost volume seller have focused on whether the seller had the capacity to supply the breached units in addition to what it actually sold. In reality, however, the relevant questions include, not only whether the seller could have produced the breached units in addition to its actual

volume, but also whether it would have been profitable for the seller to produce both units. As one commentator has noted, under

> the economic law of diminishing returns or increasing marginal costs[,] . . . as a seller's volume increases, then a point will inevitably be reached where the cost of selling each additional item diminishes the incremental return to the seller and eventually makes it entirely unprofitable to conclude the next sale. . . .

Thus, under some conditions, awarding a lost volume seller its presumed lost profit will result in overcompensating the seller, and 2-708(2) would not take effect because the damage formula provided in 2-708(1) does place the seller in as good a position as if the buyer had performed.[10]

Another situation in which the seller may seek its lost profit is when it is a jobber. A jobber functions as a middleman, buying goods and reselling them, making a profit on the spread between the buy price and the resale price. In many situations, the jobber is in the same position as a lost volume seller, because the jobber may have as many buyers as it can possible resell the goods to and is able to obtain an unlimited supply of goods for resale.

After determining that a seller is entitled to recover under section 2-708(2), the next task is to calculate the lost profit.[11] Typically, a seller's profit on a transaction would be computed as follows:

$$\text{lost profit} = \text{sale price} - \text{cost of production}$$

Costs of production come in two basic varieties: (i) fixed costs (also known as "overhead") that do not vary with the number of items produced or purchased; and (ii) variable costs that increase as the number of items produced or purchased increases.

$$\text{lost profit} = \text{sale price} - (\text{fixed costs} + \text{variable costs})$$

$$\text{or}$$

$$\text{lost profit} = \text{sale price} - \text{fixed costs} - \text{variable costs}$$

Examples of fixed costs include the rent the seller pays on its manufacturing plant and the annual salary of its chief executive officer. A typical variable cost would be the costs of raw materials used to manufacture the finished goods.

---

[10] *R.E. Davis Chemical Corp. v. Diasonics, Inc.*, 826 F.2d 678, 683–84 (7th Cir. 1987).

[11] *See* John M. Breen, *The Lost Volume Seller and Lost Profits Under UCC § 2-708(2): A Conceptual and Linguistic Critique*, 50 U. MIAMI L. REV. 779 (1996).

Determining what portion of the seller's fixed costs (overhead) should be allocated to the breached contract can be very difficult. For example, how much of the chief executive officer's annual salary should be allocated to the breached contract? Does the amount of time the officer spent negotiating the deal matter? What portion of the seller's annual insurance premiums and advertising costs should be counted? Fortunately, we need not answer these questions because the damages formula in section 2-708(2) specifically authorizes recovery for these costs by indicating in the parenthetical that the seller is also entitled to reasonable overhead. Read section 2-708(2). Thus, the statutory computation is:

$$\text{recovery} = \text{sale price} - \text{fixed costs} - \text{variable costs} + \text{fixed costs}$$

The two entries for fixed costs cancel each other out and we end up with:

$$\text{recovery} = \text{sale price} - \text{variable costs}$$

In essence, this formula calculates lost profit using the marginal cost of production. Unfortunately, by taking fixed costs (overhead) out of the calculation and leaving variable costs in, it becomes necessary to determine which of the seller's costs fall into which classification. While some costs – such as those for the chief executive officer's annual salary on one hand, and the cost of raw materials on the other – are easy to classify, other costs are not. Many expenses, such as employee wages and electricity might fall under either category, depending on the situation. For example, if the lost sale was minor in relation to the seller's normal output, the seller may have incurred no extra labor or utility costs to produce the goods that were supposed to go to the breaching buyer. However, if manufacturing the goods for the lost sale would have required the seller to pay overtime and run equipment for longer hours, such expenses would be better viewed as variable costs. One thing is clear, though: how a seller treats expenses for income tax purposes will have little or no bearing on whether they qualify as fixed costs or variable costs for the purpose of measuring damages.[12]

If you have read section 2-708(2) carefully, you may have noticed that the formula also calls for incidental damages and "due allowance for costs reasonably incurred and due credit for payments or proceeds of resale." "Due allowance for costs reasonably incurred" is a reference to reliance costs that the seller has actually expended and would normally recoup if it was getting the sale price. However, because the seller is not getting the sale price but only its profit margin, it is not able

---

[12] *See, e.g., Sure-Trip, Inc. v. Westinghouse Engineering*, 47 F.3d 526 (2d Cir. 1995).

to recoup those actual reliance expenditures without adding them on to the lost profit measure. The last part of the quoted phrase, "due credit for . . . proceeds of resale" is clearly a mistake and courts properly ignore it. The reason it is a mistake is that, if followed literally, a lost profit seller would have no recovery. Because the gross proceeds of a resale almost always exceed the seller's expected profit, subtracting those proceeds from the lost profit measure would almost always leave the seller with nothing. That does not comport with either the principle of section 1-305 or the purpose of section 2-708(2).

Keeping all this in mind, try your hand at the following problem.

Problem 9-7

On July 1, Best Woodworking Inc. contracted to purchase an industrial lathe for $90,000 from Sawtooth Supply Company, a distributor of machinery manufactured by Mammoth Machines. Delivery was to occur on October 1. Sawtooth Supply then placed an order for the lathe with Mammoth Machines for $80,000, with delivery by September 15. On August 15, and without justification, Best Woodworking repudiated the contract with Sawtooth Supply. Sawtooth Supply then promptly canceled its order with Mammoth Machines, which charged Sawtooth Supply its customary cancellation charge of $1,000.

Sawtooth Supply comes to you for advice. The market price of the equipment at the "time and place for tender," October 1, was estimated to be $90,000. Sawtooth Supply has incurred $2,000 to purchase parts that it expected to use to modify the lathe before delivering it to Best Woodworking. Sawtooth Supply expected to – but did not – spend an additional $1,500 to inspect, prepare, and install the lathe if Best Woodworking had not repudiated. Sawtooth Supply also estimates that approximately $500 of its annual overhead is allocable to each machine that it sells.

A. What is Sawtooth Supply's lost profit on this contract?

B. What damages should Sawtooth Supply recover?

What if the seller would not have made any profit on the contract that the buyer breached? Should the buyer be able to use that fact to argue that the seller is overcompensated if the seller attempts to recover damages based upon the market price or the resale price of the goods? The leading case indicates no, the lost profit measurement should not be used to limit the other measurements of the seller's expectation interest because section 2-708(2) authorizes using the seller's lost profit only if the other remedy measurements are inadequate, not if the lost profit measurement results in the least amount of damages.[13]

4. Recovering the Price

Normally when the buyer has breached by repudiating the contract or by refusing to accept the goods, the seller still has the goods and, if it chooses to seek an award of damages, uses one of the three formulas previously discussed: resale damages, market damages, or lost profits. Occasionally, however, the seller is able to recover the full contract price. We have already seen that section 2-709 authorizes the seller to recover the price when the buyer has accepted the goods. It also authorizes the seller to recover the price in two circumstances where the buyer has not accepted the goods. One of these circumstances is when the goods have suffered a casualty after the risk of loss has passed to the buyer. Issues relating to risk of loss are discussed in section 4 of this Chapter. The other circumstance is where the seller is unable to resell the goods. Re-read UCC § 2-709.

If the seller is unable to resell the goods, using the resale price of the goods is unlikely to be a reliable way to measure the seller's expectation interest. Using the market price to compute damages could work reasonably well, *provided* the seller's inability to sell implied that the market price of the goods was $0. However, the seller's inability to sell could be attributable to reasons other than a lack of buyers and, in any event, the goods may have some value even though proving what that is may be difficult. Using the lost profit measurement to calculate damages would be undesirable for the seller because it compensates the seller only for the difference between the contract price and the cost of production. If the seller is left with goods that it cannot sell, the seller would be left without any way to recoup those costs of production.

For these reasons, section 2-709 allows the seller to recover the contract price for the goods it cannot sell. Of course, if the seller obtains a judgment for the price,

---

[13] *Trans World Metals, Inc. v. Southwire Co.*, 769 F.2d 902 (7th Cir. 1985).

the seller must hold the goods for the buyer or credit against the judgment any resale price obtained for the goods if a resale becomes viable. This is consistent with the focus on the expectation interest of the seller and ensuring that the seller is not overcompensated.

The major challenge in applying this section is determining when the goods are not readily resalable. Consider one court's view:

> The evidence at trial clearly established that all of Foxco's goods were specially manufactured for the customer who ordered them and that it was difficult for Foxco to resell fabric manufactured for one purchaser to another buyer. Further, it was normally very difficult to sell Foxco's spring fabric after the spring buying season had ended; the precipitous decline of the knitted fabric market presented an additional barrier to resale. It was not until the next spring buying season returned that Foxco, in September 1975, finally sold a portion of the goods identified to Fabric World's October 1974 order.
>
> Fabric World argues that Foxco made no effort whatsoever to resell the goods during the months that intervened (between the contract breach and Foxco's eventual disposition of the fabric in September 1975) despite the presence of some market for the goods in that interim period. Thus Fabric World concludes, the requisites of § 2-709(1)(b) were not satisfied. Under § 2-709(1)(b), however, Foxco was required only to use *reasonable* efforts to resell its goods at a *reasonable* price. From the time of Fabric World's breach to September 1975 there was a 50% decline in the market price of this material. We cannot say that the jury was precluded from finding that Foxco acted reasonably under the circumstances or that there was no reasonable price at which Foxco could sell these goods. Fabric World breached its contract with Foxco, and the jury was entitled to a charge which gave Foxco the full benefit of its original bargain.[14]

Problem 9-8

Standard Shipping, Inc. contracted to sell a customized shipping container to Blaster Electronics, Inc., for use in shipping sensitive electronic cargo. The contract price was $3,000. Just as Standard Shipping was about to deliver the container, Blaster Electronics repudiated. The

---

[14] *Foxco Indus., Ltd. v. Fabric World, Inc.*, 595 F.2d 976, 984 (5th Cir. 1979).

container cost $1,800 to build. Non-customized containers generally sell for $2,000 each.

A. Standard Shipping is unable to find a buyer willing to pay $3,000 for the customized container but has an offer to buy for $1,500. Is Standard Shipping entitled to recover the contract price from Blaster Electronics?

B. No one is willing to buy the customized container but Standard Shipping could sell the container for scrap for $500. Is Standard Shipping entitled to recover the contract price from Blaster Electronics?

Problem 9-9

Review Problem 9-4 and section 2-704. May Specialty Displays recover the price from Bacchanalian Catering?

5. *Incidental Damages*

All four formulas used to measure the seller's damages – resale, market, lost profit, and price – expressly allow the seller to recover incidental damages in addition to the amount otherwise computed from the applicable formula. *See* UCC §§ 2-706(1), 2-708(1), (2), 2-709(1). Read section 2-710, which identifies some of the incidental damages that an aggrieved seller might suffer. Unlike the buyer's remedies, however, none of these provisions purports to authorize the seller to recover consequential damages for the buyer's breach. Because section 1-305(a) indicates that consequential damages are unavailable unless specifically provided for in the UCC or in other law, most courts have held that an Article 2 seller is not entitled to consequential damages.[15] Thus one of the challenges is to separate incidental (recoverable) damages from consequential (nonrecoverable) damages.

---

[15] *See, e.g., Nina Industries, Ltd. v. Target Corp.,* 2005 WL 323745 (S.D.N.Y. 2005); *cf.* Roy Ryden Anderson, *In Support of Consequential Damages for Sellers,* 11 J.L. & COM. 123 (1992). *Compare* RESTATEMENT (SECOND) OF CONTRACTS § 351, cmt. e.

Note, for this purpose it is the nature of the damages, not their amount, that matters. Incidental damages can in fact be quite large.[16]

Problem 9-10

Buyer has defaulted by failing to pay when due the price of a piece of equipment that Seller was to manufacture. Seller has begun, but not completed, manufacturing the goods. Which, if any, of the following types of harm qualify as incidental, and thus are recoverable as damages?

A. Interest on a loan Seller obtained before Buyer's breach to finance the operation of Seller's business and to purchase equipment.

B. Interest on a loan Seller obtained before Buyer's breach to finance Seller's performance on the contract with Buyer.

C. Interest on a loan Seller obtained after the breach to make a profitable investment that Seller had planned to finance with the price paid by Buyer.

D. Interest on a loan Seller obtained after the breach to finish work on the goods and to obtain a commercially reasonable resale.

6. Restitution to a Breaching Buyer

If the buyer has prepaid in whole or part for the goods before repudiating or otherwise breaching the contract, an issue arises as to whether the buyer is entitled to receive back all of its payment. One possible approach, consistent with the principle expressed in section 1-305(a), would be to say that the buyer is entitled to full restitution, but the seller may offset the damages under whichever of the damages measures applies. Another approach would be to regard the requirement

---

[16] *See Commonwealth Edison Co. v. Allied Chemical Nuclear Products, Inc.*, 684 F. Supp. 1429 (N.D. Ill. 1988) ($293 million in incidental damages – consisting of storage costs – when nuclear fuel re-processor which was supposed to take spent nuclear fuel in trade for equivalent fissile material failed to do so).

of a down payment or prepayment as a sort of liquidated damages clause – that the seller is entitled to retain the payment received, provided it passes the test in section 2-718(1).

Article 2 does neither of these. Instead, in some rather complicated provisions, it does something close to the first approach but also allows the seller to retain the lesser of $500 or 20% of the contract price. This formula functions as a type of statutory liquidated damages. Read section 2-718(2)– (4). Now try the following problem.

Problem 9-11

On July 1, Best Woodworking Inc. contracted to purchase an industrial lathe for $90,000 from Sawtooth Supply Company, distributor of machinery manufactured by Mammoth Machines. The contract called for delivery September 1. Pursuant to the contract, Best Woodworking made a down payment of $20,000. Sawtooth Supply then placed an order for the lathe with Mammoth Machines for $80,000, with delivery to be made directly to Best Woodworking. On August 1 and without justification, Best Woodworking repudiated the contract with Sawtooth Supply. Sawtooth Supply then promptly canceled its order with Mammoth Machines, which charged Sawtooth Supply its customary cancellation charge of $1,000.

At the time of the repudiation, the market price of the lathe was $85,000. Because the economy was in a mild recession, the market price declined to $80,000 on September 1.

A. If Sawtooth Supply's agreement with Best Woodworking provides Sawtooth Supply is entitled to $10,000 as liquidated damages in the event Best Woodworking repudiates, how much of the $20,000 down payment is Best Woodworking entitled to receive back?

B. If Sawtooth Supply's agreement with Best Woodworking has no liquidated damages clause, how much are Sawtooth Supply's damages and how much of the $20,000 down payment is Best Woodworking entitled to receive back? *See Neri v. Retail Marine Corp.*, 285 N.E.2d 311 (N.Y. 1972).

Problem 9-12

On March 1, Superior Equipment, Inc., located in Chicago, contracted to manufacture custom lathes for Bristol Woodworking, Inc., located in Phoenix, for $80,000, delivery F.O.B. Chicago no later than November 1. Cost of shipping was estimated at $2,000. At the time that Bristol and Superior entered into the contract, Bristol made a down payment of $20,000. Superior delivered the lathes on time. Bristol accepted the lathes but one week later demanded that Superior take the lathes back and return its down payment. Bristol's demands were unjustified because both the lathes and Superior's tender had conformed to the contract requirements. Nevertheless, Superior took the lathes back.

Superior estimated its costs of producing the lathes was $70,000. On November 1, the market price of the lathes in Chicago was $60,000. The market price in Phoenix was $55,000. Superior was looking for a buyer for the lathes in Phoenix in order to avoid having to ship the lathes again, and was expending $100 per day for storage of the lathes in Phoenix.

Two months after taking the lathes back, Superior sold the lathes in Denver for $50,000, F.O.B. Denver, and incurred $1,500 in shipping costs to send them from Phoenix to Denver. Calculate Superior's damages.

7.   *CISG and UNIDROIT Principles*

The CISG allows an aggrieved seller to recover damages based upon the either difference between the contract price and a resale price, Art. 75, or the difference between the contract price and the market price, Art. 76. Both damage remedies require that the seller has avoided the contract for fundamental breach. To avoid a contract, the buyer's breach must be fundamental, Arts. 25, 64, and the seller must notify the buyer, Art. 26. If the buyer has already paid the price for the goods, the seller's ability to avoid the contract is limited. Art. 64. In addition to the damages measured by those formulas, the seller is entitled to recover consequential damages that were foreseeable at the time the contract was made. Art. 74. Such consequential damages can include lost profits, *id.*, but are subject to a generalized obligation to take reasonable actions to mitigate loss. Art. 77. If the aggrieved seller does not or cannot avoid the contract, the seller is entitled to recover the price. Art.

62. However, a court may refuse to award that remedy if the court's local law would not permit that remedy. Art. 28.

The UNIDROIT Principles allow the seller to recover the price. Art. 7.2.1. Alternatively, an aggrieved seller may recover damages from the breaching buyer based upon what is required to "fully compensate" the seller. Art. 7.4.2. The seller's damages may be measured based upon the difference between the contract price and the resale price, Art. 7.4.5, or the difference between the contract price and the market price, Art. 7.4.6. The seller can also recover consequential damages that are reasonably certain and foreseeable. Arts. 7.4.3, 7.4.4. The seller is not able to recover damages for harm that it could have avoided. Art. 7.4.8.

SECTION 4.   SELLER'S REMEDIES FOLLOWING A CASUALTY TO THE GOODS

In Chapter Four, we learned that three principles underlie the rules on when the risk of loss passes. First, the party who controls the goods, and is thus in the best position to avoid the loss, should bear the risk. *See* UCC § 2-509 cmt. 3. Second, the party most likely to have insurance protection under the circumstances should bear the risk. *Id.* Third, the party in breach should bear the risk of loss. *Compare* UCC § 2-509 *with* § 2-510. We then saw that, absent breach, the risk of loss generally passes to the buyer when the seller makes a conforming tender of delivery, if the seller is a merchant, or upon the buyer's receipt of the goods, if the seller is a non-merchant. UCC § 2-509(3). Slightly different rules apply if the tender is to occur through a carrier or a bailee. UCC § 2-509(1), (2).

A principal corollary to the risk of loss rules studied in Chapter Four is that if the risk of loss has passed to the buyer, and within a reasonable time thereafter the goods are lost or damaged, the buyer is liable to the seller for the price of the goods. UCC § 2-709(1)(a). This situation is usually encountered in a shipment contract (where the risk of loss passes to the buyer when the seller tenders conforming goods to the carrier) and the goods are lost or damaged in transit.

We now explore how the buyer's breach affect the risk of loss. Read section 2-510(3). If the buyer unjustifiably repudiates or breaches after conforming goods have been identified to the contract but before the risk of loss would have passed to the buyer under section 2-509, the buyer will bear the risk of loss for goods lost or damaged within a reasonable time after that breach, if the seller has a deficiency in its insurance coverage. Remember that if the goods are identified to the contract, but have not yet been tendered to the buyer, both the buyer and the seller will have an insurable interest in the goods. UCC § 2-501. Whether one or both have insurance coverage for those goods depends upon construction of the insurance policies.[17]

Problem 9-13

Sterling Corp. and Bryce Industries agreed that Bryce would purchase ten standard lathes for $1,000 per lathe, FOB point of shipment, delivery November 1. On October 25, Sterling rigged the lathes for shipment to Bryce.

A. Bryce notified Sterling on October 28 that it would not take any of the lathes due to a downturn in Bryce's business. That night, the warehouse where Sterling had stored all of its lathes was destroyed by a fire caused by lightening. What are Sterling's remedies against Bryce?

B. Sterling properly contracted with Federated Carriers to deliver the lathes. Sterling made proper arrangements with Federated for shipment, and duly notified Bryce when the lathes were delivered to Federated. When the lathes were delivered two days later to Bryce, three of them were noticeably damaged beyond repair. Bryce rejected the three damaged lathes by timely notification to Sterling and accepted the other seven. Upon using the seven lathes, Bryce discovered that those seven had also been damaged in transit. Bryce notified Sterling that it was revoking acceptance of those seven lathes. Sterling has sued Bryce for the full contract price. Is Sterling entitled to the price?

---

[17] Nothing in Article 2 explicitly addresses whether the risk passes back to the seller if, after accepting the goods, the buyer attempts an unjustified revocation and the seller takes the goods back. Presumably, once the seller takes the goods back, the seller should have the risk of loss for the goods. Prior to the seller taking the goods back, the breaching buyer should probably have the obligation to at least take reasonable care of the goods, although Article 2 does not address this situation. *See* UCC § 2-602.

CISG and UNIDROIT Principles. Under the CISG, the risk of loss principles in Articles 66 through 70 do not appear to affect the seller's remedies for the buyer's breach. The UNIDROIT Principles do not address risk of loss issues.

SECTION 5.   THE STATUTE OF LIMITATIONS

As we learned in Chapter Seven, section 2-725 provides a four-year limitations period after a cause of action for breach accrues. The cause of action accrues when the breach occurs. When the seller is the aggrieved party, the seller's cause of action will often arise when the buyer fails to pay or otherwise render its required performance, wrongfully rejects the goods, or wrongfully attempts to revoke acceptance. It is a little less clear when the seller's cause of action accrues when the buyer repudiates. Recall that the seller is entitled either to treat the buyer's repudiation as a breach or to await performance for a commercially reasonable time. UCC § 2-610. Because there will usually be uncertainty as to when that commercially reasonable time expires, a cautious seller should commence any action within four years of the repudiation.

While the seller may have a breach of warranty claim if the buyer made a warranty of noninfringement when the buyer supplied specifications for the goods, review UCC § 2-312, there is very little litigation on the issue of the statute of limitations when the seller is the aggrieved party. One reoccurring issue is what statute of limitations governs when the seller has also taken a security interest in the goods and is seeking to exercise its security interest, or collect a deficiency judgment. Some courts hold that a statute of limitations other than section 2-725 applies, such as the general statute of limitations that applies to breach of contract actions,[18] whereas other courts hold that section 2-725 applies to that situation.[19]

CISG and UNIDROIT Principles. The statute of limitations issues when the seller is the aggrieved party are the same as previously discussed when the buyer is the aggrieved party. Review the material from Chapter Seven.

---

[18] *See, e.g., Orix Financial Services, Inc. v. Holmes*, 2007 WL 3143707 (S.D.N.Y. 2007).

[19] *See, e.g., D.A.N. Joint Venture III, L.P. v. Armstrong*, 2007 WL 634457 (Ohio Ct. App. 2007).

CHAPTER TEN

THIRD PARTY CLAIMS TO THE GOODS

SECTION 1. PROPERTY CONCEPTS

It is no doubt obvious that a contract for the sale of goods transfers ownership of the goods. Indeed, that is the essence of a "sale" transaction. Article 2 recognizes this effect on ownership by defining a sale as "the passing of title from the seller to the buyer for a price." UCC § 2-106(1). "Title" is an undefined term but it is useful to think of it as a shorthand for ownership, or at least nominal ownership (ownership in name).

Even though transferring title (ownership) to the goods is the purpose of an Article 2 sales transaction, the drafters attempted to reduce reliance on title concepts to determine the buyer's and seller's rights against each other in the performance of the sales contract. *See* UCC § 2-101 cmt. Thus, title issues are not generally relevant to such issues as who breached the contract, the seller's right to reclaim the goods from the buyer, or the buyer's right to specific performance. Even risk of loss analysis has been divorced from ownership concepts and instead relies largely on whether the seller has fulfilled its tender obligation. In short, Article 2 is primarily about the parties' *contract* rights, not their *property* rights.

In some circumstances, however, who has an ownership interest in the goods is very important. For those circumstances, section 2-401 provides for when title passes from the seller to the buyer. Courts use this provision to determine who has title when dealing with such issues as whether the goods are covered under an insurance policy,[1] whether the goods are part of the seller's or buyer's bankruptcy estate,[2] or who has liability for sales tax.[3]

Title and ownership concepts are also important when dealing with *property* claims to the goods.[4] As much as the Article 2 drafters tried to make title issues

---

[1] *See, e.g., Collins v. Mountjoy*, 2008 WL 746979 (Ohio Ct. App. 2008); *Concord General Mut. Ins. Co. v. Sumner*, 762 A.2d 849 (Vt. 2000).

[2] *See, e.g., In re Alofs Mfg. Co.*, 209 B.R. 83 (Bankr. W.D. Mich. 1997).

[3] *See, e.g., In re Valley Media, Inc.* 226 Fed. Appx. 120 (3d Cir. 2007).

[4] *See* Linda J. Rusch, *Property Concepts in the Revised U.C.C. Articles 2 and 9 Are Alive and Well*, 54 SMU L. REV. 947 (2001); Jeanne L. Schroeder, *Death and Transfiguration: The Myth That The U.C.C. Killed "Property"*, 69 TEMP. L. REV. 1281 (1996); William L.

irrelevant to the rights of the buyer and seller as against each other, title concepts are vital when dealing with property-based claims to the goods by persons other than the buyer or seller. This Chapter addresses these third-party, property-based claims to the goods and the buyer's and seller's rights when faced with those claims. To give some context to this point, consider the following simple hypothetical which illustrates some of the circumstances where these property claims may be asserted.

Illustration

Seller, an equipment dealer, and Buyer enter into a contract in which Buyer agrees to buy a lawn tractor for use at the golf course that Buyer runs. Assume that the lawn tractor is identified to the contract for sale. Seller is in possession of the lawn tractor. Buyer wants to get possession of the tractor but it turns out that Seller has actually sold the tractor twice and the other buyer is contending it has a superior claim to the tractor. Who has a superior claim to possession of the tractor as between the two buyers? What if instead of selling the tractor twice, Seller allowed one of its principal lenders to take a security interest in the tractor to secure a debt that Seller owes that lender? What if one of Seller's judgment creditors, in an attempt to collect on the judgment, levied on the lawn tractor, thereby obtaining an execution lien on it? Does Buyer have a property claim to the tractor that is superior to the interests of these creditors?

Now assume Seller has delivered the lawn tractor to Buyer. Does Buyer take the lawn tractor free of any pre-existing property claims asserted by Seller's creditors? Does Seller have any property claim to the tractor to the extent that Buyer has not paid for the tractor? If Seller has a property claim to the tractor, is that claim superior to the property-based claims of Buyer's creditors, such as a creditor to whom Buyer has granted a security interest? Would Seller's property-based claim, if it exists, be superior to the claim of someone who purchased the tractor from Buyer?

These questions are just some of the many issues that may arise regarding the resolution of competing property-based claims to goods that are the subject matter

---

Tabac, *The Unbearable Lightness of Title Under the Uniform Commercial Code*, 50 MD. L. REV. 408 (1991).

of the sales contract. When two or more people assert property-based claims to the same goods, it sets up a classic priority issue, posing the question of which person's claim to the goods has priority over the other.

It is important when working through these issues to have a clear understanding of the basis of each person's property claim. This is because the resolution of the priority question often hinges on how each claimant acquired its property interest. The rights of unpaid transferors, pre-paying transferees, donees, secured creditors, and lien creditors are all different. Thus, to continue the illustration above, the priority of Buyer's claim to the tractor against the claim of Seller's secured party may be resolved differently from the competing claims of the two persons who each purportedly purchased the tractor from Seller.

Most, if not all, property-based claims to the goods arise because of some interaction a third party has with either the buyer or the seller. These relationships between the parties can be diagramed as follows:

We will revisit this diagram throughout the remainder of this Chapter, as we discuss the rights of the various parties it identifies.

Once you have identified the nature of the property-based claims to the goods, the next step is to ascertain when each claim arose. A fundamental tenet of property law is that a transferor of a property right may transfer only the rights that the transferor has, or has been given power to transfer by some rule of law.[5] Like many fundamental legal principles, it is often expressed in Latin: *nemo dat qui non habet* (one cannot give what one does not have). Section 2-403 codifies this basic

---

[5] We have already looked at that concept when we examined the warranty of title in Chapter Three.

principle.[6] Although some competing property-based claims may be resolved in ways that are inconsistent with this principle, for the most part sequence matters.

Finally, the last step in the analysis is to identify the appropriate priority rule that resolves a contest between two competing property claims to the same goods. The applicable rule may be found in the UCC, in other state statutes, or in the common law. If there are three or more competing property claims, more than one priority rule may apply. For example, assume that parties A, B and C each assert a property-based claim to the same goods. To properly analyze the situation, you may need to consult three different priority rules, one for each of the following contests: (i) A v. B; (ii) A v. C; and (iii) B v. C.

Before digging into the details of property-based claims to the goods, it is important to understand when title normally passes to the buyer. Read section 2-401.

Problem 10-1

In the absence of the parties' agreement otherwise, when does title to the goods pass from the seller to the buyer in a sales transaction under section 2-401? Compare these default rules on title passage to the default rules on tender of delivery in section 2-503 and passage of the risk of loss in section 2-509. How are the tender of delivery rules and risk of loss rules similar to and different from the title passage rules?

CISG and UNIDROIT Principles. The CISG provides that "except as otherwise expressly provided in this Convention, it is not concerned with: . . .the effect which the contract may have on the property in the goods sold." CISG Art. 4. In short, the CISG does not purport to resolve any third-party's claim to the goods. As a result, courts in the United States may use Article 2 principles to

---

[6] Subsection (1) provides that a person may only transfer the rights it had and provides two circumstances in which the transferor has the power to transfer greater rights than the transferor had. In subsection (1), the transferor has power to transfer greater rights than it has if it took possession of the goods in a transaction for purchase in which the transferor obtained voidable title, and then delivered the goods to a good faith purchaser for value. In subsection (2), a merchant-seller has the power to transfer to a buyer in ordinary course of business the rights of the person who entrusted the goods to the merchant.

determine who has title, to the extent that is relevant in a contract otherwise covered by the CISG.[7] The UNIDROIT Principles do not deal with title issues.

SECTION 2.   BUYER'S RIGHTS AGAINST PERSONS WHO CLAIM AN INTEREST IN THE GOODS THROUGH THE SELLER

When goods subject to a sales contract are in the seller's possession, the seller will usually still have an ownership claim to the goods. That is because title to the goods does not usually pass to the buyer until the seller completes its tender obligation. UCC § 2-401. However, the buyer too will have property rights in the goods, even while they remain in the seller's possession, if the goods are identified to the contract. UCC § 2-501. Thus, it will often be the case that both the buyer and the seller have property rights in the goods at the same time. This should not be surprising. As you no doubt learned in property class, ownership of property can be broken out into different interests, and all of the individual property interests need not be held by the same person.

The buyer's property rights, standing alone, do not entitle the buyer to force the seller to turn over the goods. Instead, as discussed in Chapter Seven, the buyer will have the right to compel the seller to transfer possession of the goods to the buyer only if the buyer can satisfy the conditions stated in section 2-502 (pre-paying buyer) or section 2-716 (specific performance or replevin). Thus a property-rights analysis does not help us determine whether the seller or the buyer has the superior right to possession of the goods as against each other.[8]

Property rights are important, however, in resolving the claims of third parties. Given that the seller and buyer may both have property rights in the goods at the same time, and the fact that each party's rights are normally transferrable, it is fairly easy for third-party claims to the goods to exist.

In this section, we consider two basic types of property-based claims to the goods arising from interactions with the seller by people other than the buyer. In one type of property-based claim, a person is asserting rights in the goods as an owner. In the other type of property-based claim, the person is asserting a property

---

[7] *Usinor Industeel v. Leeco Steel Products Inc.*, 209 F. Supp. 2d 880 (N.D. Ill 2002).

[8] However, a pre-paying buyer could obtain a security interest in the goods to secure the seller's obligation to deliver the goods. Security interests are discussed *infra*.

interest in the goods to secure an obligation, that is, a lien. We explore how both types of claims fare against the buyer's property rights to the goods.

How could multiple ownership claims arise in the goods? The seller could have sold the goods to multiple buyers. Alternatively, the person who transferred the goods to the seller could be claiming an ownership interest in those goods because something went wrong in the transaction in which the seller acquired the goods. Part A below addresses the buyer's rights against both such claimants – people who assert an ownership interest in the goods based upon interaction with the seller. Part B then addresses the buyer's rights against creditors who assert a lien or security interest in the goods pursuant to an interaction with the seller. In each part, we identify when each property-based claim arose and the applicable priority rule used to resolve the dispute.

One last preliminary point is worth making. You may be tempted to think that the relative rights of the buyer and the seller – whether grounded in property or in contract – should be determinative of the relative rights of the buyer and a third-party claiming through the seller. In other words, you might assume that if the buyer's rights are better than the seller's, then the buyer's rights will be better than the third party's rights derived from its interaction with the seller, and that if the buyer's rights are inferior to the seller's, then the buyer's rights will be inferior to the rights of the third party derived from its interaction with the seller. Alas, it is not that simple. There is no substitute for the methodical process of identifying the basis of each party's claim to the goods, determining when that claim arose, and then isolating and applying the correct priority rule to the dispute.

A. Buyer's Right Against Persons Asserting Ownership Interests

In this section, we consider two typical priority disputes based upon competing ownership type property claims.[9] Revisiting the diagram at the beginning of this Chapter, this section is concerned with the parties that are highlighted in bold in the version below.

---

[9] To the extent there is a claim of a third party to the goods, the Buyer has a possible cause of action against the Seller for breach of a warranty of title as explored in Chapter Three. But that breach of contract right as against the Seller does not answer the question as to the priority of the potential ownership claims in the goods as between the Buyer and another person.

Let's start with the transferor's possible property claims. The transferor could be an owner from whom the Seller stole or borrowed the goods. In that situation, the Seller would not have any property rights in the goods, rather all the property rights still reside in the transferor/owner. In that circumstance, the Seller would have no rights at all to transfer to the Buyer and the Buyer should lose in a priority contest with the transferor. Review UCC § 2-403(1).

Alternatively, the transferor could have sold the goods to the Seller. Prior to delivery, the transferor would still have property rights in the goods because title would not normally have passed to the Seller. *See* UCC § 2-401. Of course, once the goods are identified to the contract, the Seller, who is buying the goods from the transferor, would have property rights under section 2-501, but would have the ability to compel delivery of the goods only to the extent so provided in section 2-502 or 2-716. Moreover, as we studied in Chapter Nine, the Seller may also be subject to the transferor's right to stop delivery under section 2-705. Even after delivery, the transferor may have the right to reclaim the goods from the Seller. UCC §§ 2-507, 2-702(2).

How do these rights of the transferor fare against the rights of the Buyer? That depends upon what rights the Buyer has. Remember, under Article 2, the earliest point in time that the Buyer could have any property right at all is when the goods are identified to the contract between the Seller and Buyer. UCC § 2-501. Until that point, the Buyer has no property-based claim whatsoever to assert against the transferor in a priority contest over the goods, and would therefore lose.

After identification, the result can differ. How soon can identification occur? Specifically, can the goods be identified to the contract between the Seller and the Buyer if the Seller does not yet have possession? Probably. Consider specially ordered goods. The Seller could be a distributor of goods who took the Buyer's order, and then placed an order for the goods from the manufacturer (*i.e.*, the transferor in the diagram) tailored to the Buyer's specifications. Once the manufacturer starts to create the goods that are designated for Buyer's order, the goods would be identified to the contract between the Seller and the manufacturer, and arguably identified to the contract between the Seller and the Buyer.

Assuming the Buyer has property rights created by identification, then we need to consult section 2-403. Subsection (1) states the basic property concept that the Seller may transfer to the Buyer only the rights the Seller has or has power to transfer. Thus, the argument is that if the rights of the transferor are superior to the rights of the Seller, and the Buyer's rights are derived from the Seller, the Buyer's rights are inferior to the rights of the transferor. However, as you may remember from our brief study in Chapter Three, section 2-403 provides for two situations when the Seller has the power to transfer greater rights than the Seller actually has. Subsection (1) deals with transferring greater rights to a good faith purchaser for value and subsection (2) allows some sellers to transfer greater rights to a buyer in ordinary course of business. Review the relevant definitions for "good faith," "purchaser" and "buyer in ordinary course of business" in section 1-201. Notice that to qualify as a buyer in the ordinary course of business (but not as a good faith purchaser for value), the buyer has to either take possession or have a right to possession under Article 2. Whether the Buyer in our situation has the right to possession (against the Seller) will depend upon application of sections 2-502 or 2-716. Alternatively, if the Buyer qualifies as a good faith purchaser for value and the Seller did what was required under section 2-403(1), the Buyer's property claim will have priority over the transferor's property claim. Similarly, if the transferor entrusted the goods to a merchant seller, and the Buyer qualified as a buyer in ordinary course of business, the Buyer would have priority over the transferor's claim.

Now try your hand at the following problem. It may help you to place each person in their relative position on the diagram, identify the type of property interest each person has, and draw a time line to reflect when each person's property interest arose. The key to analysis here is painstaking and careful attention to the details.

Problem 10-2

A. Seller, who had stolen a diamond necklace from Owner, sold it to Buyer who knew nothing of the theft. As between Owner and Buyer, who is entitled to the necklace?

B.   Seller purchased a used diamond necklace from Transferor, and a few days later sold and delivered the necklace to Buyer. Shortly thereafter, Seller and Buyer learn that Transferor had stolen the necklace from Owner. As between Owner and Buyer, who is entitled to the necklace?

C.   Seller, who had acquired a diamond necklace from Transferor by paying for it with a check that was later dishonored, sold and delivered the necklace to Buyer.
   1.   As between Transferor and Buyer, who is entitled to the necklace?
   2.   How, if at all, would the analysis change if Buyer had paid for the necklace but had not yet taken possession of it?

D.   Transferor sold a diamond necklace to Seller, promising to deliver it the next week. Seller then made an agreement to sell the necklace to Buyer and Buyer paid 25% of the purchase price to Seller.
   1.   Seller was to make a funds transfer by Friday to Transferor. Seller did not make the funds transfer and Transferor refused to deliver the necklace to Seller. As between Transferor and Buyer, who is entitled to the necklace?
   2.   Transferor and Seller had agreed that Seller would pay 50% at time of delivery and the balance in two days. Transferor delivered the necklace to Seller when Seller paid 50% of the price, but Seller did not pay the balance. Seller, in the meantime, delivered the necklace to Buyer. As between Transferor and Buyer, who is entitled to the necklace?

E.   Seller, who had borrowed a diamond necklace from Friend to wear at a party, sold and delivered the necklace to Buyer. As between Friend and Buyer, who is entitled to the necklace?

F.   Seller, a jeweler who had received a diamond necklace from Owner to repair and clean it, sold and delivered the necklace to Buyer.
   1.   As between Owner and Buyer, who is entitled to the necklace?
   2.   How, if at all, would the analysis change if Buyer had paid for the necklace but had not yet taken possession of it?

Let us now discuss the rights of a transferee. Just as the rules in section 2-403 can be useful in resolving a priority contest between the Buyer and a transferor, they can also help resolve a battle between the Buyer and a transferee. Consider the following problem. In doing so, determine whether and how section 2-403 applies to each transaction.

Problem 10-3

A. Seller, a jeweler, contracted to sell a diamond necklace to Buyer, who paid in full but asked to be allowed to pick it up the following week. Seller agreed. Two days later, Seller sold and delivered the same necklace to Transferee.
    1. As between Buyer and Transferee, who is entitled to the necklace?
    2. How, if at all, would the analysis change if Seller were not a merchant?

B. Seller, a jeweler, contracted to sell a diamond necklace to Buyer, who made a down payment and promised to pay the remainder of the purchase price the following day. Buyer agreed to allow Seller to retain possession until Buyer paid the price in full. Later that day, Seller sold the same necklace to Transferee, who paid the price in full but allowed Seller to maintain possession until Purchaser could come back to pick it up, sometime the following afternoon. Before Transferee came back to pick up the necklace, Buyer returned, paid the rest of the purchase price and took delivery of the necklace. As between Buyer and Transferee, who is entitled to the necklace?

As you may remember from our study of rejection and revocation of acceptance in Chapter Seven, the buyer may have a security interest in the goods to secure repayment of any part of the price that has been paid and some of the incidental expenses connected with the rejected goods or effecting cover. UCC § 2-711(3). In order for the buyer to claim the security interest, the buyer must be in possession of the goods and it will lose its security interest if it gives up possession of the goods to its seller.[10] The buyer may sell the goods pursuant to the sale process in section 2-706 as a method of enforcing its security interest.

If the buyer has such a security interest, what is the priority of that interest as against the potential interest of a transferor (who sold the goods to the buyer's seller)[11] or a transferee (who purchased the goods from the seller but has not taken delivery)? As we learned in completing Problem 10-2, the transferor who sold the goods to the Seller has only one Article 2 right in this circumstance, that is, the right to reclaim the goods. Both the cash and credit reclamation rights are subject to the rights of a good faith purchaser from the seller under section 2-403. UCC §§ 2-702(3), 2-507 cmt. 3. Thus in our diagram, if Buyer was asserting its Article 2 security interest against a transferor asserting a right to reclaim the goods, the Buyer would be a good faith purchaser, and the Buyer's right to enforce its security interest should be superior to the transferor's right to assert its reclamation claim.

Article 2 is less clear on the relative rights of a buyer with a security interest in the goods and a transferee with a right to specific performance or replevin under section 2-716, or the right to obtain the goods under section 2-502. However, Article 9 provides the answer. If the transferee qualifies as a buyer in ordinary course of business, *see* UCC § 1-201(b)(9), then the transferee will take free of the Buyer's security interest. UCC § 9-320(a).

B. Buyer's Right Against Seller's Creditors

Now we will consider the property-based claims to the goods of the seller's creditors. The parties we are concerned with in this section are in bold on the diagram below.

---

[10] Even though the buyer has a security interest, title to the goods will revert to the seller. UCC § 2-401(4).

[11] If the buyer's seller had no rights in the goods (for example if the seller stole the goods from the transferor), the buyer's security interest would not be effective, as seller would have not had any rights in the goods that would have transferred to the buyer in the first instance.

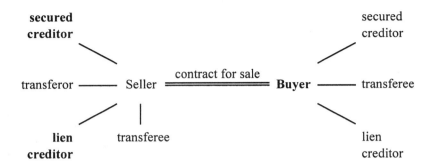

There are two general types of property-based claims to the goods made by creditors of the Seller: (i) those that arise when the creditor uses judicial process to collect a debt; and (ii) those that arise by agreement between the Seller and the creditor. The creditor that obtains a property interest in the Seller's goods using judicial process to collect on a judgment is call a lien creditor. The claim itself is variously called a judicial lien, an execution lien, or an attachment lien. The rules for determining priority between a lien creditor and the Buyer are found in the laws governing collection and in UCC Article 2.

A creditor whose property rights in the goods is based upon an agreement with the Seller is called the secured creditor. The claim itself is called a security interest. The rules for determining priority between the Buyer and a secured creditor of the Seller are found in UCC Article 9.

We explore the lien creditor versus Buyer contest first.

1.   Buyer Against Seller's Lien Creditor

Under general principles of debtor and creditor law, a creditor who has a claim against a person – whether based in contract, tort, restitution, or some other principle of law – does not generally have any property rights in the personal property of the debtor. Even if the claim is reduced to judgment, the judgment creditor typically has no property rights in the judgment debtor's goods or other personal property. Rather, under most states' law, the creditor must take additional action to obtain a lien – an interest in property that secures payment of a judgment – on the debtor's personal property. In most states, that additional step is to levy on the debtor's personal property pursuant to a legal process generally called "execution on judgments" (states may have different names for their processes, but the essential concepts have a surprising degree of uniformity). Levy generally occurs when the relevant executive authority, such as the county sheriff or U.S. marshal, acting pursuant to a judicial order,[12] takes either actual or constructive possession of the goods. Under most states' law, the creditor obtains a lien on the goods once the levy takes place, and at that point in time becomes a lien creditor. Thus in the diagram above, the lien creditor would not have a property interest in the goods that are the subject of the sales contract between the Buyer and Seller unless and until it had levied on the goods. In a few states, a judgment creditor can acquire a lien on the judgment debtor's personal property by filing a notice of the lien in a particular state office. In either case, before the lien creditor has a property interest in the goods, the lien creditor would have no basis for using property law to trump the Buyer's property rights in the goods.

Under the law of most states, a lien creditor's lien attaches only to the property rights the seller had at the time that the levy takes place. Unless some statute provides to the contrary, the lien creditor's property rights (the lien) in the goods levied upon are no greater than the rights of the debtor (the Seller in our example) in that property. This is a reflection of the fundamental property-law principle discussed earlier: a person may transfer only the rights the person has.

Now read section 2-402(1). Although the rule of this provision does not, on its face, apply to lien creditors, it does mean that a creditor's status as creditor will not be enough to defeat the property rights of the Buyer. Once we add to this rule the general principle that a lien creditors' rights are typically no greater than the rights of the judgment debtor (the Seller in our hypothetical), we see that the lien creditor is subject to whatever rights the Buyer could assert against the Seller to get the goods, provided the Buyer had those rights at the time the lien creditor levied on the goods. Thus the time when the lien creditor's lien attached to the goods will often be critical to who wins the priority battle.

Problem 10-4

Buyer, a consumer, made a $300 down payment on a new stereo at Dealer's store. Buyer and Dealer agreed that Buyer could take possession of the stereo upon payment of the remainder of the $800 purchase price. Dealer marked the stereo with Buyer's name and stored the stereo in

---

[12] If the order is entered before judgment is entered against the debtor, it is typically called a "writ of attachment"; if it is issued after judgment is entered, it is typically called a "writ of execution."

Dealer's warehouse. Creditor, who had a judgment against Dealer, had the sheriff levy on Dealer's inventory, including the stereo that was marked for Buyer. Creditor thereby acquired a judicial lien on the stereo. Buyer returned to the store with the $500 remaining purchase price and wanted the stereo. Dealer was unable to deliver the stereo because of the levy.

A. As between Creditor and Buyer, who has the superior right to possession of the stereo? *See* UCC §§ 2-402(1), 1-201(b)(13).

B. How, if at all, would the analysis in Part A change if Creditor acquired its judicial lien on the stereo – before Dealer contracted to sell the stereo to Buyer – by properly filing a notice of the judgment in the state's secretary of state's office?

C. How, if at all, would the analysis in Part B change if Buyer took delivery of the stereo before Creditor filed a notice of the judgment in the state's secretary of state's office?

Occasionally, a lien creditor can use fraudulent transfer law to nullify the Buyer's property rights and thereby claim priority in the goods. In particular, in some states, a Seller who retains possession of goods sold can be deemed to be engaged in a fraudulent attempt to mislead the Seller's creditors into believing that those goods would be available to the seller's creditors for payment in the event of a levy.[13] In short, retaining possession of goods already sold might make it appear to the Seller's creditors that the seller owns more assets – the goods – than the Seller really owns. As a result, those states effectively nullify the sale and allow the Seller's creditors to levy on the goods, and thereby permit the creditors to obtain rights to the goods superior to the Buyer who left the goods with the Seller.

Read section 2-402(2), which is a partial response to those decisions. The first clause acknowledges that there may be a rule of applicable state law that allows a creditor of the seller to treat the seller's retention of goods sold as fraudulent, and thus to invalidate the sale. The real import of subsection (2), however, is in the final clause. It creates an exception for a merchant seller's possession of goods sold for a commercially reasonable time and in good faith. Such conduct is deemed not fraudulent as against the Seller's creditors even if the state follows the general

---

[13] *See, e.g.*, Cal. Civ. Code § 3440(a).

principle that treats retention of possession as fraudulent. Applying this exception would in effect make rights of a Buyer who left the goods with the Seller superior to the lien of the Seller's lien creditor if the Buyer had the right to obtain possession of the goods from the Seller.

Now consider a different type of property right of the Buyer: the Buyer's security interest arising under section 2-711(3). The Buyer's security interest will arise upon the Buyer's rightful and effective rejection or justifiable and effective revocation of acceptance. In considering how this security interest affects the Buyer's right to the goods, bear in mind that the lien creditor's lien could arise at any of the following distinct times: (i) before identification of the goods to the contract; (ii) after identification of the goods to the contract but before delivery of the goods to the Buyer; (iii) after delivery of the goods to the Buyer.

Assume the lien creditor acquired its lien before the goods were identified to the contract for sale. At the time the judicial lien arose, the buyer would have no property interest in the goods and thus under first-in-time principles, the lien creditor's rights should be superior to the buyer's rights even if the seller subsequently delivered the goods to the buyer and the buyer is asserting a security interest in the goods under section 2-711(3). Of course, this sequence of facts is unlikely to arise if the judicial lien was created by levy because in that case the seller would not generally be able to subsequently deliver the goods to the buyer.

Now assume the lien creditor acquired its lien after the goods were identified to the contract for sale but before the seller delivered the goods to the buyer. Section 2-402(1) teaches that if the buyer had the right to force the seller to deliver the goods under section 2-502 or section 2-716, the lien creditor's rights would be subordinate to the buyer's rights. Thus, if the buyer was later asserting its security interest, that security interest should also be superior to the lien creditor's rights, although nothing in Article 2 specifically answers this question. If the buyer did not have the ability to force the seller to deliver the goods under section 2-502 or 2-716, then section 2-402(1) would not apply, and under basic first-in-time principles, the lien creditor's lien would be superior to the buyer's later arising security interest.

Now assume the seller delivers the goods and the lien creditor tries to levy on the goods in the buyer's possession. Here, the buyer's argument is that the seller no longer has a property right in the goods as title has transferred to the buyer under section 2-401 and thus there are no seller's rights to which the lien creditor can attach its property interest. Thus when the buyer asserts its security interest in the goods, there is no priority contest because the lien creditor has no property interest in the goods.

2. *Buyer Against Seller's Secured Creditors*

We now consider what happens if the Seller in our diagram has granted a security interest in the goods to a secured creditor. To be clear, the Seller has an agreement with the secured creditor that gives the secured creditor a security interest in the same goods that the Buyer has contracted to buy. In a dispute between the Buyer and the Seller's secured creditor over the goods, the priority of the parties' respective property rights in the goods will be determined not by Article 2, but by Article 9. Under Article 9, the default rule is that the secured creditor wins. *See* UCC § 9-201. There are, however, several exceptions that may come to the aid of the Buyer. Understanding those exceptions requires some knowledge of Article 9. Accordingly, what follows is a very distilled version of Article 9's basic principles. A more complete exploration of these principles must await a course on secured transactions.[14]

First, remember that merely because the Seller owes money to a creditor does not mean that the creditor has a property interest in any of the Seller's assets. To obtain a property interest in the Seller's assets – in our example, the Seller's goods – the Seller and the secured creditor must have entered into an agreement that grants the creditor a property interest in the goods to secure an obligation that the Seller owes to the creditor. The process of creating this property interest (referred to as a "security interest") is called "attachment." *See* UCC § 9-203. The intricacies of attachment are left to a secured transactions course. For our purposes, the important point is that attachment of the security interest requires the agreement of the Seller.

Second, the priority of the creditor's security interest in the goods depends on several factors, the most important of which is whether the secured creditor has "perfected" its interest. Perfection is a term of art under Article 9. Generally, when the Seller has possession of the goods subject to the security interest, the secured creditor will perfect its security interest by filing a document called a "financing statement." To be perfected, the secured creditor's financing statement must contain certain specified information and be filed in the correct public office. The details behind that summary are quite complex and also are relegated to a course on

---

[14] As we have seen many times in this course, Article 2 is merely one source of commercial law. Other Articles of the UCC, along with principles and rules of general contract law and the law governing debtor-creditor relations, are some of the other components of commercial law that can be relevant to a sales transaction.

secured transactions. For the purpose of studying sales, we will simply designate whether the secured creditor has or has not made a filing sufficient to perfect its security interest.

With this basic understanding, let's explore the two priority rules most likely to allow the Buyer to take the goods free of the Seller's creditor's security interest. The first is section 9-317(b), which deals with a secured creditor who has not made a filing sufficient to perfect its security interest. Read UCC § 9-317(b). This rule is in large measure a timing rule: it protects the Buyer if the goods are delivered to the Buyer before the secured creditor perfects its security interest, although other requirements must also be satisfied for the Buyer to prevail.[15]

Section 9-317(b) will not help the Buyer if the secured creditor has perfected its interest at the time the Buyer has taken delivery. However, the Buyer may nevertheless prevail under section 9-320(a). Read that provision. This priority rule protects a buyer in ordinary course of business from a security interest created by that buyer's seller, even if the security interest is perfected. We encountered buyers in ordinary course of business when we explored the entrustment rule in section 2-403(2). Reread the definition of buyer in ordinary course of business in section 1-201(b)(9) and review the materials covered previously as to when the Buyer becomes a buyer in ordinary course of business. Now try the following problem.

Problem 10-5

Sublime Diversions manufactures and sells gaming tables (tables with inlaid chess boards, built-in holders for poker chips, *etc.*). To finance its operations, Sublime borrowed money from First Bank and granted the bank a security interest in all its inventory (the gaming tables) and equipment (*e.g.,* manufacturing machines, computers, office furniture). Busted contracted to purchase some goods from Sublime and paid half the purchase price. Using the matrix below, determine in which of the open boxes, if any, Busted will take free of First Bank's security interest in the goods sold and identify the provision that allows Busted to do so.

---

[15] Section 9-317(e) is an exception to the priority rule stated in subsection (b). Exploration of that exception would require much more than a dip into the Article 9 scheme and thus is not covered in this course.

		First Bank's security interest is perfected	First Bank's security interest is unperfected
Busted contracted to buy a used band saw	Busted has received the goods from Sublime		
	Busted has a right to compel delivery under § 2-502 or § 2-716		
	Busted has neither received the goods nor has the right to compel delivery		
Busted contracted to buy a gaming table	Busted has received the goods from Sublime		
	Busted has a right to compel delivery under § 2-502 or § 2-716		
	Busted has neither received the goods nor has the right to compel delivery		

One more wrinkle to be added to this priority contest is the situation where the Buyer has a security interest in the goods pursuant to section 2-711(3). If the Buyer has taken free of the security interest of the Seller's creditor, then there is no priority contest. The secured creditor simply has no property interest at all.[16] If the Buyer has not taken the goods free from the creditor's security interest, then relative priority of the security interest of the Buyer and the Sellers' creditor is governed by section 9-110. Under that section, the Buyer's security interest will have priority over the creditor's security interest even though the creditor's security interest was

---

[16] This analysis may change if the security interest of the Seller's secured creditor reattaches to the goods. The Buyer's effective and rightful rejection of the goods or justified and effective revocation of acceptance cause title to the goods to revest in the Seller. UCC § 2-401(4). The secured creditor's security interest may reattach to the goods pursuant to the terms of the security agreement with the Seller. In such a case, the Buyer's security interest would have priority over the secured creditor's interest under section 9-110.

attached and perfected before the Buyer's security interest arose, as long as the Seller (the debtor) does not get possession of the goods.

So far we have assumed that the Seller has granted a security interest to a financing creditor, someone who has loaned the Seller funds and secured the obligation to repay with a security interest in the Seller's property pursuant to a security agreement with the Seller. But, that is not the only way that a security interest in the goods may arise through an interaction with the Seller. Article 2 provides for two circumstances in which security interests arise as a result of a sales contract.

First, a seller of goods may, pursuant to the terms of the sales contract, purport to "retain title" to the goods despite making delivery to the buyer. This is normally done if the buyer has not yet fully paid for the goods. However, such a clause in the sales agreement does not actually prevent title from passing to the buyer. Instead, section 2-401 provides that the seller has merely retained a security interest in the buyer's goods. *See also* UCC § 1-201(b)(35). The sales contract therefore doubles as a security agreement. The second circumstance occurs when the seller ships the goods under reservation pursuant to section 2-505. That action is also sufficient to create a security interest in the goods. Thus to return to our diagram, the transferor to the Seller may create a security interest in the goods under Article 2 by either "retaining title" or shipping under reservation.

Even though these security interests arise under Article 2, their priority is governed by Article 9. Thus sections 9-317(b) and 9-320(a) will determine whether the Buyer takes free of these security interests in the same way as if the security interest had arisen under Article 9.[17]

SECTION 3.   SELLER'S RIGHTS AGAINST PERSONS WHO CLAIM AN INTEREST IN THE GOODS THROUGH THE BUYER

We now switch to the other side of the diagram and consider how the Seller's rights to the goods fare against those who may claim a property interest in the goods based upon some interaction with the Buyer. The usual competitors with the Seller are the Buyer's transferee, secured creditor, or lien creditor. Thus the parties we are concerned with in this section are in bold in the diagram below.

---

[17] In applying these priority rules, one must take into account the effect of section 9-110 which governs security interests arising under section 2-401 or 2-505.

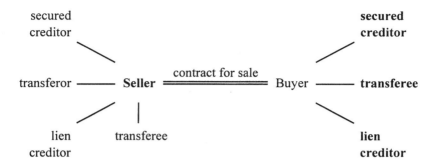

The reason such contests can arise is that a Seller, who has contracted to sell goods to the Buyer, remains the owner of the goods. As we have already seen, merely entering into the contract for sale does not divest the Seller of its ownership interest. This is true even if the Buyer has obtained property rights in the goods through identification, and then transferred those rights to someone else. Moreover, as we have previously discussed, the Seller also may have a right to stop delivery of the goods, and, if the goods have already been delivered, may have a right to reclaim them. UCC §§ 2-705, 2-702, 2-507.

The priority of the Seller's claim to the goods varies with the nature of the competing claimant's property interest in the goods. Thus, for example, the Seller's rights against the Buyer's transferee are different from the Seller's rights against the Buyer's secured creditor. We therefore discuss these three priority contests in turn: (i) Seller vs. Buyer's transferee; (ii) Seller vs. Buyer's lien creditor; and (iii) Seller vs. Buyer's secured creditor.

The Seller's rights also depend on whether the Seller is asserting merely its rights under Article 2 or whether the Seller can also claim a security interest granted by the Buyer. Often times, a buyer who has not paid the seller in full for the goods will grant the seller a security interest in the goods to secure payment of the remainder of the price. However, the priority of such a security interest is largely independent of the seller's role in the transaction as seller and in any event is likely to be fully explored in a course on secured transactions.[18] Therefore, we concern ourselves here with the Seller's rights under Article 2.

---

[18] For those who are curious, the relevant Article 9 sections are:

    Seller as secured party vs. Buyer's transferee   UCC §§ 9-317(b), 9-320;

    Seller as secured party vs. Buyer's lien creditor   UCC § 9-317(a), (e); and

    Seller as secured party vs. Buyer's secured creditor   UCC §§ 9-322(a), 9-324.

A. Seller Against Buyer's Transferee

We first consider the Seller's rights against a non-creditor transferee from the Buyer.

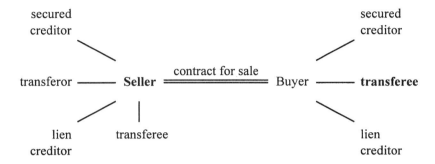

The transferee is most commonly a subsequent buyer, but could also be a donee or an entity that succeeds to the Buyer's property rights by operation of law.[19] The good news is that we have effectively already covered this priority battle when we covered the Seller's transferor's rights against the Buyer. A transferor's rights against the Buyer are the same as the Seller's rights against a transferee. There is no difference in the analysis.

If the Seller still has possession of the goods or the goods have been stopped in transit, the Buyer's transferee will not be able to force the Seller to deliver the goods to it unless the Buyer could force the Seller to deliver possession to the Buyer. UCC § 2-403(1) (the Buyer can only transfer the rights it has or has power to transfer). Once the Seller delivers the goods to Buyer, the transferee could have rights superior to the Seller by virtue of one of the two exceptions to section 2-403 that protect good faith purchasers for value and buyers in ordinary course of business. Similarly, if the Seller tried to exercise its reclamation rights under either section 2-507 or 2-702(2), the Seller would lose if the transferee qualified as a good faith purchaser for value of the goods or a buyer in ordinary course of business. Finally, if the transferee has a security interest under section 2-711(3), the transferee's status as a good faith purchaser for value or buyer in ordinary course of business should protect its security interest from the Seller's right to reclaim. We explored all of these rules in Problem 10-2 and the accompanying text.

---

[19] For example, the transferee could be the estate of a deceased Buyer.

B. Seller Against Buyer's Lien Creditor

A lien creditor of the Buyer acquires its lien – its property interest in the goods – through judicial process. Remember, in most states, that occurs when the creditor causes the sheriff or marshal to levy on the goods pursuant to a writ. In a few states, the lien can be created by filing a notice of the judgment in a public office. In either case, the lien attaches to only those rights in the goods that the Buyer has.

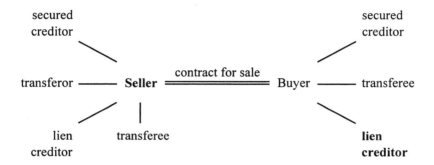

Based on these principles, the earliest point in time that a lien creditor could acquire a lien on goods that are subject to a contract for sale between the Seller and the Buyer is when the goods are identified to that contract. That is because identification is the point in time when the Buyer first obtains a property interest in the goods which could be captured by a judicial lien. While the Seller still has possession of those goods, however, the lien creditor would be able to gain priority over the Seller's property interest – that is, compel the Seller to transfer the goods – only if the Buyer would be able to so compel the Seller. Thus, a lien creditor's right to goods that are still in the Seller's possession will depend upon the Buyer's rights under section 2-502 or 2-716 to compel the Seller to deliver the goods to the Buyer. Because the Buyer must pay the Seller for the goods to exercise these rights, the lien creditor must do so as well, if the Buyer has not already paid.[20]

---

[20] The Seller's priority over a lien creditor would be further assured if the Seller had a security interest in the goods under section 2-401 or 2-505. In such a case, as long as the Buyer does not obtain possession of the goods, the Seller's security interest would be governed by section 9-110 which provides that the Seller's security interest has priority over the claims of other secured creditors. That section does not mention what the Seller's priority is over a lien creditor. However, another priority rule in Article 9 provides that the Seller's

Much the same analysis applies if the goods are in transit. Because the lien creditor's rights are no greater than the Buyer's rights, if the Seller is entitled to stop the goods in transit as against the Buyer, the lien creditor's rights in the goods are subject to that right as well. *See* UCC §§ 2-705, 9-110, cmt. 5.

After the Buyer obtains possession of the goods, the Seller may have a right to reclaim the goods under section 2-507 or 2-702(2). Those sections do not address the priority of the Seller's reclamation right as against the Buyer's lien creditor. At common law, the reclaiming Seller prevailed over the Buyer's lien creditor, regardless of the timing of the lien creditor's levy as against the Seller making the reclamation demand. Without any contrary rule in Article 2, the common law rule may be appropriate to apply. *See* UCC § 1-103. *Cf.* UCC § 2-702(3).

Problem 10-6

Sterling Manufacturing agreed to sell specially manufactured equipment to Bristol for $100,000. Sterling was to deliver on August 1. Bristol was to pay half the purchase price upon delivery and pay the balance ten days later. Sterling identified the equipment to the contract on July 1. Under the relevant state law, a creditor with a judgment may acquire a judicial lien on goods of the judgment debtor merely by filing a notice in a designated office of the county in which the debtor is located.

A. On July 15, Lacy, a creditor with a judgment against Bristol, acquired a judicial lien on Bristol's goods by filing a notice in the public records in the county where Bristol is located. On August 1, Sterling tendered delivery but Bristol did not tender the payment due upon delivery. Sterling refused to allow Bristol to take the equipment. As between Lacy and Sterling, who has superior rights to the equipment?

B. On July 15, Lacy, a creditor with a judgment against Bristol, acquired a judicial lien on Bristol's goods by filing a notice in the public records in the county where Bristol is located. On August 1, Sterling repudiated its obligation to deliver the equipment. Bristol desperately needs the equipment and cannot get any other replacement equipment,

---

security interest in these circumstances would have priority over the lien creditor's lien because the Seller's security interest is deemed perfected. *See* UCC § 9-317(a), (e).

given the specially manufactured nature of this equipment. As between Lacy and Sterling, who has superior rights to the equipment?

C. On August 1, Sterling tendered delivery of the equipment, Bristol made the required payment with a check, and Bristol took possession of the equipment. On August 5, Sterling learned that the check had been dishonored by Bristol's bank. On August 6, Lacy, a creditor with a judgment against Bristol, acquired a judicial lien on Bristol's goods by filing a notice in the public records in the county where Bristol is located. Sterling demanded that Bristol return the goods. As between Sterling and Lacy, who has superior rights to the equipment?

C. Seller Against Buyer's Secured Creditor

One of the requirements for a security interest to attach is that the debtor have rights in the collateral. Thus, unless the Buyer has a property interest in the goods, the Buyer will not be able to grant an effective security interest in the goods to its secured creditor. Therefore, until the goods are identified to the contract of sale between the Buyer and Seller, a secured creditor of the Buyer could not have a security interest in the goods. In short, prior to identification, there can be no priority contest at all. Seller has the only property interest.

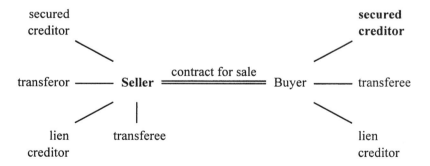

After identification of the goods to the contract, the Buyer can transfer a security interest in the goods, even if the goods remain in the possession of the Seller. Nevertheless, until the Seller delivers them, the Seller will remain the principal owner of the goods. UCC § 2-401. In such situations, the Seller's rights have priority over the rights of the Buyer's secured creditor under the derivation principle embodied in section 2-403(1): the Buyer may transfer to the secured creditor only those rights the Buyer has. Because the Buyer is subject to the Seller's rights to keep possession or stop delivery, the Buyer's secured party is subject to those rights as well. *See* UCC § 9-110, cmt. 5.

The results are substantially different if the Seller has delivered the goods to the Buyer and is seeking to reclaim them under section 2-507 or 2-702(2). Those rights of the Seller are subject to the rights of a good faith purchaser for value. *See* UCC §§ 2-403(1), 2-702(3). Because the Buyer's secured creditor – unlike a lien creditor – qualifies as a "purchaser" of the goods under section 1-201(b)(29) and (30) and because the Buyer's debt to the secured creditor constitutes value given, *see* section 1-204(2), the secured creditor will defeat the Seller's reclamation rights as long as the secured creditor has acted in good faith.

What if the Seller claims a security interest in the delivered goods under section 2-401 (retention of title) or 2-505 (shipment under reservation)? As long as the Buyer does not obtain possession of the goods, the Seller will win over Buyer's secured creditor. UCC § 9-110. After the Buyer gains possession of the goods, the relative priority of the security interests of the Seller and the Buyer's secured creditor is a matter governed by Article 9, not by Article 2. There are things the Seller may be able to do to attain priority. However, that discussion is very complex and beyond the scope of this course. Full exploration awaits you in a course on secured transactions.

Problem 10-7

Sterling Manufacturing agreed to sell specially manufactured equipment to Bristol for $100,000. Sterling was to deliver on August 1. Bristol was to pay half the purchase price upon delivery and pay the balance ten days later. Sterling identified the equipment to the contract on July 1. Bristol granted SP a security interest in all of its equipment to secure a loan that SP made to Bristol.

A. On July 2, as between SP and Sterling, who has superior rights to the equipment?

B. Sterling tendered delivery on August 1 and Bristol paid the required payment with a check. Bristol then took possession of the equipment. On August 5, Sterling found out the check had been dishonored by

Bristol's bank. As between SP and Sterling, who has superior rights to the equipment?

CHAPTER ELEVEN

LEASES

SECTION 1.   SCOPE

A. Overview

We now turn our attention to another important type of commercial transaction: leases of goods. Article 2A of the Uniform Commercial Code, as enacted by the states, governs leases of goods. It is of comparatively recent vintage (1989) compared to other articles of the UCC and is modeled on Article 2 (thus it is inserted between Articles 2 and 3). While many of the provisions in Article 2A are similar or identical to the analogous rules of Article 2, there are also many that are different. In addition, several provisions in each article have no analog in the other. The differences between the two articles are designed to account for the differences between lease and sale transactions and the business practices associated with them. Because there is so much similarity between Articles 2 and 2A, it would be overly time consuming and somewhat repetitive to now study all of Article 2A. Instead, this Chapter focuses on the differences between them.

The place to start the discussion is with the distinction between a lease and a sale. Recall that a sale is defined as the passing of title to the goods from the seller to the buyer for a price. UCC § 2-106(1). Now read the definition of a lease in section 2A-103(1)(j). Notice that instead of passing title, a lease is the transfer of more limited property rights, the right to possess or use the goods[1] for a term. The critical distinction is that in a lease transaction, the lessor has the right to get the goods back at the end of the lease term. This fundamental difference underlies all the differences in the law governing the two transactions, particularly in the parties' remedies for breach and their rights against third parties' property-based claims to the goods.

---

[1] Compare the definition of goods in section 2-105(1) with the definition of goods in section 2A-103(1)(h). Can you explain the reasons for the differences?

B. Distinguishing a Lease from a Sale

Unfortunately, the distinction between a lease and a sale is often much easier to state than to apply. Consider a transaction in which a merchant leases a new laptop computer to a customer for 99 years. The transaction *purports* to be a lease. The merchant has the *right* to get the computer back at the end of the lease term. But what are the economic realities? Putting aside the fact that both parties will likely have passed away long before the lease term ends, the reality is that the computer too will have died. Personal computers simply do not have a useful life anywhere near that long. Even if the computer still functions, it will no doubt be hopelessly antiquated due to technological advancements in the interim. We may not know now what those advancements will be, but we can predict with reasonable certainty that the computer will have minimal or no value after 99 years. Indeed, it may have negative value due to the cost of disposal. So, is the transaction a lease or really a sale?

Before trying to answer that question, it is important to understand that the consequences of the distinction are legion. First, if it is a sale, then Article 2 applies. If it is a lease, then Article 2A applies. Given the similarity between those two articles, that distinction will often not matter much. However, the following other consequences, which are noted on the chart below, may matter greatly.

First, there are significant tax and accounting consequences to the distinction. For example, if the transaction is a true lease, then the lessor is the tax owner and may claim any depreciation deduction. Moreover, the rent would be income to the lessor and potentially a deductible expense for the lessee. On the other hand, if the transaction is a sale, the putative lessee – who is really a buyer – would be the tax owner of the goods and may claim any available depreciation allowance. The rental payments would not be deductible by the lessee or income to the lessor. Instead, the lessor – as a seller – may have recognizable gain or loss on the sale.

Second, if the lessee seeks bankruptcy protection, the characterization of the transaction will greatly affect what happens to the goods. If the transaction is a lease, the goods may be retained by the lessee only if the lease contract is performed according to its terms. If the transaction is a sale, it may be possible for the lessee/buyer to keep the goods while paying the lessor/seller over time either the amounts due under the lease or the value of the goods, whichever is less.

Third, and perhaps most important, if the transaction is really a sale, then not only will Article 2 govern, but so too will Article 9. That is because of the rule of section 2-401(1). As we have already seen, reservation of title by a seller of goods is limited in effect to the retention of a security interest. In a transaction structured as a lease, the lessor retains title. If the economic realities are such that the putative lease is really a sale, then the seller's/lessor's retention of title (by structuring the transaction as a lease) is limited to a security interest.

The potential application of Article 9 to the transaction is very important, particularly to the putative lessor. That is because a true lessor need not provide public notice of its property rights in the goods to be protected against the rights of the lessee's creditors. However, if the transaction is a sale, and putative lessor is therefore really a seller and a secured party, it must perfect its security interest, typically by filing a financing statement in the designated state office.[2]

THE SIGNIFICANCE OF THE SALE/LEASE DISTINCTION

	Sale & Security Interest (structured as a lease)	True Lease
Governing Law	Articles 2 & 9	Article 2A
Tax/Accounting Depreciation Allowance	Buyer/Lessee	Lessor
Tax/Accounting Payments	No effect.	Income to Lessor and deduction to Lessee.
Rights of Creditors of Buyer/Lessee	Can potentially get goods if Lessor/Seller did not perfect a security interest.	Cannot get goods, may be able to attach rights to lessee's leasehold interest.
Effect of Bankruptcy by Buyer/Lessee	If Lessor/Seller perfected its security interest, its property rights are protected but can be modified. Lessor/Seller entitled to lesser of debt or value of goods.	Lessor entitled to have all lease obligations performed or the goods returned.

---

[2] Article 9 allows a lessor/seller to file a financing statement in order to protect itself in the event the transaction is determined to be a sale with a security interest. The filing itself cannot be used as evidence that the transaction is in fact a sale. UCC § 9-505.

The law could have allowed the parties' designation of their transaction to control. It could have provided that a transaction structured as a lease will be treated as a lease and a transaction structured as a sale will be treated as a sale. It could have, but it did not. *See* UCC §§ 2A-102, 9-109(a)(1) (both indicating that the form of a transaction is not determinative of whether the Article applies). Instead, section 1-203 contains some rather complicated rules to determine whether a transaction is a sale or a lease for the purposes of Articles 2, 2A and 9.[3] These rules are based on the economic substance of the transaction. Neither form nor intent controls.

Read section 1-203. Subsection (a) informs us that the determination is a factual one. What it fails to do is actually state what the test is. Nevertheless, based on the remainder of the section and the comments, it is clear that the key issue here is whether there is a reasonable chance that the lessor will get the goods back when the goods still have meaningful economic value.[4] If the answer is yes, then the leasing structure of the transaction will be respected and the deal will be treated as a lease. If the answer is no, either because it is very unlikely that the lessor will ever get the goods back or because the goods will have no significant value when the lessor does get them, then the transaction will be treated as a sale with a retained security interest. The rules of subsection (c), (d), and (e) occasionally provide some help in making this assessment.

Subsection (b) provides a test, that if met, means that the transaction is a sale with a retained security interest. It is a sort of safe harbor rule. If the test is not met, then the analysis reverts to the factual test in subsection (a).

Problem 11-1

Consider the following transactions in which an equipment dealer "leases" a new $200,000 skid loader to a construction company. The construction company is responsible for all maintenance and insurance on the skid loader. The construction company is obligated to pay the entire $200,000 price even if it returns the skid loader to the dealer before the end of the "lease" term. In which of these scenarios, if any, is the transaction really a sale?

---

[3] The distinction between a sale and a lease for tax purposes will be governed by tax law.

[4] *See* Edwin E. Huddleson, III, *Old Wine in New Bottles: UCC Article 2A-Leases*, 39 ALA. L. REV. 615, 625 (1988).

A. A 5-year lease at $3,900 per month (paying $3,900/month for five years amortizes, *i.e.*, pays off, a $200,000 debt with 6% interest.)
   1. The dealer gets the skid loader at the end of the "lease" term.
   2. The construction company has an option to buy for $5,000 at the end of the "lease" term.
   3. The construction company has an option to buy for $100 at the end of the "lease" term.

B. A 25-year lease at $2,000 per month. The dealer gets the skid loader at the end of the 25 years.

C. How, if at all, does the analysis change in any of the scenarios if the construction company may return the skid loader to the equipment dealer before the end of the lease term without any further obligation to make any remaining monthly payments?

C. Finance Leases

A transaction that is a true lease may also be used as a financing mechanism when it is a "finance lease." While the definition in section 2A-103(1)(g) is very long, the basic concept of a finance lease is very simple. The lessee picks out the goods from a supplier based upon the lessee's specifications. The finance lessor (typically a bank or other entity that has agreed to finance the transaction) buys the goods from the supplier. That transaction is governed by Article 2 as a sale of goods. The finance lessor then leases the goods to the finance lessee pursuant to a finance lease.[5]

Perhaps an illustration may help. In a traditional lease, the lessee deals directly with the lessor. In doing so, the lessee may obtain needed financing from a lender and may grant the lender a security interest in the leased goods to secure that loan:

---

[5] The lease between the finance lessor and the finance lessee must qualify as a "true" lease under section 1-203, or it will be treated as a sale and secured transaction.

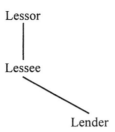

In a finance lease, the lender assumes the role of lessor, by purchasing or leasing the goods from the supplier and then leasing them to the lessee. The form of the transaction is depicted on the left below, but its substance more closely resembles the structure on the right.

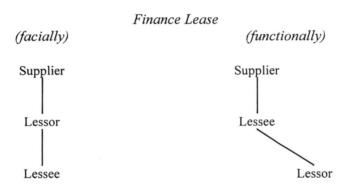

The lessor in a finance lease does not want to accept any responsibility for the quality of the goods. The lessor's role is really just to provide financing to the lessee.[6] Rather, it is the supplier to whom the lessee expects to look for the warranties and other quality assurances regarding the functioning of the goods. Article 2A accommodates this economic reality by having special rules applicable

---

[6] Although the finance lessor is in essence providing financing to enable the lessee to obtain the goods, the transaction between the lessor and lessee must be a true lease under the test in section 1-203 in order to qualify as a finance lease, that is the finance lessor must have a meaningful residual economic interest in the goods. Because the finance lessor will have that residual interest, but does not actually want the goods back, the finance lease generally provides that the lessee may purchase the lessor's interest at the end of the lease term for a fair market value price.

to finance leases. As a result, throughout Article 2A, some provisions apply to all leases and some provisions apply only to finance leases.

D. Intersection with other Laws

A lease of goods often involves motor vehicles that are subject to a certificate of title law. Article 2A generally defers to the provisions of that other law. See UCC §§ 2A-104, 2A-105. Transactions subject to Article 2A may also be covered by consumer protection law. Again, Article 2A generally defers to that other law. UCC § 2A-104.

However, it is worth noting that many of the laws we considered in Chapter Eight, such as the Magnuson-Moss Warranty Act and state lemon laws, may not apply to leases. Moreover, even if a transaction in the form of a lease would be re-characterized as a sale for the purposes of Articles 2, 2A, and 9, other law may not abide by that re-characterization and may still regard the transaction as a lease and outside the other law's scope. This is yet another reason why sellers may choose to structure their transactions as leases: to avoid application of some laws, particularly consumer protection laws. Accordingly, lawyers need to thoroughly understand whether and how other laws in their jurisdiction apply to leases or to sales structured as leases.

Until recently, leases of goods have been fairly localized transactions. Perhaps because of that, neither the CISG, which governs many international sales of goods, nor any other international convention governs leases of goods. To the extent the parties wanted to adopt the UNIDROIT Principles of International Commercial Contracts, they could do so in a lease transaction.[7]

---

[7] UNIDROIT has sponsored a project to develop a Draft Model Law on Leasing. *See* www.unidroit.org.

SECTION 2.　LEASE FORMATION

A.　Basic Formation Principles

Analogous Provisions	
Article 2	Article 2A
§ 1-201(b)(3)	§ 2A-103(1)(k)
§ 1-201(b)(12)	§ 2A-103(1)(*l*)
§ 2-204	§ 2A-204
§ 2-205	§ 2A-205
§ 2-206	§ 2A-206
§ 2-207	n/a

Article 2A contains provisions on contract formation that are very similar to the Article 2 provisions on that subject. First, the definitions of "lease agreement" and "lease contract" in section 2A-103(1)(k) and (*l*) largely mirror the definitions of "agreement" and "contract" in section 1-201. Second, the rules in sections 2-204 through 2-206 are largely replicated in sections 2A-204 through 2A-206, with one exception. Section 2A-206 does not contain an equivalent to section 2-206(1)(b) on formation following an order for prompt or current shipment. This reflects the differences between how sales agreements are formed and how leases are entered into. Rarely do prospective lessees submit orders to lease goods. Even more rare would be for a lessor to respond to such an order by simply shipping the goods. Instead, lease transactions usually involve greater interaction and negotiation between the lessor and the lessee. In particular, they need to determine the length of the lease term, which party will be responsible for maintenance and insurance, and various other terms. It is this difference in the practices surrounding formation that explains why Article 2A also has no analog to the battle-of-the-forms rules in section 2-207. Leases are usually the product of negotiation, not an exchange of standard forms.

That is not to say that a lease transaction cannot be entered into through electronic interaction. As we learned in covering Article 2, the provisions of the Uniform Electronic Transactions Act (if enacted in the relevant state) and the federal E-Sign statute (15 U.S.C. § 7001) permit parties to use electronic communications and E-Sign provides some consumer protections to ensure the consumer has assented to electronic communication. These provisions apply to transactions governed by Article 2A just as they applied to transactions governed by Article 2.[8]

With these exceptions – no equivalent to section 2-106(1)(b), section 2-207, or the CISG – all we have learned about the formation of sales contracts is relevant to the formation of a lease contract under Article 2A. Article 2A does not add any additional rules on contract formation that are unique to the lease transaction.

B. Statute of Frauds

Analogous Provisions	
Article 2	Article 2A
§ 2-201	§ 2A-201

As we learned in Chapter Two, Article 2 requires some agreements for the sale of goods (those for more than $500) to satisfy the statute of frauds in order to be enforceable. UCC § 2-201. Article 2A has a statute of frauds that is modeled on the one in Article 2, but has some significant differences. Read section 2A-201.

Problem 11-2

Identify all the differences between the statute of frauds section 2-201 and section 2A-201 other than one governs a sale transaction and the other governs a lease transaction.

C. Unconscionability

Analogous Provisions	
Article 2	Article 2A
§ 2-302	§ 2A-108(1), (3)
n/a	§ 2A-108(2), (4)

---

[8] UETA § 3; E-Sign, 15 U.S.C. § 7003(a).

The concept of unconscionability is an important control on overreaching by a contracting party. The basic principle, articulated in section 2-302, that courts need not enforce unconscionable agreements or terms, is repeated in section 2A-108(1) and (3). Article 2A adds to this basic rule some additional protections for "consumer leases," a term defined in section 2A-103(1)(e). Read that definition. The additional protections, which are found in section 2A-108(2) and (4) focus on "procedural" unconscionability and provide relief if unconscionable conduct induced the contract or occurred in collecting on a claim arising from the lease contract. In those situations, there is no requirement that the consumer lease agreement be substantively unconscionable for relief to be available. Article 2A also differs from Article 2 by expressly providing for a consumer lessee who prevails on a claim of unconscionability to recover reasonable attorney's fees. *See* UCC § 2A-108(4).

SECTION 3.   LEASE TERMS

A. Agreement and Contract

Article 2A is based upon the same fundamental concepts of "agreement" and "contract" that underlie Article 2. Thus, the bargain in fact of the parties, as augmented by the Article 2A gap fillers, will comprise the lease contract. Review the definitions of "lease agreement" and "lease contract" in section 2A-103. The concepts of usage of trade, course of dealing and course of performance are just as relevant to an Article 2A transaction as they are to an Article 2 transaction. *See* UCC §§ 1-303 and 2A-207. Similarly, every Article 2A transaction is subject to the good faith obligation stated in section 1-304.

Unlike Article 2, however, Article 2A has relatively few gap-filler provisions. Notably absent are any provisions that are comparable to the following sections of Article 2:

> § 2-304 (how price payable);
> § 2-305 (open price term);
> § 2-306 (output and requirements contracts);
> § 2-307 (delivery in single lot);
> § 2-308 (place of delivery);
> § 2-309 (time for performance);
> § 2-310 (time for payment);
> § 2-311 (cooperation respecting performance);

§ 2-503 and § 2-504 (tender of delivery); and

§ 2-505 (shipment under reservation).

Most of these omissions can be explained by the fact that lease agreements tend to be more complete than sales agreements. The parties do not generally, as a matter of practice, rely on gap fillers when entering into a lease. Instead, the parties tend to have express terms addressing the numerous items that may be addressed by the Article 2 gap fillers. Another reason why Article 2A lacks gap fillers on these subjects is that lease agreements have no nearly universal way of dealing with many of them, and thus there is no obvious choice for what the gap filler rule would be. In particular it may not make sense to apply the gap-filler provisions in Article 2 to the different rights and obligations of the parties in a lease transaction.

Remember, however, that a lease transaction is based upon contract principles, just as a sale transaction is. To the extent that Article 2A does not explicitly displace the common-law principles of contract law, those principles may help fill in the gaps in Article 2A. UCC § 1-103.

In addition to the protection for consumer lessees in section 2A-108 regarding unconscionability, Article 2A contains a restriction on two typical contract clauses: choice of law and choice of forum. Read UCC § 2A-106. This restriction is applicable to consumer leases, UCC § 2A-103(1)(e). As stated in the comment, however, this section does not restrict the parties' ability to choose a nonjudicial forum such as arbitration. Thus clauses providing that the parties have agreed to arbitrate all disputes would be enforceable, if enforceable under otherwise applicable contract law.

B. Warranties

Analogous Provisions	
Article 2	Article 2A
n/a	§ 2A-209
§ 2-312	§ 2A-211
§ 2-313	§ 2A-210
§ 2-314	§ 2A-212
§ 2-315	§ 2A-213
§ 2-316	§ 2A-214(1)–(3)

Analogous Provisions	
Article 2	Article 2A
n/a	§ 2A-214(4)
§ 2-317	§ 2A-215
§ 2-318	§ 2A-216

Article 2A contains the same three warranties of quality that are found in Article 2: express warranty, section 2A-210; implied warranty of merchantability, section 2A-212; and the implied warranty of fitness for a particular purpose, section 2A-213. There are no material differences between the express warranty provisions in section 2A-210 and section 2-313. The substance of the implied merchantability warranty and the implied warranty of fitness for a particular purpose in Article 2A are also the same as the comparable provisions in Article 2, with one exception.

In a finance lease, the finance lessor does not make either implied warranty. *See* UCC §§ 2A-212(1), 2A-213. A finance lessor could make an express warranty, including an *express* warranty of merchantability or fitness for a particular purpose, but that would be unusual. The reason that a finance lessor does not make either of the *implied* warranties, and does not normally make express warranties, is that the finance lessor is really just a lender: someone providing the funds necessary to purchase or obtain the goods from the supplier and then is charging the finance lessee for the use and possession of those goods. Instead, the finance lessee typically looks to the supplier of the goods (the party that provided the goods to the finance lessor) for its remedies. Section 2A-209 therefore provides that the implied warranties that would normally accompany the supplier's transaction with the finance lessor – whether under Article 2 or Article 2A – flow directly to the finance lessee. Review the definition of "finance lease" in section 2A-103(1)(g), read section 2A-209, and then try the following problem.

Problem 11-3

Sensational Electronics manufactures computer servers for use in networks. Lasting Data operates a data storage business that relies heavily on computer servers. Three months ago, Lasting Data began negotiating with Sensational Electronics to acquire 30 new servers. The parties had a draft agreement that included several express warranties and disclaimed any implied warranty of fitness for particular purpose. When it became clear that the cost of the servers was more than Lasting Data could afford out of its operating funds and existing bank line of credit, Lasting Data approached Boston Finance for assistance. Boston Finance agreed to purchase the servers from Sensational Electronics and then lease the servers to Lasting Data. Boston Finance reviewed the draft agreement between Sensational Electronics and Lasting Data, made a few changes to the risk of loss provisions, and then Boston Finance and Sensational Electronics executed the agreement. On the same day, Boston Finance and Lasting Data executed an agreement by which Lasting Data leased the servers from Boston Finance. After the servers were delivered and installed at Lasting Data's facility, several of the servers malfunctioned.

A. Which warranties, if any, did Sensational Finance make to Lasting Data regarding the servers?

B. Which warranties, if any, did Boston Finance make to Lasting Data regarding the servers?

C. How, if at all, would the analysis of Parts A and B change if the agreement between Sensational Electronics and Boston Finance was a lease agreement rather than a sale?

D. How, if at all, would the analysis of Parts A and B change if the agreement between Boston Finance and Lasting Data obligated Lasting Data to purchase the servers at the end of the lease term?

Just as a seller of goods may disclaim all implied warranties of quality, if it follows the requirements of section 2-316, so too may a lessor disclaim all of the implied warranties of quality in the lease transaction. To do so, the lessor must comply with section 2A-214. The first three subsections of section 2A-214 follow fairly closely the requirements found in section 2-316.

Article 2A also follows the Article 2 model on extending warranties to persons lacking privity with the lessor. *Compare* UCC § 2-318 *with* UCC § 2A-216.[9]

---

[9] This extension of warranty protection to persons other than the lessee is different from and in addition to the rules in section 2A-209, which extend a supplier's warranties to the finance lessee in finance lessee.

Under section 2A-216, if the lessee is a beneficiary of a warranty, that section determines whether someone other than the lessee has the benefit of the warranty.

A lessor in a lease transaction makes a warranty of non-infringement that is substantially similar to the warranty of non-infringement in a sale of goods. *Compare* UCC § 2A-211(2), (3) *with* UCC § 2-312(3). In addition, under section 2A-211, the lessor makes a transfer warranty that is analogous to a seller's warranty of title. Of course, because a lease transaction is not a transfer of all of the property rights in the goods, merely the right to use and possess the goods, the lessor warrants merely that no one has a claim arising from an interaction with the lessor that will interfere with the lessee's rights under the lease. Finally, unlike Article 2, Article 2A contains an explicit provision on how to disclaim the warranty of non-interference and the warranty of non-infringement. UCC § 2A-214(4).

C. Finance Leases and the Obligation to Pay

We have already seen that warranties flow somewhat differently in a finance lease than in an ordinary lease or in a sale transaction. The other important difference between an ordinary lease and a finance lease concerns the lessee's payment obligation. This difference reflects the fact that the finance lessor is really only a lender, providing the financing necessary for the lessee to acquire the use and possession of the goods from the supplier. Accordingly, unless the finance lessor makes an express warranty concerning the goods – which would be uncommon – the finance lessor has no responsibility for the functioning of the goods. A corollary to this is that the finance lessor wants to be paid by the lessee regardless of whether the goods are satisfactory or defective. The finance lessor expects the lessee to look to the supplier if there are any problems with the goods, but expects the lessee to pay regardless. Read section 2A-407. The import of that section is that, once the lessee accepts the goods, the lessee's promise to pay becomes irrevocable and independent of the promises of the supplier and the lessor regarding the functioning of the goods or of the lessor's performance obligations. This obligation to pay is called a "hell or high water" term, because the lessee has promised to pay come "hell or high water" (in other words, without exception or excuse). Section 2A-407 makes this a presumed term (a gap filler) in a finance lease that is not a consumer lease.[10] In a consumer lease, the parties may contract for a similar term unless precluded by some law other than Article 2A.

Problem 11-4

Return to Problem 11-3.

A. How does section 2A-407 affect Lasting Data's obligations under the lease with Boston Finance?

B. You represent Boston Finance and are drafting the lease agreement for the transaction with Lasting Data. Is there anything you should put in the lease agreement to supplement the rules in section 2A-407? If so, what should you put in and why? *See Wells Fargo Bank Minnesota, N.A. v. B.C.B.U.*, 49 Cal. Rptr. 3d 324 (Cal. Ct. App. 2006).

D. Remedy Limitations

Analogous Provisions	
Article 2	Article 2A
§ 2-718	§ 2A-504
§ 2-719	§ 2A-503

A lease agreement may limit the remedies normally available for breach. The rules in Article 2A regarding remedy limitations are very similar to the analogous rules in Article 2, but there are a few notable differences. First, section 2A-503(2) provides that if a remedy limitation is unconscionable, then the limitation is not enforceable. This result is implicit in Article 2, but not stated expressly. *See* UCC § 2A-503 cmt. 2. Second, section 2A-503(3) expressly provides that consequential

---

[10] Because the UCC does not displace many common-law doctrines, *see* UCC § 1-103(b), a lessee may be able to prevent enforcement of a hell-or-high-water clause in the agreement and prevent application of the rules of section 2A-407. *See Faust Printing, Inc. v. MAN Capital Corp.*, 2007 WL 4442325 (N.D. Ill. 2007) (fraudulent inducement claim may be basis to avoid liability under a "hell or high water" clause of a finance lease).

damages may be either liquidated pursuant to section 2A-504 or limited pursuant to section 2A-503. In contrast, section 2-719(3) expressly provides that consequential damages may be limited but does not expressly state that they may be liquidated, although that right is probably available under section 2-718(1).

Third, and far more significant, is that the standard for the enforceability of a liquidated damages clause is different. Section 2A-504 requires that liquidated damages be reasonable in light of anticipated harm, whereas section 2-718 allows the parties to liquidate damages as long as the measure is reasonable in light of either anticipated or actual harm and the difficulty of obtaining an otherwise adequate remedy.

E. Parol Evidence

Analogous Provisions	
Article 2	Article 2A
§ 2-202	§ 2A-202

As we learned in Chapter Five, the parol evidence rule in section 2-202 helps ensure the primacy of writings by limiting the evidence that a party to a sales contract may submit to supplement or contradict a writing that at least partially integrates the parties' agreement. Article 2A has an almost identical parol evidence rule. *Compare* UCC § 2A-202 *with* § 2-202.

F. Modification

Analogous Provisions	
Article 2	Article 2A
§ 2-209	§ 2A-208

In Chapter Three, we examined the several principles on modification contained in section 2-209. A modification needs no consideration to be binding, the parties may have an effective no-oral-modification clause (a clause that prevents subsequent modification except through a signed writing), an ineffective attempt to modify may operate as a waiver, and in certain circumstances a waiver may be retracted. *See* UCC § 2-209. Section 2A-208 contains each of these rules. The only difference between section 2A-208 and section 2-209 is that the former has no analog to section 2-209(3) on the relationship between the modification and the statute of frauds. The comment to section 2A-208 notes that the courts should resolve on a case-by-case basis the impact of an oral modification on a lease that otherwise satisfies the statute of frauds, noting that enforcing the modification might sometimes be inappropriate but that enforcing the lease as it was prior to the modification might occasionally be even worse.

SECTION 4. PERFORMANCE ISSUES

A. Insecurity and Repudiation

Analogous Provisions	
Article 2	Article 2A
§ 2-609	§ 2A-401
§ 2-610	§ 2A-402
§ 2-611	§ 2A-403

Article 2A approaches reasonable grounds for insecurity and the ability to request adequate assurance in the same manner as Article 2. *Compare* UCC § 2-609 *with* § 2A-401. The aggrieved party's ability to deal with a repudiation in a lease contract is the same as an aggrieved party's ability to deal with a repudiation in a sales contract. *Compare* UCC §§ 2-610, 2-611 *with* § 2A-402, 2A-403. Thus the concepts discussed in Chapter Six regarding insecurity, adequate assurance, and repudiation are equally relevant to the lease transaction.

B. Risk of Loss and Insurance Absent Breach

Analogous Provisions	
Article 2	Article 2A
§ 2-501	§ 2A-218
§ 2-509	§ 2A-219

The risk of loss rules for leases of goods are substantially different from the risk of loss rules for sales. This difference is probably attributable to the different types of property interests at stake. In a sales contract, the property rights to the goods pass from the seller to the buyer. While there may be a period of time when both parties have property rights in the goods, that period is likely to be relatively short (at least in relationship to the useful life of the goods). Thus, the purpose of rules on risk of loss is to determine when the risk of loss passes from the original holder of all the property rights (the seller) to the new holder of the property rights (the buyer). In lease contracts, however, both parties will have property rights in the goods for the entire lease period. So, risk of loss rules are less concerned with when risk of loss passes from one party to the other and more concerned with how to allocate the risk of loss between the parties during the term of the lease.

You might think that the logical way to handle this would be for the risk of loss to be shared between the parties, with the lessor bearing the risk to the extent of its residual interest in the goods and the lessee bearing the risk to the extent of its leasehold interest in the goods. However, that is not the approach the drafters took. You might then think that the lessee should have the entire risk of loss because the lessee is the one with custody of the goods. That might make sense, but it too is not what Article 2A provides. Instead, for leases other than finance leases, the lessor retains the risk of loss. UCC § 2A-219(1). Bear in mind, however, that the parties are free by agreement to alter this rule, *see* UCC § 1-302, and they frequently do. Many lease agreements place the risk of loss on the lessee during the lease term.

In a finance lease, however, the default rule is that the risk of loss does pass to the lessee. If neither party is in default, the risk of loss will pass to the finance lessee at one of the times stated in section 2A-219(2). These times for passage of the risk of loss are largely the same as those in section 2-509, with a couple of minor differences. First, it contains only one time for the risk of loss to pass when the goods are held by a bailee and to be delivered without being moved. *Compare* UCC § 2-509(2) *with* § 2A-219(2)(b). This may be because documents of title are not usually used in delivering goods to the lessee in a lease transaction. Second, in a finance lease, the risk of loss passes when the lessee receives the goods if the *supplier*, not the *lessor*, is a merchant. This mirrors the rule from Article 2 which focuses on the merchant status of the seller, but takes into account the supplier's role in the transaction. *Compare* UCC § 2-509(3) *with* § 2A-219(2)(c).

Irrespective of the risk of loss, the lessee acquires an insurable interest in the goods once the goods are identified to the lease contract. UCC §§ 2A-218(1), (2), 2A-217. Because the lessor retains property rights in the goods, the lessor also retains an insurable interest in the goods even if the lessee has acquired possession of them. UCC § 2A-218(3). The lessor loses its insurable interest in the goods if and when the lessee exercises an option to buy the goods. UCC § 2A-218(3). The parties may agree which party must insure the goods and who has a right to proceeds of that insurance. UCC § 2A-218(5).

C. Excuse

Analogous Provisions	
Article 2	Article 2A
§ 2-613	§ 2A-221
§ 2-614	§ 2A-404
§ 2-615	§ 2A-405
§ 2-616	§ 2A-406

In Chapter Six, we considered the ability of the seller or the buyer in a sales transaction to be excused from its contract obligations. Article 2A follows the Article 2 model with few changes. Section 2A-221, the lease analog to section 2-613, deals with the lessor's excuse when the lease contract requires the particular goods that are identified to the contract when the contract is made. The Article 2A rule appears to operate the same as the Article 2 rule except that if the lease is a finance lease that is not a consumer lease, the lessee, if it chooses to take the goods, does not get an allowance for the damage to the goods to offset against the rent due. In other words, in that situation, the finance lessee who accepts the goods is going to have to pay full rent. This result is consistent with the hell-or-high-water rule in section 2A-407.

Section 2A-404 follows the model from section 2-614 regarding shipping and payment substitutions without substantive change. Sections 2A-405 and 2A-406 follow the same principles as sections 2-615 and 2-616 in allowing a lessor, or a supplier in a finance lease transaction, to seek excuse based upon commercial impracticability. Again, the one difference in treatment between the sale transaction and the lease transaction is that in a finance lease that is not a consumer lease, the finance lessee who accepts part of the quota allocated to it is still obligated to pay the entire amount of the lease payments, instead of only an allocable share.

D. Assignment and Delegation

Analogous Provisions	
Article 2	Article 2A
§ 2-210	§ 2A-303

The lessor has two basic rights under a lease contract: the right to the residual interest in the goods and the right to the rental payments. If the lessor assigns the right to payment (with or without the residual interest in the goods), that assignment is a secured transaction subject to Article 9. *See* UCC § 9-109. Generally, clauses in the lease agreement that purport to prohibit the lessor from assigning its rights under the lease are not effective to prevent the transfer from taking effect or to create an event of default that would give the lessee remedies for the lessor's breach. UCC §§ 2A-303(2), 9-406(d), 9-407.

The lessee has the right to possession of the goods that are the subject of the lease. If the lease contract makes transfer of that right a default under the lease, but the lessee transfers that right anyway, then the lessor may exercise its remedies against the lessee. UCC § 2A-303(4)(a). If the lease contract does not make such a transfer a default, but merely prohibits it (a very unlikely circumstance), the transfer is effective unless a damage award against the lessee would not be adequate, in which case the lessor can obtain a court order disallowing the transfer. UCC § 2A-303(4)(b). The lessee of course also has the duty to pay rent. Even if the lessee effectively delegates this duty to someone else, the lessee is not released from the obligation. UCC § 2A-303(6). This is the same rule that appears in section 2-210(1).

SECTION 5.   LESSOR'S DEFAULT AND LESSEE'S REMEDIES

A. Overview

Analogous Provisions	
Article 2	Article 2A
n/a	§ 2A-502
§ 2-711	§ 2A-508

The lessee's right to exercise remedies is keyed to the lessor's default under the lease contract as determined by the parties' agreement and Article 2A. UCC § 2A-501. The lessor's typical defaults are a repudiation of a lease contract, a failure to deliver the goods, or delivery of goods that do not conform to the contract. *See* UCC § 2A-508. The lessee has no general obligation to notify the lessor of the default, but this rule is subject to several exceptions and can be modified by the terms of the agreement. UCC § 2A-502. The lessee's remedies are catalogued in section 2A-508. The lessee may also have additional remedies pursuant to the lease agreement. As is true in Article 2, the focus in Article 2A is on putting the aggrieved lessee in the same position it would have been in if the lessor had fully performed. UCC § 1-305.

B. Lessor's Failure to Deliver

Analogous Provisions	
Article 2	Article 2A
§ 2-502	§ 2A-522
§ 2-612	§ 2A-510
§ 2-712	§ 2A-518
§ 2-713	§ 2A-519
§ 2-715	§ 2A-520
§ 2-716	§ 2A-521
§ 2-723	§ 2A-507(1)–(3)
§ 2-724	§ 2A-507(4)

When the lessor fails to deliver the goods or repudiates the lease contract before the delivery date, the lessee has to choose whether to attempt to obtain the goods from the lessor or cancel the contract and seek damages. If the lessee wants to obtain the goods from the lessor, the lessee may do so through specific performance or replevin, just as a buyer in a sales contract may seek specific performance or replevin from the seller. The standard for granting such relief is largely the same. *Compare* UCC § 2-716 *with* § 2A-521. A pre-paying lessee has the right to recover identified goods if the lessor became insolvent within ten days after the lessee has made the first payment. UCC § 2A-522. This rule mirrors the rule in section

2-502(1)(b) for pre-paying buyers. However, the protection for a pre-paying consumer buyer contained in section 2-502(1)(a) has no analog in section 2A-522.

If the lease is *not* an installment lease contract, the lessee may respond to the lessor's failure to deliver by canceling the contract. UCC § 2A-508(1)(a), 2A-505. In contrast, if the lease is an installment lease contract – that is, a lease that calls for delivery in separate lots, UCC § 2A-103(1)(i) – the lessee may cancel the contract only if the lessor's default substantially impairs of the value of the entire contract. *See* UCC § 2A-510(2).

The lessee may, of course, also seek damages for the lessor's failure to deliver the goods. These remedies are very similar to a buyer's remedies for nondelivery. First, the lessee may recover the rent that has been paid. UCC § 2A-508(1)(b). In addition, the lessee may cover and obtain damages based upon the cover price, UCC § 2A-518, or may seek damages based upon a market price measurement, UCC § 2A-519. On top of this, the lessee is entitled to incidental and consequential damages. UCC § 2A-520.

Computation of the lessee's cover damages is complicated because the lessee is authorized to cover either by entering into a substitute lease or by purchasing goods similar to those called for by the breached lease. If the lessee enters into a substitute lease that is substantially equivalent to the breached lease, the damages are calculated as the present value of all the rent due under the new lease (for the period that is comparable to the breached lease) minus the present value of all the rent due under the breached lease. UCC § 2A-518(2). Added to this amount are any incidental and consequential damages. Subtracted from this amount are expenses saved as a result of the lessor's breach. If the lessee covers either by entering into a lease that is not substantially similar to the breached contract or by purchasing replacement goods, the lessee's damages are calculated, not based on the cover transaction, but using a market rent formula. UCC § 2A-518(3). Under this market rent formula, the lessee is entitled to the difference between the present value of the market rent minus the present value of the rent under the breached lease, plus incidental and consequential damages, minus expenses saved as a result of the lessor's breach. UCC § 2A-519(1). Market rent is determined at the time of default. UCC § 2A-519(1). Section 2A-507 provides guidance on how to determine the market rent.

C. Lessor's Nonconforming Tender of the Goods

Analogous Provisions	
Article 2	Article 2A
§ 2-508	§ 2A-513
§ 2-513	n/a
§ 2-601	§ 2A-509(1)
§ 2-602(1)	§ 2A-509(2)
§ 2-602(2)(b), (c)	§ 2A-512(1)(a), (c)
§ 2-603	§ 2A-511(1)–(3)
§ 2-604	§ 2A-512(1)(b), (2)
§ 2-605	§ 2A-514
§ 2-606	§ 2A-515
§ 2-607	§ 2A-516
§ 2-608	§ 2A-517
§ 2-706(5)	§ 2A-511(4)

Article 2A uses the same rejection, acceptance, cure, and revocation of acceptance model as does Article 2. If the lessor tenders goods that fail to conform to the contract, the lessee has a right to reject them. UCC § 2A-509. For non-installment contracts, Article 2A follows the perfect tender rule. UCC § 2A-509(1). In installment lease contracts, the lessee may reject the goods only if the nonconformity in the installment substantially impairs the value of that installment and cannot be cured or the lessor fails to give adequate assurance of a cure. UCC § 2A-510. Rejection of the goods must occur within a reasonable time and is ineffective unless the lessee seasonably notifies the lessor. UCC § 2A-509(2). Just as we saw in Chapter Seven when discussing the rights and duties of a rejecting buyer, a lessee who rejects the goods may in some circumstances have to state all ascertainable defects that justify rejection or the lessee will be deemed to have waived them. UCC § 2A-514. The lessee's ability to reject is countered somewhat by the lessor's right to cure. That right to cure is the same as the seller's right to cure under Article 2. *Compare* UCC § 2A-513 *with* § 2-508.

After rejecting the goods, the lessee has an obligation to hold the goods with reasonable care. UCC § 2A-512(1)(a). A merchant lessee has the obligation to follow reasonable instructions from the lessor as to dealing with the goods. UCC

§ 2A-511. In some circumstances, the lessee may sell the goods or otherwise dispose of them without liability to the lessor. UCC §§ 2A-511(2), 2A-512(1)(b). The lessee has a security interest in the goods to secure any prepayments made and may enforce that security interest by disposing of the goods. UCC § 2A-508(5). The purchaser or transferee from these sales will take the goods free of any claim of the lessor or supplier as the case may be. UCC §§ 2A-511, 2A-512. These sections parallel the rules in Article 2.

After a timely and rightful rejection of the goods, the lessor has the same right to cure that a seller has. *Compare* UCC § 2A-513 *with* § 2-508. Absent cure, the lessee will be entitled to recover damages based either upon the cost of cover or the market rent, plus incidental and consequential damages, minus expenses saved as a consequence of the breach. UCC §§ 2A-518, 2A-519, 2A-520.

A lessee has the right to inspect the goods (although there is no section in Article 2A that parallels section 2-513) and will have accepted them if after that time, it fails to timely reject the goods, or it signifies to the lessor or the supplier that the goods are conforming or it will take them in spite of a nonconformity. UCC § 2A-515. Upon acceptance of the goods, the lessee is obligated to pay the rent and may no longer reject the goods. UCC §§ 2A-516(1), (2), 2A-529(1)(a). A lessee who has accepted the goods despite a nonconformity in the goods or tender has a damage remedy for the breach, provided the lessee notifies the lessor (and in a finance lease, the supplier) of breach in a timely manner. UCC 2A-516(3). The damage remedy focuses on the diminishment in the present value of the use of the goods, because that is the loss the lessee has suffered. UCC § 2A-519(3), (4). *Cf.* UCC § 2-714. In addition, the lessee is entitled to recover incidental and consequential damages. In a lease other than a finance lease subject to section 2A-407, the lessee may deduct the damages from the rent owed. UCC § 2A-508(6). *Cf.* UCC § 2-717.

For leases that are not finance leases, the lessee has the same right to revoke acceptance of the goods that a buyer has in a sales transaction. *Compare* UCC § 2A-517 *with* § 2-608. That is, the lessee may revoke acceptance of the goods if the nonconformity substantially impairs the value of the goods and the lessee accepted the goods either on the assumption the nonconformity would be cured or without having discovered the nonconformity due to the lessor's assurances or the difficulty in discovering the problem. The lessee may also revoke acceptance of goods if the lessor defaults (*i.e.*, breaches the lease in a manner that is not related to conformity of the goods) under the lease contract and that default substantially impairs the value of the goods. UCC § 2A-517(2). Of course, the parties are free to expand or contract the lessee's right to revoke. *See* UCC § 2A-517(3).

In a commercial finance lease, the only statutory basis for revocation of acceptance is that the nonconformity substantially impairs the value of the goods and the lessee accepted the goods without discovery of the nonconformity due to the lessor's assurances. UCC §§ 2A-517, 2A-516(2). This restriction on the ability of a finance lessee to revoke acceptance is necessary in order to give effect to the hell-or-high-water rule contained in section 2A-407. In a consumer finance lease, the lessee may also revoke acceptance of goods if the lessor defaults in a way that substantially impairs the value of the goods. UCC § 2A-517(2). This right is particularly important for the consumer lessee because it avoids the obligation to pay all the rent despite the nonconformity.

A justified revocation of acceptance must take place within a reasonable time after the basis for the revocation is or should have been discovered and is effective when the lessee notifies the lessor. Revocation is not allowed if there is a substantial change in the condition of the goods that is not caused by the nonconformity that justifies revocation. A revoking lessee has the same obligation to take care of the goods as if the lessee had rejected the goods. UCC § 2A-517(4), (5).

If a lessee justifiably and effectively revokes acceptance of the goods, then the lessee has the right to recover damages based either on a cover transaction or on market rent for the goods, plus incidental or consequential damages, minus expenses saved as a consequence of the lessor's breach. UCC §§ 2A-518, 2A-519, 2A-520.

Problem 11-5

Sensational Electronics manufactures computer servers for use in networks. Lasting Data operates a data storage business that relies heavily on computer servers. Several months ago, Lasting Data began negotiating with Sensational Electronics to acquire 30 new servers, with financing from Boston Finance. Last month, Boston Finance purchased the servers from Sensational Electronics and then leased the servers to Lasting Data. Before doing so, Boston Finance sent the purchase agreement to Lasting Data for approval.

After 20 servers were installed in Lasting Data's facility, five of the servers malfunctioned. Sensational Electronics failed to deliver the remaining ten servers after Lasting Data complained about the five that had malfunctioned.

Lasting Data may be able to obtain replacement servers from another manufacturer but is not sure that it will be able to do so for the same price as Sensational Electronics offered. In any event, while it decides what to do and until it can bring its server capacity up to the desired amount, it is experiencing difficulty in servicing all of its customers on a timely basis. What are Lasting Data's remedies, if any, against both Sensational Electronics and Boston Finance?

D. Risk of Loss Following the Lessor's Breach

Analogous Provisions	
Article 2	Article 2A
§ 2-510	§ 2A-220

Section 2A-220 parallels section 2-510 on the effect of breach on the risk of loss. If the lessee has the right to reject the goods because of a nonconformity in the goods or the tender, the risk of loss remains on the lessor or the supplier until cure of the nonconformity or acceptance of the goods. If the lessee rightfully and effectively revokes acceptance, and the lessee has a deficiency in its insurance coverage for the goods, the risk of loss is treated as resting on the lessor to the extent of the deficiency. Given the very limited circumstances in which the lessee in a finance lease may be able to revoke acceptance of the goods, the comment to section 2A-220 indicates that the risk of loss in that situation should rest on the lessor, not the supplier, to the extent the lessee's insurance coverage is insufficient.

E. Statute of Limitations

Analogous Provisions	
Article 2	Article 2A
§ 2-725	§ 2A-506

Article 2A contains a four-year statute of limitations period for actions for breach of a lease contract. UCC § 2A-506(1). The four year period runs from when the cause of action accrues. So, far, this is the same as the rules applicable to sales contracts. However, whereas a cause of action for breach of a sales contract accrues in most circumstances when the breach occurs, regardless of when it is or should be discovered,[11] *see* UCC § 2-725(2), a cause of action for breach of a lease agreement accrues under a more liberal standard: when the breach takes place or when the breach is or should be discovered, whichever is later. UCC § 2A-506(2). Other law determines whether there are circumstances in which the running of the limitations period is tolled. UCC § 2A-506(4).

SECTION 6.   LESSEE'S DEFAULT AND LESSOR'S REMEDIES

A. Overview

Analogous Provisions	
Article 2	Article 2A
§ 2-703	§ 2A-523

When a lessee defaults in its obligations under the lease, the lessor's main objective is usually to recover the goods and then obtain damages for the breach. Unlike in a sales transaction, the lessor has a strong claim to the return of the goods because of the lessor's residual reversionary interest in them. However, the lessor does not have to attempt to recover the goods. The lessor has several remedial choices and those choices are catalogued in section 2A-523. The lessor may also have additional remedies pursuant to the lease agreement. As was true in Article 2, the focus in Article 2A is on putting the aggrieved lessor in the same position it would have occupied if the lessee had fully performed. UCC § 1-305.

---

[11] As you recall, Article 2 provides that a cause of action accrues when the breach is or should have been discovered when a warranty "explicitly extends to future performance of the goods and discovery of the breach must await the time of such performance." UCC § 2-725(2).

B. Lessee's Repudiation or Breach Prior to Delivery

Analogous Provisions	
Article 2	Article 2A
§ 2-704	§ 2A-524
n/a	§ 2A-525
§ 2-705	§ 2A-526
§ 2-706	§ 2A-527
§ 2-707	n/a
§ 2-708	§ 2A-528
§ 2-709	§ 2A-529
§ 2-710	§ 2A-530
n/a	§ 2A-532

If the lessee repudiates or has defaulted in its obligations under the lease prior to delivery, the lessor may withhold delivery of the goods. UCC §§ 2A-523(1)(c), 2A-525. The lessor also has that right if the lessee is discovered to be insolvent, even if that event is not technically a default under the lease. UCC § 2A-525(1). If the goods are in transit, the lessor has the right to stop the delivery as determined under section 2A-526. These sections parallel in significant part sections 2-702(1) and 2-705.

In addition to keeping the goods from the lessee, the lessor may cancel the lease contract, although in an installment lease contract, the right to cancel requires a substantial impairment of the value of the whole contract. UCC §§ 2A-523(1), 2A-510(2). *Cf.* UCC §§ 2-703, 2-612(3). In an installment lease contract, the lessor might well seek to cancel to avoid having to deliver future installments to the lessee.

A lessor who, because of the lessee's breach, has rightfully withheld or stopped delivery of the goods is entitled to recover damages from the lessee for the breach. Those damages are usually measured in one of three ways:

(i) by reference to a substitute lease transaction, UCC § 2A-527;

(ii) by reference to market rent, UCC § 2A-528(1); or

(iii) by reference to the lessor's lost profit, UCC § 2A-528(2).

In a rare case, where the lessor is unable to dispose of the goods on a reasonable basis, the lessor may be entitled to the rent due under the lease. UCC § 2A-529. These remedies thus parallel the seller's remedies in sections 2-706, 2-708, and

2-709. These remedies are alternative ways in which to measure the lessor's expectancy.

Even though these remedies are modeled on the similar Article 2 provisions, the calculation of damages is somewhat different. That is because the lease is designed to compensate the lessor for the right to use or possess the goods merely for a period of time, not for the full value or useful life of the goods. If the lessor enters into a substitute lease transaction that is substantially similar to the breached lease, the lessor is entitled to recover any unpaid rent under the breached lease that has accrued up to the time the substitute lease agreement was entered into plus the difference between the present value of the remaining payments under the breached lease and the present value of the payments under the substitute lease that will be due during the remaining term of the breached lease. UCC § 2A-527(2). To this amount incidental damages are added and expenses saved as a result of the lessee's breach are subtracted. Article 2A follows Article 2 in not providing for the lessor to recover consequential damages.

If the lessor does not enter into a substantially similar lease transaction – either because the lessor does not enter into a substitute lease at all, the substitute lease is not substantially similar, or the lessor sells the goods – then the lessor is entitled to recover damages under section 2A-528(1). Those damages are the accrued unpaid rent under the breached lease as of the date of the lessee's default plus the difference between the present value of the rental payments remaining under the breached lease term minus the present value of the market rent for the goods for the same term. Again, incidental damages are added and expenses saved as a consequence of the lessee's breach are subtracted.

If these market rent-based damages are inadequate to protect the lessor's expectancy interest, the lessor is entitled to recover the present value of the profit it would have realized on the breached lease, plus a reasonable overhead amount and incidental damages. The lessor is also allowed to recover unpaid reliance costs, but the damages must be reduced by the proceeds of a disposition, taking into account the fact that the lessor is entitled to retain the residual value of the goods. UCC § 2A-528(2).

Finally, if the lessor is unable after reasonable effort to dispose of the goods, the lessor may recover the unpaid rent that has accrued by the date of the judgment, plus the present value of the rent for any remaining term of the breached lease. Incidental damages are added to this amount and expenses saved in consequence of the breach are subtracted. UCC § 2A-529(1)(b).

If the leased goods are not yet finished, or have not yet been identified to the contract, the lessor may finish the goods, dispose of them in the unfinished state, or identify them to the contract in an effort to minimize loss. UCC § 2A-524. This is the analog to section 2-704 for an aggrieved seller.

A breaching lessee who has prepaid part or all of the rent from whom the lessor has withheld the goods or stopped delivery of the goods is entitled to at least partial restitution of that amount, after accounting for any enforceable amount of liquidated damages, or if no agreement to liquidated damages, to deduction of the lessor's damages as calculated under Article 2A. If there is no enforceable liquidated damages clause in the lease agreement, the lessor is entitled to deduct 20% of the present value of the rent the lessee was obligated to pay. That amount is capped in a consumer lease at $500. UCC § 2A-504(3), (4). These rules are very similar to the rules in section 2-718(2).

C. Lessee's Wrongful Refusal to Keep the Goods

If the lessee wrongfully rejects the goods,[12] the lessor is entitled to recover damages to the same extent as if the lessee had wrongfully repudiated prior to delivery. Thus, the lessor may recover damages based on a substitute lease transaction, market rent, lost profit, or the rent under the breached lease if the goods cannot be reasonably disposed of.

Problem 11-6

On March 1, Superior Equipment, Inc., located in Chicago, contracted to lease custom lathes to Bristol Woodworking, Inc., located in Phoenix, for $80,000 for a three-year term, delivery F.O.B. Chicago no later than November 1. Cost of shipping was estimated at $2,000. At the time that Bristol and Superior entered into the contract, Bristol made a down payment of $20,000. Superior delivered the lathes on time. Bristol accepted the lathes but one week later demanded that Superior take the lathes back and return its down payment. Bristol's demands were unjustified because both the lathes and Superior's tender had conformed to

---

[12] Or if the lessee wrongfully attempts to revoke acceptance of the goods and the lessor voluntarily takes the goods back.

the contract requirements. Nevertheless, Superior took the lathes back and stored them in Phoenix at a cost of $100 per day.

On November 8, the market rent for a three-year term for the lathes was $60,000 in Chicago, and $55,000 in Phoenix. Two months after taking the lathes back, Superior leased the lathes in Denver for $50,000 for a two-year term, F.O.B. Denver, and incurred $1,500 in shipping costs to send them from Phoenix to Denver. Calculate Superior's damages.

D. Lessee's Default While in Possession of the Goods

Now assume that the lessee has defaulted while it has possession of the goods. If the lessee has accepted the goods, the lessor has the option to pursue an action for the entire rent that is due under the lease. The lessor is entitled to the accrued and unpaid rent as of the time of the judgment, plus the present value of the remaining rent due under the breached lease, plus incidental damages, minus expenses saved as a consequence of the breach. UCC § 2A-529(1)(a).

Instead of pursuing a judgment for the rent, the lessor may seek to recover the goods coupled with damages for the lessee's breach. Because this is a lease transaction, and the lessor has a residual interest in the goods, the lessor always has a right to regain possession of the goods when the lessee has defaulted. UCC § 2A-525(2). The lessor is authorized to use self-help – that is, to take the goods without judicial process – provided the lessor can do so without breach of the peace. UCC § 2A-525(3). This "breach of the peace" standard is borrowed from Article 9 and there is a wealth of case law interpreting what it means in the context of a secured party repossessing goods after a debtor's default. It is essentially a fact intensive inquiry, but there are a few basic points on which there is general agreement. The lessor may not engage in conduct that threatens or creates a substantial risk of violence or injury. The lessor may engage in a trespass but may not break and enter, particularly into residential property. If the lessor is unable to repossess the goods without a breach of the peace, the lessor may seek a court order to get the goods from the lessee. UCC § 2A-525(3).

E. Risk of Loss Following the Lessee's Breach

The lessee is liable for the rent if conforming goods are delivered, the risk of loss has passed to the lessee, and the goods are lost or damaged within a reasonable time after that risk of loss has passed to the lessee. UCC § 2A-529(1)(a). Because the risk of loss does not usually pass to the lessee in a non-finance lease, UCC § 2A-219, this provision will have effect only in a finance lease or if the parties have made an agreement for the risk of loss to pass to the lessee in a non-finance lease.

If the lessee repudiates or defaults, regardless of whether it has the risk of loss, the lessee is treated as having the risk of loss for a commercially reasonable time after the repudiation or default to the extent the lessor's insurance coverage, or in a finance lease, the supplier's insurance coverage, is insufficient. UCC § 2A-220(2).

F. Statute of Limitations

Article 2A has a limitations period of four years from when the cause of action accrues. UCC § 2A-506(1). Article 2A contains different rules than Article 2 on when the cause of action accrues by providing for a discovery rule instead of a rule that focuses only on when the breach occurs. A cause of action for breach of the lease agreement accrues when the breach takes place or when the breach should be or is discovered, whichever is later. UCC § 2A-506(2). Other law determines whether there are circumstances in which the running of the limitations period is tolled. UCC § 2A-506(4).

SECTION 7.   PROPERTY RIGHTS IN THE LEASED GOODS

A. Overview

As we know, both the lessor and the lessee have property rights in the leased goods. The lessee has the right to possession and use of the goods during the leased term and the lessor has the residual property interest in the leased goods. For the most part, both the lessor and the lessee are free to transfer their respective interests to someone else. *Cf.* UCC § 2A-303. What we analyze here are the circumstances in which one of them can transfer some or all of the rights of the other. Put another way, this section addresses the ability of third parties to claim rights in the goods that would have priority over either the lessor's residual interest or the lessee's right to use and possess the goods.[13]

The discussion that follows is, by necessity, brief. The goal is not so much to fully explore each of the relevant rules, but to explain their different scope, so that you can later isolate the rule that would apply to a situation that may arise.

B. Lessor's Ability to Transfer Goods Free of Lessee's Rights

Analogous Provisions	
Article 2	Article 2A
§ 2-403	§ 2A-304 § 2A-307(2)

In Chapter Ten, we saw that section 2-403 contains two rules that create an exception to the general principal of property law that one cannot give what one does not have. First, section 2-403(1) allows a buyer with voidable title to transfer good title to a good faith purchaser for value. These situations could be diagramed as follows (the buyer is depicted in bold italics because the buyer is the transferor in the transactions to which the provision is speaking).

---

[13] For purposes of this discussion of property rights, we are ignoring the intersection of Article 2A and certificate of title laws. For the most part, Article 2A defers to the rules found in certificate of title statutes. *See* UCC §§ 2A-104, 2A-105. The property rights provisions in Article 2A continue this deference by providing that a third party who is asserting property based rights in the leased goods subject to a certificate of title statute gets no greater rights than that provided by Article 2A and the certificate of title statute. UCC §§ 2A-304(3), 2A-305(3).

We also do not cover third party claims to the leased goods when the goods are fixtures or accessions. Article 2A provides special rules for those types of goods to accommodate the varied interests that may arise. *See* UCC §§ 2A-309, 2A-310. These situations are too complex to explore in this course.

§ 2-403(1)

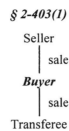

Seller

| sale

Buyer

| sale

Transferee

Second, section 2-403(2) empowers a seller to transfer the rights of an owner of goods to a buyer in ordinary course of business if the seller is a merchant who deals in goods of that kind and the owner has entrusted the goods to the seller. The following diagram illustrates this scenario (this time the seller is depicted in bold italics because the seller is the transferor in the transactions to which the provision is speaking).

§ 2-403(2)

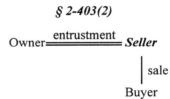

Owner ══entrustment══ ***Seller***

| sale

Buyer

Article 2A has analogous rules that apply to transfers by the lessor. Section 2A-304 deals with situations in which a person with voidable title leases the goods to a good faith lessee for value:[14]

§ 2A-304(1)

Transferor

| sale

Lessor

| lease

Lessee

---

[14] Because section 2-403(1) applies to all purchasers for value, and a lessee qualifies as a "purchaser" under section 1-201(b)(29), (30), section 2-403(1) may already protect good faith lessees for value. Nevertheless, the drafters protected them in section 2A-304(1) to remove any doubt on this point.

The same provision also purports to cover another situation: when a lessor first leases the goods to one person and then leases them again – for either the same or at least an overlapping lease term – to someone else:

§ 2A-304(1)

In general, the subsequent lessee takes subject to the original lease. There are, however, two major exceptions to this rule. First, if the lessor is disposing of the leased goods as a method of setting damages pursuant to a breach of the lease contract, the buyer or lessee from the lessor takes free of the existing breached lease contract. UCC § 2A-527(4). Second, if the lessee has entrusted the goods back to the lessor, the subsequent lessee takes the goods free of the original lessee's rights under section 2A-304(2) if the subsequent lessee is a lessee in ordinary course of business.

Another entrustment rule is apparently implicit in section 2A-307(2). Although that provision does not on its face appear to be referring to entrustment situations, comment 3 to section 2A-304 indicates that section 2A-307(2) does indeed protect a lessee in ordinary course of business in the following situation :

§ 2A-307(2)

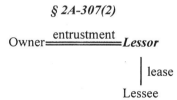

Taking the comment as true, section 2A-307(2) is closely analogous to the rule of section 2-403(2), from which it was derived. The major difference is that in the lease context the owner is not deprived of all rights to the goods, the owner simply takes subject to the lease (*i.e.,* loses the goods for the leasehold term).

C. Lessee's Ability to Transfer Goods Free of Lessor's Rights

Analogous Provisions	
Article 2	Article 2A
§ 2-403	§ 2A-305

Under normal principles of property law, lessees should be able to transfer their limited leasehold interest in the goods, but nothing more. If the law were otherwise, if a lessee could transfer both its leasehold interest and the lessor's residual interest in the goods, few owners would be willing to lease their goods to anyone other than the most saintly of lessees. The risk would simply be too great. Accordingly, a lessee should not – and generally does not – have the power to transfer rights in the goods free of the lessor's residual interest.

However, section 2A-305 provides for two situations in which the lessee may transfer greater rights than it has. The first is subsection (1), which is another analog to section 2-403(1). It allows a lessee with a voidable leasehold to transfer a good leasehold interest to a good faith sublessee or buyer. This provision does not allow the subsequent transferee to override the lessor's residual interest in the goods, it merely allows the lessee to transfer a better leasehold than what the lessee had.

§ 2A-305(1)

Lessor
    | voidable lease
Lessee
    | sale/sublease
Transferee

Second, subsection (2) is another entrustment rule. It applies if the lessee is a merchant who deals in goods of the kind leased and allows that lessee to transfer the goods free of the lessor's rights to a buyer or lessee in ordinary course of business. Thus, this rule gives the lessee the ability to eliminate the lessor's residual interest in the goods.

§ 2A-305(2)

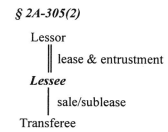

A final rule that allows a lessee to transfer more rights in the goods than the lessee itself has is section 2A-511(4). It provides that if a lessee is disposing of the goods after the lessor's breach, the purchaser takes the goods free of the lessor's interest under the lease contract. This rule too operates to eliminate the lessor's residual interest in the goods.

D. Lessee's Rights against Lessor's Creditors

A lessor's creditors may be interested in attaining an interest in the leased goods to satisfy obligations the lessor owes to those creditors. Is the lessee's interest in the goods subject to the claims of the lessor's creditors? The answer to that question depends upon what type of creditor is making the claim to the leased goods.

If the creditor is someone who has furnished services or materials to the leased goods and has a lien under other law for the value of those services or materials as long as those goods are in the creditor's possession, then the lessee's rights under the lease contract is subject to that lien, regardless of when the lien arose.[15] UCC § 2A-306.

If the creditor's lien on the goods arose prior to the lease contract being entered into, the lessee will be subject to that lien, unless the lien is an Article 9 security interest and the provisions of Article 9 allow the lessee to take free of the security interest in the goods. UCC § 2A-307(2), (3). A lessee will take free of an Article 9 security interest in the leased goods created by the lessor if the lessee qualifies as a lessee in ordinary course of business, UCC § 9-321(c), or if the lessee gives value and takes possession of the goods without knowledge of the security interest and at

---

[15] If the other law creating the statutory lien provides a different priority rule, that priority rule will govern.

a time when the security interest is not perfected, UCC § 9-317(c). This protection for a lessee from a security interest created by the lessor parallels the protection for a buyer of the goods from a security interest created by the seller. UCC §§ 9-320, 9-317(b).

If the creditor's lien on the goods arose subsequent to the lease contract being entered into, the creditor of the lessor is generally subject to the lessee's rights under the lease contract. This rule is subject to two exceptions. The first exception is for the statutory lien creditor as discussed above. The second exception is found in section 2A-308. If the creditor of the lessor is entitled to treat the lease contract with the lessee as a fraudulent transfer (as determined under other law), the lessee would be subject to the creditor's claim. *Compare* UCC § 2-402.

E. Lessor's Rights against Lessee's Creditors

The lessee's creditors generally do not have rights to the leased goods that are superior to the lessor's property rights in the goods. UCC § 2A-307(1). There is only one exception to this rule. If the creditor is someone who has furnished services or materials to the leased goods and has a lien under other law for the value of those services or materials as long as those goods are in the creditor's possession, then the lessor's rights under the lease contract are subject to that lien, regardless of when the lien arose.[16] UCC § 2A-306.

---

[16] If the other law creating the statutory lien provides a different priority rule, that priority rule will govern.

CHAPTER TWELVE

INTRODUCTION TO PAYMENT SYSTEMS

SECTION 1.   PAYMENT TRANSACTIONS

This morning you went to a supermarket to pick up some groceries. You select items and put them in a cart. You then proceed to the checkout counter where the clerk scans the items and computes a total sales prices. You now need to pay for the items. We can think of this as a fairly simply business transaction,[1] that is, the exchange of groceries for payment.

Now consider how you will pay for the groceries. You could use currency, commonly known as "money." In the United States, money consists of Federal Reserve notes, printed by the United States Bureau of Engraving and Printing, and coins, produced by the United States Mint. This payment method is quite simple. You simply hand to the clerk the amount of currency necessary to cover the price. If necessary, the clerk will give you change back if you pay more than the sales price because you do not have exact change.

Alternatively, you could use one (or more) of several other payment methods. For example, you may decide to use a credit card, which in all likelihood has been issued by a bank or financial services company. The cashier will capture information from your card and the supermarket will submit that information, along with information about the transaction, to its bank, called the "merchant bank." The merchant bank will initiate a funds transfer to the supermarket's operating bank account, thereby paying the supermarket for the items you purchased. The merchant bank will also communicate the information about the transaction, probably though a private, nationwide network of banks and financial services companies, to the card issuer. The merchant bank will receive payment from the card issuer through that same network. Within a few weeks, the card issuer will bill you for the charges you have incurred by presenting your card. At that point, you will pay your credit card bill by using a further payment mechanism, such as by

---

[1] Do not make the mistake of thinking of a business transaction as something that necessarily involves business entities, not consumers. Consumers are involved in business transactions every time they buy or sell property or services. In payments law, there are only a few circumstances where the status of the actor (consumer or non-consumer) matters. In this text, the term "business transaction" encompasses both consumer and commercial transactions.

directing your bank to transfer funds from your bank account to the card issuer, or by writing a check drawn on your bank account directing payment to the card issuer.

You could also use your debit card, generally issued by the bank at which you maintain a deposit account. The supermarket cashier will capture information from the debit card and communicate that information and the transaction information through its bank and the debit card network to your bank. That information transfer network may function in a manner very similar to the credit card network, with the following critical difference. Your bank account will be debited in a real time manner for the amount of the purchase.

You may instead use a stored value card (often called a pre-paid card or gift card), if the supermarket allows that form of payment. With a pre-paid card, you have already paid an issuer for the value that is associated with the card. The supermarket cashier captures information associated with the card and verifies with the issuer, often through an electronic network, that the card value is valid. The amount of your purchase is then deducted from the balance of available value. The supermarket will obtain its value from the card issuer, again often through the supermarket's bank and communication in a network that connects that bank to the card issuer.

You may even write a check, although for reasons we will see the supermarket may lack confidence in this payment method – if, for example, you have a history of writing checks that are later dishonored – and may refuse to accept it. If the supermarket does accept your check, the supermarket will typically deposit the check with its bank and, sometime later, either that check or information from that check will be presented to your bank. Your bank will either honor or dishonor the check. If the check is dishonored, eventually the credits that the supermarket obtained from its bank upon the deposit will be reversed and your account will not be debited for the amount of the check. If the check is honored, the credits the restaurant received upon deposit will be "firmed up" and the amount of the check will be debited from your bank account.

Alternatively, the supermarket may choose to process your check in a different manner. The cashier may scan the information from the bottom of the check (the bank routing number and your bank account number), key in the amount, and hand it back to you. The information obtained from the check is then used to initiate a debit funds transfer using the Automated Clearing House (ACH) system. In essence, the supermarket's bank will send an instruction to your bank to debit your bank account the amount of the purchase and the supermarket's bank will credit the supermarket with the amount of the purchase, minus the fee charged by the supermarket's bank. Notice that you initiated payment using one mechanism (a check) but, perhaps without your understanding, payment was effected through another mechanism (a debit funds transfer).

Given the nature of your purchase from the supermarket, you are unlikely to contact your bank while you are standing in the cashier' line and direct a credit funds transfer from your bank directly to the supermarket's bank. A credit funds transfer is usually used for business transactions with a larger dollar value. For example, assume the supermarket rents its premises. The supermarket may decide to make its monthly lease payment through a credit funds transfer in which the supermarket directs its bank to transfer the amount of the monthly rent to the bank account of the landlord. This direction is carried out through a series of instructions between the banks, or through bank-run networks, which eventually result in a debit to the supermarket's bank account and a credit to the landlord's bank account.

You are also unlikely to use a promissory note, a writing in which you promise to pay a certain sum of money either on demand or at a definite time later. While you may think that would be great (buy now, pay later), the supermarket is highly unlikely to accept that form of payment.

Another payment mechanism you are unlikely to use, given the nature of your purchase from the supermarket, is a letter of credit. A letter of credit is a letter issued by a bank stating that upon satisfaction of the conditions specified in the letter, usually the presentation of precisely defined documents, the bank will pay the beneficiary a stated amount of money. An applicant (the person wishing to use this device to make payment) requests a bank to issue such a letter, often paying the bank the stated amount of the letter of credit plus a fee, in advance. The bank will then pay the beneficiary if the beneficiary complies with the conditions stated in the letter. The supermarket may have used a letter of credit to provide payment to merchants who sold goods to the supermarket. The letter of credit mechanism allows the merchant to be virtually assured of payment if the merchant presents the correct documents because the issuing bank will be liable for payment based upon the terms of the letter of credit. This liability of the issuing bank is independent of the supermarket's obligation to pay for the goods. The letter of credit also assures the supermarket that the payment will not be made unless the merchant complies with the terms of the letter of credit.

Each manner of payment described above can be thought of as a "payment mechanism." As you think about business transactions, and the number of ways in which payment may be made, you may be curious about several things. Why are there so many different payment options? Which party gets to decide what mechanism to use and what reasons would the parties have for preferring one mechanism over another? What advantages do the payor and payee enjoy in each type of payment mechanism? What risks are attendant on the payor and what risks are borne by the payee in each payment mechanism? Do these payment mechanisms have anything in common?

These are the types of questions that will occupy this material on payment systems. Before we delve into the incredible detail of these various payment mechanisms, it is important to understand the common issues that cut across the use of these different types of payment mechanisms. This big picture will help keep you grounded on the important issues (it is easy to get overwhelmed by detail) and will help you think of how these issues should be approached as new payment mechanisms evolve.

SECTION 2.   THE LANDSCAPE OF PAYMENT SYSTEMS

A. Payment Systems Themes

Keeping in mind the simple examples above, first consider the purpose of a payment mechanism. At its most fundamental level, a payment mechanism is about transferring value from the payor to the payee. The payee has something of value – typically property or services – that the payee is willing to transfer or provide in return for some payment from the payor. The *business transaction* is about deciding whether each wants to trade with the other and arriving at an agreed price. That agreed price is normally denoted in some unit of government-recognized currency such as U.S. dollars, Canadian dollars, euros, pesos, yen, or other currency unit.[2] The *payment mechanism* is the manner in which the designated currency unit is paid. Thus if you want to buy a new car, the dealer and you will agree on the make and model of the car to be provided and the price to be paid. The dealer will deliver the car and you will pay the price in the agreed number of currency units.

---

[2] Modern business transactions do not usually designate payment in non-currency units of value, such as bales of cloth, bushels of corn, or other items that have value but are not considered to be "money" units. If goods or services are exchanged for other goods or services that are not units of value designated as money, that transaction is called a "barter" transaction.

The purchase and sale of the car is the business transaction. The method by which you remit payment of the currency units is the payment mechanism.[3]

Four factors play a key role in the parties' decision about which payment mechanism to use: access, timing, cost, and risk.

Access. Consider first the issue of access. A person buying used clothes at a yard sale is unlikely to pay by credit card. The same is true of an employer paying an employee's wages or salary. That is because neither the yard-sale seller nor the employee is likely to have a contract with a merchant bank in the credit card system for the merchant bank to process the charge. Accordingly, some other payment mechanism will have to be used. Similarly, a person without a bank account has very few options to make payment and is generally restricted to currency, stored value cards, or money orders. We will not spend much time in this book discussing issues of access, but that does not mean those issues are unimportant. The remaining three factors, and the issues associated with each, are the focus of this book.

Timing. How long will the it take for the payment mechanism to complete the transfer of value from the payor to the payee? When dealing with currency, this is not likely to be much of an issue. When using another payment method, one that uses a network of banks or financial institutions as intermediaries, it may be. Timing issues involve more than mere speed. Timing issues also include concerns about "finality," the point in the process when the transfer of value from the payor and payee is no longer reversible or retrievable through some form of specific relief. Yet another timing issue involves the concept of "discharge," the effect of the payment mechanism on the payor's obligation to the payee (in the underlying business transaction). Does initiation of a payment immediately discharge the payor's obligation to pay the payee according to the terms of the underlying business transaction? If not, when does that discharge take place and is the underlying obligation to pay in the underlying business transaction suspended while the payment mechanism is operating?

Cost. Consider now the issue of cost. This necessarily involves two related points: what are the costs and who will bear them? For example, if payment is to

---

[3] On the other side of the transaction, the substantive law governing the provision of property or services often governs the mechanism of conveying the property or providing the service to the payor. For example, in the United States, Uniform Commercial Code Article 2, as enacted by the relevant state, and the parties' contract will address how the car will be tendered.

be by check, there are the costs of printing the check and delivering the check, both likely borne by the payor. There may also be costs associated with collecting the check. For example, the payor may be charged a fee for each check written and the payee may be charged for each check deposited. Either or both parties may also be charged a monthly fee to maintain a bank account, and thereby have access to the check clearing system. Even if the payor's and payee's respective deposit accounts have no monthly fee and no per-transaction fees, they may still be paying at least part of the cost of the check collection system if the depositary bank pays no or below-market interest on the funds credited to the deposit account.

Other payment mechanisms also have costs. A merchant who accepts payments by credit card effectively pays a percentage of the face amount of each transaction to the merchant bank. The cardholder may have to pay an annual fee to the issuer to maintain the credit card account. Even if payment is with currency, there may be attendant costs involved. For example, a merchant who receives payments in cash has to pay employees for the time it takes them to count the money received, make change, and then transport the money to a bank. This may seem insubstantial but it is one of several reasons why most employers do not pay their employees in cash. They do not want to pay a payroll master to count out and hand over the proper payment to each employee, let alone the lost productivity while employees stand in line for payment or the cost of monitoring to prevent fraud, error, or loss of the currency.

In addition to the costs borne by the payor and the payee, there will invariably be other costs associated with a payment mechanism. For example, someone must pay for the printing, minting and distribution of currency. For credit cards, checks, and funds transfers, there is the cost of maintaining the network of financial institutions that process the payments. These costs may not affect the decision of the payor and payee about what payment mechanism to use, but legislators or regulators, enacting law or promulgating regulations as instruments of social policy and social justice, need to be aware of these costs.

Risk. Finally, and most important, let us consider the risks associated with a payment mechanism. What risks do the payor and payee take when using a particular payment mechanism? For example, who bears the risk of a theft of currency? Who bears the risk that currency is counterfeit? What if a check is lost in the mail or lost after delivery? When does each party bear the risk of fraud by the other? For example, does the payee bear the risk of an unauthorized use of a credit card or debit card? Can the payor stop payment on the debit card transaction if the payor finds it has been deceived by the payee?

Let us pause for a moment. All of the discussion above about risk focused on the interests of only the payor and the payee. However, they are not the only players in any payment mechanism. A payment by credit card will typically involve, in addition to the cardholder and merchant (*i.e.*, the payor and payee), the issuer, the merchant bank, and several intermediaries. A payment by check will involve at lease one bank – the drawee – and possibly several. A funds transfer will involve at least two financial institutions. Even the use of currency involves, at least peripherally, the governmental entities that print the bills or mint the coins and the banks that help distribute the money into commerce. In short, whereas the *business transaction* may involve only the payor and the payee, the *payment mechanism* will invariably involve third parties as well.

Who bears the risks of error or wrongdoing by intermediaries who process the payment mechanism? Under what circumstances should an intermediary in a payment system – *i.e.*, someone other than the payor or payee – be on the hook if something goes wrong? For example, who takes the risk of error in the clearance system, such as garbled, lost, or misdirected communication between financial institutions? Will that determination be based on fault or some other consideration? Who bears the risk of insolvency of one of the intermediaries? Who bears the risk of forgery or data security lapses?[4] Does the answer depend on what is forged (*e.g.*, a credit card or a signature), how the data lapse occurred, relative fault (failure to prevent, discover or report the forgery or data security lapse), cost considerations, or some other factor?

Easily moving value from payor to payee is essential to commerce. The mechanism for transferring value from the payor to the payee is a cost of the underlying business transaction. If a payment mechanism is costly or risky, it makes the business transaction more expensive. There is therefore a societal interest in making sure that the society's payment system has wide accessibility, functions at the lowest possible cost, operates swiftly and with finality, and minimizes the level of risk of error and wrongdoing. Of course, these goals will sometimes be in tension with each other.

One of the main challenges of any course on payments – aside from dealing with these occasionally conflicting goals – is dealing with the diversity of payment mechanisms. Each payment mechanism has its own resolution of timing issues and

---

[4] *See* Mark MacCarthy, *Information Security Policy in the U.S. Retail Payments Industry,* 2011 STAN. TECH. L. REV. 3.

each has its own allocation of costs and risks. Why do we have such diversity in the rules governing the different payment mechanisms? For at least two reasons.

First, the legal rules (statutes and regulations) governing each payment mechanism were promulgated by different governmental authorities and at different points in history. Often the rules of the particular payment mechanism were developed only after the payment mechanism became widespread and particular problems emerged in the use of the mechanism. For example, checks have been used for centuries and consequently many of the rules governing them can be traced to rules developed long ago. In contrast, the regulations governing credit cards[5] are much more recent and were adopted to deal with certain specified risks encountered in the practice and use of those cards. Debit cards and stored value cards are even newer payment mechanisms and the law has not addressed these mechanisms other than in a piecemeal manner.[6]

Second, each payment mechanism functions differently and thus each has its own level of risk for each type of error, wrongdoing or other problem. For example, checks are cleared through the banking system differently than are credit cards, and thus those two payment mechanisms present different risks to the payor, payee, and the participating banks.

Regardless of the reasons for this complexity, one thing is clear. The study of the payment system must be, in essence, a separate study of each individual payment mechanism. As we embark on that study, it is useful to keep in mind the following common themes and questions to be considered when dealing with each payment mechanism:[7]

  A. *Operation.* How does the payment mechanism transfer value? How does the payment mechanism work?

  B. *Timing.*

  (1) When is payment final?

---

[5] Reg. Z, 12 C.F.R. pt. 226 (to implement provisions of the Truth in Lending Act, codified at 15 U.S.C. §§ 1601–1667f).

[6] *See* Reg. E, 12 C.F.R. pt. 205 (coverage of consumer debit cards, and some coverage of payroll and gift cards).

[7] There are different ways to think about payment systems at a theoretical level. *See* L. Ali Khan, *A Theoretical Analysis of Payment Systems*, 60 S.C. L. REV. 425 (2008) (focusing on principles of authorization, negligence and dishonor).

(2) When does the payment mechanism discharge the payor's underlying obligation to the payee?

(3) Prior to discharge, is the payor's underlying obligation to the payee suspended?

C. *Rights & Duties.*

(1) What obligations to the payor, payee, or other parties does the use of the payment mechanism create?

(2) To the extent use of the mechanism creates additional obligations:

(i) How are those obligations satisfied?

(ii) What defenses does the obligor have to those obligations?

(iii) If there are multiple obligors created by use of the mechanism, what is the relationship among those obligors?

D. *Risk.*

(1) What effect will a party's insolvency have on the finality of the payment and the discharge of the underlying obligation?

(2) What errors might arise during use of the payment mechanism and, for each error, which party or parties bear the risk?

(3) What wrongdoing may occur during the use of the payment mechanism and, for each type of wrongdoing, which party or parties bear the risk?

As you study each payment mechanism, return to this list in order to keep focused on the big picture and to organize the detail that is to follow. In other words, begin your study of each mechanism by understanding who its participants are and how it works. Then focus on the legal rules that govern it, organizing those rules around the themes and question noted above. In so doing, it is important to think about the underlying policy issues that these questions pose. Be prepared to compare and contrast the operation and rules governing the different payment mechanisms, because that is essential both to true understanding and to a proper evaluation of the law.

But now a word of warning. While every payment mechanism deals in some way with the issues and questions identified above, each payment mechanism addresses these issues and questions in its own unique way. Generalizing across the dividing lines between these payment mechanisms or assuming that two different mechanisms will treat the same issue similarly will lead to error and confusion. Thus resist the temptation to attempt to simplify your study of payment systems into a few major principles. There is no avoiding the complexity that you are about to encounter. Rather, embrace the challenge of mastering that complexity. The ability to master complexity is a skill lawyers need in the modern age.

B. Overview of the Legal Regulation

As noted above, the legal rules governing the various payment systems have been promulgated by different government bodies, at different times in history. The following list demonstrates this incredibly complex legal environment:[8]

1. The rules regarding currency in the United States are a combination of common-law principles augmented by a few federal statutes and regulations.

2. The law governing credit cards is a mixture of contract-law principles with overlaying federal law addressing some targeted issues in the Truth in Lending Act (codified at 15 U.S.C. §§ 1601–1667f) and the implementing regulation, Regulation Z (12 C.F.R. pt. 226).

3. The law governing electronically initiated debit or credit funds transfers accessing a consumer bank account is also primarily contract law, with some overlying federal law in the Electronic Fund Transfers Act (codified at 15 U.S.C. §§ 1693–1693r) and its implementing regulation, Regulation E (12 C.F.R. pt. 205). A credit funds transfer is an order by the payor to the payor's bank to credit the account of the payee at the payee's bank. A debit funds transfer is an order by the payee (or the payee's bank) to the payor's bank to debit the payor's bank account. This category includes any electronic mechanism to access a consumer bank account, such as ATM cards, debit cards, or using on-line banking to make a funds transfer.

---

[8] This text does not address the international aspects of payments law. *See, e.g.,* United Nations Convention on International Bills of Exchange and International Promissory Notes (1988); UNCITRAL Model Law on International Credit Transfers (1992); United Nations Convention on Independent Guarantees and Standby Letters of Credit (1995); Benjamin Geva, *Payment Transactions Under the EU Payment Services Directive: A U.S. Comparative Perspective,* 27 PENN. ST. INT'L L. REV. 713 (2009); Neil M. Peretz, *The Single Euro Payment Area: A New Opportunity for Consumer Alternative Dispute Resolution in the European Union,* 16 MICH. ST. J. INT'L L. 573 (2008); Benjamin Geva, *Recent International Developments in the Law of Negotiable Instruments and Payment and Settlement Systems,* 42 TEX. INT'L L.J. 685 (2007).

4. The law governing pre-paid or stored value mechanisms is a mixture of state regulatory law, federal law in Regulation E (12 C.F.R. pt. 205) governing some types of pre-paid mechanisms, and contract law.

5. The law governing checks is primarily found in the Uniform Commercial Code (UCC) Articles 3 and 4 (law enacted by state legislatures) and two federal statutes: the Expedited Funds Availability Act (codified at 12 U.S.C. §§ 4001–4010) and the Check Clearing for the 21st Century Act (codified at 12 U.S.C. §§ 5001–5018). Each of the federal acts has spawned regulations promulgated by the Federal Reserve Board and found for the most part in Regulation CC (12 C.F.R. pt. 229). If a check is cleared through the Federal Reserve System, Regulation J, 12 C.F.R. pt. 210, will also govern. The rules governing checks now found in UCC Article 3 are built upon common law principles developed over several hundred years and previously codified in the Uniform Negotiable Instruments Act. The two federal acts were enacted in 1987 and 2004 respectively.

6. The law governing negotiable promissory notes is found in UCC Article 3. The law governing non-negotiable promissory notes is found in contract law. Some types of notes (called transferrable records) may also be subject to Uniform Electronic Transactions Act § 16 (enacted at the state level) or the federal Electronic Signatures in Global and National Commerce Act (codified at 15 U.S.C. § 7021).

7. The law governing credit funds transfers (not involving a consumer bank account) is found in UCC Article 4A, also enacted at the state level, and if the transfer is cleared through the Federal Reserve System, Regulation J, 12 C.F.R. pt. 210 .

8. The law governing debit funds transfers that are not covered by the Electronic Fund Transfers Act and Regulation E (see above), is the common law (such as contract law and tort law).

9. The law governing letters of credit is found in UCC Article 5, or in international conventions such as the Uniform Customs and Practices for Documentary Credits (UCP 600).

To the extent that any payment mechanism involves an extension of credit by a bank or other financial institution, Regulation AA, 12 C.F.R. pt. 227 regulating unfair or deceptive acts or practices, will govern as well. Finally, the recent legislation on financial regulatory reform may result in additional regulation of some payment mechanisms.[9]

After looking at this list, one should clearly question whether the various payment mechanisms truly comprise a single "payment system."[10] Very little about this landscape can be called systematic in the sense of an organized method for approaching a particular subject. It would be much easier to learn (and teach) a system of principles that governed all payment mechanisms, but alas, that is not the world in which we live.[11]

---

[9] *See* Dodd-Frank Wall Street Reform and Consumer Protection Act, Pub. L. No. 111-203, 124 Stat. 1376 (July 21, 2010) (Title VIII provisions on payment, clearing, and settlement supervision; Title X provisions on the Bureau of Consumer Financial Protection). *See also* Colin C. Richard, *Dodd-Frank, International Remittances, and Mobile Banking: The Federal Reserve's Role in Enabling International Economic Development*, 105 NW. U. L. REV. COLLOQUY 248 (2011).

[10] The number and features of mechanisms used to transfer value are limited only by the imagination of those engaging in the transactions where such movement is desired. The examples discussed so far demonstrate the myriad of different payment mechanisms you could use to pay an obligation. The mesh of imagination and electronics will certainly lead to other mechanisms evolving to facilitate commerce over the coming years.

For some examples of recent articles on issues raised by evolving payment mechanisms see, Eniola Akindemowo, *Contract, Deposit or E-value? Reconsidering Stored Value Products for a Modernized Payments Framework*, 7 DEPAUL BUS. & COM. L.J. 275 (2009); Amelia H. Boss, *Convergence in Electronic Banking: Technological Convergence, Systems Convergence, Legal Convergence*, 2 DREXEL L. REV. 63 (2009); Erik Lillquist and Sarah E. Waldeck, *Government Intervention in Emerging Networked Technologies*, 87 OR. L. REV. 581 (2008); Mark E Budnitz, *Consumer Payment Products and Systems: The Need for Uniformity and the Risk of Political Defeat*, 24 ANN. REV. BANKING & FIN. L. 247 (2005); Bradley Crawford, *New Methods of Payment and New Forms of Money*, 20 BANKING & FINANCE L. REV. 393 (2005); Ronald J. Mann, *Making Sense of Payments Policy in the Information Age*, 93 GEO. L.J. 633 (2005); James Stevens Rogers, *The New Old Law of Electronic Money*, 58 SMU L. REV. 1253 (2005); Ronald J. Mann, *Regulating Internet Payment Intermediaries*, 82 TEX. L. REV. 681 (2004).

[11] Some commentators have engaged in a debate regarding whether this diversity of rules should or could be changed. *See* David Frisch, *Commercial Law's Complexity*, 18 GEO. MASON L. REV. 245 (2011); Robert G. Ballen and Thomas A. Fox, *The Role of Private Sector Payment Rules and a Proposed Approach for Evaluating Future Changes to Payments Law*, 83 CHI.-KENT L. REV. 937 (2008); Clayton P. Gillette and Steven D. Walt, *Uniformity and Diversity in Payment Systems*, 83 CHI.-KENT L. REV. 499 (2008); Gail

This text is organized by payment mechanism as follows:

currency	Chapter Twelve
credit cards	Chapter Thirteen
checks (drafts) and notes	Chapters Fourteen through Nineteen
funds transfers	Chapter Twenty
pre-paid (stored value) mechanisms	Chapter Twenty-One
letters of credit	Chapter Twenty-Two

Within the discussion of each type of payment mechanism, the questions identified above will be addressed.

SECTION 3.   CURRENCY AS A PAYMENT MECHANISM

Before we discuss currency as a payment mechanism, we need to think about the concept of money. In human societies, a token is often used as a medium of exchange. A very small society, with perhaps only a few dozen members, could perhaps accomplish all its transfers of value through bartering. In a larger society, that is simply not practical. Imagine that you lived in a large society that did not have tokens as a medium of exchange. Not being a farmer, you want to acquire

---

Hillebrand, *Before the Grand Rethinking: Five Things to do Today with Payments Law and Ten Principles to Guide New Payments Products and New Payments Law*, 83 CHI.-KENT L. REV. 769 (2008); Sarah Jane Hughes, *Duty Issues in the Ever-Changing World of Payments Processing: Is it Time for New Rules?*, 83 CHI.-KENT L. REV. 721 (2008); Anita Ramasastry, *Confusion and Convergence in Consumer Payments: Is Coherence in Error Resolution Appropriate?*, 83 CHI.-KENT L. REV. 813 (2008); James Stevens Rogers, *Unification of Payments Law and the Problem of Insolvency Risk in Payment Systems*, 83 CHI.-KENT L. REV. 689 (2008); Linda J. Rusch, *Reimagining Payment Systems: Allocation of Risk for Unauthorized Payment Inception*, 83 CHI.-KENT L. REV. 561 (2008). *See also* Clayton P. Gillette, *Rules, Standards, and Precautions in Payment Systems*, 82 VA. L. REV. 181 (1996).

An early attempt to change that diversity of legal regimes and promulgate a more unified system of rules collapsed under a storm of protest. *See* Fred H. Miller, *A Report on the New Payments Code*, 39 BUS. LAW. 1215 (1984); Edward L. Rubin, *Efficiency, Equity and the Proposed Revision of Articles 3 and 4*, 42 ALA. L. REV. 551 (1991).

food. You go to the local store or to whoever has spare food. What would you bring with you to trade? Some books? Jewelry? An offer of services? How would you know in advance what items of yours the food seller would be willing to accept in exchange? Even if parties all trusted each other and were willing to trade based on a promise to deliver something of value later, so that you need not to carry all your spare belongings with you, every transaction would have to be individually negotiated. The parties would have to reach a shared assessment of the value of any the items proposed to be exchanged.

To avoid the inefficiencies of barter, almost all societies have adopted one or more tokens as a medium of exchange. **Read the definition of "money" in UCC § 1-201(b)(24).** Most ancient societies adopted as tokens things that people already valued, such as small pieces of rare metals. Modern societies still use metal coins, but most also used printed pieces of paper with a stated representational value.

The piece of paper that we call the U.S. dollar is a token that represents a single unit of value. Dollar bills have value not because everyone loves the feel of the paper and admires the artwork – in other words, not because the tokens are themselves something that people want to possess or amass – but because of society's faith that everyone within the society will accept these tokens as a medium of exchange. Tokens used as a medium of exchange facilitate business transactions in a very cost-effective manner. Payment mechanisms are ways in which we transfer these tokens. Thus, for example, using a check to pay for food at the grocery store ultimately results in debits or credits in amounts that represent the value in currency – the standard token. In this sense, the check too is a sort of token, or perhaps more accurately, a meta-token: a representation of the payee's right to receive from the payor tokens of a stated value.[12]

In addition to functioning as a medium of exchange, money serves as a standard of value, a store of value, and a standard for deferred payments. A "standard of

---

[12] A deposit account is also a sort of meta-token, representing the right of the depositor to receive funds from the depositary bank. So too is a casino chip. Checks, deposit accounts, and casino chips do not constitute "money" within the meaning of UCC § 1-201(b)(24) because they are not "authorized or adopted by a foreign or domestic government." Some meta-tokens circulate in the economy – *e.g.,* are used by the payees who receive them to pay obligations in connection with unrelated subsequent transactions – or are otherwise used to provide assurance of later payment. Because of this, such meta-tokens, even though they do not constitute "money" under the UCC, may be treated as a store of value for other purposes, such as measuring the nation's monetary supply.

value" means that we use money tokens to measure the value of other things. A "store of value" means that we use money in order to hoard value. A "standard for deferred payments" means that money is used as a measurement unit when borrowing value. What determines the value of money is ultimately a matter of public confidence in the token as a means of performing these three functions.[13]

How does it come to be that any particular token is recognized as money and suitable for fulfilling these purposes? The history of money in the United States is interesting for its approach to developing a medium of exchange to facilitate commerce. In its early history, the United States relied on gold and silver coinage of other countries as well as coining its own money out of those metals. Standards were set prescribing the quantity of gold or silver in each coin. Later, the government issued coins that contained less gold or silver but were redeemable for a set amount of gold or silver. Private banks also issued notes that were redeemable in gold or silver. These notes circulated as mediums of exchange and were valued based upon the level of confidence in the bank that issued the notes. However, because bank failures were not uncommon, circulating bank notes often did not fare well as mediums of exchange. Today, banks based in the United States do not generally issue circulating bank notes and United States currency is not redeemable for a set amount of gold or silver.[14]

The federal government's power to deal with monetary concerns is prescribed in the U.S. Constitution, Article I, sections 8 and 10.[15] The federal government was

---

[13] *See* THOMAS MAYER, JAMES S. DUESENBERRY, AND ROBERT Z. ALIBER, MONEY, BANKING AND THE ECONOMY (6th ed. 1997); HIRAM JOME, PRINCIPLES OF MONEY AND BANKING (1957); JAMES WILLARD HURST, A LEGAL HISTORY OF MONEY IN THE UNITED STATES, 1774-1970 (1973).

[14] *See generally* ARTHUR NUSSBAUM, A HISTORY OF THE DOLLAR (1957).

[15] U.S. Constitution, Article I, Section 8 provides in relevant part:
   Section 8. The Congress shall have Power * * * *
      To coin Money, regulate the Value thereof, and of foreign Coin, and fix the Standard of Weights and Measures;
      To provide for the Punishment of counterfeiting the Securities and current Coin of the United States; * * * * *
      To make all Laws which shall be necessary and proper for carrying into Execution the foregoing Powers, and all other Powers vested by this Constitution in the Government of the United States, or in any Department or Officer thereof.
   U.S. Constitution, Article I, Section 10 provides in relevant part:

given the power to develop the currency for the nation and the states were prohibited from coining money. The federal government did not exercise that power until 1861, when it first issued demand notes as part of the effort to finance the Civil War. As a medium of exchange, those federal bank notes – called "greenbacks" because of the color of ink used on the obverse side – were only a partial success. Many private parties did not like to accept those notes because they were not sure others would honor them.[16]

The following year, to deal with this lack of confidence, the federal government issued legal tender notes, which by law were "legal tender for all debts, public and private." After the Civil War, the federal government issued paper money that was redeemable in silver or gold. This increased public confidence in the currency but tied the supply of money to the government's reserves of those metals. Whole political parties emerged about how to deal with money. The federal reserve bank notes used as money in the U.S. today were made legal tender in 1933.[17] It was at that time that they ceased being redeemable in gold or silver.

Now that we have some understanding about the concept of money, let us return to the questions that we need to think about when dealing with money as a payment mechanism: (i) how is money used to transfer value, and (ii) when does use of money as a payment mechanism discharge the obligation arising out of the underlying business transaction.

With respect to the first question, recall the concept of money as a medium of exchange, a standard of value, and a store of value. A dollar bill has value because of the faith in the issuing government[18] and because people and business in society

---

No State shall enter into any Treaty, Alliance, or Confederation; grant Letters of Marque and Reprisal; coin Money; emit Bills of Credit; make any Thing but gold and silver Coin a Tender in Payment of Debts; pass any Bill of Attainder, ex post facto Law, or Law impairing the Obligation of Contracts, or grant any Title of Nobility.

[16] The Confederacy issued paper currency as well and those that accepted it came to regret it. After the Confederacy fell, that currency was worthless except as an historical artifact.

[17] *See* Task Force on Stored-Value Cards, *A Commercial Lawyer's Take on the Electronic Purse: An Analysis of Commercial Law Issues Associated with Stored-Value Cards and Electronic Money*, 52 BUS. LAW. 653, 665–70 (1997).

[18] This aspect of value is demonstrated on a daily basis by currency markets. The value of the U.S. dollar constantly fluctuates as against the value of other currency, such as the euro, because of the relative faith in the issuing governments and traders' assessments of among

accept it as a way to pay for property and services. A payee who receives a dollar bill in one transaction is able to then use that dollar bill as a payor in a completely different transaction with someone else. The mechanics for transferring the value represented by that token (the paper bill) are simple: transfer of physical possession of the bill.

Now consider the second question. Does the physical transfer of currency discharge the underlying obligation to pay in the business transaction? That question requires consideration of the idea of legal tender.

> "Legal tender" is a concept, not a thing. When legislation of a sovereign government provides that only certain types of paper or objects, if tendered to an obligor, will discharge indebtedness, that concept is known as legal tender. The weakest form of legal tender laws merely oblige the government to accept a particular media of exchange in satisfaction of taxes. Such laws enhance the acceptability of the paper, commonly known as money, because almost all persons will eventually be indebted to the tax collector and will, therefore, need money to discharge such indebtedness. Stronger forms of legal tender laws provide that certain media of exchange, if presented to a private party, will be deemed to satisfy debts denominated in such currency. These laws may apply unless the party specifically objects or even if the party objects. The strongest legal tender laws contain criminal sanctions against a transactor who refuses to accept the tender.[19]

As provided in 31 U.S.C. § 5103, "United States coin and currency (including Federal reserve notes and circulating notes of Federal reserve banks and national banks) are legal tender for all debts, public charges, taxes, and dues. Foreign gold or silver coins are not legal tender for debts."[20] What this means is that a tender and

---

other things, governmental stability, monetary policy, and the strength of relevant markets, such as the New York Stock Exchange.

Because payment mechanisms use currency units, all payment mechanisms suffer from the risk of value fluctuation. The dollar that you charge on your credit card today is not the same "value" as the dollar that you pay 25 days later when you pay your credit card bill.

[19] *See* Task Force on Stored-Value Cards, *A Commercial Lawyer's Take on the Electronic Purse: An Analysis of Commercial Law Issues Associated with Stored-Value Cards and Electronic Money*, 52 BUS. LAW. 653, 669 (1997) (footnotes omitted).

[20] Notice that a notation regarding legal tender is on the paper bills used as U.S. currency.

acceptance of U.S. currency and coins will discharge the underlying obligation in a transaction governed by U.S. law.

Problem 12-1

A. Tenant leases office space from Landlord. The lease agreement requires Tenant to pay rent of $3,000 on or before the first day of each calendar month using a check or funds transfer. On February 1, Tenant tenders thirty $100 bills to Landlord. Must Landlord accept the cash? *See Martinez v. Mattern*, 2006 WL 1295571 (S.D. Tex. 2006); *Croley v. Hunting Creek Club Condominium Assoc.*, 2005 WL 5269272 (E.D. Va. 2005), *aff'd*, 201 Fed. Appx. 953 (4th Cir. 2006); *Nemser v. New York City Transit Authority*, 530 N.Y.S.2d 493 (N.Y. Sup. Ct. 1988). What reasons might Landlord have for not accepting the cash?

B. Shortly after Electric Utility received regulatory approval to raise the rates it charges residential customers, Disgruntled decided to exact revenge. Instead of mailing a check in payment of his $243.87 monthly utility bill, Disgruntled went to Electric Utility's local office and tendered more than 20,000 pennies, nickels, and dimes. Must Electric Utility accept Disgruntled's tender?

Now consider the other issues that were outlined earlier. When is payment completed? The payment transaction is finished once the physical possession of the currency changes hands. This is also the moment when the underlying obligation is discharged. Thus the effect of a physical transfer of currency in a payment transaction is to make the payee the owner of the currency. This aspect of a payment mechanism is often referred to as "finality," that is, what is the point after which payment cannot be reversed. The fact that the payor may later be able to obtain a judgment against the payee for breach of the underlying contract, or rescission and restitution, does not alter the finality of the payment transaction itself.[21]

Do you think it is important for the bill to have that notation?

[21] The right to seek rescission of the underlying transaction is determined by the principles of contract law and the law of restitution, not by the law governing the payment mechanism. Some of the circumstances that may give rise to a right to rescind the underlying obligation

Does the act of using currency to pay an obligation create a further obligation on the part of the payor or the payee, or any other person? No. Currency is the most basic and simplest of payment mechanisms. Transfer of physical possession does not impose any additional obligations on either the parties to the business transaction or on any other persons.[22]

Even though using currency to make payments is simple, doing so has risks. It is to those risks we now turn. There are at least two kinds of risk that exist: (i) the currency may be counterfeit; or (ii) the currency might be damaged, lost, stolen or destroyed, before, during, or after transfer from the payor to the payee.

It should be no surprise that counterfeiting money is a crime. It should also be no surprise that if you know the paper money and coins in your possession are counterfeit, you will be subject to federal criminal penalties if you attempt to transfer those items to another person.[23] But those criminal laws do not directly address the effect of using counterfeit currency in a payment transaction. Still, the rules should come as no surprise. If the payor transfers counterfeit paper or coins to the payee, that transfer will not discharge the underlying obligation in the business transaction, even if both parties are unaware of the counterfeit nature of the currency transferred. Thus, the legal risk of counterfeit currency rests on the payor, the person attempting to use those items to pay.

Of course, the practical risk may fall on the payee. If, for example, the payee has parted with valuable property or services before discovering that the currency

---

under contract law include misrepresentation, mistake, or incapacity. Even if under the law of contracts and restitution, the payor would be entitled to specific restitution of the currency transferred, that right can be realized only if the specific currency bills or coins are "identifiable" as the same items transferred by the payor to the payee. This is usually an impossible task and thus the right to restitution of a monetary payment is the right to obtain a judgment for the value of the currency transferred, and not a replevin order to turn over the precise bills and coins originally transferred.

[22] This is unlike the use of any other payment mechanism. Each of the other payment mechanisms that are explored in this text create obligations through mere use. For example, using a credit card creates a further obligation between the card issuer and the cardholder (to pay the bill when it is due) and between the merchant and its bank (to credit the account of the merchant pursuant to their agreement) and between the merchant bank and the issuing bank (to clear the transaction according to the governing network agreement).

[23] *See* 18 U.S.C. §§ 470–492.

is counterfeit,[24] the payee will have the *legal right* to pursue the payor but may lack the *practical ability* to do so, either because the payor has disappeared or because the payor lacks the real funds needed to satisfy the obligation to the payee. In such a situation, the payee bears the real risk that the currency is counterfeit. As you should know by now in your study of law, having a legal right to collect or pursue recovery is not the same thing as succeeding on that right. Bear this point in mind as we discuss other payment mechanisms. Legals rules assign legal risk. Other factors may affect on whom the risk falls in reality.

Now consider the risk of loss or destruction of valid currency. Assume the payor is en route to the payee, clutching an envelope filled with valid U.S. currency. The payor is involved in an unfortunate accident and the currency is completely destroyed. The payor has no ability to get that currency replaced by the U.S. Treasury.[25] More to the point, the payor still owes the obligation to the payee. Because payment with currency is completed only upon the transfer of physical possession, and that has not occurred, the underlying obligation of the payor survives. In short, the rules on finality dictate, or at least greatly influence, on whom this particular risk falls. If, instead, the payor had transferred physical possession of the currency to the payee, and the currency was destroyed in an accident on the payee's way home, the result would be the reverse. The payee would have no ability to get that currency replaced by the U.S. Treasury. Moreover, because transfer of legal tender from payor to payee effected a discharge of the payor's obligation to the payee, the payee would not be able to require the payor to pay again. The owner of currency bears the risk of the currency's destruction.

What if a person loses currency and someone else finds it? Can the owner obtain the currency back from the finder? What if a thief steals currency? Can the owner obtain the currency back from the thief? The short answer to these questions is yes. The rightful owner of any property, including currency, has a legal right to recover it from a finder or thief.

But what if the finder or the thief transferred the currency to someone else in exchange for goods or services? Can the owner of the currency recover the

---

[24] Note, this may occur either before or after the act of transferring the currency.

[25] *See* 31 C.F.R. § 100.6. If more than 50% of a currency bill remains, and the holder of that remnant may be able to have the currency bill replaced through the U.S. Treasury. *See* 31 C.F.R. § 100.5. If less than 50% of a currency bill remains, the holder of that smaller remnant may be able to have the currency bill replaced only if the U.S. Treasury is satisfied that the missing portion is totally destroyed. *See* 31 C.F.R. § 100.7.

currency from the transferee? How might the owner of the currency identify what was stolen? Consider the following case.

CITY OF PORTLAND V. BERRY
739 P.2d 1041 (Or. Ct. App. 1987)

Rossman, Judge

Plaintiff brings this interpleader action to determine which of the defendants is entitled to $18,000 in $1,000 and $500 bills that its Bureau of Police acquired for use as evidence in the criminal prosecution of the thief who stole them. Defendants Berry and Kelly (appellants) seek return of the bills.[26] The trial court awarded them to defendant United States National Bank of Oregon (Bank). Berry and Kelly appeal, and we affirm.

This dispute arose after appellants' live-in attendant, Wetzel, stole nine $1,000 bills and 18 $500 bills from them.[27] Over the course of three months, Wetzel took the bills to Bank, where she converted them into smaller denominations of cash, travelers' checks, a cashier's check, savings bonds and savings accounts. During the course of its investigation and preparation for prosecution of Wetzel for theft, the Bureau of Police subpoenaed and obtained the bills.[28] After Wetzel was

---

[26] Throughout the trial and in their briefs, Berry and Kelley refer to their theory as replevin. That confuses the issue. The City's interpleader action sought a determination of who was entitled to possession of the bills. Although replevin principles are useful as a basis for analysis, we do not rely on replevin to reach the result in this case.

[27] The $1,000 and $500 bills recovered from the bank were only a part of the valuables that were stolen. In January, 1986, Berry and Kelly obtained a default judgment against Wetzel for $131,085.50 on a complaint that alleged that Wetzel took silver certificates, 50, 20, ten and two dollar bills, coins and ingots valued at $54,834 and that she failed to repay a $4,100 loan. Berry and Kelly sought to recover the value of the stolen items, repayment of the loan and $100,000 in punitive damages.

[28] When the police first requested the bills, Bank retained four $1,000 bills and 14 $500 bills in its vault. The other bills had been purchased by bank employees and customers. Bank repurchased the bills and turned them over to the police pursuant to the subpoena.

convicted of theft,[29] plaintiff initiated this action to determine whether they should be returned to the appellants as victims of the theft or to Bank.

Appellants' assignments of error raise an issue of first impression in this state. First, they argue that the trial court should have applied the general rules of replevin to reach its disposition. Bank successfully argued below that the applicable rule is the "money rule,"[30] which provides that a third party who takes stolen money in good faith and for valuable consideration obtains good title and prevails over the victim of the theft. Appellants contend that the "money rule" should not apply here, because the bills are not "money" in the sense that they are not normal cash and that, even if they are "money," the policy reason for the rule does not apply when the bills in question are of $500 and $1,000 denominations.

We reject appellants' contention that the bills are not "money." Although the United States Treasury has not printed $500 and $1,000 bills since 1945 and has been systematically taking them out of circulation and destroying them since 1969, their rarity does not affect the fact that the bills continue in circulation and are legal tender.

As a general rule, an action for replevin will lie for recovery of personal property to which the plaintiff has the right to immediate possession. Money is personal property. If the action for recovery of money fails, it is usually because the specific money is not sufficiently identifiable as the plaintiff's property. When, however,

> "specific bills and coins are identifiable because of serial numbers or special markings, or because they are located uncommingled at a specific exclusive place or contained within a [sic] identifiable container, the bills and coins, so identifiable, can be replevied."

Williams Management Enterprises v. Buonauro, 489 So. 2d 160, 164 (Fla. App. 1986).

Even assuming that the particular bills are sufficiently identifiable, appellants' argument nevertheless fails. Although generally the owner of stolen property can

---

[29] She was convicted in a stipulated facts trial to the court and was sentenced to five years in prison with a 14-month minimum and ordered to pay full restitution of $48,934.00. In addition, a default judgment was entered against her for $31,085.50 on a breach of contract and conversion action brought by Berry and Kelley.

[30] Each party asserts that the rule which it espouses is the general rule to which the opposing party's "rule" is the exception. We do not think that either rule is an exception but simply that the rules apply to different situations.

recover it from anyone who acquires it, because a thief cannot pass title to stolen property, title to currency passes with delivery to a good faith purchaser for value. *Transamerica Insurance Company v. Long*, 318 F. Supp. 156, 160 (W.D. Pa. 1970). Thus, as against the thief, appellants can assert their right of ownership. However, a third party who takes stolen money "in good faith and for good consideration will prevail over the unfortunate victim of the thief." *Kelley Kar Company v. Maryland Casualty Company*, 298 P.2d 590, 592 (Cal. Ct. App. 1956). A similar rule applies when bearer paper is lost or stolen. The victim of the loss or theft cannot recover from a good faith purchaser for value who takes the instrument in the ordinary course of business, because the purchaser is a holder in due course. *See* ORS 71.2010(20); 73.3020(1); 73.3050; 73.3060; White and Summers, UNIFORM COMMERCIAL CODE § 14-3 (1980). Although at least one state requires that the purchase be made in the ordinary course of business before a person who takes money in good faith and for value can obtain good title, *Sinclair Houston Federal Credit Union v. Hendricks*, 268 S.W.2d 290, 295 (Tex. Civ. App. 1954), because of the necessity that currency be readily acceptable as payment for debts, we conclude that the good faith and valuable consideration requirements provide ample protection from pretextual transfers of stolen money from a thief to a third party. Accordingly, if Bank took the money in good faith and for good consideration, appellants have no ownership rights that can be asserted.

Appellants argue that the policy behind the rule, that there is a "necessity that money pass freely in commercial transactions," *Sinclair Houston Federal Credit Union v. Hendricks,* 268 S.W.2d at 295, would not be furthered by its application when, as here, bills of these denominations are unusual and relatively rare. We do not agree. So long as the United States Treasury has not removed the bills from circulation and considers them to be legal tender, the policy underlying the rule remains viable. We do not accept appellants' argument that, because these specific bills were not freely flowing in commerce, the policy justification for the rule ceased to exist. Legal tender must continue to be freely acceptable without inquiry as to its source.

Appellants also challenge the trial court's factual determination that the bills "were received by the bank in good faith [and] for good consideration."[31]   In *Community Bank v. Ell*, 564 P.2d 685 (Or. 1977), the Supreme Court considered

---

[31] The trial court also determined that Bank had received the bills in the ordinary course of business. Because we do not require such a finding, we will not review the evidence supporting it.

the Uniform Commercial Code good faith requirement of ORS 71.2010(19): "honesty in fact in the conduct or transaction concerned." The court's interpretation, which we adopt in this case, is that "[t]he appropriate standard is a subjective one, looking to the intent or state of mind of the party concerned." 564 P.2d 685. The trial court heard evidence that the large denomination of the bills aroused the interest of Bank employees, that they asked Wetzel where she got them, to which she replied that the money was an inheritance, and that the employees considered the answer believable. The employees testified that they did not suspect that the money was stolen and we find nothing in the record that would lead us to conclude that Bank was not acting in good faith.

Appellants argue that Bank did not give consideration for the bills, because it paid only the face value, not the price for which they could have been purchased on the open market. Face value of legal tender is valuable consideration.

Affirmed.

Note

Are the principles the court discusses regarding cutting off the title rights of the owner of currency different from the rules regarding cutting off title claims of owners of other types of property? *See* UCC § 2-403. If they are different, what is the rationale for that difference?

Problem 12-2

A. Penny cashed a bonus check from work and received five new $100 bills from the bank. She used the bills to buy a television from Ducky Appliance Inc. When Penny got the television home and turned it on, the television did not work. Penny promptly returned the television to Ducky for a refund. Ducky offered to send her a check for $500.

    1. Does Penny have a right to return of the five $100 bills she paid to Ducky?

    2. Would it make any difference to your answer if Ducky knew that the television did not work when Ducky sold it to Penny?

B. Shortly after Thanksgiving, Penny decided to buy some holiday gifts for friends and relatives. She withdrew $900 from her deposit account at the local bank and received nine new $100 bills. While at the mall, Thief picked Penny's pocket and stole the $900.

1. Thief used four of the $100 bills to pay Landlord the past-due rent on Thief's apartment. What rights, if any, does Penny have against Landlord?

2. Thief gave three of the $100 bills to Thief's mother as a gift. What rights, if any, does Penny have against Thief's mother?

3. Thief used two of the $100 bills to buy a high-definition television from Buddy, an old friend who knows that Thief occasionally engages in larcenous activities. Just prior to the transaction, Buddy asked where Thief got the money. With a wink, Thief said, "at the mall." What rights, if any, does Penny have against Buddy? *See* UCC § 1-201(b)(20).

C. Pursuant to their agreement, Developer handed City Planner $3,000 in cash as a bribe for City Planner's assistance in getting a zoning variance Developer wanted. Fearing discovery and prosecution, City Planner did not provide any assistance and Developer never received the variance. Can Developer recover the $3,000 from City Planner?

Now that you are aware of some of the risks associated with currency, and how those risks are allocated, are you likely to alter your behavior concerning the use of currency?

As we study the use of other payment mechanisms and the legal rules that apply to each one, consider the extent to which those rules should be similar to or different from the rules relating to currency.

CHAPTER THIRTEEN

INTRODUCTION TO
CREDIT AND CHARGE CARDS

SECTION 1. INTRODUCTION

Using a credit card to pay obligations incurred in the purchase of goods or services is commonplace. Those of us who have grown up with the credit card system in place have difficulty imagining a time when you could not pull a piece of plastic from your wallet to pay for your purchases. It has not always been so.

Credit and charge cards evolved from the practice of retailers issuing charge plates to customers in order to help identify the customers to sales staff at the retailer's store. This practice spread to the oil companies and airlines. In 1950, Diners Club® issued its first card. Club members could use it to purchase food, lodging, travel, and entertainment from retailers who contractually agreed to participate in the Diners Club® system. In the later 1950s, American Express® launched its own card to compete with Diners Club®. Both of these cards were a form of *charge* card; the cardholder was required to pay the full balance of charges incurred each month. Because of this, the issuers sought cardholders who were wealthy and who could afford to pay their card balance each month.

In the 1960s, Bank of America launched its card (the precursor to Visa®) and the Interbank Card Association launched its card (the precursor to MasterCard®). These *credit* cards sought to appeal to a different market of cardholders: those with less income and the need for credit. Cardholders are required to pay a minimum amount each month, but are also permitted to pay less than the entire balance in return for incurring interest charges. In addition, major department store retailers and oil companies issue credit cards for charging purchases made at the issuer's retail outlets. These cards are often issued on easier credit terms than either charge cards or the universal credit cards in the Visa® and MasterCard® networks and serve to encourage purchasing at the issuer's outlets.

Charge cards are funded through two primary sources: cardholder fees and a merchant discount (the merchant accepting less from the issuer than the cardholder is charged). Because credit card issuers expect to make significant sums from the credit feature – *i.e.*, interest – they tend to have smaller cardholder feeds and less of a merchant discount. For this reason, many merchants prefer to accept credit cards than charge cards. However, many still accept charge cards out of fear of losing the wealthy clientele who carry such cards, if the merchants refused to accept them.[1]

Throughout the years, there has been aggressive competition for customers among the issuers of charge cards and credit cards. That is in part because this business has been extremely profitable for card issuers, particularly as the issuers have become more creative in devising ways to charge cardholders fees for the privilege of using the card or running a credit balance. Credit cards (from this point forward, references to "credit cards" include both credit cards and charge cards) have also become a very convenient payment mechanism. They are easy to use and for the most part function very well. Based upon a study of payment methods used in 2009, approximately 21.6 billion of 109 billion noncash payment transactions in the United States were made using credit cards. However, credit card transactions represented only $1.9 trillion out of $72.3 trillion transferred in noncash payment transactions.[2] Credit card transactions are therefore a high volume (20% of total number of noncash transactions) but a relatively small dollar amount (3% of total value of noncash transactions) method of transferring value.

The law that governs credit cards is, in large part, simply the contract law that governs the various relationships in a credit card transaction: (i) the cardholder and the merchant; (ii) the merchant and its bank; (ii) the cardholder and the card issuer, and (iv) the merchant's bank and the card issuer, through the clearinghouse association. Many of these contracts are private and not readily attainable. Moreover, many require arbitration of the disputes that may arise, with the result that there are few published decisions interpreting the contracts or applying traditional contract-law principles to them. Nevertheless, the fact remains that the legal rules governing most aspects of credit card use are no different than the law governing contracts in general.

---

[1] For more on the history of credit cards, see LEWIS MANDELL, THE CREDIT CARD INDUSTRY: A HISTORY (1990).

[2] 2010 FEDERAL RESERVE PAYMENTS STUDY: NONCASH PAYMENT TRENDS IN THE UNITED STATES: 2006–2009 (Dec. 8, 2010). Another recent study noted that over a third of credit card users are "convenience users," cardholders who pay off their balance in full every month. In addition, private label cards (issued by a single retailer) have a relatively low usage, with general purpose credit use rising, particularly with cards that offer rewards programs. Susan Herbst-Murphy, *Trends and Preferences in Consumer Payments: Lessons from the Visa Payment Study Panel* (May 2010) (Payment Cards Center, Federal Reserve Bank of Philadelphia).

This contract-law landscape has, however, an overlay of regulation that affects one of the contractual relationships: the relationship between the cardholder and the card issuer. That regulation is found largely in the federal Truth in Lending Act (TILA),[3] and through the implementing regulation, Regulation Z.[4] Much of the regulation of credit cards under TILA and Regulation Z can be explained by the historical development of the credit card market and the card issuers' practices. In partial response to political outrage over some issuers' practices and profits,[5]

---

[3] Codified at 15 U.S.C. §§ 1601–1667f (incorporated into the Consumer Credit Protection Act).

[4] 12 C.F.R. pt. 226. The Federal Reserve System is the independent central bank of the United States. The Federal Reserve Board is the rule making body, and promulgated Regulation Z. The twelve regional Reserve Banks provide banking services to financial institutions and the federal government. For more information about the Federal Reserve System, *see* http://www.federalreserve.gov/pf/pf.htm.

Prior to the transfer date under Dodd-Frank (scheduled for July, 2011), the Federal Reserve Board was the primary regulatory authority for the TILA. After the transfer date, the Bureau of Consumer Financial Protection will be the primary regulator. Dodd-Frank Wall Street Reform and Consumer Protection Act, Pub. L. No. 111-203, Title X, §§ 1100A(2), 1100H, 124 Stat. 1376, 2107, 2113 (July 21, 2010). Other federal agencies, including the Federal Reserve Board, have been delegated power to enforce TILA provisions through regulation. *See* TILA § 108, 15 U.S.C. § 1607. Additional regulation is in Regulation AA, 12 C.F.R. pt. 227. A careful lawyer should analyze the statute to determine whether the regulation promulgated is within the boundaries of the delegation.

In addition, prior to the transfer date under Dodd-Frank, the Division of Consumer and Community Affairs of the Federal Reserve Board issued staff commentaries on Regulation Z. These commentaries are collected in Supplement I to Regulation Z. The Supreme Court has indicated a high degree of deference to the staff commentaries to Regulation Z. *See Ford Motor Credit Co. v. Milhollin*, 444 U.S. 555, 565–66 (1980) ("deference is especially appropriate in the process of interpreting the Truth in Lending Act and Regulation Z. Unless demonstrably irrational, Federal Reserve Board staff opinions construing the Act or Regulation should be dispositive"). *See also Chase Bank v. McCoy*, 131 S. Ct. 871 (2011) (showing deference to Board interpretation of Regulation Z set forth in amicus brief).

[5] Several commentators have written about perceived abuses of the card issuer and cardholder contractual relationship. *See, e.g.*, Mark E. Budnitz, *The Development of Consumer Protection Law, the Institutionalization of Consumerism, and the Future Prospects and Perils*, 26 GA. ST. U. L. REV. 1147 (2010); Ronald J. Mann, *Unsafe at Any Price?*, 157 U. PA. L. REV. PENNUMBRA 167 (2009); Oren Bar-Gill & Elizabeth Warren, *Making Credit Safer*, 157 U. PA. L. REV. 1 (2008); Carolyn Carter, *et al.*, *The Credit Card*

Congress passed the Credit Card Accountability Responsibility and Disclosure Act of 2009 (the CARD Act),[6] which significantly changed parts of the TILA and its regulation of credit card terms. These statutory amendments required numerous amendments to Regulation Z in 2009 and 2010. Federal or state banking laws may also affect the cardholder-issuer relationship terms, depending upon whether the card issuer is a regulated entity, such as a national bank, a state chartered bank, or another type of financial services company.[7] Various state statutes governing consumers, such as the Uniform Consumer Credit Code and usury laws, may also regulate the cardholder-issuer relationship.

Given the diversity of possible statutes and regulations that may apply depending upon the identity of the card issuer or the cardholder, we will concentrate our study on the federal regulation found in TILA and Regulation Z, which applies to all card issuers and cardholders, as defined in the statute and regulation. Before we turn to these special regulatory rules, recall the issues identified in Chapter Twelve regarding any payment mechanism:

A. *Operation.* How does the payment mechanism transfer value? How does the payment mechanism work?

B. *Timing.*
   (1) When is payment final?
   (2) When does the payment mechanism discharge the payor's underlying obligation to the payee?
   (3) Prior to discharge, is the payor's underlying obligation to the payee suspended?

Market and Regulation: In Need of Repair, 10 N.C. BANKING INST. 23 (2006); Samuel Issacharoff and Erin F. Delaney, *Credit Card Accountability*, 73 U. CHI. L. REV. 157 (2006); Ronald J. Mann, *"Contracting" For Credit*, 104 MICH. L. REV. 899 (2006); Oren Bar-Gill, *Seduction by Plastic*, 98 NW. U. L. REV. 1373 (2004).

[6] Pub. L. No. 111-24, 123 Stat. 1734 (May 22, 2009). *See also* Credit Card Technical Corrections Act of 2009, Pub. L. No. 111-93, 123 Stat. 2998 (Nov. 6, 2009). For an overview of the CARD Act provisions, see Obrea Poindexter, *Update on CARD Act Rules–Credit Cards*, 66 BUS. LAW. 423 (2011); Joseph U. Schorer, *The Credit Card Act of 2009: Credit Card Reform and the Uneasy Case for Disclosure*, 127 BANKING L. J. 924 (2010); Eric A. Zacks, *Unstacking the Deck? Contract Manipulation and Credit Card Accountability*, 78 U. CIN. L. REV. 1471 (2010).

[7] *See* Adam J. Levitin, *Hydraulic Regulation: Regulating Credit Markets Upstream*, 26 YALE J. ON REG. 143 (2009).

C. *Rights & Duties.*
   (1) What obligations to the payor, payee, or other parties does the use of the payment mechanism create?
   (2) To the extent use of the mechanism creates additional obligations:
      (i) How are those obligations satisfied?
      (ii) What defenses does the obligor have to those obligations?
      (iii) If there are multiple obligors created by use of the mechanism, what is the relationship among those obligors?

D. *Risk.*
   (1) What effect will a party's insolvency have on the finality of the payment and the discharge of the underlying obligation?
   (2) What errors might arise during use of the payment mechanism and, for each error, which party or parties bear the risk?
   (3) What wrongdoing may occur during the use of the payment mechanism and, for each type of wrongdoing, which party or parties bear the risk?

SECTION 2: HOW VALUE IS TRANSFERRED FROM THE CREDIT CARDHOLDER TO THE MERCHANT

A cardholder who makes a charge on a credit card is incurring an obligation to the card issuer to pay the amount of the charge. The card issuer (for both Visa® and MasterCard®, the card issuer will be a bank) has a contractual relationship with the credit card association, such as those operated by Visa Inc. or MasterCard Worldwide. The association in turn has a contractual relationship with the merchant's bank and the merchant has a contractual relationship with its bank. These contractual relationships can be diagramed as follows:

```
Cardholder  ─────────────────────────────────────  Merchant
                        Sale Transaction

   │          Cardholder              Processing       │
   │          Agreement               Agreement        │
  Card      ────────────    Association    ────────   Merchant
 Issuing                 Association Agreement          Bank
  Bank
```

A typical credit card transaction starts with the cardholder using the credit card to pay for goods or services purchased from a merchant. Transaction information for approval of the charge is communicated electronically through the network maintained by the association. Once the transaction is approved and finalized, the merchant communicates the transaction information to its bank, the merchant bank. The merchant's bank makes funds available to the merchant based on the transaction information. The merchant's bank generally does so at a contractually discounted rate, so that the merchant receives less than the full amount that has been charged. For example, assume the cardholder made a $100 purchase at the merchant's business and the merchant bank charges a 2% fee. The merchant would receive a credit for $98 to its bank account at the merchant bank. This is the "merchant discount."

The merchant's bank then sends the transaction information to the association, which directs the transaction information to the card issuer. There is a fee charged for this information exchange – an interchange fee. Assume that the interchange fee in our hypothetical transaction is 1.5%. The card issuing bank would pay the merchant bank $98.50 instead of $100. The card issuing bank then issues a bill in the form of a periodic statement to the cardholder. On the bill, the transaction with the merchant is reflected as a $100 charge. The cardholder then pays the card issuing bank $100.

Out of that $100 in our hypothetical transaction, the merchant bank will net $.50, the card issuing bank will net $1.50, and the merchant will net $98.00. Both the merchant bank and the card issuing bank belong to the association and will pay fees to the association pursuant to their contracts with the association. The amount of the interchange fee is set by the association. The merchant discount (in the example $2.00) will capture at least as much as the interchange fee and will vary from merchant bank to merchant bank.[8] While all of the transaction information used to be communicated using paper "charge slips," in the electronic age, much of the transaction information is transmitted electronically even if the merchant collects a paper charge slip.

The merchant discount, even though only about 2%, can be quite steep for merchants in a competitive industry or with a low profit margin.[9] Nevertheless,

---

[8] For a more in-depth treatment of these multi-party relationships, see BARKLEY CLARK AND BARBARA CLARK, THE LAW OF BANK DEPOSITS, COLLECTIONS AND CREDIT CARDS, Chap. 15 (rev. ed. 2010).

[9] There have been unsuccessful antitrust challenges to the interchange fee. *See* Steven

several states prohibit merchants from recovering this cost by imposing on their customers a surcharge for payment by credit card, although some states allow the merchant to provide a discount for payment in cash.[10]

In the event a cardholder disputes a credit card charge, the transaction can be "charged back" through the system to the merchant. Thus the merchant has an incentive to employ security procedures, including obtaining a signed charge slip or its equivalent, to verify that the cardholder in fact made the charge.

Semeraro, *The Antitrust Economics (and Law) of Surcharging Credit Card Transactions*, 14 STAN. J. L. BUS. & FIN. 343 (2009); Steven Semeraro, *Credit Card Interchange Fees: Three Decades of Antitrust Uncertainty*, 14 GEO. MASON L. REV. 941 (2007); Avril McKean Dieser, *Antitrust Implications of the Credit Card Interchange Fee and an International Survey*, 17 LOY. CONSUMER L. REV. 451 (2005); Adam J. Levitin, *The Antitrust Super Bowl: America's Payment Systems, No-surcharge Rules, and the Hidden Costs of Credit*, 3 BERKELEY BUS. L.J. 265 (2005).

Whether interchange fees should be regulated is a hotly debated issue. Debate about interchange fees is in essence a debate about how the cost for the use and maintenance of the credit card system should be borne and who should profit from the use of the system. *See* Robin A. Prager, *et al.*, *Interchange Fees and Payment Card Networks: Economics, Industry Developments, and Policy Changes* (May 13, 2009) (Finance and Economics Discussion Series, Federal Reserve Board); Steven Semeraro, *The Reverse-Robin-Hood-Cross-Subsidy Hypothesis: Do Credit Card Systems Tax the Poor and Reward the Rich?*, 40 RUTGERS L.J. 419 (2009); Adam J. Levitin, *Priceless? The Social Costs of Credit Card Merchant Restraints*, 45 HARV. J. ON LEGIS. 1 (2008). The Durbin Amendment to the Dodd-Frank legislation (codified at 15 U.S.C. § 1693o-2) requires regulation of the interchange fee for non-credit card transactions. *See* Reg. II, 12 C.F.R. pt. 235.

[10] Cal. Civ. Code § 1748.1(a); Col. Rev. Stat. § 5-2-212; Conn. Gen. Stat. § 42-133ff(a), (c); Fla. Stat. § 501.0117(1); Mass. Gen. Law ch. 140D, § 28A(a); N.Y. Gen. Bus. Law § 518; Okla. Stat. tit. 14A, §§ 2-211(A), 2-417. *See also* Kan. Stat. § 16a-2-403; Tex. Fin. Code § 339.001(a) (both prohibit surcharges for use of a credit card but making no mention of cash discounts). *Contra* Minn. Stat. § 325G.051 (expressly authorizing merchants to impose a surcharge of up to 5% for payment by credit card). Some states, however, permit government agencies to impose a surcharge on people who pay fines or licensing fees with a credit card. *See* Tex. Fin. Code § 339.001(b). Some states invalidate a clause in the merchant-merchant bank contract that prohibits offering a discount for customers who pay in cash. *See* Cal. Civ. Code § 1748; Md. Com. Law § 12-509; Nev. Rev. Stat. § 97A.210; Okla. Stat. tit. 14A, § 1-110; Wis. Stat. § 422.422.

SECTION 3.   OBLIGATIONS AND RISKS IN USING A CREDIT CARD

Now that the basic scheme of the credit card value transfer mechanism is understood, return to the recurring issues identified above. First, when using a credit card, when is the underlying obligation discharged? Second, what other obligations, if any, does the cardholder incur when using the credit card and how are those obligations satisfied? Third, who bears the risk of errors or fraud arising from use of the credit card?

A. Obligations

Discharge of the underlying obligation. When the cardholder presents the card and the merchant accepts the card as a mechanism for payment, the cardholder's obligation to pay the merchant for the purchased property or service is not discharged. Rather, the merchant has implicitly agreed to seek payment through the card association and the cardholder's obligation to pay is probably suspended while payment through the card association is pursued. We say probably because no statute expressly so provides but this is the rule applicable to payment by check,[11] and it would make sense if the same rule applied to payment via credit card.

The implications of this become most apparent if the merchant does not receive final settlement of that underlying obligation through the card association. Presumably the merchant will still have recourse against the cardholder for the underlying obligation to pay for the purchased property or service. Thus, for example, if the information necessary to process the charge were lost or corrupted, or if the merchant were expelled or withdrew from the credit card system before the charge were processed, the merchant would have recourse against the cardholder for payment of the underlying contractual obligation.

The cardholder's obligation to pay the merchant presumably is discharged when the merchant's settlement through the card association becomes irrevocable. The time when this occurs is governed by the contracts between the merchant, its bank, and the association, not by the agreement between the cardholder and the card issuer.

Cardholder's obligation to pay the card issuer. When entering into the transaction with the merchant, the cardholder incurs an obligation to pay the

---

[11] *See* UCC § 3-310(b).

merchant for the price of the property or services the merchant has provided or will provide. By using the credit card to effect payment, the cardholder also incurs a separate obligation: to pay the card issuer the transaction amount pursuant to the terms and conditions in the cardholder contract with the card issuer. In that contract, the cardholder agrees to be liable to the card issuer for all authorized charges incurred using the card and all applicable fees and interest charges. The cardholder satisfies its obligation to the card issuer by engaging another payment mechanism to pay the card issuer for the amounts owed from using the card.[12]

B. Risk and Regulation

Several risks are associated with the contractual relationship between the cardholder and card issuer.[13] Perhaps the most obvious risk relates to the credit nature of the transaction. That is, the card issuer is extending credit to the cardholder to the extent the card issuer either pays or becomes obligated to pay the card association before or regardless of whether the card issuer receives payment from the cardholder. Of course, this is a risk of which the card issuer is well aware and presumably one that the card issuer assessed before issuing the card. Other risks arise out of the multi-party nature of the transaction and the number of obligations associated with the use of the credit card. These risks can be grouped into two general categories.

Risks associated with the underlying transaction. The risks associated with the underlying transaction usually relate to the property or services that the merchant has or was supposed to provide in exchange for payment. What if the property sold was defective or otherwise not as promised? Certainly ultimate responsibility for

---

[12] The cardholder may pay by writing a check to the card issuer or by authorizing a funds transfer to the card issuer. The time when the underlying obligation to the card issuer is discharged depends upon what payment mechanism the cardholder uses to pay the card issuer.

[13] In the use of any payment mechanism there are risks: credit and liquidity risks (the risk that the counter party will not settle the obligation in full when due or at anytime thereafter), operational risk (the risk that losses will be incurred because of failed operational processes such as from fire or earthquake, or from inadequate security protocols), and legal risk (the risk that law will be applied in an unexpected way or because a contract is unenforceable). *See Federal Reserve Policy on Payment System Risk* (as amended effective March 24, 2011).

that falls on the merchant. But what if payment to the merchant is final and the merchant is no longer in business or lacks the resources to provide appropriate compensation? As between the cardholder and the card issuer, who bears this risk?

Risks associated with use of the credit card. These risks typically involve a charge that the cardholder never intended to incur. For example, a thief might steal the card and use it to pay for property or services. Will the resulting loss fall on the merchant who is out the goods or services, the cardholder, or the card issuer? The cardholder may present the card to a merchant who, either intentionally or unintentionally, initiates a charge to the cardholder's account for an amount that is higher than that to which the merchant is entitled. If the merchant has been paid, will the loss fall on the cardholder or the card issuer?

Some of these risks are allocated by contract.[14] Others are allocated by law. It is to that law that we now turn.

Regulation. The TILA and Regulation Z place certain controls on the contractual relationship between the cardholder and the card issuer.[15] These controls focus, for the most part, on the credit aspects of the cardholder and card issuer relationship.[16] They require disclosure of the credit terms and prohibit some credit terms. However, a small portion of the regulation is directed at some of the risks associated with using a credit card to make a payment. To explore this portion of the regulation, we now examine three aspects of the TILA and Regulation Z:

(i) What cardholder–card issuer rights and obligations are governed by these rules?

(ii) What rights do the cardholder and the card issuer have against each other when the merchant errs in transmitting information to the card association, engages in wrongdoing in relation to a credit card transaction, or breaches its obligation in the underlying transaction with the cardholder?

---

[14] For example, the circumstances under which the card issuer can recover against the merchant or the merchant's bank if the cardholder fails to pay are specified in the card association agreement. Some commentators have questioned whether these contractual rules create incentives to reduce fraud. *See* Adam J. Levitin, *Private Disordering? Payment Card Fraud Liability Rules*, 5 BROOK. J. CORP. FIN. & COM. L. 1 (2010).

[15] Neither the TILA nor Regulation Z addresses the risks involved in the merchant–merchant bank relationship, the merchant bank–association relationship, or the issuing bank–association relationship. *But see* 12 C.F.R. § 226.12(f).

[16] *See also* Regulation AA, 12 C.F.R. pt. 227, prohibiting defined unfair trade practices in extending credit.

(iii) What are the relative rights of the cardholder and the card issuer when someone other than the merchant initiates a credit card transaction?

1.   *Scope of Regulation Z*

Read 12 C.F.R. § 226.1 and § 226.3. To determine the types of transactions that Regulation Z governs, it is important to read the operative provisions of the regulation.[17] Regulation Z regulates both "open end" credit[18] and "closed end" credit.[19] **Read the definitions of open-end and closed-end credit in 12 C.F.R. § 226.2.** A credit card may be issued as part of either an open-end or closed-end credit relationship, although it is more commonly thought of as an open-end credit device.

Notice that both types of credits are defined in relationship to "consumer credit." **Read that definition and the definitions of "consumer," "cardholder," "person," "credit card," and "charge card," all found in 12 C.F.R. § 226.2.** Both types of credit are also defined in terms of a "creditor." **Read that definition, and the definition of "card issuer," in 12 C.F.R. § 226.2 as well.**

One way to determine the scope of a regulation (in addition to reading the provision detailing its scope), is to look at who or what is being regulated. Keeping in mind the definitions you just read, now skim through the provisions of Subpart B.[20] First, notice who is being regulated: creditors and card issuers. Second, notice what is being regulated: disclosure of terms, allowed terms, and the process for changing terms.

Initially, the TILA and Regulation Z focused on protecting borrowers through disclosure, under the theory that if the terms and cost of the credit were adequately disclosed, a borrower would be able to determine if the credit being offered was in the borrower's best interest. Thus it should not be surprising to find a large proportion of Regulation Z focused on disclosure. Sections 226.5, 226.5a, 226.5b, and 226.6 all deal with the terms that must be disclosed at the start of the creditor-

---

[17] See the commentary published at 12 C.F.R. pt. 226, Supplement I. That commentary can be very helpful in understanding the application of Regulation Z.

[18] *See* Subpart B, 12 C.F.R. § 226.5 through § 226.16.

[19] *See* Subpart C, 12 C.F.R. § 226.17 through § 224.24.

[20] 12 C.F.R. § 226.5 through § 226.16.

debtor relationship in an open-end credit.[21] These sections identify the terms that must be disclosed, mandate the manner in which the terms are disclosed, and specify when those terms must be disclosed. Section 226.5a is specifically directed at card issuers, but other provisions also impact card issuers (who are a subset of the term "creditor").

Sections 226.7 and 226.8 regulate the disclosures, including transaction information, that must be provided in periodic statements, and these rules apply to card issuers. Section 226.9 regulates the disclosures a creditor, including a card issuer, must make annually, and the disclosures a card issuer must make before renewal of the credit card. As part of this disclosure model, Regulation Z also contains provisions on how creditors may advertise the terms of credit.[22] The focus of disclosure is not only on the timing of the disclosures, but also on the types of information related to the cost and terms of credit, and the form in which the information is provided. Because one of the purposes of TILA was to accurately disclose the cost of the credit, Regulation Z specifies how the annual percentage rate must be calculated.[23] Lawyers who represent card issuers will periodically review the disclosure information the card issuer provides and disclosure process the card issuer uses to make sure the card issuer is complying with the TILA and Regulation Z. Appendix G to Regulation Z contains model forms of disclosure for open-end credit and Appendix H contains model forms of disclosure for closed-end credit.

Regulation Z is not and never was, however, limited solely to disclosure. Some of its rules directly affect the substance of the creditor's relationship with the debtor. For example, section 226.12(a) bars the creditor practice of sending unsolicited credit cards.[24] Other sections specify some terms that a creditor must include and some terms that a creditor must not include in its agreement with the debtor.[25] Sections 226.10 and 226.53 address the treatment of payments. Section

---

[21] Required disclosures in a closed-end credit are set forth in 12 C.F.R. § 226.17 through § 226.20.

[22] *See* 12 C.F.R. § 226.16 (open-end credit), § 226.24 (closed-end credit), § 226.57 (marketing to college students).

[23] *See* 12 C.F.R. § 226.14 (open-end credit), § 226.22 (closed-end credit).

[24] *See Acosta v. Target Corp.*, 728 F. Supp. 2d 968 (N.D. Ill. 2010).

[25] The 2009 CARD Act resulted in a new Subpart G governing credit card accounts. 12 C.F.R. § 226.51 through § 226.59.

226.11 addresses the treatment of credit balances.[26] Sections 226.52, 226.54, and 226.55 limits fees and other charges. Section 226.56 deals with transactions over the cardholder's credit limit, which have historically been a source of fees for card issuers. Section 226.59 addresses finance rate changes. Section 226.9(c) addresses how the creditor may change the terms of the credit. Finally, 226.58 requires card issuers to submit the form agreements to the Federal Reserve Board and to make the form agreements available on the internet or available to the cardholder on request.

If a card issuer fails to comply with Regulation Z requirements, the applicable regulatory agency may pursue the card issuer for that violation. The card issuer also incurs civil liability to the cardholder under section 130 of the TILA.[27] This liability is for actual damages, statutory damages, and attorneys' fees.

Problem 13-1

To solidify your understanding of how Regulation Z applies to credit cards, write in your own words a paragraph that describes that application.

2. *Cardholder Disputes with the Merchant and the Card Issuer*

For our purposes, the most important portions of Regulation Z are sections 226.12 and 226.13. **Read those sections now.** Section 226.12(b) limits a cardholder's liability for fraud. Subsection (c) allows the cardholder to assert against the card issuer some of the cardholder's claims or defenses against the merchant. Subsection (d) prohibits setoff by the card issuer against deposited funds of the cardholder in most circumstances. Subsection (e) deals with crediting the credit card account based upon refunds and returns. Subsection (f) provides two protections to persons who honor cards from terms that a card issuer may try to impose. Section 226.13 provides for a process for resolving billing errors.

In certain types of transactions involving a secured obligation, a debtor may have the right to rescind a credit transaction. 12 C.F.R. §§ 226.15, 226.23. These provisions do not apply to the typical credit card transaction.

[26] Section 226.21 addresses treatment of credit balances in closed-end credit.

[27] 15 U.S.C. § 1640.

To understand how these provisions allocate the risks associated with using a credit card, read the following case and then work through the questions and problems that follow it.

STIEGER V. CHEVY CHASE SAVINGS BANK
666 A.2d 479 (D.C. Ct. App. 1995)

Pryor, Senior Judge

For the first time we are asked to determine whether a credit cardholder who permits use of the card by another for a specific purpose is liable for other uses not specifically authorized. The precise issue is whether, in such circumstances, the card user had "apparent authority" to use the card in the context of the provisions of the Truth-in-Lending Act, 15 U.S.C. §§ 1601 *et seq.* (1988). We agree with the Superior Court that for thirteen of the fifteen disputed charges the matching of the signature, combined with the cardholder's voluntary relinquishment of the card for a third party's use, constitutes such "apparent authority" under the Act, thereby making appellant liable for the full amount of the thirteen charges. We, therefore, affirm the decision of the Superior Court.

I.

On November 10, 1992, appellant brought suit against Chevy Chase Bank, F.S.B. ("Chevy Chase") claiming he should not be held liable for certain charges credited to his Chevy Chase Visa card. Appellant voluntarily gave his credit card to a Ms. Garrett for the limited purpose of renting a car and for hotel lodging during a business trip. Appellant contacted both the car rental agency and the hotel to determine what type of authorization would be needed for Ms. Garrett to use his Visa card. Both companies informed him that he must write a letter authorizing the charges. Appellant asserts that he wrote both companies, but was unable to produce a copy of the letter to the hotel, which he contends limited his liability to $350.00.

Shortly after the conclusion of Ms. Garrett's business trip, appellant learned that she had made several other charges he had not specifically authorized. His signature apparently had worn off the back of his credit card, and Ms. Garrett signed it as "P. Stieger" rather than Paul Stieger. On thirteen of the fifteen charges in dispute, Ms. Garrett had signed the charge slip "P. Stieger," and on the other two she signed her own name.[28] Appellant has obtained a judgment against Ms. Garrett for $3200.00, but only $750.00 has been collected, and Ms. Garrett can no longer be located. Therefore, this action was brought to contest Chevy Chase's refusal to dismiss the charges as unauthorized.

Commissioner Diaz ruled in favor of Chevy Chase on all fifteen charges. Appellant appealed to the Superior Court asserting that the charges were unauthorized under the Truth-In-Lending Act. After review of the case, a judge of the Superior Court held that the Commissioner "had a factual and legal basis upon which she could properly decide that the voluntary relinquishment of the cardholder's credit card for one purpose gives the bearer apparent authority to make additional charges."

The Superior Court judge also considered the Commissioner's reasonableness analysis. The Superior Court found that the merchants acted reasonably in accepting appellant's credit card in thirteen of the fifteen charges where the name signed ("P. Stieger") matched the signature on the card. However, the court reversed the two charges where Ms. Garrett had signed her own name. Appellant filed an application for allowance of appeal, and on April 29, 1994 we granted the application.

II.

In a broad sense, the resolution of this matter involves an economic consideration of whether the cardholder, card issuer, or merchant should bear the financial responsibility in the circumstances presented. The Truth-In-Lending Act was enacted "in large measure to protect credit cardholders from unauthorized use perpetrated by those able to obtain possession of a card from its original owner." *Towers World Airways Inc. v. PHH Aviation Systems, Inc.*, 933 F.2d 174, 176 (2d Cir.), *cert. denied*, 502 U.S. 823 (1991). The Act specifically limits liability for the cardholder to a maximum of $50 for charges made by third parties that are "unauthorized." 15 U.S.C. § 1643(a). However, the Act does not limit liability for the cardholder for third party charges made with "actual, implied or apparent authority." 15 U.S.C. § 1602(o).

The essential question on appeal is whether the disputed charges were incurred by an "unauthorized user" under the Act. The statute specifically incorporates agency concepts by defining "unauthorized use" as "a use of a credit card by a

---

[28] Twenty-two charges were made by Ms. Garrett, of which seven were dropped by the Bank prior to trial.

person other than the cardholder who does not have actual, implied, or *apparent* authority for such use and from which the cardholder receives no benefit." 15 U.S.C. § 1602(o) (emphasis added); see also 12 C.F.R. § 226.12(b)(1) n.22 (stating same). Thus, our inquiry focuses on whether the relinquishment of a credit card to another for a limited purpose, which is then expanded by the user to make additional charges not authorized by the cardholder, is an "unauthorized" use under 15 U.S.C. § 1602(o), thereby limiting cardholder liability. Since actual or implied authority are not alleged in this case, the narrower issue is whether Ms. Garrett had apparent authority to use the card.

Our cases reveal that "[a]pparent authority arises when a principal places an agent 'in a position which causes a third person to reasonably believe the principal had consented to the exercise of authority the agent purports to hold. This falls short of an overt, affirmative representation by a principal.' " *Insurance Management of Washington, Inc. v. Eno & Howard Plumbing Corp.*, 348 A.2d 310, 312 (D.C.1975) (*quoting Drazin v. Jack Pry, Inc.,* 154 A.2d 553, 554 (D.C.1959)). Specifically, in this jurisdiction "apparent authority of an agent arises when the principal places the agent in such a position as to *mislead* third persons into believing that the agent is clothed with authority which in fact he does not possess." *Jack Pry, Inc. v. Harry Drazin*, 173 A.2d 222, 223 (D.C.1961) (emphasis added).

"Though a cardholder's relinquishment of possession may create in another the appearance of authority to use the card, the statute clearly precludes a finding of apparent authority where the transfer of the card was without the cardholder's consent as in cases involving theft, loss, or fraud." *Towers,* 933 F.2d at 177. As one court has stated:

> Where a credit cardholder, who was under no compulsion by fraud, duress, or otherwise, voluntarily permits the use of his or her credit card by another person, the cardholder has authorized the use of that card and is thereby responsible for any charges as a result of that use, even if he or she requested that the other person not charge over a certain amount or make charges on it for specified purposes. The user has apparent authority to use the card even after actual authority ceases; provided, however, that the cardholder is not liable for use of the card after the issuer has been notified that actual authority for others to use the card no longer exists.

Standard Oil Co. v. Steele, 489 N.E.2d 842, 844 (Ohio Mun. Ct. 1985).

Nearly every jurisdiction that has addressed a factual situation "where a cardholder voluntarily and knowingly allows another to use his card and that person subsequently misuses the card," *Martin v. American Express,* 361 So. 2d 597, 601

(Ala. Civ. App. 1978), has determined that the agent had apparent authority, and therefore was not an "unauthorized" user under the Act limiting liability for the cardholder.

However, * * * [n]o liability can attach to the cardholder when the card was not voluntarily relinquished, but rather was stolen. In addition, if the cardholder notifies the card issuer that the card is being used in an unauthorized manner, the cardholder will not be liable for any charges made by the third party after the notice.

We agree with these general principles because the voluntary relinquishment of the credit card, as distinguished from the stolen card situation, can often "mislead third persons into believing the agent is clothed with authority which in fact he does not possess." *Drazin,* 173 A.2d at 223.

III.

Appellant argues that he had the right to expect Ms. Garrett to use the credit card only for the charges he authorized, and that he cannot be held liable for his agent acting beyond the scope of her authority. Appellant also asserts that Ms. Garrett could not reasonably present herself as Paul Stieger, and that a merchant should be required to give greater scrutiny to the person using the card.

Turning to the specific facts in this case, appellant gave Ms. Garrett his credit card to use. As the Superior Court noted, thirteen of the charges had the same signature as appeared on the back of the card. Appellant placed Ms. Garrett, by voluntarily giving her the card, "in such a position as to mislead third persons into believing that the agent is clothed with authority which in fact [s]he does not possess." *Drazin,* 173 A.2d at 223. To a merchant, voluntary relinquishment combined with the matching of a signature is generally a reasonable indication of apparent authority to utilize the credit card. *See* 15 U.S.C. § 1643(a)(1)(F); 12 C.F.R. § 226.12(b)(2)(iii) & Supp. I at 341 (requiring the card issuer to provide a means of verifying the authority of the card bearer such as a signature, photograph, fingerprint or electronic or mechanical confirmation).

We agree with the Superior Court that the Commissioner "could properly conclude that the third-party merchants' actions were reasonable," and that the "voluntary relinquishment of the cardholder's credit card for one purpose gives the bearer apparent authority to make additional charges." However, we agree with the Superior Court that the same cannot be said of the two charges where Ms. Garrett signed her own name rather than "P. Stieger." It is an unreasonable extension of the apparent authority provided to Ms. Garrett for a merchant to accept charges, where the signatures do not match, without any additional factors to mislead the merchant into believing that the person presenting the card is the agent of the cardholder.

Appellant attempted to limit his authorization exclusively to the hotel and car rental company, and to a specific dollar amount for each. He testified he did this by writing letters to the two companies limiting the amount Ms. Garrett could charge. These letters to the two companies would limit his liability to the amounts stated in the letters if they were in fact received by the companies when the credit card was offered as payment. Mr. Stieger was able to produce only a copy of the letter to the car company. The charge to the car company did not exceed the limit in the letter. However, Mr. Stieger was unable to produce a copy of the letter to the hotel that he asserts limited the amount Ms. Garrett could charge to $350. By testifying that he voluntarily gave his credit card to Ms. Garrett and wrote the hotel to authorize the charge, the bank has met its burden of showing apparent authority.[29] Since Mr. Stieger has not submitted a copy of the letter limiting his exposure to $350, we agree with the Superior Court that the Commissioner did not err in concluding that Mr. Stieger is liable for the full amount of the hotel charge in excess of the $350.

In sum, Mr. Stieger was in the best position to control the uses of his credit card by not relinquishing it to a third party he could not trust, by notifying the card issuer that his credit limit should be lowered to a specific dollar amount, thereby limiting his exposure, or by notifying the card issuer upon becoming aware of certain unapproved purchases that any further purchases are unauthorized. As one court has noted "[i]n four-party arrangements of this sort [cardholder, issuer, third party and merchant], it is totally unrealistic to burden the card issuer with the obligation to convey to numerous merchants whatever limitation the cardholder has placed on the card user's authority." *Towers,* 933 F.2d at 179. The Truth-In-Lending Act, although generally designed to protect credit cardholders, specifically reveals a congressional preference that where apparent authority exists, under the circumstances, the cardholder should bear the financial responsibility. Mr. Stieger voluntarily relinquished his credit card to an unreliable person, and thereby put Ms. Garrett in a position to mislead merchants to believe that she possessed apparent authority to utilize the card. Under the circumstances, Mr. Stieger should bear the

---

[29] This fact was uncontroverted, and thus under settled concepts, appellant created an apparent authority in Ms. Garrett to reasonably use the card. It sometimes happens, as here, that appellant provided the factual basis for appellee's burden to proceed. A remand on this point would be futile.

financial responsibility for the unauthorized charges made by Ms. Garrett as determined by the trial court.

Affirmed.

Ruiz, Associate Judge, dissenting:

I agree with the majority that under the Truth-in-Lending Act the focus of our inquiry must be on whether Garrett had "apparent authority" to make the contested charges. I part company with the majority at the point that it decides that Garrett's act of forging Stieger's signature can be used to establish apparent authority. * * * Therefore, I respectfully dissent.

I.

As the majority observes, a principal purpose of the Truth-in-Lending Act is to protect credit cardholders from unauthorized use. The Act seeks to achieve that objective by limiting the liability of credit cardholders to $50 for "unauthorized" charges to their accounts. 15 U.S.C. § 1643(a)(1) (1988). For the cardholder to have any liability at all for unauthorized use of her card, however, the card issuer must have undertaken to establish procedures to guard against unauthorized use, including providing "a method whereby the user of such card can be identified as the person authorized to use it." *Id.* § 1643(a)(1)(F).

The term "unauthorized" is defined to mean "use of a credit card by a person other than the cardholder who does not have actual, implied, or apparent authority for such use and from which the cardholder receives no benefit." 15 U.S.C. § 1602(o). The parties do not appear to dispute that Stieger received no benefit from the impugned charges. Other than with respect to one charge, a hotel charge in Oklahoma as to which Stieger testified he had authorized Garrett to charge up to $350, there is no dispute as to the existence of actual or implied authority. Therefore, the threshold legal question in determining Stieger's liability is whether Garrett was an unauthorized user or had "apparent authority" within the meaning of the statute to use Stieger's credit card.

Congress' reference to "actual, implied or apparent authority" would appear to necessarily incorporate some manner of common-law definition, whether by reference to state law or federal common law. The Federal Reserve Board, which has authority to promulgate regulations implementing the Truth-in-Lending Act, 15 U.S.C. § 1604(a), in its "Official Staff Interpretations" of Regulation Z, section 12(b) of which implements § 1643, states that "[w]hether such authority exists must be determined under state or other applicable law."[30] 12 C.F.R. pt. 226, supp. I, at 341 (1995). Consequently, it seems appropriate to look to common-law rules of agency, both generally and in the states in which Garrett made the contested charges, which are Oklahoma, Texas, Virginia and the District of Columbia.

The common-law rule permits only the acts of the putative principal to be used in establishing apparent agency. For example, the RESTATEMENT (SECOND) OF AGENCY provides:

> Apparent authority is the power to affect the legal relations of another person by transactions with third persons, professedly as agent for the other, *arising from and in accordance with the other's manifestations to such third persons.*

RESTATEMENT (SECOND) OF AGENCY § 8 (1958) (emphasis added).

Both Oklahoma and Texas have cited that provision of the RESTATEMENT with approval. The Supreme Court of Virginia has cited a comment to section 8 of the RESTATEMENT with approval, but it has not adopted the black-letter provision.

This court has never expressly adopted the RESTATEMENT definition; we have however, defined apparent authority in similar terms:

> "Apparent authority arises when a principal places an agent 'in a position which causes a third person to *reasonably believe that the principal had consented* to the exercise of authority the agent purports to hold. This falls short of an overt, affirmative representation by a principal.'"

Feltman v. Sarbov, 366 A.2d 137, 139 (D.C. 1976) (*quoting Insurance Management v. Eno & Howard Plumbing Corp.*, 348 A.2d 310, 312 (D.C. 1975) (*quoting Drazin v. Jack Pry, Inc.*, 154 A.2d 553, 554 (D.C. 1959))) (emphasis added). For example, in *Jack Pry, Inc. v. Drazin*, 173 A.2d 222 (D.C. 1961), relied upon by the majority, the facts that we found to be sufficient to establish apparent agency were all acts of the putative principal, not of the apparent agent.

---

[30] The Staff Interpretations do not appear intended to have legally binding effect, however. The introduction to the interpretations states that "[g]ood faith compliance with this commentary affords protection from liability under [a provision] of the Truth-in-Lending Act [that] protects creditors from civil liability for any act done or omitted in good faith in conformity with any interpretation issued by a duly authorized official or employee of the Federal Reserve System." Thus, the interpretations provide a safe harbor for creditors, but do not bind the courts (or other agencies) in their interpretation of the Act. Nevertheless, reference to the interpretation should serve as persuasive authority.

Thus, courts have repeatedly said that the third party must reasonably rely upon the conduct of the putative principal and not the putative agent in concluding that the putative agent had authority to bind the principal. Over a hundred years ago, the Supreme Court of the District of Columbia, sitting in general term, said that "if the fraud consists in the agent's pretending to have the authority for that which he does, the principal is not affected." *Brooke v. Barnes*, 12 D.C. (1 Mackey) 5, 11 (1880).

In the present case, Stieger, the putative principal, gave his credit card, embossed with his name, to Garrett, the putative agent. In accordance with instructions he received from the merchants for which he authorized her to use his credit card, he provided written authorization for two particular uses, and no others. He did not permit Garrett to sign the card. Thus, the question is whether a merchant, having knowledge of the putative principal's actions, could reasonably conclude that the putative agent had *carte blanche* to make charges to the credit card.

Stieger took care to find out how to authorize Garrett to make limited use of his charge card and followed the instructions given to him. The majority focuses primarily on Stieger's action in turning over the card to Garrett as if, instead of having provided the card so that she could use it only for such limited purposes, he had given her a master key that, without more, can open all doors. In this respect, however, it is important to remember that a credit card is *not* a bearer instrument. Were it otherwise, the result might be different.[31]

As the majority recognizes, however, because a credit card is not a bearer device, a third party is not reasonable in treating it as such by failing to check the identity of the user against the identity of the cardholder by at least matching the signature of the bearer with the signature on the card. This point was reinforced by the evidence adduced by Stieger regarding the industry practice of requiring written authorization of the cardholder for use by an agent.[32] The majority holds Stieger

---

[31] In this respect, it is interesting to note that "apparent authority exists only with regard to those who believe and have reason to believe that there is authority; there can be no apparent authority created by an undisclosed principal." RESTATEMENT (SECOND) OF AGENCY § 8 cmt. a. In the instant case, it appears that with respect to the thirteen charges signed "P. Stieger," it is at least arguable that Garrett did not purport to act as an agent for Stieger, but instead acted on her own behalf. If so, then she could not have bound Stieger, for his existence remained undisclosed to the merchants. The point does not appear to have been argued, however.

[32] At the hearing on his claim, Stieger testified regarding his experience with and

liable for those charges where Garrett signed Stieger's name, but not those for which she signed her own name. According to the majority, the merchants reasonably relied on her signature for the former because it matched the signature on the back of the card. However, there is no dispute that Stieger did not permit Garrett to sign his card; her signing of the card was an act of forgery, compounded each of the thirteen times that she signed the charge slips as "P. Stieger." Under the common law, the principal's liability for acts within the apparent authority of an agent is based on the merchants' reasonable reliance on an action of the principal. That was not the case here, where the merchants relied on Garrett's forgeries. Thus, Garrett did not have apparent authority, within the meaning of 15 U.S.C. § 1643(a), to bind Stieger for the thirteen charges that she unlawfully signed "P. Stieger."

I believe that this result is consistent with the purpose of the rules of agency, which as Blackstone observed, is to further commerce. *See* 1 WILLIAM BLACKSTONE, COMMENTARIES ON THE LAWS OF ENGLAND 418 (1765) ("[W]ithout such a doctrine as this, no mutual intercourse between man and man could subsist with any tolerable convenience."). In the furtherance of commerce through the use of agents, there are two interests to be balanced. The rules should not make it too risky for a principal to employ agents. But the rules also should not make the dealings of third persons with agents so uncertain of their validity that third persons will refuse to deal with agents. The law of agency balances those interests by charging the principal only with her own acts, while demanding only that third persons behave reasonably in relying upon those acts. After those rules have been exhausted, the law places the burden of fraudulent conduct outside the scope of actual agency upon the party defrauded, whether it is the principal or a third party. That is logical, because each member of society participating in commerce is

---

investigation into the practices of merchants in accepting credit cards from persons other than the cardholder. * * * Specifically, Stieger testified about his experiences with the car rental company and the hotel, which required written authorization when he called about what he should do to permit Garrett to use his card. He also testified that a hotel in California required written authorization from him before they would charge his father's room to his credit card. He testified that merchants have often required him to prove his identity in connection with his use of his own credit card. He testified that his own investigation of local merchants disclosed that several never honor credit cards presented by one other than the cardholder, and that of the remainder, all but one require a written authorization. The one exception is a drug store chain, which will accept a credit card presented by one other than the cardholder without written authorization only if it is used to pay for a drug prescription which matches the name of the cardholder.

charged with looking out for his or her own interests, and when those interests are wrongfully infringed, is given the right to proceed against at least the primary wrongdoer.

In my view, the majority's opinion upsets the balance of interests in the common law of agency by making the credit cardholder bear a disproportionate share of the risk from an activity furthering commerce that clearly benefits the card issuer and the merchants who accept the card. I disagree that the cardholder is in a better position to prevent fraud by a user with limited authority, such as Garrett perpetrated in this case. As the Truth-in-Lending Act makes clear, it is the duty of the card issuer to "provide[ ] a method whereby the user of such card can be identified as the person authorized to use it." 15 U.S.C. § 1643(a)(1)(F). Currently, it appears that most card issuers rely on a combination of embossed name and a signature provided by the cardholder. If those means of identification are too easily avoided or defeated by persons intent on fraud, it would seem that it is the card issuer that bears the burden of either improving the system or absorbing the loss.

* * *

Notes

1. In any case involving a wrongdoer, such as Ms. Garrett in the *Stieger* case, the wrongdoer will invariably be liable under some legal rule, usually a rule based in tort law or contract law. The wrongdoer's liability is therefore usually not a matter of payments law. However, often the wrongdoer cannot be found or is judgment proof, something also true of Ms. Garrett. When the remaining parties to the payment mechanism seek to put the loss on each other, that is where payments law comes into play. Payment law will assign the risk of loss from the wrongdoer to one or more of the parties.

2. Why does the TILA and Regulation Z place the bulk of the risk of unauthorized use on the card issuer?

3. Compare the majority and dissent's discussion of apparent authority with this formulation found in the RESTATEMENT (THIRD) OF AGENCY § 2.03 (2006):

   > Apparent authority is the power held by an agent or other actor to affect a principal's legal relations with third parties when a third party

reasonably believes the actor has authority to act on behalf of the principal and that belief is traceable to the principal's manifestations.

Would there be a different result if the new Restatement formulation applied? What policy should inform the meaning of the term "unauthorized use" to allocate the risk of wrongdoing in using the credit card?

4. Would Judge Ruiz reach the same result in a case in which the cardholder allows the cardholder's 18-year-old child to use the card, the child uses the card for far more than the cardholder authorized, but the cardholder and child have the same last name?

5. To whom must the card user's apparent authority be apparent, the issuer or the merchant? In answering this question, consider the case excerpt below.

DBI ARCHITECTS, P.C. V. *AMERICAN EXPRESS TRAVEL-RELATED SERVICES CO.* 388 F.3d 886 (D.C. Cir. 2004)

ROGERS, Circuit Judge

* * *

DBI is a corporation with its principal place of business in the District of Columbia. It had an AMEX corporate credit card account, which it authorized certain employees to use. On March 14, 2001, DBI appointed Kathy Moore as the Accounting Manager for its District of Columbia and Virginia offices. In that position, Moore was in charge of both approval and payment functions in the cash disbursement system: she controlled accounts receivable, accounts payable, corporate checking, corporate credit cards, and all other financial aspects of DBI's business. She had authority to issue DBI corporate checks to pay bills and invoices from vendors * * * and was responsible for the receipt, review, and payment of DBI's AMEX invoices.

On or about August 10, 2001, AMEX added Moore as a cardholder on DBI's corporate account at Moore's request and without DBI's knowledge or approval. From August 2001 to May 2002, Moore charged total of * * * $133,254.79 in unauthorized charges for clothing, travel, jewelry, and other personal items. During this period, AMEX sent DBI ten monthly billing statements, each listing Moore as a corporate cardholder and itemizing her charges. Between August 2001 and June 2002, Moore paid for these charges with thirteen DBI checks made payable to

AMEX. * * * [After discovering the Moore's fraud, DBI sued AMEX for violating 15 U.S.C. § 1643 by refusing to repay DBI for the $133,254.79 in fraudulent charges made by Moore]. * * *

AMEX cannot meet its burden to show that it is entitled to judgment as a matter of law, based solely on DBI's failure to examine its monthly billing statements. Indeed, AMEX makes no such attempt. AMEX contends, and we hold, that DBI cannot avoid liability for Moore's fraudulent charges because its repeated payments in full after notice led AMEX reasonably to believe that Moore had the authority to use DBI's corporate credit card. Imposing liability based on the cardholder's payment after notice is not inconsistent with Congress's plan for allocating loss from credit card fraud. By identifying apparent authority as a limit on the cardholder's protection under § 1643, Congress recognized that a cardholder has certain obligations to prevent fraudulent use of its card. DBI's troubles stemmed from its failure to separate the approval and payment functions within its cash disbursement process. Moore had actual authority both to receive the billing statements and to issue DBI checks for payment to AMEX. While DBI did not voluntarily relinquish its corporate card to Moore, it did mislead AMEX into reasonably believing that Moore had authority to use the corporate card by paying her charges on the corporate account after receiving AMEX's monthly statements identifying her as a cardholder and itemizing her charges. While payment may not always create apparent authority, this is not a case involving "an occasional transgression buried in a welter of financial detail." *Minskoff v. American Express Travel Related Services Co.*, 98 F.3d 703, 710 (2d Cir. 1996). Nor is this a case involving payment without notice, as might occur when a cardholder authorizes its bank to pay its credit card bills automatically each month. Where, as here, the cardholder repeatedly paid thousands of dollars in fraudulent charges for almost a year after monthly billing statements identifying the fraudulent user and itemizing the fraudulent charges were sent to its corporate address, no reasonable juror could disagree that at some point the cardholder led the card issuer reasonably to believe that the fraudulent user had authority to use its card.

* * *

Accordingly, we hold that DBI is estopped from avoiding liability to AMEX for the charges Moore incurred on the corporate account after her apparent authority arose. The question remains when Moore's apparent authority arose. * * * [N]o relevant statute sets a time period that is controlling. * * * Because the question of precisely when apparent authority arose cannot be resolved as a matter of law, we remand DBI's § 1643 claim to the district court to determine, or as appropriate to allow a jury to determine, at what point DBI's payment created apparent authority and thereby terminated DBI's protection under the statute. * * *

———————

Note

Several other courts agree with the D.C. Circuit's analysis.[33]

Problem 13-2

In January you used the Internet website of a retailer located in Michigan to order $500 worth of clothing to be shipped to you in Seattle. You used your credit card to pay for the clothing. It is now two weeks later and you have not yet received the clothing but your most recent credit card bill includes the charge for the purchase price. Your payment is due in two weeks.

A. Do you have the right to dispute the charge? If so, how is that dispute to be resolved and what rights do you have pending resolution of the dispute?

B. Would you have the right to dispute the charge if you had ordered the clothing for your employees to wear?

C. Does the TILA or Regulation Z govern your rights as against the merchant?

D. Would your analysis differ if you received the clothing but were not happy with its quality and the merchant refused to either replace the clothing or give you a refund?

———————

[33] *See Azur v. Chase Bank, USA*, 601 F.3d 212 (3d Cir. 2010); *Asher v. Chase Bank USA*, 310 Fed. Appx. 912 (7th Cir. 2009), *cert. denied,* 130 S. Ct. 148 (2009); *Permobil, Inc. v. American Express Travel Related Servs. Co.*, 571 F. Supp. 2d 825 (M. D. Tenn. 2008); *Carrier v. Citibank (South Dakota)*, 383 F. Supp. 2d 334 (D. Conn. 2005), *aff'd,* 180 Fed. Appx. 296 (2d Cir. 2006).

E. If you are not required to pay the card issuer, does Regulation Z say anything about the relative rights of the merchant and the card issuer?

F. Would your analysis differ if your monthly bill showed two charges of $500 from the same merchant but you had ordered only one shipment priced at $500?

Problem 13-3

You are the managing partner in a law firm. Some employees have credit cards issued to them under the law firm's name to pay for travel expenses incurred in the course of their employment. What processes would insure that the firm is not liable for charges made on those cards that the law firm does not intend to pay for?

SECTION 4. REVIEW

1. Summarize the rules regarding the allocation of the risk of errors and fraud in the use of credit cards. What risks does the card issuer bear? What risks does the merchant bear? What risks does the cardholder bear?

2. Compare and contrast the rules regarding errors and fraud in the use of credit cards with the rules regarding errors and fraud in the use of currency.

3. Why have different rules for two different types of payment mechanisms?

CHAPTER FOURTEEN

INTRODUCTION TO NEGOTIABLE INSTRUMENTS AS A PAYMENT MECHANISM

SECTION 1. INTRODUCTION

In Chapters Twelve and Thirteen, we introduced the concept of the payment system and considered two relatively simple payment mechanisms: currency and credit cards. In this Chapter we begin exploring a considerably more complicated payment mechanism: a negotiable instrument.

Most of us use negotiable instruments on a regular basis. Each time you write a check to pay a bill you have used this payment mechanism. When purchasing expensive property, such as a house or car, if the seller or a lender is providing credit, the buyer may sign a negotiable promissory note, another type of negotiable instrument.

Just as with other payment mechanisms, the issues we identified in Chapter Twelve are present when a negotiable instrument is used. As a reminder those issues are:

A. *Operation.* How does the payment mechanism transfer value? How does the payment mechanism work?

B. *Timing.*
   (1) When is payment final?
   (2) When does the payment mechanism discharge the payor's underlying obligation to the payee?
   (3) Prior to discharge, is the payor's underlying obligation to the payee suspended?

C. *Rights & Duties.*
   (1) What obligations to the payor, payee, or other parties does the use of the payment mechanism create?
   (2) To the extent use of the mechanism creates additional obligations:
      (i) How are those obligations satisfied?
      (ii) What defenses does the obligor have to those obligations?
      (iii) If there are multiple obligors created by use of the mechanism, what is the relationship among those obligors?

D. *Risk.*
   (1) What effect will a party's insolvency have on the finality of the payment and the discharge of the underlying obligation?

(2) What errors might arise during use of the payment mechanism and, for each error, which party or parties bear the risk?

(3) What wrongdoing may occur during the use of the payment mechanism and, for each type of wrongdoing, which party or parties bear the risk?

We will explore these issues in roughly this order. However, we will do so over the next several Chapters. That is because, unlike the relatively simple rules applicable to currency and credit cards, the rules relating to negotiable instruments are quite complex.[1]

This Chapter deals principally with the operational and timing issues. It discusses the mechanics of value transfer using a negotiable instrument, the requirements that must be met for something to qualify as a negotiable instrument, and the relationship between the use of a negotiable instrument and the underlying obligation.

Chapters Fifteen through Eighteen deal with the rights and duties associated with the use of negotiable instruments. Specifically, Chapter Fifteen addresses the contract obligations that are created through use of a negotiable instrument, including the defenses to and the satisfaction of those obligations. Chapter Sixteen explores the obligations created when the banking system is used to collect negotiable instruments. Chapter Seventeen addresses the contractual obligations among multiple obligors on a negotiable instrument. Chapter Eighteen discusses property-based obligations that arise when negotiable instruments are transferred and collected.

Finally, Chapter Nineteen addresses how the risks of error and wrongdoing are allocated when using a negotiable instrument to transfer value. The allocations of risks and wrongdoing studied in Chapter Nineteen depend upon the obligations that are studied in Chapters Fifteen through Eighteen. Thus, Chapters Fourteen through

---

[1] Some would say that the rules are also archaic and unnecessary. *See* Dale A. Whitman, *How Negotiability has Fouled up the Secondary Mortgage Market, and What to do About It*, 37 PEPP. L. REV. 737 (2010); Neil B. Cohen, *The Calamitous Law of Notes*, 68 OHIO ST. L. J. 161 (2007); Ronald J. Mann, *Searching for Negotiability in Payment and Credit Systems*, 44 UCLA L. REV. 951 (1997); Edward L. Rubin, *Learning from Lord Mansfield: Toward a Transferability Law for Modern Commercial Practice*, 31 IDAHO L. REV. 775 (1995); James Steven Rogers, *The Myth of Negotiability*, 31 B.C.L. REV. 265 (1990). *Compare* Adam J. Levitin, *Finding Nemo: Rediscovering the Virtues of Negotiability in the Wake of Enron*, 2007 COLUM. BUS. L. REV. 83.

Nineteen constitute an integrated set of material that explores the functioning of negotiable instruments as a payment mechanism.

A. Using Negotiable Instruments to Transfer Value

Assume that you want to buy a car. In a barter economy, you might find that the person who wants to sell the car is interested in obtaining something you have, in which case you could work out a swap. If you did not have something the seller wants, perhaps you could enter into swaps with several people to obtain the item or items that the car seller was willing to accept in trade for the car. In an economy that uses money tokens, you could obtain sufficient tokens to give to the car seller in exchange for the car. In common parlance, you would have paid cash for the car. However, obtaining possession of enough tokens to pay for the car may not be practical. Moreover, there may be safety concerns associated with carrying around so much currency, given the ease with which someone who comes into possession of the currency (*e.g.,* a thief) could transfer rights to the currency. We explored this problem in Chapter Twelve.

You could use a credit card to make payment, a process discussed in Chapter Thirteen. However, that too may not be feasible for a variety of reasons. Your credit limit on the credit card may be less than the price of the car. The transaction costs (*e.g.,* the merchant discount) may be more than the seller is willing to pay and thus the seller may not accept payment with a credit card. The interest rate that the issuer charges you for the extension of credit may be prohibitively expensive.

Having considered and rejected these types of payment systems, let us now consider using a negotiable instrument as a payment mechanism. Assume that you have a checking account at State Bank. You have a sufficient balance in that account to cover the price of the car you wish to purchase. You write a check drawn on the account at State Bank, payable to the car seller. As we will learn in this Chapter, the check is a special type of a contract called a "negotiable instrument."

The car seller deposits the check in the seller's account at the seller's bank. The seller's bank gives the seller a credit in the seller's account in the amount of the check deposited. The seller's bank then transfers the check to a clearinghouse which credits the account the seller's bank maintains with the clearinghouse. The clearinghouse transfers the check (or the information from the check) to State Bank (the buyer's bank) and debits State Bank's account with the clearinghouse. State

Bank then debits your checking account and returns the check to you (or an image of your check) in your bank statement for the month. The transaction can be represented graphically as follows:

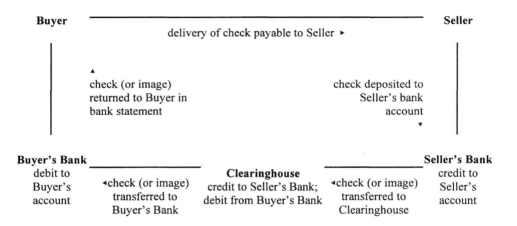

Thus, if the check is in fact paid by the buyer's bank, the check has been used as a mechanism to transfer value from the buyer to the seller through a series of debits and credits in the bank collection system.

The issuance of the check suspends the buyer's further obligation to pay for the car, and creates an obligation on the part of the buyer (the drawer) to pay the check. *See* UCC §§ 3-310, 3-414. If the check is paid by the buyer's bank, the obligation to pay for the car is satisfied. Thus, the tender of the check itself is not payment of the underlying obligation to pay for the car, rather it is a short deferment of that obligation until the check clears or is dishonored. We will return to this provision regarding the relationship between the check and the underlying obligation in Section 3 of this Chapter.

Now assume that you do not have enough credits in your checking account to pay for the car. Another option to pay for the car is to borrow the funds from someone willing to lend. Often the car seller is willing to lend you the money by selling the car to you on credit, accepting in return now your promise to pay at a later date. The car seller has you sign a negotiable promissory note in which you promise to pay the seller the amount stated, usually in installments over a specified period of time. The note is another type of negotiable instrument.

By entering into the car-purchase transaction, you have incurred an obligation to pay for the *car*. By signing that note and giving it to the car dealer in payment for the car, you have incurred an obligation to pay the *note*, which suspends your underlying obligation to pay for the car. *See* UCC §§ 3-310, 3-412. Assuming you later make all of the payments on the note, the underlying obligation to pay for the car will have been satisfied.

You may have noticed that, by itself, the note seems not to operate as a payment mechanism at all. Indeed, instead of actually paying the obligation created in the underlying transaction, you seem to be delaying payment by issuing the note. However, it is important to understand that a promissory note is an asset of the payee, which the payee may transfer in exchange for other assets, including currency. While it is true that the car seller in our example could transfer the right to receive payment from you, the buyer, under the underlying car purchase contract, even if you had not provided a promissory note,[2] the fact is that the provision of a promissory note makes it far easier for the car seller to transfer its right to payment of the price. This ease of transfer is due to one of the special attributes of negotiable instruments.

B. Special Attributes of Negotiable Instruments

Negotiable instruments law is based upon principles of both contract law and property law that English courts developed and refined over the course of hundreds of years. To facilitate commerce, the common law embraced special rules concerning two types of contracts: bills of exchange (drafts and checks in today's terminology) and notes.[3] These special rules made it easier for the holder of a bill of exchange or note to enforce and transfer the rights represented by the bill of exchange or note. To understand why, a short review of the law of contract assignment and delegation is in order.

1. *Terminology*

When two parties enter into a contract, each party promises to perform an obligation to the other party. Thus, in a contractual relationship, there are

---

[2] This would be an assignment of an account, a transaction generally governed by Article 9 of the UCC. UCC § 9-109 (scope of Article 9), § 9-102(a)(2) (definition of account).

[3] *See* JOHN BARNARD BYLES, A TREATISE ON THE LAW OF BILLS OF EXCHANGE: PROMISSORY NOTES, BANK-NOTES AND CHEQUES (1891).

reciprocal obligations. Each party is an obligor as to obligations it owes to the other party (the obligee) and each party is the obligee with respect to obligations the other party (the obligor) owes to it. Returning to the simple example above, the car seller is the obligor on the obligation to deliver the car and car buyer is the obligee as to that obligation. The car buyer is the obligor on the obligation to pay for the car and the car seller is the obligee as to that obligation.

In your contracts course you may have studied the rules relating to assignment and delegation of contractual rights and duties. When assigning a contract right, the *obligee* transfers to a person not a party to the contract (the *assignee*) the right to receive some or all of the obligee's right to receive the obligor's performance under the contract. In delegating a contract duty, the *obligor* transfers to a person not a party to the contract (the *delegatee*) the obligation to perform some or all of the obligor's contractual duties. Transferring a negotiable instrument does not generally involve the delegation of a duty and thus the remaining material will focus on assignment of contract rights.[4]

2. *Assignment of Contract Rights*

Whenever an obligee assigns its right to receive the obligor's performance, there must be at least three parties involved: the original two parties to the contract (the obligor and the obligee), plus a third party, the assignee. A typical assignment of a contractual right to payment can be illustrated as follows:

---

[4] Under contract law principles, an obligor delegates its duty to perform by manifesting an intent to do so and obtaining the delegatee's consent to the delegation. If the delegatee consents, it will have a contractual duty to perform the delegated duty, but the obligor is not released from its obligation to perform the delegated duty unless the obligee has expressly agreed to that release. An obligee may prevent an obligor from delegating its duties if a contract term so provides, or if the obligee has a substantial interest in the original obligor performing the duty. *See* RESTATEMENT (SECOND) OF CONTRACTS §§ 318, 322, 328.

Party A (obligor)	promise/obligation to pay ▸ ◂ promise/obligation to provide goods or services	Party B (obligee)

↓

C
(assignee)

For an obligee of the payment obligation – Party B – to transfer to an assignee – C – the right to receive performance of that obligation from the obligor – Party A, – the obligee must manifest the intent to transfer the rights[5] and, in most cases, C must assent to the assignment.[6] Because Party A's consent to the assignment is normally not required, the law seeks to minimize the effect of the assignment on Party A. It does this in part by making C's right against Party A the same as whatever Party B's rights were prior to the assignment.[7] If Party A had a defense to performance of the payment obligation that could be asserted against Party B, and if that defense accrued prior to the assignment, Party A generally may assert that defense against C.[8]

---

[5] *See* RESTATEMENT (SECOND) CONTRACTS § 324. In some rare circumstances, the obligor may be able to effectively preclude the obligee from validly assigning the obligee's right to receive the obligor's performance if the contract between the obligor and the obligee so provides or other principles of law make the obligee's right not assignable. *See* RESTATEMENT (SECOND) OF CONTRACTS §§ 317, 322. *But see* UCC § 9-406 through § 9-409.

[6] *See* RESTATEMENT (SECOND) CONTRACTS § 327.

[7] Once the obligor is notified of the assignment to the assignee, the obligor is obligated to render its performance to the assignee and cannot discharge its obligation by rendering performance to the obligee. *See* RESTATEMENT (SECOND) OF CONTRACTS § 338.

[8] *See* RESTATEMENT (SECOND) OF CONTRACTS §§ 336, 337. This assumes that the obligor has not made a binding promise to waive defenses against an assignee. *See* RESTATEMENT (SECOND) OF CONTRACTS § 336, cmt. f. *See also* UCC §§ 9-404(a), 9-403.

3.   Negotiable Instruments and Contract Assignment

A negotiable instrument is a type of contract.   An issuer of a negotiable instrument makes an express or implied promise to pay the obligee – henceforth referred to as a "payee," but who need not always be identified in the instrument – an amount of money specified in the instrument.   That contract (the negotiable instrument) may be assigned and the payee's right to receive payment thereby transferred to an assignee.   Of course, as with any assignment, the obligor on the instrument may have defenses to payment arising out of the obligor's contractual relationship with the payee.   However, unlike an assignment of a right to payment not represented by a negotiable instrument, many of the defenses to payment that the obligor may have against the original payee may not be valid against an assignee.   In short, the assignee of a negotiable instrument can obtain greater rights to the obligor's performance than the payee had.

The assignee of a negotiable instrument obtains these greater rights if it qualifies as a "holder in due course," a concept and a status discussed in Chapter Fifteen.   Those greater rights mean that an assignee who qualifies a holder in due course is not subject to many of the defenses the obligor can raise to payment of the negotiable instrument or to payment of the obligation incurred in the transaction that gave rise to the negotiable instrument.   A person who does not qualify as this special type of assignee, that is, an assignee who is not a holder in due course, normally obtains the same rights that any assignee of a contract right obtains.   Thus, an assignee who is not a holder in due course is subject to a defense to payment to which the payee would be subject.   The few defenses that may be asserted against both a holder in due course and a person who is not a holder in due course are discussed in Chapter Fifteen.

One of the primary effects of issuing a writing that qualifies as a negotiable instrument is to make it possible for the right to payment to be transferred to a holder in due course, who thereby takes free of most of the defenses the obligor may otherwise raise to the obligation to pay.   This advantage makes a negotiable instrument more valuable and more effective as a mechanism to transfer value from one person to another.   Contracts that do not qualify as negotiable instruments do not get the benefit of the holder in due course doctrine.

A secondary effect is that restrictions on further transfer of the negotiable instrument are generally not respected.   That means that even if the obligor on the instrument stated it was not transferrable without the obligor's permission, that restriction is not given effect.   *See* UCC § 3-206(a).

4. *Contract Rights as Property*

Another consequence of creating a contractual promise to pay that qualifies as a negotiable instrument is to provide special protection from property-based claims to the instrument. We will consider this more fully in Chapter Eighteen, but a short preview is important to understand how negotiable instruments differ from other types of contracts.

A contract right is an intangible form of personal property.[9] Thus persons other than the current holder may assert property claims to those contract rights. The common-law approach is to follow the derivative rights principle in most situations: an assignee acquires whatever rights the assignor had and purported to assign. As a result, a second assignee (from the same assignor) normally takes subject to the rights of a first assignee. Return to the diagram illustrating a typical contract assignment. Assume that Party B (the obligee) has assigned to C (the assignee) the right to receive Party A's (the obligor's) performance. Later, Party B (the obligee) purports to assign to D the same right to receive Party A's (the obligor's) performance. In most situations, D's right under the second assignment would be inferior to C's rights under the first assignment.[10]

If the contract right is represented by a negotiable instrument, however, the obligation to pay is reified in the instrument. That is, the writing does not merely *evidence* the obligation, it *embodies* the obligation. The owner of a negotiable instrument (the obligee) may grant property rights in that instrument. An assignee of that instrument who qualifies as a holder in due course or succeeds to another

---

[9] E. ALLAN FARNSWORTH, CONTRACTS § 11.9 (4th ed. 2004).

[10] In some situations under contract-law principles, a subsequent assignee can obtain superiority over the rights of a first assignee. For example, if the first assignment is voidable or revoked, the subsequent assignee may have rights superior to the first assignee. *See* RESTATEMENT (SECOND) OF CONTRACTS § 342(a). Similarly, if the subsequent assignee acquires its rights in good faith, without knowledge of the first assignee's rights, and for value, the subsequent assignee is not subject to the rights of the first assignee if the subsequent assignee obtains payment from the obligor, a judgment against the obligor, a new contract with the obligor, or possession of a writing that is customarily accepted as the evidence of the right assigned (*i.e.*, a negotiable instrument). *See* RESTATEMENT (SECOND) OF CONTRACTS § 342(b). To the extent UCC Article 9 on secured transactions applies to the priority contest between the first and second assignees of a negotiable instrument, the Article 9 rules would also trump the normal first-in-time contract assignment rule.

person's rights as a holder in due course takes that instrument free of another's property-based claim to the instrument, even if that property-based claim arose prior to the holder in due course's rights to the instrument. Conversely, someone without holder-in-due-course status generally does not take the negotiable instrument free of pre-existing property based claims to the instrument,[11] and generally will lose to a subsequent assignee who does qualify as a holder in due course. We will consider this aspect of negotiable instrument law in Chapter Eighteen.

5. Negotiability

The key principle of negotiability – in simple terms, that the rights of a transferee can be greater than the rights of the transferor[12] – is not unique to negotiable instruments. In fact, negotiability is applicable to many different types of property and modes of transfer, but in varying degrees of strength.[13] Consider, for example, the following illustration from the law governing the sale of goods, UCC Article 2.

> Customer buys a new television from a Retailer. Retailer acquired the television from Supplier but paid for the television with a check that was dishonored.

As between Retailer and Supplier, Supplier may have a right to recover the television from Retailer because the check was dishonored.[14] In essence, Retailer has *voidable title* to the television: ownership rights subject to defeasance pursuant to Supplier's right to reclaim the television. Under the derivative rights principle, Retailer could sell the television to Customer, but Customer's title would be similarly subject to defeasance by Supplier. This derivative rights principle is well

---

[11] Principles of contract law provide some limited exceptions. *See supra* note 10.

[12] *See* Gregory E. Maggs, *The Holder in Due Course Doctrine as a Default Rule*, 32 GA. L. REV. 783 (1998).

[13] *See* Curtis Nyquist, *A Spectrum Theory of Negotiability*, 78 MARQ. L. REV. 897 (1995). *See also* Edward J. Janger, *The Costs of Liquidity Enhancement: Transparency Cost, Risk Alteration, and Coordination Problems*, 4 BROOK. J. CORP. FIN. & COM. L. 39 (2009).

[14] *See* UCC § 2-507.

entrenched in commercial law.[15] It is also codified in the first sentence of UCC § 2-403(1) as applicable to purchasers of goods.

However, the second sentence of UCC § 2-403(1) codifies an exception to the derivative rights principle. This exception is an embodiment of a very weak concept of negotiability. In the example given above, if Customer is a good faith purchaser for value and has taken delivery of the television, Customer receives *good title* to the television. Customer's right to the television is not subject to defeasance by Supplier. In other words, Supplier's right to reclaim the television is not good against Customer. Because Customer has received transfer of the television free of Supplier's claim to the item, Customer's rights are better than the rights its transferor, Retailer, had. This is a type of "negotiability of goods" rule.

As you may remember from Chapter Twelve, currency is very "negotiable." Good faith transferees of currency who give value take the currency free from all claims to that currency and, in most circumstances, are not subject to an obligation to make specific restitution (*i.e.*, an obligation to give the specific currency bills back to the transferor if the underlying obligation is unwound or to return the currency to a prior owner). The rules concerning currency are the strongest example of the negotiability concept. The rules governing negotiable instruments are probably the second strongest example of the negotiability concept.

These attributes of negotiable instruments – that restrictions on transfer are invalid, that holders in due course take free of most defenses to payment, and that holders in due course take free of property-based claims to the instrument – make negotiable instruments a powerful mechanism for transferring value. They also allow negotiable instruments to flow freely in commerce and even to serve some of the functions of money. Indeed, prior to the creation of the Federal Reserve System, when many parts of the country occasionally suffered from a severe shortage of currency, notes made by particularly creditworthy entities could and did trade much like currency.

---

[15] *See* John F. Dolan, *The U.C.C. Framework: Conveyancing Principles and Property Interests*, 59 B.U.L. REV. 811 (1979); Steven L. Harris, *Using Fundamental Principles of Commercial Law to Decide U.C.C. Cases*, 26 LOY. L.A.L. REV. 637 (1993). A corollary of the derivative rights principle is the shelter principle: a transferor is able to transfer all of its rights to a transferee, that is, the transferee can take shelter in – is protected by – the transferor's rights.

C. Governing Law

Negotiable instruments are governed principally by state law. Most of the basic rules are codified in Uniform Commercial Code Article 3.[16] Article 4 of the UCC provides additional rules on the process of collecting on negotiable instruments through the banking system.[17] However, not all of the rules regarding collection through banks are found in UCC Article 4. Banks are regulated entities and much of their operations are controlled or overseen by various state and federal agencies. In particular, the process for collecting negotiable instruments through the banking system is subject to regulations promulgated by the Federal Reserve Board. For example, in 1987 Congress enacted the Expedited Funds Availability Act ("EFAA"),[18] which limits how long a bank may take to give a depositor access to funds deposited in a bank account. Pursuant to the EFAA, the Federal Reserve

---

[16] *See* UCC § 3-102(a). The Uniform Commercial Code was drafted by the National Conference of Commissioners on Uniform State Laws ("NCCUSL") and the American Law Institute ("ALI"). The drafts as promulgated by NCCUSL and ALI are proposed for enactment by each state, and may or may not be enacted in their uniform form. UCC Articles 3 and 4 were revised in 1990 and then amended in 2002. This book refers to Articles 3 and 4 as revised in 1990 and amended in 2002. As of the summer of 2011, all states but one (New York) have enacted the 1990 revisions, and 10 states have enacted the 2002 revisions.

[17] *See* UCC § 4-102 and § 4-104(a)(9) (definition of "item"). UCC Articles 3 and 4 have a relationship to other articles of the Uniform Commercial Code. The other articles in the UCC govern specific types of transactions. UCC Articles 3 and 4 could apply to one part of the transaction and another article could govern other parts of the transaction. For example, UCC Article 2 governs transactions in goods. Suppose you buy a washing machine at your local department store and pay the store with a personal check. UCC Article 2 will apply to disputes with the department store about the quality of the washing machine or other obligations under the contract for sale. UCC Articles 3 and 4 will apply to the obligations and liabilities related to the check as it travels from your hands, to the store's hands, to the store's bank, to your bank, and finally back to you in your checking account statement. Because UCC Articles 3 and 4 are part of a set of articles governing various types of transactions, various sections or concepts from other articles might be relevant to the issues under these articles. Familiarity with the other articles of the UCC is essential for a well rounded view of commercial law. To the extent there is a conflict between UCC Articles 3 and 4, Article 4 controls. *See* UCC §§ 3-102(b), 4-102(a).

[18] Codified at 12 U.S.C. §§ 4001–4010.

Board issued Regulation CC.[19] In order to facilitate the check collection process in light of developments in electronic methods of communicating data, in 2004 Congress enacted the Check Clearing for the 21st Century Act (commonly called "Check 21").[20] The Federal Reserve Board promulgated amendments to Regulation CC to implement Check 21.

These two Acts and Regulation CC govern some aspects of the check collection process and the availability of funds in banks subject to the regulation. In addition, Regulation J[21] governs some aspects of the collection process for checks collected through the Federal Reserve system. The relationship between UCC Article 4 and these federal regulations is unsurprising: the federal regulations control to the extent they conflict with a UCC Article 4 rule. *See* UCC § 4-103, cmt. 3. If there is no conflict between UCC Article 4 and the federal regulation on a particular issue, both will apply.

SECTION 2.   REQUISITES OF A NEGOTIABLE INSTRUMENT UNDER UCC ARTICLE 3

For a promise or order to pay to qualify as a negotiable instrument – and thereby allow for the principles of negotiability described briefly above to come into play – it must satisfy the requirements specified in UCC § 3-104. **Read UCC § 3-104 and the comments to that section.** A promise or order to pay that does not qualify as a negotiable instrument may nevertheless be enforceable as a contract, but there can be no holder in due course who cuts off defenses to payment or takes free of property-based claims to the right to payment.

When first approaching a statutory list such as appears in UCC § 3-104(a), it is advisable to check the conjunction that joins the last two items in the list before analyzing each provision. Notice that UCC § 3-104(a) uses the conjunction "and."

---

[19] 12 C.F.R. pt. 229. The Dodd-Frank legislation provides that after the transfer date (July 2011), the Federal Reserve Board will have joint rulemaking authority with the Bureau of Consumer Financial Protection as to matters covered by the EFAA. Pub. L. No. 111-203, Title X, §§ 1086, 1100H, 124 Stat. 1376, 2086, 2113. The Federal Reserve Board retains its existing rulemaking authority with respect to matters covered by Check 21.

[20] Codified at 12 U.S.C. §§ 5001–5018.

[21] 12 C.F.R. pt. 210.

Accordingly, *all* of the requirements listed in subsection (a) must be satisfied for the writing to qualify as a negotiable instrument. If even one requirement is not satisfied, the writing is not a negotiable instrument.

The next thing to do when analyzing a statutory provision is to break it down into its component parts. In other words, identify each word or phrase that is important to the provision's meaning. It is then necessary to determine if the statute further defines or explains the meaning of component parts. In fact, almost every word and phrase in UCC § 3-104(a) is defined or explained elsewhere in either UCC Article 3 or UCC Article 1. Problem 14-1 requires that you create an outline of all the requirements of a negotiable instrument based upon the relevant provisions from the UCC. To help get you started on that task, and to illustrate what you should do whenever you approach a new statutory provision, here is a list of the main elements along with a reference to where that element is further defined or explained.

	Element	UCC sections
1.	a promise or order;	§ 3-103(a)(8), (12)
2.	that is unconditional;	§ 3-106
3.	to pay a fixed amount of money;	§ 3-112(b)
4.	payable to bearer or order;	§ 3-109
5.	at the time of issue or when it first comes into possession of a holder;	§ 1-201(b)(21), § 3-105
6.	payable on demand or definite time; and	§ 3-108
7.	does not state any other undertaking or instruction except as allowed by § 3-104.	§ 3-104(a)(3)

The following discussion and questions will help you construct a more detailed outline of the requirements of a negotiable instrument. **Do not breeze through these questions.** To answer the questions, read the cited statutory provisions closely, along with the official comments. The comments are not enacted law but courts often treat them as persuasive authority as to the meaning of the statute and they are frequently very helpful in trying to understand what the statutory text means.

Promise or order. **Read the definitions of "order" and "promise" in UCC § 3-103.** What is the distinction between the two terms? Notice that each requires that the instruction or undertaking be "written" and "signed." In addition, the instruction or undertaking must be to pay "money." Now read UCC § 3-103(d). It refers you to Article 1 of the UCC for general definitions.[22] **Read the definitions of "written," "signed," and "money" in UCC § 1-201(b).** Drafts embody orders to pay and notes embody promises to pay. UCC § 3-104(e).

Now look at a typical check blank.

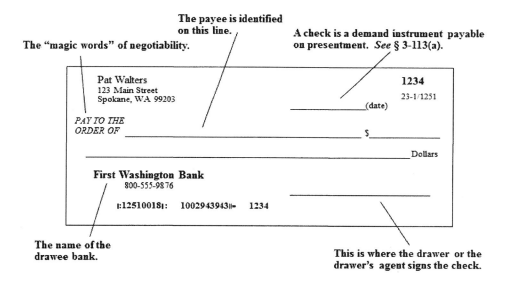

The payee is identified on this line.

The "magic words" of negotiability.

A check is a demand instrument payable on presentment. *See* § 3-113(a).

Pat Walters
123 Main Street
Spokane, WA 99203

1234
23-1/1251

PAY TO THE
ORDER OF

(date)

$

Dollars

First Washington Bank
800-555-9876

⑆125100181⑆ 1002943943⑈ 1234

The name of the drawee bank.

This is where the drawer or the drawer's agent signs the check.

The payee line contains the pre-printed phrase "Pay to the order of." There is a place for putting an amount of money in both numerical and written form and a place for a signature at the bottom right. The instruction to pay is directed to the financial institution whose name is preprinted on the lower left hand side (the "drawee"). When the blank form is filled out, this is an example of an "order" under UCC § 3-103(a)(8), a "draft" under UCC § 3-104(e), and a "check" under

---

[22] UCC Article 1 applies to any transaction covered by another Article of the UCC. UCC § 1-102. Article 1 contains definitions and other general rules. You should make it a habit to always consult Article 1 to see if it has any sections relevant to the problem at hand. This book will refer to the provisions of Revised Article 1 as promulgated in 2001.

UCC § 3-104(f). However, these three terms are not synonymous. What is the critical factual difference between a "draft" and a "check"?

Now consider the other major type of negotiable instrument, a note. Reread the definition of "promise" in UCC § 3-103. Notice that the major distinction between an "order" and a "promise" is the difference between an "instruction" and an "undertaking" to pay money.

Unconditional. Second, that promise or order must be "unconditional." What does that mean? **Read UCC § 3-106.** As you can see by reading that section, there are three ways to make a writing conditional. What is the difference between an express condition and an implied condition? What is the difference between a writing that is "subject" to another writing and one that "refers" to another writing? **Read UCC § 3-117.** How does that section relate to the effect of a separate agreement on the obligation to pay represented by an instrument? What contract doctrine does the phrase "subject to applicable law regarding exclusion of proof of contemporaneous or previous agreements" in UCC § 3-117 refer to?[23] Are the rules in UCC § 3-106(c) and (d) exceptions to the principle of an "unconditional" promise or order?

Why might it be important for the promise or order to not have any conditions to it stated in a separate writing? Why might it be important for the promise or order to not have any conditions stated in the same writing that contains the promise or order? How might this requirement of unconditional be related to the idea of transferring the instrument free of claims and defenses to payment?

Fixed amount of money. Third, the promise or order must be to "pay a fixed amount of money, with or without interest or other charges described in the promise or order." We have already looked at the definition of "money" in UCC § 1-201(b). A negotiable instrument may be payable in U.S. dollars or other currency that qualifies as "money." **Read UCC § 3-107.**

What does it mean that the amount must be fixed? Is it referring to the principal amount, interest, or the costs of collecting the obligation? **Read UCC § 3-112.** Does that help your understanding of this requirement?

---

[23] For an example of an analysis of the application of UCC § 3-117, see *Rogers v. Jackson*, 804 A.2d 379 (Me. 2002). *See also Schuyler Co-op Ass'n v. Sahs*, 755 N.W.2d 802 (Neb. 2008) (note is separate obligation from underlying agreement); *Marcovitz v. Rogers*, 752 N.W.2d 605 (Neb. 2008) (note terms cannot alter terms of divorce decree and thus the note terms that purported to do so were not enforceable).

Payable to bearer or order. Fourth, the promise or order must be "payable to bearer or to order at the time it is issued or first comes into possession of a holder." This requirement is initially confusing because it uses the word "order" in a different sense than the word "order" has been used so far. This requirement also contains two concepts: a statement of how the instrument is payable ("payable to bearer or order") and a timing rule (as of time of "issue" or first in possession of a "holder"). Start with the concept of how the instrument has to be payable. Payable to bearer or order is explained in UCC § 3-109. **Read UCC § 3-109.**

Payable to order or to bearer language is akin to "magic words." For the language on the instrument to make the instrument payable to bearer or to order, the form and syntax of the language in UCC § 3-109 must be followed. **Re-read UCC § 3-104(a)(1) and (c) and comment 2 to that section.**

A promise or order that is payable to order requires that there be an "identified person" named in the instrument. UCC § 3-110 provides rules for determining who is the person identified in the instrument. This section is very important in determining how the instrument may be negotiated (necessary to make someone a holder in due course) and who is the person entitled to payment of the instrument.

At the time of issue or when it first comes into possession of a holder. Fifth, the payable to bearer or order language must be on the instrument at the time the instrument is first issued, UCC § 3-105, or at the time the instrument first comes into possession of a holder. "Holder" is another defined term. *See* UCC § 1-201(b)(21)(A). What does it add to your understanding of the requirements for a negotiable instrument? In Chapter Fifteen, we will explore what it takes to become a "holder" of an instrument.

Demand or definite time. Sixth, the promise or order must be "payable on demand or a definite time." These phrases are further defined in UCC § 3-108. **Read UCC § 3-108.**

No other promises or orders. Finally, the last requirement is that the instrument state no "other undertaking or instruction by the person promising or ordering payment to do any act in addition to the payment of money" except as allowed in UCC § 3-104(a)(3). How is this different from the requirement that the promise or order be "unconditional?"

Problem 14-1

Construct a list of the requirements of a negotiable instrument, incorporating all of the sub-rules we have read in the text and comments of UCC §§ 1-201, 3-103, 3-105 through 3-113, and 3-117. Incorporate within your answer the answers to the questions posed in the text. This synthesis skill is critical to develop when working with a statutory scheme.

Return to UCC § 3-104 and **read UCC § 3-104(e) through (j) and comment 4.** These provisions define several related terms, each a kind of negotiable instrument. UCC Article 3 is highly technical, and treats each of these things differently for at least some purposes. Therefore you will need to understand how these terms are similar and how they are different.

Let us start with a check, the type of instrument illustrated above and with which you are most likely to be familiar. A check is a type of "draft." Various types of checks exist: ordinary checks that are drawn on a business or personal account at a bank or other financial institution, UCC § 3-104(f); cashier's checks that are issued by a bank and drawn on the same bank, UCC § 3-104(g); and teller's checks that are drawn by a bank on another bank, UCC § 3-104(h). The term "draft" also includes some things other than checks. For example, a draft may be drawn on a non-bank entity (*i.e.*, something other than a bank). A "note" is something different from a draft. Do you understand the difference between them? A traveler's check can be either a draft or a note. *See* UCC § 3-104(i) & cmt. 4. Now look at the definition of "certificate of deposit" in UCC § 3-104(j). A certificate of deposit is a "note" of the bank.

Problem 14-2

Create a Venn diagram that depicts the relationship of the following terms:

cashier's check	certificate of deposit
check	draft
negotiable instrument	note
teller's check	travelers's check

Other terms may be included in an instrument without affecting negotiability. **Read UCC § 3-111 and § 3-113.** What terms might you want in a negotiable instrument if you were the person to whom the payment of money would be made? What about a promise to pay costs and fees for collection? How about a promise by the person to whom payment is made to apply the payments first to interest and then to principal?

An instrument that does not meet the UCC § 3-104 requirements cannot be made negotiable by declaration. UCC § 3-104, cmt. 2. However, an instrument that does satisfy the requirements of negotiability can be made non-negotiable by a conspicuous declaration to that effect. UCC § 3-104(d). Why does the law have this lack of symmetry? In other words, why does it prohibit the parties from opting into the rules governing negotiable instruments if one or more of the requirements of UCC § 3-104(a) are not satisfied but allow them to opt out of the rules governing negotiable instruments even though all the requirements of negotiability are met?[24]

Recall the earlier statement that all of the requirements in UCC § 3-104 must be satisfied for an instrument to be negotiable. **Read UCC § 3-104(c).** Why does that subsection contain an exception for one of the requirements if the instrument is a check?

Now try the following problems, applying the rules you have just studied.

Problem 14-3

Evaluate whether each communication below, sent by Marla to Pete on a piece of paper, satisfies the requirements of a negotiable instrument. If so, identify whether it is a draft or a note.

A.
| I agree to pay $100 to Pete in the event Pete needs money for his rent. |
| *Marla* |

B.
| I promise to pay Betty or her order on January 10, 2010, 10,000 euros with interest at the 90-day Treasury Rate adjusted monthly plus all costs of collection. This obligation is secured as stated in a security agreement dated January 5, 2010. This amount is payable at the residence of Marla. |
| *M* |

---

[24] *But see* Jonathan Yovel, *Quasi-Checks: An Apology for A Mutation of Negotiable Instruments*, 5 DEPAUL BUS. & COM. L.J. 579 (2007).

C.

> To: Pete
> From: Marla Rhodes
>
>   Pay to bearer $1,000 30 days after sight.

D.

> I promise to pay to the order of Pete $1,000 on January 10, 2010, subject to prepayment without penalty at any time, as soon as Pete transfers his Sony high definition TV to me.
>
>   *Marla*

E.

> Pete, I would appreciate it if you would pay the $400 you owe me to the order of George on July 5, 2010.
>
>   *Marla*

Problem 14-4

It is June 1. You have agreed to lend $5,000 to Pat, your neighbor. Pat is to repay the loan within nine months but must repay immediately if Pat receives a holiday bonus of $5,000 or more from Pat's employer. Interest is to accrue at the highest rate legally allowable in your jurisdiction. Draft a note for Pat to sign that will qualify as a negotiable instrument and will, to the greatest extent possible, be consistent with these terms.

Problem 14-5

Determine whether each communication below is a negotiable instrument. If so, identify whether it is a note or a draft.

A. Fred sent the following e-mail message to Jane to pay a debt that Fred owed Jane:

> From: Fred@abc.org
> To: Jane@xyz.org
>
> Pay to the order of Jane or bearer $1,000 on January 10, 2010, subject to acceleration in the event the holder deems itself insecure.

B. Alvin and Beth had an agreement that Alvin would pay Beth pursuant to the terms of the following writing only when Alvin had sufficient funds to make the payment. The writing stated:

> I promise to pay to Beth $1,000 on April 3, 2010, subject to an extension of time at the option of the holder hereof.
>
> *Alvin*

C. Carl wrote the following on a napkin while drinking in a bar and gave the napkin to Sherry:

> I promise to pay to the order of Santa Claus $1,000. I also agree to grant a security interest in my car to secure this obligation and to execute all documents necessary for that purpose. I waive presentment and notice of dishonor.
>
> *Carl*

D. Jane wrote a note to Bill that stated:

> I promise to pay Bill all amounts I owe Bill on January 3, 2010. The amounts owed to Bill shall be calculated based upon a contract dated July 1, 2009.
>
> *Jane*

E. Betty signed a paper document that provided the following:

> The undersigned promises to pay to First Bank or bearer $10,000 plus 5% per annum interest on February 12, 2011 or on demand made before that time. This obligation is secured by collateral as stated in a security agreement dated July 2, 2010. All payments will be credited first to interest and then to principal.
>
> *Betty*

Problem 14-6

Draft a *negotiable* promissory note that encompasses the following terms. The borrower is John Merrill and the lender making the loan is State Bank.

- Principal: $15,000 payable in five years.
- Interest: 4% over the federal funds rate or 3% over the London Interbank Offered Rate, whichever is greater.
- Acceleration in the event the holder deems itself insecure.

- Prepayment with a 1% fee based upon the outstanding principal balance at time of prepayment.
- All amounts owed secured by a security interest in the obligor's inventory.
- Obligor agrees to pay all costs of collection, including attorney's fees.
- Waiver of presentment and notice of dishonor.
- Payable at the holder's offices on the due date.

SECTION 3.   EFFECT ON THE UNDERLYING OBLIGATION

A. General Rules

A negotiable instrument is usually issued or transferred in payment of an underlying obligation. That usual transaction raises several issues concerning the relationship between the underlying obligation and the contract obligation on the negotiable instrument.

First, what effect does issuance or transfer of the negotiable instrument have on the ability of the obligee to enforce the underlying obligation?

Second, what effect does payment of the negotiable instrument have on the underlying obligation?

Third, what effect does dishonor of the negotiable instrument have on the underlying obligation?

Fourth, what is the effect on the underlying obligation of a discharge of the obligation on the negotiable instrument (by a manner other than payment)?

In this segment, we will deal with the first two of these questions. We will return to the third and fourth questions in Chapter Fifteen, after we explore the rules on the obligations that are created by issuing and transferring a negotiable instrument.

Effect of issuance or transfer of the negotiable instrument on the underlying obligation. **Read UCC § 3-310.** The answer to the first question depends on the type of instrument issued or transferred. *Compare* UCC § 3-310 subsection (a) *with* subsection (b)(1) and (2). The issuance or transfer of the types of negotiable instruments specified in subsection (a) discharges the underlying obligation. In all other situations, the issuance or transfer of a negotiable instrument merely suspends the underlying obligation.

Effect of payment of the negotiable instrument. If the underlying obligation is merely suspended, when does that suspension end? Subsection (b)(1) and (2) state that the underlying obligation is suspended until payment of the instrument or dishonor. If payment of the instrument results in a discharge of the obligation on the instrument (a topic explored in Chapter Fifteen), the underlying obligation is also satisfied to the extent of the discharge of the obligation on the instrument.

Problem 14-7

A. Pat is buying Frank's house. Pat procured a cashier's check from State Bank. Pat gave the check to Frank at the closing. Frank is the payee of the check. What is the effect of that transfer of the check on the underlying obligation of Pat to pay Frank for the house?

B. Pat is buying Frank's house. Pat gave Frank a negotiable promissory note she had signed payable to the order of Frank in payment for the house. What is the effect of that transfer of the note on Pat's obligation to pay Frank for the house?

C. Arden drew a check on Bank, payable to the order of Crystal. Arden delivered the check to Crystal in payment of the price of some goods that Arden bought from Crystal.
1. What is the effect of delivery of the check to Crystal on Arden's underlying obligation to pay for the goods?
2. Crystal took the check to Bank and properly obtained payment of the check. What is the effect of that payment on the underlying obligation of Arden to pay for the goods?

D. Arden issued a $1,000 negotiable note payable to the order of Crystal in partial payment of the $3,000 price of goods that Arden bought from Crystal.
1. What is the effect of the note issuance on Arden's underlying obligation to pay Crystal for the goods?
2. Crystal properly negotiated that note to David in payment of an $800 debt that Crystal owed to David. What is the effect of the negotiation on: (i) Arden's underlying obligation to pay Crystal for

the goods; and (ii) Crystal's underlying obligation to David on the $800 debt?

3. Arden properly paid David the amount of the note when David presented the note to Arden. What is the effect of that payment on: (i) Arden's underlying obligation to pay Crystal; and (ii) Crystal's underlying obligation to pay David?

B. Exception: Accord and Satisfaction

Reread UCC § 3-310(a) and (b). Both sections state that the underlying obligation is discharged to the same extent as if the same amount had been transferred in money. This principle is subject to an exception set forth in UCC § 3-311, called accord and satisfaction.

Many people use the doctrine of accord and satisfaction as an informal method of dispute resolution. When the existence or amount of a debt is disputed, the obligor may send to the obligee a check for the amount that the obligor thinks is owing, with the expectation that if the obligee cashes or deposits the check, the obligee has agreed to the compromise of the obligation to that amount. Section 3-311 codifies an approach to accord and satisfaction that allows the payment of an instrument to be satisfaction of the entire amount of the underlying obligation even if the amount of the instrument is not the entire amount of the underlying obligation. This rule is, in effect, an exception to the general rule that payment of only part of an obligation discharges only the portion paid. However, because an accord and satisfaction is supposed to be a knowing and voluntary agreement of both parties, UCC § 3-311 contains a variety of rules to ensure that the obligee understands the significance of what the obligor is attempting to do.

Read UCC § 3-311. The requirements of an accord and satisfaction when using a negotiable instrument are stated in UCC § 3-311(a). The effect of the payment on the underlying obligation is stated in subsection (b). Subsection (c) is an exception to the rule stated in subsection (b). Subsection (d) is an exception to the rule of subsection (c). *See also* UCC § 1-308.

Problem 14-8

Alvin bought goods on credit at Department Store, charging the amount to Alvin's account with Department Store. Department Store sent an invoice to Alvin, billing Alvin for the amount due for the goods.

A. Alvin decided that the goods were not worth the amount that he had been charged for those goods. Alvin sent a check payable to Department Store for less than the invoice amount with the notation written in capital letters "IN FULL PAYMENT." Department Store cashed the check. Has there been an accord and satisfaction?

B. Assume Alvin asserted that the goods were defective and Department Store was unwilling to take the goods back. After several weeks of arguing between Alvin and the credit department of Department Store about whether the goods were defective, Alvin sent the check to Department Store for less than the invoice amount with "IN FULL PAYMENT" written on the front of check. Department Store cashed the check. Has there been an accord and satisfaction? If so, is there anything Department Store could have done prior to receiving the check or after cashing the check to make sure there was no accord and satisfaction?

C. Assume the same facts as Part B, except Alvin sent the check to the head of Customer Service with a long letter explaining the purported defect and that the check was in full satisfaction of the amount of the debt. Department Store had included with its invoice a notice that all communications regarding disputes about the invoice should be sent to the Complaint Department. Department Store cashed the check. Has there been an accord and satisfaction? Would it matter if Department Store sent the amount of the check back to Alvin several weeks later?

CHAPTER FIFTEEN

CONTRACT LIABILITY ON A NEGOTIABLE INSTRUMENT

SECTION 1. INTRODUCTION

In Chapter Fourteen we started our study of negotiable instruments as a payment mechanism. We learned how these instruments are used to transfer value and how using such an instrument affects the obligation to pay in the underlying transaction. This Chapter addresses the separate obligation that is created when a negotiable instrument is used as a payment mechanism. This obligation is referred to as the contract obligation "on" the instrument. This obligation "on" the instrument is distinct from the obligation that arises out of the underlying transaction in which the negotiable instrument is used as a payment mechanism.[1]

This Chapter explores the contract liability on an instrument. On a negotiable instrument, the obligor owes the obligation on the instrument to the obligee. The obligee is thus the person who will be the plaintiff in any action to enforce the obligation on the instrument against the obligor. In this Chapter, we will explore the obligee's case against the obligor and the obligor's defenses to the enforcement of this obligation on the instrument.

We start with the plaintiff's (obligee's) case against the defendant (obligor), which consists of proving that:

(i) the instrument is a negotiable instrument;

---

[1] As we saw in Chapter Fourteen, Section 3, the separate nature of the obligation on the instrument is evidenced by several provisions of Article 3. *See, e.g.,* UCC §§ 3-118 (providing the statute of limitations for liability on an instrument, which might be quite different from the limitations period on the underlying obligation); 3-310(b) (suspending the obligation on the underlying transaction until the instrument is paid or dishonored).

Most negotiable instruments are issued to effect payment of some sort of contractual or legal obligation. Occasionally, however, a negotiable instrument may be used to effect payment of a gift. For example, a person may send a check as a gift to a family member or charitable organization. In such a case, there may be no underlying obligation in the underlying transaction (*i.e.*, the gift or the promise to make a gift). Nevertheless, there may be an obligation on the instrument to the initial payee, *see In re Estate of Smith*, 694 A.2d 1099 (Pa. Super. Ct. 1997); *contra Woo v. Smart*, 442 S.E.2d 690 (Va. 1994), and there generally will be an obligation on the instrument to someone who qualifies as a holder in due course.

(ii) the defendant is obligated on the instrument;

(iii) the plaintiff is entitled to enforce the obligation; and

(iv) the obligation is due.

The material in Chapter Fourteen addressed the first element of the plaintiff's case: proving that the instrument qualifies as a negotiable instrument. This Chapter deals with the remaining requirements for the plaintiff to prove and enforce contract liability on the instrument.

Creation of contract liability on the instrument. The contract obligation "on" the instrument arises when the instrument is signed.[2] As we learned in Chapter Fourteen, UCC § 3-104 requires that a negotiable instrument contain a promise or order to pay money and be signed by the person promising to pay or making the instruction to pay. That signature is the basis of contract liability on the instrument.

A person signing a negotiable instrument will do so in one of four defined roles:

"maker,"	*see* UCC § 3-103(a)(7);
"drawer,"	*see* UCC § 3-103(a)(5);
"acceptor"	see UCC § 3-103(a)(1); and
"indorser,"	*see* UCC § 3-204.

The role in which the person signs the negotiable instrument determines the nature of the signer's liability on the instrument. For example, a person that signs a negotiable note as a maker will have liability on the note to the extent specified in UCC § 3-412 (a maker is an issuer of a note, UCC § 3-105). A person that signs a check as a drawer will incur liability on the check pursuant to UCC § 3-414.

In some circumstances, a person signing an instrument does so as an agent for someone else. For example, a corporate officer, acting within the scope of the officer's authority, may sign a check to one of the corporation's suppliers or a note to one of the corporation's lenders. In such a case, the corporation will generally be bound on the instrument regardless of whether the corporate officer signed the instrument using the officer's own name or the corporation's name.[3] *See* UCC § 3-402(a). Even if the corporate officer exceeded the officer's authority by signing the instrument, the corporation may still be bound pursuant to common-law

---

[2] While the signer has a defense if the signer never "issued" the instrument – that is, never voluntarily delivered the instrument, *see* UCC § 3-105(a), (b) – that defense is not valid against a holder in due course. *See* UCC § 3-305(a), (b), cmt. 2.

[3] In some cases, the corporate officer may also have liability on the instrument. *See* UCC § 3-402(b), (c). The role of agency law in determining who is liable on the instrument is explored more fully in Section 2 of this Chapter.

principles of agency. Just as in other cases, however, the extent and nature of the corporation's liability will depend on whether the corporate officer signed as maker, drawer, or indorser. We explore more fully the liability created by signing an instrument in Section 2 of this Chapter.

Persons who may enforce contract liability on an instrument. A person that signs (or whose agent signs) a negotiable instrument incurs liability to "the person entitled to enforce" the instrument, UCC § 3-301, and in some circumstances to an "indorser who has paid" the instrument. *See* UCC § 3-414 (drawer's liability), § 3-415(a) (indorser's liability owed to a subsequent indorser who has paid).[4] The person who seeks to enforce liability on the instrument must be the person to whom the contract obligation on the instrument is owed, that is be the correct obligee. These rules are explored in Section 3 of this Chapter.

When the contract obligation on the instrument is due. The contract liability on the instrument will be owed at a particular time. This time is determined both by the terms of the instrument itself and the rules of UCC Article 3. Consider what we learned in Chapter Fourteen regarding "payment on demand or at a definite time" as one of the requirements for a negotiable instrument. UCC § 3-108. If, for example, a negotiable note is payable on demand, liability on the instrument does not become due until there is a proper demand for payment. That demand for payment is called a "presentment." UCC § 3-501. If the negotiable instrument is not paid when due, the instrument has been "dishonored." UCC § 3-502. In some circumstances, such as when dealing with an indorser, a person's liability on an instrument does not become due until the person seeking enforcement gives timely "notice of dishonor." *See* UCC § 3-415 (liability of an indorser). These rules are explored in Section 4 of this Chapter.

Defenses to contract liability on the instrument and holder in due course status. The defendant may, of course, challenge any aspect of the plaintiff's case. If the defendant does so successfully, the plaintiff will lose its case based upon contract liability on the instrument. Even if the plaintiff prevails in its prima facie case, however, the defendant may raise one or more affirmative defenses. Suppose, for example, the defendant claims to have been defrauded in the underlying transaction or demonstrates a lack of capacity when entering into the underlying transaction or when signing the instrument. Remember a negotiable instrument is a type of contract, and thus defenses based upon general principles of contract law are available. *See* UCC § 3-305(a)(2).

---

[4] *See also* UCC § 3-413 (acceptor's obligation also owed to a drawer who has paid).

The extent to which the plaintiff (the person seeking to enforce contract liability on the instrument) is subject to defenses is arguably the heart of the law of negotiable instruments. In general, a plaintiff who qualifies as a holder in due course of the instrument is invulnerable to many of the common contract defenses to liability, even if the defendant could factually prove the elements of the defense. This protection for holders in due course is one of the key aspects of "negotiability," a concept explored briefly in Chapter Fourteen. While the details of holder-in-due-course status are complex, *see* UCC § 3-302, the essential requirements are that the holder has taken the instrument for value, in good faith, and without notice of either claims to the instrument[5] or defenses to payment of the instrument. If the person entitled to enforce has the rights of a holder in due course, that person will take the instrument free of many defenses to payment of the contract claim and will take free of claims to the instrument. UCC §§ 3-305, 3-306. A person entitled to enforce the instrument who lacks the rights of a holder in due course will be subject to all defenses to liability on the instrument and to all claims to the instrument.

Section 5 of this Chapter explores the defendant's defenses in detail by identifying the typical defenses to contract liability on the instrument and identifying who qualifies as a holder in due course, and thus takes free of most defenses. It then covers the very important issue of which defenses are valid against a holder in due course.

This litigation-oriented construct that deals first with the plaintiff's case (Sections 2 through 4 of this Chapter) and then with possible defenses (Section 5 of this Chapter) is set forth in UCC § 3-308. **Read that section and its comments.** Compare that section and the comments with the overview given above of the typical plaintiff's case and the defendant's response.

Enforcing the underlying obligation. Finally, Section 6 of this Chapter circles back to the relationship between contract liability on the instrument and liability in the underlying transaction. It explores how dishonor of the instrument and discharge of the obligation on the instrument affect the underlying obligation.

---

[5] Claims *to* the instrument – based upon property-based rights to obtain the instrument or its proceeds – are considered in Chapter Eighteen.

SECTION 2.   INCURRING THE CONTRACT OBLIGATION ON THE INSTRUMENT THROUGH SIGNING THE INSTRUMENT

A person is not liable for the contract obligation on a negotiable instrument unless the person has signed the instrument or is responsible for the signature. **Read UCC § 3-401.** Unfortunately, this relatively simple statement is laden with a lot of subtle meaning and is informed by several other provisions of the UCC as well as by other areas of law. Let us start with the relatively simple issue of what it means to sign a negotiable instrument. Compare the definition of "signed" in UCC § 3-401(b) with the definition of "signed" in UCC § 1-201(b)(37). Notice that while an individual may sign by writing his or her full name in script, such formality is not required. Any word, mark or symbol can be used, and it need not be handwritten. As detailed in Chapter Fourteen, absent a signature of a person promising or ordering payment, the document is not a negotiable instrument. UCC §§ 3-103(a)(8), (12), 3-104(a).

Problem 15-1

In each of the situations described below, determine whether the document has been signed.

A. Paula Andrews wrote her first initial on the typed document below and then delivered the document to John Doe.

> January 5, 2010
>
> I, Paula Andrews, promise to pay to the order of John Doe, the sum of $2,000 on demand.
>
> *P*

B. Paula Andrews typed the document below and then delivered it to John Doe.

> January 5, 2010
>
> I, Paula Andrews, promise to pay to the order of John Doe, the sum of $2,000 on demand.

C. Paula Andrews wrote the date, the payee's name, and the amount on the pre-printed document below and then mailed it to Spokane Electric Company.

Paula Andrews 123 Main St. Spokane, WA *2011*	*June 5,*
Pay to the order of *Spokane Electric Co.*	*$243.75.*
First Bank 456 State St. Spokane, WA	_____

A person can be responsible for someone else's signature in a variety of ways. Perhaps the most common way is if the law of agency makes the non-signer responsible, as a principal, for the acts of the signer, as agent.[6] UCC Article 3 refers to the principal as the "represented person" and to the agent as a "representative." When a representative (agent) signs a negotiable instrument, there are two separate questions:

(i) is the representative (agent) bound by the signature; and

(ii) is the represented person (principal) bound by the signature.

Read UCC § 3-402. Subsections (b) and (c) address the first question. Subsection (a) addresses the second question, in part by referring to common-law principles of agency and other law. If these principles bind the represented person, the signature is, by definition, an "authorized signature of the represented person." **Read UCC § 1-201(b)(41).** Note, though, that the liability of the representative and the represented person are not mutually exclusive; in some situations a single signature can bind both of them to a contract obligation on the instrument.

What liabilities do the parties have if the representative's signature is unauthorized? First, the unauthorized signer incurs liability. **Read UCC § 3-403.** For example, if X signs Y's name to an instrument and that signature is not authorized by Y under UCC § 3-402(a), X is liable on the instrument to a person who in good faith paid the instrument or took the instrument for value. Y is generally not liable on the instrument but could become so in a couple of ways.

---

[6] We briefly considered principles of agency law in Chapter Thirteen, when discussing unauthorized use of a credit card.

First, Y could ratify the unauthorized signature with post-signing words or conduct. UCC § 3-403(a). Generally, ratification requires that Y act with knowledge of X's signing of the instrument and that Y retain the benefits of the underlying transaction.[7] Second, in some circumstances Y will be precluded from denying that the signature X placed on the instrument is Y's signature. *See* UCC §§ 3-406, 4-406. These two situations regarding unauthorized signatures are explored more fully in Chapter Nineteen.

When a plaintiff seeks to enforce the contract liability on an instrument and the defendant wants to argue that the signature is unauthorized, the defendant must specifically deny in the pleadings that the signature was authentic or made with authority. **Reread UCC § 3-308(a).** Thus, to continue the example above, if the person entitled to enforce sues Y on the basis of X's signature of Y's name on a negotiable instrument, Y must specifically deny in the answer to the complaint that it is Y's signature and that X was authorized to sign Y's name. Once a defendant puts the signature's validity into question by the specific denial, the person entitled to enforce must prove that the signature is valid or that Y should be denied the ability to contest the signature based upon a rule found in UCC Article 3 or 4 or applicable common law, UCC § 1-103.

Thus the first step of the plaintiff's case is to prove that the defendant signed the instrument or is responsible for the signature. Connected with this step is to demonstrate the role of the signor (maker, drawer, acceptor, or indorser) in regard to that instrument. That role is important because the elements of the contract liability of that signor depends upon the role they have on that instrument.

As we learned in Chapter Fourteen, a negotiable instrument is either a "note" or a "draft." UCC § 3-104(e). **Now read the definitions of "maker" and "drawer in UCC § 3-103.** A maker signs a note and is referred to as an "issuer" of the note. **Read UCC § 3-105.** UCC § 3-412 specifies the nature and extent of a maker's liability on a note, and thereby sets forth the elements of a plaintiff's case against a maker. **Read UCC § 3-412.** A maker, by custom and tradition, signs a note in the bottom right hand corner of the last page of the note.

In contrast, a drawer signs a draft. A drawer's obligation is set forth in UCC § 3-414. **Read UCC § 3-414.** A drawer, by custom and tradition, signs the draft in the lower right hand corner of the piece of paper on which the order to pay is written. Notice that for certain types of drafts – cashier's checks and other types of drafts drawn on the drawer (*i.e.*, where the drawer and the drawee are the same

---

[7] *See QAD Investors, Inc. v. Kelly*, 776 A.2d 1244 (Me. 2001).

entity) – the drawer's contract liability is treated the same as the contract liability of a maker of a note and is governed UCC § 3-412, not UCC § 3-414. In reviewing those two sections, can you identify the major differences in the two statements of liability?

With respect to drafts other than cashier's checks and other types of drafts drawn on the drawer, the nature of a drawer's liability on the draft depends on whether the draft is "accepted" or "unaccepted" by the drawee. *See* UCC § 3-414(b)-(d). If the draft is accepted, the drawer's liability also depends on whether the drawee is a bank. **Read the definitions of "acceptor" and "drawee" in UCC § 3-103.** These rules regarding the *drawer's* liability on the draft are best understood when compared to the rules relating to a *drawee's* liability on the draft. A drawee who does not accept the draft incurs *no* contract liability on the draft. UCC § 3-408. A drawee who signs the draft in the manner prescribed by UCC § 3-409(a) has "accepted" the draft and thereby incurs contract liability as an "acceptor." **Read UCC § 3-409(a) and § 3-413.** As should be apparent from reading the above cited sections, "accepted draft" and "acceptance" have unique meanings and should *not* be confused with other things that may happen with or to a draft, such as negotiating the draft, presenting the draft for payment, or depositing the draft in a bank account.

There is one more type of signature used on negotiable instruments: that of the indorser. **Read the definitions of "indorsement" and "indorser" in UCC § 3-204(a) and (b).** Both notes and drafts may be indorsed. If an instrument is payable to order, the person named as payee must indorse the draft in order to negotiate the draft to another person (negotiation is discussed in Section 3 of this Chapter). When a person indorses an instrument, that person generally incurs liability on the instrument. **Read UCC § 3-415.**

One final, but important, point must be made about the contract liability that is incurred by signing an instrument. Persons signing as *drawer* or *indorser* can avoid incurring the contract obligation on the instrument by writing the words "without recourse" next to the their signature. **Read UCC § 3-414(e) and § 3-415(b).** *But see* UCC § 3-203(c) (transferee entitled to unqualified indorsement in certain circumstances). Notice, this rule does not apply to the drawer of a check (UCC § 3-104(f)). Notice also that there is no comparable provision in UCC § 3-412 or § 3-413, and thus a *maker* or *acceptor* cannot avoid liability by writing the words "without recourse."

As the foregoing few pages indicates, the rules relating to contract liability on an instrument resulting from a signature are numerous and detailed. To sort through and apply those rules, it is useful to follow the analytical steps listed below in the sequence specified. Taken together, these steps comprise a sort of algorithm for determining whether a person has incurred contract liability on an instrument.[8]

First, determine that the document is a negotiable instrument and identify the type of instrument (a note or a draft).

Second, identify the role in which the potential defendant has signed the instrument (drawer, maker, acceptor, or indorser).

Third, determine whether the mark qualifies as a signature and, if so, whether the signature is authentic and authorized.

Fourth, determine whether there is any enforceable limitation on contract liability on the instrument based upon how the instrument was signed.

Now test your understanding of the concepts discussed above by using this analytical process on the following problem.

Problem 15-2

Identify the type of instrument (note or draft), whether the instrument is "signed," the role of the person signing (maker, drawer, acceptor, indorser), and who has contract liability on the instrument.

A.

> January 5, 2010
>
> I, Martin Best, promise to pay to the order of Jane Doe, the sum of $2,000 on demand.
>
> *Martin Best,*
> *without recourse*

Assume Martin Best placed the signature on the bottom right hand corner followed by the words, "without recourse."

---

[8] These steps are only the beginning steps for determining whether a person has contract liability on an instrument. Sections 3 through 5 of this Chapter explore the additional issues that must be analyzed to give a thorough answer to the question of whether a person is liable on an instrument.

B.

> January 5, 2010
>
> To: Acme Co.
> Pay to the order of Finance Co. the sum of $2,000.
>   *Bill Dunn*

Assume that Bill Dunn did not sign the instrument, rather Ed Johnston signed Bill's name. *See* UCC § 3-402(a).

C.

> January 5, 2010
>
> To: Acme Co.
> Pay to the order of Finance Co. the sum of $2,000.
>   *Bill Dunn by Ed Johnston, agent*

Assume that Ed Johnston signed the instrument. *See* UCC § 3-402.

D.

> January 5, 2010
>
> To: Acme Co.
> Pay to the order of Finance Co. the sum of $2,000.
>   *Bill Dunn*

Assume that Bill Dunn signed the instrument on his own behalf and not as an agent for anyone else.

1. After delivery of the writing to Finance Co., Finance Co.'s treasurer applied the following stamp to the back of the writing as follows: FINANCE CO.
2. What difference, if any, would it make if, when signing his name, Bill added the words "without recourse" after his name?

E.

> Bill Dunn
> 123 Main St.
> Evans, OH   *Jan. 5, 2010*
>
> Pay to the order of ___*Finance Co.*___ $2,000   .
> *Two thousand and no/100* -- dollars
>
> First Bank
> 456 Johnson St.   *Ed Johnston*
> Evans, OH

1. Assume Ed Johnson signed the writing. *See* UCC § 3-402.

2. What difference, if any, would it make if, when signing his name, Ed added the words "without recourse" after his name?

F.

> January 5, 2010
>
> To: Acme Co.
> Pay to the order of Finance Co. the sum of $2,000.
>
> *Bill Dunn*

Assume that Bill Dunn signed his own name on his own behalf and not as agent for anyone else. After Bill delivered the writing to Finance Co., Finance Co. took the writing to Acme Co. and asked Acme's president to sign the writing. Acme's president, Sue Acme, signed the writing on the back as follows: *Acme Corp. by Sue Acme, President*

G.

> January 5, 2010
>
> The undersigned promises to pay to the order of First Bank or bearer the sum of $20,000 plus interest at 5% per annum one year from the date hereof.
>
> *Tool Supply Co., Jane Tool, President*

1. Assume that Jane Tool signed the instrument and that the instrument was executed in return for a loan of $20,000 to Tool Supply Co. from First Bank.
2. What difference, if any, would it make if Jane Tool also signed the writing on the back as follows: *Jane Tool*
3. What difference, if any, would it make if Jane had personally received the proceeds of the loan?

H.

> January 5, 2010
>
> To: First State Bank
> Pay to the order of Acme Co. $20,000.
>
> *First State Bank*

1. Assume that the instrument was signed by a clerk employed at First State Bank. *See* UCC § 3-402.
2. What difference, if any, would it make if, when signing the writing, the clerk added the words "without recourse" after the signature?

SECTION 3. TO WHOM THE CONTRACT OBLIGATION IS OWED

A. Person Entitled to Enforce

Sections 3-412 through 3-415 each set forth to whom the contract obligation on an instrument is owed. In each case, the obligation is owed to, among others, "a person entitled to enforce" the instrument. It is to that concept we now turn. **Read UCC § 3-301.** A person can qualify as "a person entitled to enforce" an instrument by falling into any one of three mutually exclusive categories:

(i) a holder;

(ii) a nonholder in possession who has the rights of a holder; or

(iii) person not in possession who is entitled to enforce.

1. *Holder*

Holder is defined in UCC § 1-201(b)(21). To qualify as a holder, a person must have possession of the instrument. But possession alone is not enough. In addition, the instrument must be in the possession of the correct person. Remember that an instrument must be either: (i) payable to bearer; or (ii) payable to the order of an identified person. *Compare* UCC § 3-109(a)(1). The implication of this rule and the definition of holder is that any person in possession of an instrument payable to bearer is a holder. However, for an instrument payable to the order of an identified person, only that identified person can be a holder.

A person may become a holder of an instrument through either of two ways: (i) issuance of the instrument; (ii) or negotiation of the instrument. **Read UCC §§ 3-301, 1-201(b)(21), 3-105, and 3-201.**

To illustrate the concepts of a "holder," "issuance," and "negotiation," consider the following example concerning a bearer instrument.

Drawer makes a check payable to the order of cash and then delivers the check to Friend. The check is a bearer instrument. UCC § 3-109. When Drawer delivered the check to Friend, the check was issued under UCC § 3-105 but not negotiated under UCC § 3-201. Do you see why from reading those two sections? Friend, who now has possession of an instrument payable to bearer, is a holder under UCC § 1-201(b)(21) and, therefore, a person entitled to enforce under UCC § 3-301.

If Friend, the initial transferee of the check, delivered possession of the check to another person, that transfer would be a negotiation under UCC § 3-201. Mere transfer of possession, even if involuntary, is a negotiation of a bearer instrument. For this reason, anyone in possession of a bearer instrument is a holder of the instrument and a person entitled to enforce the instrument.

If the instrument were instead payable to order, a different analysis would apply. Consider this second example.

Drawer makes a check payable to the order of Friend. The check is an order instrument. UCC § 3-109. When Drawer delivers the check to anyone, either Friend or someone else, that is an issuance under UCC § 3-105, but not a negotiation under UCC § 3-201. If the check were issued to Friend, the named payee, and the drawer intended that Friend be the payee of the check, then Friend is the person to whom the check is payable. *See* UCC § 3-110(a).[9] Friend would therefore be a holder under UCC § 1-201(b)(21) and a person entitled to enforce under UCC § 3-301. If the issuance were not to Friend, such as if Drawer delivered the check to Neighbor even though the check was made out to Friend, Neighbor would not be a holder under UCC § 1-201(b)(21). Do you see why?

In short, if an instrument is payable to the order of an identified person (as defined in UCC § 3-110), then – at least initially – only that identified person can be a holder of the instrument. However, a subsequent possessor of the instrument which is payable to order can qualify as a holder if the instrument becomes payable to that person or to bearer. *See* UCC § 1-201(b)(21). To make an instrument that is initially payable to the order of an identified person payable either to another person or to bearer requires that the instrument be indorsed.[10]

---

[9] The intent of the drawer is relevant even though the check identifies the payee by name for at least two reasons. First, the intended payee's name may be misspelled or otherwise improperly written on the check. Second, there may be more than person with the same name. *See* UCC § 3-110 cmt. 1.

[10] An instrument payable to bearer can also be indorsed, but it need not be indorsed to be negotiated to the next person. When a bearer instrument is indorsed, it is often for the purpose of obtaining the indorser's contract obligation on the instrument or to make a bearer instrument payable to an identified person.

Returning to the second illustration above, now assume Friend has possession of the check in which she is the named payee. In order for her to make anyone else a holder of the instrument, she has to transfer possession and indorse the instrument.

Indorsement is defined in UCC § 3-204. **Read that section.** Every indorsement will have one characteristic from each of the following three pairs of mutually-exclusive characteristics: (i) special or blank; (ii) qualified or unqualified; and (iii) restricted or unrestricted. Thus every indorsement will have one of the following sets of characteristics:

(1) blank, qualified, and restricted;

(2) blank, qualified, and unrestricted;

(3) blank, unqualified, and restricted;

(4) blank, unqualified, and unrestricted;

(5) special, qualified, and restricted;

(6) special, qualified, and unrestricted;

(7) special, unqualified, and restricted; or

(8) special, unqualified, and unrestricted.

Blank or special. Section 3-205 defines special and blank indorsements. **Read that section.** The distinction deals with to whom the instrument will be payable after the indorsement. Notice that a special indorsement need not use the "magic words" we encountered in evaluating whether an instrument was negotiable under UCC § 3-109.

Qualified or unqualified. Section 3-415(b) allows an indorsement to be made without recourse, which is called a qualified indorsement. A qualified indorsement disclaims the contract liability of the indorser on the instrument.

Restricted or unrestricted. Restrictive indorsements come into play most often in the bank collection process for instruments and address whether and how the indorsement may restrict further negotiation of the instrument. **Read UCC § 3-206.** Restrictive indorsements will be taken up more fully in the discussion of the bank collection process in Chapter Sixteen.

Problem 15-3

Assume a check is issued to the named payee in each of the scenarios described below and then indorsed as indicated. In each case, determine the steps the current holder needs to take, after the indorsement is placed on the check, to further negotiate the check so that the next person will qualify as a holder. In addition, if the type of the indorsement is not indicated, classify the type of indorsement (from the list of eight possibilities above). Before attempting the problem, **read UCC § 3-110.**

How Instrument Is Payable	Indorsement	Type of Indorsement	Action Needed to Further Negotiate
Pay to the order of Ned Smith	*Ned Smith*	Blank, unqualified, unrestricted	
Pay to the order of Ned Smith	*Ned Smith, without recourse*	Blank, qualified, unrestricted	
Pay to the order of Ned Smith	*Ned Smith, without recourse, for deposit only*	Blank, qualified, restricted	
Pay to the order of Ned Smith	Pay to Alice Jones, *Ned Smith*	Special, unqualified, unrestricted	
Pay to the order of Ned Smith	Pay only to Alice Jones, *Ned Smith without recourse*		
Pay to the order of Ned Smith	Pay to Alice Jones in trust for Carrie Bonds, *Ned Smith without recourse*		
Pay to the order of Ned Smith/John Smith	*John Smith*		
Pay to the order of Spiderman ("Spiderman" is Ned Smith's nickname)	*Spiderman without recourse*		

How Instrument Is Payable	Indorsement	Type of Indorsement	Action Needed to Further Negotiate
Pay to the order of the CFO of General Mills Co.	*Bill Jones, CFO*		

Now that we have explored indorsements and negotiation, it is appropriate to return to the subject we started with: the "holder" of an instrument. As explored above, a holder is one type of "person entitled to enforce" the contract obligation on the instrument. Being able to recognize whether someone is a "holder" is critical to understanding negotiable instruments because it often determines whether the person can enforce the instrument and is a necessary condition to qualifying as that special type of holder: a holder in due course. A holder in due course must, first of all, be a "holder." Review the definition of "holder" in UCC § 1-201, the concept of negotiation in UCC § 3-201, and the concept of issue in UCC § 3-105. Practice your understanding of these concepts in the next problem.

Problem 15-4

In each of the scenarios described below:

(i) identify whether the instrument has been issued or negotiated and, if so, when and to whom; and

(ii) determine whether the person in possession of the instrument is a holder, and if not, identify what could have been done to make the possessor a holder.

A. Abby wrote a check for $100 payable to the order of "Bill or bearer" and signed the check as drawer. Abby delivered the check to Carl.

B. Abby wrote a check for $100 payable to the order of "Bill," intending Bill to be the payee, and signed the check as drawer. Abby delivered the check to Carl.

C. Abby wrote a check for $100 payable to the order of "Bill" and signed the check as drawer. Abby delivered the check to Bill. Bill delivered the check to Carl.

D. Abby wrote a check for $100 payable to the order of "Bill" and signed by Abby as drawer. Abby delivered the check to Bill. Bill wrote on the back of the check "*Bill*" and lost the check. Carl picked up the check.

E. 1. Abby wrote a check for $100 payable to the order of "Bill" and signed the check as drawer. Abby delivered the check to Bill. Bill wrote on the back of the check "*Bill* without recourse." Bill gave the check to Carl.
    2. Does Bill have any contract liability on the check?

F. 1. Abby wrote a check for $100 payable to the order of "Bill" and signed the check as drawer. Abby wrote "without recourse" next to her signature on the bottom right hand corner of the check and then delivered the check to Bill.
    2. How, if at all, would the analysis change if the instrument were a draft but not a check?

G. 1. Abby wrote a check for $100 payable to the order of "Bill" and signed the check as drawer. Abby delivered the check to Bill. Bill wrote on the back of the check "*Bill* without recourse" and then delivered the check to Carl. Carl delivered the check to Dan.
    2. Does Carl have any contract liability on the instrument?

H. 1. Abby wrote a check for $100 payable to the order of "Bill" and signed the check as drawer. Abby delivered the check to Bill. Bill wrote on the back of the check "Pay to Carl, *Bill*" and delivered the check to Carl.
    2. What must Carl do to further negotiate the check?

I. 1. Abby wrote a check for $100 payable to the order of "Bill" and signed the check as drawer. Abby delivered the check to Bill. Bill wrote on the back of the check, "Pay to Carl if Carl paints my house, *Bill*" and delivered the check to Carl.
    2. How, if at all, can Carl transfer the check to someone else and make that next person a holder?

J. 1. Abby wrote a check for $100 payable to the order of "Bill and Ted" and signed the check as drawer. Abby delivered the check to Bill.

  2. How, if at all, would the analysis change if the check were payable to the order of "Bill or Ted"? What if the check were payable to the order of "Bill/Ted"?

2. *Nonholder in Possession with Rights of a Holder*

The second category of person entitled to enforce an instrument is a nonholder in possession who has the rights of a holder. A person can acquire this status through a voluntary transfer of possession of the instrument for the purpose of transferring the right to enforce or through the application of other principles of law. **Read UCC §§ 3-203, 1-201(b)(15).**

Section 3-203 is an expression of the concept of derivative rights: a transferee of an instrument who receives possession can acquire the transferor's right to enforce even if the transferee is not a holder. Consider the following illustration.

Avery signed as maker a negotiable note for $10,000, payable to the order of "Barbara," and delivered the note to Barbara. Without indorsing the note, Barbara delivered the note to Charley. By now you should recognize that Charley would not qualify as a "holder" of the check. If you are not sure why, review the material we just covered. However, Charley may qualify as a "nonholder in possession with the rights of a holder." Whether Charley does or does not so qualify depends on why Barbara delivered the note to Charley. If Barbara transferred possession of the note for the purpose of transferring the right to enforce, then Charley would be a nonholder in possession with rights of a holder. UCC §§ 3-203, 3-301. This would be likely if Barbara had either sold the note to Charley or hired Charley to service the note (*i.e.*, collect the note) for Barbara. Barbara would not have the requisite purpose if she had merely delivered the note to Charley for safekeeping.[11]

---

[11] On the issue of what Charley would have to show to demonstrate that the transfer was for the stated purpose as provided in UCC § 3-203, see *Nessi v. Sudovest Group, Inc.*, 57 U.C.C. Rep. Serv. 2d 417 (Minn. Ct. App. 2005).

3. Person Not in Possession

The third category of a person who is "entitled to enforce" is a person not in possession of an instrument. Because the obligation represented by a negotiable instrument is said to be "reified" – that is, the incorporeal right to payment is embodied in the tangible paper – this category of persons is rather narrow and is generally limited to situations when the instrument is not now and is unlikely in the future to be available. It extends to instruments that have been lost, stolen, or destroyed. *See* UCC § 3-309. It also applies in the relatively rare situation in which an instrument is mistakenly paid and the payment is later recovered. *See* UCC § 3-418(d). For the present, we will concentrate on the requirements for enforcing lost or stolen instruments. **Read UCC § 3-309.** We will consider UCC § 3-418 in Chapter Nineteen when we consider recovery when there are errors or wrongdoing concerning a negotiable instrument.

Practice your understanding of these three categories of a person entitled to enforce in Problem 15-5.

Problem 15-5

A. Ann signed as maker a negotiable note for $1,000, payable to the order of "Brad," and delivered the note to Brad. Brad wrote on the back of the note, "Pay to Doug, *Brad*." Brad then delivered the note to Candy.
   1. Is Candy a holder?
   2. Is Candy a person entitled to enforce Ann's contract liability against Ann?
   3. Is Candy a person entitled to enforce Brad's contract liability against Brad?

B. Ann signed as maker a negotiable note for $1,000, payable to the order of "Brad," and delivered the note to Brad. Brad wrote on the back of the note, "Pay to Doug, *Brad*." Brad then delivered the note to Candy. Candy gave the note to Doug. Doug then gave the note to Ernie.
   1. Is Ernie a holder?
   2. Is Ernie a person entitled to enforce Ann's contract liability against Ann?
   3. Is Ernie a person entitled to enforce Brad's contract liability against Brad?

4.   Does Doug have any contract liability on the instrument?

C.   Ann signed as maker a negotiable note for $1,000, payable to the order of "Brad," and delivered the note to Brad. Brad then misplaced the note.
1.   If Brad cannot find the note, can Brad nevertheless enforce Ann's contract liability against Ann?
2.   How, if at all, does the analysis change if the note had been stolen from Brad instead of being misplaced?
3.   How, if at all, does the analysis change if Brad had given the note to Candy instead of misplacing the note?

D.   Ann signed as maker a negotiable note for $1,000, payable to "Beta Corp.," and delivered the note to Clerk, Beta Corp.'s authorized representative. Pursuant to the applicable state corporations law, Beta Corp. then merged into Gamma, Inc., with the result that Gamma, Inc. succeeded to all the rights and liabilities of Beta Corp. Clerk is now an authorized representative of Gamma, Inc. and has custody of the note. Is Gamma, Inc. entitled to enforce Ann's contract liability on the note?

B.   To Whom the Contract Obligation on the Instrument is Owed in Addition to the "Person Entitled to Enforce"

In the normal course of events – to the extent that consists of timely payment by the maker of note or the drawee of a draft – the contract obligation on an instrument will not be owed to anyone other than a "person entitled to enforce" the instrument. However, as we saw in Section 2 of this Chapter, persons other than makers and drawers can have liability on an instrument. If such other persons pay the instrument, the maker, drawer, or even someone else may have liability to the person who paid. **Reread UCC §§ 3-412, 3-413(a), 3-414(b), and 3-415(a).** Each of these provisions extends liability to someone in addition to a "person entitled to enforce." The following chart details the additional person to whom liability is owed.

	Person Liable	Person To Whom Liability Is Owed
§ 3-412	Issuer	Indorser who paid
§ 3-413(a)	Acceptor	Drawer or indorser who paid
§ 3-414(b)	Drawer	Indorser who paid
§ 3-415(a)	Indorser	Subsequent indorser who paid

Problem 15-6

A. Ari signed as drawer and issued a negotiable demand draft for $100 payable to the order of "Bruce." Bruce indorsed the draft, "Pay Chris, *Bruce*," and delivered the draft to Chris. Chris indorsed the draft, "Pay Darla, *Chris*," and delivered the draft to Darla. Darla indorsed the draft, "Pay Edward, *Darla*," and delivered the draft to Edward, who presented the draft to the drawee, Xavier. Xavier refused to pay.

   1. Who, among Ari, Bruce, Chris, and Darla, has contract liability on the instrument and to whom is that liability owed?
   2. Edward demanded that Chris pay the draft. Chris did so. Who, if anyone, has contract liability on the instrument to Chris?

B. Ari signed as drawer and issued a negotiable draft for $100 payable on May 3 to the order of "Bruce." Bruce indorsed the draft, "Pay Chris, *Bruce*," and delivered the draft to Chris. Chris indorsed the draft, "Pay Darla, *Chris*," and delivered the draft to Darla. Darla presented the draft to the drawee on May 1. The drawee signed the draft on the front and returned it to Darla. Darla presented the draft again on May 3 and the drawee refused to pay.

   1. If the drawee is a bank, against whom may Darla enforce contract liability on the instrument?
   2. If the drawee is not a bank, against whom may Darla enforce contract liability on the instrument?
   3. Assume the drawee is not a bank. Darla demanded that Ari pay the draft and Ari did so. Who, if anyone, has contract liability on the instrument to Ari?

SECTION 4.   WHEN THE OBLIGATION IS DUE

After determining who owes the contract obligation on an instrument (Section 2 of this Chapter) and to whom that obligation is owed (Section 3 of this Chapter), the next task is to determine when the contract obligation on the instrument is due.

Terms of the instrument.[12] It should come as no surprise that the first place to look to determine when the obligation is due is the instrument itself. A negotiable instrument must be payable either on demand or at a definite time. UCC § 3-108. The instrument may also state the place of payment. *See* UCC § 3-111.

Other factors affecting when the obligation is due. However, the time stated on the instrument is not the only consideration. Depending on who is liable on the instrument – maker, drawer, acceptor, indorser – one or more other conditions must be satisfied for the obligation to become due. For example, we have already seen that the contract liability of a drawer under UCC § 3-414(b) and of an indorser under UCC § 3-415(a) arises after the instrument is "dishonored." Dishonor is a defined term that is based in part on another defined term: "presentment." We now turn to these two concepts: presentment and dishonor.

---

[12] The terms of the instrument will also define the amount of the obligation that is due. *See* UCC §§ 3-104(a), 3-107, 3-112. Each of the sections defining contract liability on the instrument specifies that the signor's obligation is to pay according to the terms of the instrument, which includes the amount of the obligation. *See* UCC §§ 3-412, 3-413(a), 3-414(b), 3-415(a).

Each of these sections detailing contract liability on the instrument also specifies the time at which the terms of the instrument are to be determined. For the obligation of a maker of a note or a drawer of a draft, the terms of the instrument are determined as of the time the instrument was issued, or if not issued, when it first came into possession of a holder. Thus the material covered earlier on when a person becomes a holder and when an instrument is issued is important to determining what obligation is due. If the issuer or drawer signed an incomplete instrument, in some circumstances the maker or the drawer may be liable based on the terms of the writing as completed even if that is later than when that person signed the instrument.

An acceptor's liability on the instrument is determined by the terms of the instrument at the time it was accepted or if the acceptor signed the draft while it was incomplete, in some circumstances by the terms at the time of completion. An indorser's liability on an instrument is determined by the terms of the instrument at the time of indorsement, or if the indorser signed the instrument while it was incomplete, in some circumstances by the terms of the instrument as completed.

We will explore the rules regarding incomplete instruments in Chapter Nineteen.

Presentment. **Read UCC § 3-501.** Presentment is the process of demanding payment of a draft or a note, or acceptance of a draft. The terms of the instrument may define how presentment is to be made, and in some circumstances, may contain a waiver of the requirement of presentment. UCC § 3-504. In the absence of such terms, UCC § 3-501(b) indicates how presentment for payment or acceptance is to be made and the actions that the person to whom presentment is made may take in response.

Dishonor. **Read UCC § 3-502.** When a dishonor occurs depends upon what type of instrument is used and whether the instrument makes payment due on demand or at a definite time. If presentment is a prerequisite to dishonor, such as with a demand instrument, the presentment must be "duly made," a term which incorporates the requirements of a proper presentment. Notice that UCC § 3-501(b)(3) allows the person to whom presentment is made to refuse to honor the instrument in certain circumstances without that refusal constituting a dishonor.

A. Conditions to Liability of a Drawer, Generally

Now take a closer look at the obligation of a drawer in UCC § 3-414. Notice that the obligation of a drawer of a draft that the drawee has not "accepted" (UCC § 3-409) is owed upon dishonor of the draft. If the draft is not dishonored, the drawer's obligation on an unaccepted draft is not yet due. What that means is that a drawer's obligation ripens only when the drawee refuses to honor the unaccepted draft.

The drawee may be asked to honor the draft in either of two ways: to pay the draft or to "accept" the draft. The request to pay or accept the draft is a presentment. UCC § 3-501(a). If the drawee refuses to pay or accept the draft upon a proper presentment, the draft is dishonored. **Read UCC § 3-502(b) on dishonor of an unaccepted, non-documentary draft.**[13]

---

[13] A documentary draft is a draft that is accompanied by documents relating to the underlying transaction, such as a bill of lading or warehouse receipt. *See* UCC § 4-104(a)(6). A documentary draft is often used as a mechanism for a seller of goods to transmit documents to the buyer through the banking system. The seller issues a draft drawn on the buyer and provides the draft and the documents to a bank that undertakes to deliver the draft and documents to a presenting bank in the buyer's locale. The presenting bank then takes the responsibility of providing those documents to the buyer/drawee if the drawee honors the

Notice that when dishonor occurs with respect to an unaccepted, non-documentary draft depends on:

(i) whether the draft is a check;

(ii) how the draft is presented to the drawee; and

(iii) whether the draft is payable at a definite time or on demand.

Dishonor of checks presented through the bank collection process is addressed in subsection (b)(1). The phrase "immediate payment over the counter" in that section refers to a presenter making the presentment in person to a teller at the drawee bank, an unusual situation. Most presentments of checks are made through the bank collection process, which we will study in Chapter Sixteen.

If the drawee has "accepted" the draft, the draft must have been presented once in a manner that resulted in the acceptance. UCC § 3-409. Sometime later, the accepted draft will be presented again to the drawee for payment. An accepted draft is dishonored if it is presented for payment and not paid by the time specified in UCC § 3-502(d).

Problem 15-7

A. Acme Co. is the payee of a negotiable nondocumentary draft payable on demand. Bill is the drawer of the draft. Claire is the drawee. Acme Co. sent an e-mail message to Claire demanding payment of the draft. Has Acme Co. made a proper presentment?

B. Allison is a payee of a check. Bank is the drawee and has established a cutoff hour of 3:00 p.m. for presentment of instruments. Allison presented the check at 4:00 p.m. to the teller at Bank. The teller told Allison that Bank will pay the check by the end of the next business day. Has Bank dishonored the check?

C. Acme Co. is the payee of a negotiable nondocumentary draft payable on demand. Bill is the drawer of the draft. Claire is the drawee. Acme transferred the draft for value to Doug without signing the draft. Doug presented the draft to Claire, demanding payment. Claire refused to

---

draft through payment or acceptance. *See* UCC § 4-501 through § 4-504. A non-documentary draft is a draft that has no accompanying documents.

pay because Acme had not signed the draft. Has Claire dishonored the draft?

D. Acme Co. is the payee of a negotiable nondocumentary draft payable on May 3. Bill is the drawer of the draft. Claire is the drawee. May 3 comes and goes. Has Claire dishonored the draft?

E. Acme Co. is the payee of a negotiable note payable on May 3. Bill is the maker of the note. May 3 comes and goes. Has Bill dishonored the note?

F. John is the payee of a check drawn on Bank. John exhibits the check to the teller at Bank, asking Bank to pay him the amount of the check. The teller informs John that to cash the check, he must place his thumbprint on the back of the check in addition to signing the check on the back. John signs the check on the back but refuses to place his thumbprint on the check. Bank teller refuses to pay the amount of the check to John. Has Bank dishonored the check? *See Messing v. Bank of Am.*, 821 A.2d 22 (Md. 2003).

G. John is the payee of a negotiable nondocumentary draft payable on May 3. Acme Co. is the drawer and National Insurance Co. is the drawee. On April 3, John presented the draft to National Insurance Co. and asked National Insurance to Co. "accept" the draft.
   1. If National Insurance refused to "accept" the draft, has dishonor occurred?
   2. Assume that National Insurance signed the front of the draft when John presented it. John then signed the draft and transferred it to ABC Corp. ABC Corp. then took the draft to National Insurance on May 1, demanding payment of the draft. On May 2, National Insurance refused to pay. Has National Insurance dishonored the draft?
   3. How, if at all, does the analysis change to both questions above if the draft were payable on demand?

B. Conditions to Liability of Indorser and of Drawer of Accepted Draft

Now consider the liability of an indorser in UCC § 3-415. Not only is the indorser's liability conditioned on dishonor, in most cases liability also requires that the indorser be given notice of dishonor. Notice of dishonor is governed by UCC § 3-503. That section details who must give the notice, the manner of the notice, and the time in which the notice must be given. UCC Article 1 further informs these rules by providing that notice is given when the sender takes reasonable steps to communicate the information, even if the person to whom it is directed never receives it. UCC § 1-202(d). In some circumstances, UCC § 3-504 may excuse the failure to provide notice of dishonor. **Read UCC §§ 3-503 and 3-504.**

Section 3-504 also allows for waiver of presentment by the terms of the instrument. **Read UCC § 3-502(e).** Waiver of the need for presentment and notice of dishonor is most common in notes. Drafts generally do not contain explicit waivers of these two requirements. If the terms of the instrument waive presentment and the instrument is a demand instrument, when will the instrument be considered dishonored?

Additional conditions to liability of drawer on accepted draft when acceptor is not a bank. A drawee that accepts the draft has the liability stated in UCC § 3-413. Review the meaning of acceptance as stated in UCC § 3-409. Now consider the effect of an "acceptance" of the draft by the drawee on the obligation of the drawer of the draft or an indorser of the draft. **Read UCC §§ 3-414(c) and (d), 3-415(d), and 3-410.** If the acceptor is not a bank, and the acceptor refuses to pay when the draft is due (*i.e.*, dishonors the draft), the drawer must be given notice of dishonor to be liable on the draft. UCC § 3-414(d).

Problem 15-8

A. Andy is the maker of a negotiable note payable on demand to Barbara. Barbara indorsed the note in blank and delivered the note to Carl. Carl presented the note to Andy. Andy refused to pay.
    1. What must Carl do to enforce Barbara's indorsement liability?
    2. If Carl timely mails a notice of dishonor to Barbara but Barbara does not receive it, is notice of dishonor effective? *See* UCC § 1-202.
    3. Carl gave Barbara notice of dishonor 40 days after Andy's dishonor of the instrument. The reason that Carl waited so long

was that Carl was in a location that suffered an earthquake that interrupted mail service. Can Carl enforce Barbara's indorsement liability?

B. Andy is the maker of a negotiable note payable on demand to Barbara. The note contains the following clause: "All parties to this instrument waive presentment and notice of dishonor." Must Barbara make a presentment to Andy and Andy refuse to pay before the note is dishonored?

C. Andy is the maker of a negotiable note payable on May 3 to Barbara. Barbara indorsed the note in blank and delivered the note to Carl. Carl presented the note to Andy on May 3. Andy refused to pay. The note provides that "presentment of this instrument is not required."
   1. What must Carl do to enforce Barbara's indorsement liability?
   2. How, if at all, would the analysis change if this were a demand note and, prior to Carl presenting the note to Andy, Andy told Barbara that he would not pay the note? *See* UCC § 3-504 cmt. and former UCC § 3-511. What is the difference between "waiver" and "excuse?"

D. Andy is the drawer of a negotiable nondocumentary draft payable on May 3. Barbara is the payee and First Bank is the drawee. Barbara presented the draft to First Bank on May 1. First Bank signed the draft on the front. Barbara then indorsed the draft in blank and transferred the draft to Carl. First Bank refused to pay the draft when Carl presented it on May 3.
   1. Against whom will Carl be able to enforce contract liability on the draft?
   2. Does Carl need to give notice of dishonor to anyone?
   3. How, if at all, would the analysis change if Barbara had indorsed the draft before First Bank signed the draft?
   4. How, if at all, would the analysis change if the drawee were National Insurance Co. which is not a bank?

E. Andy is the drawer of a check payable to Barbara and drawn on State Bank. Barbara indorsed the check in blank and deposited the check in her checking account at Commerce Bank. Commerce Bank then forwarded the check for collection to State Bank. State Bank dishonored the check and returned the check to Commerce Bank the next day. What must Commerce Bank do to be able to enforce Barbara's indorsement liability?

We will return to presentment, dishonor, and notice of dishonor when we study the check collection system in Chapter Sixteen.

At this point, we have explored the elements of the plaintiff's case on enforcement of the contract liability on the instrument. Those elements are:

(i) the instrument is a negotiable instrument;

(ii) the defendant is obligated on the instrument because of a signature;

(iii) the plaintiff is entitled to enforce the obligation; and

(iv) the obligation is due.

If the plaintiff cannot prove that the instrument is a negotiable instrument, the defendant may have liability under normal rules of contract law, but not under negotiable instruments law. If the instrument is a negotiable instrument, and the plaintiff cannot prove any one or more of the other elements of the plaintiff's case, the defendant will not be liable on the instrument to that plaintiff.[14]

If the plaintiff is able to prove the elements of the plaintiff's case, the defendant may nevertheless have an affirmative defense to contract obligation on the instrument.[15] It is to that subject, we now turn.

---

[14] The defendant may have no liability on the instrument at all to any person if the plaintiff is unable to prove that the defendant is responsible for the signature. The defendant may have no liability to this particular plaintiff if the plaintiff is unable to demonstrate that the plaintiff is a person entitled to enforce the instrument. Alternatively, the defendant's obligation may simply not have come due, such as if the defendant is a drawer and the plaintiff cannot show that the draft has been dishonored.

[15] UCC § 3-308 states that the plaintiff has the burden to prove its case and the defendant has the burden to prove its defenses. However, a defendant seeking to undermine the plaintiff's case has a burden of production: the defendant must introduce sufficient evidence so that a finder of fact would find that the plaintiff has not carried its burden of proof.

SECTION 5.   DEFENSES, CLAIMS IN RECOUPMENT, AND HOLDER IN DUE COURSE STATUS

A. Overview

Reread UCC § 3-308. If the plaintiff makes a prima facie showing that the defendant has contract liability on the instrument to the plaintiff, the defendant may still have either a defense to payment of the obligation on the instrument (that is, the defendant need not pay any amount at all) or a claim in recoupment (that is, the defendant has a recoupment right that reduces the amount of the defendant's contract obligation on the instrument).

Defenses. **Read UCC § 3-305(a).** This provision identifies two classes of potentially available defenses. One class is the set of defenses available under contract law. *See* UCC § 3-305(a)(1), (2). It makes sense to look to contract law for possible defenses because we are dealing, after all, with contract liability on the instrument. Thus, for example, assume that there was a mutual mistake that would justify not enforcing a contract under common-law principles. That is an example of the type of defense referred to UCC § 3-305(a)(2). *See also* UCC § 3-117. The other class of defenses contains those provided by UCC Article 3. **Read comment 2 to UCC § 3-305.** That comment lists various defenses to payment that are referred to by the language of UCC § 3-305(a)(2).

Claims in recoupment. A claim in recoupment is a counterclaim that the defendant may assert against the plaintiff and that arises out of the transaction that also gave rise to the note. **Read comment 3 to UCC § 3-305.**[16]

Defendant must own the defense or claim in recoupment. One more thing to realize about defenses and claims in recoupment. It is a cardinal rule of contract law that a person may only assert his or her own defenses to an obligation. That principle also applies to a negotiable instrument and is reflected in UCC § 3-305(c).[17] That means that if there are multiple obligors on an instrument, it is critical to identify who is able to assert the defense. To illustrate, assume a maker

---

[16] Claims in recoupment should not be confused with claims to an instrument under UCC § 3-306. Claims to an instrument – based upon an assertion of property-based rights to the instrument or its proceeds – will be discussed in Chapter Eighteen.

[17] This principle is subject to an exception in UCC § 3-305(d) regarding accommodation parties. We will consider this exception in Chapter Seventeen when we consider suretyship obligations and defenses.

issues a note to a payee and the payee indorses the note. The maker is liable on its contract obligation under UCC § 3-412 and the indorser is liable on its contract obligation under UCC § 3-415. Now assume that the maker has a contract-law defense, such as misrepresentation in the underlying transaction. The indorser may not assert the maker's contract defense of misrepresentation. Only the maker may assert that defense, in the event the maker is sued on its contract obligation as an issuer of the note.

Another illustration of this principal arises when a bank check is taken for an obligation. Assume that a person obtains a teller's check from its bank, payable to a payee. The issuing bank is the drawer and the check is drawn on another bank. UCC §§ 3-104(h), 3-103(a)(15). Assume that after delivery of the check to the payee, the remitter (the person obtaining the teller's check) determines that the payee should not be paid because of the payee's breach of contract pursuant to the underlying transaction between the remitter and the payee. The remitter asks the issuing bank (the drawer) to stop payment on the check. While the issuing bank may do so, if it is sued on its drawer's liability, it has no defense of its own to that liability. The drawer may not assert the remitter's defense to payment arising out of the underlying transaction between the remitter and the payee. **Read UCC § 3-411.**

Is the plaintiff subject to the defense or claim in recoupment? Once you have identified an argument that can serve as a defense to the contract obligation on the instrument or a claim in recoupment against the contract obligation on the instrument, the next step is to determine whether that defense or claim in recoupment may be asserted against this particular plaintiff. If the plaintiff qualifies as a holder in due course, or is able to assert the rights of a holder in due course, the defendant will not be able to assert most defenses and will not be able to assert any claims in recoupment against that plaintiff.

Reread UCC § 3-305(b). Generally, a holder in due course is subject to the defenses listed in UCC § 3-305(a)(1) (called the "real" defenses) but is not subject either to the defenses referred to in subsection (a)(2) (called the "personal" defenses) or to claims in recoupment as provided in subsection (a)(3).

This rule protecting a holder in due course is subject to an exception embodied in the phrase "against a person other than the holder," found at the end of UCC § 3-305(b). This phrase means that, even if the plaintiff is a holder in due course, the plaintiff is subject to a discharge of which it has notice, UCC § 3-601, defenses arising contemporaneously with or subsequent to the transfer of the instrument to the holder in due course, and defenses as a result of the holder in due course's own behavior.

As discussed in Chapter Fourteen, one of the hallmarks of negotiability is the possibility that the payment obligation will become payable to a holder in due course – that is, to someone who takes the instrument free from most defenses and claims in recoupment. This enables negotiable instruments to be freely transferred without the usual baggage connected to an assignment of contract rights. That is because an assignee of contract rights is generally subject to all the defenses that the obligor could assert against the assignor. The holder-in-due-course rule alters that common-law principle. Holder-in-due-course status is one of the most important concepts in the law of negotiable instruments.

Qualifying as a holder in due course. So what does it take to be a holder in due course? **Read UCC § 3-302.** In order to qualify as a holder in due course, one *must* be a "holder." Everything that we have learned about negotiation of a negotiable instrument is relevant to that inquiry. Section 3-302 sets out several additional requirements that must be met for a person to qualify as a holder in due course. *All of these elements must be met.* Thus, if the person qualifies as a holder but does not take the instrument "for value," or takes the instrument for value but does not take the instrument "in good faith," the person is not a holder in due course. Some of the terms listed in UCC § 3-302 are further explained in other sections. **Read UCC § 3-303** (value), **UCC § 1-202** (notice), **UCC § 3-304** (overdue), and **UCC § 3-103(a)(6) or 1-201(b)(20)** (good faith).[18]

---

[18] The requirement of good faith is a troublesome one. It is not clear what is meant by the requirement that the holder comply with reasonable commercial standards of fair dealing. *See* UCC § 3-103 cmt. 4. This issue has resulted in a fair amount of litigation. *See Maine Family Fed. Credit Union v. Sun Life Assurance Co. of Canada*, 727 A.2d 335 (Me. 1999) (bank did not comport with reasonable commercial standard of fair dealing when the bank did not place a hold on funds availability from deposit of large insurance checks drawn on an out-of-state bank); *Any Kind Checks Cashed, Inc. v. Talcott*, 830 So. 2d 160 (Fla. Ct. App. 2002) (check cashing store did not cash $10,000 check to businessman in good faith without verifying check with the drawer; legitimate businessmen rarely used check cashing stores because of the high fee they charge); *Mid Wisconsin Bank v. Forsgard Trading, Inc.*, 668 N.W.2d 830, 833 (Wis. Ct. App. 2003) ("it does not matter whether, as here, the account had been overdrawn previously. Mid Wisconsin's policy is to place holds on checks when it has reasonable doubt about the check based on the depositor's history. Here there was no reasonable doubt. Whenever Forsgard had been overdrawn previously, it always deposited funds to cover the overdraft when the bank alerted it to the problem. Mid Wisconsin had no

Holder-in-due-course status is determined for the most part at the time the holder "took" the instrument. *See* UCC § 3-302(a)(2). *Cf.* UCC § 3-302(a)(1) (referring to when the instrument was "issued or negotiated").[19] This timing issue is often important because, by the time the holder in due course actually sues someone on the contract obligation on the instrument, the holder in due course will typically know that there are problems with the instrument, *i.e.*, that the defendant is asserting a defense or claim in recoupment. If holder-in-due-course status were determined at the time of the lawsuit, then no one would ever qualify as a holder in due course.

Problem 15-9

Make a checklist of the elements of holder-in-due-course status, incorporating the meaning of the further definitions into your checklist.

Relationship of holder-in-due-course status to the plaintiff's case. Even if the plaintiff qualifies as a holder in due course, it is important to understand that such status is irrelevant to whether the plaintiff has proven some of the elements of plaintiff's prima facie case. Recall the four elements of a plaintiff's case:
  (i) the instrument is a negotiable instrument;
  (ii) the defendant is obligated on the instrument because of a signature;
  (iii) the plaintiff is entitled to enforce the obligation; and
  (iv) the obligation is due.
  Qualifying as a holder in due course necessarily means that the person is entitled to enforce the obligation (element (iii) above). It also implies that the instrument is a negotiable instrument (element (i) above). That is because there is no such thing as a holder in due course of a non-negotiable instrument. To be a holder (and thus a holder in due course), the instrument must be negotiable. *See* UCC §§ 1-201(b)(21), 3-302(a). Of course, the mere fact that a person took an instrument for value, in good faith, and without notice of a claim or defense does not mean that the instrument itself qualifies as a negotiable instrument.

---

reason to suspect there would be any problem if immediate credit was extended for this check. Consequently, we conclude that Mid Wisconsin observed reasonable commercial standards of fair dealing and therefore was a holder in due course.").

[19] *See Southern Bank of Commerce v. Union Planters Nat'l Bank*, 289 S.W.3d 414 (Ark. 2008).

However, holder-in-due-course status is irrelevant to whether the defendant is obligated on an instrument (element (ii) above) or whether the obligation is due (element (iv) above). Thus, even a holder in due course is subject to an argument that the defendant is not responsible for any signature on the instrument or that a required notice of dishonor was not given.

B. Analysis of Defenses and Holder-in-Due-Course Status

Method of analysis. After the plaintiff has proven its case (including that it is entitled to performance of the defendant's contract obligation on the instrument), the first issue to consider is whether the defendant has a defense or claim in recoupment. If the defendant has neither a defense nor a claim in recoupment to assert, the status of the plaintiff as a holder in due course is irrelevant.[20] If the defendant has a defense or a claim in recoupment, the next step is to determine if the plaintiff is a holder in due course or has the rights of a holder in due course. If so, then the third step is to determine if that status bars the successful assertion of the defendant's defense or claim in recoupment.

Problem 15-10 focuses on steps one and three, identifying defenses and claims in recoupment and whether those are assertable against a holder in due course. Problem 15-11 explores the elements of holder in due course status: step two of the analysis above. Problem 15-12 requires consideration of all three steps.

Problem 15-10

A. Abigail issued a negotiable note to Electronics Inc. in payment for a big screen TV. Electronics Inc. promised to deliver the TV on Tuesday.
1. Electronics Inc. failed to deliver the TV at all.
    a. Does Abigail have a defense to payment of the note or a claim in recoupment? *See* UCC §§ 2-711, 2-714, 2-709.
    b. Electronics Inc. negotiated the note to a holder in due course. Does Abigail have a defense to payment or claim in recoupment against the holder in due course?

---

[20] *See Consumer Solutions Fin. Servs., Inc. v. Heritage Bank*, 684 S.E.2d 682 (Ga. Ct. App. 2009)

2. Electronics Inc. delivered the TV on Tuesday but the TV does not work properly and therefore Electronics Inc. has breached the warranty of merchantability made in the sale transaction.
   a. Does Abigail have a defense to payment of the note or a claim in recoupment? *See* UCC §§ 2-711, 2-714, 2-709.
   b. Electronics Inc. negotiated the note to a holder in due course. Does Abigail have a defense to payment or claim in recoupment against the holder in due course?

3. Electronics Inc. delivered the TV on Tuesday and the TV worked fine. However, a computer that Abigail recently purchased from Electronics Inc. in a separate transaction does not work as promised and Abigail has a breach of warranty claim against Electronics with respect to the computer.
   a. Does Abigail have a defense to payment of the note or a claim in recoupment? *See* UCC §§ 2-711, 2-714, 2-709.
   b. Electronics Inc. negotiated the note to Supplier, who had notice of Abigail's claim with respect to the computer. Does Abigail have a defense to payment or claim in recoupment against Supplier?

B. Bob is 14 years old but appears older. He purchased a car from Acme Cars and signed a negotiable promissory note payable to the order of "Acme Cars" for $5,000, the purchase price of the car minus Bob's down payment.
   1. Does Bob have a defense to payment of the note?
   2. Acme Cars negotiated the note to a holder in due course. Does Bob have a defense to payment against the holder in due course?

C. Callista is 30 years old and a recent immigrant from Greece. She does not speak or read English. Callista decided to go into business for herself. She rented a store from Leonidas, a landlord who is fluent in both Greek and English. Leonidas put two documents in front of Callista, a lease and a negotiable promissory note. The lease obligated Callista to make reasonable rental payments for the store. The promissory note contained a promise to pay $10,000 on demand to the order of Leonidas. Both documents were written in English. Callista signed both documents without reading them.

1. Does Callista have a defense to payment of the note?
2. Leonidas negotiated the note to a holder in due course. Does Callista have a defense to payment against the holder in due course?
3. Assume Callista is fluent in English. The understanding between Callista and Leonidas was that Leonidas would not seek to collect on the note unless Callista defaulted on the lease. Leonidas negotiated the note to a holder in due course. Does Callista have a defense to payment against the holder in due course?

D. Donald issued a check to his landlord in payment of the rent for his apartment. The landlord agreed not to cash the rent check until the landlord had fixed the stove in Donald's apartment. The landlord did not fix the stove but deposited the check in his bank account. Donald stopped payment on the check so that the drawee bank dishonored the check. When the drawee bank dishonored the check, the check was returned to the depositary bank.
   1. Does Donald have a defense to payment of the check?
   2. Assume the depositary bank is a holder in due course. Does Donald have a defense to payment against the holder in due course?
   3. The depositary bank collected the amount of the dishonored check from the landlord. The landlord seeks to collect from Donald. Does Donald have a defense to payment as against the landlord? Does it matter whether the landlord qualified as a holder in due course when taking the check?

E. Elena issued a negotiable demand note to the order of First Bank in exchange for a loan. First Bank's president indorsed the note "First Bank" and transferred it to Second Bank in exchange for Second Bank's promise to pay First Bank 80% of the face amount of the note. Second Bank then transferred the note to Third Bank in exchange for a cash payment of 85% of the face value of the note. Assume Third Bank is a holder in due course. Third Bank presented the note to Elena and she dishonored it. Third Bank sued First Bank on the note for indorser's liability.

1. Third Bank did not give notice of dishonor to First Bank as required by UCC § 3-503. Does First Bank have a defense in the lawsuit by Third Bank?

2. Assume Third Bank gave timely notice of dishonor to First Bank and Second Bank had defaulted on its promise to pay First Bank. Does First Bank have a defense to payment it may assert against Third Bank?

Reread UCC §§ 3-302, 3-303, 3-304, 1-202, and 3-103(a)(6). Review the checklist you prepared in answer to Problem 15-9. Remember that in order to be a holder in due course, *all* the requirements in UCC § 3-302 must be satisfied.

Problem 15-11

Arnie issued a check to Barry in payment of wages of $100 payable to the order of "Barry." Arnie signed on the drawer's line. "Acme Inc." is imprinted on the upper left hand corner of the check. Barry indorsed the check "*Barry*" and gave the check to Carla in exchange for a lamp Carla was selling at a garage sale.

A. Assume that Barry delivered the check to Carla in exchange for Carla's promise to deliver the lamp next week to Barry's house. Is Carla a holder in due course of the check?

B. Assume that Barry kept the check for 4 months because Barry misplaced the check. When Barry found the check, he then gave it to Carla as payment for the lamp. Is Carla a holder in due course of the check?

C. Assume that Barry is 10 years old and Arnie is Barry's parent. Is Carla a holder in due course of the check?

D. At the time Carla took the check from Barry, Carla knew that Acme Inc. was on the verge of bankruptcy because Acme Inc. had a reputation for selling shoddy merchandise. Is Carla a holder in due course of the check?

E. When Carla received the check from Barry, she noticed that the payee's name was smudged and part of the line for the payee's name looked like it had been erased. Is Carla a holder in due course of the check?

F. Assume that Carla knew at the time she took the check from Barry that Arnie did not work for Acme Inc. Is Carla a holder in due course of the check?

G. Assume that the lamp from the garage sale did not work. Carla had promised Barry that it worked.
    1. What defense does Barry have, if any, to his indorser's liability on the check?
    2. Is Carla a holder in due course of the check? Does it make any difference when Carla found out that the lamp did not work, prior to or after taking the check from Barry?
    3. Even if Carla is a holder in due course, is she subject to Barry's defense to payment of his indorser's liability?

H. Assume that Barry indorsed the check "*Barry*" and delivered the check to Carla in payment of a longstanding debt that Barry owed Carla, not in payment for the lamp. Is Carla a holder in due course of the check?

I. Assume that Barry indorsed the check in blank in anticipation of depositing the check in his bank account. Barry owed Carla money from a previous transaction and Carla had obtained a judgment on that debt. Carla seized the check through a lawful execution procedure in order to collect on that judgment. Carla then bought the check at a properly conducted execution sale. Is Carla a holder in due course of the check?

J. While Barry has possession of the check and prior to any indorsement of the check, is Barry a holder in due course of the check?

Problem 15-12

Allison is 25 years old. She purchased a car from Bakerfield Cars, signing a negotiable promissory note for $10,000. The note is payable to bearer and calls for payments in equal monthly installments over the course of the next 5 years. Bakerfield Cars sold the note and transferred possession of it to First Bank for $8,000.

A. First Bank knows that, when Bakerfield Cars sells cars, its sales representatives are often not truthful in representing the cars' performance capabilities, but First Bank has no specific knowledge that Bakerfield Cars made any misrepresentation to Allison. Bakerfield Cars represented that the car sold to Allison was in perfect operating condition. In fact, as Bakerfield Cars knew, the car had a cracked engine block and needed major repairs.
   1. Does Allison have a defense or claim in recoupment effective against First Bank?
   2. Allison missed a payment. First Bank was willing to allow her to cure the default, but insisted that she make up the missed payment by paying with a cashier's check. Allison procured a cashier's check from State Bank and tendered it to First Bank. After doing so, Allison discovered the problems with the car and asked State Bank to dishonor the cashier's check. If State Bank did so, would State Bank have a defense to payment of its obligation on the check? *See* UCC § 3-411.

B. Assume that the note Allison signed contained the following language: "Any Holder of this contract is subject to all claims and defenses which the debtor could assert against the seller of goods obtained with the proceeds hereof." This language is mandated in the FTC Holder in Due Course rules. *See* 16 C.F.R. pt. 433.
   1. Is the note negotiable?
   2. Is First Bank a holder in due course of the note?
   3. Is First Bank subject to any defenses that Allison could have asserted against Bakerfield Cars?
   4. Assume the note Allison signed did not have the language quoted above even though it is mandated by the FTC Rule. Also assume

Allison has a claim in recoupment based upon a breach of warranty claim against Bakerfield Cars. May Allison assert that claim in recoupment against First Bank?

C.   Assume that Allison missed a payment on the installment note. After Allison missed the payment, First Bank negotiated the note to Second Bank for value. Is Second Bank a holder in due course?

Sheltering in holder in due course status. A person entitled to enforce the contract obligations on the instrument may not qualify as a holder in due course under UCC § 3-302. However, that person may be entitled to assert a previous holder's rights as a holder in due course.[21] This generally occurs when the person in possession of the instrument takes the instrument from a holder in due course and takes shelter in the holder in due course's rights. **Read UCC § 3-203.** This rule allows a holder in due course to transfer its rights under an instrument freely. Regardless of whether the transferee of the instrument would qualify in its own right as a holder in due course, the transferee acquires the holder-in-due-course rights that the transferor possessed.

For example, assume that Darren issued a check to Alice. Alice indorsed the check and negotiated it to Bill in a transaction in which Bill is a holder in due course. Bill then delivered the check as a gift to Carlotta. Carlotta does not qualify as a holder in due course because she has not given value for the check. UCC

---

[21] Federal law may provide that the person seeking to enforce an instrument must be treated as if it were a holder in due course, even if that person would not qualify as a holder in due course under UCC Article 3. An example of such a rule appears in 12 U.S.C. § 1823(e). Under that provision and the doctrine from the case of *D'Oench, Duhme & Co. v. FDIC*, 315 U.S. 447 (1942), the FDIC is treated as a holder in due course of all instruments that it acquires when it acquires a failed bank, even if the FDIC would not be a holder in due course under the requirements of UCC § 3-302. The status of the FDIC as a holder in due course under this doctrine was put in doubt by the Supreme Court's decisions in *O'Melveny & Myers v. FDIC*, 512 U.S. 79 (1994), and *Atherton v. FDIC*, 519 U.S. 213 (1997). *See* Jimmy L. Paul and David H. Martin, *Rights, Remedies Available in Litigation by FDIC and Its Transferees Under Federal Law*, 30-MAR AM. BANR. INST. J. 32 (2011); Cherie Stephens Bock, Comment, *Alive, But Not Quite Kicking: Circuit Split Illustrates the Progressive Deterioration of the D'Oench, Duhme Doctrine*, 42 ST. LOUIS U. L.J. 945 (1998); Jason Kellog, Comment, *D'Oench Lives, But for How Long?: The Eleventh Circuit Breathes Life into an Ailing Banking Doctrine*, 30 FLA. ST. U. L. REV. 167 (2002).

§ 3-302. But, under UCC § 3-203, Carlotta may assert Bill's rights as a holder in due course as against Alice on her indorser's liability and against Darren on his drawer's liability. A limitation on the ability to shelter in the transferor's rights is stated in UCC § 3-203(b).

While the plaintiff may assert the holder in due course rights of a previous transferor, recall as noted earlier in this Chapter, the defendant may not generally assert the defenses or claims in recoupment that belong to another obligor on the instrument. UCC § 3-305(c). Rather, the defendant may only assert its own defenses or claims in recoupment. Test your understanding of these principles in Problem 15-13.

Problem 15-13

Alvin signed a check drawn on State Bank for $1,500 payable to the order of Betty. Alvin delivered the check to Betty in payment for a table. Betty bought a new computer from Charlie and delivered the check to Charlie after indorsing it in blank. The new computer is defective and under UCC Article 2, Betty properly rejected the computer and returned the computer to Charlie. Betty told Alvin of the problem with the computer and Alvin stopped payment on the check.

Alvin ———————————→ Betty ———————————→ Charlie
Check issued   Check negotiated

A. When the check was presented to State Bank for payment, State Bank dishonored the check. Charlie now has possession of the check.
1. Is Charlie a holder in due course of the check?
2. What is Alvin's liability on the check?
3. Does Alvin have a defense to payment against Charlie?
4. If Charlie collects the amount of the check from Alvin, may Alvin enforce Betty's contract liability on the check?
5. Assuming Alvin has not paid anything, what is Betty's liability on the check?
6. Does Betty have a defense to payment against Charlie?
7. If Charlie collects the amount of the check from Betty, may Betty enforce Alvin's contract liability on the check?

B. Assume that Charlie negotiated the check to Diego. Diego presented the check to State Bank and State Bank dishonored the check. Diego now has possession of the check.

Alvin ——————▶ Betty ——————▶ Charlie ——————▶ Diego
Check issued   Check negotiated   Check negotiated

1. What is Betty's liability on the check?
2. Assume Diego is not a holder in due course.
   a. Does Betty have a defense to payment against Diego?
   b. Assume that instead of Betty returning the computer to Charlie, Betty kept the computer and has damages of $2,000 based upon Charlie's breach of warranty. Does Betty have a defense to payment or a claim in recoupment against Diego?
3. Assume Diego is a holder in due course.
   a. Does Betty have a defense to payment against Diego?
   b. Assume that Diego gave the check to Elise as a gift and Elise presented the check to State Bank and it was dishonored. Does Betty have a defense to payment against Elise?

C. Prior to Betty's rejection of the computer, Charlie negotiated the check to Diego. Diego is a holder in due course. Diego then negotiated the check back to Charlie in exchange for value, and State Bank dishonored the check when Charlie presented it. Charlie seeks to collect the amount of the check from Betty. May Betty assert her breach of contract defense against Charlie?

C. Discharge of the Contract Obligation on the Instrument: A Defense by Another Name

Contract liability on an instrument can be discharged in various ways, including any manner sufficient to discharge a contract obligation under common-law principles. **Read UCC § 3-601(a).** One example of the discharge of liability under contract-law principles would be a novation. In a novation, the parties agree to a new contract to replace a previous contract. In the context of negotiable instruments, that might be the issuance of a new note as a satisfaction of the liability under an original note.[22]   This commonly occurs when loans represented by promissory notes are refinanced.

An even more obvious manner in which an obligor may discharge contract liability on an instrument is by paying the obligation stated on the instrument. **Read UCC § 3-602.** Contract liability on the instrument may also be discharged in the ways provided in UCC § 3-603 (tender of payment) and UCC § 3-604 (cancellation).

Discharge of the contract obligation on the instrument is a "defense" in the sense that, if the facts support the basis of the discharge, and the discharge can be asserted against the plaintiff, the defendant will not be liable on its contract obligation on the instrument. However, in the nomenclature of UCC Article 3, it is not treated as a "defense." Here is why. A person cannot be a holder in due course if at the time it takes the instrument it has notice of a "defense." Treating a discharge as a "defense" for purposes of qualifying as holder in due course status would prevent a subsequent taker of an instrument that has been partially paid from qualifying as a holder in due course. **Read UCC § 3-302(b) and comment 3.** Even though a person is not prevented from qualifying as a holder in due course if the person has notice of a discharge, the person is subject to those discharges of which the person has notice of when taking the instrument. UCC §§ 3-302(b), 3-601(b). However, the key point is that the person can still qualify as a holder in due course even though the person has notice of a discharge, and be entitled to enforce the rights of a holder in due course with respect to non-discharged obligations on the instrument.

The first step in working through the discharge rules is to understand when the contract obligation on the instrument is discharged. **Read UCC § 3-601 through § 3-604.** These sections contain the basic rules on discharge of the contract obligation on the instrument.[23]   We have already considered other discharge provisions in UCC § 3-414(c), (f) (discharge of drawer); § 3-415(c), (d), (e) (discharge of indorser).

The second step is to determine the effect of that discharge against the plaintiff who is seeking to enforce the contract obligation on the instrument. **Review UCC § 3-302 and § 3-305.**

---

[22] *See Cumberland Bank v. G & S Implement Co.*, 211 S.W.3d 223 (Tenn. Ct. App. 2006).

[23] We will consider the discharge rules in UCC § 3-605 when we consider suretyship rights and obligations in Chapter Seventeen.

Problem 15-14

A. Allen drew a check on State Bank and delivered the check to Bernice,
    the payee. Bernice indorsed the check in blank and delivered the check
    to Clarissa. Clarissa presented the check to State Bank. State Bank
    paid the amount of the check to Clarissa.
    1. Is Allen's drawer's liability discharged?
    2. Is Bernice's indorser's liability discharged?

B. Allen issued a negotiable demand note payable to the order of Bank.
    Bank sold the note to Columbia Finance Co., which took possession of
    the note. Bank did not indorse the note. Columbia Finance Co.
    demanded payment from Allen. Allen paid Columbia Finance Co. the
    amount of the note. Is Allen's maker's liability discharged?

C. Allen issued a negotiable demand note payable to the order of Bank.
    While Bank had possession of the note, Allen paid the entire amount
    due on the note. No notation of payment was made on the note and
    Allen did not recover possession of the note.
    1. Bank presented the note to Allen and insisted that he pay again.
        Does Allen have a good defense against Bank?
    2. After that payment, Bank indorsed the note and transferred
        possession of the note to Columbia Finance Co., which qualified
        as a holder in due course. Columbia Finance Co. then demanded
        that Allen pay. He refused. Does Allen have a good defense
        against Columbia Finance Co.?

D. Allen issued a negotiable installment note payable to the order of Bank.
    Bank indorsed the note in blank and transferred possession of the note
    to Columbia Finance Co., which qualified as a holder in due course.
    Allen did not know that Bank had transferred the note to Columbia
    Finance Co. Thereafter, Allen made a regular installment payment to
    Bank. If Columbia Finance Co. seeks to collect that installment
    payment from Allen, does Allen have a good defense against Columbia
    Finance Co.?

E. Acme Co. issued a check to Bruce in payment of wages. Bruce indorsed the check in blank and transferred the check to Carmen in exchange for a rare book. Carmen crossed out Bruce's indorsement and transferred the check to David as payment for a debt Carmen owed to David. The check was dishonored by the drawee.
    1. May David enforce any contract liability on the check against Carmen?
    2. May David enforce any contract liability on the check against Bruce?
    3. May David enforce any contract liability on the check against Acme?

F. Acme Co. issued a check to Bruce in payment of wages. Bruce indorsed the check in blank and transferred the check to Carmen in exchange for a rare book. Carmen crossed out Bruce's indorsement and transferred the check to David as payment for a debt Carmen owed to David.
    1. David intentionally burned up the check in the fireplace. Is anyone's contract liability on the check discharged? Is UCC § 3-309 available to David to enforce liability on the check?
    2. David's house burned down as a result of a grease fire in the kitchen, completely destroying the check. Is anyone's contract liability on the check discharged? Is UCC § 3-309 available to David to enforce liability on the check?
    3. David presented the check to the drawee bank, who dishonored the check. David demanded payment from Acme and mistakenly gave the check to Acme when David made that demand even though Acme did not pay David. Is anyone's contract liability on the check discharged? Is UCC § 3-309 available to David to enforce liability on the check?

G. Allen issued a negotiable demand note payable to the order of Bank. Bank sold the note to Columbia Finance Co. Bank indorsed the note in blank and delivered the note to Columbia Finance Co. Allen tendered full payment of the note to Columbia Finance Co., which refused the tender.
    1. Is Allen's maker's liability on the note discharged?

2. Is Bank's indorser's liability on the note discharged?

SECTION 6.   THE RELATIONSHIP BETWEEN CONTRACT LIABILITY ON THE INSTRUMENT AND THE UNDERLYING OBLIGATION

Review the material in Chapter Fourteen on the relationship between the issuance or transfer of a negotiable instrument and the underlying obligation. We learned that the issuance or transfer of a negotiable instrument, other than a certified check, cashier's check, or teller's check, results in suspension of the underlying obligation until the instrument is dishonored or paid. UCC § 3-310. We also learned that if the instrument is paid, the suspended underlying obligation is paid. Thus, if the instrument is paid so that the contract liability on the instrument is discharged, UCC § 3-602, then the underlying obligation will be discharged as well.

Effect of dishonor. Now consider the effect of dishonor of the instrument on the underlying obligation. In the event the instrument is dishonored, the suspension of the underlying obligation ends. **Read UCC § 3-310(b)(3).** If the person entitled to enforce the instrument is the same person as the obligee on the underlying obligation, that person may enforce either the contract liability on the instrument or the underlying obligation.

What if the person who was the obligee on the underlying obligation is not the person entitled to enforce the instrument? For example, assume a purchase of goods from a retail store in exchange for a check. The store deposits the check into its bank account and when the check arrives at the drawee bank, the check is dishonored and returned to the depositary bank. The underlying obligation to pay for the goods is no longer suspended. The store is the obligee on the underlying obligation to pay for the goods but is not the person entitled to enforce the check (because it does not have possession of the check). The person entitled to enforce the check would be the depositary bank (because it has possession of the returned check). **Read UCC § 3-310(b)(4) and comment 3 to that section.** The store would not be able to enforce the underlying obligation unless the depositary bank returned the check to the store. If the depositary bank does so, then the store has its choice to sue on either the underlying obligation to pay for the goods or to enforce the contract liability on the check as against the drawer.

Effect of a discharge of obligation on instrument through a manner other than payment. Now consider the following situation. A negotiable note is issued in exchange for a loan. The payee indorses the note and transfers it to a transferee in order to pay an obligation that the payee owes the transferee. The transferee decides to forgive the payee its debt and rips up the note. What is the effect of that action on the maker's obligation on the note and the underlying obligation that maker owed payee? Under UCC § 3-604, the maker's obligation and the indorser's obligation on the note would be discharged by cancellation. The maker's underlying obligation to the payee/indorser and the payee/indorser's underlying obligation to the transferee is also discharged. **Read UCC § 3-310(b)(3) and comment 3.**

Problem 15-15

A. In connection with Arden's purchase of Buford's house, Arden gave Buford a negotiable promissory note payable to the order of Buford.
   1. Arden was unable to make the payments called for in the promissory note and defaulted. What are Buford's options to collect the money from Arden?
   2. Assume that Buford sold the note to City Bank for 80% of the face value of the note. Buford indorsed the note in blank and delivered the note to City Bank. Arden defaulted on the payments required on the note. Who can sue Arden and what is the cause of action?

B. Arden issued a check drawn on State Bank and payable to the order of Buford in payment for goods that Arden purchased from Buford. Buford indorsed the check in blank and delivered the check to Cleaning Co. in payment of services that Cleaning Co. rendered to Buford. Cleaning Co. presented the check to State Bank and State Bank paid the check.
   1. What is the effect, if any, of that payment on Arden's underlying obligation to Buford?
   2. What is the effect, if any, of that payment on Buford's underlying obligation to Cleaning Co.?

C. Arden issued a negotiable note payable to the order of Buford. Buford indorsed the note and transferred the note to Cleaning Co. in payment of services that Cleaning Co. rendered to Buford. Cleaning Co. demanded payment from Arden and Arden refused, dishonoring the note. Cleaning Co. failed to send notice of dishonor to Buford within 30 days of the dishonor. Presentment and notice of dishonor are not excused.

1. What is the effect, if any, of that failure on Buford's underlying obligation to Cleaning Co.? What should Cleaning Co. do?
2. Can Buford now enforce Arden's underlying obligation?

SECTION 7.   REVIEW

To put the material from this Chapter and Chapter Fourteen together, organize what you have learned according to the causes of action discussed in this Chapter.

Problem 15-16

John Smith issued the note reproduced below to First Bank on May 1, 2011. First Bank required Mary Smith, John's wife, to sign the note on the back at the same time. Mary did not know why she signed the note or what John was going do with the proceeds from the loan. The First Bank officer told Mary her signature was required merely as a formality because John and Mary were married.

First Bank sold the note on May 10, 2011 to Second Bank in exchange for $9,000. First Bank signed the note on the back as follows: "Pay to the order of Second Bank, *First Bank by Stan Frank, President*, without recourse." First Bank delivered possession of the note to Second Bank on May 10, 2011.

On June 10, 2012, Second Bank sold the note to Third Bank for $8,000. Second Bank signed the note on the back as follows: "*Second Bank*" and delivered the note to Third Bank.

PROMISSORY NOTE

Dated May 1, 2011

    For value received, the undersigned maker promises to pay to the order of First Bank, at its offices in San Francisco, California, the principal sum of $10,000 plus interest at the rate of 10% per annum, one year from the date stated hereon.

    The maker of this note may prepay in whole or part any and all amounts due under this note at any time without penalty. Such prepayment in part does not relieve the maker from making payment on the due date stated above. Any payments on this note will be applied as follows: first, to payment of any fees, costs, or assessments due under the terms of this note and any document granting a security interest or mortgage to secure the maker's obligations under this note, second, to payment of any accrued unpaid interest and then to payment of the principal balance due hereunder.

    This note is secured by a security interest in collateral as provided in the security agreement signed by the maker. In the event of default in the payment of principal or interest hereunder, the holder hereof may declare the entire unpaid balance due and payable and the maker will also be liable for all costs of collection, including reasonable attorneys' fees. Presentment for payment, demand, protest, and notice of dishonor are hereby expressly waived by the makers, and each endorser or guarantor hereof.

                                                    John Smith

---

A. Is the note a negotiable instrument?

B. Third Bank has sued John Smith, Mary Smith, First Bank, and Second Bank. Identify and analyze Third Bank's arguments to impose liability on each of those parties and each party's likely response to those arguments.

C. Second Bank brings cross-claims against John Smith, Mary Smith and First Bank. Identify and analyze Second Bank's arguments to impose liability on each of those parties and each party's likely response to those arguments.

D. First Bank brings cross-claims against John Smith and Mary Smith. Identify and analyze First Bank's arguments to impose liability on each of those parties and each party's likely response to those arguments.

CHAPTER SIXTEEN

COLLECTION OF NEGOTIABLE INSTRUMENTS THROUGH THE BANK COLLECTION SYSTEM

SECTION 1. OVERVIEW

In Chapter Fifteen we learned about the elements of contract liability on a negotiable instrument, incurred through signing the instrument. In doing so, we learned about who was entitled to enforce the contract obligation, presentment, dishonor, notice of dishonor, and discharge of that obligation. In this Chapter, we will explore these issues in fuller detail, focusing in depth on the process of collecting checks through the banking system, and considering on a limited basis the use of the banking system for collection of other types of negotiable instruments.

Consider the basic collection dilemma. A person who has signed a negotiable instrument has in effect promised to pay currency in satisfaction of that obligation at some point later in time. Given that negotiable instruments can be negotiated and that the original payee may no longer be the person entitled to enforce the instrument, there needs to be some system for letting the obligor know who to pay. This is particularly important because, as explored in Chapters Fourteen and Fifteen, in most situations, the obligor's obligation on the instrument and the underlying payment obligation is discharged only if the payments are made to the right person, that is, the person entitled to enforce the contract obligation on the instrument. UCC §§ 3-602, 3-310.

UCC Article 3 contemplates that presentment will be the mechanism by which the person entitled to enforce an instrument requests payment from the obligor or drawee. In the modern commercial world, however, the payee seldom makes a presentment through a physical exhibition of the instrument in a face-to-face setting to the obligor or drawee, as presumed by the rules in UCC § 3-501. Instead, for at least some types of negotiable instruments, the bank collection system lends a helping hand.

The bank collection system refers to the process by which one or more banks handle an item, such as a check, on behalf of a customer seeking payment of that item. *See* UCC §§ 4-102, 4-104(a)(9) (defining "item"), 4-201 (bank acting as agent of customer). For this purpose, a customer is a person who has an account at the bank and for whom the bank has agreed to collect items. *See* UCC § 4-104(a)(5) ("customer"), (a)(1) ("account"). UCC Article 4 provides many of the rules governing the bank collection system. These rules are supplemented and refined by both contract and other law, such as system agreements among participating banks and Federal Reserve regulations and operating circulars. *See* UCC § 4-103.

This Chapter explores four main questions relating to the bank collection system. First, how does this bank collection system work? Second, what obligations do banks incur by participating in this collection system? Third, what are the rights and obligations of the customer for whom an item is being collected? Fourth, what additional rights and obligations (other than those provided for in UCC Article 3) does the obligor on an instrument have if collection is sought through the bank collection system?

SECTION 2.   COLLECTION OF NOTES

As you no doubt remember, a promissory note may be either payable on demand or payable at a definite time. If it is payable on demand, a request for payment must generally be made for payment to become due. As we learned in Chapter Fifteen, this may be a formal presentment or something less formal if the presentment requirement has been waived. In either case, the maker needs to be told in some manner that the person entitled to enforce the note is requesting payment. For the most part, unless acting as the payee, banks play no role in this process: banks generally do not collect notes on behalf of their customers. For example, assume a demand note is payable to Payee, which is not itself a bank. Payee's bank may agree to present the note on behalf of Payee to the maker (or to another obligor on the note), but would not normally do that as part of the bank's routine operations and customer service. Payee may, however, sell or assign that note to Bank, and assuming the negotiation were done properly (as studied in Chapter Fifteen), the Bank would then be entitled, and likely would attempt, to enforce the note on its own behalf.[1] This kind of transaction in demand notes does not implicate the rules of UCC Article 4 because, if a bank does take a note from one of its customers – either to collect the note on the customer's behalf or as a purchaser of the note – that transaction is done on an individualized and negotiated basis.

If a note is payable at a definite time, there need not be a formal demand for payment through a presentment. The note is dishonored if it is not paid at the

---

[1] The sale of the note may be governed by UCC Article 9. UCC § 9-109.

definite times stated in the note. *See* UCC § 3-502(a)(3). Notes that are typically payable at a definite time include installment notes (which require payment to be made on a recurring, periodic basis, such as monthly) and balloon notes (which require payment of all or most of the amount due at a single specified future date). Given that a payee may transfer or negotiate a note at any time before the specified payment dates, a maker may not know at the time payment is due whom to pay, that is, who is entitled to enforce the note. As a matter of industry practice, commercial payees of notes, such as financial institutions, who transfer or negotiate notes payable at a definite time handle this situation in either of two typical manners. First, either the payee or the transferee will notify the maker that the note has been transferred and that future payments should be made to the transferee. Second, the payee and transferee may agree that the payee will act as the transferee's servicing agent and continue to collect payments from the maker and have a responsibility to remit those payments to the transferee. This practice is recognized in the 2002 amendments to UCC § 3-602 and official comments 3 and 4.

These practices regarding notes payable at a definite time are also generally outside the scope of the bank collection system that is governed by UCC Article 4. While a promise to pay, such as a note, may constitute an "item" under UCC § 4-104(a)(9), banks need not be involved in the collection process and even when they are, they typically are collecting on their own behalf or as an agent on behalf of another financial institution or a commercial lender, neither of which is typically a customer of the bank (as defined in UCC § 4-104).[2] Thus the rules of UCC Article 4 usually do not apply to these types of instruments.

---

[2] In fact, many notes payable at a definite time are transferred into special purpose entities formed for the precise purpose of buying thousands of notes in a process known as securitization. To illustrate, assume Payee is in the business of lending money and its borrowers sign promissory notes promising to repay the loans in installments over a five-year period. Payee sells the notes to SPE (Special Purpose Entity), a corporate entity that is created solely for the purpose of buying the notes. SPE issues securities *(i.e.,* stocks or bonds) through a public offering. The money raised from the issuance and sale of these securities is used to purchase the notes from Payee. The amounts collected from the makers of the notes are then used by SPE to pay dividends or other returns to the security holders. The sale of the notes to the SPE is typically a transaction governed by UCC Article 9. UCC § 9-109(a), (d).

SECTION 3.   COLLECTION OF DRAFTS: OVERVIEW

As we learned in Chapter Fourteen, the other major category of negotiable instruments is drafts. Drafts come in three primary flavors: checks, drafts drawn on a drawee other than a bank; and documentary drafts. Review the definitions of the types of drafts in UCC § 3-104 and § 4-104. UCC Article 4 is designed for the most part to deal with the process of collecting drafts, primarily checks, on behalf of customers that have an account at a bank. *See* UCC § 4-101, cmts. 1 & 2. This bank collection system is designed to take the check from the payee and make a presentment of the check to the drawee bank. This is important given that, in many circumstances, the payee is at some distance from the drawee bank and making an in-person demand for payment from the drawee would be inconvenient, expensive, or both.

Of course, the collecting bank may also be at some distance from the drawee bank, but the bank collection system takes advantage of both technology and economies of scale to make the collection process more economical and convenient. Consider the situation of an electric utility, that receives checks from its customers every day. These checks may be drawn on hundreds of different banks. For the utility to sort these checks and present each to the correct drawee would be a burdensome task indeed. Instead, the utility transfers all of the checks to its own bank for collection. That bank then takes all the checks, along with the checks it has received from its other customers, and presents them through one or more clearinghouses to the drawee banks for payment.

The bulk of this Chapter focuses on the collection of checks through the banking system (Sections 3 through 7). After covering the applicable processes and rules, it briefly discusses some special principles that apply when using the bank collection system for documentary drafts and for drafts that are neither checks nor documentary drafts (Section 8).

A. Process of Check Collection

It is helpful to keep in mind a simple example of the check collection process. Assume that you have a checking account at a Bank. You have a sufficient balance in that account to cover the price of some goods or services you wish to purchase. You write a check drawn on the checking account, payable to the seller. The seller deposits the check in the seller's account at a different bank. The seller's bank gives the seller a credit in the seller's account in the amount of the check deposited. The seller's bank then transfers the check to a clearinghouse which credits the account of the seller's bank with the clearinghouse. The clearinghouse transfers the check to your bank and debits your bank's account with the clearinghouse. Your bank then debits your checking account and returns the check to you in your bank statement for the month. This system can be represented graphically as follows:

The bank collection system illustrated above can be divided into four stages.

Forward collection. The forward collection stage consists of the process of routing either the item (usually a check) or information extracted from the item from the first bank in the process (the depositary bank) to the bank that pays the item (the drawee/payor bank). In the example above, the forward collection stage is when the seller's bank routes the check through the clearinghouse to the buyer's bank.

Funds availability. The depositary bank must, at some point, make funds available to the person who initiated the item collection process. In this hypothetical, the seller's bank, upon taking the check for deposit, must make funds available to the seller, typically by crediting the seller's deposit account at the seller's bank. The seller's bank must do this by a specified time, which may arise before the seller's bank learns whether the buyer's bank will pay the check.

Payment or return decision. In this stage of the system, the drawee bank decides whether to pay the item or return it. The drawee bank generally bases that decision on whether sufficient funds to cover the check are credited to the drawer's account. In the example above, the buyer's bank must decide whether to pay the check or return the check to the seller's bank. If the buyer's bank pays the check, the buyer's bank will make a corresponding debit to the buyer's bank account. If the check is returned, the next stage comes into play.[3]

Return and chargeback process. The item return and chargeback stage consists of the process of routing the item (or information from the item) back to the person who initiated the bank collection process and charging back the various credits given for the item during the forward collection process. Thus, in the hypothetical above, if the check (or information from the check) is dishonored, the buyer's bank will return the check (or information from the check) either through the clearinghouse or directly to the seller's bank. The seller's bank will charge back the amount of the check to the seller's account by reversing the credit previously posted to the seller's account. The seller's bank will also typically charge a fee to the seller for the returned item.

In learning about the bank collection system, we will explore the rules that apply to each stage described above. Before considering the mechanics and legal rules of each stage in detail, it is important to have a sense of the risks inherent in this process.

B.   Risks in the Collection Process

The settlement process described above has several types of risks embedded within it. First there is the credit risk. In the hypothetical above, the seller's bank take a credit risk by making funds available to the seller without knowing whether the check will be honored by the buyer's bank. The clearinghouse similarly takes a credit risk if the credit it gives the seller's bank is not covered by available funds from the account of the buyer's bank at the clearinghouse. Finally, the buyer's bank may assume a credit risk if it pays the check even though the buyer's account does not have enough available credits to cover the amount of the check (the negative balance in the buyer's account after the amount of the check is debited is commonly known as an overdraft).

A second type of risk is the risk of fraud. In the hypothetical above, when the seller takes the check from the buyer, the seller has no way of knowing that the buyer actually has an account at buyer's bank. This is different from the credit risk.

---

[3] If the drawer's bank decides to return the check, the bank will normally charge a fee to the drawer. *See Quality Bank v. Cavett*, 788 N.W.2d 629 (N.D. 2010) (bank agreement allowing for overdraft fees was not unconscionable).

The buyer may have made up "fake" checks drawn on a non-existent account or on a non-existent bank. Alternatively, the account and bank might be legitimate but the buyer might not be a person authorized to write checks on the account. These are risks associated with a scheme to defraud participants in the transaction.

Another risk is the chance of error in the process. As a check is collected, accounts are credited and debited based upon the amount of the check and the route the check takes in making its way to the drawee bank. Each bank connected with the transaction may introduce error into the collection process by garbling the information, by misdirecting the check or the information from the check, or by losing or destroying the check or information from it. For example, a drawee bank might lose all the information from a check after it has paid the check but before it has debited the drawer's account. In such a situation, unless the drawee bank can recapture the missing information or recover the payment, it will suffer a loss.

Finally, there is a risk that one of the intermediaries in this transaction may fail. In the example above, the clearinghouse (an intermediary) may become insolvent and cease operations while a check collection is in process.[4] This presents a risk to participants that deal with the intermediary. To illustrate, assume a clearinghouse fails after it has provisionally credited the seller's bank but before it has collected funds from the buyer's bank regarding the check. The clearinghouse, if insolvent, may not be able to make good on its provisional credit to the seller's bank. This intermediary insolvency is rare given that, in most instances, checks are processed through regulated entities, such as banks. The risk of intermediary failure is greater when the check is processed by an entity that is not regulated, such as a check processing service.

One of the goals of UCC Article 4 was to provide certainty on how to allocate the various types of risk inherent in the collection process. In each stage of the check collection process, legal rules provide that certain actions must be taken, in a certain amount of time, and pursuant to a certain standard of care. In addition, the consequences of failing to comply with those rules is specified. As we consider the legal rules and modern practice, ask yourself whether UCC Article 4 is still fulfilling this goal of providing certainty in risk allocation.

---

[4] This risk is not unlike the credit risk described above that the clearinghouse takes if the credit it gives the seller's bank is not covered by available funds from the account of the buyer's bank at the clearinghouse. The buyer's bank is not an intermediary in the process, however, it is the drawee/payor bank.

C. Costs of the Collection System and Electronic Processing

Checks traditionally have been transported across the country by various types of courier services and commercial carriers such as airlines and trucking companies. In addition to the risks identified above, this process of physically transporting checks from the first bank in the collection system (the depositary bank) to the drawee bank (also known as the payor bank) is expensive. To ameliorate the risks identified above and to reduce the costs of collecting the checks, the banks have every incentive in the forward collection process to get the check from the depositary bank to the payor/drawee bank as fast, as reliably, and as inexpensively as possible.

To achieve these goals in the forward collection process, banks and clearinghouses have embraced a technological change that results in something called "truncation." Truncation involves taking the paper check and converting it into electronic information in some form. Truncation may happen at any point in the collection process. For example, the depositary bank may scan the check or otherwise extract the information on it and then transmit that information electronically to a clearinghouse. The clearinghouse then continues the forward collection process by transmitting the information from the check to the payor/drawee bank and obtaining a credit transfer from the payor/drawee bank. All this occurs without having to transport the actual check, which might in fact be destroyed as part of the truncation process. Large, institutional payees that receive thousands of checks (think again of electric utility companies, for example) may initiate truncation even earlier in the process by capturing the information from the checks they receive and transmitting that information electronically to the depositary bank.

Many check clearance services, including The Clearing House[5] and the Federal Reserve Banks[6] offer "electronic check presentment" which means the capture and electronic transmission of information from the check.   The electronic

---

[5] The first and perhaps best known clearinghouse is The Clearing House (formerly the New York Clearinghouse Association). In 2008, The Clearing House cleared over 5.6 billion check images, with a total value of $8.5 billion. *See* http://www.svpco.com/press_releases/pressReleaseDocs/069622.php.

[6] In 2010, the average daily volume of checks processed through the Federal Reserve System was 30.6 million and the average daily value of those checks was $43.9 billion. *See* http://www.federalreserve.gov/paymentsystems/check_commcheckcolannual.htm.

representation of the information may be captured from the MICR (Magnetic Ink Character Recognition) line information,[7] or through a full electronic imaging of the check.[8] In either case, essential to this methodology is that the payor/drawee bank has agreed to accept electronic check presentment instead of presentment of the physical check. *See* UCC § 4-110.

A typical example occurs when a merchant accepts a customer's check in full or partial payment of some transaction. The merchant delivers the check to its bank for deposit. The check is electronically imaged at the merchant's bank and the information from the check is transmitted electronically, through a clearinghouse, to the customer's bank. The paper check is destroyed. The customer's bank account is debited based on the electronic transmission of information from the merchant bank.[9] This type of electronic conversion may happen earlier, at the seller's place of business, or at any other point prior to presentment to the drawee/payor bank.[10]

---

[7] This information consists of the amount of the check, the payor bank's numerical designation, and the drawer's account number.

[8] The image of the check must conform to certain technical standards that the industry has agreed to accept. Those technical requirements are published by ANSI (American National Standards Institute) as the X9 standard.

[9] It is estimated that forward collection is now more than 97% electronic. In fact, the only remaining processor of paper checks is the Federal Reserve Bank and paper processing has become such a low volume business that, as of 2010, only the Federal Reserve Bank of Cleveland still handles paper check processing. *See* http://www.frbservices.org/files/communications/pdf/press/030210_check_infrastructure.pdf.

[10] One of the challenges of the evolving payments landscape is the convergence of different practices without the convergence of the legal rules governing them. To illustrate, assume a merchant takes a check from the customer and runs it through the cash register to capture the data on the bottom of the check (the MICR line). The merchant then keys in the amount of the purchase and hands the check back to the customer. The electronic information is transmitted via a secure network to the customer's bank and the customer's account is debited. The secure network is often the Automated Clearing House (ACH). An ACH transaction is run through a private network managed by NACHA (National Automated Clearing House Association). An ACH transaction is an electronic funds transfer, and is not issuance of a check, and thus not governed by Article 4 (there is no "item"). *See* Stephanie Heller, *An Endangered Species: The Increasing Irrelevance of Article 4 of the UCC in an Electronics-Based Payments System*, 40 LOY. L.A. L. REV. 513 (2006); *In re Snowden*, 422

Historically, the payor bank/drawee stored and then sent paid checks to the drawer with a monthly bank statement. This now rarely occurs. Rather the payor bank/drawee will generally image any paper checks it has received, store the images of the "electronic" checks it has paid, and transmit all of those images to the drawer. This substantially reduces costs.

Using electronics to increase the speed and reduce the expense of the check collection process creates issues regarding whether the legal infrastructure designed to deal with paper checks allocates the risks inherent in this electronic process with the appropriate degree of efficiency and certainty.[11] In other words, do the rules designed to deal with risk allocation, the participants' duties in handling the checks, fraud and error in connection with paper checks, and physical presentment translate well to truncation of the paper check and the transmission of electronic information? Keep these issues in mind as we study the rules from UCC Article 4 and the operation of the bank collection system.

B.R. 737 (Bankr. W.D. Wash. 2009) (ACH transaction is not presentment of a check under 11 U.S.C. § 362(b)(11)). In an ACH transaction, information is transmitted through the private network so that the payor/drawee bank receives an instruction to debit the drawer's account for the amount of the check.

Similarly, a funds transfer and not a check is involved if the customer uses a debit card, with or without entry of a personal identification number (PIN). The information from the card and the PIN are transmitted via a secure network (such as ACH) to the customer's bank and the customer's account is debited. Even though the banks may market the card as a "check" card, it is not a check and the law of negotiable instruments and UCC Article 4 do not apply. The same card may also be used as a credit card. If the transaction is processed as a credit transaction, then the rules studied in Chapter Thirteen come into play. In contrast, NACHA has a pilot program (Deposited Check Truncation–DCT for short) designed to use an ACH transaction but apply the "check" rules, instead of the funds transfer rules, to collection of small dollar consumer checks. We will study electronic funds transfer rules in Chapter Twenty, and explore in more depth the blurring of the operational lines between check collection and funds transfer.

[11] *See* Amelia H. Boss, *Convergence in Electronic Banking: Technological Convergence, Systems Convergence, Legal Convergence,* 2 DREXEL L. REV. 63 (2009). *See also* Paul W. Bauer and Geffrey R. Gerdes, *The Check is Dead! Long Live the Check! A Check 21 Update,* ECONOMIC COMMENTARY (Federal Reserve Bank of Cleveland, June 2009) (discussing the costs of check processing).

D. The Regulatory Landscape

In addition to the UCC Article 3 rules we have already studied and the rules in UCC Article 4 that we will address in this Chapter, a variety of other rules impact the bank collection system. **Read UCC § 4-103.**

Regulation CC and Regulation J are federal rules promulgated by the Federal Reserve Board as part of its authority to regulate the banking system and pursuant to the Board's authority under the Expedited Funds Availability Act (EFAA)[12] and the Check Clearing for the 21st Century Act, known as "Check 21."[13] Two federal regulations, Regulation CC[14] (implementing both the EFAA and Check 21) and Regulation J (for checks collected or returned through the Federal Reserve Banks),[15] supplement the rules in UCC Articles 3 and 4 and preempt any of those rules that conflict with either regulation.[16] UCC § 4-103, cmt. 3.

Check 21 was instrumental in vaulting the industry into the electronic processing of checks in the forward collection process. Check 21 is very simple in concept. Under the paper check processing system, banks and others involved in the check collection system have been hampered in their ability to truncate checks and collect checks through electronic presentment. This is because, in order to do so, each bank or collection facility in the middle, as well as the drawee bank, must have agreed to accept the information electronically. *See* UCC § 4-110. The inability to obtain agreements by all parties in the collection chain presented an obstacle to using electronic means for check presentment, resulting in costly transportation and processing of paper items.

Rather than attack the problem directly by requiring all banks to allow electronic presentment of checks, Check 21 authorized a new species of negotiable

---

[12] Codified at 12 U.S.C. §§ 4001–4010.

[13] Codified at 12 U.S.C. §§ 5001–5018.

[14] 12 C.F.R. pt. 229.

[15] 12 C.F.R. pt. 210.

[16] A good lawyer, however, will also check the statute's provisions. The Federal Reserve Board's authority to promulgate regulations is limited to regulations that are consistent with the enabling statute. Starting in July 2011, the new Consumer Financial Protection Bureau will also have authority to promulgate regulations under the EFAA, jointly with the Federal Reserve Board. This change was made as part of the Dodd-Frank legislation. Pub. L. No. 111-203, Title X, §§ 1086, 1100H, 124 Stat. 1376, 2086, 2113.

instrument called the "substitute check." 12 U.S.C. § 5003; Reg. CC, 12 C.F.R. § 229.2(aaa). A substitute check is *not* an electronic representation of the original check. It is instead a paper copy of the original check that complies with four stated requirements. A substitute check is deemed to be the legal equivalent of the original check if it meets these requirements, contains a required legend, and a bank has made the warranty provided in Check 21. The legend must state "This is a legal copy of your check. You can use it the same way you would use the original check." 12 U.S.C. § 5003; Reg. CC, 12 C.F.R. § 229.51(a).

How this "substitute check" scheme allows for electronic processing and presentment of data from checks is best illustrated by an example.

Bank A, a depositary bank located in New York, receives a check for deposit to a customer's account. The check is drawn on Bank Z, located in California. Bank Z does not allow for electronic presentment of checks. Bank A may still truncate the deposited check by converting the information from the check to electronic data, and send that data for collection through the banking system with entities that have agreements with Bank A to process the data. When the data reaches the entity immediately prior in the collection chain to Bank Z, that entity may convert the data to a paper "substitute check" with legal equivalence and present it to Bank Z. Bank Z must treat that "substitute check" as the legal equivalent of the original check and pay or dishonor it accordingly. After we explore the bank collection system, we will return to a discussion of Check 21 and the challenges it creates for the system and its participants.

The Federal Reserve Board also promulgates operating circulars that may vary the effect of UCC Article 4 provisions. *See* UCC § 4-103(b) and cmt. 3. Operating circulars are periodically revised as processes evolve. Operating Circular 3 governs collection of "cash" items through the Federal Reserve system.[17] Checks are generally processed as cash items. In addition to the Board's role as a regulator, as previously noted, the Federal Reserve Banks play a major role in processing checks for collection and return.

In addition to the Federal Reserve System, private organizations called clearinghouses, consisting of a group of banks or other institutions, have been formed to facilitate collection of items. These organizations promulgate rules governing the clearing of items through the clearinghouse. Pursuant to UCC § 4-103, clearinghouse rules may vary the effect of UCC Article 4 rules.

---

[17] Operating circulars are available at http://www.frbservices.org.

Clearinghouses may also use the Federal Reserve Banks to process items that need to move outside the clearinghouse membership. The Electronic Check Clearing House Organization (ECCHO) is an example of an association that has promulgated a rule set for banks who join the organization to use to exchange electronic check images.

Another method for processing items is for banks to exchange the items directly pursuant to direct agreements with each other. This is usually referred to as a correspondent banking relationship. Correspondent banks may enter into agreements that vary the effect of the provisions of UCC Article 4.

Finally, the effect of the provisions of UCC Article 4 may also be varied by agreements between the bank and its customer. Remember that in the bank collection system, there is a bank at each end of the process: the initial collecting bank (or depositary bank) at the front end, and the payor bank (*i.e.*, the drawee) at the back end. Each bank will have an agreement with its respective customer regarding taking and paying items.

Because of all of these different sources of rules, in analyzing any question that involves collecting an item through the banking system, you need to be familiar with the rules from UCC Articles 3 and 4, Regulation CC, Regulation J, operating circulars, the clearinghouse rules, the agreements between banks, and the agreements between banks and their customers.

As you study this complex system, consider the effect of UCC § 4-103. Why would the parties involved in this process want to vary the effect of the rules in UCC Article 4? What is encompassed within a bank's obligation of "good faith" and "reasonable care" in this process which cannot be disclaimed but may be defined as long as that definition is not "manifestly unreasonable"? Does this variation by agreement structure provide enough certainty to deal with the risks presented by electronic collection and return of checks?

UCC Article 4 has its own nomenclature. **Review the definitions in UCC §§ 4-104 and 4-105** before you start the next section so that you have a working idea of the labels used for the various players in the bank collection system.

SECTION 4.   COLLECTION OF CHECKS: FORWARD COLLECTION, FUNDS AVAILABILITY

A. Forward Collection

Recall that collecting an item through the banking system is the process of giving the item to the first bank in the collection chain (the depositary bank) and transferring the item to successive entities (collecting banks, clearinghouses, or a Federal Reserve Bank) until the item is presented to the bank on which the item is drawn (the drawee/payor bank).

Agency. **Read UCC § 4-201.** The presumption is that the banks in the collection process are acting as agents of the owner of the item.[18] The bank that receives the item from the owner for deposit in the owner's bank account gives provisional credit to the owner's account for that item. Thus, if you deposit a check in your checking account and that check is drawn on another bank, your bank (the depositary bank and also a collecting bank), gives your account provisional credit for that check. You are still the owner of the item and your bank is acting as your agent in forwarding the item for collection.

Your bank will then forward the check or the information from the check to either the payor bank directly or to an intermediary that will, directly or indirectly, forward the check or the information to the payor bank.[19] Because of the credit, fraud, and insolvency risks identified earlier in this Chapter, the banks have every incentive to move the check or the information from the check as quickly and reliably as possible from the bank of first deposit to the payor bank.

Settlement. Each bank that receives the check or the information from the check will settle with the entity that transferred the check or the information to it. *See* UCC § 4-104(a)(11) (defining "settle"). To illustrate this settlement process, assume that the depositary bank, First Bank, transferred the check to a collecting bank, Second Bank. Second Bank will transfer value to First Bank in exchange for

---

[18] Occasionally a bank will actually purchase an item it has taken for collection or payment. In such a case, the relevant provisions of UCC Article 4 will continue to apply. *See* UCC § 4-201(a) and cmts. 2 through 4.

[19] There could be an infinite number of intermediaries. A collecting bank typically attempts to ascertain the most efficient route for the information in light of the relationships it has with a clearinghouse, correspondent banks, or other intermediaries such as the Federal Reserve Bank for its district.

the check. That settlement may be by crediting an account of First Bank held by Second Bank or by First Bank debiting an account of Second Bank held by First Bank. Second Bank may also give a settlement to First Bank by giving First Bank a cashier's or teller's check. *See* UCC § 4-213. Similarly, when the check is presented to the payor bank, the payor bank will give the presenter a provisional credit for the check as well. **Read UCC § 4-301(a)**. These provisional credits are called provisional settlements. If the check is not finally paid by the payor bank, the provisional settlements that have been made in the forward collection process will be revoked. **Read UCC § 4-214.**

Do not be mislead by this example to think that the banks are transferring one check at a time. Most information from checks is transferred in large batches at least once each banking day, with settlement for all the transfers netted against each other. For example, Bank A may transfer thousands of items for forward collection to its Federal Reserve Bank. The Federal Reserve Bank credits Bank A's account for the value of all those items, and sorts those items either for presentment to the payor bank or for transfer to another Federal Reserve Bank, which will then make the presentment. Assume among the batch of check images transferred to the Federal Reserve Bank, 100 of the checks are drawn on Bank B. The Federal Reserve Bank will debit Bank B's account at the Federal Reserve Bank for the value of the checks and make presentment of the check images to Bank B. Meanwhile Bank B has also transferred to the same Federal Reserve Bank thousands of items for forward collection, 50 of which are drawn on Bank A. Bank B's account at the Federal Reserve Bank will be credited with the value of the thousands of items, and the Federal Reserve Bank will debit Bank A's account at the Federal Reserve Bank for the value of the 50 items it presents to Bank A.[20]

---

[20] Regulation CC makes one change to the forward collection process by providing that provisional settlements made in the forward collection process are final when made. Reg. CC, 12 C.F.R. § 229.36(d). However, the impact of this is relatively minor. In UCC parlance, a provisional settlement can be revoked and a final settlement cannot be. *See* UCC § 4-214(a). But by making provisional settlements final, Regulation CC does not limit the ability of the collecting bank to revoke the settlement under UCC § 4-214 or the ability of a payor bank to revoke a provisional settlement under UCC § 4-301. *See* Reg. CC Commentary to § 229.36(d). Instead, the Regulation CC rule is merely designed to acknowledge that the path an item takes in the forward collection process may be different from the path it takes when returned. Accordingly, the credits and debits issued in the forward collection process are not necessarily revoked when the item is returned. Instead, credits and debits will be issued based on the return path the item actually takes.

Obligations of collecting banks. UCC Article 4 imposes several obligations on collecting banks. A collecting bank must send an item for collection by a reasonably prompt method. **Read UCC § 4-204.** More important, a collecting bank must send the item within a specified amount of time and must act with a certain standard of care. **Read UCC § 4-202** (and the definition of midnight deadline in UCC § 4-104). To determine whether the collecting bank has acted within the allotted time and with the proper level of care, you must take into account several additional sections:

UCC Provision	Content
§ 4-108	Time items are received
§ 4-107	A branch of a bank is a separate bank for purposes of time deadlines
§ 4-109	Excuses for delay
§ 4-103	Bank's ability to define ordinary care and the obligation of good faith
§ 4-104(c) & § 3-103(a)	Definition of ordinary care

Read those sections. A person harmed by a collecting bank's failure to forward an item in accordance with the duties stated in UCC § 4-202 and § 4-204 has a cause of action for the damage caused by that failure. **Reread UCC § 4-103.**

In the collection process, each bank is responsible for its own actions, UCC § 4-202(c), and must follow instructions from its transferor, UCC § 4-203. Once an item is in the collection chain, notations must be made on the item to identify the banks that have handled the item. UCC § 4-206.

Warranties. Each transferor of an item in the forward collection process – whether a customer or a collecting bank – makes two types of warranties, in addition to any obligation incurred under UCC Article 3 by signing the item (as discussed in Chapter Fifteen). First, a transferor makes *transfer* warranties to transferees of the item. **Read UCC § 4-207.** Notice that there are two sets of transfer warranties: the six warranties in subsection (a) and the additional warranty in subsection (b). Second, presenters and prior transferors make *presentment* warranties to the drawee who pays the item. **Read UCC § 4-208.** As to checks, these transfer and presentment warranties cannot be disclaimed. UCC §§ 4-207(d), 4-208(e). Regulation CC imposes additional warranties in the forward collection process. 12 C.F.R. § 229.34(c), (d). These warranty liabilities of a collecting bank are in addition to the collecting bank's obligations under UCC § 4-202 and § 4-204.

Encoding. When a check is taken for collection, the first bank in the collection chain usually encodes the check. Encoding is a process of putting the MICR information on the bottom of the check using a special type of machine-readable ink. This encoding allows for the automated routing of checks and the automated posting of checks to the drawer's account at the payor bank. The encoded information consists of the amount of the check, the payor bank's numerical designation, and the drawer's account number.[21] However, because the payor bank's designation and the drawer's account number are usually already encoded when the check forms are printed, the depositary bank typically encodes only the amount. **Read UCC § 4-209 and Regulation CC, 12 C.F.R. § 229.34(c)(3).** These sections provide for warranties concerning the accuracy of the encoding. Who makes the encoding warranty? To whom is the encoding warranty made? What are the damages for breach of the warranty?

Electronic presentment and forwarding electronic information. We have already considered the use of electronics in the collection process. UCC Article 4 allows for electronic presentment agreements. **Read UCC §§ 4-110, 4-209(b), (c).** The difficulty with this authorization is that it rests on "agreement." *See* UCC § 1-201 (definition of agreement). In a multi-party environment dealing with millions of instruments, it is extremely difficult to obtain agreements with all of the involved entities. Federal Reserve Operating Circular 3 allows for electronic images of checks to be sent through the Federal Reserve System and also allows for electronic presentment through submission of the MICR line information. The Clearing House also has a service through which banks that are members may electronically clear checks based upon the system rules of The Clearing House. In addition, ECCHO's rule set is used to govern image exchange programs for its members. These are three examples of organizations that rely on UCC § 4-103 and § 4-110 to create rules that allow for presentment of electronic information regarding checks instead of the actual physical paper.

Using an intermediary. The obligations of collecting banks are augmented by the system rules of any clearinghouse, Federal Reserve Bank, or other intermediary, if those intermediaries are used in the forward collection process. In addition, if a collecting bank engages in a direct presentment, without using an intermediary, the

---

[21] *See* W. David East, *Check Encoding Warranties Under Revised Uniform Commercial Code Article 4 and Regulation CC*, 51 U. MIAMI L. REV. 97 (1996).

collecting bank and the payor bank will have usually entered into an agreement regarding that activity, particularly given the need to have a set of protocols regarding presentment of an electronic image or MICR line information. The ECCHO rules are an example of a model set of such protocols for check image exchange. Such system rules and interbank agreements are allowed under UCC § 4-103 as long as the obligations of good faith and reasonable care are not disclaimed.

If a check is sent through the Federal Reserve System, Regulation J, 12 C.F.R. part 210, is applicable (in addition to UCC Articles 3 and 4, Regulation CC, and the operating circulars). **Read Regulation J, 12 C.F.R. §§ 210.3, 210.4, 210.5, 210.6, 210.7.** What are the obligations of a bank that sends the item to the Federal Reserve Bank? What are the obligations of the Federal Reserve Bank? What are the obligations of a bank that receives an item from the Federal Reserve Bank?

Relationship to UCC Article 3. When a customer deposits a check with a depositary bank, the depositary bank will generally become a holder of the check as defined in UCC § 1-201. *See also* UCC § 4-205. Thus, if the check is dishonored and returned to the depositary bank, the depositary bank will have rights as a holder to enforce the contract liability of drawers and indorsers on the check.[22] We will consider this aspect of the bank collection system when we discuss the check return process.

Problem 16-1

At 4:00 p.m. on Monday, Paul Payee took a check payable to him to First National Bank, indorsed the check in blank, and deposited it in his checking account at First National Bank. The check was drawn on Third National Bank.

A. First National Bank forwarded the check to Second National Bank on Wednesday at 9:00 a.m. using an electronic image of the check.
    1. Did First National Bank act properly? What else do you need to know?
    2. How, if at all, would the analysis change if First National Bank had a 2:00 p.m. cutoff for handling of checks?

---

[22] *See Consumer Solutions Fin. Servs., Inc. v. Heritage Bank*, 684 S.E.2d 682 (Ga. Ct. App. 2009).

    3.   How, if at all, would the analysis change if First National Bank had a computer failure on the day that it received the check?

    4.   When Paul deposited the check to his account, did he make any warranties to any person?

B. Assume that the branch of First National Bank at which Payee deposited the check was in a small town. The branch sent the check to First National Bank's main office in a city 20 miles away. The main office received the check at 3:30 p.m on Tuesday. How long does the main office have to send the check or information from the check on to another bank?

C. Assume First National Bank notified Second National Bank on Tuesday at 10:00 a.m. that Second National Bank could access an electronic image of the check on a secure website. How long does Second National Bank have to either make a presentment to Third National Bank or make the image available to another collecting bank?

D. If First National Bank has a banking relationship with Third National Bank, is sending the check image to Second National Bank an unreasonable action? If it is, what is First National Bank's liability and to whom is First National Bank liable?

E. First National Bank forwarded the check to Second National Bank on Tuesday at 9:00 a.m. by placing the check in the first class mail, properly stamped and addressed to the payments processing center of Second National Bank.

    1.   Did First National Bank act properly?

    2.   Did First National Bank make any warranties to any person?

F. First National Bank forwarded the check to Second National Bank on Tuesday at 9:00 a.m. by private courier service. Assume that Payee forgot to indorse the check and no one at First National Bank noticed because no one inspected the check. Has First National met its standard of care? Was First National Bank a holder of the check when it had possession of the check? UCC § 4-205.

G. Assume that Payee indorsed the check: "For deposit only, Paul Payee."
   What effect does that indorsement have on the forward collection
   process? UCC § 3-206(c), (e).

H. First National Bank forwarded an electronic image of the check to the
   Federal Reserve Bank in its district on Tuesday at 9:00 a.m. What
   obligations does First National Bank have? What obligations does the
   Federal Reserve Bank have?

Problem 16-2

To organize this material, create a checklist of all of the obligations of
a collecting bank set forth in UCC Article 4, Regulation CC, and
Regulation J regarding the handling of a check in the forward collection
process. Your checklist should differentiate between when a Federal
Reserve Bank is an intermediary in the forward collection process and
when it is not. For each obligation, identify the content of the obligation,
who is a potential plaintiff (*i.e.*, to whom the obligation is owed), the
applicable measure of damages, and any procedural steps that must be
taken in order to bring a legal action for a breach of the obligation.

B. Funds Availability

When a customer deposits a check to its account at a depositary bank, the bank
will give the customer a provisional credit to the customer's deposit account for the
amount of the check. Giving the customer that provisional credit does not
necessarily make those funds available to the customer, either to make payments or
to withdraw in currency. In fact, UCC Article 4 provides little guidance about when
the depositary bank must make funds available to its customer, indicating merely
that the bank must do so after settlement has become final and a reasonable time has
passed without the item being returned. UCC § 4-215(e). This may be due to the
fact that banks had a substantial role in promulgating UCC Article 4 and a
depositary bank that does makes funds available to its customer before it is sure that
the check will be honored takes a credit risk (if the check is dishonored, the bank
will not be able to recover either the funds made available to its customer or the
amount of the check from someone with liability on the instrument), a fraud risk

(that the check is not properly drawn on the drawee bank), and an insolvency risk (that an intermediary will fail before the depositary bank collects the funds that check represents).

To fill this gap and to decrease the amount of time it takes for depositary banks to make deposited funds available to their customers, Congress passed the Expedited Funds Availability Act (EFAA) and the Federal Reserve Board promulgated Regulation CC to implement the EFAA. Regulation CC establishes a variety of deadlines by which a depositary bank must make deposited funds available to its customers, although these deadlines do not preempt pre-existing state laws that require funds to be made available sooner. *See* Reg. CC, 12 C.F.R. § 229.20. A bank that fails to follow the funds availability rules can be liable for that failure. *See* Reg. CC, 12 C.F.R. § 229.21.

Read Regulation CC, 12 C.F.R. § 229.10, § 229.12 and the applicable definitions. These sections establish the deadlines for making funds available, making numerous distinctions based on how the funds were deposited. The rules are almost byzantine in complexity. One exercise that might help you understand the rules would be to make a chart of them. This would entail addressing the following issues in the order presented.

1. The time line starts to run from the day of deposit. So first determine what day the item is considered deposited. *See* Reg. CC, 12 C.F.R. § 229.19(a).
2. Then determine what type of item has been deposited. Does the deposit consist of cash or a check? If a check, is it a local check or a nonlocal check? Is it a government check? Is it a cashier's check?
3. Then determine in what type of facility the item has been deposited. Is it over the counter at the depositary bank, at an ATM on the bank premises, at an ATM in a shopping mall, at a night deposit box, or by mail?
4. Then identify the appropriate funds availability rule in either Regulation CC, 12 C.F.R. § 229.10 or § 229.12.
5. Then consider whether all or only part of the funds must be made available, at what time of day the funds must be made available, and whether the funds must be made available for withdrawal in all ways or only some. *See* Reg. CC, 12 C.F.R. § 229.19(b), § 229.2(d), § 229.12(d).

Needless to say, creating the chart would consume considerable time and effort.

We do not believe that the benefit in understanding would be worth the expense in time and effort. That is because three major developments have accelerated funds availability in practice. First, electronic presentments of check images or MICR line information in forward collection has cut down the time lag between initial deposit and presentment. Thus the credit, fraud, and insolvency risks that a depository bank assumes in making funds available before an item is finally paid have been significantly reduced. Second, because the Federal Reserve system has consolidated down to one paper check processing Federal Reserve Bank, there are no longer "nonlocal" domestic checks. All checks are in the same check processing region, which consists of the domestic United States. Thus, all domestic checks are now "local." Third, the banking industry has engaged in competition for deposits and as a result, many banks have more generous funds availability policies than that mandated by Regulation CC.[23] Given these industry practices and changes, Regulation CC has become increasingly irrelevant regarding funds availability.

That said, one portion of Regulation CC remains important. **Read 12 C.F.R. § 229.13.** It contains exceptions for situations when a bank need not comply with the otherwise applicable deadlines. When a dispute arises about funds availability, it is likely to be about whether one or more of these exceptions is available, even if the bank has a funds availability policy that is more generous to the customer than that prescribed by Regulation CC.

Relationship of funds availability to other concepts. The funds availability obligation of the depository bank is a separate obligation owed to its customer. The depository bank's obligation to make the funds available to the depositor has nothing to do with whether:

1. final payment has been made by the payor bank after presentment of the item (discussed *infra* in Section 5);
2. the depository bank (a collecting bank) can exercise rights of chargeback against its customer under UCC § 4-214 if the item is returned by the payor bank (discussed *infra* in Section 6);[24]
3. timely notice of dishonor has been given to any indorser; and
4. either the payor bank or any collecting bank has met the UCC Article 4 requirements for check return or the Regulation CC requirements for an

---

[23] On this point, it is worth noting that Regulation CC requires the depository bank to disclose its funds availability policy to its customers. Reg. CC, 12 C.F.R. § 229.15 through § 229.18. You may wish to ask your bank for its funds availability policy and then compare that policy to the requirements of Regulation CC.

[24] Indeed, often the depository bank will be required to make the funds available to the customer before the payor bank makes final payment and before the depository bank's right of chargeback terminates.

expeditious return and large check return notice. These topics are discussed *infra* in Section 6.

SECTION 5.   COLLECTION OF CHECKS: PAYOR BANK'S DECISION TO PAY OR RETURN AND THE RELATIONSHIP WITH ITS CUSTOMER

A.   Payor Bank's Decision to Pay or Return

Final payment. When the item is presented to the payor bank, the bank must decide whether to pay or dishonor the item. There are two main methods of presentment contemplated by UCC Article 4. The first method is presentment "over the counter." The paradigm example is when a payee of a check takes the check to the payor bank and presents the check to the teller "over the counter." If the teller pays the amount of the check to the presenter, the payor bank has made "final payment." **Read UCC § 4-215(a) and compare UCC § 4-301(a).**

The second method of presentment is more common. The payee deposits the check at a depositary bank, which forwards the check to the payor bank either directly or indirectly through an intermediary bank, a Federal Reserve Bank, or a clearinghouse. When the payor bank receives the check, it normally makes a provisional settlement for the check. To preserve a right to revoke that provisional settlement, the payor bank must make the provisional settlement by midnight of the banking day it received the check. **Read UCC § 4-301(a).** A timely provisional settlement is not "final payment" because the payor bank retains the right to revoke the settlement. UCC § 4-215(a)(3). To revoke the provisional settlement, the payor bank must return the check before the midnight deadline. *See* UCC § 4-301(a). The midnight deadline is midnight of the banking day following the banking day of receipt.[25] UCC § 4-104(a)(10).

If the payor bank timely returns the check after a timely provisional settlement, the check has been dishonored. **Read UCC § 3-502(b)(1).** A return is effectuated as provided in UCC § 4-301, which requires that the check be "sent" by the

---

[25] Determining when the payor bank receives the check is critical to determining whether the return of the check is timely. *See Heartland State Bank v. American Bank & Trust,* 791 N.W.2d 638 (S.D. 2010) (checks mailed to payor bank were received when they arrived at payor bank).

midnight deadline. UCC § 1-201(b)(36). If the payor bank makes a provisional settlement but does not return the check by its midnight deadline, then it has made final payment for the check. UCC § 4-215. Thus, final payment for checks not presented over the counter occurs with the passage of time after the payor bank's provisional settlement.

Has the payor bank made final payment if it fails to make the provisional settlement by midnight of the banking day of receipt? No, final payment has not been made. Instead, the check has been dishonored but the payor bank has become "accountable" for the item. **Read UCC § 4-302 and comment 4 to UCC § 3-502.**

Thus, events following presentment (other than by over the counter) will proceed along one of the following paths:

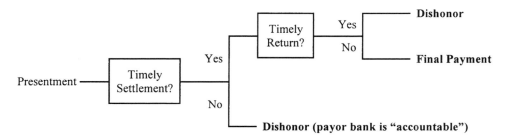

To determine whether a payor bank has acted within a required time frame, several additional sections must be consulted. *See* UCC §§ 4-107, 4-108, 4-109. One note of caution about terminology. While any bank in the forward collection process can *settle* or make a *settlement* for a check, and such settlements can be either provisional or final, only the payor bank makes *final payment* on a check.

Related to this caution is an important point to remember. Unless the payor bank has "accepted" the draft (UCC § 3-409), it incurs no liability to anyone other than its customer for a dishonor of the draft after the payor bank makes a timely provisional settlement. UCC § 3-408. We will consider the customer's right (the drawer) against its own bank (the drawee/payor bank) in subsection B of this section.

Midnight deadline. The time frames set out for the payor bank in UCC § 4-301 are not generally subject to alteration by agreement between the payor bank and its customer. That is because, as we shall see, the primary effect of final payment is not on the payor bank's customer, but on those parties upstream in the collection process. Moreover, because final payment occurs passively, with the passage of time – when the payor bank fails to return an item after giving the provisional settlement – and requires no communication to the depositary bank or other signaling event, it would be very difficult for the depositary bank to know whether an item has been finally paid if the deadlines could be altered by agreement. The deadlines set by UCC § 4-301 thus provide a measure of certainty to the process that would be lacking if the deadlines could be altered by an agreement to which the depositary bank was not a party.

Having said that, however, Regulation CC allows a short extension of the payor bank's midnight deadline if the payor bank complies with 12 C.F.R. § 229.30(c). **Read that section.** One of the main goals of Regulation CC is to create a structure that gets returned checks back to the depositary bank as fast as possible in order to reduce the risks arising from making funds available at the times mandated by the EFAA. Remember that for a payor bank to "return" an item and thus not make final payment, the payor bank must "send" the item. "Send" does not mean the same thing as "receipt." **Review the definitions in UCC § 1-201 and § 1-202.** The extension of the midnight deadline allowed by Regulation CC is keyed to the receiving bank's receipt of the item in the time the recipient would have normally received the item if the payor bank had complied with the midnight deadline in sending the item.[26] Put simply, Regulation CC creates a "no harm, no foul" rule regarding the midnight deadline rule. If the return is after the UCC Article 4 midnight deadline but sent in a manner to arrive on the following banking day, it is still a timely return.

Warranties. A payor bank that pays an item presented to it is the beneficiary of presentment warranties. **Read UCC § 4-208.** The payor bank is also the beneficiary of the warranties in Regulation CC, 12 C.F.R. § 229.34(c) and (d) and, if presentment is by a Federal Reserve Bank, the warranties in Regulation J, 12 C.F.R. § 210.6.

Item return. A payor bank that returns an item makes warranties about that item. Those warranties are not imposed by UCC Article 4 but by Regulation CC, 12 C.F.R. § 229.34, and Regulation J, 12 C.F.R. § 210.12. These warranties are discussed *infra* in Section 6.

Final payment and relationship to other concepts. Final payment is a watershed event in the check collection process with three important consequences.

    1. *Dishonor.* After final payment, the item can no longer be dishonored.

---

[26] *See U.S. Bank v. HMA, L.C.*, 169 P.3d 433 (Utah 2007); *Oak Brook Bank v. Northern Trust Co.*, 256 F.3d 638 (7th Cir. 2001).

2. *Chargeback.* Final payment firms up the provisional credits granted by the collecting banks and makes those credits final settlements. UCC § 4-215(c). Upon final settlement, a collecting bank is liable to its customer for the amount of the item, UCC § 4-215(d), and loses the right to exercise its statutory right of charge back against its customer. UCC § 4-214(a). This aspect is discussed *infra* in Section 6.

3. *Discharge of the contract obligation on the instrument and the underlying obligation.* A payor bank's final payment on the item will often, but not always, discharge the contract liability on the item of the drawer and any indorser. Final payment and discharge are separate concepts, however, and the latter does not always accompany the former. *See* UCC § 3-602. The same is true with respect to the underlying obligation for which the item was issued or transferred. *See* UCC § 3-310.

However, it is also important to understand what final payment does not mean or imply.

4. *Properly payable.* The fact that the payor bank has made final payment on an item does not mean that the item was properly payable from the drawer's account. A payor bank may make final payment of the item but not have a right to charge the customer's account under UCC § 4-401. The rules regarding when an item is properly payable from the account of the customer of the payor bank are dealt with *infra* in subsection B of this section.

5. *Funds availability.* As previously discussed, the depositary bank's obligation to make funds available to its customer is independent of, and typically arises before, final payment by the payor bank.

If there is nothing wrong with a check (no forgeries, no alterations, no unauthorized signatures), the payor bank that makes final payment will also be able to charge the drawer's account, because the check will be properly payable from the drawer's account. The payor bank will have paid a person entitled to enforce the item and thus discharged the drawer's and indorser's contract liability on the instrument. That payment will discharge the underlying obligation for which the instrument was issued or transferred. It is when there is something wrong with the instrument that the analysis gets more interesting. In Chapter Nineteen, we will consider how these issues play out when there is fraud and wrongdoing.

For now, it is important to understand the concept of final payment and the effect of the payor bank's actions in deciding to pay or return the item.

Problem 16-3

Patty Payee received a check payable to her and drawn on State Bank.

A. Payee took the check to a teller window at State Bank, indorsed the check, and requested the teller pay her the amount of the check. The teller did so. Has State Bank made a provisional settlement? Has State Bank made final payment?

B. Payee indorsed the check in blank and deposited the check in her checking account at First Bank. First Bank sent the check to State Bank for payment.
   1. State Bank received the check on Monday at 4:00 p.m. but did not give a provisional settlement for the check to First Bank. On Wednesday at 2:00 p.m., State Bank returned the check to First Bank because the drawer's account had insufficient funds to cover the amount of the check. Has State Bank made final payment? Has State Bank dishonored the check?
   2. State Bank received the check on Monday at 4:00 p.m. and gave a provisional settlement for the check to First Bank. State Bank has a cutoff time of 3:00 p.m. for receipt of checks for payment. On Wednesday at 2:00 p.m., State Bank sent the check to First Bank because the drawer's account had insufficient funds to cover the amount of the check. Has State Bank made final payment? Has State Bank dishonored the check?
   3. State Bank received the check on Monday at 4:00 p.m. and gave a provisional settlement for the check to First Bank. On Tuesday at 11:00 p.m., State Bank sent the check to the Federal Reserve Bank because the drawer's account had insufficient funds to cover the amount of the check. First Bank received the check from the Federal Reserve Bank on Wednesday at 2:00 p.m. Has State Bank made final payment? Has State Bank dishonored the check?
   4. State Bank received the check on Monday at 4:00 p.m. and gave a provisional settlement for the check to First Bank. On Wednesday at 1:00 p.m., State Bank sent the check to First Bank because the drawer's account had insufficient funds to cover the amount of the check. First Bank received the check on Wednesday at 2:00 p.m.

Has State Bank made final payment? Has State Bank dishonored the check?

C. How, if at all, does the analysis of each of the questions in Part B change if First Bank imaged the check and presented the image to State Bank?

B. Payor Bank's Relationship with Its Customer

The payor bank and the drawer of a check (the customer of the payor bank) have a relationship founded on contract and supplemented by the rules from UCC Article 4. When opening a checking account, the payor bank usually has the customer sign a signature card account agreement. This customer-bank agreement will often vary the effect of the UCC Article 4 rules, subject to the limitations in UCC § 4-103.

1. *Properly Payable*

When a check is presented to the payor bank, the bank must decide whether to pay or return the item. Obviously, one factor in making that decision will be whether there is a sufficient balance in customer's account to cover the amount of the item or, if not, whether the payor bank has agreed to honor items that create an overdraft. Another factor in making that determination is whether the item is properly payable from the customer's account. If the payor bank pays an item that is not properly payable, then the payor bank may not charge the customer's account. **Read UCC § 4-401.**

An item is properly payable if "it is authorized by the customer and is in accordance with any agreement between the customer and bank." UCC § 4-401(a). Thus, the bank-customer agreement may specify the items that are – or, perhaps more to the point, are not – properly payable from the account.[27] For example, the

---

[27] *See Spear Ins. Co., Ltd. v. Bank of America*, 40 U.C.C. Rep. Serv. 2d 807 (N.D. Ill. 2000) (corporate customer authorized bank to pay checks bearing facsimile signatures that matched the signatures of certain identified persons; the corporation failed to change that authority when an officer was fired; counterfeit checks with officer's facsimile signature were properly

bank-customer agreement for a corporate client may specify that no checks above a specified dollar amount are properly payable, as a way of protecting the corporation from misconduct by the employees authorized to sign checks. The agreement will no doubt also specify whose signature or signatures will be required to make a check properly payable.[28]

Nevertheless, in the absence of something specific in the bank-customer agreement, a lot of questions remain about what "properly payable" means. Some of these questions have a fairly certain answer. For example:

1. Is a check properly payable if paying would result in an overdraft in the customer's account? The answer is yes, at least to the extent that properly payable means permitted to charge the customer's account. *See* UCC § 4-401(a), (b).[29] The payor bank need not pay an item that will create an overdraft, unless it has agreed to do so, *see* UCC § 4-402(a), but if the payor bank does pay the item it may charge the customer's account for it.

2. Is a check properly payable if it is postdated (*i.e.*, presented before the date listed on the check)? Again the answer is yes, unless the customer has given notice of the postdating to the payor bank. *See* UCC § 4-401(c). *Cf.* UCC § 3-113.

3. Is a check that is more than six months old still properly payable? Yes. A payor bank is under no obligation to pay such a check, but is permitted to do so as long as it acts in good faith. *See* UCC § 4-404. Given the automated nature in which checks are processed, payor banks can in good faith pay checks that are years old, provided the customer has not issued a stop-payment order.[30]

---

payable by virtue of bank-customer agreement).

[28] Note, this is potentially different from whether the customer has "authorized" the check. For example, the president of a corporation may have the power, under applicable corporations law, to authorize a check but nevertheless not be someone permitted to do so under the bank-customer agreement.

[29] Notice the subtle shift in phrasing. UCC § 4-401(a) provides that a payor bank may charge its customer's account for an item that is properly payable. Here we are saying that the item is properly payable because the bank is authorized to charge the customer's account for it.

[30] *See IBP, Inc. v. Mercantile Bank of Topeka*, 6 F. Supp. 2d 1258 (D. Kan. 1998) (customer had no cause of action against bank for paying check that was nine years old).

Other questions about the meaning of "properly payable" do not have a clear answer. These include:

1. What is the relationship between "properly payable" and "person entitled to enforce"? Is a check properly payable (i.e. authorized by the customer) to any person entitled to enforce, only certain kinds of persons entitled to enforce (*e.g.*, holders), or even to some who do not qualify as a person entitled to enforce?

2. Is a check that has been altered (such as by changing the payee name or by changing the amount) properly payable? *See* UCC § 4-401(d).

On a more practical level, what actions must the payor bank take to determine if the item is properly payable? Must the payor bank compare the signature on the check to the signature of the customer on file with the bank? *See* UCC § 4-104(c) and § 3-103(a)(9) (definition of "ordinary care"). Does the customer have any obligation to discover and notify the bank that an item was not properly payable? *See* UCC § 4-406. What other issues do you see that may affect whether the item is properly payable?

Remember two things. First, just because a check is properly payable under UCC § 4-401, that does not mean that the payor bank has made final payment (UCC § 4-215). Second, the fact that a check is properly payable does not mean that a discharge has occurred of either the contract obligation on the check or the underlying obligation for which the check has been issued or negotiated. UCC §§ 3-602, 3-310.

Problem 16-4

Arnold issued a check for $50 payable to the order of Bridget, drawn on Arnold's checking account at State Bank. Bridget gave the check to Claire. Claire took the check to State Bank and presented the check for payment over the counter.

A. Although Bridget had not endorsed the item, State Bank gave Claire $50 when she presented the check. Is the check properly payable from Arnold's account?

B. Prior to giving the check to Claire, Bridget indorsed the check as follows: "*Bridget*, without recourse." State Bank gave Claire $50 when she presented the check.

1. Is the check properly payable from Arnold's account?
2. Did the payment of the check result in a discharge of the contract obligations on the check? *See* UCC § 3-602.
3. Did the payment result in a discharge of the underlying obligation that Arnold owed to Bridget or that Bridget owed to Claire? *See* UCC § 3-310.

C. Prior to giving the check to Claire, Bridget indorsed the check as follows: "*Bridget*, without recourse." Claire then lost the check and David picked it up and presented it to State Bank. State Bank gave David $50.
   1. Is the check properly payable from Arnold's account?
   2. Would the result be different if Bridget indorsed the check as follows: "Pay to Claire, *Bridget*, without recourse."

D. Bridget indorsed the check in blank when she gave the check to Claire. When Claire presented the check to State Bank, Arnold's account had a balance of only $10. State Bank paid the check anyway. Was the check properly payable from Arnold's account? What may State Bank do now?

E. Arnold issued the check on July 1, but he dated the check July 5. Bridget indorsed the check in blank and gave the check to Claire. Claire presented the check to State Bank on July 3. State Bank gave Claire $50 when she presented the check. Is the check properly payable from Arnold's account? Does it matter if payment on July 3 created an overdraft? What should Arnold have done to prevent payment prior to July 5?

F. Arnold issued the check on May 1. Bridget indorsed the check in blank and gave the check to Claire. Claire presented the check to State Bank on January 15 of the next year. Is the check properly payable?

G. Arnold issued the check, drawn on a joint account with his wife, Cindy. They are currently separated, but not divorced. Bridget indorsed the check in blank and gave the check to Claire. When Claire presented the check to State Bank, the account had a balance of only $10. State

Bank paid the check anyway. Can State Bank collect the amount of the overdraft from Cindy?

H. Instead of Claire taking the check directly to State Bank, she deposited it to her account at First National Bank. First National encoded the amount as $500, and made a provisional credit of $50 to Claire's account. When First National Bank forwarded the check to Second National Bank, Second National Bank credited First National Bank for $500. When Second National Bank presented the check to State Bank, State Bank credited Second National Bank with $500 and debited Arnold's account for $500.

1. For what amount is that check properly payable? Who bears the liability for that mistake and who can recover for that mistake? *See* UCC § 4-209; Reg. CC, 12 C.F.R. § 229.34.

2. How, if at all, would the analysis be different if First National had made a provisional credit of $500 to Claire's account?

Problem 16-5

You are corporate counsel for State Bank and are in the process of revising the bank's standard bank-customer agreement. What language would you like to include in the agreement regarding overdrafts? *See* UCC § 4-401(b) & cmt. 2.

If a payor bank pays an item that is not properly payable, and is therefore not permitted to charge its customer's account, the payor bank has in essence paid the item with its own funds, not the customer's funds. In such a case, the payor bank will usually attempt to recover the amount of the payment from someone who handled the item earlier in the process, such as the entity that presented the item to the payor bank, the payee, or someone in between them. The payor bank that has made final payment has three methods for attempting to recover from someone who handled the item earlier: breach of warranty, restitution, and subrogation.[31]

---

[31] UCC § 4-302(b) provides an avenue for recovery by the payor bank but that avenue applies only if the payor bank is "accountable" for the item, not when the payor bank has made final payment.

Warranty. Let us digress for a moment and talk about warranties more generally. Warranties are generally obligations that are created by contract or imposed by law (statute, regulation, or common law) on a transferor that run to the benefit of a transferee. If you have taken a course discussing UCC Article 2, you are familiar with the warranty of title that, unless disclaimed, is imposed on every seller of goods. Pursuant to that warranty, the seller covenants that the buyer will become the rightful owner of the goods. *See* UCC § 2-312. Thus, for example, if a particular good has been the subject of four successive sale transactions (A → B → C → D → E), then each seller (A, B, C, and D) will have warranted to its buyer that the buyer is getting good title.

If it turns out that the first seller, A, was a thief who had stolen the goods from the rightful owner, and the rightful owner is able to recover the goods from the last buyer, E, then E will have a cause of action against D. D in turn will have a cause of action against C, C will have a cause of action against B, and B will have a cause of action against A. The end result of this is that liability flows all the way back to the culprit, A. If A cannot be located or is judgment proof, then the loss, as a practical matter, will fall on B, the person who dealt directly with the thief.

Of course, a number of things may interfere with this scheme. Any one or more of the intermediate parties may be dead or insolvent. The statute of limitations may have expired on some or all of the causes of action. There may be a problem getting personal jurisdiction or one of the sellers may have disclaimed the warranty. Nevertheless, this legal structure generally works.

Now let us return to the warranties associated with the forward collection process. As we study them, consider whether they operate in the same manner. Do these warranties put ultimate liability on the wrongdoer or, failing that, on the person who dealt with the wrongdoer?

Read UCC § 4-208. The presenter of a draft and all previous transferors of that draft make presentment warranties to a payor bank that has paid or accepted an item.[32] Based on the UCC Article 4 presentment warranty, who in the collection process bears the risk that a draft has been altered, has a forged or unauthorized necessary indorsement, or has a forged or unauthorized drawer's signature? What does the payor bank have to do to pay in "good faith"? **Now review the**

---

[32] Review UCC § 3-409 on the meaning of acceptance. *See* UCC § 4-104(c). "Paid" as used in UCC § 4-208 does not mean the same thing as "pay" or "paid" in UCC § 3-602 or § 3-310. If it did, the warranty in UCC § 4-208(a)(1) would rarely be breached. Rather, it probably refers to final payment. *See* UCC § 4-215.

Regulation CC and the Regulation J warranties in 12 C.F.R. § 229.34 and 12 C.F.R. § 210.6. What additional risks do these warranties cover?

Restitution. A payor bank may also argue that it is entitled to restitution from the person to whom payment was made. **Read UCC § 3-418.** To illustrate this section, assume that the payor bank made payment on a check on which the drawer's signature was forged. The drawer successfully argues that the check was not properly payable from the drawer's account because it was not "authorized" by the drawer (due to the forgery of the drawer's signature). Under UCC § 4-208, the payor bank may recover from the person making presentment, or a prior transferor, if that person had knowledge that the drawer's signature was unauthorized. If the presenter or prior transferor did not know that the drawer's signature was unauthorized, the payor bank may attempt to pursue a cause of action for restitution. Under UCC § 3-418(a), paying an item based upon a forged drawer's signature gives rise to a claim for restitution against the person who received the payment. The difficulty with this claim is that the person receiving payment often has a defense under UCC § 3-418(c) because the person either took the instrument in good faith and for value or in good faith changed its position in reliance upon the payment.

Subrogation. A third method of recovery is for the payor bank to be subrogated to someone else's rights on the instrument. **Read UCC § 4-407.** This will not work in the case of a forged drawer's signature, however. The purported drawer is not liable on the instrument (as we learned in Chapter Fourteen) because the purported drawer did not sign the instrument. Therefore, subrogating the payor bank to the rights of a holder or the payee in that case will not help the payor bank as against the purported drawer. Nevertheless, subrogation may be helpful in other circumstances, where the drawer's signature is not forged. Consider a situation in which the payor bank paid over a valid stop order. Might the drawer be unjustly enriched so that the payor bank should be subrogated to rights against the drawer? We will come back to the payor bank's subrogation rights after we consider stop payment orders.

Problem 16-6

A. Allan issued a check for $50 payable to the order of Betty, drawn on Allan's checking account at State Bank. Betty did not indorse the check. She lost it and Clara picked up the check. Clara signed Betty's name on the back of the check. State Bank paid Clara $50 when she presented the check at the teller's window. Allan objected to the charge against his account after Betty told Allan she had lost the check. What are State Bank's obligations and options as to Allan, Betty, and Clara?

B. Allan issued a check for $50 payable to the order of Betty, drawn on Allan's checking account at State Bank. Betty indorsed the check in blank and lost it. Clara picked up the check, and altered the amount to $500. State Bank paid Clara $500 when she presented the check at the teller's window. Allan objected to the charge against his account. What are State Bank's obligations and options as to Allan, Betty, and Clara?

C. Darren stole Allan's checkbook, wrote a check for $1,000 payable to the order of "cash" drawn on Allan's account at State Bank, and signed "Allan" on the drawer's line on the bottom right-hand corner. Darren deposited the check in his bank account at National Bank. National Bank presented the check to State Bank. State Bank paid the check. Allan objected to the charge against his account. What are State Bank's obligations and options as to Darren, Allan, and National Bank?

Because it is difficult for the payor bank to succeed on the theories identified above, payor banks have asserted other causes of action such as negligence or violation of the obligation of good faith in order to try to pass liability to those entities in the collection chain that handled the item prior to presentment. Courts have not been sympathetic to those arguments.[33]

---

[33] *See Frost Nat'l Bank v. Midwest Autohous, Inc.*, 241 F.3d 862 (7th Cir. 2001) (no good faith obligation of depositary bank to let payor bank know there is a possible check kite taking place); A. Brooke Overby, *Allocation of Check Kiting Losses Under the UCC, Regulation CC, and the Bankruptcy Code: Reconciling the Standards*, 44 WAKE FOREST L. REV. 59 (2009). As explained by the judge in *First Nat'l Bank in Harvey v. Colonial Bank*, 898 F. Supp. 1220, 1222-23 (N.D. Ill. 1995):

> Check kiting is a form of bank fraud. The kiter opens accounts at two (or more) banks, writes checks on insufficient funds on one account, then covers the overdraft by depositing a check drawn on insufficient funds from the other account.
>
> To illustrate the operation, suppose that the defrauder opens two accounts with a deposit of $500 each at the First National Bank and a

2. *Wrongful Dishonor*

If the payor bank returns (*i.e.*, dishonors, UCC § 3-502) an item that is properly payable from the drawer's account, it has wrongfully dishonored the item. **Read UCC § 4-402.** Thus to analyze whether an item is wrongfully dishonored, one must

---

distant Second National Bank. (A really successful defrauder will have numerous accounts in fictitious names at banks in widely separated states.) The defrauder then issues for goods or cash checks totaling $3000 against the First National Bank. But before they clear and overdraw the account, he covers the overdrafts with a check for $4,000 drawn on the Second National Bank. The Second National account will be overdrawn when the $4,000 check is presented; before that happens, however, the defrauder covers it with a check on the First National Bank. The process is repeated innumerable times until there is a constant float of worthless checks between the accounts and the defrauder has bilked the banks of a substantial sum of money.

John D. O'Malley, "*Common Check Frauds and the Uniform Commercial Code,*" 23 RUTGERS L.REV. 189, 194 n. 35 (1968-69). By timing the scheme correctly and repeating it over a period of time, the kiter can use the funds essentially as an interest-free loan. *Williams v. United States*, 458 U.S. 279, 281 n.1 (1982) (*quoting* Brief for the United States).

* * * *

A kite crashes when one of the banks dishonors checks drawn on it and returns them to the other banks involved in the kite. Clark, *supra*. Usually, such a dishonor occurs when one bank suspects a kite. *Id.* However, an individual bank may have trouble detecting a check kiting scheme. "Until one has devoted a substantial amount of time examining not only one's own account, but accounts at other banks, it may be impossible to know whether the customer is engaged in a legitimate movement of funds or illegitimate kiting." JAMES J. WHITE & ROBERT S. SUMMERS, UNIFORM COMMERCIAL CODE § 17-1 (3d ed. 1988 & Supp. 1994). But each bank is usually able to monitor only its own account, and "[t]here is no certain test that distinguishes one who writes many checks on low balances from a check kiter." White & Summers § 17-2. Even if a bank suspects a kite, it might decide not to take any action for a number of reasons. First, it may be liable to its customer for wrongfully dishonoring checks. § 4-202. Second, if it reports that a kite is operating and turns out to be wrong, it could find itself defending a defamation suit. White & Summers § 17-1 (Supp.1994). Finally, if it errs in returning checks or reporting a kite, it may risk angering a large customer. *Id.*

first determine if it is properly payable. If the item is not properly payable, the payor bank is under no obligation to honor the item.

Wrongful dishonor is a cause of action that the customer of the account has as against the payor bank. This is an important, and often misunderstood, point. Only the customer – *not the payee or holder of the check* – can have a cause of action against the payor bank for wrongful dishonor. *See* UCC § 4-402 cmt. 5.[34]

Wrongful dishonor can wreck havoc on a customer's financial life. For that reason, UCC § 4-402 makes the payor bank liable for all damages proximately caused by the wrongful dishonor. Such damages may be far more than the amount of the dishonored item. Consider the following case, in which the payor bank dishonored several checks issued by a cattle dealer, Maryott, because it was concerned that several checks made payable to the cattle dealer had been dishonored. The bank, without consulting Maryott, decided to dishonor the checks drawn by Maryott, thinking that something "suspicious" was taking place. The bank froze Maryott's account and refused to honor another outstanding check, even though the account had sufficient funds. A payee of one of the dishonored checks made a claim against Maryott's bond, which eventually resulted in Maryott going out of business. The jury awarded "$600,000 in damages for lost income, lost value of [the dealer's] business and emotional distress."

MARYOTT V. FIRST NATIONAL BANK OF EDEN
624 N.W.2d 96 (S.D. 2001)

Gilbertson, Justice

* * *

Bank argues that the evidence fails to establish the necessary elements for recovery of damages for emotional distress. Bank notes that damages for emotional distress are recoverable in South Dakota only when the elements of either

---

[34] The payor bank has no obligation to the payee (or other person entitled to enforce) unless the payor bank has incurred acceptor's liability on the item. *See* UCC §§ 3-408, 3-409, 3-413. If the payor bank has incurred acceptor's liability on the check, the cause of action of the person entitled to enforce is determined by UCC § 3-413, not UCC § 4-402.

Do not confuse the payor bank's *acceptor's liability* on an item – derived from its acceptance of the item – with the payor bank's *accountability* for an item, which arises from its failure to make a timely settlement. *See* UCC § 4-302.

intentional or negligent infliction of emotional distress are proven. According to Bank, Maryott has failed to establish the elements of either cause of action. Maryott argues that his emotional damages are recoverable under [UCC § 4-402], which provides that a bank is liable for "actual damages proved and may include . . . other consequential damages." Maryott argues that damages for emotional distress are part of his consequential damages, and he is therefore not required to establish the elements of intentional or negligent infliction of emotional distress. In the alternative, Maryott claims he has nevertheless met those requirements.

Our initial inquiry must be whether [UCC § 4-402] has created a new breed of emotional damages or whether those damages are commensurate with theories of recovery already recognized under South Dakota law. This inquiry requires statutory interpretation, which is reviewed de novo as a question of law. The text of [UCC § 4-402] provides no assistance on this issue. Nor does the official comment to the U.C.C. offer guidance as to the requirements to establish emotional damages.

In support of his claim, Maryott directs us to *Twin City Bank v. Isaacs*, 672 S.W.2d 651 (Ark. 1984). That case involved a wrongful dishonor under U.C.C. § 4-402. The plaintiffs sued their bank and the jury awarded them damages for mental anguish. On appeal, the Supreme Court of Arkansas stated, "[i]n general, the type of mental anguish suffered under § 4-402 does not need to rise to the higher standard of injury for intentional infliction of emotional distress." *Id.* at 654.

However, a number of courts have not interpreted § 4-402 so broadly. In *Farmers & Merchants State Bank of Krum v. Ferguson*, 617 S.W.2d 918 (Tex. 1981), a bank froze its customer's checking account, without informing the customer, causing several checks to be wrongfully dishonored. The court stated that, in accordance with Texas law, "[d]amages for mental anguish [under § 4-402] cannot be recovered absent a showing of an intentional tort, gross negligence, willful and wanton disregard, or accompanying physical injury." *Id.* at 921. Likewise, the court in *First Nat'l Bank of New Castle v. Acra*, 462 N.E.2d 1345 (Ind. Ct. App. 1984), examined a claim of emotional damages for wrongful dishonor in light of its state law requirements for intentional or negligent infliction of emotional distress. The *Acra* court noted that Indiana allowed recovery of damages for emotional distress only when intentionally inflicted or accompanied by a physical injury. In addition, the California courts require a plaintiff to prove either physical impact and resulting injury or intentional wrongdoing by the defendant before damages for emotional distress can be recovered under § 4-402. *Lee v. Bank of America*, 267 Cal. Rptr. 387, 390 (Cal. Ct. App. 1990). Furthermore, the New

Jersey Supreme Court applies a more stringent test, requiring proof of intentional infliction of emotional distress before emotional damages are recoverable under § 4-402. *Buckley v. Trenton Sav. Fund Soc.*, 544 A.2d 857, 864 (N.J. 1988).

Like those jurisdictions just discussed, South Dakota allows recovery of emotional damages only when intentionally inflicted or accompanied by actual physical injury. *Stene v. State Farm Mut. Auto. Ins. Co.*, 583 N.W.2d 399, 404 (S.D. 1988). The U.C.C. provides that our common-law is effective in commercial transactions unless specifically displaced by a particular Code section. [UCC § 1-103]. Because § 4-402 does not define the consequential damages that may be recovered and does not clearly indicate an independent right of recovery of emotional damages, we must interpret that section in light of our precedent which requires a plaintiff to prove either intentional or negligent infliction of emotional distress to recover emotional damages. In *Wright v. Coca Cola Bottling Co.*, 414 N.W.2d 608, 610 (S.D. 1987), we noted that:

> three principal concerns continue to foster judicial caution and doctrinal limitations on recovery for emotional distress: (1) the problem of permitting legal redress for harm that is often temporary and relatively trivial; (2) the danger that claims of mental harm will be falsified or imagined; and (3) the perceived unfairness of imposing heavy and disproportionate financial burdens upon a defendant, whose conduct was only negligent.

These concerns are equally applicable today. The best way to balance these concerns while still providing adequate relief for injured plaintiffs is to require plaintiffs to meet the standards already established in this state for the recovery of emotional damages. The simple statement that consequential damages are recoverable under § 4-402 will not convince us otherwise. Therefore, while emotional damages may be recoverable under § 4-402, they are not recoverable unless the plaintiff can establish the requirements of either intentional or negligent infliction of emotional distress.

We must now determine if the evidence introduced by Maryott is legally sufficient to satisfy the requirements of either of those causes of action. * * *

To recover for intentional infliction of emotional distress, Maryott must show:

1) an act by defendant amounting to extreme and outrageous conduct;

2) intent on the part of the defendant to cause plaintiff severe emotional distress;

3) the defendant's conduct was the cause in-fact of plaintiff's distress;

4) the plaintiff suffered an extreme disabling emotional response to defendant's conduct.

For conduct to be deemed "outrageous," "it must be so extreme in degree as to go beyond all possible bounds of decency, and to be regarded as atrocious, and utterly intolerable in a civilized community." *Stene,* 583 N.W.2d at 404. While Bank's actions were illegal and irresponsible, they do not rise to the level of outrageous conduct. Nor was any evidence introduced that Bank acted with the requisite intent. Indeed, Maryott did not even argue in his brief that he met the requirements of intentional infliction of emotional distress. Therefore, the issue is waived.

We have repeatedly held that negligent infliction of emotional distress requires "manifestation of physical symptoms." Maryott argues that his clinical depression and the symptoms thereof that resulted from Bank's wrongful dishonor are sufficient to establish "manifestation of physical symptoms." The physical symptoms of his depression included shame, interruption of sleep, and humiliation. We discussed a similar claim in *First Nat'l Bank in Sioux Falls v. Drier,* 574 N.W.2d 597 (S.D. 1988), where the trial court refused to instruct the jury that physical injury included a diagnosed severe mental illness. We affirmed the trial court's decision, stating "Driers' proposed instruction is not consistent with South Dakota law because it expands the definition of 'physical injury.' " *Drier,* 574 N.W.2d at 600.

Likewise, Maryott's claim that clinical depression satisfies the requirement of physical symptoms is inconsistent with our established law. Nor can shame and humiliation be classified as physical symptoms. Finally, interruption of sleep on its own cannot be considered a physical symptom that would allow for recovery of emotional damages. Because Maryott has failed to establish the elements of either intentional or negligent infliction of emotional distress, his claim for emotional damages under § 4-402 must fail as a matter of law.

[The court then went on to evaluate the verdict to determine if it was excessive and to determine whether Maryott's request for punitive damages should have been submitted to the jury – ed.]

After the jury's verdict, Bank moved for a new trial * * *, claiming the damages were awarded "under the influence of passion or prejudice." Bank now appeals the denial of that motion. A motion for a new trial based upon an excessive damages award

> is addressed to the sound discretion of the trial court and a denial of the motion will not be reversed absent an abuse of that discretion.... If the jury's verdict can be explained with reference to the evidence rather than by juror passion, prejudice or mistake of law, the verdict should be affirmed.

Berry v. Risdall, 576 N.W.2d 1, 4 (S.D. 1998). In addition, "it must be remembered that the amount of damages to be awarded 'is peculiarly a question for the jury.' " *Id.* Finally, "[t]he trial court is best able to judge whether the damages awarded by a jury are the product of passion or prejudice." *Id.*

The jury awarded Maryott $250,000 damages for lost income and $200,000 for the lost value of his business. After reviewing the record, we cannot conclude that the jury's verdict could only have been reached through passion or prejudice. Maryott's expert, Don Scholten, first estimated Maryott's lost income based on the average number of cattle sold in the previous four years; 42,334. As a conservative figure, he used 40,000 head per year, with average weight of 700 pounds, earning $.50 per hundred weight. At that rate, Maryott could expect an annual income of $140,000 per year. At the time of trial, three and a half years had elapsed since the wrongful dishonor, so the annual revenues multiplied by 3.5 years amount to $490,000. Scholten also calculated Maryott's damages assuming that Maryott would switch to a consignment based business. This type of business model would produce fewer sales because, according to Maryott's testimony, not as many producers want to use that system. Scholten used Maryott's estimate that sales would be reduced by one-half. Using the same weight and commission assumptions, Maryott's income would be reduced to $70,000 per year, which multiplied by 3.5 years amounts to $245,000. Based on these calculations there is sufficient evidence by which the jury's verdict can be explained.

Nevertheless, Bank contends that Scholten failed to take into account various factors including the failure to include 1995 sales, Maryott's health problems, the fact that he spent winters in Arizona, and the possibility that Maryott could continue to work in some other capacity in the cattle industry. Each of these concerns was raised by Bank during cross-examination, and was taken into account by the jury. Scholten testified that the 1995 sales were not included in the average number of cattle sold because Maryott was working in a salaried position with Central at that time and was not actively brokering cattle through his business. Each of Bank's claims essentially go to the weight that should be given to Scholten's testimony. The jury determined Scholten's estimates were credible. When reviewing a jury verdict, we are "not free to reweigh the evidence or gauge the credibility of the witnesses." The trial court did not abuse its discretion in denying Bank's motion for a new trial as to damages for lost income.

The jury also awarded Maryott $200,000 for the lost value of his business. Bank challenges this award, claiming that Maryott's business had value only because of Maryott's ability to buy and sell cattle and the contacts he had developed in the industry. This argument relies heavily on Bank's previous assertion that the loss of Maryott's bond did not proximately cause any damages. As we have determined that claim to be without merit, this argument also fails. Bank's actions caused the forfeiture of Maryott's bond, which effectively put him out of business. On October 27, 1995, after inspecting the property, Bank valued Maryott's business at $300,000. Hofer later estimated the value to be only $100,000. There was also testimony from Brett Bunger that in early 1996, he entertained an offer to buy Maryott's business for $324,000. The jury's verdict comports to the evidence on valuation and was not the result of passion or prejudice. The trial court did not abuse its discretion in denying Bank's motion for new trial on lost value of Maryott's business.

* * *

Our initial inquiry must be whether punitive damages are recoverable under [UCC § 4-402]. That section is silent on the issue, but as discussed above, allows for recovery of consequential damages. Whether punitive damages are included under § 4-402 is therefore determined by non-U.C.C. state law. *See* [UCC §§ 1-103, 1-106; 4-402, cmt 1]. A majority of states that have examined this issue allow punitive damages under § 4-402, but only when a bank's conduct has been malicious, intentional, or fraudulent.

In South Dakota, punitive damages are permitted in actions other than breach of contract, when a defendant acts with oppression, fraud or malice. S.D. Codified Laws § 21-3-2. The breach of a statute, such as [UCC § 4-402], is an action "not arising from contract." *Groseth Int'l, Inc. v. Tenneco Inc.*, 440 N.W.2d 276, 279 (S.D. 1989). In light of our statutory authority, we agree that punitive damages are recoverable under § 4-402, but only when there is oppressive, fraudulent or malicious conduct by the bank. Because we have determined that punitive damages are recoverable, we must resolve whether the trial court should have submitted the issue to the jury * * *.

Under S.D. Codified Laws § 21-1-4.1, the trial court must find by "clear and convincing evidence, that there is a reasonable basis to believe that there has been willful, wanton or malicious conduct on the part of the party claimed against." The trial court found that Maryott had failed to satisfy that burden. Before we will reverse the trial court's finding to the contrary, Maryott must show the trial court was clearly erroneous. * * *

We have previously examined the issue of punitive damages in the banking context. In *Vreugdenhil v. First Bank of South Dakota*, 467 N.W.2d 756 (S.D. 1991), the bank's president requested the sheriff break down the door of

Vreugdenhil's business so the bank could take possession of its collateral. These actions were a clear violation of Vreugdenhil's constitutional due process rights and we reversed the trial court's decision denying a claim for punitive damages. *Id.* at 760. The bank in *Brandriet v. Norwest Bank*, 499 N.W.2d 613 (S.D. 1993), fraudulently misrepresented that Brandriet's loan had been denied, when the application had in fact never been processed. This Court affirmed the trial court's decision allowing a claim for punitive damages. *Id.* at 618. In addition, punitive damages were allowed against a bank when its employee embezzled a customer's funds. *Olson v. Tri-County State Bank*, 456 N.W.2d 132, 135 (S.D. 1990). However, we refused to allow punitive damages where there was no evidence that the bank acted with bad faith, ill will or malice toward its customer. *Yankton Prod. Credit Ass'n v. Jensen*, 416 N.W.2d 860, 863 (S.D. 1987).

Maryott argues Bank acted with malice when it violated the midnight deadline rule and because of "irregularities" in Maryott's checking account. According to Maryott, these actions show that Bank acted with reckless disregard of his rights. The violation of a statute, on its own, is insufficient to support punitive damages; there must also be oppression, fraud, or malice. *Groseth,* 440 N.W.2d at 279. There is no evidence that Bank acted with oppression, fraud, or malice when it violated the midnight deadline rule. On the contrary, it consulted an attorney as well as officials with the Federal Reserve before dishonoring the checks. These parties did not admonish Bank's proposed actions as being oppressive or fraudulent.

The "irregularities" involve an alleged discrepancy between Maryott's monthly statement and Bank's daily activity report. While Bank noted the credits and debits associated with the dishonored checks on its daily activity report, there was no corresponding credits or debits shown on Maryott's monthly statement. According to Maryott, this creates "the logical inference" that Bank was covering itself and acting with presumed malice. However, that inference is not supported by the testimony at trial. Mehlhaff testified that when items are returned, the transaction is removed from the customer's account. Although Bank's internal records would record the appropriate credits and debits, those transactions would not be shown on the customer's monthly statement, because for purposes of account records, the transaction never occurred. There is no reason to believe Bank was acting with malice simply because it did not record a credit and debit for each returned check on Maryott's monthly statement.

Bank suspected Maryott was involved in or the victim of fraudulent activity when it dishonored the checks. Although later events did not support Bank's beliefs, its conduct did not rise to the level of willful, wanton or malicious conduct.

In light of our precedent, Maryott has failed to show that the trial court was clearly erroneous in not submitting the issue of punitive damages to the jury. * * *

Sabers, Justice (concurring in part and dissenting in part)

The citizens of South Dakota, represented by this Marshall County jury, found that the bank's wrongful dishonor was the cause of Maryott's mental anguish. The majority opinion jumps in the jury box and reverses the jury's award of $150,000 for Maryott's emotional damage which was clearly precipitated by the bank's wrongful conduct. In so holding, the majority opinion sidesteps the legislative pronouncement that when a bank chooses to wrongfully dishonor a properly payable item it is liable for any "actual damages." As the jury's determination is supported by law and fact, it should stand and not be overturned on a whim.

[UCC § 4-402] provides in part:

A payor bank is liable to its customers for damages proximately caused by the wrongful dishonor of an item. Liability is limited to *actual damages proved* and may include damages for an arrest or prosecution of the customer or other consequential damages. *Whether any consequential damages are proximately caused by the wrongful dishonor is a question of fact to be determined in each case.*

(Emphasis added). This determination is supposed to be made by a jury on proper instructions, not by the Supreme Court.

The instructions to this jury properly stated that the Bank was liable for the foreseeable consequences proximately caused by its conduct. The jury was instructed that emotional distress "means mental suffering, mental distress or mental anguish. It includes all highly unpleasant mental reactions, such as fright, nervousness, horror, grief, shame, anxiety, humiliation, embarrassment, mortification, anger, worry and stress, as well as physical pain." Additionally, "the measure of damages is the amount which will compensate the party aggrieved for all detriment proximately caused thereby." The jury properly found that Maryott suffered emotional damages as a result of the Bank's wrongful conduct.

First National Bank of Eden and the majority opinion urge the view that emotional damages are never available unless the torts of negligent infliction of emotional distress or intentional infliction of emotional distress are independently asserted. Though this view is not without support in other forums, I concur with the commentators and courts that maintain that recovery for "actual damages proved" encompasses the mental suffering caused by a wrongful dishonor. The majority opinion's requirement for an independent tort theory of emotional distress to safeguard against baseless claims is an outdated approach supported only by jury distrust. I submit the juries of this state are capable of discerning when actual damages include mental anguish, as they did here.

In *Twin City Bank v. Isaacs*, 672 S.W.2d 651 (Ark. 1984), the Supreme Court of Arkansas recognized that "the type of mental anguish suffered under § 4-402 does not need to rise to the higher standard of injury for intentional infliction of emotional distress." *Id.* at 654. It further compared these intangible injuries to those types of damages recognized in defamation actions. *Id.* In addressing this issue, we are faced with the economic reality that "embarrassment and humiliation" suffered from the bank's wrongful acts are very real, though sometimes intangible harms. *See id.* The damage to Maryott's reputation and the ensuing effect on his credit, a lifeline in his type of business, created very real and incredible damage. The jury recognized it based on proper instructions and so should we.

Leading commentators on the U.C.C. have addressed the issue. "Might one argue that 'actual damages' excludes recovery for mental distress? We think not." White & Summers, HANDBOOK OF THE LAW UNDER THE UNIFORM COMMERCIAL CODE § 17-4 p. 675 (2d Ed 1980). Explaining further, White & Summers note: "It is inconsistent to allow recovery for embarrassment and mental distress deriving from arrest and prosecution and to deny similar recovery in other cases. Moreover, cases under the predecessor to 4-402, the American Banking Association Statute, held that 'actual damages' includes damages for mental distress." *Id.*

This rationale, coupled with the evidence adduced by Maryott and the jury's findings on proper instructions, demonstrate that the award was proper. Inability on the part of some members of this appellate court to appreciate or recognize these damages is no reason to vacate them. Therefore, I respectfully dissent.

Problem 16-7

To what extent may a payor bank alter its liability for wrongful dishonor, either by disclaiming liability entirely or modifying the measure of damages? *See* UCC § 4-103 and § 4-402 cmt. 2.

A payor bank may receive many items in a single day to be charged against a particular account. Sometimes payment of one item will deplete the account to such a degree that other items, if paid, would create an overdraft. In that situation, the customer of the account may argue that items that were returned were wrongfully dishonored because the dishonored items should have been paid first. **Read UCC §§ 4-303, 3-408**. These sections give the payor bank discretion regarding the order in which to honors items. However, a bank may engage in wrongful action under state consumer protection laws by posting items in a manner designed to maximize overdraft fees.[35]

Problem 16-8

Albert issued a check for $50 payable to the order of Beatrice, drawn on Albert's checking account at State Bank. Beatrice gave the check to Camille. Camille took the check to State Bank and presented it for payment.

A. Prior to Beatrice giving the check to Camille, Beatrice indorsed the check as follows: "*Beatrice.*" State Bank did not pay the check when Camille presented it to State Bank even though there were sufficient credits available in Albert's account.
  1. Is this a wrongful dishonor? If so, what is Albert's remedy? Does Camille have any remedies?
  2. How, if at all, does the analysis change if State Bank did not pay the check because Albert did not have sufficient credit in his account to cover the $50 check?

B. Albert issued the check on July 1 but he dated the check July 5. Beatrice indorsed the check in blank and gave it to Camille. Camille presented the check to State Bank on July 3. State Bank did not pay the check but dishonored it. Is that a wrongful dishonor?

C. Albert issued the check on May 1. Beatrice indorsed the check in blank and gave the check to Camille. Camille presented the check to

---

[35] *See Gutierrez v. Wells Fargo Bank*, 730 F. Supp. 2d 1080 (N.D. Cal. 2010), motion to amend denied, 2010 WL 4072240 (N.D. Cal. 2010). *See also* Reg. E, 12 C.F.R. § 205.17 (regulating overdraft fees regarding ATM and debit card transactions). *Cf. Hassler v. Sovereign Bank*, 374 Fed. Appx. 341 (3d Cir. 2010) (account agreement allowed bank to determine order of posting items to an account).

State Bank on January 15 of the next year. State Bank did not pay the check. Has it wrongfully dishonored the check? *See* UCC § 4-404.

D. Assume that Beatrice indorsed the check in blank prior to giving it to Camille. Camille deposited the check in her account at National Bank. National Bank presented the check the next morning to State Bank. State Bank's employee checked the account at 12:00 p.m. and determined that Albert's account had insufficient funds to pay the check. The employee put the check aside and made a notation that the account should be checked later that day to determine whether the check should be dishonored. The employee went home sick and no one else checked the account balance. The check was dishonored. If the account had been checked later that day, enough funds would have been present to pay the check. Is this a wrongful dishonor?

Problem 16-9

On March 20, drawee bank received the following three items for payment at the time listed:

10:00 a.m.	check for $200
11:00 a.m.	check for $300
12:00 p.m.	check for $100.

The balance in the account at the beginning of the day was $800. No deposits were made that day. The bank has a valid setoff claim against the debtor based on an overdue promissory note for $400. The bank officer decided to set off the bank debt of $400, pay the $100 check and the $200 check and dishonor the $300 check. Does the payee of the $300 check have a cause of action against the bank? Does the drawer have a cause of action against the bank under UCC Article 4?

Finally, consider how the funds availability question might relate to the question of whether there is a wrongful dishonor of an item drawn on the account. Assume that Customer has a checking account at Bank. Customer deposited a check for $1,000. Assume under the applicable funds availability rule, Bank must make the funds fully available to the customer on Wednesday. On Wednesday, the account balance is $1,200 (counting the value from the $1,000 check). The next day, Thursday, a check for $800 drawn on the account with Customer as the drawer is presented to Bank. If Bank pays the check the account balance will be $400. However, Bank is concerned about whether the $1,000 check deposited earlier will actually clear. Thus Bank dishonors the $800 check at a time when the funds availability rules would lead to a determination that Customer had sufficient available funds on deposit so that the $800 check was properly payable. Bank may be liable for wrongful dishonor of the $800 check and may be liable for failure to follow the funds availability rules in Regulation CC.

3. *Stop Payment Orders*

Sometimes a customer has reason to stop payment on an item that the customer has already issued. The customer may realize that the item was issued in error or may have a dispute with the initial payee about the underlying traction that gave rise to the item. The reason is largely immaterial to the check collection process. **Read UCC § 4-403**.

Section 4-403 imposes two conditions on the efficacy of a stop payment order. First, the person who issues the order must be one entitled to do so. This can be any person authorized to draw on the account, regardless of whether that person issued the check. *See* UCC § 4-403(a). Second, the stop payment order must be issued in time for the drawee/payor bank to act on it and remains effective for a limited period of time *See* UCC § 4-403(a), (b).

If a stop payment order is issued in a timely manner by a person authorized to do so, then presumably the item is no longer properly payable from the customer's account. *See* UCC § 4-403 cmt. 7. However, even a valid stop payment order is not determinative of the parties' rights. Rather, it is a starting point in the analysis of those rights. **Reread UCC § 4-407** and then consider the following scenarios.

1. Drawer issues a check to Payee. Drawer gives Payor Bank a timely and effective stop order that the check should not be paid. Meanwhile, Payee indorses the check and deposits it at Depositary Bank. Depositary Bank presents the check to Payor Bank. Payor Bank, in accordance with the stop payment order, dishonors the check. At this point, Payor Bank has no further responsibility. Instead, Drawer's underlying obligation to Payee, if there is one, which was suspended when the check was issued, is now revived. *See* UCC § 3-310(b). In addition, Drawer has liability on the check. *See* UCC § 3-414(b). If Depositary Bank is a holder in due course, UCC § 3-302, many of the

defenses to payment that Drawer might have against Payee will be cut off. *See* UCC § 3-305. Thus, a stop payment order that the payor bank follows may be effective to actually stop payment but has little direct affect on the liability of the drawer.

2. Drawer issues a check to Payee. Drawer gives Payor Bank a timely and effective stop order that the check should not be paid. Meanwhile, Payee indorses the check and deposits it at Depositary Bank. Depositary Bank presents the check to Payor Bank. In spite of the stop payment order, Payor Bank pays the item and debits Drawer's account. Drawer objects and insists that Payor Bank re-credit its account. Payor Bank refuses.

    Using UCC § 4-407(1), Payor Bank is subrogated to Depositary Bank's rights against Drawer. If Depositary Bank qualifies as a holder in due course of the check, most defenses to payment that Drawer has against Payee are cut off. UCC § 3-305. Drawer would have to pay the amount of the item to Depositary Bank. Because Payor Bank is subrogated to the rights of Depositary Bank, Payor Bank need not re-credit Drawer's account.

    Alternatively, using UCC § 4-407(2), Payor Bank is subrogated to Payee's rights against Drawer. If Drawer does not have any defenses to payment that could be asserted against Payee, again Payor Bank need not re-credit Drawer's account.[36] Because being subrogated to the rights of a holder in due course will cut off most defenses, Payor Bank will generally avail itself of the subrogation rights under UCC § 4-407(1) whenever Depositary Bank qualifies as a holder in due course.

3. Same facts as scenarios #2 except that Payor Bank re-credits Drawer's account. Payor Bank is now subrogated to Drawer's rights against Payee. *See* UCC § 4-407(3). If Drawer did not actually owe an obligation to Payee – as might be the case if Drawer issued the check by mistake or has a defense to payment in the transaction that gave rise to issuance of the check – Drawer would likely have a restitution right

---

[36] Technically, for this subrogation section to work, we have to pretend that the check was dishonored, not paid. That is because the drawer's obligation on the check only arises upon dishonor, not upon payment. UCC § 3-414(b).

as against Payee. Because Payor Bank is subrogated to the Drawer's rights against Payee, Payor Bank would be able to recover from Payee.

A payor bank's rights of subrogation are in addition to whatever rights it may have based upon breach of presentment warranties, UCC § 4-208, (or the warranties under Regulation CC or Regulation J) or based upon restitution under UCC § 3-418. However, in the scenarios above, the warranties would not be helpful to the payor bank because none of them was breached. The right of restitution might be helpful as long as the person to whom the payment was made does not have the defense in UCC § 3-418(c).

As you consider the stop payment order and how it works, consider also whether the effect of UCC § 4-403 may be altered by the bank-customer agreement pursuant to UCC § 4-103.

Problem 16-10

Acme Company purchased new equipment from Supplier. Acme Company has a checking account at State Bank. Pursuant to the bank-customer agreement, Acme's treasurer and president must both sign any checks drawn on Acme's account. Acme issued to Supplier a properly signed check in full payment for the equipment, drawn on Acme's checking account at State Bank. When Acme received the equipment, some of it appeared to be defective. Acme's president called State Bank and instructed the bank not to pay the check.

A. Is that an effective stop order? May State Bank charge Acme's account a fee for the stop order?

B. State Bank received the check at 10:00 a.m. on Friday. The next banking day was the following Monday. The oral stop order was given at 12:00 p.m. on that Monday.
   1. Was the stop order given in time to allow State Bank to stop payment on the check? UCC § 4-303.
   2. Assume State Bank had established a cutoff hour of 10:00 a.m. for receipt of stop payment orders. Was the stop order given in time to allow State Bank to stop payment on the check?

C. Would the stop order have been effective if the vice president, instead of the president, called State Bank?

D. Assume State Bank received the stop order in time to allow it to act on the order. The regular clerk who usually dealt with stop orders was not at work that day. The temporary clerk failed to properly process the stop payment order. State Bank made final payment for the check.
    1. What are Acme's rights against State Bank?
    2. Can State Bank defend on the basis that the drawer will have to pay the payee anyway, therefore the drawer is not damaged? UCC § 4-407.
    3. How, if at all, would the analysis change if paying the check so depleted Acme's account that State Bank dishonored three other checks Acme had written, causing Acme to suffer extensive harm to its business?

E. Assume the equipment is not defective and Acme had no basis for stopping payment to Supplier Company. Does that fact preclude Acme from issuing a stop order to State Bank?

A reoccurring issue is whether a person who procures a cashier's or teller's check (a remitter) or obtains a bank acceptance on a check (a certified check) is able to stop payment on the check.[37] **Read UCC § 3-411.** Is a cashier's or teller's check drawn on the customer's account within the meaning of UCC § 4-403?

4. *Customer Death or Incompetence*

Are items still properly payable if the customer dies or is incompetent? **Read UCC § 4-405.** May the payor bank alter the effect of this provision by terms in the bank-customer agreement? UCC § 4-103.

---

[37] *See Transcontinental Holding Ltd. v. First Banks, Inc.*, 299 S.W.3d 629 (Mo. Ct. App. 2009) (under UCC § 3-411, a bank may refuse to pay a cashier's check to assert its own defenses to payment, not the remitter's defense to payment). *See also MidAmerica Bank v. Charter One Bank*, 905 N.E.2d 839 (Ill. 2009).

Problem 16-11

Joe Drawer died on March 10. The administrator of his estate notified the payor bank on March 12 that Joe had died but to continue paying checks written before March 10. The payor bank continued to honor checks. On March 15, a man named Ed told the payor bank's officer that he was Joe's long lost nephew and that the bank should stop paying checks. The payor bank's officer had never seen this person before, and calls you. What is your advice? Should the payor bank continue paying checks?

SECTION 6.   COLLECTION OF CHECKS: CHECK RETURN AND CHARGEBACK

If the payor bank decides to return an item, the item must eventually be returned to the first bank in the collection chain. Prior to the passage of the Expedited Funds Availability Act (EFAA) and the promulgation of Regulation CC, a returned item would follow the same route – in reverse – that it followed in the forward collection process, and each provisional credit granted in that process would be revoked as the item traveled all the way back to the first bank in the collection chain. This revocation of the provisional credit is called a chargeback. Because the first bank in the chain would not know for some time whether final payment had occurred, the bank would put a long "hold" on the funds, preventing the person who had submitted the item for collection from having access to the funds until the first bank was quite sure that enough time had passed to ensure that the check would not be returned.

As discussed earlier in Section 4 of this Chapter, Congress passed the EFAA in an effort to limit the time that banks could place a hold on funds. To reduce the resulting risk that banks faced by allowing access to funds with respect to a check that might later be returned, the check return process had to be faster. To achieve this goal, Regulation CC obviates the need for returned items to follow the path they took in the forward collection process. Instead, the item may follow a shorter path, even going directly from the payor bank to the depositary bank. *See* Reg. CC Commentary to 229.30, XVI.A.8; UCC § 4-214 cmt. 4. Because of this, intermediary banks may have no way of knowing whether an item has been paid or returned, and thus whether a provisional credit has become final. That is why

Regulation CC makes all provisional settlements final in the forward collection process. Reg. CC, 12 C.F.R. § 229.36(d).

UCC Article 4 requirements. Let us begin by considering the UCC Article 4 rules on check return. We already know that the payor bank starts the check return process by sending the check to someone that preceded it in the collection chain, including directly to the depositary bank. UCC § 4-301. UCC Article 4 allows for return of an image of the item if the parties have agreed to that method of return. UCC § 4-301(a)(2). It also allows for a notice of return if the item is unavailable for return. UCC § 4-301(a)(3). If returning to the presenting bank, the payor bank revokes the provisional credit that the payor bank had given to the entity that presented the item to the bank. UCC § 4-301(a). If returning to an entity other than the presenting bank, the payor bank will obtain settlement from the entity to which it returns the check. A timely check return in accordance with UCC § 4-301(a) is a dishonor of the check. UCC §§ 4-301(c), 3-502.

Once the payor bank has returned the check to a collecting bank, the collecting bank must exercise "ordinary care" in handling the item that has been returned. As we learned in the forward collection process, a collecting bank has exercised ordinary care if it takes the required action by its midnight deadline. **Review UCC § 4-202.** Because the payor bank will revoke the provisional settlement it previously gave the collecting bank for the item it is returning (or obtain a settlement from the bank to which the item is returned), the collecting bank will want to recover that amount from someone else. Hence, the collecting bank may charge back against its customer's account or obtain a refund from the customer. **Read UCC § 4-214.** A collecting bank will also usually be a person entitled to enforce the item (assuming the item is a check or other negotiable instrument). Thus, it may alternatively enforce the contract obligations on the instrument using the principles from UCC Article 3.   Remember that to enforce the contract obligation of an indorser on a dishonored item, the indorser must be given timely notice of dishonor. **Review UCC § 3-415 and 3-503.** A collecting bank may also have a viable cause of action for breach of transfer warranties under UCC§ 4-207. If there is a problem with the encoding on the check, the collecting bank may have a viable cause of action for breach of the encoding warranty under UCC § 4-209.

The point of these "pass the loss" provisions in UCC Article 4 is to move the loss to the person who introduced the item into the bank collection system, if at all possible.

Regulation CC requirements.   Regulation CC provides additional rules governing the check return process. The Regulation CC provisions do *not* displace the UCC Article 4 rules explained above. Rather, Regulation CC imposes additional obligations on the banks in the check return process.

Remember, the goal of Regulation CC is to get the check back to the depositary bank as quickly as possible. Regulation CC facilitates this faster return by imposing an obligation of expeditious return on the payor bank (paying bank in Reg. CC terminology), 12 C.F.R. § 229.30, and on collecting banks (returning banks in Reg. CC terminology), 12 C.F.R. § 229.31. If the amount of the check returned is large, then the payor bank has an additional notice obligation as described in 12 C.F.R. § 229.33. The depositary bank has the obligations stated in 12 C.F.R. § 229.32.

Read each of those sections and the related commentary. In each section, the primary concerns are the time in which the bank has to act and the requirement of settlement for the returned item. Regarding settlement for the check, see 12 C.F.R. § 229.36(f). **Now read 12 C.F.R. § 229.38 and the related commentary.** That section imposes liability only for failure to exercise ordinary care or good faith in complying with the obligations imposed in Regulation CC. Thus, the liability of banks for failure to comply with these additional requirements of expeditious return and the large check return notice is not absolute.

In the return process, the payor and returning banks make warranties specified in 12 C.F.R. § 229.34. These warranties are an additional source of liability. They do not substitute for the obligation of the payor bank and collecting banks to make an expeditious return or for the payor bank to give the large check return notice.

Do the expeditious return and large check return notice constitute adequate notice of dishonor for purposes of UCC § 3-503 if given to an indorser of the item?

Problem 16-12

Make a checklist of the obligations that Regulation CC imposes on the payor bank and on the collecting banks in the return process. Specify the content of the obligation owed and who would be seeking to recover on those obligations.

Regulation J. Regulation CC applies no matter which banks are involved in the check return process. Regulation J applies when checks are returned through a Federal Reserve Bank. When a Federal Reserve Bank is involved, there are two basic avenues of inquiry. First, what is the obligation of the bank that returns an item to the Federal Reserve Bank? Second, what is the obligation of the Federal

Reserve Bank when it receives a returned item? With those two questions in mind, **read Regulation J, 12 C.F.R. §§ 210.12, 210.13, 210.14**.

Distinct obligations.   It is important to realize that the UCC Article 4 obligations in the return process are separate and distinct from the Regulation CC requirements of expeditious return and the large check return notice. All of those duties are also separate and distinct from the payor bank's decision to pay or return the check. The payor bank's decision to return the check and thus not make final payment is done in accord with UCC § 4-301. If the payor bank returns the check, the payor bank is obligated to make the return in such a manner so as to meet the expeditious return requirements and the large check notice requirements. It is also important to realize that each bank in the return process has its own obligation to meet the expeditious return deadlines in addition to the obligations under UCC Article 4. Finally, the Regulation J obligations also apply when the check is being returned through a Federal Reserve Bank.

Impact of all domestic checks are "local." Given that the Federal Reserve System has consolidated all paper check processing at one Federal Reserve Bank, returns of paper checks are in effect "local" checks and subject to the shorter time period stated in Regulation CC. While over 97% of forward collection of checks is accomplished through transmission of electronic images or data, electronic return of checks has not been as easy to accomplish. Industry estimates are that approximately 60% of returns are made using electronic image or data returns. Whether this comports with the Regulation CC requirements is unclear. *See* 12 C.F.R. §§ 229.30(f), 229.31(f). Paper returns are often made using a substitute check with legal equivalence as allowed under Check 21, given that the presentment is often done with electronic data. However, it is quite clear that the significantly compromised paper processing infrastructure is not sufficient to allow compliance with Regulation CC expeditious return requirements with a return of a paper check. Amendments to Regulation CC to deal with this issue have been proposed. 76 Fed. Reg. 16862 (Mar. 25, 2011).

Problem 16-13

On Friday, a check for $3,000 was presented for payment to State Bank, the drawee. The check was drawn on an account with insufficient funds to pay the check. State decided to return the check. The depositary bank was First National Bank.

A. 1. What should State Bank do to make a timely and rightful return of the check in a manner that will avoid final payment of the check and not make State Bank accountable for the check under UCC Article 4?

   2. Assume that State Bank made a timely provisional settlement for the check but missed its midnight deadline under UCC § 4-301. State Bank still wants to return the check. Can it do so and avoid liability for the item under UCC § 4-215? *See* Reg. CC, 12 C.F.R. § 229.30(c).

B. Assume that State Bank properly returned the check before its midnight deadline to the Federal Reserve Bank in its area.

   1. Has State Bank made an expeditious return under Regulation CC? Even if State Bank has made such a return, has it met all of its Regulation CC obligations?

   2. What is State Bank's liability to the Federal Reserve Bank under UCC Article 4, Regulation CC and Regulation J?

   3. What is the Federal Reserve Bank's obligation under UCC Article 4, Regulation CC and Regulation J?

C. Assume that State Bank timely and properly returned the check to Second National Bank. What is Second National Bank's obligation under UCC Article 4 and under Regulation CC?

D. State Bank properly returned the check to Second National Bank by its midnight deadline under UCC § 4-301.

   1. Despite meeting its midnight deadline, State Bank failed to meet the deadline for an expeditious return under Reg. CC because the paper check could not reach First National Bank within the required time period. Who can recover against State Bank and for what can they recover?

   2. Despite meeting its midnight deadline, State Bank failed to make an expeditious return of an electronic image of the check due to a computer failure, even though Second National Bank and First National Bank both agreed to handle electronic image returns. Is that an acceptable excuse for failing to meet the UCC Article 4 and Regulation CC deadlines?

E. State Bank properly and timely returned the check to First National Bank. First National Bank received the returned check in a timely manner. What are First National's rights and duties with respect to:
1. State Bank; and
2. First National Bank's customer?

F. Assume that State Bank's customer contends that the check was not authorized because the customer did not sign the check and thus the item was not properly payable and State Bank cannot charge the customer's account under UCC § 4-401. State Bank does not return the check by its midnight deadline but returned the check when its customer told the bank the item was unauthorized. Will State Bank be successful in passing the liability upstream to a previous bank or to the payee of the item?

G. State Bank properly returned the check by its midnight deadline and made an expeditious return directly to First National Bank.
1. May First National Bank seek to collect from the drawer or any indorsers on contract liability on the instrument? What should it do to preserve its rights against signers of the check?
2. Assume the drawer has a defense to contract liability based upon failure of consideration in the transaction for which the check was issued. Can First National Bank qualify as a holder in due course and take free of that defense? Review the relevant parts of Chapter Fifteen and *see* UCC §§ 4-205, 4-210, 4-211.

SECTION 7.   CHECK 21 AND SUBSTITUTE CHECKS

It is now time to examine how the bank collection system deals with the substitute check scheme allowed by Check 21 and Regulation CC. Recall that a substitute check is a paper object, typically created from an electronic image of the check.

The illustration in this Chapter of a situation involving a substitute check is very simple in that it contemplates the creation of a single substitute check. There is no limit, however, on the number of substitute checks that may be created in the collection chain with respect to single item, and each of those substitutes will have "legal equivalence" to the original. For example, Bank A may truncate the original check to electronic data and transfer that data to Bank B. Bank B may create a "substitute check" and send that item to a check collection service that truncates the "substitute check" into electronic data for transfer to Bank C. Bank C may then create a "substitute check" to present the item to Bank Z for payment. Each "substitute check" that meets the requirements for legal equivalence is deemed to be the legal equivalent of the original check. This scheme violates one of the primary hallmarks of the concept of negotiable instruments: that the obligation to pay is reified into **one** piece of paper so that the person obligated to pay will know that it is paying the right person upon presentment of that one piece of paper.

Obviously, one of the risks of the substitute check with legal equivalence scheme is that the customer who issued the original check must be vigilant to avoid paying more than once. This problem is addressed in Check 21 by the creation of a warranty. Any bank that transfers, presents, or returns a substitute check and receives consideration for that check warrants that no depositary bank, drawee, drawer, or indorser will have to pay twice because of the substitute check. **Read Regulation CC, 12 C.F.R. § 229.52(a).** Non-banks do not make this warranty even when they are the entities that create a substitute check. Banks dealing with non-banks in the collection process must use contractual agreements to pass on losses caused by the non-bank's actions in creating or dealing with substitute checks. The banking industry has also developed operational controls to minimize the risk that multiple items created out of the original item will find their way to presentment for payment from the customer's account.

Notice that the warranty is made only when a substitute check is created. What about the entity that truncates the original check and forwards on only electronic data (such as MICR line information or an electronic image of the check)? Check 21 does *not* provide any rights as against the truncating entity. Neither does UCC Article 4, which deals only with "items" transferred through the banking system. Electronic data is not an item. UCC § 4-104(a)(9). Now look at Regulation J, 12 C.F.R. § 210.5 and § 210.6. The Federal Reserve Banks receive and give transfer warranties as to electronic data. The bank collection system relies on system rules (such as those promulgated by ECCHO or The Clearing House) to give warranties regarding double payment or other problems in the creation of the electronic data.

Another risk associated with substitute checks is that a bank may in fact be wrong in thinking that it is dealing with a substitute check that is the legal equivalent of the original check. For example, a drawee bank that treats an item as a substitute check with legal equivalence, and thus regards it as properly payable from the customer's account, may learn later that the substitute check did not meet the requirements for legal equivalence or was not in fact a substitute check. To deal with this risk, any bank that transfers, presents, or returns a substitute check for consideration warrants that the substitute check is in fact a substitute check that meets the requirements for legal equivalence. Reg. CC 12 C.F.R. § 229.52. However, there is something of a chicken-and-the-egg problem here. That warranty applies only if the paper document meets the requirements for a substitute check (or a paper or electronic representation of a substitute check) in the first instance. So if a paper document is not a substitute check, Check 21 imposes no liability on a bank that handles that item.[38]

Check 21 contains a general liability provision that persons injured by the breach of either warranty may recover the amount of the loss up to the amount of the substitute check plus interest and expenses, including attorney's fees. Reg. CC, 12 C.F.R. § 229.56. In addition, an indemnity provision operates to pass losses caused by receiving a substitute check instead of the original check back to the bank that created the substitute check. **Read 12 C.F.R. § 229.53.** The amount recoverable through the indemnity depends upon whether there is a breach of one or both of the above warranties that caused a loss. If there is a breach of one of the warranties provided for in Regulation CC, 12 C.F.R. § 229.52, the indemnity amount is any loss, including attorney's fees, caused by the breach of warranty. Presumably this could include consequential damages suffered by a customer whose account was debited more than once due to the substitute check creation. If there is no breach of warranty, the indemnity amount is limited to the amount of the loss but no more than the amount of the substitute check plus interest and expenses including attorney's fees. The ability to recover under the indemnity provision is subject to a comparative negligence analysis that may reduce the amount recoverable. An indemnifying bank may reduce its liability by producing the original check or a sufficient copy of the check necessary to determine the validity of the claim of loss.

The other major pieces of Check 21 are the expedited re-credit process for consumers in Regulation CC, 12 C.F.R. § 229.54 and the expedited re-credit process for banks in Regulation CC, 12 C.F.R. § 229.55. Notably non-consumer bank customers have *no* re-credit rights at all. The re-credit right is somewhat limited

---

[38] Are substitute checks without legal equivalence, or paper that does not qualify as a substitute check, "items" for purposes of UCC Article 4 or "checks" for purposes of the Regulation CC requirements regarding funds availability and expeditious return?

because it is predicated on the assumption that the problem will require production of the original check in order to determine whether the substitute check was properly charged to the consumer's account or whether the consumer has a warranty claim with respect to the substitute check. Production of the original check will be somewhat irrelevant if the issue is that multiple substitute checks or the original and a substitute check have both been charged to the customer's account. Production of the original check will likely be most helpful with regard to issues such as forgery, alteration, MICR encoding errors and the like where information on the original check needs to be examined. Whether the original check can be produced is a problem, given that industry practice has become to image the check and then destroy the original.

To analyze the following problems, ask yourself these questions. First, was a substitute check created? Second, if so, did that substitute check qualify for legal equivalence? Third, what was the problem with the paper document that was created? Fourth, how is the risk of that problem occurring allocated as between the banks and as between the bank and its customer?

Problem 16-14

Bank A in California received a check for $1,500 from its customer for deposit into her checking account. The check was drawn on Bank C located in Iowa. Bank A forwarded the check to the Check Clearing Association. Check Clearing Association took possession of the check and converted the check to electronic data and forwarded that electronic data to Bank B in Nebraska. From that data, Bank B created a paper copy of the check inscribed with the legend "This is a legal copy of your check. You can use it the same way you would use the original check." The paper copy met all of the requirements for a substitute check under Check 21 except that the MICR line on the paper copy stated the amount was $15,000. The paper copy was presented to Bank C and the drawer's account was debited $15,000. The drawer's account then had insufficient funds to pay other checks drawn on the account, resulting in checks totaling approximately $4,000 being returned for insufficient funds. What are the drawer's rights under the UCC and Regulation CC?

Problem 16-15

Bank A in California received a check for $1,500 from its customer for deposit into her checking account. The check was drawn on Bank C located in Iowa. Bank A forwarded the check to the Check Clearing Association. Check Clearing Association took possession of the check and converted the check to electronic data and forwarded that electronic data to Bank B in Nebraska. From that data, Bank B created a paper copy of the check, which was a valid substitute check and met the requirements for legal equivalence under Check 21. Bank B forwarded the substitute check to Bank C for payment. Bank C honored the check. Through a processing error, Check Clearing Association also forwarded the original check directly to Bank C and Bank C honored the check. What are the drawer's rights under the UCC and Regulation CC?

Because of widespread industry practice adopting electronic images for presentment purposes, the use of substitute checks in forward collection is not the usual practice. Where substitute checks seem to have most use is in the return process, if the depositary bank to which the check is to be returned does not accept electronic returns.

Problem 16-16

What risks does a bank take in using a substitute check to return a check to a depositary bank? What risks does a depositary bank take in taking a substitute check as a return item?

SECTION 8.   COLLECTION OF DRAFTS OTHER THAN CHECKS

A draft may be drawn on a bank – in which case it is a check – or drawn on any other person. If a draft is drawn on a non-bank, a bank may handle the draft for purposes of making presentment to the non-bank. One common example of this type of draft is a draft "payable through" a particular bank. When the named bank receives the check, it will present it to the drawee for payment. Some large non-bank institutions, such as insurance companies, issue payable-through drafts as a way of maintaining control over payments to ensure that the proper signatures have been obtained.

If a draft is payable through a named bank, the named bank is a collecting bank, not a drawee bank, for purposes of the duties in UCC Article 4. **Read UCC § 4-106.** However, under Regulation CC, the named bank is a paying bank, and that bank has the paying bank's responsibilities for expeditious return and notice of large check return. Reg. CC, 12 C.F.R. §§ 229.2(z)(4), 229.36.

Another type of draft is a documentary draft. **Read the definition in UCC § 4-104(a)(6).** A documentary draft is often a draft that is payable through a bank and which must be accompanied by other documents when presented for payment or acceptance. You may have encountered a documentary draft transaction in a course on sales of goods because such drafts are often used in delivery of and payment for goods. This type of draft is best understood through working through an example.

> Seller agrees to sell goods to Buyer, who is located at some significance distance from Seller. Pursuant to the parties' agreement, Seller will furnish documents, such as a bill of lading, invoices and insurance certificates, to Buyer. Seller draws a draft on Buyer (naming Buyer as the drawee), signs the draft as drawer, and names itself (Seller) as the payee. The draft is payable through Buyer's bank, located near Buyer. Seller gives the draft and documents to Seller's bank, which will use the bank collection system to transfer the draft and documents to Buyer's bank. *See* UCC § 4-501. Buyer's bank then presents the draft and the documents to Buyer for payment or acceptance within a reasonable time after the goods have arrived at Buyer's location. *See* UCC §§ 4-502, 4-503. If Buyer pays the draft or accepts the draft (review UCC § 3-409), Buyer's bank releases the documents to Buyer and Buyer is able to obtain the goods from the carrier using the documents, particularly the bill of lading. If Buyer does not pay or accept the draft as required, Buyer's bank will often seek instructions about what to do with the goods and the documents, and if it does not receive instructions, may deal with the goods in any reasonable manner. *See* UCC § 4-504.

Thus in a documentary draft transaction, the bank collection system is used as a mechanism for transporting documents from a seller to the buyer, in addition to the use of a draft as a payment mechanism.

SECTION 9.   REVIEW

To bring the concepts of this Chapter together, organize the obligations of each bank in the collection chain.   What are the obligations of a depositary bank, a collecting bank other than a depositary bank, and a payor bank?   Separate these obligations according to the phases of the collection process: forward collection, funds availability, payment or return decision, and the return and chargeback process.   Add in the obligations created by Check 21.   In setting out those obligations, identify the content of the obligation, to whom the obligation is owed, and the liability for failure to fulfill the obligation.   Use this outline and your knowledge of the various causes of action studied in Chapters Fourteen and Fifteen to analyze the following problem.

Problem 16-17

Sue issued a check for $5,000 drawn on her account at Second Bank payable to Value Hardware in payment for a lawn tractor.   Value Hardware indorsed the check "Value Hardware, by *James*, without recourse, for deposit only" and deposited the check in its account at First Bank on Monday.

Monday evening, First Bank sent the check image to the Federal Reserve Bank for the region.   Tuesday morning, the Federal Reserve Bank sent the check image to Second Bank.   Second Bank received the check image on Tuesday morning, and checked Sue's account which did not have a sufficient balance to pay the check.   Later that day, Sue deposited a cashier's check for $10,000 providing enough credit in her account to pay all checks including the $5,000 check to Value Hardware.   Second Bank returned the check image to the Federal Reserve Bank at 12:30 a.m. Thursday morning by sending an electronic file to the designated server at the Federal Reserve Bank.   The Federal Reserve Bank printed a substitute check with legal equivalence from the check image and mailed that print to First Bank on Thursday at 10:00 a.m.   First Bank received the returned substitute check on the following Monday in its morning mail.

Prior to First Bank receiving the substitute check back in the mail, Value Hardware decided to close its account at First Bank on Friday.   The clerk at First Bank certified a check, payable to the order of Value Hardware, that Value Hardware drew on its account in order for Value

Hardware to take the funds to another bank. When First Bank received the returned substitute check, Value Hardware's account was already closed with a zero balance. First Bank calls you to advise it of its rights.

CHAPTER SEVENTEEN

MULTIPLE OBLIGORS ON A NEGOTIABLE INSTRUMENT

SECTION 1. INTRODUCTION

We saw in Chapter Fifteen that a person who signs a negotiable instrument incurs contract liability on the instrument to a person entitled to enforce the instrument. Recall that liability can be incurred in any of four particular roles: maker, indorser, drawer, or acceptor. Chapter Sixteen then addressed how the instrument is actually collected using the bank collection system. In this Chapter, we deal with what happens when there are multiple people with liability on the instrument. In so doing, we address two issues: (i) the relationship between the person entitled to enforce and the multiple obligors on the instrument, and (ii) the relationship among the multiple obligors on an instrument.

We have already touched on this subject (Chapter Fifteen, Section 3.B) in discussing the liability of a drawer or maker to an indorser, or of an acceptor to a drawer or indorser. For example, when a drawer issues a draft to a payee, the payee may indorse the draft as part of the negotiation of that draft to another person. When that occurs, both the drawer and the indorser have an obligation on the draft to the person entitled to enforce the draft. The drawer owes its obligation not only to the person entitled to enforce the draft (such as the payee or the person to whom the payee negotiated the draft) but also to the indorser, if the indorser pays the person entitled to enforce the draft. The indorser owes its obligation not only to the person entitled to enforce the draft but also to any subsequent indorser who pays the draft.

Sometimes, however, more than one person may sign an instrument in the same role, such as when there are two or more makers on a note. Whenever this occurs, the baseline rules regarding the signers' obligations and rights are: (i) the signers who sign in the same role (other than some indorsers) are jointly and severally liable for the entire obligation on the instrument; and (ii) those who have joint and several liability are, in the absence of an agreement to the contrary, entitled to contribution from each other. **Read UCC § 3-116 and compare UCC § 3-415(a).**

Problem 17-1

In return for a loan to both of them, Auguste and Botticelli signed a negotiable note payable "to the order of Cassatt and Degas." Cassatt and Degas each signed the back of the note as follows "Pay to Ernst, *Cassatt* and *Degas*" and jointly delivered the note to Ernst. Ernst subsequently signed the back of the note as follows "*Ernst*" and delivered the note to Fouquet.

A. Who has liability on the note to Fouquet? Are there any conditions to that liability?

B. If only one of the persons liable on the note pays Fouquet, what rights, if any, does that person have against each of the others who also had contract liability on the note? *See* UCC §§ 3-116, 3-412, 3-415.

Alas, these baseline rules are merely the starting point in the analysis. They are modified and complicated by the law of suretyship and the concept of an accommodation party.[1] It is to these matters we now turn. After exploring how a suretyship relationship is created and who qualifies as an accommodation party, we will consider how these concepts affect: (i) the liability of the multiple obligors that is owed to the person entitled to enforce an instrument, and (ii) the liability among the multiple obligors on an instrument.

SECTION 2. CREATING SURETYSHIP RELATIONSHIPS

Under the common law, a suretyship relationship is created whenever: (i) pursuant to contract, an obligee has recourse against a person (the secondary obligor) or that person's property with respect to the obligation owed by another person (the principal obligor), and (ii) as between the secondary obligor and the principal obligor, it is the principal obligor who ought to perform.[2] For example, when a draft is signed by a drawer, and then indorsed, there are two obligations on

---

[1] Indeed, the baseline rule providing a right of contribution is itself part of the law of suretyship, and that law is part of the "applicable law" to which UCC § 3-116(b) refers.

[2] RESTATEMENT (THIRD) OF SURETYSHIP AND GUARANTY § 1, cmt. b.

the instrument owed to the person entitled to enforce the instrument: the obligation of the drawer and the obligation of the indorser. If the indorser actually makes payment to the person entitled to enforce the note, the indorser has a right of recourse against the drawer. *See* UCC § 3-414 (drawer owes its obligation to an indorser who has paid). Accordingly, as between the drawer and the indorser, the drawer is primarily liable and the indorser is secondarily liable. Thus, there is a suretyship relationship between them. **Now read the definitions of "secondary obligor" and "principal obligor" in UCC § 3-103.**

Do not be mislead by the labels "principal" and "secondary" into thinking that this indicates the order in which the obligee must seek recovery from the obligors. Returning to our example of the indorsed draft, the holder may not pursue the indorser unless the drawee has dishonored the note and the holder has given timely notice of dishonor to the indorser (unless there is a waiver of presentment and notice of dishonor). However, once the draft has been dishonored, the holder may seek to recover from either the drawer or the indorser. As long as the draft has been dishonored, the holder need not actually attempt to collect from the drawer before seeking to collect from the indorser. Indeed, the holder may simultaneously seek to collect from both the drawer and the indorser, although the holder is of course entitled to only one satisfaction.[3] In short, the labels "principal" and "secondary" deal with the relationship of the obligors between or among themselves, not their relationship to the obligee.

With this basic understanding of the concepts of principal and secondary obligations, now consider the variety of ways in which such suretyship relationships can be created and defined by signing a negotiable instrument.

Suretyship relationships created by signing as a drawer of an accepted draft or an indorser. Review UCC § 3-412 through § 3-415. As should be readily apparent, the drawer of a draft accepted by a non-bank drawee is a secondary obligor and the acceptor is a principal obligor.[4] Similarly, as we have already seen, the indorser of a draft or note is a secondary obligor, whereas the principal obligor is the drawer (of a draft) or maker (of a note).[5]

---

[3] *See, e.g.,* RESTATEMENT (THIRD) OF SURETYSHIP AND GUARANTY § 52, cmts. a, b.

[4] In contrast, if a bank drawee accepts the draft, the drawer is discharged on its obligation. UCC § 3-414(c).

[5] The indorser may also have recourse against an acceptor. UCC §§ 3-413, 3-415(d).

Suretyship relationship created by multiple obligors signing the instrument in the same capacity. Now consider the example of two co-makers of a negotiable note who shared equally in the proceeds of a loan for which they gave the note in exchange. The two co-makers have joint and several liability on the note. *See* UCC § 3-116(a). That means each of them is obligated on the contract liability for the full amount of the note to a person entitled to enforce the note. However, each may also be entitled to contribution from their co-party. If one co-maker paid more than half of the obligation on the note to the holder, that co-maker would likely be entitled, pursuant to some express or implied agreement, to contribution from the other co-maker.[6] For example, assume that the principal amount of the note is $10,000 and the two co-makers agreed that each would be liable, as between themselves, for half the amount. Co-maker 1 then pays $8,000 to the person entitled to enforce the note. Co-maker 1 would have a right of recourse against Co-maker 2 for $3,000 because Co-maker 1's liability as between the two makers should be no more than $5,000. Accordingly Co-maker 1 is a secondary obligor as to Co-maker 2 to the extent of $3,000, the amount for which Co-maker 1 has a right of contribution against Co-maker 2.[7]

Suretyship relationship created by signing as an accommodation party. Yet another way to create a suretyship relationship is through becoming an accommodation party, a concept unique to negotiable instruments. The definitions of "principal obligor" and "secondary obligor" in UCC § 3-103 refer respectively to an "accommodated party" and an "accommodation party." An accommodation party is a kind of secondary obligor. Specifically, it is a person who signs an instrument for the purpose of incurring liability on the instrument (on which someone – the accommodated party – also has contract liability) but who did not directly receive the value given for the instrument. **Read UCC § 3-419(a).**

An accommodation party may sign in any role: maker, drawer, acceptor, or indorser. **Read UCC § 3-419(b).** That role determines the accommodation party's

---

[6] *See Collection Center, Inc. v. Bydal*, 795 N.W.2d 667 (N.D. 2011) (presumption of proportionate liability and co-surety status unless the parties have agreed to another arrangement).

[7] A right to contribution arises only when a co-surety pays more that its allocable share of the liability. Assuming that co-sureties are to share liability in proportion to their number, *see* RESTATEMENT (THIRD) OF SURETYSHIP AND GUARANTY § 57(1), no right would arise in this scenario if Co-maker 1 had paid only $4,000 (because Co-maker 1's allocable share of the liability was $5,000). *See Lestorti v. DeLeo*, 4 A.3d 269 (Conn. 2010).

liability to the obligee (the person entitled to enforce)[8] but does not fully determine the accommodation party's relationship with or rights against the accommodated party. Rather the accommodation party has rights as against the accommodated party in addition to the rights against that party inherent in the role in which the accommodation party signed. To illustrate this, consider the following two illustrations.

1. In return for a loan, Student issues a negotiable note payable to Bank. At Bank's insistence, Parent signs the note as co-maker. The only reason for Parent to sign the note is to incur liability on the note as a maker. Parent receives no direct benefit of the proceeds of the loan Bank made to Student. Parent has the liability of a maker of the note. Parent is also an accommodation party and has the rights of such a party set forth in UCC § 3-419. These rights include a right of reimbursement from Student. UCC § 3-419(f).[9]

2. Same facts as illustration 1 except that Parent signed the note as an indorser. Parent has the rights and obligations of an indorser. Therefore, Parent's liability to Bank is conditioned on dishonor and notice of dishonor, UCC § 3-415, unless waived, UCC § 3-504. Parent is also an accommodation party and has the rights of such a party set forth in UCC § 3-419. Note, this scenario also illustrates the concept of anomalous indorsement. *See* UCC § 3-205(d). An anomalous indorsement is usually made for the purpose of becoming an accommodation party. *See* UCC § 3-419(c).

Suretyship relationship created by separate agreement. A person may also become a surety for an obligation represented by a negotiable instrument without signing the instrument. A common example arises when a maker executes a negotiable note and a guarantor signs a separate document obligating itself as a

---

[8] An accommodation party may limit the ability of the person entitled to enforce the instrument to seek recovery against the accommodation party before pursuing the accommodated party if the accommodation party unambiguously indicates that it is guaranteeing collection only. UCC § 3-419(d).

[9] An accommodation party's right of reimbursement differs from a co-surety's right of contribution. As discussed *supra*, a co-surety is entitled to contribution only if and to the extent the co-surety pays more that its allocable share of the obligation. An accommodation party is entitled to be reimbursed by the accommodated party for the full amount that the accommodation party has paid.

guarantor of the debt evidenced by the note. Such a surety (the guarantor) is not an accommodation party. As the comments to UCC § 3-419 point out, an accommodation party is always a surety, but a surety is not always an accommodation party. The rights of an obligee against a surety who has signed a separate guarantee document are not determined by UCC Article 3, but by the common law of suretyship and guarantees.[10] The remainder of this Chapter will be concerned with suretyship relationships created through multiple signatures on a negotiable instrument, and not on suretyship relationships created through a party executing a separate guarantee contract.

In order to understand these suretyship relationships and the rights and obligations that flow from them, it is important to be able to identify when suretyship relationships arise. Try your hand at this task in the following problem.

Problem 17-2

A. Apollo issued a demand draft, payable to the order of Bacchus, drawn on Ceres. Bacchus indorsed the draft in blank and delivered the draft to Diana. Who is a secondary obligor? Who is a principal obligor? Is anyone an accommodation party?

B. Apollo issued a demand draft, payable to the order of Bacchus, drawn on Ceres. Bacchus obtained Ceres's signature on the draft. Ceres is not a bank. Who is a secondary obligor? Who is the principal obligor? Is anyone an accommodation party?

C. Apollo issued a demand draft, payable to the order of Bacchus, drawn on Ceres. Bacchus would only take the draft if Apollo obtained the signature of Eros on the draft. Eros signed the draft on the back and then Bacchus took the draft. Who is a secondary obligor? Who is the principal obligor? Is anyone an accommodation party?

---

[10] *See Belden v. Thorkildsen*, 197 P.3d 148 (Wyo. 2008). In 2002, several Article 3 provisions were amended to conform the rules in Article 3 concerning accommodation parties and suretyship to the common law rules of suretyship. One expression of the common law rules can be found in the RESTATEMENT (THIRD) OF SURETYSHIP AND GUARANTY (1996).

D. Apollo issued a demand draft, payable to the order of Bacchus, drawn on Ceres. Bacchus indorsed the draft. Bacchus offered to transfer the draft to Eros in satisfaction of a debt he owed to Eros. Eros was unwilling to take the draft unless Diana indorsed the draft. Bacchus requested that Diana indorse the draft and Diana did so, signing her name on the back of the draft. Bacchus then delivered the draft to Eros. Who is a secondary obligor? Is anyone an accommodation party? If someone is an accommodation party, in what capacity did that person sign the instrument and who is the accommodated party?

E. Aphrodite issued a negotiable note payable to the order of First Bank in exchange for a loan of funds. Bank required Aphrodite to have a co-signor in order to obtain the loan. Chronos signed the note when Aphrodite asked him to, on the front right under the signature line where Aphrodite signed the note. First Bank indorsed the note in blank and transferred the note to Second Bank for value. Who is a secondary obligor? Who is the principal obligor? Is anyone an accommodation party? If someone is an accommodation party, in what capacity did that person sign the instrument and who is the accommodated party?

F. Aphrodite issued a negotiable note payable to the order of First Bank in exchange for a loan of funds, signing the note on the front right hand corner. First Bank required Aphrodite to obtain a surety for the loan. Aphrodite convinced Chronos to sign the note on the back. After both Aphrodite and Chronos signed the note, First Bank indorsed the note in blank and transferred possession of the note to Second Bank for value. Who is a secondary obligor? Who is the principal obligor? Is anyone an accommodation party? If someone is an accommodation party, in what capacity did they sign the instrument and who is the accommodated party?

Once you determine that there is a suretyship relationship between or among the signatories to an instrument – something that occurs pretty much any time two or more parties have contract liability on the instrument – two main questions must be addressed. First, how, if at all, does suretyship status affect the secondary obligor's liability to the person entitled to enforce the instrument? Second, how, if at all, does suretyship status affect the secondary obligor's rights against the principal obligor or other secondary obligors? These issues are explored below, in Sections 3 and 4, respectively.

SECTION 3.   EFFECT OF SURETYSHIP RELATIONSHIP ON SECONDARY OBLIGOR'S LIABILITY TO PERSON ENTITLED TO ENFORCE THE INSTRUMENT

A secondary obligor who signs a negotiable instrument in some role (maker, drawer, indorser, or acceptor) may be able to assert any or all of three different types of defenses against a person entitled to enforce the instrument:

> (i) defenses based upon the role in which the party signed the instrument, regardless of whether the person is a secondary obligor;
>
> (ii) suretyship defenses available to secondary obligors, *see* UCC § 3-605; and
>
> (iii) defenses based upon the secondary obligor's status as an accommodation party, *see* UCC §§ 3-305(d), 3-419(d), (e).[11]

We explored the first category of defenses in Chapter Fifteen. *See* UCC § 3-412 *through* § 3-415. To review, assume a maker issues a negotiable note payable on demand to a payee. The payee indorses the note and negotiates it to a holder. The holder presents it to the maker and the maker dishonors the note. The holder sues the maker and the indorser on their respective contract liabilities. As should already be apparent, the indorser is a secondary obligor because it has a right of recourse against the maker if it pays any amount on the note to the holder. The maker of the note is the principal obligor.

Assume further that the holder did not give timely notice of dishonor to the indorser and there was no excuse or waiver of the obligation to give notice of dishonor. The indorser may assert the lack of notice of dishonor as a defense to payment. That defense is available even if the holder is a holder in due course. Demonstrating timely notice of dishonor is part of the holder's prima facie case against the indorser. UCC § 3-415. That defense of lack of notice of dishonor is

---

[11] A secondary obligor who is an accommodation party on an instrument will be liable to the obligee for contract liability on the instrument based upon the capacity in which the accommodation party signed the instrument. UCC § 3-419(b). Thus, a person could be an accommodation maker, accommodation drawer, accommodation indorser, or accommodation acceptor.

based upon the parameters of the contract liability of the indorser, not the fact that the indorser is a secondary obligor.

Let us now move to the second category of defenses, those based on the indorser's status as a secondary obligor. Assume that the holder releases the maker from its obligation on the instrument. If the maker could use this release as a defense against the indorser's assertion of the maker's liability to the indorser under UCC § 3-412 (after the indorser pays the holder), the holder's release of the maker has impaired the indorser's right of recourse as against the maker.

Read UCC § 3-605(a). The second sentence of paragraph (1) provides that, unless the release specifies otherwise, the holder's release of the maker (the principal obligor) also discharges the maker from its liability to the indorser (the secondary obligor). The first sentence of paragraph (2) then provides that, unless the release specifies otherwise, the release of the maker also operates to release the indorser from its obligation to the person entitled to enforce.

This defense based on a release of the principal obligor is a codification of traditional suretyship principles that discharge a secondary obligor to the extent actions of the obligee have impaired the secondary obligor's right of recourse against the principal obligor.[12] The same is true for subsection (b), which deals with an extension of time for the principal obligor to pay the instrument, subsection (c), which deals with a modification (other than a release or an extension of time) of the principal obligor's obligation, and subsection (d), which deals with actions that impair the value of any collateral securing the obligation to pay the instrument. **Read UCC § 3-605(b)-(d).**

Notice that any secondary obligor, even if it is not an accommodation party, may use these suretyship defenses. Thus, an indorser will have these defenses even if it is not an accommodation party, as will a drawer who is a secondary obligor in relationship to an acceptor. However, not all suretyship defenses are found in UCC

---

[12] *See* UCC § 3-605 cmt. 1. *See also* RESTATEMENT (THIRD) OF SURETYSHIP AND GUARANTY § 39.

The holder may prevent the release from discharging the indorser in either of two ways. First, the holder may expressly reserve the right to enforce the instrument against the indorser. However, such a reservation does not work at all if the instrument is a check, *see* UCC § 3-605(a)(2), and is not effective to the extent that the indorser's loss of recourse against the maker would cause the indorser to suffer a loss, *see* UCC § 3-605(a)(3). Second, the holder could expressly reserve both the holder's right to enforce the instrument against the indorser and the indorser's recourse against the maker. If that is done, and the instrument is not a check, the liability of the indorser will not be discharged.

§ 3-605. *See* UCC § 3-603(b) (discharging indorsers and accommodation parties when tender of payment refused). The UCC provisions on suretyship defenses do not "displace" other common-law principles of suretyship and those other principles supplement UCC Article 3. *See* UCC § 3-605 cmt. 1.

In some circumstances, a secondary obligor will not be entitled to an otherwise available suretyship defense. **Read UCC § 3-605(f).** That subsection allows for a secondary obligor to waive the right to assert suretyship defenses. Waivers of suretyship defenses are commonly found in negotiable promissory notes. In addition, the person entitled to enforce the instrument must generally know that the person is a secondary obligor in order to be subject to a suretyship defense. **Read UCC § 3-605(e).**

Finally, a secondary obligor that is also an accommodation party has two potential defenses to the contract obligation on the instrument, in addition to the defenses based upon the capacity in which it signed the instrument and the suretyship defenses discussed above. **Read UCC §§ 3-305(d), 3-419(d), (e).** First, an accommodation party may assert against a person entitled to enforce the instrument the defenses or claims in recoupment that the principal obligor (the accommodated party) could assert against the person entitled to enforce. This is an exception to the rule stated in UCC § 3-305(c) that a person may assert only its own defenses or claims in recoupment against the person entitled to enforce the instrument. Second, if an accommodation party unambiguously indicates that it is guaranteeing collection only, not payment, then the person entitled to enforce the instrument must first exhaust efforts to collect against the accommodated party or show why those efforts would be unavailing. *See* UCC § 3-419(d).[13] These two additional defenses are not available to a secondary obligor on a negotiable instrument that is not an accommodation party.

---

[13] Subsection (d) provides for a specific type of accommodation, "collection guaranteed," rather than payment guaranteed. UCC § 3-419(d) thus operates as a limited exception to the general rule of subsection (b). New subsection (e) (added by the 2002 amendments) addresses the usual situation where the accommodation party does not limit its liability on the instrument to "collection guaranteed."

Problem 17-3

Apollo issued a negotiable note payable to the order of Bacchus in exchange for a loan of funds. Bacchus required Apollo to obtain a surety for the loan. Apollo convinced Ceres to sign the note on the back. After Apollo signed the note on the front and Ceres signed the note on the back, Bacchus indorsed the note in blank and transferred possession of the note to Diana for value.

A. Assume that the note was originally payable on May 1 and Diana gave Apollo until June 1 to pay the note. On May 20, Diana demanded Apollo pay the note. Apollo refused, citing the previous extension given. Diana gave timely notice of dishonor to Ceres and demanded that Ceres pay the note. Does Ceres have any defense to payment? If Diana had given timely notice of dishonor to Bacchus and demanded payment from Bacchus would Bacchus have a defense to payment?

B. Assume that the note is secured by a security interest in collateral provided by Apollo. Diana released the collateral from the security interest. Apollo subsequently dishonored the note. Diana gave timely notice of dishonor to both Bacchus and Ceres. Diana then demanded that Bacchus and Ceres pay the amount of the note. Does either Bacchus or Ceres have a defense to payment?

C. Assume that Diana presented the note to Apollo and Apollo paid the note. Apollo did not get the note back from Diana. Diana then sold the note to Eros, transferring possession of the note to Eros. Eros demanded payment from Apollo who refused because he had previously paid. Eros gave timely notice of dishonor to Bacchus and Ceres and then demanded payment from Bacchus and Ceres. Do either of them have a defense to payment?

Problem 17-4

Archimedes issued a negotiable note payable to the order of Bernoulli in exchange for a loan of funds. Bernoulli required Archimedes to have a co-signor in order to obtain the loan. Condorcet signed the note when

Archimedes asked him to, on the front right under the signature line where Archimedes signed the note. Bernoulli indorsed the note in blank and transferred the note to Descartes for value.

A. When the note became due, Descartes demanded that Condorcet pay the amount of the note. Does Condorcet have any defenses to payment?

B. Assume the note was payable on May 1. The note was not paid when due. Six months later, Descartes demanded that Archimedes, Condorcet and Bernoulli pay the note. Does any of the three have any defenses to payment?

C. Assume the note was payable on May 1. After the note was transferred to Descartes, Archimedes obtained a discharge in bankruptcy of all Archimedes' obligations, including liability on the note. Descartes demanded that Condorcet and Bernoulli pay the note. Does either Condorcet or Bernoulli have any defense to payment?

D. Archimedes issued the note to Bernoulli in exchange for goods that Bernoulli sold Archimedes. The goods were defective and breached a warranty that Bernoulli gave regarding the quality of the goods. Archimedes refused to pay the note when Descartes presented it to Archimedes. Descartes sought payment from Bernoulli and Condorcet.
   1. Does either of them have a defenses to payment if Descartes does not qualify as a holder in due course of the note?
   2. Does either of them have a defenses to payment if Descartes does qualify as a holder in due course of the note?

E. In any situation above where there is a possible defense to contract liability, what language in the instrument could have prevented successful assertion of that defense?

SECTION 4.   EFFECT OF SURETYSHIP RELATIONSHIP ON LIABILITY AMONG SIGNERS OF THE INSTRUMENT

Consider first the rights of a secondary obligor against the principal obligor. The whole concept of a secondary obligor is that it is a person who has liability and rights: liability to the obligee but a right of recourse against the principal obligor. Hence, the law of suretyship provides secondary obligors with the right to recover from the principal obligor. The three primary remedies that a secondary obligor has against a principal obligor are: (i) reimbursement; (ii) subrogation to the obligee's rights against the principal obligor; and (iii) exoneration (forcing the principal obligor to perform its obligation). These rights are expressly recognized in UCC Article 3. For example, if the secondary obligor is an indorser who paid, the indorser has the right to enforce contract liability on the instrument against the principal obligor. *See* UCC § 3-412 *through* § 3-415. If the secondary obligor is a drawer with liability that survives the drawee's acceptance of the draft, the drawer has a similar right of recourse against the acceptor. UCC § 3-413. These statutory provisions essentially codify rights to reimbursement of a secondary obligor that has paid the obligation on the instrument. A secondary obligor who pays not only has a right to be reimbursed by the principal obligor, but also a right to be subrogated to the obligee's position against the principal obligor, including the obligees's interest in any collateral that secures the obligation.[14]

Now consider what rights two or more secondary obligors may have among themselves. In the beginning of this Chapter we saw the baseline rule on how to deal with multiple people who have incurred contract liability on an instrument by signing the instrument. Those who signed in the same capacity are, in the absence of an agreement or principle of law to the contrary, entitled to contribution from

---

[14] *See* UCC § 3-605 cmt. 7; RESTATEMENT (THIRD) OF SURETYSHIP AND GUARANTY §§ 27, 28(1)(c).

UCC § 3-419(f) specifies the rights an accommodation party (secondary obligor) has against the accommodated party (principal obligor). In addition to reimbursement from the principal obligor and subrogation to the obligee's position against the principal obligor, the accommodation party is entitled to the right of exoneration. These rights for an accommodation party are separately stated in the event that the accommodation party is not already a secondary obligor by virtue of the role in which the secondary obligor has signed the instrument (such as a drawer with rights against an acceptor and an indorser).

each other. UCC § 3-116. Suretyship principles frequently change this baseline rule.

Two or more secondary obligors who have signed an instrument may either be co-sureties or sub-sureties. In general, co-sureties have joint and several liability to the obligee, a right of reimbursement against the principal obligor, and a right of contribution as against the other. UCC § 3-116. The scope of their right of contribution will be determined by any agreement between them or, in the absence of such an agreement, by common-law suretyship principles.[15]

A surety and sub-surety have no right of contribution against each other. Instead, the sub-surety has a right of reimbursement against the surety. In essence, between themselves, the sub-surety stands as a secondary obligor to the surety, who stands as the principal obligor. We have already seen an example of a sub-surety relationship: the relationship created through a series of indorsements on the instrument. Later indorsers who have paid the instrument may recover from earlier indorsers. UCC § 3-415. Thus, the later indorsers are sub-sureties in relation to the earlier indorsers.

Whether someone is a co-surety or a sub-surety is a factual question based upon the order of signing (if indorsers) or the agreement of the parties.[16] For example, assume three makers sign a note. The agreement of the parties is that Maker A is the principal obligor and Makers B and C sign as accommodation parties. Makers B and C could agree that each will be liable for half of the debt (co-surety) or that Maker C will be a sub-surety for Maker B.

Problem 17-5

Avogadro issued a demand draft, payable to the order of Bohr, drawn on Curie. Bohr indorsed the draft and offered to transfer it to Einstein in satisfaction of a debt Bohr owed. Einstein was unwilling to take the draft unless Doppler indorsed the draft. Bohr requested that Doppler indorse the draft and Doppler did so, signing his name on the back of the draft. Bohr then delivered it to Einstein. Einstein presented the draft to Curie who dishonored the draft.

---

[15] *See Schwetschenau v. Whitfield*, 894 N.E.2d 96 (Ohio Ct. App. 2008).

[16] *See Irish v. Woods*, 864 N.E.2d 1117 (Ind. Ct. App. 2007).

A. Einstein sought payment from Avogadro. Avogadro and Einstein agreed that if Avogadro paid ½ the amount of the draft, Einstein would delete Avogadro's name from the draft. After Einstein received payment from Avogadro, Einstein crossed out Avogadro's name on the draft. Did Einstein's action discharge Bohr or Doppler from their contract liability on the draft? Will Einstein's actions prevent Bohr or Doppler from recovering from Avogadro in the event one of them pays Einstein?

B. Assume Bohr paid the amount of the draft to Einstein. Does Bohr have any rights against Doppler?

C. Assume Doppler paid Einstein the amount of the draft. Does Doppler have any rights against Bohr?

Problem 17-6

In return for a loan, the president of Armstrong Corp. signed on behalf of the company a $100,000 negotiable note payable to the order of State Bank. At State Bank's insistence, the three shareholders of Armstrong Corp. – Basie, Calloway, and Duke – all signed the note as co-makers. Armstrong Corp. failed to pay the note when it became due.

A. State Bank then demanded payment from Calloway, who paid the note in full. To what extent, if any, may Calloway recover from Armstrong Corp., Basie, and Duke?

B. Assume that instead of demanding payment from Calloway, State Bank demanded payment from Armstrong Corp., which paid the note in full. To what extent, if any, may Armstrong Corp. recover from Calloway, Basie, or Duke?

SECTION 5.   REVIEW

Problem 17-7

Alberta issued a negotiable demand note in the amount of $15,000 payable to bearer in return for a business loan from Brunswick Bank. Approximately one year later, Brunswick Bank demanded payment and Alberta refused to pay. Brunswick Bank then sold the note to Columbia Bank for $8,000, and gave Columbia Bank possession of the note. Brunswick Bank did not disclose to Columbia Bank that Alberta had dishonored the note, and there was no indication on the note that there had been a dishonor. As one of the terms of the sale of the note, Columbia Bank required that Brunswick Bank indorse the note in blank. Brunswick Bank represented that there were no defaults at the time the note was sold to Columbia Bank. Columbia Bank then sold the note to National Bank for $7,000. Columbia Bank did not sign the note and transferred possession of the note to National Bank.

National Bank demanded that Alberta pay the note. National Bank and Alberta negotiated that Alberta could satisfy her entire liability by paying National Bank $10,000, which she paid in full. National Bank then sued Brunswick Bank and Columbia Bank for $5,000.

A. Analyze Brunswick Bank's obligation to National Bank including any defenses it may have to that obligation.

B. Analyze National Bank's rights against Columbia Bank and any defenses that Columbia Bank may have.

C. Analyze Brunswick Bank's rights against Alberta and any defenses that she may have.

CHAPTER EIGHTEEN

NEGOTIABLE INSTRUMENTS
AS PERSONAL PROPERTY

SECTION 1.   INTRODUCTION

Chapter Fifteen explored the contract obligation created when a negotiable instrument is issued and Chapter Sixteen addressed collecting on that contract obligation through the bank collection system. Chapter Seventeen then covered the relationship between the obligee and multiple obligors who have incurred that contract obligation and the relationship among the multiple obligors. A common theme in all three of these Chapters was the obligor's contract obligation on the instrument.

This Chapter changes focus a bit by looking at the aspects of the negotiable instrument that are governed by property law. As a result, it looks primarily – but not exclusively – at the rights of people other than the obligor.

A negotiable instrument is a kind of personal property; it represents a valuable right, the right to payment of the contract liability on the instrument (*i.e.,* the reified obligation discussed in Chapter Fourteen). As with other types of personal property, the owner of an instrument may sell or gift those rights to someone else or may transfer something less than complete ownership, such as a consensual lien, to another person. Issues associated with property rights to an instrument include:

(i) identifying the owner(s) of the instrument and who else, other than an owner, may have a property-based claim to the instrument;

(ii) understanding the methods for transferring property rights to the instrument;

(iii) identifying the remedies available to those with a property-based claim to the instrument; and

(iv) understanding the warranties made by a transferor of the instrument (whether an owner, a person with a property-based right, or someone without any property-based right at all) to a transferee and how those warranties protect and define the rights that the transferee obtains.

SECTION 2.   CREATING AND TRANSFERRING PROPERTY RIGHTS IN AN INSTRUMENT

Return to UCC § 3-105. A negotiable instrument is "born" when it is first issued. Once a maker signs a note or a drawer signs a draft, and delivers that note or draft to a person for purposes of giving anyone rights in the instrument, the reified obligation is created and the instrument becomes an asset of the owner of the instrument. However, identifying the owner of an instrument is not an easy task. The owner need not be the initial payee, the person to whom the instrument is first delivered, or a person who later has possession of the instrument. Rather, who owns the instrument is determined by common-law principles of property.

To illustrate the difference between ownership and possession generally, consider the following example. You lend your car to a friend. You are still the owner, even if your friend possesses the car. The same thing is true for a negotiable instrument. Consider the simple situation of a supermarket customer who writes a check payable to cash to pay for groceries and hands the check to the cashier. The check is a bearer instrument and the cashier, as the person in possession, may be the person entitled to enforce the instrument. But the check is no doubt owned by the supermarket. Thus, the person entitled to enforce the contract liability on an instrument (the possessor) is not necessarily the owner of the instrument under property law principles. **Read comment 1 to UCC § 3-203.** Thus, to determine who in fact has ownership of the instrument at the time the instrument is "born" requires an understanding of the transaction in which the instrument is issued. Now consider this scenario.

> You sign and deliver a note to Bank One, payable to the order of Bank One, in return for a loan. To raise funds, Bank One later sells the note to Bank Two. Bank One does not indorse or deliver the note to Bank Two. Instead, the parties sign a written agreement memorializing the sale transaction and specifying that Bank One will act as Bank Two's agent in collecting from the obligor any and all payments on the note. There has been no negotiation of the note (review UCC § 3-201), and thus Bank One is still entitled to enforce the note (review UCC § 3-301). However, Bank Two is the owner of the note. It is a serious mistake to equate either possession or entitlement to enforce of the instrument with ownership or property rights in the instrument. *See* UCC § 3-203(b) & cmt. 1.

Once you determine who is the owner of the instrument, it is necessary to determine if other property interests have been created in the instrument. As with other personal property, the owner may grant a consensual lien (*i.e.*, a security interest) on the instrument to a creditor of the owner to secure a debt. A creditor of the owner may also attempt to obtain a non-consensual lien (*e.g.*, a judgment lien) on an instrument, typically through judicial process. Both consensual and non-consensual liens are a kind of property interest.[1]

UCC Article 3 does not address how to transfer ownership of or create a lien on an instrument, leaving these matters to other law. Much of this other law will be found in UCC Article 9, which governs the creation of a consensual lien on both notes and drafts and many sales of promissory notes (defined to include negotiable notes). *See* UCC § 9-109. However, UCC Article 9 does not cover sales of drafts or the creation of non-consensual liens on instruments. The sale of a draft will be governed by common-law principles of contract. The creation of a non-consensual lien on a note or draft will be governed by the relevant state's law regarding civil process for judgments and other types of judicial process.

To illustrate the application of UCC Article 9 in creating property interests in an instrument, consider this example. Assume Alice is the payee of a negotiable promissory note with Payor as the maker. This note is an asset of Alice. Now assume Alice wishes to borrow money from First Bank, perhaps because payment on the note is not yet due and Alice needs money now. First Bank insists that Alice provide collateral to secure repayment of requested loan. So, Alice grants First Bank a security interest in the negotiable promissory note, an item of her personal property that has value (because of Payor's maker's obligation to pay the note). First Bank's security interest is a type of property interest in the negotiable promissory note.[2]

In addition to ownership or lien interests in an instrument, a property interest in a negotiable instrument could also arise if an instrument is given as payment in

---

[1] There may, of course, be other types of property-based rights in an instrument. For example, assume that a negotiable note is issued by a maker to two payees jointly. Under principles of property law (not merely because they are joint payees under UCC Article 3), the two payees are likely to be tenants in common (co-owners) of the note, and each would have a property right in the note based upon its rights as a tenant in common.

[2] Whether First Bank's security interest is perfected may be relevant to the priority of First Bank's security interest in the note as against other parties who claim security interests or liens in the note, but perfection is not relevant to whether First Bank has a property interest in the note. As to how First Bank would perfect its security interest in the note, *see* UCC §§ 9-310, 9-312(a), and 9-313(a).

a transaction that is later rescinded under contract law. For example, assume that a negotiable promissory note is negotiated as payment for an item in a transaction where there is a misrepresentation sufficient to avoid the transaction for fraud under contract law principles.[3] If a transaction is avoided because of fraud, the usual remedy is to allow restitution of the benefit provided to each side.[4] The benefit provided to the party who committed the fraud is the negotiation of the negotiable promissory note to them. Under UCC § 3-202, rescission of the negotiation of the negotiable promissory note is allowed if allowed under other law. The person entitled to rescind the negotiation of the instrument would have a property-based right to get the instrument back.

While UCC Article 3 does not specify how property interests in instruments are created or transferred, it does recognize those interests. It calls such property-based rights "claims" to the instrument.[5] **Read UCC § 3-306.** The first key to analyzing property rights in an instrument (claims) is to determine who has them and what type of property right is at issue.

Problem 18-1

A. Arnold issued a negotiable demand note payable to the order of State Bank. State Bank used the note as collateral for a loan from National Bank. National Bank took possession of the note after State Bank indorsed the note in blank. According to the agreement between State Bank and National Bank, National Bank is entitled to collect on the note only if State Bank defaults on the loan.
    1. Who is entitled to enforce the note?
    2. Who has a claim to the note?

B. Anna issued a negotiable demand note payable to the order of Bank Two in return for a loan from Bank One. Bank One intends to sell the

---

[3] RESTATEMENT (SECOND) OF CONTRACTS § 164.

[4] RESTATEMENT (SECOND) OF CONTRACTS § 376.

[5] Article 3 uses the term "claim" to refer to property-based rights in an instrument and the term "claims in recoupment" to refer to defenses to payment that may reduce the amount owed on an instrument. UCC § 3-305(a)(3). As the comment to UCC § 3-306 points out, these two terms refer to two different concepts.

note to Bank Two but that sale has not yet been completed. Bank One is in possession of the note.

1. Who is entitled to enforce the note?
2. Who has a claim to the note?
3. Bank One and Bank Two execute the necessary documents to sell the note to Bank Two. Bank One is still in possession of the note, which Bank One has not indorsed. Now who has a claim to the note and who is entitled to enforce the note?

C. Ashton issued a check payable to bearer and delivered possession of the check to Betty, for Betty to deliver to Creek, Inc. in payment for goods that Ashton purchased from Creek, Inc.
1. Who is entitled to enforce the check?
2. Who has a claim to the check?

SECTION 3.   ASSERTING PROPERTY-BASED CLAIMS TO AN INSTRUMENT

Once the claims to the instrument are identified, there are at least three initial questions to consider. First, if someone has a claim to the instrument, what action may that person take to assert that claim? Second, if a person is entitled to enforce the instrument but someone else asserts a rightful property claim to the instrument, what effect does that have on the rights of the person entitled to enforce the instrument? Third, if someone other than a person entitled to enforce the instrument has a rightful property claim to the instrument, does this alter the rights or obligations of the a person with contract liability on the instrument?

A. Remedies Used to Enforce a Claim to an Instrument

A person with a claim to an instrument has, in general, the same remedies that protect property-based interests in any type of personal property. Those remedies are not provided in UCC Article 3 but come from other law. For example, if an instrument is stolen, the owner could of course report the theft and seek to have the thief prosecuted under criminal law. More to the point, the owner could enforce its property rights in the instrument by using a replevin action to recover possession of the instrument, bringing an action for conversion to recover damages,[6] or seeking injunctive relief to prevent collection of the payment obligation. **Read UCC § 3-202.** All three of these possible remedies arise out of the law governing personal property, not out of Article 3. Article 3 merely does not *prevent* these remedies. UCC § 3-202, cmt. 2.

UCC Article 3 does explicitly provide for one type of property-based cause of action: conversion. **Read UCC § 3-420.** The first sentence of subsection (a) brings into Article 3 the common law regarding the tort of conversion of personal property. The rest of subsection (a) then specifies an additional situation in which an instrument is deemed converted. We will consider this provision in depth in Chapter Nineteen when we consider fraud and wrongdoing with respect to instruments. But for now, keep in mind this simple illustration of the second sentence of section 3-420(a). Assume that a negotiable note is issued payable to the order of Payee. Payee is the owner of the note. Payee does not indorse the note. We learned in Chapter Fifteen that in order to make the next person a holder, Payee must indorse the note. UCC § 3-301. Assume that Ted steals the note from Payee and forges Payee's indorsement. Ted is not a person entitled to enforce the note. Ted then sells the note and transfers possession of it to an unsuspecting Mary. Mary is not a person entitled to enforce because Payee has not indorsed the note. Ted's forgery of Payee's name is not Payee's indorsement. UCC § 3-403. Ted has converted the note under the first sentence of section 3-420(a). Mary has converted the note under the second sentence of section 3-420(a).

UCC Article 3 addresses conversion in another circumstance as well. **Read UCC § 3-206(c).** In Chapter Fifteen we briefly addressed the concept of restrictive indorsements. A common type of restrictive indorsement is when a person entitled to enforce deposits a check in a bank account and indorses the check "for deposit only." Once a check is indorsed in that manner, a non-bank purchaser of the check will have converted the check unless the amount of the check is received by the indorser. A depositary bank that takes that check will have converted the check unless the proceeds are paid to the indorser or applied consistently with the indorsement.

---

[6] Replevin (sometimes called by different names, such as claim and delivery) is a state-law process that seeks to recover possession of identified personal property. Conversion is the common-law tort for interference with property rights in personal property. It is often defined as the wrongful deprivation of another of the use and possession of personal property. BLACK'S LAW DICTIONARY (9th ed. 2009).

B. Effect of a Claim to an Instrument on Rights of Person Entitled to Enforce

Given that the person who has a property claim in the instrument may not be a person entitled to enforce, we must consider yet another issue. Is the person entitled to enforce the instrument subject to another person's property-based claim to the instrument? **Reread UCC § 3-306.** Whether the person entitled to enforce the instrument is subject to the claim depends upon whether that person is a holder in due course. Consider this example.

Payee indorses a check in blank and loses the check. Finder picks up the check. Finder is a person entitled to enforce because she is in possession of a bearer instrument. Payee's ownership interest is a claim to the check. As between Payee and Finder, Payee would be able to assert its claim to the check using the remedies discussed earlier in this Chapter. Finder is a holder, but not a holder in due course (no value given for the check).

Now assume that Finder negotiated the check for value to Anne, who qualifies as a holder in due course under UCC § 3-302. If Payee attempts to assert his claim to the check using the remedies discussed earlier in this Chapter, Anne will win. She is a holder in due course and takes the negotiable instrument free from claims to the instrument. UCC § 3-306. What that means is, in a lawsuit between Payee and Anne in which Payee is asserting a property claim to the instrument, Anne would win and get to keep the check (and be entitled to enforce it against the drawer, and the indorser, Payee). Anne has no liability to Payee for conversion.

This is a somewhat remarkable result. Typically, a person that acquires an item of personal property from a finder or thief acquires no greater property rights than the finder or thief had. This rule of derivative property rights to goods is codified in the first sentence of UCC § 2-403. As we learned in Chapter Twelve, however, this rule does not apply to currency. As the *Berry* case illustrated, a person that takes currency in good faith and for value from a thief obtains good title to the currency even though the thief had no title to give. The commercial need for the free transferability of currency outweighs a fundamental principle of property law. That same philosophy is behind the rule that protects a holder in due course from property-based claims to a negotiable instrument.

Recall that in order to qualify as a holder in due course, a person must not have notice of a claim to the instrument when the holder takes the instrument. UCC

§ 3-302(a)(2)(v).   Whether someone has notice of a claim is the same as determining whether someone has notice of a defense. **Review UCC § 1-202.** How might a person taking an instrument have notice of a claim to the instrument?

It is important to understand that holder-in-due-course status is an all-or-nothing prospect: someone either qualifies or does not qualify as a holder in due course. Notice of any claim or defense will prevent a holder from becoming a holder in due course. This in turn could make the holder subject to another claim or defense of which the holder had no notice. So, for example, if a holder is not a holder in due course because the holder had notice of a claim to the instrument, the holder will take subject to a defense to payment that is unrelated to the claim. Similarly, if a person is not a holder in due course because the person has of notice of a defense, and it so happens that someone else has a claim, the holder is subject to that claim even if the holder did not have notice of that claim. To illustrate how this works, consider the following.

> Assume that Maker signed a negotiable promissory note as maker and issued the note to Payee in exchange for a delivery of goods. Payee indorsed the note in blank and gave possession of the note to State Bank as security for a loan from State Bank. When State Bank took the note, it had notice the note was overdue and thus did not qualify as a holder in due course. When State Bank sues Maker to enforce the note, Maker asserts a claim to the note based on a right to rescind the transaction due to Payee's fraud in the underlying transaction. Because State Bank is not a holder in due course based upon its notice of the fact that the note was overdue, State Bank is subject to Maker's claim to the note based upon the alleged fraud of Payee. Of course whether Maker will actually win on that ground depends upon whether there was sufficient fraud in Maker's transaction with Payee to justify rescission for fraud. That question will be determined as a matter of contract law outside of UCC Article 3. What UCC § 3-306 means in this context is that State Bank would not be able to avoid a determination of the merits of that fraud dispute by asserting holder-in-due- course status as to the note. Because State Bank is not a holder in due course, it is subject to all claims and defenses that Maker may assert regarding this note even though the basis of Maker's defense has nothing to do with why State Bank is not a holder in due course.

One thorny question related to this is whether a person with a security interest in an instrument can ever qualify as a holder in due course of the instrument. A creditor who has a consensual lien on the instrument to secure an obligation of its debtor will always have notice that its debtor still has a property interest in the instrument,[7] and thus would seem always to have notice of a claim. This would seem to prevent the secured party from qualifying as a holder in due course. But it is not clear that notice of the debtor's retained ownership interest is the type of claim which should prevent a secured party who is a holder from qualifying as a holder in due course. **Now read UCC § 3-302(e).** Is that rule predicated on the assumption that a secured party can qualify as a holder in due course or is it a rule that grants to a secured party some (but not all) of the rights of a holder in due course?

C. Effect of a Claim to an Instrument on the Obligation of an Obligor

In general, a person who owes the contract obligation on an instrument cannot assert another person's claim to the instrument as a defense to payment. Return to the scenario on page 694 in which Bank One sells the note to Bank Two but retains possession. Assume Bank One then seeks to enforce the maker's liability on the note. The maker is not permitted to raise Bank Two's claim to the note. The maker may join Bank Two to the action so that Bank Two can raise its claim, but in the end the maker will still have to pay someone. **Read UCC § 3-305(c).**

The last sentence of subsection (c) has is an exception if the obligor can prove the instrument is lost or stolen and the person entitled to enforce does not have the rights of a holder in due course. To illustrate this, return to the illustration involving Payee and the Finder given on page 699. Assume further that Payee has informed the drawer that the check was lost. The drawer notifies the drawee not to pay the check when it is presented. The drawee dishonors the check and Finder (who still has possession) sues to enforce the drawer's obligation. If the drawer can prove that Payee lost the check, the drawer will have a defense to payment. In other words, even though the drawer has no defense to drawer's liability, the drawer may assert the fact that the check was lost and that Payee has a claim to the check to avoid payment of the drawer's obligation to Finder. However, the result will be different if Anne, the person to whom Finder negotiated the check, sues to enforce

---

[7] For those who have not yet studied UCC Article 9, taking a consensual lien interest in a piece of property to secure a debt does not extinguish the debtor's ownership interest in the property subject to the lien. It is only upon default, and after following the prescribed legal process for foreclosing the lien, that the debtor's ownership interest will be eliminated.

the drawer's obligation. Anne qualifies as a holder in due course and the drawer cannot raise as a defense to paying her that the instrument was lost.

There is one corollary to the rule that the obligor generally cannot raise a third party's claim to the instrument as a defense. The obligor is discharged of contract liability on the instrument by paying a person entitled to enforce the instrument even if the obligor knows or has notice of a third party's claim. **Read UCC § 3-602.** There are exceptions, however, if the obligor pays while knowing either that payment has been enjoined by a court of competent jurisdiction or that the instrument was stolen and that the person paid had possession wrongfully. *See* UCC § 3-602(e).

Problem 18-2

Adam issued a negotiable demand note payable to the order of Belinda. Belinda pledged the note to City Bank to secure a loan that City Bank gave to Belinda. Belinda indorsed the note in blank on the back. City Bank took possession of the note. According to the terms of the security agreement between City Bank and Belinda, City Bank may collect on the note only if Belinda defaults on her obligation to repay the loan from City Bank.

A. Assume that Adam issued the note in the principal amount of $10,000 to Belinda in exchange for goods. The goods were defective and breached a warranty that Belinda gave regarding the quality of the goods. The value of the breach of warranty claim was $7,000. Belinda defaulted on her loan from City Bank and owes City Bank $6,000. City Bank sought to enforce its security interest in the note by making a demand on Adam for payment. Does Adam have a defense to payment that he can assert against City Bank? UCC § 3-302(e).

B. Assume that City Bank sold the note to Downtown Bank, and delivered possession of the note to Downtown Bank. Downtown Bank paid Bank 80% of the face value of the note and did not know about the security arrangement with Belinda. The sale to Downtown Bank violated the terms of the security agreement between City Bank and Belinda.
   1. What can Belinda do?
   2. When it bought the instrument from City Bank, Downtown Bank had notice that Belinda had provided defective goods to Adam in

the transaction that gave rise to the note. How, if at all, does this fact change Belinda's rights?

Problem 18-3

Alice issued a check to Betty, drawn on State Bank. Betty indorsed the check in blank and then lost the check on the street. Chris found the check and presented the check over the counter to the teller at State Bank.

A. The teller paid the check amount to Chris. Is Alice's or Betty's contract liability on the check discharged?

B. Alice notified State Bank that the check was lost and gave State Bank a timely stop payment order.
   1. State Bank paid the check anyway. Is there a discharge of Alice's or Betty's contract liability?
   2. State Bank dishonored the check. Chris seeks to collect from Alice for the amount of the check. May Alice raise the fact that Betty is the owner of the check as a defense to payment of the check? Does Betty have any rights that she can assert in this situation?

C. Assume that Chris did not present the check for payment to the drawee, State Bank. Instead, Chris transferred the check for value to David, who qualifies as a holder in due course. Alice stopped payment on the check after Betty told Alice the check was lost. State Bank dishonored the check. David sued Alice and Betty on their contract liabilities on the instrument. What result?

D. Assume that Betty did not indorse the check before she lost it. Chris found the check, indorsed it with Betty's name and deposited the check to Chris's account at National Bank. The check was paid by the drawee bank, State Bank, when National Bank presented the check. Does Betty have any rights against Chris or National Bank?

E. Assume that Betty indorsed the check in blank and with the words "for deposit only." Then Betty lost the check. Chris found the check and deposited it to Chris's account at National Bank. The check was paid by the drawee bank, State Bank, when National Bank presented the check. Does Betty have any rights against Chris or National Bank?

D. Claims Based on Wrongful Actions of a Fiduciary

A reoccurring fact situation regarding claims to a negotiable instrument involves embezzlement by an employee or other person with authority to sign or deal with instruments on behalf of someone else. UCC Article 3 contains a special provision to deal with these situations. That provision imputes, in some situations, notice of a claim to an instrument to a person who takes an instrument, thereby preventing the holder from becoming a holder in due course. **Read UCC §§ 3-307 and 3-206(d).**

Consider the following illustration.

George is the treasurer of Inventions, Inc. For some reason – greed, spitefulness, personal need – George decides to embezzle funds from Inventions, Inc. One of George's responsibilities as treasurer is to receive checks payable to Inventions, Inc., stamp them with the indorsement of Inventions, Inc., and deposit those checks to Inventions' deposit account at National Bank. George takes a check payable to Inventions, Inc., stamps it with the blank indorsement of Inventions, Inc., and deposits the check at an ATM to George's personal bank account at State Bank. The check is paid by the drawee bank. The president of Inventions, Inc. discovers what George has done and makes a claim against State Bank to recover the funds that State Bank credited to George's account due to the check deposit.

The basis of Inventions' lawsuit against State Bank is conversion. *See* UCC § 3-420(a). George in effect stole the check which belonged to Inventions. Under the common law of conversion, a person need not know that the property was stolen to have liability. To avoid liability for conversion, State Bank will have to show that it was a holder in due course of the check so that it took the check free of Inventions' property-based claim to the check. *See* UCC § 3-306. Whether State Bank qualifies as a holder in due course will depend, in part, on whether it took the check with notice of Inventions' claim to the check.[8] Section 3-307 addresses State

---

[8] State Bank will, of course, also need to prove that it gave value and took the check without notice of the facts listed in UCC § 3-302. State Bank will have given value by crediting George's deposit account for the amount of the check. *See* UCC §§ 4-211, 4-210.

Bank's notice of Inventions' property claim to the check based upon George's actions in stealing the check.

For UCC § 3-307 to apply and impute notice to State Bank in this situation, several factual determinations must be made. First, George must be a "fiduciary" with respect to the check. Second, State Bank must have taken the instrument from George for payment, collection, or value. Third, State Bank must have knowledge that George is a fiduciary. Fourth, Inventions must make a claim to the check or its proceeds based upon George's breach of fiduciary duty. These factual prerequisites are based upon UCC § 3-307(a) and the first clause of subsection (b) (before the colon and paragraph (1)). If these four prerequisites are true, then the rules in paragraphs (1) through (4) of subsection (b) apply.

Subsection (b)(1) provides that if the taker of the instrument has notice of the breach of the fiduciary duty, the taker has notice of the claim of the represented person. That notice relates back to the requirements of holder-in-due-course status. Notice of the claim of the represented person would preclude the taker from being a holder in due course, UCC § 3-302, and make the taker vulnerable to the conversion cause of action, or other causes of action that are based upon the property rights of the represented person. UCC § 3-306.[9] Paragraphs (b)(2) through (b)(4) then describe different situations in which the taker is deemed to have notice of the breach of fiduciary duty. In sum, the provision works as follows. If the four factual predicates are true, and any one of paragraphs (b)(2) through (4) is also true, then the taker has notice of the breach of the fiduciary duty, which in turn is notice of the claim of the represented person, which prevents the taker from qualifying as a holder in due course.

Now consider how UCC § 3-307 applies to the hypothetical. Is George a fiduciary with respect to the check? Generally if an employee has responsibility with respect to instruments, such as indorsing them or writing them, most courts would find that person to be a fiduciary with respect to the instrument. If an employee does not have job-related responsibilities with respect to that type of instrument, a court may conclude that the employee is not a fiduciary with respect to the instrument.

Did State Bank take the check for collection, payment, or value? Yes. When George deposited the check into his deposit account at State Bank, State Bank is taking the instrument for collection. As we learned in Chapter Sixteen, the

---

[9] It will also make the taker vulnerable to any defenses to payment of the instrument that may be asserted by persons who have contract liability on the instrument. *See* UCC § 3-305.

collection process is started by that deposit and State Bank's processes will result in eventual presentment of that check for payment to the drawee bank.

Did State Bank have "knowledge" of the fact that George was a fiduciary? **Read the definition of knowledge in UCC § 1-202.** What facts would give State Bank actual knowledge that George was a fiduciary for Inventions, Inc.? State Bank must have "knowledge" not merely "notice" of that fact. Inventions could have a hard time demonstrating that State Bank had such knowledge from the mere deposit of the check payable to Inventions Inc. and indorsed in blank.[10]

Is the basis of Inventions' cause of action against State Bank a claim to the check or proceeds based upon George's breach of fiduciary duty? Yes. Inventions is claiming conversion of the check and its proceeds. The basis of the conversion cause of action is George's action in stealing the check, *i.e.,* converting it, a breach of his fiduciary duty (assuming George is a fiduciary).

Assuming that Inventions can surmount the hurdle of demonstrating that State Bank knew of George's fiduciary status, UCC § 3-307(b)(2) would apply. The check was payable to the represented person, Inventions, Inc. and it was deposited to an account other than the account of the fiduciary as a fiduciary or an account of the represented person. George deposited the check to his personal account, not to an account he maintains as the fiduciary of Inventions. State Bank would have "notice" of the breach of fiduciary duty and thus notice of a claim. That notice of a claim prevents State Bank from being a holder in due course and thus subject to Inventions' conversion claim.

If you step back and think about it, this makes perfect sense. If a bank knows that a person is a fiduciary, and then nevertheless allows the fiduciary to deposit a check into the fiduciary's personal account, the bank should be on notice that something is amiss. It is not normal for an instrument payable to a represented person to be used for the personal benefit of the fiduciary. UCC § 3-307 cmt. 3.

As should now be apparent, the result in this scenario hinges on one critical question: did State Bank have actual knowledge of George's fiduciary status? If the answer is yes, Inventions will be successful in its conversion action against State Bank. If the answer is no, and State Bank otherwise qualifies as a holder in due course, Inventions will be unsuccessful in its conversion action against State Bank.

---

[10] *See Western Ohio Colt Racing Ass'n v. Fast,* 2009 WL 737776 (Ohio Ct. App. 2009) (organization logo on check with the name of the treasurer noted on the check not sufficient to give taker actual knowledge of fiduciary status of treasurer).

The other subparagraphs of UCC § 3-307(b) focus on other situations in which a fiduciary might deal with instruments. Paragraph (b)(3) addresses instruments issued by the fiduciary or represented person and payable to the fiduciary personally. Paragraph (b)(4) addresses instruments issued by the fiduciary or represented person and payable to the taker.

Problem 18-4

Why does UCC § 3-307(b)(3) require the taker to "know" of the breach of fiduciary duty whereas the standard used in paragraphs (2) and (4) is mere notice (*i.e.*, reason to know)? *See* UCC § 1-202.

Consider another example of wrongdoing by a fiduciary. Suppose a negotiable note states it is payable to the order of Mary. Mary indorses that note "Pay to George, in trust for Inventions, Inc." George indorses the note in blank and sells it to First Bank. UCC § 3-206(d) deals with this issue. **Read UCC § 3-206(d).**

Do UCC § 3-307 and § 3-206(d) address all the ways in which someone may attempt to embezzle funds? What if the embezzler is not a fiduciary, does that mean the taker of the instrument from the embezzler does not have to worry about claims to the instrument? Consider the following case.

MUTUAL SERVICE CASUALTY INSURANCE CO. V. ELIZABETH STATE BANK
265 F.3d 601 (7th Cir. 2001)

Rovner, Circuit Judge

In the course of his employment with Jo Daviess Services, Inc. ("Jo Daviess," or "the company"), Arlyn Hemmen managed to misappropriate more than $80,000 from the company's bank account at the Elizabeth State Bank ("ESB" or "the bank"). Mutual Service Casualty Company ("Mutual"), which insured Jo Daviess, compensated the company for its loss. Mutual then filed suit against ESB, contending that the bank had breached its contractual obligations to Jo Daviess by allowing Hemmen to abscond with its funds. The case proceeded to trial, and after both parties had presented their cases, Judge Reinhard entered judgment as a matter of law in favor of Mutual. ESB appeals, contending that Mutual was not entitled to judgment as a matter of law * * *. We affirm the judgment in Mutual's favor * * *.

I.

During the period of time relevant to this case, Jo Daviess was a farm service cooperative located in the northwestern Illinois community of Elizabeth, a town of approximately 700 people. Among other things, Jo Daviess sold animal feed, seed, fertilizer, and fuel to its members.

Late in 1991, the company hired Hemmen to serve as its controller. Hemmen previously had worked at a number of banks. In his capacity as controller, Hemmen maintained the company's books and accounts, reviewed and reconciled its bank statements, prepared monthly operating statements and other financial reports, and supervised his co-workers in the absence of the office manager.

While Hemmen was employed with the company, Jo Daviess maintained two accounts with ESB: an operating account, into which the company deposited all of its revenue and out of which it paid for its day-to-day expenses and any products the company purchased, and a second account reserved for the company's payroll. ESB maintained another account, referred to as the treasury tax and loan ("TT & L") account, into which the bank's commercial customers deposited the federal income tax that they withheld from their employees' paychecks; funds from this account were forwarded to the federal government on a daily basis. As needed, Jo Daviess periodically transferred funds out of its operating account into either the payroll or the TT & L account.

Pursuant to the terms and conditions of the agreement governing the operating account at ESB, only authorized signers could withdraw or transfer funds from that account. Hemmen was never a signer on the operating account. He did have the authority to sign checks drawn on the payroll account – a power that company officials could not recall him ever having exercised – but witnesses from ESB as well as Jo Daviess agreed that Hemmen's status as a signer on one account did not authorize him to make withdrawals or transfers from another account.

Although Hemmen was not a signer on the operating account, he regularly prepared checks drawn on that account, both to pay Jo Daviess' suppliers and to transfer funds into one of the other accounts. These checks would be presented to the company's general manager for signature. On occasion, for purposes of transferring funds into the TT & L account, Hemmen would prepare a check payable to the order of ESB. Jo Daviess did not owe any money to the bank so the only legitimate reason for making a check payable to the bank would be to accomplish a transfer of funds from the operating account to the TT & L account.

The company kept a small amount of petty cash ($50 to $100) on hand in the office. This fund was primarily used to handle small, incidental expenses.

Periodically a check would be drawn on the operating account to replenish that fund. Typically these checks were made out to "cash," "petty cash," or "Jo Daviess Service Company petty cash." On occasion, the check might be made payable to the bank, but if so, the check would bear a notation indicating that it was issued in order to "replenish petty cash." In practice, Jo Daviess allowed both Hemmen and office secretaries to cash these checks, although none was a signer on the operating account. Company officials never had any discussion with Hemmen regarding the limits of this authority. However, the amount of such checks never exceeded the total amount of the petty cash fund; they typically ranged from $25 to $50.

Beginning in January 1992, Hemmen began to embezzle money from Jo Daviess. Periodically, he would prepare a check on the company's operating account payable to the order of ESB, as if he were making a deposit into the TT & L account. He would then present the check to the general manager, who signed the check assuming that the proceeds were, indeed, destined for the TT & L account. So far as company officials were concerned, that was the only legitimate reason for preparing a check payable to the bank. In fact, however, Hemmen would divert the proceeds of the checks to his own use in one of several ways. On some occasions, Hemmen presented the check to an ESB teller and requested that a portion of the check be deposited into the TT & L account, with the balance to be disbursed to him either in cash or one or more cashier's checks payable to Hemmen's creditors. On other occasions, Hemmen would present the check and have the entirety of the proceeds issued to him, again either in the form of cash or a cashier's check. Bank personnel did not realize that Hemmen was diverting the proceeds to his own use; Hemmen would explain that the cash and cashier's checks were necessary in order to pay for supplies, parts or some other legitimate company expense. In case anyone at Jo Daviess should notice that not all of the check proceeds were being deposited into the TT & L account, Hemmen would make a false entry in Jo Daviess' internal records indicating that the cash or cashier's check issued to him was used to pay for something like postage, for example. "It was just a total fake, [a] total lie," Hemmen testified. Indeed, Jo Daviess paid its obligations with cash or cashier's checks only on rare occasions.

ESB was aware, of course that Hemmen was not an authorized signer on Jo Daviess' operating account, and Jo Daviess never indicated to the bank that Hemmen had authority to withdraw funds from that account. Nonetheless, the bank acceded to Hemmen's requests for cash and cashier's checks without first consulting with Jo Daviess to confirm his authority to receive the proceeds of these checks, and without even asking him to endorse the checks. In fact, it was the bank's custom during this period of time to honor such requests. So long as bank personnel knew the presenter, and so long as the check was signed by an authorized individual, the bank would disburse the proceeds of the check to the presenter notwithstanding the fact that the presenter himself was not an authorized signer. "We didn't question it if we knew them," explained one bank employee. And the bank's personnel knew Hemmen – shortly after Jo Daviess had hired Hemmen, a company secretary who once had worked at ESB took him down to the bank and introduced him to the bank's staff. In short, there was nothing that Jo Daviess did or said that induced the bank to comply with Hemmen's requests; the bank simply did so in compliance with its usual practice. On the other hand, Jo Daviess officials had never discussed with ESB whether Hemmen could legitimately receive the proceeds of any checks payable to the bank. "We weren't instructed whether he did or did not have authority to do that," said a bank official. "There were no instructions."[11]

Banking experts who testified on behalf of Mutual and ESB disagreed as to whether it was proper for ESB to honor the checks that Hemmen presented. Mutual's expert, Charles Malony, a banking official from the Chicago area, opined that it is bad form for a bank to negotiate a check that is payable to the bank's own order and that is presented to the bank by someone who is not a signer on the account. The proper course of action for a bank to take in this situation, Malony believed, would be to send the presenter away or to contact an official of the drawer with signature authority in order to confirm the propriety of the transaction. If the

---

[11] Bank teller Kathy McCall testified that when Hemmen first presented one of these checks to her and asked for a cashier's check in return, she sought approval from Marvin Wurster, the bank's vice-president, because the request struck her as unusual. According to McCall, Wurster approved the request, and from that point forward she and the other tellers allowed Hemmen to negotiate checks payable to the bank in this way, although they believed it was "a little different." (McCall would later go to work for a different bank in Elizabeth. At that bank, she said, an individual who presented a corporate check payable to the bank could not receive cash back if he was not an authorized signer, unless the transaction was authorized by the company.)

We note McCall's testimony but do not take it into consideration in assessing the propriety of the district court's decision to enter judgment as a matter of law in Mutual's favor. As noted above, we are obligated to construe the evidence in ESB's favor. Wurster himself could not recall having had such a conversation with McCall, and other bank personnel, who described McCall as a malcontent, doubted that the conversation had occurred.

presenter is given cash, he ought in the least be required to sign the back of the check. Moreover, the presenter's position with the drawer should have no bearing on his ability to receive the proceeds of such checks, Malony testified. Malony was willing to acknowledge, however, that in practice, a bank that knows its customer well is more likely to be liberal in its policies.

On the other hand, ESB's expert, Jeffrey Snyder, a banking official who had worked at a number of small-town banks, indicated that it is common for banks in small communities to rely on individuals who are not authorized signers for instructions as to the appropriate disposition of checks drawn to the bank's order. Snyder acknowledged that "the bank has a responsibility to post [a] transaction as the drawer expects[.]" But in practice, Snyder explained, the authorized signer typically is the owner of a business, who has better things to do with his or her time than to traipse down to the bank. Typically, a bookkeeper or another employee is sent instead of an authorized signer. In a larger metropolitan area, where a bank has no way of knowing each of the many persons who will transact business with it, bank employees will naturally be unwilling to accept instructions from non-authorized employees. But in a small community like Elizabeth, "we know all of these people," Snyder observed. "We probably know who their parents were."

> "And because we have that knowledge of our customers, it allows us to facilitate some of these transactions with the confidence that we're acting according to the instructions of the drawer. And we also know how these businesses – people run their businesses, and, you know, we have the confidence that if the business didn't intend to have that person tell us what to do with the item, they wouldn't have signed it and sent them down there with it."

Thus, so long as the bank is familiar with the presenter and knows that he is the drawer's employee, and in the absence of any suspicious circumstances, a small town bank in practice likely will honor the presenter's instructions – including an instruction to issue cash to the presenter himself. This amounts to a judgment call on the part of the bank employee to whom the item is presented, Snyder said, turning on such factors as one's familiarity with the presenter, the length of time he has been employed by the drawer, his position with the drawer, and the amount of money involved in the transaction.

Taking advantage of the small-town practice that Snyder described, Hemmen managed to embezzle approximately $83,000 from Jo Daviess over a three-year period. There was nothing irregular on the face of the checks themselves, and the monthly bank statements that the bank mailed to Jo Daviess revealed appropriate debits to the company's operating account. As far as Jo Daviess personnel knew, 100 percent of the proceeds of these checks were being transferred into the TT & L account. Company officials did no checking of their own to make sure that the proceeds of the checks were being handled as Hemmen had led them to believe; they trusted him. Because the bank never notified Jo Daviess that Hemmen was instead receiving cash and cashier's checks, and did not confirm his authority to do so, the company remained ignorant of Hemmen's embezzlement. Not until an outside audit was performed in February of 1995 did Jo Daviess discover what Hemmen had done. After coming across a check that had been recorded as a deposit to the TT & L account, auditors discovered that some cash had been returned to the presenter. The disbursement of cash struck the auditors as unusual, and they undertook a comprehensive review of all checks that culminated in the discovery of Hemmen's malfeasance.

Jo Daviess submitted a claim to its insurer, Mutual, which paid the company a total of $82,963. Mutual, as Jo Daviess' subrogee, in turn filed this action against the bank, seeking reimbursement on alternative theories of breach of contract (based on the deposit agreement) and negligence. * * * [Mutual conceded its negligence claim was barred by the Illinois economic loss rule and that claim was dismissed – eds.] The breach of contract claim proceeded to trial.

ESB attempted to pursue a number of defenses to the contract claim that the district court, in advance of trial, determined not to be viable as a matter of law. *First*, ESB wished to show that it had taken the checks underlying Mutual's claim as a holder in due course, and that as a result it took those checks free of all claims – including Mutual's claim for breach of contract. Judge Reinhard determined, however, that the bank could not qualify as a holder in due course because the checks were drawn to the order of the bank, and ESB had distributed the proceeds of the checks to a presenter who lacked authority to withdraw funds from the account. *Second*, ESB sought to prove that Hemmen was a fiduciary who was empowered to instruct the bank as to the disposition of proceeds of checks made payable to the bank, and that, consequently, under the Illinois Fiduciary Obligations Act, ESB was not liable for Hemmen's misdeeds unless it acted in bad faith. This defense was not viable, the district judge reasoned, because there was no evidence that would permit the jury to find Hemmen qualified as a fiduciary vis à vis checks drawn to the bank's order. Hemmen was not an authorized signer on the operating account, and thus had no authority to receive the proceeds of these checks. *Third*, under a theory of pure comparative negligence, ESB wished to show that Jo Daviess' own negligence in employing Hemmen, placing him in charge of the company's financial record-keeping, and in its handling of the checks that Hemmen made payable to the bank's order, was a substantial cause of the company's (and hence Mutual's) loss and therefore reduced ESB's liability. But Judge Reinhard concluded that a defense based on comparative negligence was not available to ESB given its written deposit agreement with Jo Daviess, which agreement did not authorize Hemmen to withdraw funds from the operating account. * * *

With these defenses eliminated, ESB resisted liability at trial on two principal theories. First, in the bank's view, the facts did not establish a breach of any contractual duty owed to Jo Daviess. ESB pointed out that nothing in the deposit agreement specifically addressed the bank's responsibility with respect to checks payable to itself. It further relied on the testimony of Snyder, as well as the testimony of its own officials, for the proposition that reasonable banking practice in small communities permits a bank to release funds to a known employee of the drawer even when that employee is not formally authorized to withdraw funds from an account. Second, ESB contended that Hemmen had either actual or implied authority to receive funds from Jo Daviess' operating account and that the bank had reasonably relied on that authority in disbursing the proceeds of the checks in question to him.

At the close of evidence, and before the case was submitted to the jury, Judge Reinhard concluded that Mutual was entitled to judgment as a matter of law. As a threshold matter, he determined that ESB had a duty, founded on the terms of the deposit agreement as well as the case law, not to disburse the proceeds of a check drawn to the bank's order to anyone other than an authorized signer. Thus, when Hemmen presented such a check to ESB, the bank ought either to have refused the check altogether, accepted it for deposit only, or held the check until such time as an authorized signer presented the check with instructions as to the appropriate disposition of the check proceeds. By electing instead to honor Hemmen's requests for cash and cashier's checks, ESB had breached that duty. Judge Reinhard rejected the notion that a bank's duty vis à vis checks payable to its own order might be different in a small town than it was elsewhere. The same rule must apply everywhere, he reasoned, lest the law of negotiable instruments be placed in jeopardy. Finally, he found that the facts precluded ESB's attempted resort to the theory that Hemmen had actual or implied authority to receive the proceeds of the checks in question. The testimony revealed that ESB made it a practice to release funds to the known employees of its commercial customers, the judge pointed out. Consequently, the bank could not show that it relied on any authority Hemmen might have possessed in releasing the check proceeds to him.

With the question of ESB's liability resolved, the parties quickly stipulated as to the amount of damages. Mutual had claimed total damages of $83,790.48, an amount slightly greater than the sum it paid to Jo Daviess. At trial, questions had arisen as to whether two of the checks that Hemmen had prepared and for which cash had been disbursed – in the amount of $1,000 and the other for $89--might have been for legitimate company purposes. Mutual agreed to drop these checks from its claim and ESB stipulated that the balance of $82,701.48 represented the amount for which it was liable. The court entered judgment in that amount.

* * *

II.

The bulk of ESB's arguments on appeal fall into two principal categories – those directed at the validity and sufficiency of Mutual's claim for breach of contract and those focused on the defenses that the district court rejected. Within the first category, there are three contentions that ESB makes: (1) that the Uniform Commercial Code has displaced the common-law underpinnings of Mutual's claim; (2) that Mutual's claim for breach of contract is at bottom a negligence claim, and as such is barred by the Illinois Supreme Court's decision in *Moorman Mfg. Co. v. National Tank Co.*, 435 N.E.2d 443 (Ill. 1982); and (3) that the evidence with respect to banking practice in small communities at the very least raised a question of fact as to whether ESB breached any duty to Jo Daviess by negotiating the checks drawn to its own order. As for the second category, ESB argues that Judge Reinhard erred in summarily rejecting [two] of its proffered defenses: (1) the holder-in-due-course defense; [and] (2) its defense under the Illinois Fiduciary Obligations Act * * *.

A.

The commercial deposit agreement that governed Jo Daviess' operating account with the bank permitted only authorized signers to withdraw funds from that account. Hemmen, of course, was not an authorized signer; so had the bank, for example, negotiated checks on the operating account that Hemmen had signed, there would be no question that it would be liable for breach of the deposit agreement. But instead, Hemmen used a time-honored method of circumnavigating the signature requirement, by preparing checks payable to the bank and having them signed by an authorized company official, and then directing the bank to issue cash or cashier's checks to him in return.

Although the deposit agreement did not specify how the bank was to handle checks made payable to its own order, implicit in the duty of care that the bank owed to Jo Daviess by virtue of the deposit agreement, was an obligation to verify that Hemmen had the authority to receive the proceeds of such checks and that his instructions vis à vis those proceeds conformed to Jo Daviess' wishes. The rule is well-recognized:

> Where a check drawn to the order of a bank is presented to such bank, and the drawer owes no [debt] to the bank, the bank must see that the proceeds are not misapplied, and cannot without justification divert the proceeds to the use of one other than the drawer, and is authorized to pay the proceeds only to persons specified by the drawer. The bank takes a risk in treating the check as being payable to the bearer, and is placed on inquiry as to the authority of the drawer's agent to receive payment. The duty to inquire of the drawer is not satisfied by making inquiry of the bearer. If the bank assumes without investigation that the instructions of the presenter are those of the drawer, it takes a risk. Where the drawer's agent or one representing himself or herself to be such is not in fact authorized, the bank is liable to the drawer for paying the check to such person.

9 C.J.S. BANKS AND BANKING § 327, at 316-17 (1996). This rule derives from the position of trust that the bank occupies with respect to funds that it has invited its customers to place in its custody.

> The public is invited to use [the bank's] conveniences as places of deposit; it holds itself out as trustworthy for such purposes; when it is named as the payee in a check by a party not indebted to it, it will be presumed that it accepts the same subject to the directions of the drawer and not to the directions of a stranger to the paper who happens to present it.

Douglass v. Wones, 458 N.E.2d 514, 522 (Ill Ct. App. 1983), quoting *Milano v. Sheridan Trust & Sav. Bank*, 242 Ill. App. 362, 368 (1926). Put another way, when a drawer owes nothing to a bank but writes a check payable to the bank's order, the drawer places that check in the bank's custody, with the expectation that the bank will negotiate the check according to the *drawer's* wishes; the bank may not, therefore, treat the check as bearer paper and blindly disburse the proceeds according to the instructions of any individual who happens to present the check to the bank. As *Wones* reflects, Illinois has long embraced this common-law rule. The Land of Lincoln is by no means an exception in that regard. "This general proposition enjoys the unwavering support of a vast body of judicial opinion originating both before and after the creation of the U.C.C." *Bullitt County Bank v. Publishers Printing Co.*, 684 S.W.2d 289, 292 (Ky. Ct. App. 1984).

The evidence admits of no doubt that ESB breached its obligation to ensure that the proceeds of the checks payable to the bank's order were not misapplied. Never did the bank bother to inquire of a Jo Daviess official (someone other than Hemmen himself, of course) whether Hemmen's instructions as to the disposition of these checks were appropriate. Conversely, Jo Daviess never gave the bank any reason to believe that Hemmen was empowered to receive the proceeds of checks made payable to the bank. The bank, aware that Hemmen was the company's controller, simply assumed that he was acting within the scope of his authority. Yet, as the Illinois Supreme Court has observed in a similar context:

> Persons dealing with an assumed agent are bound, at their peril, to ascertain, not only the fact of the agency, but the extent of the agent's authority. They are put upon their guard by the very fact that they are dealing with an agent, and must, at their peril, see to it that the act done by him is within his power.

Paine v. Sheridan Trust & Savings Bank, 174 N.E. 368, 370 (Ill. 1931). This the bank failed to do.

B.

The bank suggests that the common-law duty of care on which Mutual's claim is based has been superseded generally by the Uniform Commercial Code, but we find nothing in the UCC, as adopted by the Illinois legislature, that displaces the common-law rule. The Code itself provides for supplementation by common-law principles, "[u]nless displaced by the particular provisions of this Act." [UCC § 1-103]. Although the scheme perpetrated by Hemmen is a common one, no provision of the Code delineates what a bank's rights and obligations are when a person presents a corporate check payable to the bank and instructs the bank to divert the proceeds of the check to his own benefit. *See Bullitt*, 684 S.W.2d at 291. As we noted earlier, the common-law rule governing this situation springs from the duty of care that the bank owes its depositors. The Code provisions governing the relationship between a bank and its customer recognize and embrace that duty. *See, e.g.*, [UCC §§ 4-103, 4-406]; *see also* [UCC § 3-103(7)] (defining "ordinary care"); *Bullitt*, 684 S.W.2d at 291-92. Indeed, although the Code permits contracting parties to vary the effect of those provisions by agreement, it expressly disallows any term which purports to "disclaim a bank's responsibility for its lack of good faith or failure to exercise ordinary care or limit the measure of damages for the lack or failure." [UCC § 4-103(a)]. Accordingly, courts throughout the country have continued to apply the common-law rule on which Mutual's claim is founded notwithstanding the advent of the UCC. No court that we are aware of has found the rule to be inconsistent with any provision of the Code.

* * *

D.

In an effort to fend off a finding that the bank had breached its contractual duty of care, ESB emphasized below that Elizabeth is a small town and posited that the duty of care on which Mutual's claim is founded must be defined with reference to small-town norms. Recall that Snyder, the bank's expert, testified that is a common practice for banks in small communities to honor a check drawn to the order of the bank when the presenter is known to the bank's staff. Informal practices like this one serve to facilitate the transaction of business by the bank's customers, he explained. Thus, in ESB's view, a small-town bank ought not be obliged to verify the presenter's authority to receive or disburse the proceeds of a check payable to the bank when bank personnel know the presenter, as they did in this case.

Judge Reinhard properly rejected the effort to modify or limit the bank's duty of care when he found, as a matter of law, that ESB had breached its contract with Jo Daviess. The bank cites no case which recognizes an exception to the common-law rule based on the size of the community, the idiosyncrasies of local banking practice, or the bank's familiarity with the presenter, and we have found none. Judge Reinhard reasoned that the rule must be uniform and he was right. The duty of care underlying the rule is one which inheres in every agreement between a bank and its depositor, and over the past century courts have given that rule a clear, simple, and consistent meaning with respect to checks payable to the order of the bank. Indeed, the UCC, to which the bank looks for a number of its appellate arguments, states that one of its purposes is "to make uniform the law among the various jurisdictions." [UCC § 1-102(c)]; *see also* Official UCC Comment regarding 1990 Revision of Article 3 (immediately preceding [UCC § 3-101]) ("The law for payments through checks and which governs other negotiable instruments . . . should be uniform and up-to-date, either through state enactments or Federal preemption. Otherwise, checks as a viable payment system in international and national transactions will be severely hampered and the utility of other negotiable instruments impaired."). The obligation imposed by the common-law rule is not onerous. The very face of the check – payable, as it is, to a bank which is owed nothing by the drawer – alerts the bank to the need for caution. The rule simply requires the bank "not [to] ignore the danger signals inherent in such an attempted negotiation." *Sun 'n Sand, Inc. v. United California Bank*, 582 P.2d 920, 937 (Cal. 1978). We are given no reason to believe that a small-town bank will have a more difficult time than any other bank in verifying the presenter's authority to receive or disburse the proceeds of such a check – if anything, it ought to be easier for a bank in a small community to do so.

E.

Generally speaking, one who takes a negotiable instrument for value, in good faith, and without notice of any claim or defense to the instrument, acquires the rights of a holder in due course. *See* [UCC § 3-302]. As such (with certain exceptions), he holds the instrument free of all claims either to the instrument or its proceeds. *See* [UCC §§ 3-302, 3-306]. In the court below, the bank wished to establish that when it negotiated the Jo Daviess checks that Hemmen presented, it became a holder in due course and was therefore shielded from Mutual's common-law claim. More particularly, it was the bank's theory that Hemmen had breached a fiduciary duty to Jo Daviess by diverting the proceeds of the checks to his own use. In the bank's view, Hemmen's status as a fiduciary brought UCC section 3-307 into play. The terms of that section would have protected the bank so long as it lacked knowledge of the facts constituting his breach of fiduciary duty. *See* [UCC 3-307(b)(4)]. However, the district judge ruled in advance of trial that section 3-307 was inapplicable, because Hemmen did not have authority to receive the proceeds of checks payable to the bank under any circumstance, and so was not a fiduciary in that regard. Judge Reinhard also concluded that the holder-in-due-course defense is not available when a bank permits an individual like Hemmen to divert the proceeds of a check payable to the bank to the use of someone other than the drawer.

On appeal, the bank relies on the holder-in-due-course provisions of the Code to make two arguments. The bank suggests first that three provisions of the Code – sections 3-302, 3-306, and 3-307 – comprehensively address the fraudulent-check scenario presented here and so foreclose Mutual's common-law claim. Alternatively, the bank contends that these provisions supply it with a meritorious defense to the claim, and that Judge Reinhard erred when he excluded the holder-in-due-course concept from the case. Before we turn to these arguments, a brief overview of the provisions on which the bank relies is appropriate.

Each of the three Code provisions that the bank invokes relates either to the rights that a holder in due course enjoys or the conditions under which he qualifies as a holder in due course. Section 3-306 sets forth a basic rule addressing competing claims to a financial instrument or its proceeds:

> A person taking an instrument, other than a person having rights of a holder in due course, is subject to a claim of a property or possessory right in the instrument or its proceeds, including a claim to rescind a negotiation and to recover the instrument or its proceeds. A person having the rights of a holder in due course takes free of the claim to an instrument.

[UCC § 3-306]. Section 3-302(a) in turn spells out the criteria for identifying a holder in due course:

> "[H]older in due course" means the holder of an instrument if:
>
> (1) the instrument when issued or negotiated to the holder does not bear such apparent evidence of forgery or alteration or is not otherwise so irregular or incomplete as to call into question its authenticity, and
>
> (2) the holder took the instrument (i) for value, (ii) in good faith, . . . [and] (v) without notice of any claim to the instrument described in Section 3-306.

Finally, section 3-307 deals with a subset of claims under section 3-306 involving a fiduciary who causes the proceeds of an instrument to be misapplied. *See* [UCC § 3-307 cmt. 2]. Specifically, this provision spells out the various circumstances under which the holder of an instrument (including a bank) can be said to have taken the instrument with notice of the breach of fiduciary duty, such that the holder cannot assert the rights of a holder in due course. As relevant here, the provision requires the holder to have knowledge of (1) the fiduciary status of the person from whom it took the instrument and (2) the facts indicating a breach of fiduciary duty.

As we have said, the bank's first contention is that these interacting provisions of the Code specifically address the scenario presented in this case, and in so doing displace the common-law claim that Mutual has asserted. This particular displacement argument is not one that the bank made below, however, and so we need not, and do not, undertake to resolve this argument on its merits. We do take the opportunity to make two observations in this regard. First, although the three provisions that the bank has cited describe in some detail the circumstances under which the holder takes an instrument free of claims, they are largely silent as to the types of claims that may be asserted when the holder-in-due-course criteria are not satisfied. Section 3-306, for example, indicates simply that a person who is not a holder in due course takes an instrument "subject to a claim of a property or possessory right in the instrument or its proceeds." The commentary to section [3-307] reveals that a claim founded on a breach of fiduciary duty would be one that could be asserted under section 3-306, *see* [UCC § 3-307, cmt. 2], but the Code otherwise offers little elucidation as to the scope of the claims that may be characterized as claims "of a property or possessory right in the instrument or its proceeds," and it does not undertake to identify the elements of such claims. Moreover, assuming that the facts in this case would permit Mutual to assert a claim under section 3-306, the bank has made no attempt to show how and why the common-law claim that Mutual has asserted might be inconsistent with relief under the Code. In short, the case for displacement is anything but obvious, as the courts' continued reliance on the common-law rule itself suggests.

As for the bank's alternative argument, we agree with Judge Reinhard that the nature of Mutual's claim renders the holder-in-due-course defense inapplicable as a matter of law. In order for the bank to qualify as a holder in due course, it must have negotiated the checks without notice of Jo Daviess' (and hence Mutual's) claim. The premise of the common-law claim, however, is that a bank *does* have notice of potential foul play when the employee of a drawer attempts to negotiate a check payable to the order of the bank, and the drawer owes no debt to the bank. The check itself poses an unanswered question as to whom the bank is to pay. The bank knowingly risks liability, then, when it honors the instructions of the presenter without verifying that his instructions reflect the wishes of the drawer. Courts in Illinois and elsewhere have therefore rejected efforts to assert holder-in-due-course status as a defense to this type of claim.

The bank acknowledges that the cases are against it on this point but asserts they are out of date. A substantial re-write of [Article] Three took effect in 1992, and among the new provisions was section 3-307, on which the bank places such emphasis. The bank posits that Hemmen was a fiduciary, and therefore section 3-307, which spells out the level of notice required before a holder is subject to a claim for breach of fiduciary duty, controls the resolution of this case. But section 3-307 defines a "fiduciary" as "an agent, trustee, partner, corporate officer or director, or other representative owing a fiduciary duty *with respect to an instrument*" (emphasis ours). It is undisputed in this case that Hemmen had no authority to direct the proceeds of checks drawn on Jo Daviess' operating account and payable to the bank's order anywhere but into either the payroll account or the TT & L account. The only Jo Daviess account on which Hemmen was an authorized signer was the payroll account, and witnesses testifying on behalf of both parties agreed that Hemmen's authority vis à vis the payroll account did not give him authority to disburse funds from any other account. Hemmen on occasion did negotiate checks on the operating account to replenish the company's petty cash fund, but these checks were always in small amounts ($25 to $50, typically), and the checks were either payable to "cash" or a variant thereof or they contained notations indicating that their purpose was to replenish the petty cash drawer. In sum, as Judge Reinhard recognized, Hemmen may have been a fiduciary for some purposes, but he did not qualify as a fiduciary with respect to checks drawn on the operating account and made payable to the bank's order.

F.

The bank argues next that even if it was contractually obliged to see that the proceeds of checks payable to its own order were not misapplied, the Illinois Fiduciary Obligations Act, 760 ILL. COMP. STAT. 65/1, *et seq.* (the "FOA"), supplies it with a viable defense which, at a minimum, precluded the district court from granting judgment as a matter of law in favor of Mutual. As with its UCC defense, the bank's resort to the FOA rests on the premise that Hemmen was a fiduciary.

"The purpose of the [FOA] is to facilitate banking and financial transactions and place on the principal the burden of employing honest fiduciaries." *County of Macon v. Edgcomb*, 654 N.E.2d 598, 601 (Ill. Ct. App. 1995). Section 1 of the FOA defines "fiduciary" to include a "partner, agent, officer of corporation, public or private, . . . or any other person acting in a fiduciary capacity for any person, trust or estate." 760 ILL. COMP. STAT. 65/1. The statute then goes on to provide, in relevant part:

> A person who in good faith pays or transfers to a fiduciary any money or other property which the fiduciary as such is authorized to receive, is not responsible for the proper application thereof by the fiduciary.

760 ILL. COMP. STAT. 65/2. Broadly speaking, a person will be deemed to have acted in "good faith" for purposes of this provision even if his actions are negligent, so long as he acts honestly and is unaware that the fiduciary is breaching the duty he owes to his principal. *See* 760 ILL. COMP. STAT. 65/1(2). In appropriate circumstances, then, the FOA will supersede the common-law rule and relieve the bank of the duty to see that the proceeds of a check are properly applied, even if the check at issue is one payable to the bank itself.

In *Stephen's Evangelical Lutheran Church v. Seaway Nat'l Bank*, 350 N.E.2d 128 (Ill. Ct. App. 1976), for example, Ferguson, the treasurer of his church, wrote multiple checks on the church's account payable to the bank's order, the bank issued the proceeds to him, and Ferguson then used the funds for his own benefit. The church sued the bank for negligence and conversion and prevailed at trial. The appellate court reversed, however, concluding that because Ferguson qualified as a fiduciary who was authorized to receive and disburse church funds, the FOA absolved the bank of liability for releasing money to him. Naturally, as treasurer, Ferguson maintained the church's financial books and records, including its checking account. More importantly, the church had executed a bank resolution that not only authorized Ferguson to sign checks on the bank's behalf, but also authorized him, and only him, to supply the bank with directions as to disbursement of church funds. The resolution also expressly authorized the bank to honor checks drawn to Ferguson's order, without further inquiry concerning his authority or the designated use of the check proceeds. 350 N.E.2d at 129. This made application of the FOA straightforward. * * *

The bank suggests that this case is no different than *St. Stephen's*. In its view, the undisputed facts establish that Hemmen was Jo Daviess' agent, thus rendering him a fiduciary for purposes of the FOA. The bank points out that Hemmen handled the bookkeeping for the company, made deposits, had signature authority over the payroll account, had authority to cash checks drawn on the operating account in amounts of up to $100 to replenish the petty cash fund, and, most importantly, had actual authority to tell the bank how to distribute the proceeds of checks made payable to the bank. Hemmen regularly exercised the latter authority when he presented checks, drawn on the operating account and payable to the bank's order, and directed that the proceeds be deposited into the TT & L account, for example.

However, it is the agent's specific authority to receive the proceeds of checks drawn to the bank's order which is crucial to the bank's ability to invoke the FOA. The very language of the statute highlights this point. Section 1 defines the term "fiduciary" as, inter alia, an "agent . . . or any other person *acting in a fiduciary capacity* for any person." 760 ILL. COMP. STAT. 65/1 (emphasis ours). The reference to the capacity in which the agent is acting suggests that his status as a fiduciary depends upon the particular activity in which he is engaged. Moreover, section 2 grants a person protection when he distributes to a fiduciary in good faith "any money or other property *which the fiduciary as such is authorized to receive.*" 760 ILL. COMP. STAT. 65/2 (emphasis ours). This language reiterates the need to focus on the agent's authority with respect to the particular transaction at issue. In other words, as Judge Reinhard recognized, the fact that Hemmen may have been a fiduciary for some purposes did not render him a fiduciary for all purposes. Section 2 will not absolve the bank of liability for the presenter's misapplication of the check proceeds unless the evidence reveals that he was authorized to receive those proceeds. In *St. Stephen's*, the treasurer was so authorized. The same was true in *Johnson v. Citizens Nat'l Bank of Decatur*, 334 N.E.2d 295 (Ill. Ct. App.

1975), where an individual who was authorized to draft checks in his employer's name made a series of them payable to the bank's order and deposited the proceeds into his personal checking account. (Citation omitted). By contrast, in *Empire Moving & Warehouse Corp. v. Hyde Park Bank & Trust Co.,* 357 N.E.2d 1196, 1202 (Ill. Ct. App. 1976), the errant bookkeeper who took a series of checks issued to his employer, endorsed them over to a bank with a rubber stamp, obtained cash in exchange, and then absconded with the proceeds, was not an authorized signer on his employer's bank account. He did have the authority to make deposits into the account; moreover, company employees would often endorse their paychecks over to the company, and the bookkeeper's routine and accepted practice was to endorse them with the same rubber stamp that he eventually put to his own use, present them to the bank, and receive cash in return. In the court's view, however, the bookkeeper's authority in these respects was not sufficient to render him a fiduciary and therefore to relieve the bank of responsibility for cashing the checks that he had made payable to the bank:

> The record shows that he was employed as a bookkeeper and that his authority extended only to depositing checks payable to plaintiff in plaintiff's bank account. He had no authority to cash checks payable to plaintiff or to receive cash proceeds of such checks. . . . Any negotiation of checks payable to plaintiff would necessarily be governed by the corporate resolution lodged with [the bank]. To exonerate [the bank] here it would be obliged to prove that [the bookkeeper] came into possession of the proceeds of the checks as a fiduciary and that he had authority to endorse the checks.

357 N.E.2d at 1202.

Here, no evidence demonstrates that Hemmen was ever given broad authority to receive cash on checks drawn to the bank's order, or to divert funds from the operating account to anywhere but the payroll or TT & L accounts, and it is Hemmen's lack of authority in this regard that precludes the bank's resort to Section 2. The fact that Hemmen could order funds moved from the operating account to one of the company's other accounts is of no moment; what is key is his authority to have funds from the operating account issued to himself. The simple fact is that Hemmen was never an authorized signer on the operating account. That he had signature authority on Jo Daviess' payroll account may have rendered him a fiduciary as to that account, but no other. The witnesses were in agreement on that point. The sole manifestation of Hemmen's authority to receive money from the operating account was his occasional negotiation of checks made out to petty cash, which were invariably for $100 or less. We see nothing in the informal practice of cashing checks to replenish the petty cash fund that would have signaled to the bank that Hemmen had the equivalent of signature authority on the operating account. The checks at issue here were payable to the bank's order--a fact which, as we have discussed, put the bank on notice of the need to inquire into the presenter's authority – and in contrast to the checks for petty cash, they contained no indication that their purpose was to replenish the petty cash fund. Also unlike the petty cash transactions (the largest of which involved a check for $87.02), these checks typically involved substantial sums of money. The first of the checks at issue in this case, for example, was for the sum of $2,997. The entire amount of that check was disbursed to Hemmen in the form of two cashier's checks payable to his creditors. In short, whatever limited authority Hemmen may have enjoyed with respect to petty cash withdrawals did not give him authority to receive or disburse the proceeds of any and all checks payable to the bank's order. The bank thus took a risk in negotiating the checks for which it may now be held to account. As Judge Reinhard recognized, the fact that Hemmen may have been a fiduciary for some purposes did not render him a fiduciary for all purposes. Because he had no signature authority on the operating account, he cannot be treated as a fiduciary with respect to checks made payable to the bank's order. * * *

III.

For the foregoing reasons, we AFFIRM the district court's decision to grant judgment as a matter of law in favor of Mutual on its contract claim against ESB. * * * Mutual shall recover its costs of appeal. We commend Judge Reinhard for his able handling of this case.

––––––––––––

Now consider the application of property-based claims to instruments, the ability to bring a conversion cause of action, and the provision on notice of breach of fiduciary obligations, to analyze the following problem.

Problem 18-5

Terry is the trustee for a trust of a minor child, Bruce. On occasion, Terry has to deposit checks to the trust bank account maintained at State Bank. Terry is listed as the trustee on the account and the account is designated as a trust account for benefit of Bruce. Terry also maintains Terry's personal bank account at State Bank.

A. Terry took a check made payable to Bruce, indorsed the check on the back as follows: "Bruce, by *Terry*, trustee." Terry deposited the check to his personal bank account. State Bank gave Terry credit in Terry's account for the amount of the check. Terry withdrew the funds and disappeared. The new trustee, Natalie, asserted a right to return of the check or the proceeds from State Bank. Is State Bank a holder in due course of that check?

B. Terry wrote a check on the trust account, payable to Terry, signed as follows: "Bruce by *Terry*, trustee." Terry indorsed the check in blank and without recourse, deposited the check to his personal bank account, and withdrew the credited funds from the account. The new trustee, Natalie, asserted a right to return of the check or the proceeds from State Bank. Is State Bank a holder in due course of that check?

C. Terry wrote a check on the trust account payable to Tailor, signed as follows: "Bruce by *Terry*, trustee." Terry gave the check to Tailor to pay for some suits that Terry purchased for himself.
    1. State Bank honored the check when it was presented for payment and debited the trust bank account. Is the new trustee, Natalie, entitled to have State Bank re-credit the account for the amount of the check?
    2. State Bank dishonored the check when it was presented because the new trustee, Natalie, stopped payment on the check. Tailor sued Bruce on the drawer's contract. Natalie asserted that Bruce does not have to pay the check. Is she correct? Is Tailor a holder in due course of the check?

D. Annabel wrote a check drawn on Annabel's account payable to Barney. Barney indorsed the check as follows: "Pay to Terry in trust for Bruce, *Barney*." Terry indorsed the check, deposited the check into his personal bank account, withdrew the funds, and disappeared. The new trustee, Natalie, asserted a claim to the check or the proceeds. Is State Bank a holder in due course of that check? *See* UCC § 3-206(d).

Problem 18-6

Belinda has a checking account at State Bank. Francis is Belinda's financial advisor. Francis convinced Belinda to place some funds in a long term certificate of deposit being offered by State Bank. Belinda wrote a check payable to the order of State Bank. Francis took the check to State Bank, obtained cash but did not buy a certificate of deposit with the cash. Instead, Francis absconded with the cash. Belinda has sued State Bank to recover the loss. Is State Bank a holder in due course of the check?

SECTION 4. WARRANTY LIABILITY

As we have already learned in Chapter Fifteen, the right to payment reified in a negotiable instrument may be transferred to another person through transfer of the instrument. Because the negotiable instrument is an item of personal property, the usual rules that govern transfers of personal property also govern instruments. The usual rule for transfer of personal property is that the transferee takes all the rights that the transferor has, and no more. We have already encountered this concept of derivative rights – a fundamental feature of the law of personal property – when we examined UCC § 3-203.

Just as a person who transfers goods ordinarily makes a warranty of title and may make one or more warranties of quality relating to the goods transferred, *see* UCC §§ 2-312 through 2-315, a person who transfers a negotiable instrument ordinarily makes warranties about the title and quality of the instrument. UCC Article 3 provides for two different types of warranties: transfer warranties and presentment warranties. UCC §§ 3-416, 3-417. We have already considered transfer and presentment warranties in Chapter Sixteen when discussing the bank collection system. *See* UCC §§ 4-207, 4-208. Here we explore the transfer and presentment warranties provided in UCC Article 3. As we do so, identify the differences, if any, between the transfer warranties provided in UCC § 3-416 and in UCC § 4-207. In addition, identify the differences, if any, between the presentment warranties provided in UCC § 3-417 and in UCC § 4-208.

Warranty liability arising out of the transfer or presentment on an instrument is a separate obligation unconnected to contract liability on an instrument. A person need not sign an instrument to incur the warranty liability. As you study the transfer and presentment warranties in UCC Article 3, make sure that you can answer the following questions: Who has made the warranty? Was the warranty adequately disclaimed? To whom was the warranty made? What warranty was made? What warranty was breached? Who breached the warranty? What must the person to whom the warranty was made do to preserve a cause of action for breach of warranty?

A. Transfer Warranties

Transfer warranties are made upon a transfer of the instrument. **Read UCC § 3-416.** Review UCC § 3-203, which defines "transfer." To make a transfer warranty, there of course must first be a transfer. Notice that to make a transfer warranty under UCC § 3-416, the transfer has to be for consideration. Review UCC § 3-303(b), which defines "consideration." In addition, for the transfer to "run with the negotiable instrument" to subsequent transferees beyond the first transferee, the transferor must indorse the instrument.

The transfer warranties are stated in UCC § 3-416(a). These warranties are promises made without regard to what the transferor knows or has reason to know. For example, the transferor warrants that the transferor is a person entitled to enforce the instrument, and does so even if the transferor has no reason to suspect that the transferor has failed to achieve that status. This is a form of strict liability.

Subsection (b) addresses the damages available for breach of a transfer warranty and subsection (d) addresses when a cause of action for breach of a transfer warranty accrues. Note that the statute of limitations on a claim for breach of a transfer warranty claims is provided in UCC § 3-118(g). UCC § 3-416(c) provides that notice of a claim for breach of a transfer warranty must be given to the warrantor within a certain time period or the liability is discharged to the extent the delay caused a loss. Subsection (c) also addresses in abbreviated form the ability of a transferor to disclaim warranty liability. *See* UCC § 3-416, cmt. 5. The transferor may not disclaim transfer warranties if the instrument is a check. The use of the phrase "without recourse," which is sufficient to disclaimer contract liability on an instrument, is not sufficient to disclaim the transfer warranties. *See* UCC § 3-416, cmt. 3.

B. Presentment Warranties

Presentment warranties are made to the person paying the instrument or accepting a draft. **Read UCC § 3-417.**

Subsection (a) addresses presentment warranties made to a drawee regarding an unaccepted draft. Review the meaning of "acceptance" in UCC § 3-409(a). UCC § 3-417(d) addresses presentment warranties that arise in presentations made to persons obligated to pay the instrument. The only persons obligated to pay an instrument (that is, have contract liability on an instrument) are a drawee of an accepted draft, drawer, maker, or indorser. Presentment of an instrument is *not* a transfer of an instrument. **Review UCC § 3-501 on presentment and UCC § 3-203 on transfer.** Thus presentment warranties are *not* made to transferees. Transfer warranties are *not* made to drawees, drawers, makers, and indorsers when the instrument is presented to them for payment.

Presentment warranties are made only when the person to whom presentment is made actually pays the instrument, or in the case of a drawee to whom presentment is made for acceptance, when the drawee actually accepts the draft. The person presenting the negotiable instrument and all prior transferors of the instrument make the presentment warranties. The drawee of a draft that pays, or accepts, the draft is the beneficiary of the warranties stated in UCC § 3-417(a). All other persons to whom presentment is made and who pay their contract obligation on the instrument get the warranty stated in subsection (d)(1). Notice that the warranties in subsection (a) are more extensive than the simple warranty in subsection (d).

Subsections (b) and (c) further address the rights of a drawee to whom a presentment warranty is made including certain defenses that the warrantor may assert to the breach of warranty claim and the amount the drawee may recover on the breach of warranty claim. Subsection (d) addresses the rights of a payor of a dishonored draft or other instrument. Subsection (e) and (f) address notice of the breach of warranty claim and accrual of the cause of action. Just as with transfer warranties, presentment warranties may be disclaimed by specific language to that effect except as limited by subsection (e).

Problem 18-7

Alyssa wrote a check payable to Barry drawn on First Bank. Barry signed his name on the back and lost the check. Claire picked up the check, went to Downtown Check Cashing, Inc. and received cash for the check. Downtown presented the check to First Bank for payment.

A. Assume that First Bank did not pay the check because Alyssa stopped payment when Barry told Alyssa that the check was lost. Downtown has possession of the check after First Bank dishonored the check.
    1. Who has contract liability on the check and to whom is such contract liability owed?
    2. Who, if anyone, made transfer warranties and to whom were such warranties made?
    3. If transfer warranties were made, were any of them breached?
    4. Who, if anyone, made presentment warranties? If anyone did make presentment warranties, were they breached?
    5. Does Barry have a cause of action against Claire or Downtown?

B. Assume that First Bank paid the check when Downtown presented the check to First Bank because Alyssa did not stop payment. How, if at all, does that change your analysis of the questions in Part A?

C. Assume that instead of losing the check, Barry gave it to Claire in exchange for a table. He forgot to indorse the check, so Claire wrote *"Barry"* on the back of the check, without Barry's permission or authority. Claire gave the check to Downtown and received cash for the check. First Bank paid the check when it was presented. Who has made transfer and presentment warranties, to whom were they made, and were any warranties breached?

Problem 18-8

Andrew issued a demand negotiable note for $500 payable to the order of Buy More Co. in payment of a debt owed to Buy More. Buy More sold the note to City Bank for $400, indorsing the note on the back as follows: "Pay to the order of City Bank, Buy More by *Teresa*, Treasurer, without recourse." Victor, the vice president of City Bank skillfully altered the amount of the note to $800, and sold the note to Downtown Bank for $700, pocketing $200, and turning $500 over to City Bank. Victor indorsed the note as follows, "City Bank." Downtown Bank presented the note to Andrew.

A. Has anyone made or breached any transfer warranties to anyone else?

B. Has anyone made or breached any presentment warranties to anyone else?

C. What procedural requirements must be met to bring a lawsuit for breach of transfer or presentment warranties? What is the amount of the recovery?

We will return to presentment and transfer warranties when we learn about fraud, forgery, and alteration of instruments in Chapter Nineteen.

SECTION 5.   REVIEW

Problem 18-9

Connie is the chief financial officer of Auto Resellers, Inc. ("ARI"). Connie is authorized to write checks on behalf of ARI. Connie wrote three checks drawn on ARI's checking account at State Bank. Each check was imprinted with ARI's name and address. Connie signed each check on the drawer's line as follows: "Connie, CFO."

Check No. 9000 was payable to the order of Connie for $5,000. Connie took the check to National Bank and deposited it to a checking account she holds jointly with her husband, Sean.

Check No. 9001 was payable to the order of Sean for $6,000. Sean is Connie's spouse. Sean indorsed the check in blank and deposited it to their joint checking account at National Bank.

Check No. 9002 was payable to the order of First Bank for $9,000. Connie owed First Bank $3,000 on a personal loan. Connie took the check to First Bank and paid off the loan and received $6,000 back from First Bank.

Neither Connie nor Sean was owed any funds by ARI. ARI's president found out what Connie had done and, after firing Connie, sued National

Bank and First Bank to recover the funds. Evaluate ARI's causes of action against each defendant.

In the event that National Bank or First Bank is liable to and pays ARI, what rights would the liable bank have under UCC Article 3 to recover from Connie or Sean?

CHAPTER NINETEEN

ALLOCATION OF LOSS FROM WRONGDOING WHEN USING NEGOTIABLE INSTRUMENTS

SECTION 1.   INTRODUCTION

This Chapter addresses how the rules studied in Chapters Fourteen through Eighteen allocate the loss when there is wrongdoing in connection with a negotiable instrument. In one sense, this Chapter is a review. For example, we dealt with unauthorized or forged signatures in Chapters Fifteen, Sixteen and Eighteen. We also dealt with lost or stolen instruments in each of those Chapters. However, in another sense this Chapter is new. We now take the rules studied in those previous Chapters and see how they operate collectively to allocate the loss or risk of wrongdoing. This is – unfortunately but necessarily – a complex process. The key point to understand at the outset is that we are, with a few exceptions, not exploring new rules; instead we applying rules previously studied in a systematic manner. In short, this Chapter introduces a methodology to follow when dealing with wrongdoing in connection with a negotiable instrument. To correctly and reliably determine who bears the associated loss, it is important to follow this methodology. To illustrate this methodology, we will work through two simple examples.

> *Example 1.* A thief steals a blank check from Abbot, forges Abbot's signature as drawer and makes the check payable to cash. The thief takes the check to the drawee bank and obtains payment. The drawee bank debits Abbot's checking account for the amount of the check. Abbot naturally protests. Does the drawee bank have to re-credit Abbot's account? If the drawee bank does re-credit the account, does it have rights against anyone else to recover the amount the thief stole?

Step One: Determine who has the loss. At present, the loss has fallen on Abbot. Abbot's checking account has been debited for the amount of the check and Abbot has received nothing in exchange. The loss will remain with Abbott unless he is able to recover the amount of the forged check from someone else.

Step Two: Consider the rights of the person bearing the loss as against the wrongdoer or other entities. First consider the rights of Abbot against the thief, who has done two things: (i) stolen a check blank; and (ii) used that check blank to forge a check and acquire cash, thereby causing Abbot to suffer a loss. Abbot's rights against the thief would be based on common-law claims for conversion or theft. Review Chapter Eighteen, Section 3. No doubt Abbot's legal claim against the thief would be a strong one. However, in most situations involving wrongdoing, the wrongdoer will be liable but will also either be missing (having absconded with the fruits of the wrongdoing) or have no recoverable assets (be in jail, insolvent, *etc.*). Thus while Abbot has common-law rights against the thief, enforcing those rights is unlikely to lead to recovery. As a result, the loss will ordinarily fall on someone who is not the wrongdoer.

Now consider a person other than the thief to whom the loss can be passed and a legal theory for passing that loss. The loss in this scenario will either stay with Abbott (because his account has been debited) or Abbot will seek to pass the loss to the drawee bank. Abbott's legal theory is based upon the properly payable rule, *see* UCC § 4-401 (Chapter Sixteen). The forged drawer's signature provides Abbott an argument as against the drawee bank that the check was not properly payable and thus the drawee bank should recredit Abbott's account for the amount of the forged check.

Step Three: Identify the possible defenses to that liability. Does the drawee bank have any defenses to the properly payable argument? One defense that we considered in Chapter Sixteen is that the deposit agreement between Abbott and the drawee bank may modify the parameters of what is "properly payable," UCC § 4-103, so that the check is properly payable as defined by the bank-customer agreement.[1]

Another defense that we considered in Chapter Fifteen is based upon ratification of the unauthorized drawer's signature. *See* UCC § 3-403(a) and cmt 3. If that defense were factually viable – and nothing in the brief facts provided suggests that it is – Abbot would be deemed to have adopted the thief's signature as his own, thereby making the check properly payable.

---

[1] One of the ways drawee banks attempt to shift losses on drafts that are paid but have a forged drawer's signature is through the use of positive pay agreements. A positive pay agreement is an agreement between the drawee bank and its customer that the customer will send a list of authorized checks and the drawee bank will only pay checks that are on that list. If a check is not on the list, the drawee bank reports the check presented for payment as an exception. The customer then instructs the drawee bank whether to pay that check. If the drawee bank follows the positive pay process and pays a check according to the process, the agreement usually provides that the drawee bank is not liable for the payment even if other law would put that liability on the bank. *See* Subcommittee on Payments, UCC Committee Business Law Section, American Bar Association, *Deterring Check Fraud: The Model Positive Pay Services Agreement and Commentary*, 54 BUS. LAW. 637 (1999).

Now consider two additional defenses that we have not previously considered that the drawee bank may assert. First, the drawee bank may defend on the basis that Abbott is precluded from asserting a claim based on the forged signature because Abbot was negligent and that negligence substantially contributed to the forgery. **Read UCC § 3-406(a).**[2] This provision operates like a statutory form of estoppel, preventing the negligent person from asserting the forgery or alteration against anyone who paid the instrument or took the instrument in good faith and for value or collection.[3] What facts would support an argument that Abbott failed to exercise ordinary care and that failure substantially contributed to the forgery? Presumably, if Abbot left his checkbook on a table in the food court of a crowded mall shortly after reading a newspaper story about rampant check forgeries at the mall, Abbot's action would have been a "failure to exercise ordinary care" that "substantially contribute[d]" to the forging of Abbot's signature. But what if Abbot left the checkbook in an unlocked door of his desk at home, from where it was taken by a roommate, houseguest, or babysitter?[4] As you may suspect, determinations about negligence are rather idiosyncratic and depend heavily on the particular facts of each case.[5]

Even if the drawee bank proves that Abbot acted negligently and that his negligence substantially contributed to the forgery, if Abbot can show that the drawee bank was also negligent, then the loss will be apportioned among them in proportion to which their negligence contributed to the loss. **Read UCC § 3-406(b) and the definition of "ordinary care" in UCC § 3-103.** This provision imposes a comparative negligence rule. What types of action by the drawee bank would

---

[2] Notice that UCC § 3-406 refers to "forged" signatures, not "unauthorized" signatures. Although all forged signatures are unauthorized, not all unauthorized signatures are forgeries. *See* UCC § 3-406, cmt. 2.

[3] Common law principles such as waiver and estoppel may also come into play. UCC § 1-103.

[4] *See Walker v. First Home Sav. Bank*, 274 S.W.3d 609 (Mo. Ct. App. 2009) (considering failure to safeguard checks as lack of ordinary care); *Bank of Texas v. VR Elec., Inc.*, 276 S.W.3d 671 (Tex. Ct. App. 2009) (same). *Cf. Chesler v. Dollar Bank, Fed. Sav. Bank*, 2011 WL 1346948 (Ohio Ct. App. 2011) (keeping check book in unlocked drawer was not lack of ordinary care).

[5] *See Distributor Label Prods., Inc. v. Fleet Nat'l Bank*, 950 A.2d 939 (N.J. Super. A.D. 2008) (employer's failure to supervise employee was negligent, and thus employer precluded from asserting forgery that would make check not properly payable).

demonstrate a failure to exercise ordinary care? Given the number of checks that a drawee bank must process daily, what steps should it be expected to take to discover a forged drawer's signature?

A final defense for the drawee bank comes from the "bank statement rule." **Read UCC § 4-406.** If the drawee bank "sends or makes available"[6] to the drawer a statement of the customer's account, the drawer fails to notify the drawee bank with reasonable promptness of any forged drawer's signature or alteration relating to the items paid, and this failure caused the drawee bank to suffer a loss, the drawer is precluded from asserting the forged drawer's signature or alteration as a reason why the check was unauthorized and therefore not properly payable. This preclusion is also subject to the loss-sharing principle stated in subsection (e).[7] Preclusion is not available at all unless the drawee bank acted in good faith.

To illustrate how this provision operates, assume Abbot received his bank statement and failed to notify the bank of the forged check for three months. Under UCC § 4-406(d)(1), if the drawee bank can demonstrate that Abbot's failure to notify the bank was a breach of Abbot's obligation under UCC § 4-406(c) and that such failure caused the drawee bank a loss, then Abbot is precluded from asserting the forgery, subject to the loss-sharing principle stated in subsection (e) if the drawee bank was in good faith but failed to exercise ordinary care which substantially contributed to the loss. How could the delay have caused the drawee bank to suffer the loss, given that the drawee bank had paid the check before sending the statement to Abbot? Perhaps the drawee bank would may have been able to track down and recover from the thief if Abbot had provided prompt notice. Absent that or something similar, though, the drawee bank will have difficulty using the preclusive effect of UCC § 4-406(d)(1). It is more common for drawee banks to use UCC § 4-406(d)(2), which applies when the same wrongdoer forges or alters

---

[6] Remember, "sent" does not mean "received." *Compare* UCC § 1-201(b)(36) (defining "send") *with* UCC § 1-202(e) (indicating when notice or notification is "receive[d]"). In addition, courts have held that making statements available for pickup by the customer is sufficient. *See Union Planters Bank v. Rogers*, 912 So. 2d 116 (Miss. 2005); *Spacemakers of Am., Inc. v. SunTrust Bank*, 609 S.E.2d 683 (Ga. Ct. App. 2005); *Tatis v. US Bancorp*, 473 F.3d 672 (6th Cir. 2007); *Jefferson State Bank v. Lenk*, 323 S.W.3d 146 (Tex. 2010).

[7] *See L & B Real Estate v. Wells Fargo Bank*, 2008 WL2486815 (Cal. Ct. App. 2008) (bank exercised ordinary care when it set at first a $35,000 threshold and later a $25,000 threshold for physical examination of checks based upon national banking practices).

multiple items, and the drawee bank pays some after the drawer should have notified the drawee bank of the earlier forgeries or alterations.

The bank statement rule of UCC § 4-406 also includes something like a statute of a limitations. Pursuant to subsection (f), the drawer has one year to discover and report an unauthorized signature or be precluded from asserting the lack of authorization as a basis for recovery.[8] Subsection (f) is independent from subsection (d), and thus is not subject to the comparative fault rule of subsection (e).[9] Moreover, the one-year period can be reduced by agreement. *See* UCC § 4-103(a). To illustrate how this works, assume that Abbot's agreement with the drawee bank provided that "the customer must report any unauthorized transactions within 30 days of when the bank statement is made available to the customer" and that failure to do so bars any action to re-credit the account. Abbot would be precluded from asserting the forgery and contesting the properly payable nature of the check if he failed to meet the 30-day deadline.

Step Four: If the loss is likely to be passed from the initial loss holder to another entity, evaluate whether that entity can pass the liability to another person and that person's defenses to that liability. Now assume that Abbot was successful in his action against the drawee bank based upon the analysis above. The drawee bank re-credits Abbot's deposit account for the amount of the check. Now the drawee bank is left holding the loss. So, we must consider against whom (other than Abbot, whose rights against the drawee bank we have already analyzed) the drawee bank may have a right to recover and what the basis of that recovery would be.

As we learned in Chapter Sixteen and reviewed again in Chapter Eighteen, a drawee bank that has paid a draft has received presentment warranties from the presenter and prior transferors. UCC §§ 3-417, 4-208. Unfortunately for the

---

[8] Courts have consistently upheld shortening this time period through provisions in the bank-customer agreement. *See Stowell v. Cloquet Co-op Credit Union*, 557 N.W.2d 567 (Minn. 1997); *American Airlines Employees Fed. Credit Union v. Martin*, 29 S.W.3d 86 (Tex. 2000); *National Title Ins. Corp. v. First Union Nat'l Bank*, 559 S.E.2d 668 (Va. 2002); *Freese v. Regions Bank*, 644 S.E.2d 549 (Ga. Ct. App. 2007); *Peters v. Riggs Nat'l Bank*, 942 A.2d 1163 (D.C. 2008); *Groue v. Capital One*, 47 So. 3d 1038 (La. Ct. App. 2010); *Napleton v. Great Lakes Bank*, 945 N.E.2d 111 (Ill. Ct. App. 2011).

[9] At least one court has held that the bank need not have acted in good faith to take advantage of the preclusion in subsection (f). *Pingis v. Regions Bank*, 977 So. 2d 446 (Ala. 2007).

drawee bank in our simple example, the only person who is a potential defendant here is the thief. Even if the drawee bank found the thief, the thief did not breach the presentment warranties.[10]

A better avenue for recovery for the drawee bank against the thief is restitution, UCC § 3-418(a). Review Chapter Sixteen. The thief will not be able to successfully assert the defense found in UCC § 3-418(c). If the thief can be found and has assets, the drawee bank will be successful in moving the loss to the thief. Absent that success, the drawee bank will be left holding the loss.

Methodology. This short example – with a long explanation – models the analysis required to determine on whom the loss from misconduct involving a negotiable instrument will fall. Let us break down the steps and restate them in general terms.

First, start with the person who has initially suffered a loss as a result of the wrongdoing and identify all potential defendants. In the example above, Abbot suffered the loss and had two potential defendants: the thief and the drawee bank.

Second, identify and evaluate the plaintiff's potential causes of action (note the plural, each cause of action must be evaluated) against each defendant. In the example above, Abbot had a common-law cause of action against the thief for theft or conversion. Abbot's cause of action against the drawee bank was for debiting Abbot's deposit account for the unauthorized check, in violation the properly payable rule of UCC § 4-401(a). Note, in evaluating each cause of action, be sure to ascertain whether the plaintiff can prove all the essential elements of the claim. For example, only a "customer" has a cause of action against the drawee bank based upon the properly payable rule. Thus, if Abbot were not a customer of the drawee bank, Abbot could not have a claim based on that rule.

STOP! Review the causes of action covered in Chapters Fourteen through Eighteen. *For each cause of action, identify who is the correct plaintiff and who are the potential defendants.*

Third, for each meritorious cause of action, identify and evaluate the defendant's potential affirmative defenses to that cause of action. For example, the thief is unlikely to have a viable defense to Abbot's cause of action for theft or conversion (other than a statute of limitations defense). However, as outlined

---

[10] While the drawee bank also has the ability to be subrogated to rights of the drawer or a holder, UCC § 4-407, those subrogation rights do not afford the drawee any significant advantages in this scenario.

above, the drawee bank has at least four potential defenses to the claim that a check was not properly payable.

STOP! *For each cause of action you have identified, list all possible defenses that could be asserted by a defendant to that particular cause of action. Review UCC § 3-305 cmt. 2.*

Fourth, if the person who initially held the loss can pass the loss along to one or more defendants, return to step one and treat each such defendant as the person on whom the loss has fallen. As demonstrated in the discussion of Example 1, if the drawee bank ends up having to re-credit Abbot's account, the drawee bank will undoubtedly seek to pass the loss to someone else. So, the analysis starts anew. What causes of action does the loss-holding defendant have against the other actors involved in the drama (other than the initial plaintiff)? What are the potential affirmative defenses to the causes of action and are those defenses viable?

This loss-passing approach to allocating the risks of wrongdoing resembles the game of "hot potato" you may have played as a child. No one wants to hold the loss (the "hot potato") and thus when the loss is passed to a person, that person attempts to pass the loss on to someone else. The one left holding the "hot potato" bears the ultimate loss on the instrument. Unlike the game of "hot potato," however, where the passer has to pick a single person to whom to throw, plaintiffs playing the "pass the loss" game usually sue as many people as possible at the same time, hoping to be able to pass the loss to at least one of the defendants. Savvy plaintiffs will not only sue multiple defendants, they will also assert multiple causes of action against each defendant. Such a strategy helps to increase the plaintiff's likelihood of success in passing the loss.

Example 1 is relatively simple because it involved only three actors: Abbot, the drawee bank, and the thief. In most cases involving wrongdoing, the facts and the analysis are more complex because there are more actors, and in each relationship there may not only be multiple causes of action, but the defendant may also have counterclaims against that plaintiff. Consider the following more complex problem.

Example 2. Alice signs a check as drawer, payable to Payee. Payee loses the check. Finder finds the check, forges Payee's indorsement, and deposits the check at Finder's bank. Payee notifies Alice that the check was lost and Alice stops payment through a timely stop order at the drawee bank. When the check is presented at the drawee bank, the check is dishonored and eventually returned to Finder's depositary bank.

Analysis. There are at least the following actors in this problem: Alice, Payee, Finder, the depositary bank, and the drawee bank. In all likelihood, though, other banks or intermediaries would be interposed between the depositary bank and the drawee bank on both the forward collection path and the check return path. However, we will ignore these intermediaries for sake of this illustration.

There are ten two-party relationships among the five actors,[11] and each relationship is one that must potentially be analyzed. In each relationship, there may be multiple causes of actions, each with multiple possible defenses. It is extremely easy to get confused and to arrive at a wrong conclusion unless the analysis is conducted carefully and methodically. There are no shortcuts, although there is typically only one "right" place to start, that is, with the person that is initially holding the loss. That is because if that person cannot recover from anyone else, then you can stop; you need not analyze the relationship between any two other parties.

In this example, the depositary bank is holding the loss because it will have had to settle with the returning bank when the check is returned. The depositary bank has at least four possible defendants: Alice, Payee, Finder, and the drawee bank, with different causes of action against each. If you created an outline of the depositary's bank's potential claims against those four defendants, it may look something like this.

Defendant	Potential Causes of Action & Counterclaims
Alice	Drawer's contract liability on instrument (Chapter Fifteen)
Payee	Indorser's contract liability on instrument (Chapter Fifteen) Payee's counterclaim based upon a claim to instrument (Chapter Eighteen)
Finder	Indorser's contract liability on instrument (Chapter Fifteen) Liability for charge back of dishonored item (Chapter Sixteen) Liability for breach of transfer warranty (Chapter Sixteen)

---

[11]   Depositary bank v. Alice,   Alice v. Payee
         Depositary bank v. Payee   Alice v. Finder
         Depositary bank v. Finder   Alice v. Drawee bank
         Depositary bank v. Drawee bank

                                            Payee v. Drawee bank
         Finder v. Drawee bank   Payee v. Finder

For those who are mathematically inclined, the number of two-party relationships in a group of n people is: $(n^2 - n)/2$.

Defendant	Potential Causes of Action & Counterclaims
Drawee bank	Final payment (Chapter Sixteen) Accountability (Chapter Sixteen) Failure to return expeditiously (Chapter Sixteen)

For each cause of action, the plaintiff (the depositary bank) would have to prove the elements of the prima facie case. The defendant may attempt to rebut one or more of those elements. In addition, the defendant might raise affirmative defenses to each cause of action or assert one or more counterclaims (to which the plaintiff may have defenses).

Each defendant, if it has the loss passed to it, will then have an incentive to pass the loss to someone else. Thus a careful analysis may need to consider the causes of action and counterclaims available in each of the following other relationships: Alice v. Payee, Alice v. Finder, Alice v. Drawee bank; Finder v. Drawee bank, Finder v. Payee; and Drawee bank v. Payee. In addition, as to each cause of action or counterclaim, the opposing party's defenses will need to be considered.

Only after completely analyzing the causes of action, counterclaims, and defenses relating to each of the ten relationships will you be able to reliably determine who bears the loss for this type of wrongdoing, when recovery against the wrongdoer is not likely. Note, you might be inclined to think that some relationships can be ignored, if say the loss cannot be passed by the party who bears it initially. However, the chance of error or confusion is sufficiently high that it is advisable to consider all the relationships. A survey of the published decisions bears this out. It also suggests that litigants often overlook their best claims and fail to pursue the party against whom they have the greatest chance of success.

Obviously, the analysis can rapidly become an organizational and conceptual challenge. The key is to stay focused and methodical as you work through each relationship.

In contrast to Chapters Fifteen through Eighteen, which were organized around rights and obligations, the remainder of this Chapter is organized around types of wrongdoing. The types of wrongdoing are: (i) unauthorized signatures; (ii) incomplete or altered instruments; and (iii) or lost or stolen instruments (without any unauthorized signatures or alterations).[12] Most of these types of wrongdoing

---

[12] Another type of wrongdoing – embezzlement – was covered in Chapter Eighteen. Embezzlement often takes place without any unauthorized signatures or alterations of a negotiable instrument because the principal has authorized the wrongdoer to deal with

can occur alone or in combination. For example, a person may steal an instrument, place an unauthorized signature on the instrument, and alter the instrument. For each type of wrongdoing, the problems in this Chapter will require you to use what you have learned in Chapters Fifteen through Eighteen to allocate the loss from that wrongdoing.

SECTION 2.   UNAUTHORIZED SIGNATURES

As we saw in Chapter Fifteen, a person incurs contract obligation on a negotiable instrument through signing the instrument. UCC §§ 3-401, 3-402. The authenticity of the signature and authority to sign are presumed unless specifically denied in the pleadings in an action to enforce liability on the instrument. *See* UCC § 3-308(a). If the authenticity of the signature or authority to sign is placed in issue, the person seeking to enforce contract liability on the instrument has the burden of proof to establish the signature is authentic and authorized. However, as we just saw in the previous section of this Chapter, a person whose signature is not authentic or authorized may be precluded from asserting that fact using one or more of the following sections: UCC §§ 3-403, 3-406, 4-406. There are two more preclusion sections to explore.

Read UCC § 3-404. This section applies to unauthorized indorsements. To illustrate how this section works consider another example.

Example 3. Aaron is approached by Barker, who tells Aaron that she represents Best Estates, Inc., an existing company. In fact, Barker does not represent Best Estates, Inc. and is a scam artist. Barker induces Aaron to issue a negotiable demand note payable to Best Estates, Inc. as an investment in the company. Barker takes the note, forges the indorsement of Best Estates, Inc. and sells the note to Carlotti. Aaron discovers that he has been fooled by Barker. Carlotti demands that Aaron pay the note.

Analysis: When Carlotti demands that Aaron pay the note, Carlotti is seeking to enforce Aaron's maker's contract liability on the note as a person entitled to enforce. UCC § 3-412. However, Barker forged the indorsement of Best Estates, Inc. Aaron's argument is that Carlotti is not a person entitled to enforce the note

---

negotiable instruments in some manner.

because of the forgery of a necessary indorsement, and thus Aaron's liability as maker under UCC § 3-412 is not owed to Carlotti.[13]

Carlotti's rejoinder is to use UCC § 3-404 to preclude Aaron from asserting the forged indorsement. Barker, the impostor, induced Aaron to issue a note to Barker.[14] Under UCC § 3-404(a), any indorsement in the name of the payee is deemed effective in favor of a person that takes the instrument in good faith and for value. Assuming Carlotti meets those criteria (*i.e.* Carlotti took the note in good faith and for value), Aaron is effectively precluded from winning the argument that Carlotti is not a holder and thus not entitled to enforce Aaron's maker's liability. Aaron's only defense will be to argue that Carlotti should share the loss under UCC § 3-404(d) if Carlotti failed to exercise ordinary care and that failure substantially contributed to the loss.

What if Best Estates, Inc. is a fictitious entity? **Read UCC § 3-404(b)** which governs that situation to the same effect as UCC § 3-404(a), subject to the loss-sharing principle stated in subsection (d). In both these situations, Aaron will bear the risk of being fooled by the imposter, with some mitigation of that risk if the person seeking to enforce contract liability on the instrument against Aaron was negligent in a manner that substantially contributed to the loss. In this situation, Carlotti may be negligent if it failed to ascertain the relationship between Best Estates, Inc. and Barker, the scammer.

Now read UCC § 3-405. This section also concerns forged indorsements, but in a situation where an employer entrusts an "employee" with "responsibility" with respect to instruments. To illustrate the application of this section, return to Example 2 in the introduction and change one fact.

> *Example 2a.* Alice signs a check as drawer, payable to Payee. Finder, an employee of Payee, steals the check, forges Payee's indorsement, and deposits the check at Finder's bank. Payee notifies Alice that the check was lost and Alice stops payment through a timely stop order at the drawee bank. When the check is presented at the drawee bank, the check is dishonored and eventually returned to Finder's depositary bank.
>
> *Analysis:* Finder is an "employee" (as defined in UCC § 3-405(a)(1)) of Payee. Assume Finder had "responsibility" (as defined in UCC § 3-405(a)(3)) with respect

---

[13] Note, this is not an affirmative defense, it is instead an attempt to disprove an element of Finance Co.'s cause of action. Nonetheless, if the authenticity of the signature is to be challenged, it must be placed in issue as prescribed in UCC § 3-308.

[14] Remember, issuance need not be to the payee. *See* UCC § 3-105.

to the check issued to Payee. Finder made a "fraudulent indorsement" of Payee's name (as defined in UCC § 3-405(a)(2)). The effect of UCC § 3-405(b) is to make the indorsement of Payee's name effective in favor of the depositary bank (a person who took the instrument in good faith for collection). If the depositary bank seeks to enforce contract liability on the instrument against either the drawer (Alice) or the indorser (Payee), the depositary bank would be deemed to be a person entitled to enforce as the indorsement is deemed to be Payee's indorsement. This ability of the depositary bank to recover from either the drawer or indorser is subject to the loss-sharing principle stated in the last sentence of UCC § 3-405(b) if negligence of the depositary bank substantially contributes to the loss.

If the depositary bank recovers from Alice on her drawer's liability, Alice will have discharged her obligation to Payee, by paying the depositary bank on the instrument. UCC §§ 3-602, 3-310. If the depositary bank recovers from Payee on the indorsement contract, Payee will have a right to recover from Alice on her drawer's liability. However, that will merely return Payee to even, and Alice's underlying obligation to Payee again will be extinguished. UCC §§ 3-602, 3-310. The end result of this is that Payee will end up bearing the loss because it will not receive the proceeds of the check, will have no rights as against any other party (other than Finder), and Alice's liability on whatever underlying obligation prompted Alice to issue the check to Payee will be discharged.

With these five provisions that may prevent a successful challenge to a signature as unauthorized in mind (UCC §§ 3-403, 3-404, 3-405, 3-406 and § 4-406), it is time to examine the effect of various types of unauthorized signatures in more depth. The consequences are different depending on what type of signature is unauthorized.

At the beginning of each section is a diagram of the path the instrument took among the parties. It is advisable to make such a diagram to help ensure that you do not overlook relevant issues. You may also find it useful to note on the diagram what happened in each transfer. On the diagram below, the signer (forger) is denoted with a solid line and the purported signer (the person whose signature was forged) is denoted with a dotted line.

A. Unauthorized Maker's Signature

1. Purported Maker Resisting Payment

Contract obligation on the negotiable note. Typically, the first indication of trouble when there is an unauthorized maker's signature is either when a demand is made on the purported maker to pay the note or when a person sues purported the maker to enforce contract liability on the note. In either case, the purported maker's obligation to pay is governed by UCC § 3-412.

To contest contract liability on the note, the purported maker needs to place the unauthorized signature in issue. Review UCC § 3-308. If the purported maker does place the authority of the signature in issue, the person seeking recovery from the purported maker has the burden of proving that the purported maker's signature was authorized under UCC § 3-402 or that the purported maker is precluded from asserting the unauthorized signature either because of ratification under UCC § 3-403 or because of negligence under UCC § 3-406.[15] As we learned in Chapter Fifteen, the plaintiff's status as a holder in due course will not prevent the purported maker from defending on the basis that the signature was unauthorized.

If the purported maker prevails on the signature issue (*i.e.,* the plaintiff cannot show that the signature is authentic, authorized or ratified), the case against the purported maker based on contract liability on the instrument is over. The purported maker will not have liability under UCC § 3-412. If the person who signed the maker's name can be found, the person entitled to enforce the instrument will of course be entitled to bring that action against the signer, based on the signer's contract liability under UCC § 3-403 and § 3-412.

If the person asserting contract liability against the purported maker prevails on the signature issue (*i.e.,* the signature is authentic, authorized or ratified, or the purported maker is precluded from asserting that the signature is not authentic or

---

[15] UCC § 3-404 and § 3-405 apply only to indorsements. UCC § 4-406 applies to a drawer's unauthorized signature, not to a maker's unauthorized signature.

authorized), the consequence of that will depend upon the reason that the purported maker lost on that issue. If the purported maker lost because the signature was in fact authentic, authorized or ratified, the purported maker is liable under UCC § 3-412 , but may nevertheless assert some affirmative defense to contract liability (based on a ground other than the forged signature) or a claim in recoupment to offset contract liability. *See* UCC § 3-305. If that occurs, the person seeking to enforce the maker's contract liability may then claim holder-in-due-course status under UCC § 3-302 and, with it, immunity from the asserted defense or claim in recoupment. If the person seeking to enforce contract liability on the note is not a holder in due course or cannot assert that status to bar an asserted defense, *see* UCC § 3-203, the purported maker will not have to pay at all if it has a valid defense. Alternatively, the purported maker will be entitled to some reduction in liability if it has a claim in recoupment. Review Chapter Fifteen.

If the reason that the purported maker lost on the signature issue was because it was precluded under UCC § 3-406 from challenging the signature due to the purported maker's negligence, the purported maker nevertheless still may assert an affirmative defense or a claim in recoupment as described above (subject to the rights of the plaintiff as a holder in due course, of course). In addition, the purported maker may claim that the person seeking to enforce the maker's obligation was also negligent in a manner that substantially contributed to the loss, so as to trigger the comparative loss-allocation rule of UCC § 3-406(b). Even a holder in due course is subject to that comparative negligence analysis.

Warranty liability. If the person seeking to enforce the note against the purported maker loses in whole or part based upon the arguments above,[16] that person will look to other parties to attempt to transfer the loss it has incurred (by giving value for a note that it cannot enforce against the maker). For example, if the note had been transferred by the initial payee, whether or not through one or more intermediaries, to the person now holding the note, the person holding the note may assert that those previous transferors breached transfer warranties, notably the warranty that all signatures are authentic and authorized. Review UCC § 3-416.[17]

---

[16] Other arguments may come into play, such as the person seeking to enforce the note is not a person entitled to enforce due to a missing or unauthorized necessary indorsement. For purposes of this analysis, the assumption is that the only thing "wrong" with the note is that the maker's signature is unauthorized.

[17] A person need not be person entitled to enforce the instrument in order to bring a transfer warranty cause of action, rather, the plaintiff need only be a transferee of the instrument.

The correct defendant in such an action for breach of the transfer warranty is not the maker, it is instead any person that transferred the note after the note was issued.[18]

Underlying obligation. In addition to a cause of action based on the note, the person entitled to enforce the note may have a cause of action against its counter party (the person from whom it received the note) based upon the underlying transaction (*i.e.*, the transaction in relation to which the plaintiff took the note). Review UCC § 3-310.

2. *Purported Maker Makes Payment and Seeks Recovery After Payment*

What if the purported maker pays the note when a demand is made, not realizing until later that its signature was unauthorized? In such a case the purported maker usually has a right to payment from the unauthorized signer and a very limited ability to recover the payment from the person paid.

Enforcing the instrument against the unauthorized signer. If the purported maker paid when it was neither bound by the signature nor precluded from asserting that the signature was unauthorized, the payment will probably not constitute discharge of the obligation on the instrument. That is because only payment by or on behalf of someone obligated to pay constitutes payment of the instrument so as to result in a discharge of the obligation on the instrument. *See* UCC § 3-602(a). As a result, the purported maker may be able to seek payment on the instrument from the unauthorized signer, at least if the purported maker qualifies as a person entitled to enforce the instrument. *See* UCC § 3-403(a). In essence, the purported maker could be treated as if it purchased the note from the person paid, and has succeeded to the rights of that person. *See* UCC § 3-203. Of course, even if the purported maker qualifies as a person entitled to enforce the unauthorized signer's contract liability on the note, the purported maker may have difficulty recovering. As already discussed, finding and recovering from wrongdoers is often quite difficult.

Warranty. Review the provisions on presentment warranties in UCC § 3-417(d). The only warranty made to a maker is that the person obtaining payment and all prior transferors were in fact entitled to enforce the obligation on the note.[19] That warranty is not breached merely because the maker's signature is

---

[18] Presentment warranties are not relevant in this situation. Presentment warranties are made *to* the maker and become relevant only if the maker pays. *See* UCC § 3-417(d).

[19] As explored in Chapters Sixteen and Eighteen, transfer warranties are not made to the

unauthorized because a person entitled to enforce the note has recourse against either the purported maker (if, as discussed above, the maker either ratified the signature or is precluded from asserting that the signature is unauthorized) or against the unauthorized signer. *See* UCC § 3-403. As discussed in Chapters Sixteen and Eighteen, the warranty that the person presenting to the maker is entitled to enforce is concerned with whether the presenter meets the criteria of that status as provided in UCC § 3-301.

Restitution. Someone who makes a payment by mistake generally has a right to restitution of that payment, subject to certain limitations.[20] Thus, for example, if a purported maker of a note was in fact not bound by the signature or precluded from asserting that the signature is unauthorized, but nevertheless mistakenly paid the note, the purported maker will have a right to restitution against the person it paid. That right to restitution is expressly recognized in UCC § 3-418(b). However, the right to restitution is subject to significant limitations set forth in UCC § 3-418(c). Restitution is unavailable against a person who took the instrument in good faith and for value or who, in good faith, changed position in reliance on the payment. These limitations generally prevent a successful restitution claim.

Property claim to instrument or its proceeds. A maker of a note is generally not the owner of the note. A note represents an *obligation* of the maker, not an *asset* of the maker.[21] Hence, the maker does not generally have a property-based claim to the note. However, when a purported maker's signature is unauthorized (and the purported maker is not precluded from asserting that lack of authority), but the purported maker nevertheless mistakenly pays the note, the note has in effect been used as an mechanism for obtaining funds from the purported maker that it was not obligated to pay. In such a case, UCC § 3-306 recognizes that a person may have a property-based claim to either the instrument or, more likely, its proceeds. Such a property-based claim to the proceeds would seem to be based on a right to restitution, and thus is probably still subject to the limitations in UCC § 3-418(c).

---

maker and thus do not provide a basis for the maker to recover what it mistakenly paid out. *See* UCC § 3-416.

[20] *See* RESTATEMENT (THIRD) OF RESTITUTION AND UNJUST ENRICHMENT § 5.

[21] UCC § 3-420 recognizes this point by providing that the maker does not have a claim for conversion of the instrument.

Moreover, as stated in UCC § 3-306, a holder in due course would not be subject to that claim to the proceeds.[22]

Problem 19-1

Arnold and Ben are brothers. Ben was being hounded by his creditors and convinced Claire, a creditor, to take a negotiable demand note purportedly signed by Arnold and payable to bearer in payment of Ben's debt to Claire. Arnold knew nothing about what Ben was doing. Claire sold the note to Bank One for half of its face amount. Bank One demanded Arnold pay the note.

A. Assume Bank One is a holder in due course of the note.
   1. What are Arnold's best arguments for resisting Bank One's demand?
   2. If Arnold is successful in resisting payment, what are Bank One's options for recovering from someone else?

B. How, if at all, does the analysis of Part A change if Bank One is not a holder in due course of the note?

C. How, if at all, would the analysis of Parts A and B change if Arnold and Ben were partners and Claire were a creditor of the partnership?

D. How, if at all, would the analysis of Parts A and B change if Ben used a signature stamp for Arnold's signature, which Arnold kept in his unlocked desk drawer?

E. Arnold paid Bank One, and later realized that Ben had forged Arnold's signature. Arnold seeks to recover from Bank One. What result?

---

[22] Similarly, a holder in due course is not subject to a claim to rescind the initial issuance or subsequent negotiations of the instrument based upon fraud. *See* UCC § 3-202.

B. Unauthorized Drawer's Signature

Consider now the unauthorized drawer's signature on a draft. Critical to the loss-allocation analysis is whether the drawee paid the draft (as in Example 1) or dishonored it.

1. *Drawee Did Not Pay*

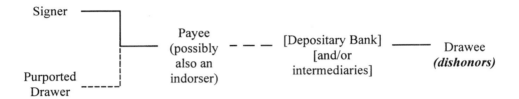

Contract obligation on the draft. If the draft is dishonored, the person who is holding the loss may sue the purported drawer for contract liability on the instrument. Review UCC § 3-414. The person seeking to enforce the drawer's obligation will have to demonstrate that it is either a person entitled to enforce the instrument or an indorser who paid the draft.[23]

To contest its contract liability on the draft, the purported drawer needs to place the unauthorized signature in issue. UCC § 3-308. If the purported drawer does place the authority of the signature in issue, the person seeking recovery from the purported drawer will have the burden of proving the purported drawer's signature was authorized under UCC § 3-402 or that the purported drawer is precluded from

---

[23] The typical plaintiff suing a purported drawer based on the drawer's contract liability on the dishonored check is a depositary bank that has some difficulty in collecting from its customer (the payee or a subsequent taker from the payee) using the right of chargeback or refund under UCC § 4-214, usually because the customer's account has insufficient funds. The depositary bank may also try to collect from an indorser of the draft based upon the indorser's contract liability on the instrument (UCC § 3-415). To collect from an indorser, the depositary bank will have to give timely notice of dishonor (UCC § 3-503 and § 3-504). Whether the drawer's signature is authorized is of no consequence to the indorser's contract liability on the instrument. Thus, the indorser will have to find a different defense to assert against the depositary bank. A depositary bank may qualify as a holder in due course, which would preclude many of an indorser's typical defenses. UCC § 3-302 and § 3-305.

asserting the unauthorized signature either because of ratification under UCC § 3-403 or because of negligence under UCC § 3-406.[24] The plaintiff's status as a holder in due course will not prevent the purported drawer from defending on the basis that the signature was unauthorized. Proving that the purported drawer should be held responsible for the signature is part of the prima facie case of the person seeking to enforce the drawer's liability under UCC § 3-414.

If the purported drawer prevails on the signature issue, the purported drawer will not have drawer's liability under UCC § 3-414. However, the person who signed the purported drawer's name will have drawer's liability on the instrument to a person who took the draft in good faith and for value. *See* UCC § 3-403.

If the person asserting contract liability against the purported drawer prevails on the signature issue, the purported drawer will have liability as the drawer under UCC § 3-414. If the purported drawer lost because the signature was in fact authorized under UCC § 3-402 or ratified under UCC § 3-403, the purported drawer may nevertheless assert some affirmative defense to contract liability (on a basis other than the forged signature) or a claim in recoupment to offset contract liability. *See* UCC § 3-305. If that occurs, the person seeking to enforce the drawer's contract liability may then claim holder-in-due-course status under UCC § 3-302 and, with it, immunity from the asserted defense or claim in recoupment. If the person seeking to enforce contract liability on the note is not a holder in due course or cannot assert that status to bar an asserted defense, *see* UCC § 3-203, the purported drawer will not have to pay at all if it has a valid defense or will be entitled to some reduction in liability if it has a claim in recoupment.

If the reason that the purported drawer lost on the signature issue was because the it was precluded from challenging the signature by UCC § 3-406, the purported drawer may claim that the person seeking to enforce the drawer's obligation was also negligent in a manner that substantially contributed to the loss, so as to trigger the comparative loss-allocation rule of UCC § 3-406(b). Even a holder in due course is subject to that comparative negligence analysis.

Warranty. A person who has suffered a loss due to dishonor of the draft may also seek to collect for breach of a transfer warranty[25] from previous transferors of

---

[24] UCC § 3-404 and § 3-405 apply only to indorsements. UCC § 4-406 only applies to the contest between the drawee bank and the drawer regarding charges to the drawer's account with the drawee bank.

[25] Presentment warranty liability is not relevant to this situation. Presentment warranty liability is liability owed *to* the drawee under UCC § 3-417(a) and arises only if the drawee

the check. Review UCC § 3-416 and § 4-207. Transferors that make the transfer warranties to subsequent transferees warrant that all signatures are authentic and authorized. If the drawer's signature is unauthorized or not authentic, that warranty will have been breached and the previous transferor will be liable regardless of the transferor's lack of knowledge of any problem with the drawer's signature or of the application of UCC § 3-406.

Underlying obligation. If the check is an unaccepted draft, the person entitled to enforce the instrument may also have a cause of action on the underlying obligation against its counter-party. Review UCC § 3-310.

Additional obligations arising out of the bank collection process. Because many drafts are collected through the banking system, it is important to consider how the obligations arising in that system affect the analysis of a dishonored draft with an unauthorized drawer's signature.

First consider the effect of bank accountability under UCC § 4-302. Assume that when the check was presented to the drawee bank, the drawee bank failed to make a provisional settlement and is therefore accountable for the item. Review UCC §§ 4-301, § 4-302. The check is considered dishonored. Review UCC § 3-502. Now, in addition to pursuing the purported drawer or the actual signer (or both), the person entitled to enforce may enforce the payor bank's liability under UCC § 4-302. Of course, that person should be entitled to only one recovery of the amount of the instrument.

In the lawsuit asserting payor bank accountability under UCC § 4-302, the payor bank may assert as a defense that there would have been a breach of a presentment warranty (if the drawee bank had paid the draft) or that there was fraud by the person seeking to hold the payor bank accountable. Review UCC § 4-302(b), § 4-208. For an unauthorized drawer's signature, however, the presentment warranties are not very robust defenses for the payor bank.

If the payor bank is accountable under UCC § 4-302, the payor bank would seek to subrogate to the rights of a holder in due course against the purported drawer or the wrongdoer who signed the drawer's name. Review UCC §§ 3-403, 3-414, 4-407.

Effect of lack of expeditious return. Recall that a drawee bank (the paying bank in Regulation CC terminology) that returns a check must do so expeditiously and, if the check is large ($2,500 or over), must give notice of that return as well. If the

---

pays or accepts the draft. A presentment warranty made to the drawer arises only if the drawer pays. UCC § 3-417(d). *See also* UCC § 4-208.

paying bank fails to do so, it may have liability if it failed to exercise ordinary care or good faith in compliance with those obligations. *See* 12 C.F.R. §§ 229.30, 229.33, 229.38. Review Chapter Sixteen, Section 6.

Effect of Regulation CC return warranties. Remember that a bank returning a check makes the return warranties in Regulation CC, 12 C.F.R. § 229.34. Would those warranties be breached if the check is returned with an unauthorized drawer's signature?

Try your understanding of these provisions in analyzing the following problem.

Problem 19-2

Xavier has a checking account at Evergreen Bank. One night, Xavier lost his checkbook. Aaron picked up the checkbook, took a check, wrote the check payable to cash for $100, and forged Xavier's name as drawer. Aaron delivered the check to Bill for $50. Bill took the check to Check Cashing Inc., which paid Bill $90 for the check. Check Cashing deposited the check in its account at Downtown Bank, which credited Check Cashing's account for $100 and sent the check to Evergreen Bank for payment. Evergreen Bank made a timely provisional settlement for the check but then returned the check by its midnight deadline directly to Downtown Bank. Evergreen Bank returned the check because Xavier had stopped payment on all checks drawn on his checking account. Downtown Bank debited Check Cashing's account for the amount of the check and returned the check to Check Cashing Inc.

A. Check Cashing seeks to recover the amount of the check from Xavier, Bill, and Aaron. What causes of action does Check Cashing have against each defendant and what defenses, if any, does the defendant have to each cause of action?

B. Does Check Cashing have any rights against Evergreen Bank?

C. Assume that Check Cashing recovered the amount of the check from Bill. What causes of action does Bill have against Aaron and Xavier and what defenses, if any, do Bill and Xavier have to each of those causes of action?

D. Assume that in an action by Check Cashing against Xavier, Check Cashing can prove that Xavier was negligent in losing his checkbook and that this negligence substantially contributed to Aaron's signing of Xavier's name.
   1. How, if at all, does such negligence affect the outcome of Check Cashing's action against Xavier?
   2. How, if at all, does such negligence affect the outcome of Check Cashing's action against Bill?

E. Assume that Evergreen Bank failed to make a provisional settlement for the check but returned the check anyway after its midnight deadline. Who will bear the ultimate liability for the check?

F. Assume that Evergreen Bank timely and properly returned the check under UCC Article 4, but did not meet the requirements for expeditious return under Regulation CC. How, if at all, does this affect the analysis of Check Cashing's rights?

2. *Drawee Made Payment*

Now consider the more usual situation where the drawee has made final payment of the check with the unauthorized drawer's signature. We have already explored some of the issues in the discussion of Example 1 earlier in this Chapter. How does this happen? Remember that in most circumstances the drawee will either not examine the drawer's signature for authenticity or authorization or, even if it does examine the signature, will not be able to determine whether the signature is authentic or authorized. Thus, the drawee's decision to honor the draft will depend upon whether the drawee is indebted to the drawer (such as when the drawee bank has the drawer's deposit account) or the drawee has the ability to obtain value from a participant in the transaction (as in a documentary draft transaction).

Purported drawer's arguments against the drawee bank. If the draft is a check that is not timely returned, and thus final payment is made, the purported drawer will typically be the person initially holding the loss because the drawee bank will have debited the purported drawer's deposit account. The purported drawer will complain[26] to the drawee that the check should not have been paid because the drawer's signature was unauthorized. The drawee bank will often respond by asserting that the item was properly payable because the purported drawer's signature was authorized or ratified. Review UCC §§ 3-401, 3-402, and 3-403. In addition, the drawee bank may assert that the purported drawer is precluded from asserting the unauthorized signature because of the purported drawer's negligence or because of the bank statement rule. Review UCC §§ 3-406, 4-406.

If the drawee bank wins the argument that the check was in fact authorized or ratified, the purported drawer is left with the entire loss because the check was properly payable. If the drawee bank wins the argument that the purported drawer's negligence precludes assertion of the forged signature, or the bank statement rule precludes assertion of the unauthorized signature, the purported drawer has the ability to attempt the loss-sharing argument based upon the drawee bank's failure to exercise ordinary care. UCC § 3-406(b), 4-406(e). We explored these rules in the discussion of Example 1 earlier in this Chapter.

Purported drawer's arguments against other parties. If the drawee bank wins any of those arguments regarding the purported drawer's signature, the purported drawer is left, at least temporarily, with either the entire loss or, if loss is allocated on the basis of comparative negligence, part of the loss. The purported drawer will then look to others who handled the item in an attempt to pass the loss on to one of them. The usual causes of action that the purported drawer has are conversion, review UCC § 3-420, and common-law negligence. These two causes of action are typically against the depositary bank which took the check for deposit, or the payee of the check who took the check from the thief who forged the drawer's signature.[27]

---

[26] In the case of the documentary draft transaction, the drawee (generally the buyer) is the one likely to complain as it has paid the draft but has not gotten the goods. The remaining discussion will focus on checks that are paid with an unauthorized drawer's signature.

[27] The purported drawer's claim against the wrongdoer who signed the check as the drawer (in effect using the check as a mechanism for stealing value from the drawer) will be a matter governed by law outside the UCC.

The depositary bank or payee will typically respond to a conversion claim with two arguments. First, UCC § 3-420 precludes a drawer of a check from suing for conversion *of the check*.[28] However, consider whether the purported drawer should have a cause of action for conversion of the *proceeds* of the check. After all, the check has been used as a mechanism for extracting value from the purported drawer's deposit account. Should the purported drawer be able to recover the proceeds from those who have taken the proceeds?[29]

Second, even if the purported drawer has an action for conversion of the proceeds of the check, the depositary bank or other taker from the thief is a holder in due course who takes free of such a conversion claim.[30] UCC § 3-306. The thief (the person who placed the unauthorized signature on the check) would not be a holder in due course and thus the purported drawer should be able to exercise common-law remedies against the thief. If a person who took the check from the thief was not a holder in due course, there is an argument that the purported drawer should be able to pursue a remedy for conversion of the proceeds of the check.[31]

---

[28] *Compare Heche v. Chase Manhattan Bank*, 45 U.C.C. Rep. Serv. 2d 549 (Conn. Super. Ct. 2001) (cause of action for conversion by drawer against depositary bank allowed)*with Amzee Corp. v. Comerica Bank-Midwest*, 48 U.C.C. Rep. Serv. 2d 833 (Ohio Ct. App. 2002) (cause of action by drawer against payee of check not allowed); *Conder v. Union Planters Bank*, 384 F.3d 397 (7th Cir. 2004) (same); *Mid-Continent Specialists, Inc. v. Capital Homes, L.C.*, 106 P.3d 483 (Kan. 2005) (same); *Borg v. Chase Manhattan Bank, U.S.A*, 247 Fed. Appx. 627 (6th Cir. 2007) (same).

[29] Note that, as discussed in Chapter Eighteen in learning about misbehaving fiduciaries, UCC § 3-307 contemplates that a represented person who is a drawer (or maker) of an instrument will have a claim against a taker of the instrument when the fiduciary violates its duty. This claim is based upon property law or restitutionary principles. Of course, the depositary bank or other taker from the thief will also argue that the drawer's signature is not unauthorized, particularly if an employee is the forger. *See Redland Co. v. Bank of America Corp.*, 568 F.3d 1232 (11th Cir. 2009) (corporation authorized embezzling employee to draw on corporate bank account and failed to detect embezzlement for a decade, depositary bank was not liable for that harm).

[30] *See also United Catholic Parish Schools of Beaver Dam Educ. Ass'n v. Card Servs. Center*, 636 N.W.2d 206 (Wis. Ct. App. 2001) *rev. denied*, 643 N.W.2d 93 (Wis. 2002).

[31] Should the purported drawer be able to sue to rescind the issuance of the check with its forged signature? *See* UCC § 3-202.

As to a common-law negligence action, the depositary bank or payee will typically argue that such an action is preempted by UCC's rather detailed loss-allocation rules. Courts are divided on this question.[32] At stake is whether the purported drawer will be permitted to pass the risk of the unauthorized drawer's signature to the depositary bank or payee, who is often the first taker of the check from the thief. How would you rule on this issue? Should the answer depend on the parties' relative degrees of fault?

The purported drawer may also have a cause of action for restitution due to mistake. However, such a claim is not likely to be very helpful to the purported drawer given the protection in UCC § 3-418(c) for the likely defendants.[33]

Drawee bank's arguments against parties other than purported drawer. If the purported drawer is able to pass all or part of the loss to the drawee bank based upon the arguments already considered, the drawee bank will likely seek to pass that loss to one of the parties who handled the check before the drawee bank paid it. These include the depositary bank, if there is one, or the payee. The drawee bank has four main avenues of attack: (i) subrogation to someone else's rights under UCC § 4-407; (ii) breach of presentment warranties under UCC § 3-417 and § 4-208; (iii) restitution under UCC § 3-418; and (iv) breach of warranty regarding remotely created checks. Review Reg. CC, 12 C.F.R. § 229.34(d) and the definition of remotely created check in 12 C.F.R. § 229.2(fff).

Other participants' arguments. If the drawee bank (or the purported drawer) is successful in passing the loss upstream to a previous entity, that entity will often use transfer warranty liability to pass the liability to the first taker from the thief. Review UCC § 3-416, § 4-207.

---

[32] *Compare White Sands Forest Prods., Inc. v. First Nat'l Bank of Alamogordo*, 50 P.3d 202 (N.M. Ct. App. 2002) (negligence cause of action not allowed), *Halifax Corp. v. Wachovia Bank*, 604 S.E.2d 403 (Va. 2004) (same); *Burns v. Neiman Marcus Group, Inc.*, 93 Cal. Rptr. 3d 130 (Cal. Ct. App. 2009) (same); *Innovative Hospitality Systems, L.L.C. v. Abe's, Inc.*, 52 So. 3d 313 (La. Ct. App. 2010) (same) *with Mutual Service Casualty Ins. Co. v. Elizabeth State Bank*, 265 F.3d 601 (7th Cir. 2001) (negligence cause of action allowed when check payable to depositary bank and no debt is owed by the drawer to the depositary bank); *Cassello v. Allegiant Bank*, 288 F.3d 339 (8th Cir. 2002) (negligence cause of action against depositary bank allowed).

[33] *See City Rentals, Inc. v. Kesler*, 946 N.E.2d 785 (Ohio Ct. App. 2010) (taker of check with forged drawer's signature was holder in due course and not subject to purported drawer's unjust enrichment claim).

In general, though, in a case involving a forged drawer's signature on a check that is not timely dishonored, the loss most often falls on the drawee bank (or on the purported drawer if that person is precluded from asserting the forgery). The likelihood of success in passing the loss upstream to other parties is usually very small.

Problem 19-3

Xavier has a checking account at Evergreen Bank. One night, Xavier lost his checkbook. Aaron picked up the checkbook, took a check, wrote the check payable to cash for $100, and forged Xavier's name as drawer. Aaron delivered the check to Bill for $50. Bill took the check to Check Cashing Inc., which paid Bill $90 for the check. Check Cashing deposited the check in its account at Downtown Bank, which credited Check Cashing's account for $100 and sent the check to Evergreen Bank for payment. Evergreen Bank made a timely provisional settlement for the check.

A. Evergreen Bank did not return the check. When Xavier received his monthly statement from the bank, he immediately noticed the check that Aaron wrote. The signature that Aaron wrote looks nothing like Xavier's signature. The next day, Xavier called Evergreen Bank and told the clerk that he did not write the check.
    1. Must Evergreen Bank re-credit Xavier's account?
    2. If Evergreen Bank re-credits Xavier's account, may Evergreen Bank recover the amount of the check from anyone else?
    3. How, if at all, would the analysis change if Xavier did not call and tell the bank about the check until three months after receiving the monthly bank statement?
    4. How, if at all, would the analysis change if Aaron had forged Xavier's name on four checks, one each month for four months, and Xavier waited three months after receiving the first monthly statement, reflecting the first forged check, to tell the bank?

B. Evergreen Bank did not return the check. The next monthly statement Xavier received from the Evergreen Bank included several checks that Aaron had written, forging Xavier's signature as drawer. However,

Xavier did not look at this statement until several months later. When he did, he noticed the forged checks but put off calling the bank about them. Thirteen months after Xavier received the bank statement with the forged checks, he finally informed Evergreen Bank. Because Evergreen Bank valued Xavier's business, it re-credited his account. May Evergreen Bank recover from anyone else?

C. Evergreen Bank returned the check after its midnight deadline. Who will bear the ultimate liability for this check? Review Chapter Sixteen, Section 5. [Hint–Has Evergreen Bank made final payment or a timely return?]

Problem 19-4

Gullible received a phone call from a telemarketer who convinced Gullible to give the telemarketer Gullible's bank account information. Gullible eventually declined to purchase any product. Much to Gullible's surprise, Gullible's next monthly bank statement showed that a check was written by the telemarketer for $1,000 drawn on Gullible's account. The drawer's line contained the notation "authorization on file with payee." Gullible called State Bank, the drawee, to complain. How will this be resolved? Who will ultimately bear the liability?

C. Unauthorized Indorsements

Now consider the case of an unauthorized indorsement. The first thing to ascertain when dealing with a potentially unauthorized indorsement is whether the indorsement was necessary for further negotiation of the instrument. After making that determination, determine whether the indorsement was in fact unauthorized under UCC § 3-401 and § 3-402. If unauthorized, determine if it has been ratified under UCC § 3-403. If not ratified (and thus retroactively authorized), then ascertain if a person has paid the instrument on behalf of itself (because it was obligated) or on behalf of another who is obligated on the instrument (as when a drawee pays on behalf of the drawer).

1. Instrument with unauthorized necessary indorsement is not paid when due or on demand

Maker or Drawer	——————	Payee	— — — —	Unauthorized Signer	——————	Maker or Drawee *(dishonors)*

To illustrate the issues, the following example will be used throughout this section.

Example. A negotiable note is issued by the maker payable to the order of the payee. The note is stolen from the payee and the payee's indorsement is forged. The forger sells the note to an unsuspecting buyer for value. The note buyer is in possession of the note. What are the note buyer's rights when the maker dishonors the note?

Maker's contract liability on the note. The note buyer will attempt to enforce the maker's contract liability on the note. Review UCC § 3-412. The maker's obligation is owed to a person entitled to enforce. The note buyer is not a person entitled to enforce because the necessary indorsement of the payee has been forged. Review UCC §§ 3-301, 3-204, 3-205. If the maker is successful in proving the forged necessary indorsement, the note buyer will not be able to enforce the maker's contract liability on the instrument. Moreover, because the forged indorsement prevents the note buyer from qualifying as a holder, the note buyer also cannot be a holder in due course.

To avoid this roadblock to recovery, the note buyer may seek to preclude the maker from arguing that the indorsement of payee is unauthorized, using one or more of the following section: UCC § 3-403 (ratification); UCC § 3-406 (negligence); UCC § 3-404 (imposters and fictitious payees); or UCC § 3-405 (fraudulent indorsement by employee).

If the note buyer can show that the payee ratified the unauthorized indorsement, then the note buyer will become a person entitled to enforce the maker's contract obligation on the note. UCC § 3-403.

For the note buyer to successfully assert that the *maker* is precluded from asserting the payee's forged indorsement under UCC § 3-406, the maker's negligence (not the payee's negligence) has to substantially contribute to the making of the forged indorsement. That is extremely unlikely because the forged indorsement necessarily was made after the maker issued the note to the payee.

Similarly, on these facts, UCC § 3-404 does not look promising. The note was not issued to an imposter, a fictitious person, or to someone who was not intended to have an interest in the instrument. UCC § 3-405 also does not look very promising. For it to apply in this hypothetical, the thief would have to be an employee of the payee of the note, the employee would have to have responsibility with respect to this note,[34] and the employee would have had to make a fraudulent indorsement on the note. If all of these elements are met, then UCC § 3-405 deems the indorsement "effective as the indorsement of the named payee." However, if any one of these elements is not met, UCC § 3-405 will provide no assistance to the note buyer.

If the note buyer is able to use UCC § 3-404, § 3-405 or § 3-406 to preclude the maker from asserting that the payee's indorsement is forged, the note buyer would qualify as a holder and be entitled to enforce the maker's contract liability on the note. In addition, the note buyer might also be a holder in due course (if it otherwise meets the requirements of UCC § 3-302) and take free of the maker's defenses and claims in recoupment arising out of the transaction between the maker and the payee. *See* UCC § 3-305. However, even if the note buyer does qualify as a holder in due course, the loss could be apportioned between the maker and note buyer if the note buyer was negligent in taking the instrument and that negligence substantially contributed to the loss. UCC §§ 3-406(b), 3-404(d), 3-405(b).

Purported indorser's contract liability on the instrument. Now consider the note buyer's rights against the purported indorser (the one whose unauthorized indorsement was placed on the instrument). In the example, the purported indorser is the payee from whom the note was stolen. Again, the first step is to determine whether the purported indorser is bound to that signature under either UCC § 3-402 or § 3-403. If not, the purported indorser will have contract liability on the instrument *only if* it is precluded from asserting the forgery or the forged indorsement is deemed to be the payee's indorsement.

Consider UCC § 3-406. If the payee's negligence substantially contributed to the forgery, the payee will be precluded from asserting its signature is forged and the note buyer will be able to assert the indorser's contract liability against the payee. Of course, the payee will be entitled to timely notice of dishonor unless that right is waived or the obligation to provide notice is excused. UCC §§ 3-503, 3-504. The purported indorser (the payee) may assert as a defense to indorser's liability that it has a claim to the note (the payee is the owner) and that the note was lost or stolen. UCC § 3-305(c). However, that defense and claim will be precluded

---

[34] *See Schrier Bros. v. Golub*, 123 Fed. Appx. 484 (3d Cir. 2005) on the meaning of responsibility with respect to an instrument.

if the note buyer qualifies as a holder in due course (which it can do if the payee is precluded from asserting the forged necessary indorsement). UCC §§ 3-305(c), 3-306. Even if the note buyer is a holder in due course, the comparative negligence rule may result in the payee being able to place some of the loss on the note buyer. UCC §§ 3-406(b).

UCC § 3-404 and § 3-405 do not look promising to preclude the payee from contesting the forged indorsement for the same reasons they did not look promising in enforcing the maker's liability.[35]

Forger's indorser liability on the instrument. Now return to UCC § 3-403. The thief – who forged the indorsement – is bound to the signature as against a person who takes the instrument in good faith and for value. Thus, the thief is liable as an indorser. However, even if the thief is liable as an indorser, the payee has not indorsed, and the payee's indorsement is necessary to make the note buyer a person entitled to enforce. Arguably, the forger should be precluded from asserting that the note buyer is not a person entitled to enforce due to the forgery of the payee's necessary indorsement. However, UCC § 3-406 provides for preclusion based on negligence, not wrongdoing, and thus it would not seem to make preclusion available on these facts.

Warranty liability. The note buyer will have an action against the thief based upon breach of a transfer warranty: all signatures are not authorized or authentic. Review UCC § 3-416. The note buyer will not, however, have a warranty action against the maker or payee because neither of them transferred the note. *See* UCC § 3-203(a).

If there were an intermediary between the thief and the note buyer (for example if the thief transferred the note to an intermediary, who transferred it to the buyer) the note buyer would have an action for breach of the transfer warranties against that intermediary as long as the instrument was transferred from the intermediary to the buyer for consideration.

Underlying obligation. Upon the maker's dishonor of the note, the underlying obligation for which the note was transferred to the note buyer is revived and the note buyer would have the rights allowed under UCC § 3-310. Those rights are only as against the person who transferred the note to the buyer (the thief if there was no intermediary between them, otherwise the intermediary) to recover the value given for the transfer of the note. There is no underlying obligation between the note buyer and the maker.

---

[35] UCC § 3-404 and § 3-405 are explored more in depth later in this Chapter.

The maker's dishonor of the note also revived the underlying obligation between the maker and the payee. The payee would not be able to enforce the underlying obligation against the maker unless the payee was also able to enforce the note. *See* UCC § 3-310(b)(4). The payee's right to do so is considered next.

Payee's rights. The payee has two primary avenues in this situation: its property rights in the note and the signers' contract obligations on the note.

Payee's property rights. The payee owns the note and should be able to recover from the note buyer either the note itself, *see* UCC § 3-202, or damages for conversion of the note under UCC § 3-420.[36] Review Chapter Eighteen. The note buyer would not qualify as a holder in due course because it is not a holder, unless as discussed above the payee were precluded from asserting the forgery of the payee's name.

If the payee were precluded from asserting the forged indorsement under § 3-402 through § 3-406, the note buyer might qualify as a holder in due course because it would be deemed a holder. If the note buyer were a holder in due course (assuming it met the other requirements of UCC § 3-302), the note buyer would take free of the payee's claim to the note or its proceeds. UCC § 3-306. Even so, the payee could still employ the comparative negligence analysis to apportion the loss

---

[36] A significant limitation on the payee's cause of action for conversion is the requirement that it has received delivery of the instrument before the instrument is converted. This requirement presents problems when the instrument is intercepted in transit between the issuer (maker or drawer) and payee. *See Jenkins v. Wachovia Bank*, 711 S.E.2d 80 (Ga. Ct. App. 2011); *Robertson v. Sun Life Fin.*, 40 So. 3d 507 (La. Ct. App. 2010); *Ludwig v. Fifth Third Bank*, 908 N.E.2d 992 (Ohio Ct. App. 2009).

Damages for conversion are presumed to be the face amount of the instrument. UCC § 3-420(b). *See Saxon Mtg. Servs., Inc. v. Harrison*, 973 A.2d 841 (Md. Ct. App. 2009) (presumption of damage amount applies even when a joint payee's indorsement is forged and action is brought by only one joint payee).

If the intended payee receives the proceeds, even if the indorsement has been forged, the payee has not suffered harm from the conversion. *See Aces A/C Supply North v. Security Bank*, 231 P.3d 761 (Okla. Ct. App. 2010); *Cameron v. Charter One Bank*, 2009 WL 2426206 (Mich. Ct. App. 2009); *Sutcliffe v. FleetBoston Fin. Corp.*, 950 A.2d 544 (Conn. Ct. App. 2008). On the other hand, someone who does not have a property interest in the instrument does not have a conversion claim based on a forged necessary indorsement. *See American Nat'l Ins. Co. v. Citibank*, 543 F.3d 907 (7th Cir. 2008), *cert. denied*, 129 S. Ct. 1679 (2009).

with the note buyer.[37] That comparative negligence analysis is not available to the payee if the indorsement was in fact authorized under UCC § 3-402 or ratified under UCC § 3-403.

   Contract liability on the instrument. If the payee recovers the note from the note buyer, the payee could then enforce the contract liability on the note against the maker. UCC §§ 3-412, 3-308. If the payee does not recover possession of the note, the payee may nevertheless still be a person entitled to enforce contract liability on the instrument against the maker by satisfying the requirements of UCC § 3-309. *See* UCC § 3-301. **Read UCC § 3-309.** If the payee is able to satisfy those requirements, the payee may have to post security to protect the maker from being forced to pay twice. That could happen if the note buyer is successful in an action against the maker or the maker unwittingly (without knowing of the forged indorsement) paid the note buyer.

2. Instrument with unauthorized necessary indorsement is paid when due or demanded

Maker or Drawer	————	Payee	— — — —	Unauthorized Signer	————	Maker or Drawee *(pays)*

   In the discussion above, the loss initially fell on the note buyer. It had paid the thief and was seeking to enforce rights on the note against the purported signers. Now consider what happens if the note buyer obtains payment from the maker when the buyer presents the note for payment. The maker may not know that the payee's indorsement is forged and would normally have no reason to inquire as to how the note buyer obtained the note. For this reason, the maker is unlikely to know that it has paid someone not entitled to payment until the payee (the one from whom the note was stolen) shows up seeking to enforce the instrument under UCC § 3-309.

   The maker's obligation to the payee on the note and the underlying obligation has not been discharged when it paid the note buyer because the maker paid a person not entitled to enforce the note. *See* UCC §§ 3-602(a), 3-310(b). Of course, the maker might be able to change that result if the payee is bound by the signature under UCC § 3-402 or § 3-403 or is precluded from asserting the forgery under

---

[37] *See Rodrigue v. Olin Employee's Credit Union,* 406 F.3d 434 (7th Cir. 2005).

UCC § 3-404, § 3-405, or § 3-406. If the maker successfully advances any of those arguments against the payee, the maker's obligation on the note would be discharged (because the note buyer would be deemed to be a person entitled to enforce), and the maker's underlying obligation to the payee would be discharged as well.

If the maker must pay the payee after having already paid the note buyer, the maker has three potential avenues for recovery against the note buyer. The maker's best claim is for breach of presentment warranty. Review UCC § 3-417(d). The note buyer has warranted to the maker that it was a person entitled to enforce the note. The note buyer is not such a person, unless the maker can be precluded from asserting the forged indorsement. Thus, we circle back to the arguments regarding UCC 3-401 through § 3-406 above.[38] If the maker is so precluded from asserting the forged indorsement based upon UCC § 3-404, § 3-405 § 3-406, the loss-sharing principle in those sections may allocate some of the loss to the note buyer.

The maker's second-best argument for recovery from the note buyer is a right to restitution based on mistake. *See* UCC § 3-418(b). However, this right is subject to the limitations in UCC § 3-418(c), which will prevent recovery if the note buyer took the note in good faith and for value. The maker's final basis for recovery from the note buyer is a claim to the proceeds of the note under UCC § 3-306 (or alternatively, conversion of the proceeds).[39] However, this is subject to the rights of a note buyer that qualifies as a holder in due course of the note. As noted previously, the note buyer could only qualify as a holder in due course only if the maker is precluded from asserting the forgery of the indorser's signature under UCC § 3-401 through UCC § 3-406.

---

[38] It is unlikely that the maker would be precluded from asserting the forged indorser's signature in the warranty action under UCC § 3-417(d) with the note buyer based upon UCC § 3-406. The maker was not negligent in a manner that contributed to the making of the forged indorser's signature. *See Bank of Nichols Hills v. Bank of Oklahoma*, 196 P.3d 984 (Okla. Ct. App. 2008) (presenter liable for breach of presentment warranty to drawee bank regarding entitlement to enforce unless the presenter can demonstrate that drawee bank was negligent in a manner that substantially contributed to the forged indorsement).

Note that UCC § 3-417(c) does not apply to the presentment warranty given under subsection (d). Is that a drafting glitch?

[39] See the previous discussion in this Chapter regarding whether a maker or drawer has a claim to ownership of the proceeds of the instrument or a conversion action to enforce that claim.

3. *Unauthorized indorsement is not necessary for further negotiation*

Maker or	_____	Payee	_ _ _ _	Unauthorized	_____	Maker or
Drawer		(indorses in		Signer		Drawee
		blank)				

The analysis changes if the unauthorized indorsement is irrelevant to further negotiation of the instrument. Return again to the example and change the facts as follows:

> *Example.* A negotiable note is issued by the maker payable to the order of the payee. The payee indorses the note in blank. The note is stolen from the payee. The thief sells the note to an unsuspecting buyer for value and in that transaction indorses the note by forging another person's name.

On these facts, the forged indorsement is irrelevant to the liability of the maker to the note buyer. Again, the analysis differs depending upon whether the maker honors or dishonors the note when the note buyer presents the note to the maker.

Assume the maker pays the note buyer. The maker's payment to the note buyer will discharge the maker's obligation on the note and the maker's underlying obligation to the payee because the note buyer qualifies as a person entitled to enforce due to the payee's blank indorsement. UCC §§ 3-301, 3-602, 3-310. The maker will not have a viable cause of action for breach of presentment warranty because the note buyer is a person entitled to enforce (a holder), even if not a holder in due course. UCC § 3-417(d). The payee's property claim to the note proceeds under UCC § 3-306 or § 3-420 as against the note buyer will be precluded if the note buyer qualifies as a holder in due course. If the note buyer does not qualify as a holder in due course, the payee will have a claim to the note proceeds against the note buyer.

Now assume that the maker does not pay the note buyer. The note buyer, as a person entitled to enforce, may sue the maker on its contract obligation on the instrument. UCC § 3-412. The payee's claim to the note may be asserted as a defense by the maker to its contract liability on the instrument as long as the note buyer is not a holder in due course and the payee is joined in the action and asserts its claim to the instrument. UCC § 3-305(c). If the note buyer is not a holder in due course, the maker can assert any defenses or claims in recoupment it has, UCC § 3-305(a), and, in addition, can use the last sentence of UCC § 3-305(c) to avoid paying its obligation if it can prove that the instrument was a lost or stolen. If the note buyer qualifies as a holder in due course, the maker will be liable to the note buyer on its maker's liability on the note subject only to the real defenses in UCC § 3-305(a)(1).

If the maker dishonors the note, the note buyer will also be able to assert indorser's liability against the payee, assuming timely notice of dishonor. The payee's defense will be its claim to the instrument, which will be precluded if the note buyer qualifies as a holder in due course. UCC §§ 3-305(c), 3-306. The note buyer will also be able to assert contract liability against the thief (the forger) on the forged indorsement, UCC § 3-403, or against the person whose signature was forged if that person is unable to contest the signature under UCC § 3-401 through § 3-406.

In addition to its rights against the signers of the note for contract liability on the note, the note buyer will have a breach of transfer warranty case against the thief because not all signatures were authentic and authorized. UCC § 3-416. The buyer will not have a transfer warranty claim against the maker or against the payee because neither the maker nor the payee transferred the note. *See* UCC § 3-203.

Thus in the usual situation where the note buyer would qualify as a holder in due course, and obtain payment from the maker, either right away or after a lawsuit, the payee ends up bearing the loss because it indorsed the note in blank. Only if the note buyer does not qualify as a holder in due course will the payee be able to recover, either from the note holder, if the maker pays, or from the maker (after obtaining the note back from the note holder).

4.   *Additional considerations when the instrument is a check*

The types of issues discussed above apply equally to a draft. Just as with a note, it is important to determine if the drawee has dishonored the draft or paid the draft. It is also important to determine if the unauthorized indorsement was necessary to further negotiation of the draft. Answering those two questions is critical to going down the right path of analysis to determine where the loss should come to rest.

If the draft is collected through the bank collection system, additional considerations will come into play. For example, if the drawee bank has paid a check with an unauthorized necessary indorsement, is the check properly payable from the drawer's account? *See* UCC § 4-401. What are the rights of a drawee bank to recover from others once it has made final payment on a check with a forged necessary indorsement? If a bank has breached a duty or warranty in the forward collection or return process as provided in UCC Article 4, Regulation CC, or Regulation J, or failed to meet a particular deadline, how does that affect the loss that may be incurred due to the unauthorized necessary indorsement? Review Chapter Sixteen.

As with an unauthorized signature of a drawer or maker, the best place to start in an unauthorized indorsement case is with the person on whom the loss initially rests. Evaluate all of the causes of action that the person initially bearing the loss might have against everyone else who handled the instrument. If the person initially bearing the loss can pass the loss to another person, then evaluate that second person's causes of action against everyone else who handled the instrument. Continue the process until the relationships among all the actors are fully analyzed.

The explanation above used a note to illustrate the analytical process to follow. The problems below require you to apply the same analytical method to transactions involving a check.

Problem 19-5

Ashton has a checking account at Franklin Bank. Ashton wrote a check for $100 payable to the order of Bianca. Bianca lost the check. Chris found the check, forged Bianca's signature and delivered the check to Downtown Money Store ("Downtown") for $90. Downtown deposited the check in its account at Evergreen Bank, which credited Downtown's account for $100 and sent the check in a timely manner to Franklin Bank for payment. Franklin Bank made a timely provisional settlement for the check.

A. Ashton stopped payment on the check when Bianca told him the check was lost. Franklin Bank timely returned the check to Evergreen Bank, meeting all UCC Article 4 and Regulation CC deadlines. Evergreen Bank debited Downtown's account for the amount of the check and returned the check to Downtown. UCC § 4-214. Downtown wants to pass the loss to someone else. Analyze and evaluate all of Downtown's potential causes of action against each possible defendant, along with all possible defenses to each of those causes of action.

B. Franklin Bank did not return the check. Five days after Franklin Bank made final payment, Ashton called Franklin Bank to stop payment of the check because Bianca had informed Ashton that she had lost the check.

1. What are Franklin Bank's rights against and obligation to Ashton?

2. How, if at all, would the analysis change if Ashton had waited three months to call Franklin Bank? *See* UCC §§ 4-406, 4-111, 3-118.

3. If Franklin Bank re-credits Ashton's account, will Franklin Bank be able to pass the loss to any other person? Analyze and evaluate all potential causes of action against each possible defendant, along with all possible defenses to each of those causes of action.

4. Who is likely to bear this loss if Chris cannot be found or has insufficient assets to pay a judgment?

Problem 19-6

Ashton has a checking account at Franklin Bank. Ashton wrote a check for $100 payable to Bianca. Bianca indorsed the check in blank and then lost the check. Chris found the check and sold the check to Downtown Money Store ("Downtown") for $90. Downtown required Chris to indorse the check. Chris indorsed the check "*Bill Smith.*" Downtown deposited the check in its account at Evergreen Bank, which credited Downtown's account for $100 and sent the check in a timely manner to Franklin Bank for payment. Franklin Bank made a timely provisional settlement for the check.

A. Ashton stopped payment on the check when Bianca told him the check was lost. Franklin Bank timely returned the check to Evergreen Bank, meeting all UCC Article 4 and Regulation CC deadlines. Evergreen Bank debited Downtown's account for the amount of the check and returned the check to Downtown. Who is likely to bear the loss for this check if Chris cannot be found or has insufficient assets to pay a judgment?

B. Franklin Bank did not return the check. Five days after Franklin Bank made final payment, Ashton called Franklin Bank to stop payment of the check because Bianca had informed Ashton that she had lost the check.

1. What are Ashton's rights against Franklin Bank?
2. On which party is the loss likely to rest if Franklin Bank does not re-credit Ashton's account?
3. Assume Franklin Bank returned the check to Evergreen Bank after Ashton's call. Evergreen Bank debited Downtown's account for the amount of the check. On which party should the loss now rest?

Problem 19-7

Ashton has a checking account at Franklin Bank. Ashton wrote a check for $100 payable to Bianca. Bianca indorsed the check "for deposit only, *Bianca*" and then lost the check. Chris found the check and sold the check to Downtown Money Store ("Downtown") for $90. Downtown required Chris to indorse the check. Chris indorsed the check "*Bill Smith.*" Downtown deposited the check in its account at Evergreen Bank, which credited Downtown's account for $100 and sent the check in a timely manner to Franklin Bank for payment. Franklin Bank made a timely provisional settlement for the check.

A. Ashton stopped payment on the check when Bianca told him the check was lost. Franklin Bank timely returned the check to Evergreen Bank, meeting all UCC Article 4 and Regulation CC deadlines. Evergreen Bank debited Downtown's account for the amount of the check and returned the check to Downtown. Analyze and evaluate all of Downtown's potential causes of action against Franklin Bank, Bianca, Chris, Ashton, and Bill Smith, along with all defenses to each of those causes of action. *See* UCC § 3-206(c) and (e).

B. Franklin Bank did not return the check. Five days after Franklin Bank made final payment, Ashton called Franklin Bank to stop payment of the check because Bianca had informed Ashton that she had lost the check.
1. What are Ashton's rights against Franklin Bank?
2. What are Bianca's rights against each relevant party?

5. *An in-depth look at UCC § 3-404 and § 3-405*

Human ingenuity and gullibility have combined to generate many fraudulent uses of negotiable instruments. UCC § 3-404 and § 3-405 address some paradigm examples of such fraud. We briefly considered both provisions at the beginning of this Section in discussing unauthorized indorsements. We return to them now for a more thorough exploration.

Reread UCC § 3-404. It deals with certain forged indorsements and operates in three different fact situations:

(i) the issuer is fooled into issuing an instrument to someone impersonating the payee or an agent of the payee (subsection (a));

(ii) the issuer issues an instrument to someone who is not intended to have any interest in the instrument (subsection (b)); and

(iii) the issuer issues the instrument to a fictitious person (subsection (b)).

In each of these situations, a forged indorsement made in the name of the payee[40] is deemed effective in favor of a person who in good faith pays the instrument or takes it for value or collection. In the last two situations, any person in possession is also a holder.

These provisions have several effects. First, a taker of the instrument will almost always be a person entitled to enforce.[41] Second, as a result, the transfer warranty that the transferor is a person entitled to enforce, and the similar presentment warranty made by a presenter,[42] will not be breached. *See* UCC § 3-404, cmt. 3.[43] Third, the forged indorsement that is deemed effective will make

---

[40] UCC § 3-404(c) defines what it means to have an indorsement made in the name of the payee. Notice that it includes within that definition an instrument that is *not* indorsed but deposited to an account in the name of the payee.

[41] In rare circumstances the taker would not qualify as a person entitled to enforce, but such a result would not relate to the forged nature of the indorsement. For example, if the forger or a subsequent holder of the instrument made a special indorsement, so that the instrument became payable to the order of a real, named person, then only that named person could be a holder. *See* UCC § 3-205(a).

[42] *See* UCC §§ 3-416(a)(1), 3-417(a)(1), (d).

[43] Making the forged indorsement effective, however, does not mean that the transfer warranty that all signatures are authentic and authorized has not been breached. UCC §§ 3-416(a)(2).

a draft properly payable from a drawer's account (at least if the only ground for objection is the forged indorsement).

The intended effect of the UCC § 3-404 scheme is to make the issuer (a drawer or maker) bear the risk of being fooled by the imposter or other person who induced the issuer to make the instrument.[44] This risk is mitigated to some effect if subsection (d) applies. Under subsection (d), if the indorsement is deemed effective under UCC § 3-404 and the taker or payor failed to exercise ordinary care and that failure substantially contributed to the loss, the loss is allocated between the issuer and the taker or payor based upon comparative negligence.[45]

Notice that the forged indorsement is deemed "effective." Compare that to UCC § 3-406 which precludes a negligent party from asserting the forgery. Consider the following potential difference in analysis.

> Scammer induces Drawer to issue a check to Payee, by impersonating someone authorized to act for Payee. Payee really exists but has no idea that Scammer has engaged in this behavior. Scammer forges Payee's signature. Scammer deposits the check to Depositary Bank, which forwards the check through normal processes to Drawee. Drawee dishonors the check because Drawer's account has insufficient funds, and the check is returned to Depositary Bank. Scammer has taken all the credited funds from her account at Depositary Bank. Depositary Bank is left holding the loss and is unable to find Scammer.

Applying UCC § 3-404(a), Depositary Bank would be a person entitled to enforce and able to pursue Drawer on its contract liability on the check. But, would Depositary Bank also be entitled to pursue Payee on the indorsement contract? If UCC § 3-406 applied, the answer would be no. Payee was not negligent and would not be precluded from asserting the forgery so that Payee would not be bound to the signature and Depositary Bank would not be a person entitled to enforce. But now consider the application of UCC § 3-404(a). By deeming the forged indorsement "effective," does that mean that Payee would have indorser's liability (deemed to be Payee's indorsement) and would therefore be obligated to Depositary Bank (a

---

[44] *See State Sec. Check Cashing, Inc. v. American Fin. Servs. (DE)*, 972 A.2d 882 (Md. 2009).

[45] *But see Siemans Building Techs., Inc. v. PNC Fin. Servs. Group, Inc.*, 226 Fed. Appx. 192 (3d Cir. 2007) (comparative negligence did not apply when bank employee was participant in fraud and bank employee's actions were not attributable to bank as a matter of agency law).

deemed person entitled to enforce)?[46] Does that make any sense, given that payees have absolutely no control over who may be impersonating them or one of their agents? Nothing in the comments speak to this issue, perhaps suggesting that this was not the intended result. Yet the language of the statute seems clear.

Now consider the following additional hypothetical.

An attorney representing a plaintiff settles a case but does not obtain the client's approval for the settlement. The attorney takes the check made payable to the client, forges the client's signature and obtains payment of the check. The defendant in the case has no idea that the attorney has acted without the client's approval or consent.

Is this a situation to which UCC § 3-404 applies? Specifically is the attorney "impersonating" a person authorized to act for the client or misrepresenting the extent of the attorney's agency authority? If the latter, what is the effect of the indorsement of the client's name?[47] Does it make sense to distinguish between impersonating someone else and misrepresenting the extent of one's agency authority? As a matter of policy regarding the allocation of loss from wrongdoing, why should a misrepresentation of agency authority be treated differently from an impersonation?

Problem 19-8

Bob told Antonia that he was the attorney for Utility Company and that her bill for electricity was overdue. Antonia wrote a check on her account at Downtown Bank payable to Utility Company and delivered the check to Bob. Bob indorsed the check "*Utility Company*" and deposited the check in his account at City Bank. Downtown Bank received the check, made a timely provisional settlement for the check, and did not return it. Bob withdrew in cash the entire credit balance of his account at City Bank, including the credit for Antonia's check.

---

[46] *Cf.* UCC § 3-403 (providing that an unauthorized signature is ineffective as a signature of the person whose name was signed "[u]nless otherwise provided in this Article").

[47] *See King v. White*, 962 P.2d 475, 481 (Kan. 1998) ("There must be an impersonation of an actual agent; a misrepresentation of agency authority is generally not sufficient to invoke the defense.").

A. Bob is not an attorney for Utility Company because that company does
    not really exist.
    1. Analyze and evaluate all of Antonia's potential causes of action
        against each possible defendant, along with all defenses to each of
        those causes of action.
    2. What are City Bank's rights if Downtown Bank re-credits
        Antonia's account and then attempts to recover against City Bank?
    3. Assume that Downtown Bank made a timely provisional settlement
        for the item and returned the check by its midnight deadline to City
        Bank because Antonia had issued a timely stop payment order.
        What are City Bank's rights? What are Antonia's rights?

B. Utility Company exists and Antonia purchases electricity from the
    company, Bob Smith is really Bob Smith. Bob Smith is not an attorney
    for the company, and is lying when he states he represents the
    company.
    1. What are Antonia's rights against Downtown Bank?
    2. What are City Bank's rights if Downtown Bank re-credits
        Antonia's account and then attempts to recover against City Bank?
    3. Assume that Downtown Bank made a timely provisional settlement
        for the item and returned the check by its midnight deadline to City
        Bank because Antonia had issued a timely stop payment order.
        What are City Bank's rights? What are Antonia's rights?

Problem 19-9

Ulysses told Antonia that he was Bob, the attorney for Utility
Company, and that her bill for electricity was overdue. Antonia wrote a
check on her account at Downtown Bank payable to Utility Company and
delivered the check to Ulysses. Ulysses indorsed the check *"Utility
Company"* and deposited the check in his account at City Bank. Downtown
Bank received the check, made a timely provisional settlement for the
check, and did not return it. Ulyssess withdrew in cash the entire credit
balance of his account at City Bank, including the credit for Antonia's
check.

A. What are Antonia's rights against Downtown Bank?

B. What are City Bank's rights if Downtown Bank re-credits Antonia's account and then attempts to recover against City Bank?

C. Assume that Downtown Bank made a timely provisional settlement for the item and returned the check by its midnight deadline to City Bank because Antonia had issued a timely stop payment order. What are City Bank's rights? What are Antonia's rights?

Reread UCC § 3-405. This section deals with forged indorsements by employees. As with UCC § 3-404, this section makes forged indorsements effective in certain situations. The principle underlying this section is that an employer should bear the risk of the fraudulent activities of its employees to whom the employer has entrusted responsibility to deal with instruments. Notice that pursuant to the definitions in subsection (a), the term "employee" includes independent contractors, the term "fraudulent indorsement" covers two situations in which employees tend to forge indorsements,[48] and "responsibility" is keyed to the particular instrument at issue.[49]

As with the other preclusion sections we have studied, when UCC § 3-405 applies, it makes the forged indorsement effective. As a result, the person in possession of the instrument can qualify as both a holder and a person entitled to enforce.[50] Moreover, if the instrument is a check, the forged indorsement will not prevent the check from being properly payable from the employer's bank account. The purpose and net effect of this is to protect good faith transferees who take the instrument for value and good faith payors. If the section makes an indorsement effective, the comparative negligence rule of subsection (b) may result in some loss being allocated to the entity that took or paid the instrument.[51]

---

[48] UCC § 3-405(c) defines what it means to have an indorsement made in the name of the payee. Notice that it includes within that definition an instrument that is *not* indorsed but deposited to an account in the name of the payee.

[49] *See Dean Classic Cars, L.L.C. v. Fidelity Bank and Trust Co.*, 978 So. 2d 393 (La. Ct. App. 2007) (mere access to corporate checks does not equate with responsibility for the checks under UCC § 3-405).

[50] This section does, however, not make the forged indorsement authorized and authentic for purposes of transfer warranty liability. *See* UCC §§ 3-416(a)(2).

[51] A common scenario in which the taker's negligence is at issue involves a depositary bank

Now consider this situation.

Employer writes a check to Supplier, a real payee. Employee, who has responsibility with respect to the check, steals the check before it is sent to Supplier, forges Supplier's name and deposits the check in Employee's account at Depositary Bank, which forwards the check through normal processes to Drawee. Before the check reaches the Drawee, Employer discovers Employee's scheme and stops payment on the check, so that it is dishonored. Drawee returns the check to Depositary Bank. Predictably, Employee has withdrawn the entire credit balance in Employee's account at Depositary Bank and disappeared. Depositary Bank is, at least initially, left holding the loss.

Few would quarrel with the result that the employer should bear the risk of the bad employee and the depositary bank should be able to have the indorsement deemed effective under this section so that the depositary bank can sue the employer on its drawer's liability on the check. But what of the payee? Is the payee, who had nothing to do with this scheme and has not received payment of the obligation that the employer owes to it, be subject to indorser's liability on the instrument? Should the words in UCC § 3-405(b) that the "indorsement is effective as the indorsement of the person to whom the instrument is payable" be applied to allow the depositary bank sue the payee on the indorsement contract? Does that make any sense?

Problem 19-10

Barbara is an employee who works for Acme Company. On occasion, she submits invoices to the company treasurer for payment. Barbara does not otherwise handle any money or checks for the company. She submitted an invoice showing that Acme owes $200 to Supplier. Supplier exists and

---

that opens deposit accounts in the name of the employer (but without the employer's authorization), and the embezzling employee steals checks payable to the employer, forges the employer's indorsement and deposits the check into that account. *See Auto-Owners Ins. Co. v. Bank One*, 879 N.E.2d 1086 (Ind. 2008) (depositary bank not negligent). *Compare LaComb v. Bank One Corp.*, 953 So. 2d 161 (La. Ct. App.), *writ denied*, 957 So. 2d 177 (La. 2007) (bank negligent in taking checks payable to a sole proprietorship for deposit into another individual's account). *See also Rodriquez v. Bank of the West*, 75 Cal. Rptr. 3d 543 (Cal. Ct. App. 2008) (bank did not owe duty of care to victim of identity theft where bank opened accounts in victim's name in furtherance of embezzlement scheme).

occasionally does business with Acme, but Acme does not really owe Supplier any money. Acme's treasurer, who was authorized to do so on Acme's behalf, signed and issued a check payable to Supplier and drawn on Acme's account at Downtown Bank. Barbara obtained the check from the stack of outgoing mail and indorsed the check "*Supplier.*" Barbara then deposited the check in her bank account at City Bank. Downtown Bank received and made a timely provisional settlement for the check.

A. Downtown Bank did not return the check. Five days after Downtown Bank made final payment, Acme discovered that the check should not have been issued and called Downtown Bank to complain.
   1. Analyze and evaluate all of Acme's potential causes of action against each possible defendant, along with all defenses to each of those causes of action.
   2. What are City Bank's rights if Downtown Bank re-credits Acme's account and then attempts to recover against City Bank?

B. Downtown Bank returned the check in a timely manner to City Bank, complying with all UCC Article 4 and Regulation CC deadlines. What are City Bank's options?

C. How, if at all, would the analysis of Parts A and B change if Supplier did not exist?

D. How, if at all, would the analysis of Parts A and B change if Acme really owed Supplier the amount of the check?

E. How, if at all, would the analysis of Parts A and B change if Barbara did not decide to steal the check until after she submitted the invoice?

F. How, if at all, would the analysis of Parts A and B change if Barbara did not prepare the invoice resulting in the check issuance?

Problem 19-11

Barbara is an employee who works for Acme Company. Barbara delivers the internal mail for the company. Barbara stole a check made payable to Acme Company from the stack of incoming mail. She indorsed that check in the name of "Acme Company" and deposited the check in her account at City Bank. That check was paid by the drawee bank. In due course, Acme contacted the drawer to complain that it had not been paid. The drawer sent Acme a copy of the cancelled check showing that it had been paid by the drawee bank. What are Acme's rights against Barbara, City Bank, and the drawee?

D. Unauthorized Acceptor's Signature

Just as with other signatures, an acceptor's signature can be unauthorized or forged. Just as with other signatures, the first step is to determine if the signature is in fact authorized under principles of agency law, UCC § 3-402, and if not, whether it has been ratified, UCC § 3-403. If the acceptor's signature is not authorized or ratified, then the purported acceptor (the drawee who purportedly signed the draft) is not liable on the signature for the acceptor's contract liability. UCC § 3-413. The purported acceptor may be precluded from asserting a forgery of its signature if it was negligent and that negligence substantially contributed to the forgery, UCC § 3-406, subject to the comparative negligence analysis provided in that section. Sections 3-404, 3-405, and 4-406 do not apply to an acceptor's signature.

SECTION 3.   INCOMPLETE INSTRUMENTS AND ALTERATIONS

So far we have focused on forged signatures and the allocation of the risk associated with them. Now we turn to instruments that are missing some critical information, so-called incomplete instruments, and instruments that are altered.

The first step in analysis is to determine if the instrument is incomplete or altered. **Read UCC § 3-115 and § 3-407.** These sections define what is an incomplete instrument and what is an alteration. Notice that if an incomplete instrument is completed without authority, the instrument is treated as if altered.

The second step is to consider the effect of filling in the missing information or altering the instrument. In general, filling in missing information in a manner authorized by the maker or drawer simply completes the instrument and binds the maker or drawer to the same extent as the maker or drawer would have been bound had the information been completed all along. Filling in information in a manner that is not authorized constitutes a type of alteration.

If an item has been altered, the third step is to determine the liability of the various signers (makers, drawers, indorsers, acceptors) on the instrument. In general, a fraudulent alteration discharges a party whose obligation is affected by that alteration. *See* UCC § 3-407(b). However, a person who in good faith pays or takes the instrument for value can enforce the instrument according to its original terms. *See* UCC § 3-407(c). *See also* UCC § 4-401(d). Moreover, the signer may be precluded from asserting the alteration as a defense if the signer failed to exercise ordinary care and that failure substantially contributed to the alteration, *see* UCC § 3-406, or pursuant to the bank-statement rule of UCC § 4-406.[52] Finally, a holder in due course will take free of this defense. *See* UCC § 3-305(a), (b). Of course, someone with notice of the alteration cannot qualify as a holder in due course. *See* UCC § 3-302(a)(2).

With respect to the liability of those who signed after the alteration, review the transfer and presentment warranties. UCC §§ 3-416, 3-417, 4-207, 4-208; Reg. J, 12 C.F.R. §§ 210.5, 210.6; Reg. CC, 12 C.F.R. § 229.34. Notice that UCC § 3-404 and § 3-405 apply only to forged indorsements.[53]

Now try your hand at working through how the risk is allocated when there is an incomplete or altered instrument.

Problem 19-12

Adam went to Bank for a $1,000 loan. While there, Adam signed a promissory note and delivered the note to the loan officer with instructions to complete the note payable to the order of Bank once the loan is approved and the loan amount is credited to Adam's account at Bank.

---

[52] *See J. Walter Thompson, U.S.A., Inc. v. First BankAmericano*, 518 F.3d 128 (2d Cir. 2008).

[53] Given the difference between an altered item and an item with a forged drawer's signature with respect to how loss is allocated, the burden of proof is critical. *See Wachovia Bank v. Foster Bancshares, Inc.*, 457 F.3d 619 (7th Cir. 2006) (check was destroyed under normal check truncation processes, presumed alteration); *Chevy Chase Bank v. Wachovia Bank*, 208 Fed. Appx. 232 (4th Cir. 2006) (treated as forged check when drawee failed to carry burden of proof that there was an alteration).

A. To what extent, if any, will the note be enforceable in each of the scenarios described below?

   1. The note states that it is "payable to the order of _____."

   2. The note states "payment is due one year from the date hereof" but the note is undated.

   3. The amount of the note is blank.

   4. The note states that "interest on the unpaid balance will accrue at a rate of _____ percent per annum, compounded daily."

B. How, if at all, will the analysis of Part A change if, after the loan is approved and the loan amount is credited to Adam's account, the loan officer properly completes the note pursuant to Adam's instructions?

C. How, if at all, will the analysis of Part A change if, after the loan is approved and the loan amount is credited to Adam's account, the loan officer completes the note in a manner contrary to Adam's instructions?

Problem 19-13

Annabel went shopping. She decided to pay for her purchases with a check. She made the check payable to the store, Boffo Clothiers, handed the check to the sales clerk, and asked the clerk to fill in the correct amount of $200. The clerk filled in $800 instead of $200. Boffo Clothiers deposited the check at City Bank, which forwarded the check in a timely manner to Downtown Bank, the drawee. Downtown Bank received the check, made a timely provisional settlement for the check, did not return it, and debited Annabel's account for $800. When Annabel received her next monthly bank statement, she promptly notified Downtown Bank and demanded that it re-credit $600 to her account. Must Downtown bank do so? If Downtown Bank does re-credit Annabel's account for $600, will Downtown Bank be able to recover that amount from someone else?

Problem 19-14

A. Arlene signed a note that stated, "I promise to pay to Best Co. $200 on June 5." Arlene delivered the note to Zeb, a Best Co. employee. Zeb added "to the order of" in front of Best Co.'s name. Zeb indorsed the note "Best Co. by *Zed*, President" and then sold and delivered the note to City Bank for $180. City Bank presented the note to Arlene for payment. Arlene refused to pay because the product she bought from Best Co. was defective. Is City Bank subject to that defense?

B. Arlene signed a note that stated, "I promise to pay to the order of _____ $200 on June 5." Arlene delivered the note to Zeb, a Best Co. employee. Zeb was supposed to stamp "Best Co." in the blank, but instead put in his own name. Zeb indorsed the note "*Zeb*, without recourse" and then sold and delivered the note to City Bank for $150. City Bank presented the note to Arlene for payment. Arlene refused to pay because the product she bought from Best Co. was defective. Is City Bank subject to that defense?

Problem 19-15

Alex wrote a check for $200 payable to Best Co. drawn on First National Bank. Chris, the president of Best Co., indorsed the check as follows: "Best Co. by *Chris*, President." Chris has the authority to indorse checks for Best Co. Chris then skillfully changed the amount of the check to $800 and used the check to buy a new fishing rod at Downtown Sports Shop. Downtown Sports Shop deposited the check in its account at Evergreen Bank, indorsing the check as follows: "For deposit only, *Downtown Sports Shop*, without recourse." Evergreen Bank sent the check in a timely manner to the Federal Reserve Bank. The Federal Reserve Bank then sent the check in a timely manner to First National Bank.

A. First National Bank made a provisional settlement for the check, debited Alex's account for $800, and did not return the check. Promptly after receiving her monthly bank statement from First National Bank, Alex objected claiming that the check had been altered. Starting with First National Bank, explain how the loss from this event will be allocated.

B. Assume that Alex timely stopped payment on the check because the goods she purchased from Best Co. were defective. First National timely returned the check to the Federal Reserve Bank. Each bank in the return process fully complied with Regulation CC, Regulation J, and UCC Article 4. Evergreen Bank debited Downtown Sports Shop's account for $800 when the item was returned to Evergreen. Starting with Downtown Sports, explain how the loss from this event will be allocated.

SECTION 4. LOST OR STOLEN CERTIFIED, CASHIER'S, AND TELLER'S CHECKS

In Chapter Fifteen and earlier in this Chapter, we examined UCC § 3-309, which provides a mechanism for a person not in possession of an instrument to enforce the contract obligation on the instrument. This section comes into play when an instrument has been lost or stolen and is often used in the case of lost negotiable notes, although it is not limited to that particular situation.

Now consider how the UCC deals with the special case of cashier's, teller's and certified checks. Review the definition of a cashier's check and a teller's check in UCC § 3-104 and the definition of a certified check in UCC § 3-409. The bank incurs contract liability on a cashier's check (review UCC § 3-412), a teller's check (review UCC § 3-414), and a certified check (review UCC § 3-409, § 3-413 and § 3-414). In addition, if such a check is taken for an obligation, that underlying obligation is discharged at that time, not merely suspended. Review UCC § 3-310(a).

So what happens if one of these special types of checks is issued but then lost or stolen? One of the first things to consider is whether the bank that is liable on such a check can be successfully instructed to stop payment on the check.[54] Neither the remitter of a cashier's check or teller's check (review the UCC § 3-103(a)(15) definition of remitter) nor the drawer of a certified check has the authority to stop payment of the check. The remitter is not the customer authorized to draw on the account on which a cashier's or teller's check is drawn. *See* UCC § 4-403. Similarly, the drawer of a draft accepted by the bank (a certified check) is discharged from its contract liability and does not have the ability to order the acceptor to breach its contract obligation on the check. Review UCC § 3-411. That

---

[54] Review the discussion in Chapter Sixteen on stop payment.

section is designed to discourage the obligated bank from dishonoring these types of checks as an accommodation to the remitter or the drawer.[55]

In some circumstances, a remitter of a teller's or cashier's check or the drawer of the certified check may want to obtain funds from the obligated bank. After all, the remitter of the teller's or cashier's check or the drawer of a certified check will have already parted with funds in order to get the bank to issue or certify the check. **Now read UCC § 3-312.** This section gives a "claimant" a mechanism for obtaining value from the obligated bank. While the section includes a drawer of a certified check and the remitter as persons who may file a declaration of loss, it is not entirely clear that those folks qualify as "claimants" under the section,[56] although they probably should be.

Notice that this section is not the exclusive manner of obtaining funds from the obligated bank. A person seeking enforcement of the bank's contract obligation on the check may also use UCC § 3-309. *See* UCC § 3-312(d).

With these principles in mind, consider the following problem.

Problem 19-16

Anderson bought a house. In preparation for the closing the next day, he requested that City Bank certify a check drawn on Anderson's account at the bank. Anderson wrote out a check for $4,000 payable to the order of Scott and Marion Brown. The teller at City Bank checked Anderson's account balance. Anderson had $10,000 in available funds. The teller certified the check by writing on the face of the check: "Certified by City

---

[55] A bank that refuses to honor a cashier's check, teller's check, or a certified check has contract liability on that check but is able to assert its own defenses to its contract liability on the check. UCC § 3-305. If the holder of the check is a holder in due course, UCC § 3-302, the bank's defenses will be barred unless they are the types of defenses to which a holder in due course is subject. *See Gentner and Company Inc. v. Wells Fargo Bank*, 90 Cal. Rptr. 2d 904 (Cal. Ct. App. 1999).

[56] The comments to UCC § 3-301 were amended in 2002 to provide that a remitter who has not yet transferred or negotiated the instrument may be a person entitled to enforce the instrument. Is this comment enough to make a remitter a "claimant" under UCC § 3-312? *Compare In re Cohen*, 300 F.3d 1097 (9th Cir. 2002) (remitter was not a person entitled to enforce a cashier's check and thus had no interest in the check for purposes of determining the initial transferee under 11 U.S.C. § 550).

Bank on June 2, 1996 for $4,000." The teller then debited Anderson's account for $4,000.

A. Later that day, Anderson was in a car accident. When he awoke in the hospital, the check was gone, along with his wallet and credit cards. What are Anderson's options with regard to the certified check and the house closing? What are the Brown's options with regard to the certified check and the house closing?

B. Anderson took the check to the closing and gave the check to Scott and Marion Brown. Thereafter, the Browns lost the check. What are the Brown's options with regard to the certified check? Can the Browns require Anderson to pay them $4,000?

SECTION 5.   REVIEW

It is usually helpful when organizing your thoughts to take each instrument and to draw a time line based upon the route the instrument took. That will help you visualize the relationships between the various actors and help you think through which causes of action should be asserted against which actors, what defenses could be asserted, and what the responses may be to the defenses.

Problem 19-17

Carpenter Enterprises Inc. is a closely-held corporation run by majority shareholder Jonathan Carpenter, who is president of the company. Carpenter Enterprises Inc. has a checking account, held by Sacramento Savings Bank. Jonathan used this checking account to pay all expenses of the business, including both operating expenses and payroll. Jonathan was the only authorized signatory on the account.

On March 1, Jonathan hired Brad Peterson as a salesperson for Carpenter Enterprises Inc. On April 2, Peterson used the routing and account information at the bottom of one of his payroll checks from Carpenter Enterprises to create a new check drawn on Carpenter Enterprises Inc.'s account at Sacramento Savings Bank and payable to "cash" for $8,000. Peterson signed the name "Jonathan Carpenter" on the drawer's line in the bottom right hand corner of the check. Peterson presented that check at Sacramento Savings Bank over the counter. The clerk thought it was odd to have such a large check presented over the counter, but after checking with the bank manager, gave $8,000 to Peterson in exchange for the check. The clerk required that Peterson sign the back of the check, which he did with the name "Bryce Peterson".

Peterson took a payroll check payable to him for $2,000 and altered the amount to $20,000. That check was deposited to his personal account at Sterling Bank, which credited $20,000 to the account. Approximately three days after that deposit, Peterson withdrew the entire credit balance in the account in the form of a cashier's check payable to Brad Peterson and closed the account. One day after he closed the account, Sterling Bank received the $20,000 back with the notation "NSF" stamped on it. (That means the check was dishonored by the drawee because of insufficient funds in the account on which the check was drawn.)

Peterson also stole from Carpenter Enterprises' incoming mail a check payable to Carpenter Enterprises for the amount of $5,000. The check was signed by the president of Anderson Consulting in payment of an debt owed to Carpenter Enterprises. Peterson deposited the check in an account Peterson had previously opened at National Bank in the name of Carpenter Enterprises. He represented to the bank officer at National Bank that he was the owner of Carpenter Enterprises at the time he opened the bank account. He indorsed the check "Carpenter Enter." The check was not returned by State Bank, the drawee. Approximately a week later, Peterson closed his account at National Bank, withdrawing in cash the full credit balance of the account (which included the credit from the $5,000 check).

At the time he opened the account at National Bank, Peterson also borrowed $10,000 from National Bank, signing as maker a negotiable demand note with the name Jonathan Carpenter. The note was payable to bearer for $10,000 plus 5% interest. National Bank sold the note to City Bank for $8,000.

Peterson quit his job and fled town, with the proceeds from all three checks, and the loan proceeds, as described above. Peterson had obtained cash from the cashier's check by presenting it at a branch of Sterling Bank a day after the cashier's check was issued.

A month later Jonathan contacted Anderson Consulting requesting that it pay its bill. Anderson Consulting refused to pay, stating its bank had already debited its account and that it no longer owed Carpenter Enterprises any debt. Banning Bank contacted Jonathan and demanded payment of the note amount. Jonathan refused to pay the note and with the help of a private investigator discovered all of the above.

Evaluate all parties' rights and liabilities.

CHAPTER TWENTY

FUNDS TRANSFER

SECTION 1. INTRODUCTION

The previous Chapters have worked through the relatively simple rules governing payments using cash and credit cards and the complex rules that govern payments using negotiable instruments. This Chapter addresses the rules that govern the mechanisms for making payments through funds transfer between deposit accounts held by financial institutions. Before proceeding to a discussion of the rules, however, it is important to understand how a funds transfer mechanism operates. At the simplest level, a funds transfer is an instruction to a bank to debit or credit a deposit account held at a financial institution and credit or debit a recipient's deposit account.

An instruction given by a person to its financial institution to transfer funds from the person's deposit account to the deposit account of another entity is known as a "push" or credit transaction. Consider a simple example of a push transaction. An individual uses an online bill paying program offered by that individual's bank to pay its utility bill. The individual instructs her bank to debit the individual's deposit account and transfer funds to the credit of the deposit account of the utility company. If the utility company's deposit account happens to be at the same bank, the bank will handle the transfer internally using its computer system. If the utility's deposit account is maintained at another bank, the individual's bank uses a third-party communication and settlement network to transfer the value from the individual's deposit account to the utility company's designated deposit account for incoming payments.

An instruction given by a person to another person's financial institution to debit a deposit account of that other person, and transfer funds from that other person's deposit account to the instructor's deposit account is known as a "pull" or debit transaction. Consider a simple example of a pull transaction. An individual seeks to purchase groceries at a local market. Instead of using a credit card to pay for the purchase, the buyer uses a "debit card" issued by the buyer's bank. The card is scanned at a terminal in the check out lane. The information from the card, the amount of the purchase, and the merchant's identifying information is transmitted to the merchant's bank, and then through a communication network, to the buyer's bank. The buyer's bank verifies the buyer's deposit account balance and, assuming a sufficient available balance, authorizes the transaction. The transaction is then cleared through the network which results in value being transferred from the buyer's deposit account to the merchant's deposit account. The merchant, through its bank, and the network, is issuing an instruction to the buyer's bank to debit the account of the buyer and transfer that value to the merchant's deposit account.

Other examples of funds transfer include automatic deposit of payroll amounts to the wage earner's deposit account, automatic bill payment through authorized deductions from a deposit account, or authorizing a commercial "wire transfer" from one financial institution to another.

What all of these transactions have in common is that the authorization and settlement of the transaction takes place through the banking system and proprietary networks used in the communication process.[1] The instruction to debit or credit the deposit account is initiated through a mechanism other than a check, and is often, but not necessarily, through an electronic means of communication.

This statement may leave the impression that it is easy to determine whether a particular transaction is a "check" transaction or a funds transfer. However, often a check is "converted" to an instruction that is then processed through a funds transfer network, or a check is used as a source document for the information to begin a funds transfer, the lines between these various mechanisms are quite blurred.[2] We will explore this convergence issue in this Chapter.

---

[1] Funds transfer transactions based upon communication to a bank to debit or credit a deposit account in order to credit or debit a different deposit account held at a bank are distinguished from what are called pre-paid or stored value transactions. In a pre-paid or stored value transaction, value typically has been deposited with non-bank entities. An example of a stored value card is a card used to make copies at a photocopy machine in a library. Other merchant networks, such as Visa®, may issue stored value cards. Gift cards are another example of a type of stored value system. The value available for use with the card may be encoded on the card itself or may be accessed when the card is run through a reader. E-cash is a type of system where the provider takes deposits of value into a web-based account and the user can then spend that value at various merchant web sites. An example of this type of system is http:/www.paypal.com. Both of these systems (stored value and e-cash) do not require settlement of transactions through the banking system. We will consider these types of pre-paid payment mechanisms in Chapter Twenty-One.

[2] *See* Amelia H. Boss, *Convergence in Electronic Banking: Technological Convergence, Systems Convergence, Legal Convergence*, 2 DREXEL L. REV. 63 (2009). The recent European Union payment services directive is designed to harmonize the legal framework for payments in Europe. *See* Agnieszka Janczuk, *The Single Payments Area in Europe*, 16 COLUM. J. EUR. L. 321 (2010); Benjamin Geva, *Payment Transactions Under the EU*

As electronic means of communication improve and evolve, new mechanisms of making funds transfers will also evolve. For example, currently there are smart phone applications that can be used to initiate a funds transfer communication.

Some examples of these networks include those currently used to clear credit card transactions (such as Visa® and MasterCard®), which have adapted to also process funds transfers initiated by debit cards, and others used specifically for funds transfers, such as the Automated Clearing House (ACH) network governed by National Automated Clearing House Association (NACHA), Fedwire (run by the Federal Reserve Banks), or the Clearinghouse Interbank Payments System (CHIPS) run by The Clearing House.[3]

The number and amount of funds transfer payments cleared annually in the United States is staggering. In 2009, approximately 37.9 billion transactions were cleared through debit card networks. Over 19 billion ACH transactions constituting $37.2 trillion were processed in 2009. Fedwire reported an average of almost 500,000 transfers per day with an average amount of over $5 million per transfer for 2009. CHIPS reported an average of $1.445 trillion per day in transfers in 2009. Funds transfer mechanisms for making payments outpace payments made using both checks and credit cards. In 2009, based upon the total number of payment transactions, checks accounted for 22%, debit cards for 35%, ACH for 18%, and credit card for 20%.[4]

Payment Services Directive: A U.S. Comparative Perspective, 27 PENN ST. INT'L REV. 713 (2009).

[3] Just as with credit cards, the networks used for transmitting information for authorization and clearing of the funds transfer transactions charge interchange and other fees to the participants. As found in a recent survey conducted by the Federal Reserve Board, interchange fees in debit (pull) transactions range from over 1% of the transaction amount to half a percentage of the transaction amount. The fees consist of both a fixed amount and a variable amount based upon the transaction amount. *See* Debit Card Interchange Fees and Routing, 75 Fed. Reg. 81722 (Dec. 28, 2010). The Dodd-Frank Wall Street Reform and Consumer Protection Act, Pub. L. No. 111-203, § 1075 (2010) amended the Electronic Fund Transfer Act, 15 U.S.C. §§ 1693–1693r, by adding a provision giving the Federal Reserve Board the ability to regulate the amount of the interchange fee for debit transactions as "reasonable and proportional" to the cost incurred with respect to the transaction. This provision is codified at 15 U.S.C. § 1693*o*-2, and has been implemented in Regulation II, 12 C.F.R. pt. 235.

[4] *See* Debit Card Interchange Fees and Routing, 75 Fed. Reg. 81722 (Dec. 28, 2010); 2010

Using a funds transfer as a payment mechanism raises the same concerns as other payment mechanisms. As outlined in Chapter Twelve, these concerns center around the following issues:

A. *Operation.* How does the payment mechanism transfer value? How does the payment mechanism work?

B. *Timing.*
   (1) When is payment final?
   (2) When does the payment mechanism discharge the payor's underlying obligation to the payee?
   (3) Prior to discharge, is the payor's underlying obligation to the payee suspended?

C. *Rights & Duties.*
   (1) What obligations to the payor, payee, or other parties does the payment mechanism create?
   (2) To the extent use of the mechanism creates additional obligations:
      (i) How are those obligations satisfied?
      (ii) What defenses does the obligor have to those obligations?
      (iii) If there are multiple obligors created by use of the mechanism, what is the relationship among those obligors?

D. *Risk.*
   (1) What effect will a party's insolvency have on the finality of the payment and the discharge of the underlying obligation?
   (2) What errors might arise during use of the payment mechanism and, for each error, which party or parties bear the risk?
   (3) What wrongdoing may occur during the use of the payment mechanism and, for each type of wrongdoing, which party or parties bear the risk?

Unfortunately, these questions are difficult to answer because funds transfer mechanisms are not governed by a comprehensive system of legal rules. The two main sources of statutory and regulatory law that do apply are:

• The Electronic Fund Transfer Act (EFTA) (codified at 15 U.S.C. §§ 1693–1693r) and its implementing regulation, Regulation E (12 C.F.R.

Federal Reserve Payments Study (Dec. 8, 2010); CHIPS Annual Statistics (http://www.chips.org/about/pages/001221.php); Fedwire Annual Statistics (http://www.federalreserve.gov/paymentsystems/fedfunds_ann.htm).

pt. 205), which govern funds transfers involving debits or credits to consumer accounts held at a financial institution.[5]

- UCC Article 4A, which governs credit transfers (not debit transfers) that are not covered in any part by the EFTA, *see* UCC §§ 4A-108, 4A-103(a)(1), and cmt. 4. **Read the Prefatory Note to UCC Article 4A.**

Debit funds transfers that do not involve consumer accounts are not governed by a comprehensive sets of federal or state laws. They are instead subject to idiosyncratic state statutes and the general common law of contract.[6] Thus, the law governing electronic funds transfers can be depicted as follows:

Transaction	Governing Law[7]
Credit funds transfer to or debit funds transfer from a consumer account	EFTA and Reg. E
credit funds transfer (other than above)	UCC Article 4A and Reg. J
debit funds transfer (other than above)	common law of contract

In addition, system and network rules promulgated by the particular network used to authorize and clear the funds transfer transaction also govern. NACHA has rules that govern both debit and credit funds transfers made through the ACH network. Funds transfers made through Fedwire are governed by Regulation J, 12

---

[5] Starting July 21, 2011, except for a few designated provisions in the EFTA, the new Consumer Financial Protection Bureau will have authority to promulgate rules under the EFTA.

[6] As the existing funds transfer rules are explored, consider whether the EFTA and Regulation E model or the UCC Article 4A model, or some combination thereof, would be appropriate for these otherwise unregulated debit funds transfers. Because debit funds transfers that fall outside the scope of the EFTA and Regulation E are not the subject of uniform state or federal law, but rather are regulated by contract and system rules (such as the NACHA rules), the material in this Chapter does not address those types of funds transfers in any depth.

[7] State and federal consumer protection laws may also apply. *See* Regulation AA, 12 C.F.R. pt. 227. *See also* Uniform Money Services Act (promulgated by the Uniform Law Commission).

C.F.R. pt. 210 and Operating Circular 6. CHIPS also has operating rules for transactions using that network.[8]

As should now be apparent, the regulations governing any particular funds transfer depends upon what type of deposit account is credited or debited, whether the transaction is a debit or credit funds transfer, and what network is used to process the funds transfer. Given the diversity of regulation, the material in this Chapter provides merely a starting point for analysis. A full legal analysis of any particular issue must also involve an analysis of any applicable system rules and agreements between the parties. The remainder of this Chapter addresses funds transfers made either to or from a consumer deposit account in Section 2 and credit funds transfers governed by UCC Article 4A in Section 3.

SECTION 2. FUNDS TRANSFER INVOLVING CONSUMER DEPOSIT ACCOUNTS

A. Scope of EFTA and Regulation E

The first step is to identify whether the EFTA and Regulation E apply. To begin that inquiry, **read the definition of "electronic fund transfer" in the EFTA, 15 U.S.C. § 1693a, and Regulation E, 12 C.F.R. § 205.3**. Make sure and read the other definitions in both the EFTA, 15 U.S.C. § 1693a, and Regulation E, 12 C.F.R. § 205.2, in order to understand the definition of "electronic fund transfer." Official staff interpretations of Regulation E found in Supplement I to Regulation E are helpful in understanding the application of the regulation.

In some instances, Regulation E applies to entities that are not financial institutions or to transfers that do not meet the definition of electronic funds transfer in Regulation E. *See* Reg. E, 12 C.F.R. §§ 205.14, 205.15, 205.18.[9] **Read UCC**

---

[8] The NACHA Operating Rules and Guidelines are available in a yearly publication, available by order from http://www.nacha.org. The Federal Reserve Board has also issued Operating Circular 4 to govern ACH items. The Rules and Administrative Procedures for CHIPS are available at http://www.chips.org.

The ACH network is used to process consumer and business funds transfers (both credit and debit). Fedwire and CHIPS are primarily used to process business credit funds transfers although on occasion those networks may be used for larger consumer transactions.

[9] The Dodd-Frank Wall Street Reform and Consumer Protection Act, Pub. L. No. 111-203,

§ 4A-108 regarding the relationship between the EFTA and Article 4A. Read UCC § 4A-102 and § 4A-104(a).

In addition to determining whether UCC Article 4A or the EFTA apply, another challenge is distinguishing a "check" transaction from a "funds transfer" transaction. As explored in Chapter Sixteen, a check may be imaged at the depositary bank and then collected using the electronically captured image. A check may be used as a source document in which the MICR line information is captured, either at the point of sale or at the payee's location (or lockbox location), and that MICR line information used to obtain value from the drawer's deposit account. A check may be deposited at an ATM machine, and then collected by transmitting an image to the payor bank. A payor may use an electronic bill paying program to instruct its bank to pay a payee, with the bank debiting the payor's deposit account and the bank then issuing its own check to the payee. Are these transactions a "check" transaction," a "funds transfer" or both?

At stake in this inquiry about governing law will be the parties' rights and obligations in the event something goes wrong.

Problem 20-1

For each of the following transactions, determine whether it is governed by the EFTA and Regulation E, UCC Article 4A, or other law.

A. Olive went into her bank to request that the bank transfer funds from her personal checking account to her daughter's savings account at another bank. The bank teller had Olive fill out a funds transfer slip, indicating Olive's account number, the name and address of her daughter's bank, and her daughter's account number.

---

§ 1073 (2010) amended the EFTA, 15 U.S.C. §§ 1693–1693r, by adding a provision governing a "remittance transfer." 15 U.S.C. § 1693o-1. A remittance transfer is defined as a funds transfer to a person located in a country other than the United States and that person is deemed to be "not a consumer" for purposes of the EFTA. If a remittance transfer also meets the definition of an "electronic fund transfer" (*i.e.*, a covered funds transfer to or from a consumer's asset account at a financial institution), the other provisions of the EFTA will apply in addition to the new provision regarding a remittance transfer. 15 U.S.C. § 1693o-1(e). The Federal Reserve Board has issued a proposed regulation to deal with a remittance transfer. 76 Fed. Reg. 29902 (May 23, 2011).

B. Using a smart phone application, Olive accessed her bank account and instructed the bank to transfer $9,000 from her personal checking account to her daughter's savings account at another bank. In doing so, Olive electronically filled out a form indicting the name and address of her daughter's bank and her daughter's account number. Her bank used Fedwire to transfer the funds to her daughter's bank.

C. Olive accessed her bank account through a web access program on her personal computer and instructed her bank to transfer $500 from her personal checking account to her daughter's savings account at the same bank every month on the fifth day of the month.

D. Mary owns a small business and has authorized her property and liability insurer to draw the amount of the premium from the business checking account each month. The insurer does so by an automated instruction to the bank holding the business checking account.

E. Sarah sent a check for $200 drawn on her personal checking account to her local utility company to pay her monthly bill. The utility company used the information from the MICR line to create a message, transmitted by the utility to its bank and then transmitted by that bank to Sarah's bank, instructing Sarah's bank to debit Sarah's deposit account on which the check had been drawn and credit the utility company's account.

F. At the grocery store, Sarah used a debit card to pay for her groceries.

G. Sarah used a card at an ATM in the local mall to deposit a check and withdraw $100 from her personal checking account.

H. Sarah's employer, Best Donuts, Inc., deposits her monthly wages through an instruction to Best Donuts' bank to credit Sarah's personal checking account at her bank.

I. Sarah's deposit account agreement with her bank provides for automatic overdraft protection. Pursuant to that protection, the bank transferred funds from her personal savings account to her personal checking account (both maintained by the same bank) to cover a check drawn on the checking account.

J.   Sarah went to her local telephone company's website and used the bill paying feature to authorize the telephone company to withdraw the amount of her monthly bill from her savings account.

K.   Bigtime Inc. decided that to pay its employees, it would set up an account at its bank for each employee and give each employee a card to access the amount of the employee's net pay (after withheld taxes). Benjamin, an employee, used an ATM card issued by the bank to withdraw $200 from th account established in his name by Bigtime.

L.   Benjamin used his WEBpay account to pay for music that he downloaded from an online music retailer. To access his WEBpay account and authorize payment, he entered his username and password on the music retailer's online checkout page. WEBpay is not a bank but allows its members to fund an account by charging a credit card for an amount and then use the charged amount to make payments to participating vendors, one of which is the online music retailer. Benjamin funded the WEBpay account by a $100 charge to his credit card six months ago, which he has since paid in the normal course.

As noted above, if a funds transfer is governed by the EFTA and Regulation E, UCC Article 4A does not apply to the transfer. One of the difficulties this state of affairs presents is that the EFTA and Regulation E govern only a few issues that may arise in a funds transfer. For other issues, because UCC Article 4A does not apply, common-law principles have to fill the gap.[10]

---

[10] A court could decide to apply UCC Article 4A by analogy as part of the development of the jurisdiction's common law. In addition, funds transfer system rules may provide an avenue for recovery against other participants in the funds transfer. *Security First Network Bank v. C.A.P.S., Inc.*, 47 U.C.C. Rep. Serv. 2d 670 (N.D. Ill. 2002) (an account holder could maintain a breach of warranty action based on the NACHA rules against a bank that originated an allegedly unauthorized ACH debit from the account holder's bank account). *But see* 2011 NACHA Operating Rules, Rule 1.9 (no third party beneficiary of NACHA rule rights and obligations).

B. Obligations in a Transaction Governed by EFTA and Regulation E

Funds transfer and the underlying obligation. When a payor authorizes either a debit or credit funds transfer instruction to pay an obligation, that authorization alone is not sufficient to discharge the obligation that the payor owes to the payee. It is not clear that the authorization suspends the underlying obligation to pay the payee because neither the EFTA or Regulation E so provide, although if the payee has agreed to accept payment through a funds transfer, suspension of the underlying obligation is a fair inference that could be supported as part of the agreement of the parties as a matter of contract law.

If the payee receives final settlement of the funds transfer through crediting of the value, the payor's underlying obligation to the payee is discharged although, again, that is an inference based upon the parties' agreement, not a rule found in either the EFTA or Regulation E. If the payee does not receive settlement of the funds transfer instruction by the actual crediting of value to its bank account, the payee will probably be able to pursue the payor on the underlying obligation. This ability may be subject to an exception if the network through which the funds transfer is executed provides to the contrary based upon its system rules. These issues regarding the relationship of the funds transfer to the underlying obligation are not dealt with in either the EFTA or Regulation E.

Funds transfer and obligations to the involved financial institutions. The EFTA and Regulation E govern the relationship between the financial institution and the consumer whose deposit account is being debited or credited, but only as to certain aspects of the funds transfer.[11] Other aspects of the funds transfer are governed by the agreement between the consumer and the financial institution. For example, the methods by which the consumer is permitted to initiate a funds transfer and the consumer's obligation to have sufficient available funds to support a debit funds transfer are matters governed by the agreement between the customer and its financial institution. Similarly, the financial institutions's obligation, if any, to the customer to carry out the funds transfer is also governed by the parties' agreement, subject to the few mandatory rules in the EFTA and Regulation E.

Much of the EFTA and Regulation E concern disclosure of terms and various forms of transaction receipts. Thus the financial institution must give initial disclosures before engaging in a covered funds transfer, Reg. E, 12 C.F.R. § 205.7,

---

[11] Regulation CC provides when funds from an electronic funds transfer must be made available to the customer. Reg. CC, 12 C.F.R. § 229.10(b).

and must give notice of change of terms, Reg. E, 12 C.F.R. § 205.8. In addition, receipts must be given at most transactions conducted at electronic terminals such as ATM machines, Reg. E, 12 C.F.R. §§ 205.9, 205.16, and the account holding institution must provide periodic statements of account activity, Reg. E, 12 C.F.R. § 205.9. The disclosures and receipts must be provided in a particular form and may be combined with disclosures required under other law, such as Regulation Z. Reg. E, 12 C.F.R. §§ 205.4, 205.12.

In addition to disclosure requirements, some aspects of funds transfers are singled out for particular prohibitions or requirements. Similar to Regulation Z, there is prohibition on issuing unrequested, validated access devices such as a debit card. **Read Regulation E, 12 C.F.R. § 205.5.** Regulation E also addresses some aspects of preauthorized transfers. Reg. E, 12 C.F.R. § 205.10. Recent additions to Regulation E govern disclosures and terms regarding overdraft services. Reg. E, 12 C.F.R. § 205.17.

Notice that some entities other than financial institutions may be subject to the disclosure requirements and other aspects of Regulation E, and for some types of covered transfers, the requirements of Regulation E noted above are modified. Reg. E, 12 C.F.R. §§ 205.14, 205.15, 205.18.

Problem 20-2

John has both a savings and a checking account at National Bank. Both accounts are for his personal use.

A. Every quarter, John has a dividend payment deposited automatically in his savings account. Every two weeks, he has his pay deposited automatically in his checking account. What obligations, if any, does National Bank have to John regarding these transfers?

B. John has a life insurance premium paid monthly by a direct withdrawal from his checking account.
   1. What obligations, if any, does National Bank have to John regarding these transfers?
   2. If John decided to cancel his life insurance policy, how does he stop future withdrawals? Does the answer depend on whether the withdrawals are push or pull transactions? If National Bank failed to honor a timely stop payment order, what is the bank's liability?

3. If the life insurance premium is paid by a monthly preauthorized negotiable draft on his account, do the EFTA and Regulation E apply?

4. The computer at National Bank had a total systems failure. As a result, the payment of the premium to John's life insurance company was two days late. May the insurance company cancel the policy due to the late payment?

C. John's employer requires that all employees have their paychecks deposited directly to their bank accounts. John does not want direct deposit. May he refuse direct deposit of his paycheck?

C. Risks and Regulation

What are the risks that arise in using a funds transfer? If a funds transfer is used to pay an obligation to a third party, there are risks associated with the underlying transaction. Such risks may include the payor's dissatisfaction with the products or services provided or the payee's failure to provide the product or service at all. There are also risks associated with the funds transfer mechanism itself, such as an intermediary's insolvency, misdirection or garbling of the communication, failure to settle the funds transfer, or an unauthorized communication.

If an electronic funds transfer is within the scope of the EFTA and Regulation E, there are two primary provisions that address these types of problems. First, Regulation E provides a mandatory error-resolution process for electronic funds transfers, similar to what Regulation Z provides for credit card transactions. Reg. E, 12 C.F.R. § 205.11. Second, Regulation E addresses liability for unauthorized electronic funds transfers in Regulation E, 12 C.F.R. § 205.6. *See* Reg. E, 12 C.F.R. § 205.2(m) (definition of unauthorized electronic fund transfer).

Problem 20-3

Deb has a personal checking account at National Bank and a debit card to access the account.

A. Deb's most recent monthly bank statement failed to reflect an ATM deposit of $1,000.

1. Advise Deb how to best correct that error and what National Bank's obligations are.
2. National Bank has advised Deb that an error did occur. What are its obligations?
3. National Bank has advised Deb that no error occurred. What should Deb do?

B. Assume Deb paid for a new chair with her debit card. The price was $500. Her bank statement reflected a charge of $700. How, if at all, does the process for correcting this error differ from the process for correcting other types of errors?

Problem 20-4

State Bank issued Chad a debit card to access his personal checking account at State Bank.

A. Chad threw the card away because he did not want it. Ted picked the card out of the trash, went to the bank, impersonated Chad and received a PIN number to use to access Chad's account. Ted withdrew $1,000 over the course of five days ($200 per day). Chad discovered the theft when he was notified that the bank had dishonored several checks that Chad had drawn on the account. Must State Bank re-credit Chad's account with $1,000?

B. Chad lost the card after he had received the personal identification number (PIN) for the card. Chad had written PIN on the card so that he would not forget it. Ted found the card and withdrew a total of $1,000 from Chad's account, $200 each day for five days.
1. Chad notified State Bank of the loss of the card on the same day that he noticed the loss. Must State Bank re-credit Chad's account for all or any portion of the amount Ted withdrew?
2. Chad noticed he lost the card on the same day that he actually lost the card. Chad notified State Bank of the loss three days later. Must State Bank re-credit Chad's account for all or any portion of the amount Ted withdrew?

3. Chad did not notice that he had lost the card for a week. He immediately notified State Bank when he noticed the card was gone. Must State Bank re-credit Chad's account for all or any portion of the amount Ted withdrew?

4. Chad notified State Bank only after he received the periodic statement on which the five transfers were reflected. Must State Bank re-credit Chad's account for all or any portion of the amount Ted withdrew?

C. Chad lent the card to his son to withdraw $50. The son withdrew $200. Is that an unauthorized electronic funds transfer?

D. State Bank issued the card without Chad's request. This card was pre-validated and was not a renewal of an existing card. Harry intercepted the card in the mail and used it to withdraw $3,000 from Chad's account. Must State Bank re-credit Chad's account for all or any portion of the amount Harry withdrew?

Notice that these provisions on error resolution and unauthorized transactions are both similar and dissimilar to the Regulation Z provisions. As with Regulation Z, Regulation E does not cover all issues that may arise in a funds transfer within its scope and primarily governs the relationship between a financial institution and its consumer. As we explore the provisions of UCC Article 4A, consider whether any of them would be useful in the context of an electronic funds transfer within the scope of the EFTA and Regulation Z.

SECTION 3. CREDIT FUNDS TRANSFERS UNDER UCC ARTICLE 4A

As already noted, UCC Article 4A applies to credit funds transfers that are not within the scope of the EFTA and Regulation E. **Reread the Prefatory note to UCC Article 4A**. That note provides a simple explanation of the funds transfers that are the subject of UCC Article 4A. **Read the comment to UCC § 4A-102**, which sets forth the policy behind UCC Article 4A.[12]

---

[12] For discussion of international funds transfers, see PEB Commentary No. 13 and the UNCITRAL Model Law on International Credit Transfers (1992). *See also* Carl Felsenfeld,

The rules of UCC Article 4A may be varied by Federal Reserve regulations and operating circulars. **Read UCC § 4A-107.** Regulation J, 12 C.F.R. pt. 210 governs funds transfers that go through the federal reserve system (Fedwire) and the Federal Reserve has issued Operating Circular 6 for Fedwire funds transfers. **Read Regulation J, 12 C.F.R. § 210.25.**

UCC Article 4A also recognizes that parties to a funds transfers may vary many of the rights and obligations that UCC Article 4A creates and that associations may promulgate rules for funds transfers between members of the association. **Read UCC § 4A-501.** Two examples of such association rules are those issued by the National Automated Clearing House Association (NACHA), which covers ACH (Automated Clearing House) transactions and those issued by The Clearing House, which covers CHIPS (Clearinghouse Interbank Payments System) transactions. Participants in a funds transfer system agree to abide by the rules of the system.

Thus to fully analyze the rights and obligations of the parties to a funds transfer that falls within the scope of UCC Article 4A, one must consider the rules of the system used to make the funds transfer (*e.g.,* Fedwire, ACH, CHIPS) and the agreements of the parties, in addition to the provisions of UCC Article 4A.

A. The Mechanics of a Credit Funds Transfer

To understand how credit funds transfers work, it is useful to consider a typical transaction. That requires first familiarity with the relevant defined terms. **Read UCC § 4A-103, § 4A-104, and § 4A-105.** Now consider the following example.

Acme, Inc. owed Supplier a debt for goods that Acme previously purchased. Acme instructed First Bank to send $100,000 to Third Bank, to be credited to Supplier's account at Third Bank. First Bank issued that instruction to Second Bank, which in turn issued a corresponding instruction to Third Bank. Third Bank credited Supplier's account.

In this scenario, Acme was a "sender" and an "originator." First Bank was an "originator's bank," a "receiving bank," and a "sender." Second Bank was a "receiving bank," an "intermediary bank," and a "sender." Third Bank was a "receiving bank" and a "beneficiary bank." Supplier was the "beneficiary." The funds transfer can be illustrated graphically as follows:

The Compatibility of the Uncitral Model Law on International Credit Transfers with Article 4A of the UCC, 60 FORDHAM L. REV. S53 (1992).

As you can see from the definition of "payment order" in UCC § 4A-103, a payment order is an instruction to pay money to a beneficiary. The payment order must be to pay a fixed amount of money to a beneficiary and there must not be any condition to the payment other than the time of the payment.[13] Using the example above, Acme sent a payment order to First Bank. First Bank accepted that payment order by executing its own payment order to Second Bank. Second Bank accepted First Bank's payment order by executing its own payment order to Third Bank. Third Bank accepted Second Bank's payment order by crediting the account of the beneficiary, Supplier. This process of sending and receiving the payment order is distinct from actually paying, or settling, the payment order.

Once the payment orders are made and accepted, payment by virtue of credits and debits must be made. Using the example above, when First Bank accepted the payment order from Acme, Acme became obligated to pay First Bank. Generally that payment would take place by First Bank debiting Acme's account at First Bank. When Second Bank accepted First Bank's payment order, First Bank became obligated to pay Second Bank. The payment would generally take place by either a debit to First Bank's account at Second Bank or a credit to Second Bank's account at First Bank. Payment could also take place through some other payment mechanism, such as a check. When Third Bank accepted Second Bank's payment

---

[13] The key to the funds transfer system is having clear and definite instructions without conditions. The system is intended to be a low cost and efficient system for moving value. The drafting of UCC Article 4A was designed to give clear rules to facilitate that operational presumption. *See BSB Constr., Inc. v. Pinnacle Bank*, 776 N.W.2d 188 (Neb. 2009) (letter to bank was not a payment order when it stated a period of time for payment and was not an instruction to pay at a definite time).

order, Second Bank became obligated to pay Third Bank. Payment of this obligation could also occur through a debit or credit to a bank account, by check, or through some other payment mechanism. When Third Bank accepted the payment order, Third Bank became obligated to Supplier. Third Bank's payment to Supplier, the beneficiary, would generally occur by crediting the beneficiary's bank account.

B. Obligations of Senders and Receiving Banks in a Funds Transfer

Based upon the typical staging of the funds transfer, is helpful to divide the process into three distinct conceptual parts: (i) sending the payment order; (ii) accepting the payment order; and (iii) paying the payment order. Each stage creates rights and obligations on the parties that are part of the funds transfer.

1. Sending and Receiving Payment Orders

A credit funds transfer starts when a person issues a payment order to the bank holding the person's deposit account to cause funds from that account be transferred to a deposit account at the same or another bank. Although the first question is whether the first sender had authority to issue the payment order, we will defer that issue until we consider the allocation of risk of unauthorized payment orders. For purposes of the discussion that follows, assume that the bank receives an authorized payment order from the account holder.

Once a receiving bank receives a payment order, it must decide whether to accept or reject the payment order. A receiving bank has no duty to accept a payment order unless it has agreed otherwise. *See* UCC § 4A-212. *See also* UCC § 4A-209 cmt. 3; § 4A-210 cmt. 3. This is true even if the originator's account has sufficient funds to cover the payment order.[14] There are rules, however, on what

---

[14] Although UCC § 4A-212 seems to give the receiving bank complete discretion to accept or reject a payment order provided there is no express agreement otherwise between the bank and its customer, the court in *Banco De La Provincia De Buenes Aires v. Baybank Boston*, 985 F. Supp. 364 (S.D. N.Y. 1997), arguably subjected the decision to some judicial review. However, the court was not clear as to the standard to be used in that review; instead it merely noted somewhat summarily that the bank's decision was neither unreasonable nor in

qualifies as acceptance and rejection of a payment order and when those acts occur. **Read UCC § 4A-209, § 4A-210, and § 4A-212**. UCC Article 4A also contains rules on how a receiving bank is to execute a payment order. **Read UCC § 4A-301, § 4A-302, § 4A-305, and § 4A-106**.

The following problem should help you flesh out the obligations of a receiving bank, other than a beneficiary's bank, when it receives and executes a payment order.

Problem 20-5

By telephone on Monday June 1, Acme Inc. instructed its bank, First Bank in New York, to transfer $100,000 to Paradise Sellers, Inc. in payment for some real estate. At that time, Acme's account at First Bank had a balance in excess of that amount. Paradise Sellers, Inc. maintains its account at State Bank in San Francisco. Pursuant to the agreement between Acme and Paradise, the payment must be credited to Paradise's account by the end of the day, Thursday, June 4.

A. What should First Bank do if it wishes to reject Acme's payment order?

B. What liability, if any, does First Bank incur if it simply fails to respond to Acme's instruction?

C. Assume First Bank wishes to accept Acme's payment order.
   1. By when must First Bank execute the payment order? Does it matter if First Bank received Acme's instruction at 3:00 p.m. and First Bank has a 12:00 noon cutoff time for payment orders?
   2. If Acme's payment order to First Bank did not specify otherwise, could First Bank execute the payment order by instructing the Federal Reserve Bank of New York to make payment to the Federal Reserve Bank of San Francisco, in order to then make payment to Paradise's account at State Bank?

---

bad faith. In contrast, the court in *Chino Commercial Bank v. Peters*, 118 Cal. Rptr. 3d 866 (Cal. Ct. App. 2010), stated that UCC Article 4A precluded a negligence cause of action against the originating bank in accepting and executing a payment order.

   3. If Acme instructed First Bank to use Second National Bank, located in Minnesota, to execute the transfer, must First Bank do so?

   4. What method of communication must First Bank use to execute the transfer? If Acme instructed First Bank to use a wire transfer, must First Bank do so?

D. First Bank executed the payment order but did not act in time to get the payment to Paradise by June 4. As a result, Acme's real estate purchase agreement fell through. What liability, if any, does First Bank have to Acme as a result?

E. First Bank executed Acme's payment order by properly issuing a payment order to Second Bank on June 2, containing the instructions to credit Paradise's account at State Bank in San Francisco with $100,000 by June 4. What are Second Bank's obligations?

Note that UCC § 4A-305 governs liability for improper execution of a payment order. This section governs some of the types of errors that can occur when a payment order is accepted. We will return to this provision when addressing the risks of error and wrongdoing later in this Chapter.

When an originating or other receiving bank executes a payment order, the goal is to communicate – directly or indirectly – to the beneficiary bank that the beneficiary bank should credit the beneficiary's account with the amount of the payment order. Let us now consider the rights and obligations of the beneficiary bank.

The beneficiary bank must decide whether to accept or reject the payment order it has received from its sender. Is the beneficiary bank obligated to accept the payment order? How does the beneficiary bank accept the payment order? How does the beneficiary bank reject the payment order? If the beneficiary bank accepts the payment order, what are the consequences of that acceptance? **Read UCC § 4A-404, § 4A-405 and Regulation CC, 12 C.F.R. § 229.10**.

Problem 20-6

By telephone on Monday June 1, Acme Inc. instructed its bank, First Bank in New York, to transfer $100,000 to Paradise Sellers, Inc. in payment for some real estate. Paradise Sellers, Inc. maintains its account at Third Bank in San Francisco. Pursuant to the agreement between Acme and Paradise, the payment must be credited to Paradise's account by the end of the day, Thursday, June 4. On June 2, First Bank properly executed Acme's instruction by issuing a payment order to Second Bank instructing payment to Paradise's account at Third Bank on June 4. Second Bank properly executed a payment order to Third Bank on June 3 at 3:00 p.m. to credit the account of Paradise.

A. Must Third Bank accept the payment order to credit Paradise's account?

B. What should Third Bank do if it wishes to reject Second Bank's payment order?

C. What liability, if any, does Third Bank incur if it simply fails to respond to Second Bank's payment order? How, if at all, would the analysis change if Third Bank has a 12:00 noon cutoff time for funds transfers?

D. Third Bank accepted the payment order. What are its obligations to Paradise?

E. What risk is Third Bank taking when it accepts the payment order?

2. *Payment of Payment Orders*

The acceptance of payment orders creates an obligation on the part of the sender to pay the amount of the payment order. Remember, for this purpose the originator and every receiving bank other than the beneficiary's bank is a "sender." *See* UCC § 4A-103(a)(5). Thus, the participants in each stage of the transaction before the payment order reaches the beneficiary's bank incurs liability for the amount of the payment order. The transmission of the payment order creates an obligation of the sender to pay the order. To settle that obligation, actual value moves from the originator to the beneficiary through a series of debits and credits in deposit accounts. In the language of UCC Article 4A, this process is called payment of the payment order or settlement of the payment order obligation. **Read UCC § 4A-401, § 4A-402, § 4A-403, § 4A-404, and § 4A-405**.

Problem 20-7

By telephone on Monday June 1, Acme Inc. instructed its bank, First Bank in New York, to transfer $100,000 to Paradise Sellers, Inc. in payment for some real estate. Paradise Sellers, Inc. maintains its account at Third Bank in San Francisco. Pursuant to the agreement between Acme and Paradise, the payment must be credited to Paradise's account by the end of the day, Thursday, June 4. On June 2, First Bank properly executed Acme's instruction by issuing a payment order to Second Bank. Second Bank issued a payment order to Third Bank. Third Bank accepted the order.

A. What obligations, if any, does Third Bank have to Paradise?

B. What obligations, if any, does Second Bank have to Third Bank and Paradise?

C. What obligations, if any, does First Bank have to Second Bank, Third Bank, and Paradise?

D. What obligations, if any, does Jill have to First Bank, Second Bank, Third Bank, and Paradise?

E. How are the various payments to be made to satisfy these obligations?

F. Assume Third Bank did not accept the payment order. What obligations, if any, do the parties have?

3. *Satisfying the Underlying Obligation*

As was true in each of the preceding three problems, most payment orders are given to settle an underlying obligation. The beneficiary bank's acceptance of a payment order has an effect on the originator's underlying obligation to the beneficiary. **Read UCC § 4A-406**. Notice that the underlying obligation is discharged even if the settlement of the payment order does not take place.

Problem 20-8

By telephone on Monday June 1, Acme Inc. instructed its bank, First Bank in New York, to transfer $100,000 to Paradise Sellers, Inc. in payment for some real estate. Paradise Sellers, Inc. maintains its account at Third Bank in San Francisco. Pursuant to the agreement between Acme and Paradise, the payment must be credited to Paradise's account by the end of the day, Thursday, June 4. On June 2, First Bank properly executed Acme's instruction by issuing a payment order to Second Bank. Second Bank issued a payment order to Third Bank. Third Bank accepted the order and notified Paradise of the receipt of that order.

A. What is the effect, if any, of Third Bank's acceptance of the payment order on Acme's obligation to Paradise?

B. How, if at all, would the analysis of Part A change if Paradise refused the payment?

C. How, if at all, would the analysis of Part A change if the amount credited to Paradises' account is $75 short due to fees charged by First Bank, Second Bank, and Third Bank?

4. Canceling or Amending a Payment Order

Once a payment order is issued, it may be canceled or amended. **Read UCC § 4A-211**. However, because payment orders are generally executed promptly upon receipt by the receiving bank, the ability to cancel or amend the order is quite limited.

Problem 20-9

By telephone on Monday June 1, Acme Inc. instructed its bank, First Bank in New York, to transfer $100,000 to Paradise Sellers, Inc. in payment for some real estate. Paradise Sellers, Inc. maintains its account at Third Bank in San Francisco. Pursuant to the agreement between Acme and Paradise, the payment must be credited to Paradise's account by the end of the day, Thursday, June 4.

A. One hour after Acme issued the payment order, Acme decided not to go through with the transaction with Paradise and called First Bank to cancel the payment order.
   1. If First Bank had not executed the order when Acme called to cancel the payment order, what are Acme's rights?
   2. If, prior to Acme's call, First Bank had already executed Acme's payment order by sending a payment order to Second Bank, what are Acme's rights?
   3. First Bank refused to cancel the payment order because it had already executed the payment order. Acme then called Third Bank and asked it not to credit Paradise's account. What result?

B. What will Acme's rights and obligations be if Acme's cancellation of the payment order is timely but First Bank nevertheless mistakenly executed the order shortly afterwards and Third Bank subsequently credited Paradise's account?

C. Assume that on June 1, after giving the initial payment order to First Bank, Acme filed bankruptcy. Can First Bank still execute that payment order? *See* 11 U.S.C. § 362.

5. *Funds Transfers and Rights Related to the Deposit Account*

Just as in UCC Article 4, the timing of credits and debits to an account can be critical. UCC Article 4A has its own provisions on this issue. **Read UCC § 4A-502, § 4A-503, and § 4A-504.**

Problem 20-10

Best Rugs issued to First Bank a $100,000 payment order identifying as the beneficiary Textile Company, which has an account at Second Bank. Best Rugs' account at First Bank has a $150,000 credit balance.

A. One of Best Rug's creditors served a writ of garnishment on First Bank to enforce a judgment for $200,000 against Best Rugs.
   1. First Bank accepted the payment order. What liability, if any, does First Bank have to the garnishor?
   2. First Bank did not accept the payment order. What liability, if any, does First Bank have to the garnishor?

B. One of Textile Company's creditors served a writ of garnishment on First Bank to enforce a judgment for $75,000 against Textile Company. First Bank has not yet accepted the payment order from Best Rugs. What liability, if any, does First Bank have to the garnishor?

Problem 20-11

Best Rugs issued to First Bank a $100,000 payment order identifying as the beneficiary Textile Company, which has an account at Second Bank. Best Rugs' account at First Bank has a $150,000 credit balance. First Bank issued a payment order to Second Bank. Prior to Second Bank's acceptance of the payment order, Textile Company's account had a credit balance of $50,000. Textile Company owed Second Bank $100,000. One of Textile's creditors served a writ of garnishment on Second Bank to enforce a $200,000 judgment against Textile Company.

A. Second Bank wants to accept the payment order for $100,000, credit Textile's account, then set off its $100,000 debt against the account, before it honors the creditor's garnishment. Assuming Second Bank is entitled to exercise its setoff rights, is that a permissible course of action?

B. May the garnishor obtain an injunction against First Bank or Second Bank to stop payment of the payment order to Textile Company?

C. On the day that Best Rugs issued its payment order, First Bank received checks totaling $70,000, drawn against Best Rugs' account. Must First Bank accept the payment order and dishonor the checks?

6. Funds Transfers Through Fedwire

Funds transfers do not always go directly from one bank to another bank. Often the banks will use funds transfer intermediaries. As previously mentioned, those intermediaries may be private associations of banks or may be the Federal Reserve System. The next problem focuses on the use of Fedwire and the extent to which the participants' rights and obligations may vary because Fedwire is used. **Read UCC § 4A-206, § 4A-501, § 4A-107, and Regulation J, 12 C.F.R. pt. 210, Subpart B**.

Problem 20-12

Plumbing Supply Company issued a payment order to First Bank in New York to pay $100,000 to Wholesaler's account at Last Bank in San Francisco. First Bank issued a payment order to the Federal Reserve Bank of New York.

A. Must the Federal Reserve Bank accept the payment order?

B. If the Federal Reserve Bank accepts the order, when is First Bank obligated to pay the order?

C. May First Bank require the Federal Reserve Bank to use Central Bank as an intermediary bank?

D. If First Bank identified Last Bank in San Francisco by number and name, but the number is wrong, may the Federal Reserve Bank rely on the number in executing the payment order?

E. Federal Reserve Bank of New York issued a payment order to the Federal Reserve Bank of San Francisco. Federal Reserve Bank of San Francisco issued a payment order to Last Bank. How will the Federal

Reserve Bank of San Francisco make payment of its payment order? When will it make its payment?

C. Allocation of the Risks of Wrongdoing and Error

The funds transfer system is designed to be a low-cost, efficient system of transferring value. To fulfill that goal, UCC Article 4A was drafted to clearly allocate the risk of errors and wrongdoing.[15] The types of errors or wrongdoing that may occur in a funds transfer include: unauthorized payment orders; errors in designating the beneficiary or the beneficiary's bank (or an intermediary bank); errors related to the wrong amount (either to much or too little); and delayed transmission of payment orders. When determining who bears the risk of errors or wrongdoing, organize your analysis by the type of problem that has taken place.

1. *Unauthorized Payment Orders*

As with other payment systems, one type of recurring problem is an unauthorized payment order. **Read UCC § 4A-201, § 4A-202, § 4A-203, and § 4A-204**. In dealing with a claimed lack of authorization, the starting point in the analysis is to determine if the purported sender of the payment order is responsible for the payment order under principles of agency. If yes, then it is an authorized payment order. Only if that analysis leads to the conclusion that the payment order was not authorized, need one go further and determine whether it is a verified payment order pursuant to a commercially reasonable security procedure.[16] If it is

---

[15] One of the tensions is whether other principles, such as conversion and negligence, can be used to supplement the loss allocation principles in UCC Article 4A. The relationship between common-law causes of action, equitable principles, and the UCC is set forth in UCC § 1-103. Reread the comment to UCC § 4A-102, which suggests that neither the common law not equitable principles should be used to subvert the allocation of risk as set out in UCC Article 4A. Subverting or supplementing the risk-allocation scheme is not an easy line to draw. For examples of courts wrestling with this issue, see *Schlegel v. Bank of America*, 628 S.E.2d 362 (Va. 2006); *Fitts v. AmSouth Bank*, 917 So. 2d 818 (Ala. 2005); *Regions Bank v. The Provident Bank, Inc.*, 345 F.3d 1267 (11th Cir. 2003).

[16] *See Hedged Investment Partners, L.P. v. Norwest Bank Minnesota*, 578 N.W.2d 765

a verified payment order, the payment order is enforceable against the purported sender under UCC § 4A-202(b), subject to a limited exception in UCC § 4A-203.

Problem 20-13

Sam, an employee of Acme Inc., called First Bank and instructed the bank to transfer $100,000 from Acme's account to Jill's account at Second Bank. First Bank required Sam to identify both Acme's account number and Jill's account number, and to give Acme's authorization code. Sam was not authorized to issue payment orders on behalf of Acme. Assume that the EFTA does not apply.

A. Has First Bank used a commercially reasonable security procedure?

B. Assume that the requirement to identify the account numbers and give an authorization code is a commercially reasonable security procedure.
  1. If First Bank executed the payment order and that order is accepted by Second Bank, must Acme pay the amount of the order?
  2. Assume that Sam is not an employee of Acme. Sam broke into Acme's office building and ordered First Bank to transfer the money using Acme's computer system. If the funds transfer is completed by Second Bank's acceptance of the payment order, must Acme pay the amount of the order?
  3. How, if at all, would the analysis of the preceding two questions change if Acme negotiated an agreement with First Bank providing that Acme is not responsible for any unauthorized payment orders?

C. Assume that the requirement to identify the account numbers and the authorization code is not a commercially reasonable security procedure and that Sam is not an employee of Acme.
  1. Must Acme pay the amount of the payment order?
  2. First Bank debited Acme's account for the amount of the payment order. The day after receiving notification of the payment order and the debit, Acme informed First Bank that the payment order

---

(Minn. Ct. App. 1998); J. Kevin French, *Article 4A's Treatment of Fraudulent Payment Orders–The Customer's Perspective*, 42 ALA. L. REV. 773 (1991).

was unauthorized and requested that First Bank re-credit its
account. What liability, if any, does First Bank have to Acme?

3. How, if at all, would the analysis of the preceding question change
   if Acme did not notify First Bank of the unauthorized transfer until
   30 days after receiving notification of the payment order and debit?

4. How, if at all, would the analysis change if First Bank had a
   written agreement with Acme expressly provided that Acme bears
   all the risk of unauthorized payment orders?

Problem 20-14

Plumbing Supply Company issued a payment order to First Bank in
New York to pay $100,000 to Wholesaler's account at Last Bank in San
Francisco. First Bank issued a payment order to the Federal Reserve Bank
of New York. The Federal Reserve Bank of New York issued a payment
order to Last Bank. Last Bank accepted the payment order, crediting
Wholesaler's account. Plumbing Supply Company's original order was
completely unauthorized and Plumbing Supply Company and First Bank
had no security procedure in effect. Plumbing Supply Company discovered
the unauthorized order 45 days after its account was debited. Who will
bear the ultimate liability for this problem? Explain fully.

2. Errors

In any process involving multiple parties, mistakes are inevitable. UCC Article
4A was designed to allocate the risk of error in a manner that avoids factual disputes
about the relative fault of each party. Typical errors are misdescription of the
beneficiary, misdescription of an intermediary or beneficiary bank, executing
payment orders in the wrong amount, issuing duplicate payment orders, failure to
follow instructions in executing the payment order, and delay in executing the
payment order. Given the attempt to clearly delineate the consequences of each
type of error, the first step in the analysis is to identify what went wrong and then
identify the correct section of UCC Article 4A that specifies the consequences of
that type of error. **Read each of the following sections.**

UCC § 4A-207   Misdescription of beneficiary

UCC § 4A-208   Misdescription of intermediary or beneficiary bank

UCC § 4A-303   Errors in execution

UCC § 4A-304   Reporting errors in execution

UCC § 4A-305   Liability for errors in execution

UCC § 4A-505   Objections to account debits

A sender and receiving bank may agree to a security procedure designed to detect certain types of errors. *See* UCC § 4A-201. Those errors are beneficiary misdescription, wrong amounts, and duplicate orders. **Read UCC § 4A-205**.

Problem 20-15

In a transaction not covered by the EFTA, Adam ordered First Bank to transfer $10,000 from his account to Betty's account at Second Bank. Adam and First Bank have agreed that all transfers of an amount greater than $5,000 will have the letter X preceding the amount. Adam's order did not have the letter X preceding the amount. Adam intended to order First Bank to transfer $1,000. First Bank debited Adam's account for $10,000 and instructed Second Bank to credit Betty's account at Second Bank for $10,000. Second Bank accepted First Bank's payment order.

A. The day after receiving notification of the payment order and the debit, Adam informed First Bank of the error and requested that First Bank re-credit his account. Who will ultimately bear the liability for this mistake? Explain fully.

B. How, if at all, would the analysis of Part A change if Adam did not notify First Bank of the error until 60 days after receiving notification of the payment order and debit?

Problem 20-16

A. Acme Inc. ordered First Bank to transfer $1,000 to Best Supply's account at Second Bank. To execute that order, First Bank sent a payment order to Second Bank. First Bank's employee mistakenly identified the beneficiary as Better Supply in the payment order to Second Bank. Second Bank accepted the payment order and credited Better Supply's account. Best Supply and Better Supply are two different, unrelated entities. Who will ultimately bear the liability for this mistake? Explain fully.

B. Acme Inc. ordered First Bank to transfer $1,000 to Best Supply's account at Second Bank. Acme identified Best Seller as the beneficiary and gave First Bank the account number of 12345 as Best Supply's account. However, Best Supply's correct account number is 12347. First Bank executed that order by issuing a payment order to Second Bank to credit account number 12345, beneficiary Best Supply. Second Bank credited account 12345, which belonged to Vento, Inc. Who will ultimately bear the liability for this mistake? Explain fully.

C. Acme Inc. ordered First Bank to transfer $100,000 to Best Supply's account at Second Bank. To execute that order, First Bank sent a payment order to Second Bank instructing Second Bank to credit Best Supply's account for $1,000,000. Second Bank accepted the payment order and credited Best Supply's account with $1,000,000.
   1. Who will ultimately bear the liability for this mistake? Explain fully.
   2. How, if at all, would the analysis change if Acme actually owes Best Supply $2,000,000? *See First National Bank & Trust Co. v. Brant,* excerpted in relevant part below.

FIRST NATIONAL BANK & TRUST CO. V. BRANT
398 F.3d 555 (6th Cir.), *cert. denied,* 546 U.S. 824 (2005)

Gilman, Circuit Judge

This case arises out of a botched electronic wire transfer from Calumet Farm, Inc. to Peter M. Brant and White Birch Farm, Inc. (collectively, White Birch). On

Friday, March 8, 1991, Calumet initiated the wire transfer of $77,301.58 by a payment order to its bank, First National Bank & Trust Company. This amount was calculated by Calumet as a payment of interest on its outstanding debt of over $1 million due to White Birch. When Calumet received written confirmation of the wire transfer from First National on the following Monday, March 11, 1991, it learned that $770,301.58, rather than $77,301.58, had mistakenly been transferred. White Birch refused to return the additional $693,000, and Calumet subsequently declared bankruptcy.

First National is now seeking restitution from White Birch for the excess payment. Both the bankruptcy court and district court ruled in favor of White Birch. The key issue on appeal is whether White Birch established the elements of the "discharge-for-value" defense to First National's restitution claim. For the reasons set forth below, we reverse the judgment of the district court and remand the case for the entry of judgment in favor of First National.

I. BACKGROUND

Most of the facts of this case were previously set forth by this court in *In re Calumet Farm, Inc.*, 1997 WL 253278, at *1-2 (6th Cir. May 14, 1997), as follows:

White Birch is a thoroughbred horse farm in Connecticut owned by Peter Brant. In 1986, Calumet purchased a one-half interest in the thoroughbred stallion Mogambo from White Birch and executed a $6,500,000 promissory note ("the Mogambo note") evidencing the obligation. On October 31, 1990, Calumet defaulted in making its annual principal payment of [$1,300,000] on the debt. Brant and J.T. Lundy, president of Calumet, reached an agreement whereby Calumet would make the payment on or before March 15, 1991. Calumet also defaulted in making several intervening interest payments and, as of March 7, 1991, owed White Birch approximately $103,057.50 in interest and penalties.

On March 8, 1991, Lundy instructed Calumet's bookkeeper, Angela Holleran [properly, "Hollearn"], to pay the interest due to White Birch as of January 31, 1991, amounting to $77,301.58. Holleran thereupon called First National to arrange payment by wire transfer, and also called White Birch to inform it that a wire transfer payment was forthcoming; however, the substance of these conversations is disputed as to the amount that White Birch was to receive. The wire transfer, referenced as "MOGAMBO INT," was made to White Birch's account at Citibank in New York on March 8, 1991.

On March 11, 1991, Holleran received written confirmation of the wire transfer from First National and realized that $770,301.58, rather than $77,301.58, had been transferred. Holleran notified First National of the mistake and First National contacted Citibank to request reversal of the wire transfer. Because the money already had been credited to White Birch's account, Citibank refused to reverse the wire transfer. Thereafter, First National requested that Brant return the additional $693,000 erroneously transferred to him, but Brant refused to return the money unless First National acknowledged in writing that it had made the error in transferring the funds.

On March 27, 1991, Calumet filed suit against First National in Scott County Circuit Court alleging negligence and breach of contract with respect to the mistaken wire transfer. Because of Calumet's precarious financial condition, Calumet and First National reached a partial settlement whereby First National agreed to lend Calumet $500,000, secured by Calumet's interest in the Mogambo note. Calumet also assigned to First National any right of recovery that it might possess against White Birch and agreed to release First National from any liability arising from the wire transfer. Although First National and Calumet had partially settled the state court action, First National filed an answer and counterclaim [actually, a third-party complaint] on April 4, 1991, asserting claims against White Birch. In the meantime, White Birch filed a complaint against Calumet in the United States District Court for the Eastern District of Kentucky, seeking the principal and interest due on the Mogambo note.

On June 11, 1991, Calumet filed a bankruptcy petition in the United States Bankruptcy Court for the Eastern District of Kentucky. In October 1991, the state court actions were removed to the Bankruptcy Court as adversary proceedings, and on December 12, 1991, the district court action was referred to the bankruptcy court.

Upon cross-motions for summary judgment, the bankruptcy court entered partial summary judgment in favor of White Birch on December 22, 1993. The court held that First National lacked standing to assert a restitution claim against White Birch, reasoning that the amount of a wire transfer, once debited from a depositor's account, belongs solely to that depositor; accordingly, the court held that only Calumet possessed standing to recover the transferred funds from White Birch. However, because Calumet owed White Birch a sum well in excess of the amount of the wire transfer, the court held that White Birch had not been unjustly enriched and was not obligated to make restitution. The court then denied First National leave to file a second amended counterclaim to include claims for conversion and intentional interference with a contract, but allowed First National to assert other state-law claims.

On September 6, 1994, the bankruptcy court entered summary judgment in favor of White Birch on all remaining claims and entered its final order on October 27, 1994. [As part of the final settlement, First National agreed to pay Calumet $50,000 in addition to the $500,000 loan, which Calumet never repaid.] First National appealed the bankruptcy court's grant of summary judgment in favor of White Birch and the court's denial of leave to amend its counterclaim. The district court affirmed the bankruptcy court's decision in its entirety on June 13, 1995.

In May of 1997, this court reversed the grant of summary judgment in favor of White Birch, but also affirmed the denial of First National's motion for leave to amend its counterclaim. The case was remanded to the district court with instructions to return the matter to the bankruptcy court for further proceedings. This court held that "the bankruptcy court should make additional factual findings as to whether White Birch had notice that the funds transfer had been made in error and, thus, determine whether White Birch [could] successfully assert [the 'discharge-for-value'] defense to First National's restitution claim." 1997 WL 253278, at *5.

In resolving cross-motions for summary judgment, the bankruptcy court determined on remand that there was insufficient evidence in the record to support a finding that White Birch had notice of the error in the amount transferred before the funds were credited to its account at Citibank. It therefore held that White Birch had satisfied the required elements of the discharge-for-value defense to First National's restitution claim. Accordingly, the bankruptcy court granted summary judgment in favor of White Birch and denied the cross-motion filed by First National. In March of 2003, the district court affirmed both determinations. First National now appeals, claiming that the lower courts failed to properly interpret and apply the discharge-for-value defense asserted by White Birch.

II. ANALYSIS
* * *

B. The discharge-for-value defense

In its earlier opinion, this court held that First National had standing to assert a claim for restitution under U.C.C. § 4A-303(a). . . . This provision authorizes a bank to seek restitution from the beneficiary of the excess payment if the bank committed an error in executing the payment order. In the prior opinion, this court noted that § 4A-303(a) incorporates the discharge-for-value defense. The RESTATEMENT OF RESTITUTION defines the discharge-for-value defense as follows:

> A creditor of another or one having a lien on another's property who has received from a third person any benefit in discharge of the debt or lien, is under no duty to make restitution therefor, although the discharge was given by mistake of the transferor as to his interests or duties, *if the transferee* made no misrepresentation and *did not have notice of the transferor's mistake.*

RESTATEMENT OF RESTITUTION § 14(1) (emphasis added). Thus, when a creditor receives what appears to be a payment on a debt from someone other than the debtor, the creditor becomes a bona fide purchaser and may keep the mistaken payment if the creditor discharges the obligation of its debtor prior to becoming aware of the mistake.

Section 14(1) of the RESTATEMENT, however, does not specify the point in time by which notice of the mistake must be received. Nor did this court's prior opinion in the present case address the issue. And the two other appellate courts that have concluded that the discharge-for-value rule applies to wire transfers also failed to focus on the timing question. *See General Elec. Cap. Corp. v. Central Bank*, 49 F.3d 280, 284 (7th Cir. 1995) (GECC); *Banque Worms v. BankAmerica Int'l*, 570 N.E.2d 189, 196 (N.Y. 1991).

Isolated language in both of the above cases, however, indicates that the notice must occur before the funds arrive. *See GECC*, 49 F.3d at 284 (holding that "a creditor should be able to treat funds credited in apparent payment of a debt as irrevocably his, unless news of the error precedes arrival of the funds"); *Banque Worms*, 570 N.E.2d at 196 (explaining that "[w]hen a beneficiary receives money to which it is entitled and has no knowledge that the money was erroneously wired, the beneficiary should not have to wonder whether it may retain the funds; rather, such a beneficiary should be able to consider the transfer of funds as a final and complete transaction, not subject to revocation"). But the question in each case (as in this court's prior decision) was whether the discharge-for-value rule applies in this setting, not how it applies. Nor, at any rate, does the quoted language squarely address the point. In a wire transfer setting, is the relevant event when the beneficiary's bank receives the money, or when the beneficiary learns that the money is in its account, or when the beneficiary credits the money to the debtor's account? Neither this court's prior decision, *GECC*, nor *Banque Worms* purports to consider the question, much less answer it.

Traditionally, the U.C.C. provides that payment in discharge of an obligation occurs under the first option – "at the time a payment order for the benefit of the beneficiary is accepted by the beneficiary's bank in the funds transfer." U.C.C.

§ 4A-406(a). But this approach does not square with the notice exception to the discharge-for-value rule. Application of this U.C.C. definition of discharge would mean that the entity that must receive notice (here White Birch) is an entity other than the entity to whom the funds were wired (here Citibank). To divide the "receipt of payment" and "notice of error" elements between different entities makes little sense and at any rate is a recipe for reading the notice exception out of the rule.

Equally unpersuasive is the argument that the discharge-triggering event necessarily occurs only when the beneficiary has actual notice that funds have been placed in its account. Such notice may not connect the funds to a given debtor or to the size of the debtor's outstanding obligation. Furthermore, while actual notice of a mistake may of course be independently disclosed by the originator to the beneficiary, constructive notice of a mistake may also occur simply as a result of the size of the transfer when considered in connection with the name of the originator. In this case, for example, White Birch assuredly would have had constructive notice of the mistake if the transfer had been, say, for $7.7 million – if, in other words, First National had made a two-digit error rather than a one-digit error in transmitting Calumet's payment order. Any sensible application of the discharge-for-value rule in this unique setting must account for constructive as well as actual notice of a mistake.

That leaves what seems to us to be the most desirable option-that the discharge-for-value defense will apply unless the beneficiary receives notice of a mistake before the beneficiary of the transfer credits the debtor's account. In addition to aligning the entity that receives notice of any mistake with the entity that receives the payment, and permitting constructive notice to trigger the rule, this approach is consistent with one of the underlying principles of the discharge-for-value rule; namely, that the creditor has given value for the mistaken payment. Nor, despite White Birch's suggestion to the contrary, will this approach undermine the discharge-for-value rule on the theory that the rule will kick in only after the beneficiary on its own terms makes an accounting of how the transfer should be credited. The time value of money being what it is, most commercial recipients of such transfers can be counted on to promptly credit the debtor's account. As in most settings, at any rate, the rule applies only to commercially reasonable accountings.

We note that a district court decision directly on point followed a similar analysis. In *NBase Communications v. American National Bank & Trust*, 8 F. Supp. 2d 1071 (N.D. Ill.1998), the court held that notice was sufficient so long as the beneficiary of the payment learned of the mistake before recovering the check from a lock box. In reaching that conclusion, the court noted that the creditor must give value for the mistaken payment-by crediting the debtor's account-before receiving notice of the mistake in order to invoke the discharge-for-value defense. *Id.* at 1076-77. Checks and wire transfers, we acknowledge, do not offer a perfect analogy. The former are governed by state law, the latter by federal law, and the two are governed by different sections of the U.C.C. But in the unique setting of applying the notice exception to the discharge-for-value rule, the reasoning of *NBase* aptly respects the principles of the rule and the realities of applying it to checks and wire transfers: "[I]t is difficult to see what is unfair about requiring a bank to return money if it was notified of the mistaken payment before it gave value for the payment. For example, only *after* the crediting would it be unfair to require the innocent creditor to make restitution." *Id.* at 1077 (emphasis in original). So it is here.

Both the bankruptcy court and the district court, in taking up the case on remand, erred in focusing on when White Birch received the funds rather than on when White Birch credited Calumet's account. In doing so, both courts effectively wrote out the element of "discharge" from the discharge-for-value defense. The undisputed record shows that White Birch did not credit the funds to Calumet's account until the afternoon of March 11, 1991. First National offered the testimony of Calumet employee Angela Hollearn to prove that White Birch was aware well before then that Calumet had intended to wire only $77,301.58 to White Birch for the payment of accrued interest. The bankruptcy court ruled against First National on the basis that Hollearn's testimony was equivocal on the issue of to whom she spoke and what was said on March 8, 1991 when she allegedly conveyed to White Birch the fact that a wire transfer had been sent, the amount of the transfer, and how that amount had been calculated.

The district court likewise dismissed Hollearn's testimony on this point as too speculative. It therefore determined that First National had not established that White Birch had notice of the error before receiving the funds. Without deciding whether the lower courts erred in excluding the disputed testimony as a matter of law, . . . , we note that there is no dispute that Hollearn notified White Birch of the error on the morning of March 11, 1991.

Furthermore, White Birch's behavior establishes that it was aware of the error as soon as it was informed of the wire transfer by its own bank. When White Birch discovered on the morning of March 11, 1991 that Citibank had credited its account for $770,301.58, it immediately transferred the additional $693,000 to Brant's personal account at Citibank, ostensibly so that "everything could be sorted out." It did not apply that amount to reduce Calumet's debt on the Mogambo note until later that day. If White Birch did not know or at least suspect that it had erroneously received the additional funds, it would have had no reason to segregate them into its owner's personal account. The fact that it segregated the precise amount of the overage, moreover, is strong evidence that White Birch knew exactly how much it was supposed to receive from Calumet. Even the wire transfer itself, after all, was referenced as "MOGAMBO *INT.*" (emphasis added.)

Thus, even if the bankruptcy court and district court correctly determined that White Birch did not have notice of the error before receiving the funds, White Birch certainly had notice before crediting Calumet's account. We therefore hold as a matter of law that White Birch had prior notice of the mistake in the funds transfer for purposes of the discharge-for-value rule and cannot avail itself of that defense. First National is therefore entitled to restitution from White Birch.

Under normal circumstances, the amount of restitution would be the $693,000 overpayment. But here First National was able to settle Calumet's claim against it for a total of $550,000. First National conceded at oral argument that this is the true extent of its loss, and thus the measure by which White Birch has been unjustly enriched at the bank's expense. Although White Birch has argued that $500,000 of the bank's claim was in the form of a loan to Calumet, the record makes clear that First National credited this amount to Calumet's account solely to settle the lawsuit filed against it as a result of the mistaken wire transfer. If the bank has in fact recovered any of this "loan" in the Calumet bankruptcy proceedings, the district court on remand can take this into account in rendering the final judgment against White Birch. The district court is also free to consider whether First National is entitled to prejudgment interest on its restitution claim.

As a final point, we note that allowing White Birch to keep funds that no one intended for it to have when it received them would constitute a windfall to White Birch at the expense of First National. Returning the $550,000 paid out by First National to extricate itself from its transmission error will, however, put the parties in the same position that they would have been in had the error in transferring the funds not occurred. Although these equitable considerations do not trump the discharge-for-value defense in situations where the defense is applicable, they are pertinent here. White Birch should, in fact, consider itself fortunate that it is having to return only $550,000 of the $693,000 excess it received because First National was able to settle with Calumet for less than the amount of the mistaken transfer.

III. CONCLUSION

For all of the reasons set forth above, we reverse the judgment of the district court and remand the case for the entry of judgment in favor of First National.

———————

Many of the provisions of UCC Article 4A dealing with allocation of loss from error refer to the ability to recover under the law of mistake and restitution. The discharge-for-value rule is part of the law of restitution and mistake. For a modern statement of restitution principles, see RESTATEMENT (THIRD) OF RESTITUTION AND UNJUST ENRICHMENT.

Problem 20-17

A. Acme Inc. ordered First Bank to transfer $100,000 to Best Supply's account at Second Bank. First Bank executed a payment order to Second Bank for $10,000, instead of $100,000. Second Bank accepted the payment order and credited Best Supply's account with $10,000. How will liability for this error be allocated? Explain fully.

B. Acme Inc. issued a payment order to First Bank for $100,000 identifying the beneficiary by account number, 678910, at Third Bank. Acme's payment order did not provide a number for Third Bank. Third Bank's correct identifying number is 134. First Bank sent a payment order to Second Bank. First Bank's payment order to Second Bank identified Third Bank only by number 143. Second Bank sent a payment order to bank number 143 (which is Last Bank), identifying the beneficiary's account as 678910. Last Bank credited the amount of the order to account 678910.

   1. How will liability for this error be allocated?

   2. How, if at all, would the analysis change if First Bank's payment order provided "Third Bank, #143"?

   3. How, if at all, would the analysis change if Acme's payment order had stated the wrong number for Third Bank?

REGATOS V. NORTH FORK BANK
838 N.E.2d 629 (N.Y. 2005)

Rosenblatt, J.

The United States Court of Appeals for the Second Circuit, by certified questions, asks us whether a commercial bank customer can recover funds that the bank improperly transferred out of his account, even though he did not notify the bank of the unauthorized transfer until well after the time limit stated in his account agreement. This issue requires us to decide whether the one-year period of repose in our Uniform Commercial Code § 4A-505 may be modified by agreement. We also resolve whether U.C.C. § 4A-204(1) requires the bank actually to send the customer notice of an unauthorized transfer in order to trigger the running of a "reasonable time" within the meaning of that section, or whether a private agreement to hold a customer's mail can allow constructive notice to start that period. These are questions of first impression in this Court, and apparently in every other court of last resort in states that have adopted the relevant statutes.

In accord with the United States District Court for the Southern District of New York, we hold for the customer on both questions. The one-year period of repose in U.C.C. § 4A-505, governing the customer's time in which to notify the bank of the unauthorized transfer, may not be modified by contract. Furthermore, both the one-year statute of repose and the "reasonable time" referred to in section 4A-204(1), which determines the customer's ability to recover interest on the misallocated money, begin to run when the customer receives actual notice of the improper transfer.

I.

Tomáz Mendes Regatos held a commercial account with Commercial Bank of New York, the predecessor to North Fork Bank. His agreement with the bank required him to notify the bank of any irregularity regarding his account within 15 days after the bank statement and items were first mailed or made available to him.[17]

---

[17] The relevant part of the account agreement stated that

"[t]he depositor will exercise reasonable care and promptness in examining such statement and items to discover any irregularity including, but not limited to, any unauthorized signature or alteration and will notify the Bank promptly in writing of any such discovery, and in no event more than fifteen (15) calendar days subsequent to the time that such statement and items were first mailed or available to the

The agreement did not provide for notice to him of electronic funds transfers, except to the extent those transfers appeared on his monthly statements. The bank adopted a practice of holding Regatos's bank statements rather than mailing them to him, and expected him to request the statements when he wanted to see them.

On March 23, 2001, the bank received a funds transfer order from someone it believed to be Regatos, but failed to follow agreed security procedures[18] to confirm the order. Without authorization, the bank then transferred $450,000 out of his account. On April 6, 2001, the bank received another transfer order, again failed to follow its security procedures and without authorization transferred an additional $150,000 out of his account. Together, these transfers represented most of the value of the account.

Regatos did not learn of the unauthorized transfers until he checked his accumulated account statements on August 9, 2001. The transfers were reflected on statements issued on March 23, 2001 and April 25, 2001, but the bank held these statements until he asked for them, following its standard practice in relation to him. He informed the bank of the unauthorized transfers on the day he learned of them, August 9, 2001.

When the bank refused to reimburse Regatos for the lost funds, he sued in the United States District Court for the Southern District of New York. In a comprehensive, well-reasoned opinion, District Judge Shira Scheindlin denied the bank's motion for summary judgment and held that the one-year statute of repose may not be shortened by agreement. The court ruled that, in any event, the 15-day notice period set by the account agreement was unreasonable and invalid. The Federal District Court further held that the U.C.C. § 4A-505 period to notify the

---

depositor. In those situations in which the depositor has authorized the Bank to hold his correspondence, this section shall apply as if the depositor received such statement on the date shown on the statement."

[18] The security procedures here involved nothing more than checking Regatos's signature against the signature on the faxed transfer order and calling him to confirm (*cf.* U.C.C. § 4A-201 ["Comparison of a signature on a payment order or communication with an authorized specimen signature of the customer is not by itself a security procedure"]). Apparently, the bank did not require any password, even for large sums. Here, the bank compared the signature on the fax to its signature on file, but did not realize that the fax signature had been forged. The jury found that the bank did not telephone Regatos to confirm that the order was legitimate.

bank began to run when Regatos received actual notice of the error on August 9, 2001.

A federal jury found in favor of Regatos. Following U.C.C. § 4A-204, the court awarded him both the principal ($600,000) and the interest from the date the bank improperly transferred the funds.

The bank appealed, and the United States Court of Appeals for the Second Circuit determined that the legal issues necessary to dispose of the case were novel, important questions of New York law. (Footnote omitted) The Second Circuit certified to this Court, and we accepted, the following questions:

"[1] Can the one-year statute of repose established by U.C.C. [§ 4A-505] be varied by agreement? If so, are there any minimum limits on the variation thereof (such as 'reasonable time') that estop [the bank] from denying Regatos recovery in this case? ...

"[2] In the absence of agreement, does U.C.C. Article 4A require actual notice, rather than merely constructive notice? If so, can this requirement be altered by agreement of the parties and was such achieved here?"

We answer the first part of the first question "no," rendering the second part academic. We answer the first part of the second question "yes" and the second part of the second question "no."

II.

U.C.C. § 4A-204 establishes a bank's basic obligation to make good on unauthorized and ineffective[19] transfers and, with one exception, forbids any variation of that obligation by agreement. * * *

Regatos argues that the one-year statutory period [provided in U.C.C. § 4A-505] is an integral part of the bank's "obligation ... to refund payment" under U.C.C. § 4A-204(1) and so, pursuant to U.C.C. 4A-204(2), "may not ... be varied by agreement." The bank and its supporting amici point out that the notice provision is in section 4A-505, not section 4A-204(1), and rely on U.C.C. § 4A-501(1), which declares that "[e]xcept as otherwise provided ... the rights and obligations of a party to a funds transfer may be varied by agreement of the affected party."[20] The bank

---

[19] Ineffective transfers are those in which the bank has not properly executed security procedures (U.C.C. 4A-202).

[20] In support of this position, the amici urge that article 4A is not a consumer protection statute, especially considering that it applies solely to presumably sophisticated commercial parties. While this is true to some extent, the provision in section 4A-204 refusing to allow

maintains that the customer's duty to notify the bank of the error before recovering misallocated funds is an "obligation" separate from that created by section 4A-204(1) and therefore modifiable.

We agree with Regatos's reading of the statutes. In context, the policy behind article 4A encourages banks to adopt appropriate security procedures. Only when a commercially reasonable security procedure is in place (or has been offered to the customer) may the bank disclaim its liability for unauthorized transfers (U.C.C. § 4A-202). Permitting banks to vary the notice period by agreement would reduce the effectiveness of the statute's one-year period of repose as an incentive for banks to create and follow security procedures.

While the issue is close, we cannot accept the bank's argument that the customer's responsibility to notify the bank of its error is modifiable. U.C.C. § 4A-204(1) states that "[t]he bank is not entitled to any recovery from the customer on account of a failure by the customer to give notification as stated in this section." Accordingly, a bank has an obligation to refund the principal regardless of notice, provided such notice is given within one year in accordance with U.C.C. § 4A-505. Moreover, as the District Court pointed out, section 4A-505 (the one-year notice period) appears in the "Miscellaneous Provisions" part of the article, not the parts touching upon substantive rights and obligations (*Regatos*, 257 F. Supp. 2d 632, 644 n. 19 [2003]). The period of repose in section 4A-505 is essentially a jurisdictional attribute of the "rights and obligations" contained in U.C.C. § 4A-204(1). To vary the period of repose would, in effect, impair the customer's section 4A-204(1) right to a refund, a modification that section 4A-204(2) forbids.

Article 4A was intended, in significant part, to promote finality of banking operations and to give the bank relief from unknown liabilities of potentially indefinite duration (*see Banque Worms v. BankAmerica Intl.*, 570 N.E.2d 189 [1991]). This legislative purpose does not suggest that those interests alter (or should alter) the statute's fine-tuned balance between the customer and the bank as to who should bear the burden of unauthorized transfers.

Therefore, we hold that the one-year repose period in section 4A-505 cannot be modified by agreement. By notifying the bank on August 9, 2001, the day he received actual notice, and four or five months after the statements were available, Regatos acted either way within the year-long period of repose. This clearly

---

parties to modify the bank's basic obligation to refund unauthorized transfer funds contradicts the amici's argument because the provision clearly protects consumers, even commercial consumers, from bearing the burden of this type of bank error.

satisfied the statutory requirement and he is entitled to recover at least his $600,000 principal.

III.

The Second Circuit next asks whether actual notice is required under article 4A (or whether mere constructive notice will do) and, consequently, whether Regatos is also entitled to recover interest on the misdirected funds.

The bank made Regatos's monthly account statements available for his review, but waited for him to request them rather than send them to him. According to its agreed security procedures, the bank was to reach him by telephone immediately after it received a funds transfer order, to confirm that he had actually authorized the transfer. Other than that call, which the jury found was never made, the only notice available to him would come from his own perusal of the account statements.

In his earlier dealings with the bank, Regatos tended to check his statements regularly. By 2001, however, he reviewed the bank's statements only intermittently. In that year, he asked to see his statements some time before the unauthorized transfer on March 23, 2001 and did not ask again until August 9, 2001, after the bank had generated statements on March 23, 2001 and April 25, 2001. These two statements revealed the unauthorized transfers, but the bank continued to hold the statements until Regatos asked for them. As discussed, he immediately notified the bank of its error when he discovered it on August 9, 2001.

The bank argues that Regatos obtained constructive notice of the transfers on March 23, 2001 and April 25, 2001, when the statements disclosing them were first generated. U.C.C. 4A-204 requires a customer seeking to recover interest on funds lost due to an unauthorized transfer "to notify the bank of the relevant facts within a reasonable time not exceeding ninety days after the date the customer received notification from the bank that the order was accepted." We agree with Regatos that this requirement may not be waived.

Under the bank's reading of the statute, an agreed 15-day notice period could run before a bank statement was even available for the customer's review. If the burden of checking whether the bank has wrongfully transferred funds out of the customer's account were to fall on the customer, as it would under a constructive notice interpretation, the customer's duty to check would presumably arise as soon as the data became available for review. In electronic funds transfers, the bank would be able to inform an inquiring customer of the transfer well before the formal monthly statement is compiled. Conceivably, the crucial information could be sitting in the bank's possession for weeks, awaiting discovery by the customer. If the customer did not inquire, and the agreement's 15-day period ran, the customer would lose the transferred funds even though the error was entirely the bank's. This seems to us both the logical consequence of a constructive notice system and an unreasonable view of actual banking relationships. Because interpretation of the U.C.C. is always conducted with an eye toward business realities and the predictable consequences of legal rules, we reject a statutory interpretation that conflicts with reasonable business practices.

Policy arguments support an actual notice requirement. An invariable statutory rule provides a bright line for banks and their customers, bringing reliability and certainty to these dealings. Constructive notice is far less exact, leaving too much room for varying interpretation and disorder. If the bank had complied with its security procedures, it would have called Regatos the same day it received each purported transfer order, thereby providing him with actual notice of the events.

Even where customers enter "hold mail" agreements with their banks, the actual notice rule still applies. Just as the one-year notice limitation is an inherent aspect of the customer's right to recover unauthorized payments, the actual notice requirement provides the bedrock for the exercise of that right. Permitting banks to enforce "agreements" to accept constructive notice would defeat article 4A's guarantee of recovery for unauthorized payments.

In response to the second certified question, we answer that article 4A requires actual notice, and that this requirement cannot be varied by a "hold mail" agreement, neither to begin the statute of repose, nor to begin "reasonable time" under the account agreement. Regatos notified the bank of his loss within an indisputably reasonable time after receiving actual notice, and is therefore entitled to recover the interest on his lost principal (U.C.C. § 4A-204).

Accordingly, the first part of certified question 1 should be answered in the negative and the second part not answered as unnecessary, and the first part of certified question 2 should be answered in the affirmative and the second part in the negative.

Questions

Should the reasoning in *Regatos* be applied to UCC § 4-406? Do you think the *Regatos* court came to the correct result in interpreting UCC Article 4A?

Problem 20-18

Acme, Inc. ordered First Bank to pay $100,000 to Best Supply's account at Second Bank. First Bank sent a payment order to Second Bank for $1,000,000, instead of $100,000. First Bank sent Acme a notice that its account was debited $1,000,000 instead of $100,000. Sixty days later, Acme notified First Bank that an error had occurred.

A. How will liability for this error be allocated? Explain fully.

B. How, if at all, would the analysis change if Acme did not notify First Bank of the error until two years later?

C. How, if at all, would the analysis change if the agreement between Acme and First Bank provided that Acme must object to all errors in funds transfers within 30 days after receiving notice of the transfer?

SECTION 4.   REVIEW

Problem 20-19

On November 25, David ordered First Bank to send $1 million to Ethel at Last Bank. David gave First Bank Ethel's account number at Last Bank as #8642. David's order stated a payment date of December 5. On December 1, First Bank sent a payment order to Federal Reserve Bank providing for a $1 million credit to Ethel, Account #8642, at Last Bank, and that same day, the Federal Reserve Bank sent a payment order to Last Bank for a $1 million credit to Ethel, Account #8642. Last Bank credited account #8642 on December 2 with $1 million. Account # 8642 is not Ethel's account, it is Quick's account. Ethel's account number at Last Bank is #8641. Quick withdrew the $1 million and is nowhere to be found.

On December 2, David realized his mistake and sent a message to First Bank cancelling his November 25 payment order and sending a new payment order for $1 million with the correct account number of Ethel at Last Bank. First Bank did nothing in response to the second payment order because David did not have a sufficient credit balance in his account to cover the order. First Bank refused to accept the attempted cancellation of the November 25 payment order. Because Ethel did not get paid on December 5, David lost his option to purchase valuable real estate. David is threatening to sue everyone involved for the $1 million and the value of the lost option. Analyze all parties' rights and liabilities. Explain fully.

Problem 20-20

Alice purchased $100 worth of groceries at the local Big Supermarket. After Alice had filled out a check for $100 payable to Big Supermarket, the clerk took the check and ran it through the cash register and then returned the check to Alice. The clerk keyed in an amount and Alice left with her groceries. When Alice received her bank statement, there was a debit from her checking account to Big Supermarket for $120, not $100. Alice also noticed that there were three more debits to her account for $120 each to Big Supermarket. Alice is sure she did not make those three other charges. Alice has called her bank to complain about the debits and her bank told her she was liable based upon her agreement in her deposit agreement and refused to re-credit her account for any amounts. What are Alice's rights? Explain fully.

CHAPTER TWENTY-ONE

PREPAID PAYMENT MECHANISMS

SECTION 1. INTRODUCTION

A. Overview

The concept of a prepaid payment mechanism is relatively simple. A user transfers value to the issuer of the mechanism, creating a credit balance on the records of the issuer. When the user wants to buy something, the user presents the prepaid mechanism to the merchant. If the merchant is the issuer of the prepaid payment mechanism, the merchant will simply deduct the purchase price from the user's balance. If the merchant is not the issuer, the merchant will, directly or indirectly, obtain value from the issuer, which will in turn deduct the transaction amount from the user's credit balance with the issuer.

Prepaid payment mechanisms have been around for quite a long time and come in many forms. Prior to the issuance of national paper currency, many banks accepted deposits and issued demand or time notes that circulated freely, at least among people who had confidence that the bank could repay. Below is an illustration of one such note.[1]

These notes are in essence a prepaid payment mechanism.

---

[1] This picture was provided and reprinted with permission of Denly's of Boston.

Merchants too accepted prepayment and issued paper certificates representing the bearer's right to receive goods or services in return. Also, when coinage was scarce, some merchants issued scrip as a means of providing change. Customers could later redeem the scrip for currency if they did so in whole-dollar amounts. Below is one example.[2]

Similarly, in many mining and logging camps, the company scrip was used to acquire goods at the company store.

In recent years, the use of prepaid payment mechanisms has expanded greatly, with over a 20% growth in both number and amount of these types of payments between 2006 and 2009.[3] If you have used a gift card or gift certificate at a retailer, then you have used a prepaid payment mechanism (sometimes called a stored value card). If you have used a device called a "prepaid debit card," issued by a participant in the Visa® or MasterCard® network, then you have also used a prepaid payment mechanism. A prepaid payment mechanism differs from a credit card because the issuer is not granting credit to the user at the time the user makes a purchase. Instead, the user has prepaid the value necessary to make the desired purchase with the prepaid payment mechanism. A prepaid payment mechanism also differs from a funds transfer because the issuer of the prepaid mechanism is typically not holding the prepayment in a way that subjects the issuer to banking

---

[2] This picture was provided and reprinted with permission of Denly's of Boston.

[3] 2010 Federal Reserve Payments Study: Noncash Payment Trends in the United States: 2006-2009, at 17.

regulation, *i.e.*, the value deposited with the issuer is not held in a deposit account as defined under banking law.[4]

While the concept of a prepaid payment mechanism is simple, this arrangement raises the same set of issues that have been addressed in this book regarding other payment mechanisms.

A. *Operation.* How does the payment mechanism transfer value? How does the payment mechanism work?

B. *Timing.*
   (1) When is payment final?
   (2) When does the payment mechanism discharge the payor's underlying obligation to the payee?
   (3) Prior to discharge, is the payor's underlying obligation to the payee suspended?

C. *Rights & Duties.*
   (1) What obligations to the payor, payee, or other parties does the payment mechanism create?
   (2) To the extent use of the mechanism creates additional obligations:
       (i) How are those obligations satisfied?
       (ii) What defenses does the obligor have to those obligations?
       (iii) If there are multiple obligors created by use of the mechanism, what is the relationship among those obligors?

D. *Risk.*
   (1) What effect will a party's insolvency have on the finality of the payment and the discharge of the underlying obligation?
   (2) What errors might arise during use of the payment mechanism and, for each error, which party or parties bear the risk?
   (3) What wrongdoing may occur during the use of the payment mechanism and, for each type of wrongdoing, which party or parties bear the risk?

---

[4] But see discussion of Regulation E provisions *infra*.

B. Transferring Value through a Prepaid Payment Mechanism

The process of using a prepaid payment mechanism typically begins when the user transfers value – the prepayment – to the issuer. That transfer may occur in cash, by check, by funds transfer, or through the use of a credit card or other payment device. In return, the issuer provides the user with a card or other device that the user can present to redeem or otherwise access the value that the user previously provided to the issuer. The prepaid payment mechanism does not have to be a physical object, such as a card. It might merely be an alphanumerical code (often used with online gift certificates). When the user presents the device to the merchant in the checkout process, the device is used to determine whether there is sufficient value associated with the device to pay for the purchase. That authentication of value is typically done in real time, either through communication to an electronic database or because adequate information is encoded on the device itself.

A prepaid payment mechanism issued by or for use at an individual retailer is generally referred to as a closed-loop system. The retailer (or a related entity) is the issuer and maintains through its own processes the information concerning the amount of value associated with the mechanism. An open-loop system is run on networks such as the Visa® and MasterCard® networks. An issuer is a participant in the network system and the mechanism is typically honored by all the merchants who honor the cards processed through that network. The issuer maintains the information regarding the value associated with the device, and the payment to the merchant is cleared through the network systems. In a hybrid system, the device is honored by numerous merchants, but not the number participating in the nationwide (indeed worldwide) networks run by Visa® or MasterCard®. An example of a hybrid system is a prepaid device issued by a mall owner and accepted by all the merchants in the mall. The mall owner is the issuer and maintains the records regarding the value associated with each card or other device. Payments to the merchants are cleared through a process set up by the issuer.

A prepaid payment mechanism may be limited to a specific amount that cannot be augmented later. Alternatively, the mechanism may be "reloadable." That is, that additional value can be added to device associated with the mechanism by transferring additional value to the issuer.

C. The Regulatory Landscape

The study of prepaid payment mechanisms is challenging. This is largely due to the fact that such mechanisms are not governed by a comprehensive code but by a hodgepodge of federal and state statutes, supplemented by the common law of contracts.

For example, the federal laws explicitly govern only some types of prepaid mechanisms.[5] The state laws vary significantly in scope and content.[6] For example, some states have limits on whether or when a stored value card may expire.[7] Some limit the fees that may be imposed.[8] Some require that the stored value be redeemable in cash while others expressly reject such a requirement.[9] These

---

[5] One of the significant issues in this mix of state and federal law is the degree to which state law is preempted if an issuer of a prepaid payment device is a federally regulated entity, such as a national bank. The answer to the preemption question is not simple nor static. *See* Michael Hamburger, *The Dodd-Frank Act and Federal Preemption of State Consumer Protection Laws*, 128 BANKING L. J. 9 (2011).

In addition, the new federal Bureau of Consumer Financial Protection has jurisdiction to regulate many types of prepaid payment devices (defined as a financial product or service, 12 U.S.C. § 5481(15)). *See* 12 U.S.C. § 5491. What regulation will come from the Bureau is not yet clear.

[6] *See* Philip Keitel, *The Laws, Regulations, Guidelines, and Industry Practices that Protect Consumers Who Use Gift Cards*, 63 CONSUMER FIN. L.Q. REP. 163 (2009); Regulation E 12 C.F.R. § 205.20. For a listing of the variety of state laws governing the various types of prepaid mechanisms, see the National Conference of State Legislatures website. That organization has collected and summarized the state laws governing gift cards and gift certificates at http://www.ncsl.org/default.aspx?tabid=12474.

[7] *See, e.g.*, Cal. Civ. Code § 1749.5 (unlawful to sell gift certificate with expiration date); Minn. Stat. § 325G.53 (same); Ky. Rev. Stat. § 367.890 (gift card cannot expire earlier than one year after issuance); Md. Com. Law § 14-1319 (gift certificate cannot expire within four years of purchase); Ill. Rev. Stat. ch. 815, ¶ 505/2SS (gift certificate cannot expire earlier than five years after issuance); Kan. Stat. Ann. § 50-6,108 (same).

[8] *See, e.g.*, Colo. Rev. Stat. § 6-1-722 (prohibiting service, dormancy, inactivity and maintenance fees); Wash. Rev. Code § 19.240.040 (dormancy fee permitted under specified conditions).

[9] *See, e.g.*, Colo. Rev. Stat. § 6-1-722 (redeemable in cash if remaining value is $5 or less); Vt. Stat. Ann. tit. 8, § 2704 (redeemable in cash if remaining value is less than $1); Kan. Stat.

variations are compounded by the significant choice-of-law problems that can arise when the issuer, merchant, and user all are located in different states and the transactions involving the mechanism – both the loading of value and the redemption of value – are done electronically between the parties.

The contract law applicable to prepaid payment mechanisms is complicated by the fact that there are multiple contractual relationships: the one between the issuer and the user, the one between the user and the merchant, and, if the merchant is not the issuer, the one between the merchant and the issuer. In addition, there may be system rules, to which parties are bound by contract, governing the settlement and clearing process used in open-loop or hybrid systems.

Finally, laws other than those explicitly directed to prepaid payment devices may apply.[10] This is because it is often difficult to distinguish prepaid payment mechanisms from other payment mechanisms. To illustrate, consider the assertion made on page 834 that allegedly separates a prepaid payment mechanism from a funds transfer: that the value paid to the issuer was not being held by a bank in a deposit account.[11] While UCC Article 4A clearly only applies to credit fund transfers from traditional banking institutions, UCC § 4A-105(a)(2) (definition of bank), Regulation E is not so limited.

The application of Regulation E to electronic fund transfers depends upon debiting or crediting a consumer's account. Reg. E, 12 C.F.R. § 205.3(b)(1). An account is defined to include an asset account "held directly or indirectly by a financial institution" and "established primarily for personal, family or household purposes." Reg. E, 12 C.F.R. § 205.2(b)(1). A financial institution is defined to include institutions that are commonly thought of as banks as well as "any other person that directly or indirectly holds an account belong to a consumer, or that issues an access device and agrees with a consumer to provide electronic fund transfer services." Reg. E, 12 C.F.R. § 205.2(i). An electronic fund transfer

---

§ 50-6,108 (redemption in cash not required).

[10] A common example is a state's escheat laws regarding the disposition of abandoned property which may apply if the value is not accessed or "spent" in a set period of time.

[11] Sometimes the funds used to purchase prepaid payment mechanisms are in fact held in deposit accounts at a bank. *See* FDIC General Counsel's Opinion No. 8, 73 Fed. Reg. 67155, 67157 (Nov. 13, 2008) (indicating that stored value cards and other nontraditional access mechanisms will be treated as "deposits" to the extent that the funds have been placed at an insured depository institution because the form of the access mechanism is unimportant).

includes point of sale transactions initiated in an electronic manner for the purpose of debiting a consumer's account. Reg. E, 12 C.F.R. § 205.3(b)(1).

Based upon those definitions, if a consumer purchased a prepaid card from a retailer, and the retailer agreed to debit purchases at the retailer against the value associated with the card, would the user's purchase transaction at the retailer's store by using the card in a point of sale electronic terminal subject that transaction to Regulation E as an electronic fund transfer? Is the value associated with the card a "demand" account?[12] There are no easy or clear answers to these questions.

---

[12] In promulgating the amendments that added payroll accounts to the definition of "account" in Regulation E, 12 C.F.R. § 205.2(b), the Federal Reserve Board stated:

> Gift cards issued by merchants that can be used to purchase items in the merchant's store are not covered by Regulation E. The regulation also does not cover general spending cards to which a consumer might transfer by direct deposit some portion of the consumer's wages. Although consumers might choose to send some or all of their salary or other compensation by direct deposit into a general spending card account, the consumer also may use these products for other purposes or for limited periods of time, like gift cards or other stored-value, or prepaid, cards. Consumers would derive little benefit from receiving full Regulation E protections for cards that may only be used for limited purposes or on a short-term basis, and which may hold minimal funds, while the issuer's costs of compliance with Regulation E might be significant. In contrast, for payroll card accounts that are established through an employer, there is a greater likelihood that the account will serve as a consumer's principal transaction account and hold significant funds for an extended period of time.

71 Fed. Reg. 51437, 51441 (Aug. 30, 2006). Would the consumer using a prepaid payment mechanism benefit from the protections regarding unauthorized transfers even if the other aspects of Regulation E would be less beneficial? Should these comments in the release of the final rules regarding payroll accounts override the seemingly plain meaning of the regulatory text?

For an argument that such prepaid amounts are not "deposits" and are merely contractual rights against the card issuer relating to a service, see Enoila Akindemowo, *Contract, Deposit or E-value? Reconsidering Stored Value Products for a Modernized Payments Framework*, 7 DEPAUL BUS. & COM. L.J. 275 (2009). Unfortunately, this argument ignores the character of a deposit account, which is merely a set of contractual rights against the bank for a service regarding the deposited value, regulated by banking law principles. *See* Dwight L. Greene, *Deposit Accounts as Bank Loan Collateral Beyond Setoff to Perfection–The Common Law is Alive and Well*, 39 DRAKE L. REV. 259, 267 (1989/90).

In an open-loop system, where prepaid payment devices are issued by a participating bank and cleared through a national network such as Visa® or MasterCard®, should transactions using those devices for consumer payments or for consumers to obtain cash withdrawals from ATMs be treated as funds transfers under Regulation E?[13] Should the issuers of prepaid payment devices be subject to reserve requirements and similar oversight placed on banks designed to meet a primary objective of bank regulation, the safety and soundness of the deposit holding entity?

Assuming the dividing line between the concept of funds transfer and prepaid payment device could be ascertained, these prepaid payment devices have raised other concerns, including money laundering,[14] the continued availability of the prepaid value,[15] and unfair and deceptive trade practices concerning failure to disclose applicable terms and imposition of onerous terms.[16]

---

[13] The definition of account in Regulation E includes "payroll accounts." Reread that definition in Regulation E, 12 C.F.R. § 205.2(b)(2). Prior to this inclusion in Regulation E, payroll cards were a common "prepaid" payment device in which the employer paid for the employee's services and then the employee could use the device to make purchases from merchants or to extract cash from an ATM device. In bringing payroll cards expressly into the scope of Regulation E, the definitions of "financial institution" and "account" were broadened so that payrolls disbursed through nonbank intermediaries were covered.

Another example of a use of a "prepaid" payment device that functions as an electronic funds transfer is the federal Electronic Benefits Transfer, whereby the federal government deposits into an account at an insured financial institution federal benefits owed to an individual and which the individual may access by a prepaid debit card. *See* 31 C.F.R. pt. 208. Reg. E, 12 C.F.R. § 205.15.

[14] See the Department of Treasury regulations of prepaid access devices to detect money laundering activity, 76 Fed. Reg. 45403 (July 29, 2011).

[15] *See* Judith Rinearson and Kristine A. Andreassen, *Developments in the Regulation of Prepaid Payment Products Under State Money Transmitter Licensing Laws*, 65 BUS. LAW. 271 (2009) (discussing state licensing laws directed to maintaining the safety and soundness of prepaid payment devices).

[16] *See* Philip Keitel, *The Laws, Regulations, Guidelines, and Industry Practices that Protect Consumers Who Use Gift Cards*, 63 CONSUMER FIN. L.Q. REP. 163 (2009).

SECTION 2.   OBLIGATIONS AND RISK IN USING PREPAID PAYMENT DEVICES

Discharge of the underlying obligation. As with other payment devices, a prepaid payment device is generally used to make payment in connection with an underlying transaction. As we saw when studying credit card transactions and a Regulation E funds transfer, without a comprehensive scheme of regulation, there is no ascertainable rule on whether the underlying obligation to pay is suspended or discharged when a prepaid payment device is used. As with both of those other types of transactions, it is reasonable to infer that a payee has agreed at least to a suspension of the underlying obligation when it accepts a prepaid payment device. It is also reasonable to infer an agreement to a discharge the underlying obligation if an when the payee receives final settlement of value through the clearing process used for the prepaid payment device. If the payee does not receive final settlement through the clearing process, the issue of discharge of the underlying obligation would likely be determined under contract law, after looking at: (i) the contract between the issuer and the device owner; and (ii) the contract between the payee and the issuer or the network through which the payee has agreed to accept the prepaid payment device.

Obligations of the issuer and the prepaid payment device owner. Assume that the prepaid payment device does not fall within the definition of electronic fund transfer in Regulation E. It still may be governed in part by Regulation E, 12 C.F.R. § 205.20. *See* EFTA § 915, codified at 15 U.S.C. § 1693*l*-1. This new provision focuses on certain types of prepaid payment devices (gift certificate, store gift card, and general-use prepaid card as defined in Regulation E, 12 C.F.R. § 205.20(a) and not excluded under subsection (b)). The scope of this new rule is limited to consumer prepaid payment devices. Regulation E requires disclosure of information concerning fees and expiration dates. Reg. E, 12 C.F.R. § 205.20(c) through (f). These provisions also contain some restrictions on the imposition of fees and expiration dates.

Risks. The risks in using a prepaid payment device are similar to the risks in using a funds transfer. Thus an owner of such a device may wish to "stop payment" if dissatisfied with the purchased product or may wish to recover payment from the issuer if engaged in a dispute with the payee.

In addition to risks regarding the underlying transaction, such as dissatisfaction with the purchased product, there are risks associated with the prepaid payment device itself. For example, the issuer may become insolvent and thus the device may become worthless (in essence, no longer honored by the potential payees because the issuer will not be able to make final settlement of the payment).[17] Alternatively, the prepaid payment device may be lost, stolen, or used in an unauthorized transaction. Although less likely, the merchants may simply refuse to honor the device as a payment mechanism (in essence, breaching a contact obligation owed to the device issuer or the participating network). Finally, errors may occur when using a prepaid payment device to pay in a transaction, resulting in the inability to complete the transaction, or completion of the transaction in an incorrect amount. Assuming that the prepaid payment device is not within the scope of Regulation E and no state statute addresses the issues, there is no law governing these issues other than the web of contractual agreements and any system rules that may apply to any particular prepaid payment device.

Problem 21-1

You are a staff member to a Senator on the Senate Banking Law Committee. She has asked you to craft a concept proposal for federal legislation regarding prepaid payment devices. Identify all the issues you think the federal law should address and a proposed solution to each identified issue.

---

[17] Indeed, one of us had a few dollars remaining on a Borders card when that business ceased operations.

CHAPTER TWENTY-TWO

LETTERS OF CREDIT

SECTION 1.   INTRODUCTION

So far we have studied several different payment systems: currency, credit cards, negotiable instruments, funds transfers, and prepaid mechanisms. Most people use one or more of these payment systems at some point in their lives. This Chapter addresses a payment system with which many students are unfamiliar: letters of credit. This payment system is similar to others already studied in that it addresses the same issues that concern other payment systems. Before we get to a detailed look at those issues, however, it is important to understand the concept of a letter of credit.

A.   Mechanics of Value Transfer by a Letter of Credit

A letter of credit is an undertaking by an issuer to a beneficiary to honor a documentary presentation by delivering an item of value. *See* UCC § 5-102(a)(10).[1] Put more simply, the issuer promises to deliver something of value upon presentation by the beneficiary of the documents specified in the letter of credit. That something of value is almost always funds (typically provided via a funds transfer or a bank check), but in rare cases is something else, such as a stock certificate.

To issue a letter of credit, the issuer creates and delivers a record (such as an electronic file or a writing) that sets forth a description of the documents that the named beneficiary must present to be entitled to delivery of the item of value. The issuer does this at the request of an "applicant." The documents described in the letter of credit typically relate to an underlying transaction between the beneficiary and the applicant. When the applicant requests the issuer to issue the letter of credit, the applicant specifies the terms that it wants included in the letter of credit.

To illustrate how this works, consider the following scenario.

A seller of goods wants to sell to a particular buyer located some distance away and with whom the seller has not previously conducted

---

[1] Examples of letters of credit can be found in John F. Dolan, COMMERCIAL LAW: ESSENTIAL TERMS AND TRANSACTIONS (2d ed. 1997).

business. The seller does not want to extend credit to the buyer, and thus will not take a note in payment for the goods. The seller does not want to accept a check on delivery because the seller is not willing to trust that the buyer's check will be honored when presented for payment. An electronic funds transfer is not feasible because the buyer does not want to release the money without proof that the goods have been shipped and the seller does not want to ship the goods without proof that funds for payment are available. Obtaining a letter of credit from a bank will allow this transaction to go forward and solve the problem of the parties' distrust of each other.

The seller and the buyer will negotiate what documents the seller needs to present to the issuing bank in order for the bank to honor the letter of credit. Typically, the documents are shipping documents (such as a bill of lading) stating that the goods have been placed in the carrier's hands, invoices listing the type and amount of goods shipped, a negotiable demand draft drawn on the bank that will issue the letter of credit, and an insurance certificate noting that insurance has been purchased for the buyer's benefit in the event the goods are lost or damaged in shipment. The buyer (the applicant) will then request its bank to issue a letter of credit for the benefit of the seller (the beneficiary) based on the terms agreed to between the buyer and seller.

The letter of credit is the *bank's* engagement to pay according to the terms of the credit, which lists the documents required to be presented. The buyer will, in turn, either pay the bank that issues the letter of credit the principal amount of the letter of credit when the letter is issued or will be obligated to reimburse the bank when the seller draws on the letter of credit. In addition, the bank will normally charge the buyer a fee for issuing the letter of credit.

Once the letter of credit is drafted, the bank issues the letter by sending a written or electronic record (the letter of credit) to the beneficiary, the seller. The seller will ship the goods, gather the documents that the letter of credit requires, and present those documents, along with the letter of credit, to the bank for payment. The bank will examine the documents to determine if the documents and the presentation comply with the terms of the letter of credit. If the documents and the presentation do comply with the letter of credit terms, the bank will pay the amount of the credit to the seller. The bank will then usually forward to the buyer the documents that the seller presented to the bank (or, if the bank, has not already been paid, hold the documents until the buyer pays for the letter of credit). The buyer will use the shipping documents to retrieve the goods from the carrier. The seller has been paid and the buyer has the goods.

If the documents or presentation do not comply with the terms of the letter of credit, the bank must notify the seller of the problem and return the documents to the seller. If the letter of credit permits, the seller may then cure the error and re-present the necessary documents. If the letter of credit does not permit this or the seller otherwise fails to make a proper presentation of conforming documents, the seller will have the shipping documents and can use them to prevent the buyer from obtaining the goods.

This transaction, which involves what is known as a *commercial* letter of credit, can be illustrated as follows:

Another type of letter of credit is called a *standby* letter of credit. Standby letters of credit are issued for the purpose of guaranteeing a payment obligation of the applicant. To illustrate the way a standby letter of credit works, assume a municipality wishes to build a parking garage. To finance construction, the municipality wishes to borrow money by selling bonds to the public. The bonds will be repaid from the revenue generated by the parking garage. To make the bonds more desirable – *i.e.,* to obtain a better credit rating and a lower interest rate – the municipality applies for a letter of credit from a bank. Under the terms of the letter of credit, the bank agrees to pay the municipality's obligation on the bonds if the revenues from the parking garage are insufficient to do so. To draw on the letter of credit, the bondholders' agent must typically present a notice of default, perhaps accompanied by a demand draft drawn on the issuing bank.

The standby letter of credit in this situation can be illustrated by the following diagram:

B. Governing Law

The law governing letters of credit is part statutory, part contractual. The domestic statutory regime is contained in UCC Article 5, as revised in 1995 and adopted by all 50 states. However, UCC Article 5 is quite short and lacks rules on many issues that affect liability in a letter-of-credit transaction. As a result, it is far from comprehensive. *See* UCC § 5-103 cmt. 2. Parties may, and frequently do, expressly agree to supplement or supercede UCC Article 5 with the rules in the Uniform Customs and Practices for Documentary Credits No. 600 (UCP600), its predecessor (UCP500), or the International Standby Practices (ISP98), each issued by the International Chamber of Commerce (ICC).[2] Alternatively, a letter of credit in an international transaction may be governed by the United Nations Convention on Independent Guarantees and Stand-by Letters of Credit.

This Chapter is designed to explore the rules in UCC Article 5. Keep in mind, however, that if the parties have agreed to incorporate UCP600 or ISP98, if the transaction falls within the UN convention, or if the parties simply so agree among themselves under UCC § 5-103(c), the rules of UCC Article 5 may be altered. **Read UCC § 5-101 and § 5-103.**

---

[2] The ICC also has an eUCP for purposes of electronic letters of credit.

C. Understanding UCC Article 5 Terminology and the Independence Principle

Return to the two examples given above. In each transaction, there are three relationships: applicant–beneficiary (based on the underlying transaction between them); applicant–issuer (based on the application for the letter of credit); and issuer–beneficiary (based on the letter of credit). **Read UCC § 5-102(a)(2), (3), and (9).**[3]

In some letter of credit transactions, the issuer will request that another bank take on the obligations of the letter of credit (confirm the credit) or advise the beneficiary that the letter of credit was issued. **Read UCC § 5-102(a)(1), (4), and (11).** Return to the example of the commercial letter of credit given above. The issuing bank may contact a bank in the seller's geographical region with whom the issuing bank has a relationship to have that second bank confirm the credit. This second bank, if it undertakes to honor the letter of credit, is known as a confirming bank. The confirming bank will examine the letter of credit and the documents. If the documents and presentation comply with the terms of the letter of credit, the confirming bank will pay the beneficiary the amount of the credit. The confirming bank will then send the documents to the issuing bank for reimbursement. If the second bank is requested to merely notify the beneficiary of the letter of credit, the second bank is not undertaking to honor the letter of credit and is known as an advisor, or advising bank. **Read UCC § 5-107.**

A letter of credit is different than any other type of obligation. It is not a negotiable instrument.[4] **Read UCC § 5-102(a)(10) and § 5-104.** Indeed, there are very few formal requirements for a letter of credit, in contrast to a negotiable instrument. A letter of credit is also not a guarantee obligation, even though it may operate much like a guarantee. One reason for this is that the issuer is deemed to have primary liability for the obligation undertaken, not secondary liability. A more

---

[3] The parties' rights and obligations are the same in both commercial and standby letters of credit even though the transaction details and the documents required are different in each transaction.

[4] If you are not sure why that statement is true, review the requirements of a negotiable instrument in Chapter Fourteen.

important reason rests on something known as the "independence principle." **Read UCC § 5-103(d) and comment 1.**[5]

Stated simply, the independence principle is a rule of law that the obligation of the issuer is independent of the obligations arising out the transaction underlying the letter of credit. What the independence principle means in the context of a commercial letter of credit is that the obligation of the issuer to the beneficiary is independent of the obligation of the applicant to the beneficiary and not subject to the same defenses. Thus, returning to our sale of goods example, if the goods that the seller shipped to the buyer do not conform to the sale contract between the seller and the buyer, the seller will nevertheless be entitled to payment on the letter of credit from the issuing or confirming bank upon a complying presentation of the correct documents in the correct form. The buyer may have a claim for breach of warranty against the seller, but the issuer must nevertheless honor its obligation on the letter of credit. In addition, the buyer will no doubt, as a matter of contract, have an obligation to reimburse the issuer. As a result, the buyer takes the risk that the money will be paid to the seller for nonconforming goods. The issuing or confirming bank has no obligation – or right – to determine whether the seller has properly performed its duties under the contract with the buyer.

Similarly, in the context of a standby letter of credit example, if the agent for the bondholders makes a conforming documentary presentation to the issuer, the agent is entitled to be paid on the letter of credit regardless of what the bonds themselves provide as to the bondholder's or agent's rights against the municipality.

One corollary to the independence principle is that a letter of credit is not a contract between the issuing bank and the applicant. **Read UCC § 5-105.** The issuing bank and the applicant will have a contract based upon the application and the bank's agreement to issue the letter of credit. *See* UCC § 5-102, cmt. 3. However, the letter of credit itself is not the contract. Instead, issuance of the letter of credit is a component of the bank's performance of its contractual obligations to the applicant.

Similarly, a letter of credit is also not a contract between the applicant and the beneficiary. Rather, the relationship between the applicant and the beneficiary is based upon the underlying transaction (such as a purchase and sale agreement, or a loan agreement), and will be governed by the law that governs that type of transaction. The applicant's procurement of the letter of credit is typically part of

---

[5] *See also* RESTATEMENT (THIRD) OF SURETYSHIP AND GUARANTY § 4(2) (indicating that the Restatement does not apply to letters of credit).

the applicant's performance of a contract obligation owed to the beneficiary. *See* UCC § 5-102, cmt. 3.

The issuance of a letter of credit is also not a "contract" between the issuer and the beneficiary. It does create an obligation of the issuer to the beneficiary but because there is no reciprocal obligation of the beneficiary to the issuer, it is generally regarded as something other than a contract. *Cf.* UCC § 5-105.[6] Accordingly, the issuer's obligation on the letter of credit is governed by its own unique set of rules, not by contract law.

SECTION 2. OBLIGATIONS UNDER THE LETTER OF CREDIT

The issuer owes its obligation to the beneficiary once the letter of credit is issued. **Read UCC § 5-106(a).** That obligation is to honor a conforming presentation of documents by delivering the item of value stated in the letter of credit. **Read UCC § 5-108(a).** A bank that confirms the credit has that same obligation to the beneficiary. UCC § 5-107(a).[7]

The terms of the letter of credit determine the scope of the issuer's obligation. The letter of credit will contain not only the list of documents required, but also the amount of the credit, the name of the beneficiary, the place of presentment and deadline for the presentation. UCC Article 5 contains a limited number of rules that fill in missing terms if the letter of credit does not state them. **Read UCC § 5-106.** Specifically, a letter of credit is deemed irrevocable unless it states it is revocable. To amend or cancel the letter of credit, the beneficiary, applicant, issuer, and confirmer (if any), must all consent, unless the letter of credit states it can be amended or cancelled without consent. A letter of credit without a stated expiration date is deemed to expire after a year. If the letter of credit states it is perpetual, it nonetheless expires in five years.[8]

---

[6] *But cf.* RESTATEMENT (SECOND) OF CONTRACTS § 1 & cmt. c (indicating that a contract can consist of a single promise as long as that promise is enforceable). Generally, a promise that is enforceable as a contractual promise requires consideration, which may consist of a return promise or other act, or forbearance to act. *See* RESTATEMENT (SECOND) OF CONTRACTS § 71 & cmt. b.

[7] An advisor's obligations are set forth in UCC § 5-107(c).

[8] *See Golden West Refining Co. v. SunTrust Bank*, 538 F.3d 1233 (9th Cir. 2008) (letter of

If the issuer rightfully honors the letter of credit, it is entitled to reimbursement from the applicant of the amount paid under the letter of credit and has discharged its obligation on the letter of credit. **Read UCC § 5-108(i).** UCC Article 5 does not address whether honor of the letter of credit satisfies either the underlying obligation the applicant owes to the beneficiary or any obligation that the issuer may owe the applicant.

An issuer who honors a letter of credit is subrogated to the rights of both the applicant and the beneficiary. **Read UCC § 5-117(a).** As protection for the issuer and the applicant in this process, the beneficiary makes warranties to the issuer and the applicant upon the issuer's honor of the letter of credit. **Read UCC § 5-110.** The issuer who honors a letter of credit also has a security interest in the documents presented under the letter of credit to secure the right of reimbursement. **Read UCC § 5-118.** If the issuer dishonors the letter of credit, it must return or hold the documents at the disposal of the presenter. **Read UCC § 5-108(h).**

If the issuer wrongfully honors the letter of credit (pays when it should not), the issuer has liability to the applicant for a wrongful honor and does not have the rights stated in UCC § 5-108(i). **Read UCC § 5-111(b).** If the issuer wrongfully dishonors the letter of credit (does not pay when it should), the issuer has liability to the beneficiary for a wrongful dishonor. **Read UCC § 5-111(a).** The issuer in either case is not responsible for consequential damages, but will be liable for incidental damages, interest, and attorneys' fees.

By far, the most important issue concerning a letter of credit is to determine what constitutes a conforming presentation, so that the issuer will be required to honor the letter of credit. The principal standard, as expressed in UCC § 5-108, is that the presentation must "strictly comply" with the terms of the letter of the credit, as determined by "standard practice." **Read UCC § 5-108(a), (e), (f), and (g).** As should be immediately apparent, this standard uses two concepts that are at odds with each other. In other words, the phrase "as determined by . . . standard practice" modifies and ameliorates somewhat the requirement of strict compliance. The result is a rather vague standard on which very large amounts of money may depend. Fortunately, UCP600 and ISP98 do much to identify and define standard practice for many letters of credit.

If a presentation strictly complies with the terms of the letter of credit, the only way for the issuer to avoid the obligation to honor the letter of credit is if: (i) one

---

credit stating it expired in one year but was automatically renewed each year unless terminated was not "perpetual").

of the presented documents was forged or fraudulent; or (ii) honor of the letter of credit would facilitate a fraud on the applicant or issuer. **Read UCC § 5-109.** These exceptions are more narrow than may seem and are explored more fully in Section 3 of this Chapter.

When a presentation is made under a letter of credit, the issuer has a limited period of time to determine whether to honor the letter of credit. If the issuer dishonors the letter of credit, the issuer must so notify the presenter and disclose the discrepancies that justify its decision. **Read UCC § 5-108(b) through (d).** Because of the relationship between rightful honor and reimbursement from the applicant, the issuer may ask that the applicant waive discrepancies between the presented documents and the terms of the letter of credit. The applicant is not under any obligation to do so, but often will waive minor discrepancies.

Review the comments to UCC § 5-108 dealing with the strict-compliance standard and then consider the following brief case excerpt.

VOEST-ALPINE TRADING USA CORP. V. BANK OF CHINA
167 F. Supp. 2d 940 (S. D. Tex. 2000),
aff'd, **288 F.3d 262 (5th Cir. 2002)**

* * *

The Court notes the wide range of interpretations on what standard banks should employ in examining letter of credit document presentations for compliance. Even where courts claim to uphold strict compliance, the standard is hardly uniform. The first and most restrictive approach is to require that the presentation documents be a mirror image of the requirements.

Second, there are also cases claiming to follow the strict compliance standard but support rejection only where the discrepancies are such that would create risks for the issuer if the bank were to accept the presentation documents.

A third standard, without much support in case law, is to analyze the documents for risk to the applicant.

The mirror image approach is problematic because it absolves the bank reviewing the documents of any responsibility to use common sense to determine if the documents, on their face, are related to the transaction or even to review an entire document in the context of the others presented to the bank. On the other hand, the second and third approaches employ a determination-of- harm standard that is too unwieldy. Such an analysis would improperly require the bank to evaluate risks that it might suffer or that might be suffered by the applicant and could undermine the independence of the three contracts that underlie the letter of credit payment scheme by forcing the bank to look beyond the face of the presentation documents.

The Court finds that a moderate, more appropriate standard lies within the UCP 500 itself and the opinions issued by the International Chamber of Commerce ("ICC") Banking Commission. One of the Banking Commission opinions defined the term "consistency" between the letter of credit and the documents presented to the issuing bank as used in Article 13(a) of the UCP to mean that "the whole of the documents must obviously relate to the same transaction, that is to say, that each should bear a relation (link) with the others on its face." INT'L CHAMBER OF COMMERCE, BANKING COMM'N, PUBLICATION NO. 371, DECISIONS (1975-1979) OF THE ICC BANKING COMMISSION R. 12 (1980). The Banking Commission rejected the notion that "all of the documents should be *exactly* consistent in their wording." *Id.* (emphasis in original).

A common sense, case-by-case approach would permit minor deviations of a typographical nature because such a letter-for-letter correspondence between the letter of credit and the presentation documents is virtually impossible. While the end result of such an analysis may bear a strong resemblance to the relaxed strict compliance standard, the actual calculus used by the issuing bank is not the risk it or the applicant faces but rather, whether the documents bear a rational link to one another. In this way, the issuing bank is required to examine a particular document in light of all documents presented and use common sense but is not required to evaluate risks or go beyond the face of the documents.

* * *

Questions

What do you think of the court's standard in *Voest-Alpine Trading*? If you were counsel for a bank that had issued a $50 million letter of credit, would the decision give you comfort or consternation?

Sometimes the beneficiary of a letter of credit will want to give the right to draw on the letter of credit to someone else, or will assign the right to receive proceeds of the letter of credit. **Read UCC § 5-112 and § 5-114.** There is a key difference between making someone a transferee beneficiary of a letter of credit and assigning the right to receive the proceeds of the letter of credit. That difference is the right to draw on the letter of credit (*i.e.*, make the demand to the issuer to honor the letter of credit). Only a transferee beneficiary has the right to draw on the letter of credit. To be a transferee beneficiary, the issuer must agree to the transfer of the beneficiary's rights to the transferee. An assignee of the right to receive the proceeds does not have the right to make the documentary presentation to the issuer and demand the issuer pay on a complying presentation. Rather, the assignee merely has a right to the proceeds if and when the issuer honors the letter of credit after the beneficiary makes a complying presentation.

Problem 22-1

Acme Computer Company ordered computer chips from Binary Bits, Inc. As a condition of the sale, Binary Bits required that Acme have a letter of credit for $100,000 issued in Binary Bits' favor. Acme asked its bank, Interstate Bank, to issue a letter of credit to Binary Bits. Interstate Bank sent a fax to City Bank (located in Binary Bits' community) asking City Bank to either advise or confirm to Binary Bits that Interstate Bank would pay $100,000 to Binary Bits when Binary Bits presented a sight draft, a clean on-board bill of lading showing shipment to Acme Computer, a commercial invoice, and a certificate of insurance for the benefit of Acme.

A. 1. Is the fax that Interstate Bank sent to City Bank a letter of credit as defined in Article 5?

2. May Acme change its mind about the transaction and revoke or cancel its application to Interstate Bank after Interstate Bank sent the fax to City Bank?

3. Assume Acme and Binary Bits renegotiated the sale transaction so that Binary Bits will be selling Acme only $50,000 worth of goods. How can Acme change its application to Interstate Bank after Interstate Bank sent the fax to City Bank?

4. If Interstate Bank has issued a letter of credit in the transaction, for how long is Interstate Bank obligated to the beneficiary?

5. Binary Bits needs funds now and wishes to sell its rights against Interstate Bank under the letter of credit. May Binary Bits do so and, if it may, how?

B. City Bank sent a notification to Binary Bits.
   1. The notification stated that City Bank had received a letter of credit in Binary Bits' favor. Label the parties to this transaction using the Article 5 terms.
   2. How, if at all, would the answer to Part B.1 change if the notification stated that City Bank will honor Interstate Bank's letter of credit?
   3. What is the difference, if any, between City Bank's liability in B.1 and B.2 above? *See* UCC § 5-107.

C. City Bank sent a notification to Binary Bits that Interstate Bank issued a letter of credit in Binary Bits' favor and that City Bank would honor that letter of credit. Binary Bits presented the required documents to City Bank.
   1. Must City Bank pay Binary Bits?
   2. City Bank paid the letter of credit amount to Binary Bits. What are the parties' rights and obligations?

Problem 22-2

Archimedes Industries, Inc., an Illinois manufacturer of GPS tracking devices, contracted to purchase 500,000 specialized computer chips from Bangkok Electronics, Inc., located in Thailand. The purchase price was $2.2 million, with $200,000 paid in advance and the balance due after shipment. Pursuant to the contract, Archimedes Industries applied for a $2 million letter of credit from International Bank. On December 1, 2011 International Bank issued the letter of credit to Bangkok Electronics. The letter of credit stated that International Bank will pay on sight at its New York office a draft for $2 million presented on or before January 15, 2012 by Bangkok Electronics and accompanied by the following documents:
   1. An invoice to Archimedes Industries, Inc. for 500,000 computer chips;
   2. A bill of lading or airbill showing shipment of the invoiced goods; and
   3. A certificate of insurance showing that the goods are insured for at least $2 million and naming Archimedes Industries as the loss payee.

Bangkok Electronics presented to International Bank at its New York office a draft for payment of the letter of credit accompanied by a bill of lading and insurance certificate, each of which complied with the terms of the letter of credit.   In each of the situations described below, determine whether International Bank should honor the draft.

A. The presentation was made on January 10, 2012 and includes an invoice from Bangkok Electronics, Inc. to Archimedes Industries, Inc. for 500,000 computer chips. The invoice is not signed.

B. The presentation was made on January 10, 2012 and includes an invoice from Bangkok Electronics, Inc. to Archimedes Industries, Inc. for 499,995 computer chips. Assume that the incorrect quality is not a fundamental breach of the contract between Archimedes Industries and Bangkok Electronics, *see* CISG Art. 51, with the result that Archimedes Industries is required to accept the goods.

C. The presentation was made on January 10, 2012 and includes an invoice from Bangkok Electronics, Inc. for 500,000 computer chips. The invoice is made out to Archimedes Industries North America, Inc., a trade name occasionally used by Archimedes Industries, Inc.

D. The presentation was made on January 17, 2012 and includes an invoice from Bangkok Electronics, Inc. to Archimedes Industries, Inc. for 500,000 computer chips.

As noted above, many parties will designate UCP600 as the governing rules for a letter of credit. How would the issues in Problem 22-2 be resolved if the letter of credit was subject to UCP600?

SECTION 3.   ALLOCATION OF THE RISK OF FRAUD

Fraud – or an allegation of fraud – in the underlying transaction between the applicant and the beneficiary presents a troublesome and reoccurring problem for the law governing letters of credit. To prevent the beneficiary from drawing on a letter of credit, the applicant will often allege that the beneficiary is engaged in some type of fraud. If courts readily enjoined payment by the issuer, the main function of letters of credit – providing assurance of payment – would be seriously undermined. In addition, both the strict compliance standard and the independence principle might be stretched to the breaking point. On the other hand, neither courts nor banks want to enable truly fraudulent conduct, and thus applicants must have some recourse available to them. **Read UCC § 5-108(d) and § 5-109**.

In general, the issuer is permitted – but not required – to dishonor a presentation because a required document is forged or honor of the presentation would facilitate a "material fraud" by the beneficiary on either the applicant or the issuer. Of course, it may be difficult or impossible for an issuer to know if the applicant's allegations of fraud are true. It will also often be difficult to assess whether an alleged fraud is material. Not every breach of contract by the beneficiary is fraudulent, but the line between breach and fraud can be difficult to discern and apply. For these reasons, and because an issuer can be liable for wrongful dishonor, most issuers will choose to honor a presentation despite an applicant's allegation of fraud. *See* UCC § 5-109 cmt. 2. The applicant's normal recourse is therefore to seek a court injunction. The analysis courts use when asked to enjoin a letter of credit draw under UCC § 5-109(b) is illustrated by the following case.

ARCHER DANIELS MIDLAND CO. v. JP MORGAN CHASE BANK
2011 WL 855936 (S.D.N.Y. 2011)

Jed S. Rakoff, District Judge

On February 14, 2011, the Court granted the request of plaintiffs, Archer Daniels Midland Co. and ADM Rice, Inc. (collectively "ADM"), for an order temporarily restraining defendant JP Morgan Chase Bank, N.A. ("Chase") from honoring a payment request by the Trade Bank of Iraq ("TBI") under a standby letter of credit ("the Letter of Credit") in the amount of $6,926,850. * * * Having carefully considered the parties' submissions, the Court, for the reasons specified below, hereby grants the motion and preliminary enjoins Chase from honoring TBI's request for payment under the Letter of Credit.

* * * ADM Rice, a wholly-owned subsidiary of Archer Daniels Midland Co., purchases rice and wheat, and exports these commodities to various countries around the world, including Iraq. Since 2005, ADM Rice has sold extensive amounts of rice and wheat to Iraq – in shipments totaling approximately 4.4 millions tons – through the Grain Board of Iraq ("GBI"), an entity under the supervision of the Iraqi Government's Ministry of Trade. As a condition of its

transactions with GBI, ADM Rice agrees to post a performance bond which guarantees the quality of the rice or wheat. Until the events that precipitated the instant motion, however, GBI had never demanded payment under any of these performance bonds. Instead, GBI's occasional issues regarding the quality of ADM Rice's products were handled on an informal, commercial basis between the parties, with ADM agreeing to satisfy "every claim that [GBI] has made against ADM . . . in full," and GBI thereby not having to resort to invocation of its rights under the performance bonds.

On August 25, 2010, GBI accepted ADM Rice's offer to sell it 120,000 metric tons of rice at a rate of $549.75 per metric ton, for a contract price of roughly $69 million. In typical fashion, the contract required ADM Rice to arrange for a performance bond through an Iraqi bank equivalent to 10% of the contract price. The next day, on August 26, 2010, ADM applied for a letter of credit in the sum of $6,926,850 with defendant Chase. Issuance of the Letter of Credit was contingent on the issuance by TBI – which, like GBI, is an Iraqi governmental entity – of a performance bond to GBI guaranteeing ADM's performance of the contract (the "Performance Bond").

On August 27, 2010, Chase issued the Letter of Credit, with ADM Rice as the account holder and TBI as the beneficiary. The Letter of Credit further states that TBI may draw funds as follows:

[Funds are] . . . available against your authenticated Swift/Tested Telex that you have duly issued your Performance Bond as requested by ourselves and that you have received a claim in accordance with the terms of the performance bond.

The Letter of Credit also expressly incorporates the terms of the Performance Bond itself, which was issued by TBI on or about September 2, 2010. The Performance Bond states, in relevant part, that:

All claims made under this performance bond must be accompanied by an SGS original laboratory report specifically certifying that the quality of the purchased commodity does not meet the contractual specifications.

SGS, formerly Societe Generale de Surveillance, is an international quality inspection company. However, the Letter of Credit does not require that TBI submit a copy of the SGS report for Chase's review in order to request payment under its terms, but merely that GBI provide TBI with that report.

On September 6, 2010, the sales transaction between GBI and ADM Rice was memorialized in a written contract (the "Contract"). As directed in that contract, ADM Rice shipped 120,000 tons of rice (the "Cargo") from the United States to

Iraq on three vessels. The first vessel, the CAPTAIN HARRY, loaded its cargo of 40,000 tons of rice in Darrow, Louisiana between November 19 and November 23, 2010. After a nearly three month, transoceanic voyage, the CAPTAIN HARRY completed unloading at Umm Qasr, Iraq, on February 14, 2011. As of February 18, 2011, the remaining two vessels were still en route to Iraq.

Before the Cargo left the United States, the quality of the rice was certified by both SGS and the U.S. Department of Agriculture. With regard to the rice shipped on the CAPTAIN HARRY, Peter Legemaate, Business Manager for SGS's U.S. Agricultural Trade Services division, testified that SGS employees were in "complete supervision" during the loading of the rice. After its loadport inspection, which included laboratory analysis of rice samples taken from the cargo, SGS issued a Certificate specifically certifying that the rice was in accordance with contractual specifications regarding its quality. Further, on January 5-6, 2011, in accord with standard procedure for ADM Rice's shipments to Iraq, the CAPTAIN HARRY stopped in Fujairah, U.A.E., prior to its discharge in Iraq, for additional inspection and sampling of its rice cargo. During its stop in the U.A.E., "[s]ampling and sample preparation was [sic] performed" on the cargo "in presence of Ms. Iraqi Grain Board, jointly with Ms. Survey & Inspection Services (SIS), vessels chief officer and SGS surveyors." After an analysis of the sampled cargo, as well as a visual inspection, the SGS inspectors concluded that the "[c]argo [on the CAPTAIN HARRY] was ... in good condition."

The CAPTAIN HARRY then proceeded to Umm Qasr, Iraq, where it arrived on January 8, 2011. Upon arrival, "[r]esampling [of the cargo] was performed at anchorage at Umm-Qasr pilot station area on 18/1/2011 at 1630 hrs." After the inspection was complete, under the supervision of SGS inspectors, the rice was discharged over a period of eleven days, ending on February 14, 2011. The SGS inspection report issued the following day, February 15, 2011, contains no indication that the condition of the rice cargo on the CAPTAIN HARRY was any different at Umm Qasr than it had been upon loading in Louisiana or upon inspection and sampling in Fujairah.

Nonetheless, on February 10, 2011, Chase received an authenticated Swift notice from TBI stating that it had received a claim from GBI in accordance with the terms of the Performance Bond and seeking to draw down the entire amount of the Letter of Credit. On Friday, February 11, 2011, Chase notified ADM that it had received what was, in Chase's view, "an in compliance drawing" under the Letter of Credit, and, accordingly, that Chase intended to honor the request. Because ADM was not aware of any issues regarding the quality of the Cargo, Christian

Bonnesen, President of ADM Rice, immediately contacted Danny Kim, a Vice-President of Chase's Global Trade Division, and communicated ADM Rice's position that the demand was "wrongful and not in compliance with the terms of the Performance Bond." The next day, on February 12, 2011, ADM Rice, through its employee Ashish Mathur, contacted the Iraqi Branch of SGS by e-mail and asked:

> Can you please advise me urgently whether or not SGS have issued a laboratory report in relation to [the] cargo certifying that the quality of the purchased rice does not meet the contractual specifications.

In an e-mail response that same day, Amjad Majdoubeh, the Branch Manager of SGS in Iraq, simply stated "We never issued such report." Mr. Legemaate also made several inquiries within SGS to determine if the company had issued a laboratory report with respect to the Cargo. First, he checked SGS's worldwide electronic system for any such report, either existing or forthcoming. Finding none, he then contacted SGS's technical governance office in Geneva, Switzerland, which confirmed that SGS had not issued any adverse quality reports in connection with the Cargo. Finally, he spoke with Majdoubeh, whose approval is required for any quality certificate to be issued by SGS personnel in Iraq. Majdoubeh confirmed that no adverse quality reports had been issued with respect to the Cargo, nor were any forthcoming.

On February 14, 2011, James Alonzo, an Assistant Vice President at Chase, reiterated Chase's position to ADM that – despite the foregoing – because TBI's request for payment facially complied with the terms of the Letter of Credit, Chase felt obliged to honor the request. That same day, ADM filed the instant action seeking to preliminary enjoin Chase from so doing.

To obtain a preliminary injunction in the Second Circuit, the movant must show (1) that it will suffer irreparable harm absent the injunction and (2) either (a) that it is likely to succeed on the merits or (b) that the motion presents sufficiently serious questions going to the merits to make them a fair ground for litigation and a balance of hardships tipping decidedly toward the party requesting the preliminary relief. Accordingly, the Court first turns to whether ADM would suffer irreparable harm absent an injunction. * * * On the basis of the unrebutted assertions made in the Al-Mukhtar declaration, the Court concludes that ADM has no adequate alternative forum in which it could reasonably pursue its claims against TBI and GBI. Moreover, given the legal hurdles (discussed *infra*) that ADM would confront in pursuing post-payment remedies against Chase, the issuer of the Letter of Credit, which in these circumstances is effectively just a stakeholder, it seems almost certain that, absent an injunction, ADM would be left with no legal recourse whatsoever. Accordingly, the Court concludes that ADM would suffer irreparable harm in the absence of its requested injunction.

As to ADM's likelihood of success on the merits, it is true that New York law (which here governs) requires strict compliance with facially valid requests for payment under a letter of credit. This is because New York courts follow the "independence principle," pursuant to which an issuing bank's obligations under a letter of credit are separate from, and independent of, the rights and obligations of the parties to the underlying commercial transaction. Therefore, under New York law, a bank that issues a letter of credit is not required to look beyond the payment documents presented by the beneficiary in order to ascertain whether the parties to the underlying transaction have complied with their respective duties and obligations.

Here, TBI complied with the express terms under which payment is available under the Letter of Credit by sending Chase an authenticated, facially valid Swift Notice stating that it had received a claim in accordance with the terms of the performance bond. Accordingly, Chase was under no obligation to independently verify that the conditions in the Performance Bond had been met before rendering payment to TBI under the Letter of Credit.

Notwithstanding the above, "fraud in the transaction" constitutes a "well established exception to the rule that banks must pay a beneficiary under a letter of credit when documents conforming on their face to the terms of the letter of credit are presented." *Semetex Corp. v. UBAF Arab American Bank*, 853 F. Supp. 759 (S.D.N.Y. 1994). This exception has been codified in the New York Uniform Commercial Code, which provides that an issuing bank may refuse to honor documents which "appear on [their] face strictly to comply with the terms and conditions of the letter of credit" but which are "forged or materially fraudulent," or if "honor of the presentation would facilitate a material fraud by the beneficiary on the issuer or applicant." N.Y. U.C.C. § 5-109(a) (McKinney 2000).

However, because the smooth operation of international commerce requires that requests for payment under letters of credit not be routinely obstructed by pre-payment litigation, the fraud exception to the independence principle "is a narrow one" that is only available on a showing of "outright" and "intentional fraud." *See All Service Exportacao, Importacao Comercio, S.A. v. Banco Bamerindus do Brazil, S.A.*, 921 F.2d 32, 35 (2d Cir. 1990); *see also Banque Worms, New York Branch v. Banque Commerciale Privee*, 679 F. Supp. 1173 (S.D.N.Y. 1988) (the fraud exception "is limited to situations in which the wrongdoing of the beneficiary has permeated the entire transaction."). As a consequence, Courts in this Circuit enjoin payment under letters of credit "only rarely" and only upon a strong showing that the request for payment was fraudulently made.

Here, however, just such a strong showing has been made. Indeed, ADM has adduced an array of unrebutted evidence that, taken collectively, strongly supports an inference that the rice aboard the CAPTAIN HARRY was in full compliance with the Contract's quality specifications. As this evidence (detailed above) demonstrates, TBI's representation to Chase that SGS had issued a laboratory report certifying problems with the Cargo's quality is almost certainly false. As Mr. Legemaate testified, and the documents corroborate, no record of an adverse quality report could be located in SGS's electronic records or by SGS's technical governance office, and the Branch Manager of SGS in Iraq confirmed that his office had not issued, nor was it planning to issue, such a report.

Further, absent an adverse SGS quality report, it is difficult to perceive a set of circumstances by which GBI or TBI could have otherwise determined that the Cargo did not meet the Contract's quality specifications, thereby warranting their demand for payment under the Letter of Credit. At the time TBI made its request, on February 10, 2011, two-thirds of the Cargo had not even reached Iraqi shores, and the portion of the Cargo that had arrived, aboard the CAPTAIN HARRY, was still in the process of being unloaded. Moreover – over the course of the CAPTAIN HARRY'S journey from Darrow, Louisiana to Umm Qasr, Iraq – SGS sampled, analyzed, and inspected the Cargo several times, and issued at least three reports certifying its quality. None of the several SGS reports issued with regard to the Cargo indicates any problem with the rice's quality, let alone a problem that would justify a full draw down on the Letter of Credit.

Based on the foregoing, the Court fails to perceive a "plausible or colorable basis under the contract" for TBI's request for payment under the Letter of Credit, and therefore concludes that the most reasonable interpretation of the relevant circumstances is that TBI's request was made in an attempt to effectuate a fraud.

For the foregoing reasons, the Court concludes that ADM will be irreparably harmed absent an injunction, and is likely to succeed on the merits of its claims. Accordingly, the Court hereby grants ADM's motion for a preliminary injunction and enjoins Chase from rendering any payment to TBI under the Letter of Credit.

* * *

Problem 22-3

Reconsider Problem 22-1. Assume that Acme Computer has learned from several sources that Binary Bits is in desperate financial shape, it has been shipping substandard parts to several customers, and that its president and majority stockholder is now "vacationing" in a country which has no extradition treaty with the United States. Acme Computer fears that Binary Bits has or will ship substandard parts to Acme Computer, try to collect on the letter of credit, and then transfer the money to the company president. Does Acme Computer have an adequate basis for enjoining honor of the letter of credit? If Acme can show that Binary Bits has shipped parts that are substandard and do not conform to the sales contract with Acme, is that a fraud justifying dishonor or an injunction against honor?

SECTION 4. REVIEW

Problem 22-4

Jane Engineer, owner of Design, Inc., wanted to buy some equipment from International Design Equipment ("IDE"). IDE demanded as a condition of sale that Jane provide a letter of credit to pay for the equipment. Jane asked Finance Bank to issue the letter of credit. Finance Bank agreed to do so if Jane signed a promissory note to pay for the credit. Jane signed a promissory note that provided:

> "The undersigned promises to pay to Finance Bank or its order the sum of $100,000 plus interest at 10% per annum on demand. This note is secured by a security interest as provided in the security agreement dated February 1, 2010. The undersigned also promises to give additional collateral if Finance Bank deems itself insecure."

The note was dated February 1, 2010, and signed on the bottom right hand corner "Design, Inc. by *Jane Engineer*" and signed on the back "*Bob Smith.*" Bob is Design, Inc.'s vice president. On February 10, 2010, Finance Bank sold the note to State Bank. Finance Bank signed the note on the back as follows: "*Finance Bank* without recourse" and delivered the note to State Bank.

On February 2, 2010, Finance Bank issued an irrevocable letter of credit for $100,000 with IDE as the beneficiary and sent an advice of credit to IDE. The letter of credit required a negotiable bill of lading showing shipment of the equipment to Design, Inc. and presentation of a sight draft drawn on the buyer and signed by the seller. The letter of credit stated it expired on March 1, 2010.

IDE was short of cash and could not make the shipment to Design, Inc. by March 1, 2010. IDE's president decided to forge the bill of lading and presented the forged bill of lading and the sight draft to Finance Bank on February 20, 2010. Finance Bank paid IDE $100,000. Design, Inc. never received the equipment. State Bank presented the note to Design, Inc. and demanded payment. Design, Inc. refused to pay the note because it never received the equipment from IDE.

Explain fully all of the parties' rights and liabilities.